The Twelve

The Twelve Minor Prophets

Translated from the original Hebrew
with a critical and exegetical commentary

Ebenezer Henderson

BAKER BOOK HOUSE
Grand Rapids, Michigan

Reprinted 1980 by
Baker Book House Company
from the 1858 edition issued by
Hamilton, Adams, and Company
ISBN: 0-8010-4217-8

PHOTOLITHOPRINTED BY CUSHING - MALLOY, INC.
ANN ARBOR, MICHIGAN, UNITED STATES OF AMERICA
1980

CONTENTS

GENERAL PREFACE

THE Minor Prophets are first mentioned as the Twelve by
Jesus the Son of Sirach.[1] Under this designation, they also
occur in the Talmudic tract, entitled Baba Bathra;[2] and
Jerome specifies, as the eighth in the second division of the
sacred books of the Jews, The Book of the Twelve Prophets,
which, he says, they call *Thereasar*.[3] Melito, who is the first
of the Greek Fathers that has left us a catalogue of these
books, uses precisely the same language.[4] That they were
regarded as forming one collective body of writings at a still
earlier period, appears from the reference made by the proto-
martyr Stephen to the Book of the Prophets,[5] when quoting
Amos v. 25—27. The same style is employed by the Rabbins, who call Isaiah, Jeremiah, Ezekiel, and the Twelve, the
Four Latter Prophets.[6] They are also spoken of as one book

---

[1] Καὶ τῶν δώδεκα προφητῶν τὰ ὀστᾶ ἀναθάλοι ἐκ τοῦ τόπου αὐτῶν. Ecclus.
xlix. 10.

[2] שנים עשר.

[3] תרי עסר; or, as it is generally contracted, תריסר.

[4] τῶν δώδεκα ἐν μονοβίβλιῳ.

[5] Καθὼς γέγραπται ἐν Βίβλῳ τῶν προφητῶν, Acts vii. 42.

ארבעה נביאים אחרנים.

by Gregory Nazianzen, in his poem, setting forth the component parts of the sacred volume.[1]

At what time, and by whom they were collected, cannot be determined with certainty. According to Jewish tradition, the collection of the sacred books generally is attributed to the men of the Great Synagogue, a body of learned Scribes, said to have been formed by Ezra, and continuing in existence till the time of Simon the Just, who flourished early in the third century before Christ. In the opinion of many, Nehemiah completed this collection, by adding to those books which had already obtained a place in the canon, such as had been written in, or near his own times.[2] If this actually was the case, it cannot be doubted that he must have availed himself of the authority of Malachi in determining what books were really entitled to this distinction; and this Prophet, who was the last in the series of inspired writers under the ancient dispensation, may thus be considered to have given to the canon the sanction of Divine approbation. Within a century and a half afterwards, they were translated into Greek, along with the rest of the sacred books, and have ever since obtained an undisputed place among the oracles of God.

To these twelve prophetical books the epithet " Minor " has been applied, simply on the ground of their size, compared with that of those which precede them, and not with any view

---

[1] Μίαν μέν εἰσιν ἐς γραφὴν οἱ Δώδεκα·
    Ὡσηὲ κ' Ἀμ 's, καὶ Μιχαίας ὁ τρίτος,
    Ἔπειτ' Ἰωὴλ, εἶτ' Ἰωνᾶς, Ἀβδίας,
    Ναούμ τε, Ἀμβακούμ τε, καὶ Σοφονίας,
    Ἀγγαῖος, εἶτα Ζαχαραίας, Μαλαχίας,
    Μία μὲν οἶδε. *Carmen* xxxiii.

[2] ——Καὶ ὡς καταβαλλόμενος βιβλιοθήκην, ἐπισυνήγαγε τὰ περὶ τῶν βασιλέων καὶ προφητῶν, καὶ τὰ τοῦ Δαυὶδ, καὶ ἐπιστολὰς βασιλέων περὶ ἀναθεμάτων. 2 Macc. ii. 13.

of detracting from their value, or of representing them as in any respect inferior in point of authority.

The books are not arranged in the same order in the Hebrew and Septuagint texts, and in neither is the chronology exactly observed, as may be seen from the following table, in which the mean time is assumed as the basis of the calculation :—

HEBREW.	LXX.	CHRONOLOGICAL ORDER.
1. Hosea.	1. Hosea.	1. Joel . . . . . about 865 B.C.
2. Joel.	2. Amos.	2. Jonah . . . . — 810
3. Amos.	3. Micah.	3. Amos . . . . — 790
4. Obadiah.	4. Joel.	4. Hosea . . . . — 750
5. Jonah.	5. Obadiah.	5. Micah . . . . — 730
6. Micah.	6. Jonah.	6. Nahum . . . — 710
7. Nahum.	7. Nahum.	7. Zephaniah . — 630
8. Habakkuk.	8. Habakkuk.	8. Habakkuk. — 606
9. Zephaniah.	9. Zephaniah.	9. Obadiah . . — 590
10. Haggai.	10. Haggai.	10. Haggai . . . — 520
11. Zechariah.	11. Zechariah.	11. Zechariah . — 520
12. Malachi.	12. Malachi.	12. Malachi . . — 440

Newcome, Boothroyd, and some other translators, have adopted the order which appeared to them to be chronologically correct; but in the present work that is retained which is found in the Hebrew Bible, and followed in the Vulgate, in all the authorized European versions, and in those of Michaelis, Dathe, De Wette, and others, simply on the ground of the facility of reference, which the other arrangement does not afford, but which is practically of greater importance than any advantage derivable from the change.

The Minor Prophets have generally been considered more obscure and difficult of interpretation than any of the other prophetical books of the Old Testament. Besides the avoidance of a minute and particular style of description, and the

exhibition of the more general aspects of events only, which
are justly regarded as essentially characteristic of prophecy, and
the exuberance of imagery, which was so admirably calculated
to give effect to the oracles delivered by the inspired Seers,
but which to us does not possess the vividness and perspicuity
which it did to those to whom it was originally exhibited,
there are peculiarities attaching more or less to each of the
writers, arising either from his matter, or from the manner of
its treatment, which present difficulties of no ordinary magnitude to common readers, and many that are calculated to
exercise the ingenuity, and, in no small degree, to perplex the
mind of the more experienced interpreter.   We are frequently
left to guess historical circumstances from what we otherwise
know of the features of the times, and sometimes we have no
other means of ascertaining their character than what are
furnished by the descriptive terms employed in the predictions
themselves.   Though in such cases general ideas may be
collected respecting the persons or things which are presented
to view in the text, yet we want the historical commentary
which would elucidate and give point to its various particulars.
The accounts contained in the books of Kings and Chronicles
are frequently too brief to furnish us with a key to many of
the prophecies which were fulfilled during the period which
they embrace ; while the pages of profane history only
slightly touch, if they touch at all, upon events which the
scope and bearing of the predictions determine to periods
within the range of subjects professedly treated of by its
authors.

Against none of these prophets has the charge of obscurity
been brought with greater appearance of justice than against
Hosea, whose prophecies are obviously, for the most part,

mere compendia, or condensed notes of what he publicly delivered, though preserving, to a considerable extent, the logical and verbal forms which characterised his discourses. Besides a profusion of metaphors, many of which are derived from sources little accordant with the dictates of occidental taste, we find in his book a conciseness of expression, an abruptness of transition, a paucity of connecting particles, and changes in person, number, and gender, to which nothing equal occurs in any of the other prophets. The visions of Zechariah also are not without their difficulties; but these arise, not from the language, which is remarkably simple in its character, but from the symbols which represent certain historical scenes and events.

The period of time within which the authors of the books flourished, includes the entire prophetic cycle of more than four hundred years—Isaiah, Jeremiah, Ezekiel, and Daniel, having also lived in it. It is unquestionably the most eventful in the history of the Hebrews. It embraces the introduction of image-worship, and that of Phœnician idolatry, with all its attendant evils, among the Israelites; the regicidal murders and civil wars which shook their kingdom to its centre; the corruptions of the Jewish state in consequence of its adoption of the idolatrous practices of the northern tribes; the Assyrian and Egyptian alliances; the irruption of the Syrian, Assyrian, and Chaldæan armies into Palestine; the Assyrian and Babylonian captivities; the Persian conquests; the release of the Jews, and their restoration to their own land; and the state of affairs at Jerusalem during the governorship of Nehemiah. Upon all these various events and circumstances, the predictions, warnings, threatenings, promises, and moral lessons, have, in a multiplicity of aspects, a more or less pointed and important bearing. Events subsequent to this period likewise form the subjects of prophetic announcement—such as the progress of Alexander the Great; the successes of the Maccabees; the corruptions which prevailed in the last times of the Jewish state; the destruction of Jerusalem by the Romans; the dispersion, future conversion, and restoration of the Jews; and the universal establishment of true religion throughout the world. Intermingled with these topics, and giving to each a significance and interest which it could not otherwise have possessed, are some of the clearest and most illustrious predictions respecting the Messiah, in his divine and human, his sacerdotal and suffering, and his regal and all-conquering character, that are to be found in the Old Testament.

It is impossible seriously to peruse this collection of prophetical writings without discovering the Omniscient Eye to which all future events, with the most minute of their attendant circumstances, are present; the Omnipotent Arm, which, in the most difficult cases, secures the accomplishment of the Divine purposes; the glorious attributes of Jehovah as the Moral Governor of the universe, and the special Friend and Protector of his people; the deep depravity of the human heart; the multiform phases of moral evil; and the just retributions which befal mankind in the present state of existence. These, and numerous subjects of a kindred nature, furnish abundance of matter " profitable for doctrine, for reproof, for correction, for instruction in righteousness," which, while it is able to make men " wise unto salvation, through faith which is in Christ Jesus," is also admirably fitted to " make the man of God perfect, throughly furnished unto all good works." 2 Tim. iii. 15—17.

The principles on which the Author has proceeded in preparing the present work are the same by which he was guided in composing his Commentary on the Prophet Isaiah. It has been his great aim to present to the view of his readers the mind of the Spirit as expressed in the written dictates of inspiration. With the view of determining this, he has laid under contribution all the means within his reach, in order to ascertain the original state of the Hebrew text, and the true and unsophisticated meaning of that text. He has constantly had recourse to the collection of various readings made by Kennicott and De Rossi; he has compared the renderings of the LXX., the Targum, the Syriac, the Arabic, the Vulgate, and other ancient versions; he has consulted the best critical commentaries; he has availed himself of the results of modern philological research; and he has conducted the whole under the influence of a disposition to place himself in the times of the sacred writers—surrounded by the scenery which they exhibit, and impressed by the different associations, both of a political and a spiritual character, which they embody. In all his investigations he has endeavoured to cherish a deep conviction of the inspired authority of the books which it has been his object to illustrate, and of the heavy responsibility which attaches to all who undertake the interpretation of the oracles of God.

In no instance has the theory of a double sense been permitted to exert its influence on his expositions. The Author is firmly convinced, that the more this theory is impartially examined, the more it will be found that it goes to unsettle the foundations of Divine Truth, unhinge the mind of the biblical student, invite the sneer and ridicule of unbelievers, and open the door to the extravagant vagaries of a wild and unbridled imagination. Happily the number of those who adhere to the multiform method of interpretation is rapidly diminishing; and there cannot be a doubt, that, in proportion as the principles of sacred hermeneutics come to be more severely studied, and perversions of the word of God, hereditarily kept up under the specious garb of spirituality and of a more profound understanding of Scripture, are discovered and exposed, the necessity of abandoning such slippery and untenable ground will be recognised, and the plain, simple, grammatical and natural species of interpretation, adopted and followed.

*** A Second Edition of this work being in demand, it has been revised for the purpose, but is otherwise only a reprint. The Author would have been glad to enrich it by adding references to those new discoveries at Nineveh, and still more recently at Memphis, which forcibly serve to illustrate the meaning and evidence the truthfulness of the prophetic writings; but being precluded by the infirmities of advancing years from making such attempt, he must rest content to re-issue the volume in its original form.

HOSEA

PREFACE

RESPECTING the origin of this prophet nothing is known beyond what is stated in the title, ver. 1. If, as is now generally agreed, Jeroboam II. died about the year B.C. 784, and Hezekiah began to reign about B.C. 728, it would appear from the same verse that the period of his ministry must have embraced, at the very least, fifty-six years. To some this has seemed incredible, chiefly on the ground that his prophecies are comprised within the compass of fourteen brief chapters. It must be remembered, however, that the prophets were not uninterruptedly occupied with the delivery of oracular matter. Sometimes considerable intervals elapsed between their communications, although there can be no doubt that, having once been called to the office of public teachers, they devoted much of their time to the instruction of the people among whom they lived. Besides, there is no reason for believing that the contents of the book are all that he ever uttered. They constitute only such portions of his inspired communications respecting the Israelites, as the Holy Spirit saw fit to preserve for the benefit of the Jews, among whose sacred writings they were incorporated.

Hosea was cotemporary with Isaiah, Micah, and Amos, and, like the last-mentioned prophet, directed his prophecies chiefly against the kingdom of the ten tribes.

From the general tenour of his book, and from the history of the times contained in the Books of Kings, it is manifest that he lived in a very corrupt age. Idolatry, a fondness for foreign alliances, civil distractions, and vice of every description abounded, the impending judgments on account of which he was commissioned to announce.

Though he occasionally mentions Judah, yet the entire scene is laid in the land of Israel, where, there can be little doubt, he lived and taught.

With the exception of the first and third chapters; which are in prose, the book is rhythmical, and abounds in highly figurative and metaphorical language. The diction is exceedingly concise and laconic; so much so, that Jerome justly describes him as " commaticus et quasi per sententias loquens." The sentences are in general brief and unconnected; the unexpected change of person is of frequent occurrence; number and gender are often neglected; and the similes and metaphors are frequently so intermixed, that no small degree of attention is required in order to discover their exact bearing and force. He is more scanty in his use of the particles than the other prophets, which adds not a little to the difficulty of interpreting his prophecies. In many instances he is highly animated, energetic, and sublime. Of all the prophets he is, in point of language, the most obscure and hard to be understood.

CHAPTER I

This chapter contains the inscription, ver. 1; a representation of the idolatrous kingdom of Israel under the image of a female, whom the prophet was ordered to marry, but who should prove false to him, 2, 3; and of the punishment with which it was to be visited, by the symbolical names of the prophet's children, together with a distinct intimation, that the kingdom of Judah should not be involved in the same destruction, 4—8. It concludes with a gracious promise of the joint restoration of all the tribes, and their flourishing condition in the land of their fathers, subsequent to the Babylonish captivity, 9—12.

---

1 THE word of Jehovah which was communicated to Hosea, the son of Beeri, in the days of Uzziah, Jotham, Ahaz, and Hezekiah, kings of Judah; and in the days of Jeroboam, the son of Joash, king of Israel.

2 The beginning of the word of Jehovah by Hosea. Jehovah said to Hosea: Go, take thee a lewd woman, and lewd children,

---

1. The kings here mentioned are those specified in the inscription to the prophecies of Isaiah, with the addition of Jeroboam, the son of Joash, commonly called Jeroboam the Second, to distinguish him from the son of Nebat. This monarch carried on very successful wars with his northern neighbours, and recovered out of their hands the territories of which they had taken possession; but though thus signally prospered, as an instrument in the hand of Jehovah, he was a wicked character, and greatly promoted idolatry in Israel. See 2 Kings xiv. 23—28.

By דָּבָר, *word*, is meant the prophetic matter contained in the book. Thus the Targ. נְבוּאָה.—הָיָה is commonly rendered "came" in such connexion, but it seems preferable to retain its usual sig-

nification, only adding another verb, as *communicated, imparted,* or such like, to suit the English idiom.

2. דִּבֶּר is equivalent to דָּבָר, and is rendered as a noun in the LXX., Targ., and Syr. It occurs in the absolute form הַדִּבֵּר, Jer. v. 13, with a similar reference to inspired matter. Some have attempted to show from the words תְּחִלַּת דִּבֶּר יְהֹוָה בְּהוֹשֵׁעַ that Hosea was the first of the prophets employed to convey Jehovah's messages to his ancient people; but contrary to the import of the words, which merely refer to the commencement of the prophecies of Hosea. For the use of the preposition בְּ in such connexion, see Numb. xii. 2; 2 Sam. xxiii. 2. Comp. ἐν προφήταις, Heb. i. 1.

The transaction here described, and that narrated chap. iii. 1, are clogged

for the land hath committed great lewdness, in a state of separation from Jehovah.

with almost insuperable difficulties; and, as may be expected, have given rise to very different modes of interpretation. By most commentators, the things specified are considered to have actually taken place in the outward history of the prophet. Others, as Abarbanel, Kimchi, Maimonides, Ruffinus, Œcolampadius, Marckius, Pococke, and recently Hengstenberg, regard the whole in the light of internal prophetic vision; while Calvin, Luther, Osiander, Rivetus, Danæus, Rosenmüller, Hitzig, and others, treat it as a species of parabolical representation, in which the prophet appropriates to himself imaginary circumstances, aptly fitted to impress the minds of those whom he addressed with a sense of their wickedness, and the punishment to which it exposed them.

To the last of these opinions it may justly be objected that the language, "And Jehovah said to Hosea, Go," &c. is identical with that used Is. vii. 3 ; viii. 1 ; xx. 2 ; Jer. xiii. 1—7; xviii. 1, 2; xix.; Ezek. iv. v. xii. xxiv.; and in many other passages, which cannot without violence be understood parabolically. Not the slightest hint is given, in the present case, that the circumstances are fictitious. Besides, it has been observed, that there is no instance of any of the prophets ever making himself the subject of a parable.

The same objection lies with equal force against the assumption, that the things described were merely exhibited internally to the mind of the prophet. The Divine mandate was doubtless internal ; but there is no intimation that what follows was in vision, any more than in the instances above quoted. On the contrary, it is set forth as real matter of fact. When internal scenic representations were granted, the verbs חָזָה or רָאָה, to see, are always employed to describe the experience of the person who viewed them, which is not the case here. See Is. vi. ; Jer. xxiv. 1 ; Ezek. ii. 9—iii. 3 ; Zech. i. 8 ; ii. iii. &c. Comp. also the phraseology of the Apocalypse.

We are, therefore, shut up to the literal interpretation, according to which the transactions, though symbolical, were real and outward in the history of Hosea. Those, however, who adopt this view, are not agreed on the subject of the females specified :—some being of opinion that only one is intended in both passages ; others, two: some, that Gomer was not a lewd character before the prophet took her, but became such afterwards ; others, that she was originally unchaste : some, as Thomas Aquinas, that he did not marry her at all, but merely lived with her as a concubine ! Lyra and Newcome think that nothing more is meant by "a wife of lewdness," than an Israelitess—one of those who had become guilty of spiritual fornication or idolatry. The position that Hosea was commanded to marry an impure female cannot be sustained, for two reasons. First, the children were clearly those afterwards described as born to the prophet, and are spoken of as lewd as well as their mother. Secondly, on the supposition that Gomer had been guilty of acts of impurity previous to her connexion with the prophet, there would be no congruity in constituting her a type of Israel, who is represented as lewd because she had lapsed into idolatry, in violation of the marriage contract entered into at Sinai. See Gesen. Lex. זָנָה, No. 2. Consistency of interpretation absolutely requires the adoption of this view of the subject, as is admitted both by Hengstenberg and Hitzig. The objections otherwise produced by the former of these authors against the literal character of the transactions are more specious than real. Besides being the most obvious and natural, it has much to recommend it on the ground of the public notoriety which infidelity on the part of the wife of a prophet must have created, and its aptness to typify the conduct of the Israelites towards Jehovah. It may indeed be said, that his marrying a notoriously lewd character must have produced a much greater sensation. True ; but besides the encouragement which it must have been calculated to give to the formation of unhallowed and irreligious connexions, it would not, as was just observed, have been in accordance with the design of the transaction, which was,

3　So he went and took Gomer, the daughter of Diblaim, and
4　she conceived, and bare him a son. And Jehovah said unto
him, Call his name JEZREEL; for yet a little while, and I will
avenge the blood of Jezreel upon the house of Jehu, and will
5　cause the kingdom of the house of Israel to cease. And it shall
come to pass in that day, that I will break the bow of Israel in
the valley of Jezreel.

not to represent the character of the
Hebrews before the period of their national reception into alliance with Jehovah, but their conduct as exhibited in the
pages of their subsequent history. The
phrases אֵשֶׁת זְנוּנִים וְיַלְדֵי זְנוּנִים, *a lewd woman
and lewd children,* have the same import,
and are not to be interpreted as if the
mother alone were guilty, and the children merely the product of her guilty
conduct. Comp. the phrase יַלְדֵי פֶשַׁע *children of transgression,* i. e. transgressors,
Is. lvii. 4. Thus as to sense the Targ.;
and the Syr. ܣܟܢܠ ܘܒܢܝ, *and children that commit lewdness.* Thus also
Rosenmüller. Both are anticipative as
to the relation of the prophet, though
typical of what had already taken place
on the part of the ten tribes. Viewed
as a kingdom, they are represented as a
mother; and as individual subjects of
that kingdom, they are spoken of as her
children. The plural זְנוּנִים is emphatic,
as דָּמִים in אִישׁ דָּמִים, &c. Comp. זְנוּנִים.רוּחַ,
chap. iv. 12, and ii. 4. That they are
otherwise to be identified appears from
the use of קַח, *take,* which properly applies
only to the female, but here governs both
nouns, as Jerome observes, ἀπὸ κοινοῦ.
The reason of the symbolic action is
assigned at the close of the verse—the
atrocious conduct of the Israelites in
renouncing the pure worship of Jehovah,
and addicting themselves to idolatry.
Comp. Lev. xvii. 7; xx. 5, 6; Hos. iv. 12.
הָאָרֶץ, *the land,* is put, by metonymy, for
its inhabitants. The preposition מִן has
here the force of a negative, which
strongly expresses the state of separation
which had taken place.
3. That the names *Gomer* and *Diblaim*
are to be taken symbolically, as Hengstenberg interprets, does not appear.
His exposition of them is fanciful, as is
that of Jerome, who takes pretty much
the same view. The use of לוֹ, *to him,* i.e.

to Hosea, proves that the child was not
of spurious origin. The word is wanting,
indeed, in three of Kennicott's MSS.,
and one of De Rossi's, the Complut.
edition of the LXX., the Itala, and the
Arab.; but the omission in all probability originated in an attempt to render
the phraseology conformable to that of
verses 6 and 8.
4, 5. יִזְרְעֶאל, *Jezreel,* i. e. God will *scatter,* from זָרַע, to *scatter, disperse,* as in
Zech. x. 9; Targ. מְבַדְּרָיָא. It was otherwise the proper name of a city in the
tribe of Issachar, on the brow of the
central valley in the great plain of the
same name, and the royal residence of
Ahab and his successors. It was here
Jehu exercised acts of the greatest cruelty, 2 Kings x. 11, 14, 17. These acts
were speedily to be avenged in the extinction of the royal family, and the
entire cessation of the Israelitish state.
It had been announced to Jehu that his
sons should occupy the throne till the
fourth generation, 2 Kings x. 30. Two
of these generations had passed away by
the time of the prophet—Jeroboam being
the great grand-son. In the following
generation, the prediction received its
accomplishment. By the "bow of
Israel" is meant her military prowess,
which was completely subdued by the
Assyrian army. The valley here mentioned, afterwards called *Esdraelon,* was
famous for the battles fought there from
the most ancient times. It consists of
the broad elevated plain which stretches
from the Jordan to the Mediterranean,
near Mount Carmel, and is well adapted
for military operations. Accordingly,
Dr. E. D. Clarke observes, "Jews, Gentiles, Saracens, Christian Crusaders, and
Anti-Christian Frenchmen, Egyptians,
Persians, Druses, Turks, and Arabs,
warriors out of every nation which is
under heaven, have pitched their tents
upon the plains of Esdraelon, and have

6 And she conceived again, and bare a daughter; and He said to him, Call her name LO-RUHAMAH; for I will no more have mercy upon the house of Israel, but will utterly take them away.

7 But I will have mercy upon the house of Judah, and will save them by Jehovah their God, and will not' save them by bow, nor by sword, nor by battle, nor by horses, nor by horsemen.

8 And she weaned LO-RUHAMAH, and conceived, and bare a

9 son. And He said, Call his name LO-AMMI; for ye are not my

10 people, and I will not be yours. Nevertheless the number of the children of Israel shall be as the sand of the sea, which can neither be measured nor numbered; and it shall be, that instead

---

beheld the various banners of their nations wet with the dews of Tabor and Hermon." It was, therefore, natural that the Israelites should endeavour to make a stand against the Assyrians in this valley; but being overpowered by numbers, they were obliged to succumb to the enemy. Of this discomfiture, and the consequent dispersion of the ten tribes, the name of the prophet's son was symbolical.

6, 7. לֹא רֻחָמָה, LO-RUHAMAH, i. e. *unpitied.* נָשָׂא ? elsewhere signifies *to forgive;* and were the verb preceded by the copulative וְ, it might be so rendered here, only supplying the negative לֹא from the preceding clause; but as כִּי *but,* excludes such repetition, the phrase must be rendered as in the translation. LXX. ἀντιτασσόμενος ἀντιτάξομαι αὐτοῖς. Syr. ܘܠܐ ܐܬܠ ܠܗܘܢ ܪ̈ܚܡܐ. Vulg. *oblivione obliviscar eorum*—reading נָשָׂא which is found in De Rossi's MS. 596, at first hand, instead of נָשָׂא. The kingdom of Israel was never more to be restored, though, in conjunction with the Jews, the scattered Israelites were to return to Canaan after the Babylonish captivity, ver. 11. It was to be very different with the Jewish power. Though likewise attacked, and threatened with utter extinction by Sennacherib, they were mercifully delivered by a divine interposition, without all human aid. And though they were afterwards carried away to Babylon, their civil polity was restored, which was not the case with the Israelites. מִלְחָמָה, *war,* stands elliptically for אַנְשֵׁי מִלְחָמָה, *warriors.*

8. The mention here made of the weaning of Lo-Ruhamah, seems designed rather to fill up the narrative, than to describe figuratively any distinct treatment of the Israelites.

9. לֹא עַמִּי, LO-AMMI, i. e. *not my people,* further sets forth the rejection of the ten tribes by Jehovah. Nothing could have been better calculated to make an impression upon the minds of his countrymen, than for the prophet thus to give to one child after another a name strongly significant of the disastrous circumstances to which they should be reduced. Instead of לֹא אֶהְיֶה לָכֶם, *I will not be yours,* i. e. your God, Houbigant and Newcome would read לֹא אלהיכם, *I am not your God:* but though the antithesis is common, it admits of an ellipsis, just as in Ezek. xvi. 8, there is an ellipsis of לְאִשָּׁה. Comp. Ps. cxviii. 6. The MSS. and versions exhibit no variation.

10, 11. These verses contain a gracious promise of the recovery of the descendants of the Israelites, along with those of their brethren the Jews, at the termination of the Babylonish captivity. Though entirely and for ever broken up as a distinct kingdom, yet, during the period of their residence in the regions of the East, whither they were to be transported, they should greatly multiply, and afterwards be reinstated in the privileges of adoption, as members of the theocracy. The eleventh verse teaches the reunion of all the tribes, and their return under Zerubbabel to their own land. That this prince is meant by the רֹאשׁ אֶחָד, *one head,* must be maintained, since the Messiah, who is by many sup-

of its having been said to them, Ye are not my people, it shall
11 be said to them, Ye are the children of the living God. Then
shall the children of Judah, and the children of Israel, be
gathered together, and they shall appoint for themselves one
12 head, and shall come up out of the land. For great shall be
the day of Jezreel. Say ye unto your brethren, AMMI; and to
your sisters, RUHAMAH.

posed to be intended, is nowhere spoken of as appointed by men, but always as the choice and appointment of God. אֶרֶץ, *land,* signifies, in this connexion, the country of Babylon, not excluding those other regions of the East in which the descendants of the different tribes were found. יִזְרְעֶאל, *Jezreel,* is obviously used here in a different acceptation from that in which it is taken ver. 4. That of *sowing* is alone appropriate. Illustrious should be the period when the tribes should again be sown in their own

country. Comp. chap. ii. 22, 23; Jer. xxxi. 27.

The principle on which part of ver. 10, and chap. ii. 23, are quoted, Rom. ix. 25, 26, and 1 Pet. ii. 10, seems to be that of analogy. As God had taken pity upon the ten tribes, who had become heathens as it respects idolatrous and other practices, so he had pitied the Gentiles who had been in the same circumstances. What was said of the one class was equally descriptive of the other.

CHAPTER II

The prophet proceeds in this chapter to apply the symbolical relation described in
the preceding. He calls the Israelites to reform their wicked conduct, 1, 2;
threatens them with a series of calamities, the effect of which should be their
repentance and return to the service of Jehovah, 3—15; and promises a
gracious restoration to His favour, and the enjoyment of security and prosperity
in their own land, 16—23.

---

1 CONTEND with your mother, contend;
2 For she is not my wife,
　Neither am I her husband:
　That she may remove her lewdness from her face,
　And her adulteries from between her breasts.

1, 2. The individual members of the Israelitish state are here summoned to urge upon their nation the consideration of its wickedness in having departed from God. Of these the *nation* of the ten tribes was the אֵם, *mother.* Cocceius, Dathe, Kuinoel, and Rückert, render כִּי,

that, and interpret: Argue the point with your nation, and show her that in consequence of her wicked conduct all relations between us have ceased. The causal signification of the conjunction, however, seems preferable. The words which it introduces form a parenthesis;

3 Lest I strip her naked,
   And set her as in the day when she was born,
   And make her as the desert,
   And set her like a dry land,
   And cause her to die with thirst.
4 And upon her children I will have no mercy,
   For they are lewd children;
5 Because their mother hath committed lewdness,
   Their parent hath acted shamefully;
   For she said: I will follow my lovers,
   That give me my bread and my water,
   My wool and my flax, my oil and my wine.

and וְהָסֵר, which, though future, is to be rendered potentially, *that she may remove,* connects with רִיבוּ, *contend ye.* The וְ is, as frequently, to be taken τελικῶς. The repetition of רִיבוּ is emphatic, as *ducite* in Virgil:—

"Ducite ab urbe domum, mea carmina, ducite Daphnin."

By זְנוּנִים וְנַאֲפוּפִים, *fornications and adulteries,* are meant the tokens or indications of lewd character:—boldness of countenance, and an immodest exposure of the breasts. Both forms are reduplicate, to express the enormity of the evil. What the prophet has in view is the reckless and unblushing manner in which the Israelitish nation practised idolatry. The LXX. have read מִפָּנַי, "from *my* face;" improperly in this connexion, though a similar phrase occurs elsewhere.

3. A striking accumulation of synonymous denunciations for the purpose of describing the state of complete destitution to which the idolatrous Israelites would be reduced by the infliction of divine judgments. They should be placed in circumstances analogous to those in which they had originally been in Egypt. Comp. Ezek. xvi. 4; xxiii. 25, 26, 28, 29. For מִדְבַּר comp. Jer. ii. 6.

4. Individuals might expect that they would escape, and not be treated as the nation in its collective capacity; but Jehovah here declares, that he would treat them according to the demerits of their individual wickedness. For בְּנֵי וְזְנוּנִים comp. יַלְדֵי וְזְנוּנִים, ch. i. 2. The second noun is, as frequently, used adjectively.

5. כִּי, *since* or *because* and לָכֵן, *therefore,* ver. 6, correspond to each other, the former marking the protasis, the latter the apodosis. The second כִּי introduces parenthetically an illustration of the statement made at the beginning of the verse. הוֹרָה is the feminine participle of הָרָה, *to conceive, be pregnant.* Comp. הוֹרָתִי, Song iii. 4. According to the Jewish exegesis, הוֹרִי, Gen. xlix. 26, is used of male progenitors. The Targ. and Jarchi suppose teachers to be here meant; but the term is merely a synonyme of אֵם, *mother,* in the preceding hemistich. Interpreters are not agreed respecting the rendering of הוֹבִישָׁה. In most instances in which the word occurs it certainly has the transitive signification; but here the intransitive seems more appropriate. Comp. Jer. vi. 15, where it is explained by כִּי תוֹעֵבָה עָשׂוּ. Comp. also הִתְעִיב, הֵרַע, הֵיטִיב, as Hiph. intransitives. The paragogic ה in אֵלְכָה, elongating the future, is expressive of a decided purpose, desire, or bent of mind; it is my settled determination to follow those who richly supply my wants in return for my religious services. מְאַהֲבִים, *lovers,* which is here employed metaphorically to denote *idols,* is seldom used except in a bad sense. This interpretation, which is that of Joseph Kimchi and Abarbanel, is more in keeping with the symbolical character of the prophecy, than that suggested by the Targ. בֵּין רִשְׁעָן אָמִין, which takes the word in the sense of idolaters, or idolatrous nations, such as Assyria, &c. Comp. as strictly parallel, Jer. xliv. 17—19. The language indicates complete alienation of

6 Therefore, behold! I will hedge up thy way with thorns,
　And will raise a wall, that she may not find her paths.

7 And she shall eagerly pursue her lovers, but she shall not over-
　　take them;
　And shall seek them, but shall not find them:
　Then shall she say: I will go and return to my first husband,
　For it was better with me then than now.

8 　Because she knew not that it was I that gave her
　The corn, and the new wine, and the oil;
　And furnished her abundantly with silver and gold,
　Which they made into images of Baal:

9 Therefore I will take back my corn in its time,

---

heart from Jehovah, the only giver of all good, and a blind confidence in, and devotion to the service of idols. The articles specified comprehend both the necessaries and the luxuries of ancient Hebrew life. שֶׁמֶן, *oil*, is much in use among the Orientals, both in its simple state, and as compounded with other ingredients. It is specially applied as ointment to the body after bathing. Comp. Psalm xxiii. 5; Prov. xxi. 17. שִׁקּוּי denotes here all kinds of artificial drink, being used in distinction from *water*. The Aldine edition of the LXX. reads ὁ οἶνός μου; but the usual reading is πάντα ὅσα μοι καθήκει, with which the Targ. and Syr. agree. The word occurs, Ps. cii. 10; Prov. iii. 8; and is evidently derived from שָׁקָה; Arab. سقى;

Eth. ០ᎩᏢ : *to make to drink, to water.*

6. For דַּרְכֵּךְ in דַּרְכֵּךְ the LXX., Arab., and Syr., read דַּרְכָּהּ, but most likely in order to produce uniformity in the use of the affix. The metaphor here employed is borrowed from the condition of a traveller whose progress is interrupted by a hedge thrown across his path, or who can no longer pass through the gap of an enclosure which used to be in his way; and who is consequently reduced to straits and difficulties. Turned out of his accustomed course, he is bewildered, and strives in vain to extricate himself. Comp. Job xix. 8; Lam. iii. 7, 9. גְּדֵרָה, *a wall*, is pointed גְּדֵרָה, in the editions of J. H. Michaelis, and Jahn,

and this punctuation Hengstenberg attempts, without success, to defend. The wall means the external hindrances which the captivity interposed between the ten tribes and the objects of their idolatrous attachment.

7. Convinced by bitter experience of the folly of idolatry, the Israelites would renounce it, and return to the service of Jehovah. רִדְּפָה is intensive, and expresses the ardour of the pursuit. The Vau in וְאָמְרָה, marking the apodosis, points out the consequence or result of the failure —a resolution to turn from idols to serve the living God. It might be rendered *so that*, but not *in order that*, as Manger proposes. אָז, *then*, designates the period previous to the apostasy of the ten tribes, when in reward for external obedience, they enjoyed temporal blessings. Thus the Targ. אֲרֵי טָב לִי כַּד הֲוֵיתִי פָלְחָא קֳדָמוֹהִי מִכְּעַן לָא אֶפְלַח לְטַעֲוָתָא.

8, 9. וְ and לָכֵן at the beginning of these verses stand in the same relation to each other as פִּי and לָכֵן, verses 5th and 6th. Before עָשׂוּ supply אֲשֶׁר. By בַּעַל, *Baal*, the prophet means "images of Baal," the singular being used collectively for the plural. Comp. ch. viii. 4, where עֲצַבִּים, *idols*, correspond to בַּעַל in the present case. Hitzig would restrict אֲשֶׁר, understood, to זָהָב, *gold*, supposing the golden calves set up at Bethel and Dan to be meant; but, as it does not appear that the name of Baal was ever applied to them, his interpretation is groundless. See chap. viii. 4; which also clearly proves that by עָשׂוּ לַבַּעַל we are not to understand the consecration

And my new wine in its season;
And I will recover my wool and my flax,
Designed to cover her nakedness.

10 And now I will expose her vileness before her lovers,
And none shall deliver her out of my hand.

of the silver and gold to the service of
Baal, but the actual conversion of these
precious metals into images of that idol,
or at least into plating with which to
cover such as were made of wood.
2 Chron. xxiv. 7, to which Secker appeals
in favour of the former meaning of the
phrase, is also to be so understood. The
rendering of Gesenius, " which *they*
offered to Baal," is equally objectionable;
the phrase ? עָשָׂה, when thus used, being
referred to sacrificial victims. Targ.
מְנֵיה עֲבַדוּ לְמַעְמָא. Hengstenberg attempts
to support the position that consecration
is meant; but his reasons are altogether
futile. The very passage which he quotes
as parallel (Ezek. xvi. 17, 18,) is directly
opposed to the exegesis of the phrase.
Baal was perhaps the most ancient of
all the gods worshipped in the East. He
was, according to Dr. Münter, the representative of the sun, the generative
power in the Eastern mythology, and
had associated with him Astarte, the
female power, which was viewed as representing the moon. Gesenius, however, is of opinion, that under these
names the planets Jupiter and Venus
were worshipped. See on Isaiah xvii.
8. From the frequency with which his
name occurs in compound Phœnician
names, as Hannibal, Hasdrubal, &c., the
worship of Baal appears to have been
common among that people; and from
them, especially the Tyrians, it was
borrowed by the Israelites. Mention is
made of this idolatry in the time of the
Judges, see chap. ii. 11, 13; iii. 7;
vi. 25; it became prevalent even in
Judah in the days of Ahaz; and, though
abolished by the pious king Josiah, was
revived by Manasseh. In Israel it rapidly gained ground after the introduction of the worship of the golden
calves by Jeroboam, and reached its
height in the reigns of Ahab and Hoshea.
The verb שׁוּב, *to return, turn back*, is
frequently used adverbially. So here
אָשׁוּב וְלָקַחְתִּי, *I will again take away*, or

take back, i.e. deprive of. The meaning
is, that instead of reaping the fruits of
the earth, &c. as they expected at the
usual season, they should be trodden
down, consumed, or taken away by the
Assyrian army under Shalmaneser.
Jehovah vindicates his right to the
various articles specified, because they
had been bestowed by his providence;
calling them *his*, with obvious reference
to ver. 5, in which Israel had called
them *hers*. The land and all it contained were specially his. נָצַל; Arab.

نصل, *liberatus fuit*, expresses the idea
of *rescuing* or *recovering* what was unjustly held. The ל in לְכַסּוֹת denotes end
or purpose, and is quite in its place; so
that there is no necessity, with Houbigant,
Dathe, Horsley, Newcome, Boothroyd,
and others, to change it into מ, out of
deference to the LXX. who render τοῦ
μὴ καλύπτειν.

10. נַבְלֻת occurs only in this place,
but is obviously equivalent to נְבָלָה, *atro-*
cious, shameful, detestable wickedness.
Targ. קְלָנָה, *her shame*; LXX. τὴν ἀκαθ-
αρσίαν αὐτῆς; Syr. ܩܒܚܘ, nudatio
in malum, pudenda. Castel.; Arab.
عورتها, *her nakedness.* Occurring in
immediate connexion with the preceding
עֶרְיָה, *nudity*, it conveys the superadded
idea of obscenity, *i.e.* by metonymy, the
results or consequences of idolatrous
conduct, a complete destitution of all
the necessaries of life. Comp. Jer. xiii.
26; Nah. iii. 5. This exposure was to
be made in the very presence of the
idols which Israel had served, none of
which should be able to afford deliverance. By a prosopopœia, the idols are
first endowed with the faculty of vision,
and then their utter imbecility is strikingly set forth. אִישׁ, not only signifies
man, but *any one*, and is frequently used
of inanimate objects. In connexion
with לֹא, it signifies *none*.

11 And I will cause all her joy to cease ;
   Her festivals, her new moons, and her sabbaths,
   And all her appointed assemblies.

12 I will also lay waste her vines and her fig-trees,
   Of which she said : They are my hire
   Which my lovers have given me :
   I will turn them into a forest,
   And the beasts of the field shall devour them.

13 I will avenge upon her the days of the Baals,
   On which she burned incense to them ;
   And decked herself with nose-rings and trinkets,
   And followed her lovers,
   And forgat me, saith Jehovah.

11, 12, explain the denouncement made ver. 10. The country was to be desolated by the invading armies, and all the festivities and seasons of religious observance were to cease. The different terms here employed are those by which the seasons of worship, &c. appointed by Jehovah in the Mosaic law, are designated ; but it is not hence to be inferred that such were observed according to his appointment. The Israelites professed to worship him, but, at the same time, served other gods. While from habit they continued to keep them as portions of time unappropriated to the ordinary occupations of life, they doubtless converted them into seasons of carnal indulgence. The nouns are those of multitude, and must be rendered in the plural. גֶּפֶן, and תְּאֵנָה, are likewise to be taken as collectives, or rather, as Horsley suggests, plantations of vines and fig-trees. These should be left uncultivated on the removal of the inhabitants into foreign regions. Comp. Is. v. 6 ; vii. 23, 24. אֶתְנָה, like אֶתְנַן, is used only of the hire of a harlot, and is peculiarly appropriate in this connexion. Thus

Tanchum on chap. viii. 9 :—هو ما يبدل

للزانية من الجعل Comp. Is. xxiii.

17, 18. The wild beast is here to be taken literally, and not figuratively, as Abarbanel does,—supposing the heathen invaders to be meant.

13. הַבְּעָלִים, the Baals, i.e. the idols which they had set up to Baal in the cities and different parts of the country, as well as in their private houses. Hence the names Baal-Gad, Baal-Hermon, Baal-meon, &c. By אֶת־יְמֵי הַבְּעָלִים, are meant the days specially devoted to the celebration of idolatrous rites. To cause grateful odours to ascend from the altars, was considered peculiarly acceptable to the objects of worship. It appears to have originated partly in the gratification afforded by agreeable smells, and partly in the custom of burning perfumes in rooms, &c. with a view to purify them from noxious vapours. נֶזֶם and חֶלְיָה appear to be employed here to denote female ornaments generally ; though strictly taken, the former commonly signifies such rings as the Oriental females wear in the nostril. See on Is. iii. 21. חֶלְיָה, from חָלָה, to be smooth, polished : Arab. حلي, ornavit monilibus mundove

suo (mulierem,) حلية, mundo ornata, denotes a trinket, necklace, or the like.

According to Firuzabad : ما يزين به من مصبوغ المعدنيات او الحجارة

quodcunque ornamentum vel e metallis conflatum, vel e lapidibus pretiosis confectum. Rosenm., the Syr., and Targ., have pearls. That courtesans decked themselves with the most costly orna-

14   Nevertheless, behold! I will allure her,
And, though I lead her into the desert,
Yet I will speak soothingly to her.

15   And I will grant her her vineyards from thence,
And the valley of Achor for a door of hope:
And she shall sing there, as in the days of her youth,
Even as in the day when she came up from the land of Egypt.

ments they could command is mentioned by Juvenal, Sat. vi.:—

" Mœchis foliata parantur;
   Emitur his quicquid gracilis huc mittitis Indi."

The prophet has in view the gay ornaments in which the Israelites decked themselves on idolatrous holidays. Their entirely abandoning themselves to the service of idols, and their dereliction of the God of their fathers, are brought forward at the conclusion of this description of their conduct, in order to heighten the aggravation of their guilt, and render the announcement of the kindly disposition of Jehovah towards them, at the beginning of the following verse, the more surprising.

14. לָכֵן cannot with any propriety be rendered "therefore" in this connexion, if the following words are to be regarded as promissory of good, and not as containing a further threatening of punishment. And that they are to be so regarded, the subsequent context sufficiently shows. This particle must therefore possess the force of the Arab. لٰكِنْ, *verumtamen, but yet, notwithstanding, nevertheless.* It thus marks the unexpected transition from threats to promises, as Is. vii. 14; x. 24; xxvii. 9; xxx. 18, *et freq.*—פָּתָה, of which מִפְתֶּה is the Piel participle, signifies *to open, be open, easily persuasible;* hence in Piel, both in a good and a bad sense, *to persuade, allure, prevail upon* by suitable inducements. It is here necessarily to be taken in the sense of inducing or gaining over to that which is good, by the use of soothing and persuasive means, as the concluding words of the verse וְדִבַּרְתִּי עַל־לִבָּהּ abundantly prove. As the Israelites were to be forcibly removed from their land by the king of Assyria, there is a

singular want of propriety in assigning to וֹ, in וְהֹלַכְתִּיהָ, its usual copulative power. It is obviously to be understood exceptively, or as introducing a kind of parenthetical sentence, expressive of what was to take place in the history of the ten tribes previously to their conversion from idolatry; and which, though it might seem severe, was indispensable for the attainment of that object. For this signification of וֹ, see Ruth ii. 13; 1 Sam. i. 5; Eccles. ix. 16; Mal. ii. 14; and other instances in Noldius, No. 46. Bauer thinks the desert between Assyria and Judæa is meant, through which the Israelites were to be conducted on their release: Döderlein, Theol. Biblioth. explains it of Judæa itself, at that time desolate and waste. I imagine the country of Babylon is intended. Jehovah is here said to do what he would employ the Assyrians in doing. For the phrase דִּבֶּר עַל לֵב, see Is. xl. 2. When reduced to circumstances of affliction in the countries of the East, whither they were to be carried, Jehovah declares that he would administer consolation to them; holding out to them the cheering prospect of restoration, on their repentance, to their native land.

15. The Israelites had altogether forfeited their possessions; nor could they acquire a new right to them except in the way of a fresh grant from the Lord. This grant he here promises them, as he had of old promised Canaan to their fathers when in the wilderness. מִשָּׁם, *thence,* means, returning from the wilderness; just as שָׁמָּה indicates the homeward direction of the exiles. To take מִשָּׁם as a particle of time, which Gesenius proposes, is less suitable. " The valley of Achor" lay in the vicinity of Jericho, and was noted in the sacred history for the judgment inflicted upon Achan. From Is. lxv. 10, it appears to have been

16 And it shall be in that day, saith Jehovah,
   That thou shalt call me, Ishi;
   And shalt no more call me, Baali.
17 For I will take away the names of the Baals from her mouth,
   And they shall no more be remembered by their name.
18 And I will make a covenant for them in that day
   With the beasts of the field, and with the fowls of heaven,

a fertile and pleasant region; and on this account alone it is thought by Calvin, Zanchius, Rivetus, and others, to be referred to by our prophet. Most of the Rabbins, however, and, after them, many Christian interpreters, consider allusion to be made to the name, which signifies *trouble* or *molestation*, and to this I incline. This valley had proved very inauspicious to the Hebrews on their former entrance into Canaan. They had been forced to turn their backs before the native inhabitants, and their hearts melted, and became as water, Josh. vii. 5, 8, 12, 24, 26. But on their return from the captivity, the exiles would pass through it with the undisturbed expectation of a peaceable and joyful occupation of the country. By פֶּתַח תִּקְוָה, *a door of hope*, is meant a *hopeful entrance* into the holy land.—עָמֵק, the LXX., Syr., Arab., and Symm., take in the signification *to be humbled* or *afflicted;* and this idea is adhered to by Grotius, who combines it with that of singing: "Intellige autem carmen fletûs et precum;" but that of celebrating the Divine goodness in songs of gratitude and joy better suits the connexion. The ה in שָׁמָּה, as before observed, indicates the homeward direction of the exiles—yet not without special reference to their approach to the valley of Achor. The point of comparison, as it respects the singing, seems to be the Song of Moses at the Red Sea. As the people then united in celebrating the goodness of Jehovah displayed in their deliverance, so should the returning Israelites do, on again taking possession of their native land.

16, 17. The word בַּעַל, *Baal*, had originally been used in its unexceptionable acceptation of *husband*, and is thus applied to Jehovah, Is. liv. 5; but as it had become common in its application by the Israelites to the heathen deities which they had worshipped, and, besides, conveyed the idea of *possession* and *rule*, rather than that of *affection*, God here declares that in future he would be called אִישׁ, *Ish*, the name more usually employed to express the relation of husband, and which was not liable to the same objections:—

"Sic mihi servitium video, dominamque paratam,
   Jam mihi libertas illa paterna vale."
                    Tibullus, lib. ii. Eleg. 4.

Before אִישִׁי, two MSS., the LXX., Aq, and Syr., insert לֹ; while two MSS., and originally seven more, and four printed editions, omit it after תִּקְרְאִי.—בְּעָלִים, is not here to be taken as a plural of excellency, but is used, according to its strict import, to denote the different images of Baal worshipped by the Israelites, such as *Baal-Gad, Baal-Ammon*, &c. Comp. Exod. xxiii. 13; Zech. xiii. 2. The prophecy was fully accomplished at the return from the Babylonish captivity.

18. Such should be the security of the returned exiles under the immediate care and protection of Jehovah, that every thing capable of injuring them should be rendered perfectly harmless. The irrational animals should be restrained, as if under the bond of an inviolable compact; and the Assyrian armies should no more attack them. Some understand the former part of the verse figuratively—the different creatures there specified denoting men corresponding to them in disposition; but the language is rather to be regarded as hyperbolical, being merely intended to heighten the effect. Comp. Job v. 23; Ezek. xxxiv. 25. Before מִלְחָמָה, supply כְּלִי, or אַנְשֵׁי, as in chap. i. 7. Targ. עָבְדֵי קְרָבָא.—אֶשְׁבּוֹר מִן is a pregnant phrase, meaning, *I will break and remove away from.* שָׁבַר is here expressive of the

And with the reptiles of the ground;
The bow also, and the sword, and the battle, I will break and
remove from the land,
And will cause them to recline securely.
19 I will also betroth thee to myself for ever;
I will even betroth thee to myself with righteousness and with
justice,
And with kindness, and with tender compassion.
20 Yea, I will betroth thee to myself with faithfulness:
And thou shalt know Jehovah.
21 And it shall be in that day,

reclining posture in which the Orientals indulge whenever they are released from active exertion. At the time predicted there would be no enemy or danger to break in upon their repose.

"Ipsæ lacte domum referunt distenta
    capellæ
Ubera, nec magnos metuent armenta
    leones.
Ipsa tibi blandos fundent cunabula
    flores.
Occidet et serpens, et fallax herba
    veneni
Occidet: Assyrium vulgò nascetur
    amomum."   *Virgil*, Eclog. iv.

19, 20. אֵשׂ signifies to contract a matrimonial alliance, and is here specially selected in order to impress the minds of the Israelites with a sense of the distinguished character of the Divine benignity. Though they had rendered themselves totally unworthy of his regard, he declares that he would treat them as if they had never apostatised to idolatry. He would form a new conjugal relation, as with a female in her virgin state. The triple repetition of the verb expresses intensity of desire, and gives the strongest assurance to the party to whom the promise is made. לְעוֹלָם, *for ever*, is to be taken as Gen. xiii. 15; Exod. xxxii. 13; Is. xxxv. 10. The several particulars here enumerated further discover, by the amplification which they form, the great kindness of Jehovah to his people. By "righteousness" and "justice," is meant every equitable obligation which God could be expected to place himself under in

the new conjugal relation—all that the Israelites could possibly expect in the way of supply from their Divine protector. To these, however, are added "kindness," and "tender compassion," which express the strong internal affection from which the former should proceed, and the high degree of interest which God would take in his recovered people. To remove every doubt from their minds, he crowns the whole by a gracious assurance that his engagements should be "faithfully" performed. רַחֲמִים, τὰ σπλάγχνα, lit. *the bowels*, but commonly employed figuratively to denote tender affection or love. Horsley's interpretation of the terms in application to our Saviour, is, like most of his exegesis, in the highest degree fanciful, being totally unsupported by the scope and connexion of the passage. The knowledge of Jehovah here predicated is not speculative, or a bare intellectual acquaintance with his character, but experimental, or that which results from the actual enjoyment of his love. Instead of אֶת־יְהוָה, twenty-six MSS., originally thirteen more, now two, perhaps other two, and two editions, supported by the Vulg., read כִּי אֲנִי יְהוָה, *i.e.* thou shalt know *that I am Jehovah.*

21, 22. One of the most beautiful instances of prosopopœia to be found in Scripture. Comp. the address to the Nile in Tibullus, lib. i. Eleg. vii. ver. 25 :—

"Te propter nullos tellus tua postulat
    imbres,
Arida nec pluvio supplicat herba Jovi."

While second causes have here their

I will respond, saith Jehovah,
I will respond to the heavens,
And they shall respond to the earth,

22 And the earth shall respond to the corn, and the new wine, and
    the oil,
And they shall respond to Jezreel.

23 For I will sow her for myself in the land,
And will have mercy upon Lo-Ruhamah,
And will say to Lo-Ammi, Thou art my people;
And they shall say, My God!

appropriate place allotted to them, as so many connected links in the chain of Divine Providence, the sovereign influence of the Great First Cause is strongly asserted by the emphatic repetion of אֶעֱנֶה, *I will respond to,* or *answer.* It must, however, be observed, that this verb does not occur the first time in one of Kennicott's MSS.; it has originally been wanting in another of De Rossi's; and is omitted in the LXX., Syr., and Arab. One of De Rossi's MSS. omits אֶעֱנֶה נְאֻם יְהוָה entirely; and another, the second אֶעֱנֶה originally.—יִזְרְעֶאל, *Jezreel,* here means *that which God hath sown,* i. e. his people whom he had *scattered,* but whom he would again restore to their native soil. Comp. chap. i. ver. 4, and 11.

23. י is causal, introducing a declaration which is designed to account for the appropriation of the name Jezreel at the end of the preceding verse. The metaphor is agricultural. The rest of the verse contains a repetition of what is promised, chap. i. 10.

CHAPTER III

This chapter contains a new symbolical represention of the regard of Jehovah for his people, and of their condition at a period subsequent to their re-establishment in Canaan at the return from Babylon. The prophet is commanded to become reconciled to Gomer, though she had proved unfaithful to him, (as predicted chap. i. 2,) ver. 1. He obeys the command, and purchases her from the individual with whom she was living in adultery, but stipulates that she was to wait for a lengthened period before she could be restored to the enjoyment of her conjugal rights, 2, 3. In the two last verses, the symbolical proceeding is explained of a long period during which the Hebrews were to live without the celebration of their ancient rites, and at the same time be free from all idolatrous practices. The direct prediction respecting their conversion to the Messiah, ver. 5, clearly proves, that their condition during the present dispersion is intended.

1 And Jehovah said unto me: Go again, love a woman beloved by
   a friend, yet an adulteress, according as Jehovah loveth the children
   of Israel, though they have turned to other gods, and love grape
2 cakes.   So I bought her to myself for fifteen pieces of silver, and

1. עוֹד, *again*, obviously refers back to
chap. i. 2. The transaction here commanded, bearing so near a resemblance
to what is enjoined in that chapter, has
occasioned nearly the same diversity of
interpretation. To me there appears no
consistent method of explaining it but
that which assumes an identity of the
female here specified with Gomer, whom
the prophet had previously married.
For, first, such construction is absolutely
required by the analogy. It was Israel
that stood in the relation of wife to
Jehovah from first to last. No other
nation was admitted to the same relation.
Secondly, the female is one already
married, but who had proved unfaithful;
which was precisely the case with Israel.
Thirdly, except she had been the prophet's own wife, who had become unfaithful to him, there would be no point
in comparing his love to her with that
borne by Jehovah to idolatrous Israel.
Fourthly, a command to love the wife of
another man, who, notwithstanding her
infidelity, was still attached to her, would
be totally repugnant to every idea of
moral justice and propriety. Lastly, the
command is not קַח, *take*, as in the
former instance, chap. i. 2, the usual
formula by which marriage is expressed;
but אֱהַב, *love*, i. e. renew thy kindness to
her; receive her back into thy house
and make kind provision for her. This
view of the passage is decidedly adopted
by Ewald in his *Propheten des Alten
Bundes*, recently published.
The words לֵךְ אֱהַב אִשָּׁה אֲהֻבַת רֵעַ וּמְנָאָפֶת,
are equivalent to, " Go, love thy wife, to
whom, though an adultress, thou art
attached;" but the indefinite form אִשָּׁה,
a wife, is purposely selected, instead of
אִשְׁתְּךָ, *thy wife*, in order to intimate the
state of separation in which they lived.
For the same purpose רֵעַ, *a friend*, or
companion, is used, and not אִישָׁהּ, *her
husband;* it being here employed not so
much as a term of endearment, as indicating that, whatever might be his disposition towards her, they were not living

on the same terms as formerly. Comp.
for this acceptation of רֵעַ, Jer. iii. 20.
The LXX. mistaking the word for רַע,
evil, and taking אהבת for the Benon. אַהֲבַת,
render ἀγαπῶσαν πονηρά; for which the

Syr. has ܐܝܕܐ ܕܪܚܡܐ ܘܓܝܪܐ

ܚܣܝܬܐ, *an adulterous woman who
loveth evil things.* The words כְּאַהֲבַת
יְהוָֹה וגו׳, are to be connected with אֲהֻבַת
רֵעַ, and not with אֱהַב. The kind feeling
of the prophet towards his faithless
wife corresponded, as a type, to the
love of God towards the idolatrous
Israelites. The sentence just quoted in
part, as well as the words פֹּנִים אֶל־אֱלֹהִים
אֲחֵרִים, form only two out of numerous
instances in which Hosea uses the language of the Pentateuch, as Hävernick
has shown in his *Handbuch der histor.-
crit. Einleit. in das A. T.* 1 Theil. 2 Ab-
theil. p. 608. אֲשִׁישֵׁי עֲנָבִים, have been
variously interpreted. LXX. πέμματα
μετὰ σταφίδος or σταφίδων, *baked meats
with raisins.* Aq. renders the former
word by παλαιά, evidently reading יְשִׁישֵׁי.
According to the Hexap. Syr., Theod.

adopts the same rendering: ܠܚܡܐܕܒܣܝܡ

ܠܚܡܐ ܕ. Symm. ἀκάρπους; Vulg.

vinacia uvarum; Syr. ܐܦܩܐ ܘܐܒܫܡܐ

placenta uvis passis condita. Junius,
Tremellius, and others, have *flagons of
wine*, as in our common version. The
word אֲשִׁישָׁין is employed by Jonathan in
his Targ. on Exod. xvi. 31, to express
the meaning of צַפִּיחִית, *a flat cake.* The
most probable derivation is from אָשַׁשׁ, *to
press, compress;* and the meaning will
be, pressed cakes of dried grapes. Such
cakes are highly esteemed in the East,
on account of their sweet taste, and
doubtless formed part of the offerings
presented to idols, and afterwards eaten
at idolatrous feasts.
2. Because the purchase of wives was, as

3 for an homer and an half of barley. And I said unto her: Thou
   shalt remain for me many days; thou shalt not commit lewdness,
4 nor become any man's: and I also will remain for thee. For the
   children of Israel shall remain many days without a king, and

it still is, no uncommon thing in Eastern
countries, (see Michaelis on the Laws of
Moses, Art. LXXXV.; Grant's Nestorians, p. 214; Perkins's Eight Years in
Persia, p. 236,) most expositors have
supposed that such a transaction is intended in this place. The fact, however,
that the price here specified, one half in
money, and the other half in grain, was
the exact amount of what was allowed
for a female slave, Exod. xxi. 32, induces
the belief that the payment was made
by the prophet for the liberation of his
own wife, who had become the property
of the person with whom she had been
living in adultery. The sum was too
parsimonious to have been given as a
dowry. The signification of *buying* as
attaching to כָּרָה, is sufficiently established by Deut. ii. 6, and Job xl. 30,
(Eng. version, xli. 6,) and the use of the

Arab. كَرَى, Conj. vi. and viii., *conduxit,
rem*, LXX. ἐμισθωσάμην. Hengstenberg's attempt to explain it here of
digging, in the sense of boring the ear
in token of a state of slavery, is unsuccessful. A לֵתֶךְ, *lethek*, according to the
Rabbins, contained fifteen seahs, or half
an homer. Theod. γομὸρ ἀλφιτῶν;
Symm. θύλακος κριθῶν; but the other
Greek versions, ἡμίκορον, *half a cor*,
which was equal to an homer. The
LXX. unaccountably have νέβελ οἴνου.
The repetition of שְׂעֹרִים, is not unusual
in Hebrew, but the abbreviated form of
expression is better English.

3. יָשַׁב, properly signifies *to sit*, but
likewise *to dwell, remain*, &c. לֹא תִזְנִי
explains its meaning here to be a re-
fraining from all cohabitation with others.
לְ, and אֵלַיִךְ, are correlates; and וְגַם אֲנִי
forms an antithesis; "while I, on the
other hand," &c. As the wife of the
prophet was to continue for a long time
in a state of separation equally from
paramours and from her husband, and
he was likewise to form no connexion
with any other woman, so the Israelites
should long live without serving either

false gods or Jehovah; while, on his
part, he would enter into no national
relationship to any other people. This
application of the symbol is distinctly
marked by לְ, and by the resumption of
יָשַׁב, ver. 4. The choice of the fuller
preposition אֶל, in אֵלַיִךְ, in preference to לְ,
seems designed to express the strength
of affection with which the symbolical
female was still to be regarded; consequently the powerful inclination of the
Lord towards his unfaithful people.

4. This verse describes a period of
great length, during which the Israelites
were to have no civil polity, either under
regal or princely rule; no sacred sacrifice; no idolatrous statue; no mediating
priest; and no images or tutelary deities.
This period cannot be that of their dispersion previous to the return from
Babylon; for the restoration of the wife
of the prophet prefigured the restoration
which took place on that return; agreeably to chap. ii. 19, 20, 23. It is true
that when they were brought back
along with the Jewish exiles, the Israelites had no more any civil or ecclesiastical polity of their own; neither did
they relapse into idolatry; but still, as
in common with their brethren, they
were subject to the same political rule,
and offered their sacrifices to Jehovah at
Jerusalem, it follows that the days here
predicted must be those which have succeeded to the times of the Asmoncæan
dynasty, or the dispersion consequent
upon the final destruction of Jerusalem.
During the protracted period of more
than eighteen centuries, (יָמִים רַבִּים) they
have been precisely in the circumstances
here predicted—separated from idolaters,
and professedly belonging to Jehovah,
yet never acknowledged by him in a
church relationship. They have neither
had a civil ruler, nor any of the consecrated offices and rites of their ancient
economy. Thus Kimchi on the passage,
ואלה הם ימי הגלות שאנחנו בו היום ואין לנו לא מלך
ולא שר מישראל כי ברשות הגוים אנחנו וברשות
מלכיהם ושריהם—"And these are the days
of our present captivity, for we have

without a prince, and without a sacrifice, and without a statue, and
5 without an ephod, and without images. Afterwards the children
of Israel shall return, and shall seek Jehovah their God, and

neither king nor prince of Israel, but
are under the rule of the nations, even
under the rule of their kings and their
princes." This interpretation, which
alone suits the views furnished by the
subject by the prophet, overturns the
hypothesis of Dr. Grant, that the Nestorian Christians are the remains of the
ten tribes. It cannot properly be said of
them that they have continued רַבִּים יָמִים,
in a state of separation from God, for they
received the gospel in the earliest ages
of Christianity. Some explain זֶבַח, both
of legitimate sacrifices and of such as
were offered to false gods; but the
grouping of this term with מַצֵּבָה, a statue,
as אֵפוֹד, ephod, following, is with תְּרָפִים,
teraphim, clearly shows that the prophet
meant the former restrictively. Kimchi
briefly explains : אין זבח לאל ואין מצבה לע״ז,
"without sacrifice to God, and without
an image for idolatrous worship." From
the prohibition Lev. xxvi. 1; Deut. xvi.
22, and the history, 2 Kings iii. 2; xvii.
10; x. 26, 27, it is manifest that מַצֵּבָה
does not stand for altar, as the ancient
versions render it, but denotes a statue
or image of some false deity. Comp.
Micah v. 13 (Hebr. 12.) אֵפוֹד, the ephod,
was that part of the high priest's dress
which was worn above the tunic and robe.
It consisted of two pieces which hung
down, the one in front over the breast,
and the other covering the back, and
both reaching to the middle of the thigh.
They were joined together on the shoulders by golden clasps, set in precious
stones, and fastened round the waist by
a girdle. In the breast-part was the
חֹשֶׁן, or pectoral, containing the Urim
and Thummim, by which divine responses
were vouchsafed to the Hebrews. According to the Jews, the ephod in its
complete state ceased with the captivity:
for they specify the Urim and Thummim
among the five things with respect to
which the first temple differed from the
second. LXX. ἱερατεία, priesthood,
which I doubt not the Hebrew term was
intended metonymically to denote in this
place. תְּרָפִים, the teraphim, were penates,
or household gods. They were used at

a very early period, as appears from the
history of Rachel, Gen. xxxi. 19, 30,
32, 34, 35. Comp. 1 Sam. xix. 13;
2 Kings xxiii. 24; Ezek. xxi. 21 (Hebr.
26); Zech. x. 2. That they were not
only kept as tutelary deities, but also
consulted for the purpose of obtaining
a knowledge of future events, appears
from several of the passages just quoted.
Hence the rendering of the LXX. δήλων.
The etymology of the word is altogether
uncertain.

5. At a period still subsequent to that
of their existence in the state just described, the Israelites (now amalgamated
with the Jews) are to be converted to
the true worship and service of Jehovah,
under the spiritual reign of our Saviour,
the promised Messiah. To him they
will then submit themselves, and richly
enjoy the blessings of divine grace,
communicated through his mediation.
That דָּוִיד, David, here means neither the
royal house of David, nor any human
monarch of that name who is yet to
reign over the Jews, as some have imagined, but the great Messiah himself,
appears evident from Scripture usage.
See Is. lv. 3, 4; Jer. xxx. 9; Ezek.
xxxiv. 23, 24; xxxvii. 24, 25. As the
name properly signifies The Beloved, it
quite accords with ὁ ἀγαπητὸς, Matt. iii.
17, and ὁ ἠγαπημένος, Eph. i. 6. Thus
the Targ. וְיִשְׁתַּמְעוּן לִמְשִׁיחָא בַר דָּוִד, "And
they shall obey Messiah the Son of
David." The following is the Rabbinical
interpretation :— אמרין אהן מלכא משיחא אם
מן חייא דוד שמיה ואם מן]רמכיה[הוא דוד שמיה
"The Rabbins say, that He is the king
Messiah; whether he be of the living,
his name is David, and whether he be
of the slain, his name is David." Be-
rachoth Jerus. in Raym. Martini Pugio
Fidei, fol. 277. See also the Rabbinical
Commentaries on the above passages in
Ezekiel. The use of אֶל, in the phrase
וּפָחֲדוּ אֶל־יְהוָה, and not מִן, or מִפְּנֵי, the
usual form, is intended to show that the
fear here specified is not of the kind
which "hath torment," and which causes
those who are under its influence to
recede from its object, but such fear as

David their king; and they shall tremblingly hasten to Jehovah
and to his goodness in the latter day.

attracts or induces them *to approach to
it.* This the addition וְאֶל־טוּבוֹ, "and *to*
his goodness," clearly shows. Comp.
Micah vii. 17. As, however, the idea
of fleeing or hastening from danger is
also implied in verbs signifying to fear,
I have rendered the word so as to
include both. In this way Rabbi Tanchum: ويقزعون اليه من كل ما يخاف
"they shall flee to him for help from all
that may be feared." Comp. Jer. xxxi.
12. LXX. ἐκστήσονται ἐπὶ τῷ Κυρίῳ
καὶ ἐπὶ τοῖς ἀγαθοῖς αὐτοῦ. Ewald
renders, *und werden beben zu Jahve und*

zu seinem Gute, u.s.w.; and Hitzig
explains, *bebend in freudiger Erwartung
werden sie herbeieilen.* While on the
one hand the Jews, under the influence
of alarm, shall be excited to flee from
the wrath to come, they shall be attracted
by the display of the divine goodness in
the mediation of Christ, to confide in
Him for all the blessings of salvation.
אַחֲרִית הַיָּמִים, *the last of the days,* i.e. the
days of the Messiah, as the Rabbins
interpret the phrase. See on Is. ii. 2,
where Kimchi says expressly, כל מקום
שנאמר באחרית הימים הוא ימות המשיח
"wherever it is said, 'In the last of the
days,' it means the days of the Messiah."

CHAPTER IV

The prophet now addresses himself more directly to the castigation of the flagrant
evils which abounded in the kingdom of Israel during the interregnum which
followed upon the death of Jeroboam, and the reigns of Zechariah, Shallum,
Menahem, and Pekahiah. He calls the attention of his countrymen to the
divine indignation, and the causes of it, 1, 2; denounces the judgments which
were about to be executed upon them, 3; describes their incorrigible character,
especially that of the priests, 4—11; and expatiates on the grossness of their
idolatrous practices, 12—14. A solemn warning is then given to the members
of the Jewish kingdom not to allow themselves to be influenced by their wicked
example, 15—19.

---

1 HEAR the word of Jehovah, ye children of Israel!
  For Jehovah hath a controversy with the inhabitants of the land;
  Because there is no truth, nor kindness, nor knowledge of God
  in the land.

1, 2. The initiatory words are those
of Hosea, summoning attention to the
divine message which he was commissioned to deliver. בְּנֵי יִשְׂרָאֵל is equivalent
to בֵּית יִשְׂרָאֵל, ch. v. 1; שִׁבְטֵי יִשְׂרָאֵל, ch. v. 9;

and frequently to יִשְׂרָאֵל and אֶפְרַיִם; and
all these different epithets are used of
the kingdom of the ten tribes in contradistinction to יְהוּדָה and בֵּית יְהוּדָה,
which designate the tribes of Judah

2   There is nothing but swearing and lying,
    And murder, and theft, and adultery ;
    They have burst forth,
    And blood reacheth to blood.

3   Therefore shall the land mourn,
    And every one that dwelleth in it shall languish ;
    With the beasts of the field and the fowls of heaven ;
    And the fishes of the sea also shall be removed.

4   Yet let no man contend with, nor reprove another ;
    For thy people are like those that contend with the priest.

5   Therefore thou shalt fall by day,
    And the prophet also shall fall with thee by night ;
    And I will destroy thy mother.

and Benjamin. רִיב signifies here *ground of complaint*, or *judicial proceeding.* LXX. κρίσις. The wickedness which abounded is first set forth negatively, and then positively, under certain items; and the infinitive absolute is employed with great effect, as expressing more emphatically, by its abstract form, the heinousness of the evils described. The force of this I have given in a free translation. Ewald improperly limits the signification of the verb פָּרַץ in this place to the act of *breaking into* houses; but the metaphor seems rather to be taken from the bursting forth of a torrent, which, in its progress, spreads wider and wider, and sweeps all before it. The plural form דָּמִים, *blood*, has also a degree of emphasis, signifying much bloodshed. What the prophet means is, that murder was so common, that no space was left as it were between its acts. LXX. αἵματα ἐφ᾽ αἵμασι μίσγουσι. Coverdale, *one bloudgiltynes foloweth another.* And Rittershusius powerfully in his poetical metaphrase :—

    "—— sic sanguine sanguis
    Truditur, et scelerum nullus finisve
    modusve est."

See 2 Kings xv.; Micah vii. 2.

3. Comp. Is. xix. 8; xxiv. 4; Joel i. 10, 12. אֻמְלַל, in the Pulal Conj., is usually employed after אָבַל, in order more forcibly to describe the calamitous state of a country. בְּ here signifies *with, extending to, accompanied by,* and includes what follows in the general predicate. Comp. Gen. vii. 21. אָסַף, is cognate with סוּף, and signifies *to gather up, away, back, take away,* as well as simply to collect together, Zeph. i. 2, 3. LXX. ἐκλείψουσιν ; Syr. ܢܣܘܦܘܢ ; Targ. יְעֻרוּן.—יָם, signifies not only what we call the *sea,* but any lesser collection of water, as pools, and even rivers. See Is. xix. 5.

4. אַל is here prohibitory, and not simply negative, as some have rendered it. The introduction of the sentence by אַךְ, *yet, nevertheless,* is designed to show the hopeless character of the persons spoken of. All reproof on the part of their friends or neighbours generally would prove fruitless, seeing they had reached a degree of hardihood, which was only equalled by the contumacy of those who refused to obey the priest, when he gave judgment in the name of the Lord, Deut. xvii. 12. The passage is thus quite plain, and requires no transposition or emendation of the words as adopted by Houbigant, Newcome, and Boothroyd. מְרִיבֵי כֹהֵן is the same as if it were מְרִיבִים אֶת הַכֹּהֵן. Comp. כִּמְסִינֵי, גְּבוּל, chap. v. 10. All the ancient versions, except the LXX. and Aq. read עַמֶּךָ. The Hexap. Syr. has ܟܣܐ ܘܡ ܘܡܠܟ.

5. By a sudden transition to the second person, the prophet addresses

6 My people is destroyed for lack of knowledge :
  Because thou hast rejected knowledge,
  I will also reject thee, so that thou shalt not be a priest to me ;
  Because thou hast forgotten the law of thy God,
  I also will forget thy children.
7 According to their increase, so they sinned against me ;
  I will change their glory into shame.
8 They devour the sin-offering of my people,
  And long for their iniquity.

himself directly to his guilty people, and predicts their utter destruction. הַיּוֹם, Kimchi, Drusius, Œcolamp., Grotius, and Ewald, improperly render "to-day." As contrasted here with לַיְלָה, *night*, it is equivalent to בַּיּוֹם, *by day*. Comp. Neh. iv. 16, (Eng. Version, 22.) That the article is not repeated before לַיְלָה, may be owing to the common adverbial use of this noun without it. The false prophets by whom the Israelites had been encouraged in wicked practices should render them no assistance in the season of calamity, but should be themselves involved in the same common ruin. דָּמִיתִי, the LXX. renders ὡμοίωσα ; and several translate, "I have reduced to silence ; " but the verb is obviously used in the sense of *destroying*, as נִדְמוּ is, ver. 6. Comp. Zeph. i 11. By אִמֶּךָ, *thy mother*, the Israelitish state is meant, of which the citizens were the children. See chap. ii. 1. Thus Kimchi, Jerome, Grotius, Michaelis, Rosenmüller, and Maurer. Others, as Cornelius à Lapide, Houbigant, Capellus, Pococke, Bauer, and Newcome, suppose the metropolis to be intended.

6. מִבְּלִי הַדַּעַת, having here the article before the noun, and occurring in connexion with הַדַּעַת, immediately following, is not to be taken in the sense of *unexpectedly*, as מִבְּלִי דַעַת is, Is. v. 13, but strictly means that destitution of the true knowledge of God which was the source of the sins now about to be punished. This ignorance is principally charged upon the religious teachers of the nation, each of whom is directly addressed in אַתָּה הַדַּעַת מָאַסְתָּ. Thus Pagninus, *O sacerdos ;* which Dathe also inserts in his text. The persons addressed pretended to be priests of

Jehovah, though they taught the people to combine with his worship that of pagan deities, or at least that of the golden calves, which, no doubt, paved the way for the universal spread of idolatry in Israel. The position adopted by Horsley, that the Jewish high-priest is intended, does not suit the connexion. The third א in אֶמְאָסְאֵךָ, is not found in a great number of Kennicott's and De Rossi's MSS., nor in some of the earlier printed editions ; in others it is marked as redundant, and some few have אמאסך קרי. The antitheses in this verse are pointed and forcible. כִּי is understood as repeated in וַתִּשְׁכַּח, and וְ before אֶשְׁכַּח.

7. As the priests are obviously the nominative to the verbs in the three following verses, and form the subject of discourse in that which precedes, they must likewise be the persons spoken of in this. It has been queried whether the increase was in number or in wealth, power, &c. Michaelis thinks the latter is meant ; still the former may be included, in harmony with the mention made of their children, ver. 6. In proportion as they multiplied in numbers and grew in influence, they promoted the increase of idolatry ; but the wealth and dignity (כָּבוֹד) which they acquired, and which they thus prostituted, should be destroyed by foreigners, by whom they would be carried into captivity. כְּרֻבָּם, and כִּבְנֹדָם, form a slight paronomasia.

8. הַטָּאת here signifies *sin-offering*, as it frequently does in the Levitical code. So Kimchi ; and it is thus rendered in Pococke's Arab. MS. قربن خطاء قومي

, ياكلون and Castalio, *piaculo*. The

9   Therefore it shall be, like people, like priest;
    I will even punish them according to their ways,
    And requite them for their deeds.
10 For they shall eat, but shall not be satisfied;
    They shall commit lewdness, but shall not increase:
    Because they have ceased to regard Jehovah.
11   Lewdness and wine and new wine take away the heart.
12 My people consult their stock;
    Their staff also announceth to them:

priests greedily devoured what the people brought for the expiation of their sins; and instead of endeavouring to put a stop to abounding iniquity, only wished it to increase, in order that they might profit by the multitude of the victims presented for sacrifice. נָשָׂא נֶפֶשׁ, *to lift up the animal soul* for any thing, means to *lust after it*, long, or have a strong desire for it, Deut. xxiv. 15; Jer. xxii. 27. וֹ in נַפְשׁוֹ, is used distributively to express the fact that such was the character of each of the priests. The reading נַפְשָׁם, found in ten MSS., originally in seven more, and perhaps in one, and supported by the LXX., Syr., Targ., Vulg., and Arab., most probably originated in emendation. Not unfrequently a proposition commences with the plural, and ends with the singular, and *vice versâ*.

9. Comp. Is. xxiv. 2. The rank and wealth of the priests would not exempt them from sharing the same fate with the rest of the nation.

10. וְאָכְלוּ is a resumption of יֹאכְלוּ, ver. 8.—הִזְנוּ is here used intransitively, as in ver. 18; v. 3, and is to be understood literally of the sensual indulgences of the Israelitish teachers, as the verb יִפְרֹצוּ shows. For the signification *to abound in children*, as attaching to this verb, see Gen. xxviii. 14. Saadius, Arnoldi, (Blumen alt-hebraisch. Dichtk.) and Horsley, disjoin לִשְׁמֹר from the preceding verb, and connect it with the following nouns, thus:—

"They have forsaken Jehovah,
    Giving heed to fornication," &c.

But, notwithstanding the apparent force of the bishop's remarks, there is something so repugnant to Hebrew usage in the combination לִשְׁמֹר זְנוּת וְיַיִן וְתִירוֹשׁ, *to*

observe fornication, and wine, and new wine, that it is altogether inadmissible. Though the verb שָׁמַר may in no other passage take יְהוָה for its object, yet it takes הַבְלֵי שָׁוְא, *lying vanities,* i. e. idols, Ps. xxxi. 7; Jonah ii. 9; in which latter passage it is connected with עָוֶן, as in the present case. The division of the words found in our common version is that of the Hexap. Syr. ܘܐܡܪ ܠܐܘܢ ܐܠܗܐ; and the Slavonic; and is approved by Michaelis, Tingstadius, Newcome, Dathe, Boothroyd, De Wette, Hitzig, and Ewald.

11. This verse has the appearance of a moral adage. The influence of habits of impurity and intoxication in blunting the moral feelings, and weakening the intellectual powers, is a well-established fact in the history of man.

"Nox et amor vinumque nihil moderabile suadent:
    Illa pudor vacat, liber amorque metu."
                                Ovid.

"Nox, vinum, mulier; nihil perniciosius adolescentulo."
                                Plaut.

There can be little doubt that the prophet has specially in view the impure and bacchanalian orgies which were connected with the Syrian idolatry. For the prevalence of drunkenness in Ephraim, see Is. xxviii. 1; Amos iv. 1.

12. The LXX., and most versions which follow them, connect עַמִּי with לֵב, at the end of the preceding verse; a mode of construction adopted by Michaelis and Dathe, but otherwise disapproved by modern translators. The Syr., Targ., and Vulg. divide properly. Hosea here adduces proofs of the mental hebetude to which the sinful practices of

For a lewd spirit hath caused them to err;
And they have lewdly departed from under their God.

13 They sacrifice on the tops of the mountains,
And offer incense upon the hills;
Under the oak, and the poplar, and the terebinth,
Because their shade is pleasant:
Therefore your daughters commit lewdness,
And your daughters-in-law adultery.

14 I will not punish your daughters when they commit lewdness,
Nor your daughters-in-law when they commit adultery;
For they themselves go aside with harlots,

the Israelitish people had reduced them —their application to their wooden idols and images for oracular counsel, and their use of rhabdomancy or divination by rods. Leo Juda: "ligno suo oracula quærit." That by עֵץ, *wood*, is here meant an idol made of such material, the connexion shows. Comp. Jer. ii. 27; x. 8; Hab. ii. 19. מַקֵּל is properly *a shoot* or *twig*, then a *rod*, *walking staff*, &c. Occurring as it does here, in reference to an idolatrous or superstitious practice, it denotes such a staff employed for purposes of divination. Some have been of opinion that it is to be taken as strictly parallel to עֵץ, and that a staff is meant which had the image of some god carved upon it; but the use of the phrase יַגִּיד לֹו, *announceth, pointeth out*, shows that a divining rod is meant. Rhabdomancy (ῥαβδομαντεία) was very common among the ancient idolaters, as it has been in later times in different countries of the East. The ancient Arabs consulted their gods in this way, taking two rods, on one of which was inscribed *God bids*, and on the other *God forbids*, drawing them out of the case into which they were put, and acting agreeably to the direction which first came forth. See Pococke, Specimen. Hist. Arab. p. 327. Maimonides quotes an ancient book entitled Siphri, in which a diviner is defined to be one who takes his staff, and inquires, Shall I go? or, Shall I not go? The Runic wands of the Scandinavian nations, on which were inscribed mysterious characters, and which were used for magical purposes, appear to have originated in the more ancient divination of Asia. רוּחַ

וּנוּנִים, lit. *a spirit of whoredoms*, i. e. a powerful impetus to commit acts of idolatry. Instead of the simple form הִתְעָה, some few MSS., the Babyl. Talmud, the Syr., Vulg., and Targ. read הִתְעָם; while the LXX. and Arab. read הִתְעוּ. For מִתַּחַת אֱלֹהֵיהֶם, comp. Numb. v. 19, 20; Ezek. xxiii. 5; and ὕπανδρος, Rom. vii. 2.

13. Mountains and hills were selected by idolaters on which to erect their altars, and offer their sacrifices, on account of their supposed proximity to the host of heaven, which they worshipped. That this custom was very ancient, appears from the prohibition, Deut. xii. 2. For imitating it, the Hebrews are frequently reproved, Is. lxv. 7; Jer. iii. 6; Ezek. xviii. 11. יְזַבֵּחוּ, being in Piel, expresses the eagerness and frequency with which the Israelites offered their idolatrous sacrifices. They also selected groves of oak, terebinth, &c. for purposes of superstition and idolatry, under whose umbrageous cover they might at once be screened from the heat of the sun, and indulge in lascivious practices. The sacrifice of female virtue which was required in the religious service of the Phœnician goddess Astarte, seems clearly to be referred to in this and the following verse. לִבְנֶה, LXX. λεύκη, *the white poplar*, from לָבַן, *to be white*.

14. Kuinoel, and others, taking לֹא, as standing for הֲלֹא, read the first part of the verse interrogatively, which is not unsupported by examples in Hebrew usage. It seems better, however, to understand it here as a simple negative, and the meaning to be that, as the

And sacrifice with prostitutes :
And as for the undiscerning people, they shall be overthrown.

15   Though thou, O Israel, art lewd,
Yet let not Judah be found guilty ;
Yea, come ye not to Gilgal,
Neither go ye up to Beth-aven,
Nor use the oath, " Jehovah liveth."

parents and husbands indulged in the flagitious practices here described, Jehovah would not make examples of the females, or suffer them to be punished, as if they alone were guilty ; but would visit with condign punishment their natural protectors, who not only abandoned them to seduction, but themselves rioted in the same wickedness. Thus Munster : "Durissimè animadvertam in parentes et sponsos, ut filiæ et sponsæ eorum punitæ videantur esse extra pœnam." The transition from the second to the third person, for the purpose of more graphically exhibiting the subject of discourse, is not without examples. See Is. xxii. 16. The use of the separate pronoun הֵם, also adds to the emphasis of the language. פָּרַד, in Piel, strongly marks the studied withdrawment of the Israelites from the assembled throngs, to such places as were devoted to scenes of impurity ; while זָנָה, in the same conjugation, signifies in this connexion, to commit lewdness as an act of idolatrous devotion. Between זנות, and קְדֵשׁוֹת, there seems to be this difference, that the former were ordinary females, who prostituted themselves for gain, but the latter those who devoted themselves to the service of Astarte, by offering their persons to be violated in her temples at the sacred festivals. See Selden de Diis Syris, Synt. ii. cap. 2 ; Herodot. lib. i. cap. 199 ; Euseb. Vit. Constantin. lib. iii. cap. 35 ; Spencer de Leg. Heb. lib. ii. cap. 22 and 23 ; Lucian de Dea Syra. Of this latter term, the mas. קְדֵשִׁים, catamites, occurs, 1 Kings xiv. 24 ; xv. 12 ; xxii. 47 ; and in the ancient book of Job, chap. xxxvi. 14, which shows at how very early a period such abominations obtained. It likewise occurs in both genders in the prohibition, Deut. xxiii. 18. To these practices the LXX. doubtless had respect in rendering the

word τετελεσμένων, initiated. Its derivation from קָדַשׁ, to be sacred, consecrated, or destined to the service of the temple, confirms our interpretation.—לָבַשׁ ; Syr.

ܚܒܠ, concitavit ; Arab. لَبَط, conjecit

in terram aliquem ; in Niph. to be cast down, overthrown, or the like. The verb occurs only here, and Prov. x. 8, 10, where see Schultens.

15. A solemn warning to the Jewish kingdom to beware of mixing itself up with that of Israel in the practice of idolatry. Here זָנָה, to commit lewdness, is again used figuratively. אָשַׁם, properly signifies to contract guilt, or become subject to its consequences. גִּלְגָּל, Gilgal, was a town situated between the Jordan and Jericho, near the confines of the kingdom of Samaria. It was regarded as a holy place as early as the days of Joshua, chap. v. 15 ; and sacrifices were offered there to Jehovah in those of Samuel, 1 Sam. x. 8, 13 ; xv. 21, 33. In process of time, however, it came to be converted into a place of idolatrous worship, Amos iv. 4, 5 ; Hos. ix. 15 ; xii. 11. בֵּית אָוֶן, Beth-aven, i. e. the house of vanity or idols, a name given by the minor prophets, by way of contempt, to Bethel, i. e. the house of God, a place sacred to true religion in the time of the patriarchs, and the judges ; but afterwards selected by Jeroboam as the principal seat of the worship of the golden calves, 1 Kings xii. 29, 32, 33 ; xiii. 1 ; Amos iii. 14 ; vii. 10, 13 ; Jer. xlviii. 13. It originally belonged to the tribe of Benjamin, but was taken by that of Ephraim, Judges i. 22—25. That there was a city of the name of Beth-aven near to Bethel, appears from Josh. vii. 2, which may have suggested the appropriation of the name to the latter. LXX. οἶκον Ὤν, reading אָן, the native

Since Israel is refractory, like a refractory heifer;
Jehovah will now feed them, like a lamb in a large place.

17 Ephraim is joined to idols;
Leave him to himself.

18 When their carousal is over, they indulge in lewdness;
Her shields are enamoured of infamy.

name of Heliopolis. Aq. and Symm. οἶκον ἀνωφελῆ; Theod. οἶκον ἀδικίας; and with this the Arab. agrees بيت الظلم, *the house of iniquity*. Comp. Amos iv. 4; v. 5. From the warning here given to the Jews not to participate with the Israelites in their idolatry, it is evident the prophecy was delivered at a time when they were comparatively free from that evil. The prohibition not to swear by the formula חַי יְהוָֹה, respects the combination of the divine name with those of idols, or the profession of attachment to Jehovah, if the persons addressed were guilty of idolatry. Comp. Zeph. i. 5. That it was otherwise lawful to use it, appears from Jer. iv. 2. Comp. Deut. x. 20.

16. The metaphor is here taken from a heifer that obstinately refuses to be yoked. Thus the Syr. ܥܶܓܠܳܐ ܡܳܪܳܕ. For the force of סָרַר, comp. Deut. xxi. 18. The latter hemistich contains the language of irony. As lambs are fond of ranging at large, but are in danger of being lost or devoured, so God threatens to remove the Israelites into a distant and large country, where they would be separated from those with whom they associated in idolatrous worship, and thus be left solitary and exposed as in a wilderness. The phrase רָעָה בַּמֶּרְחָב, *to feed in a large place*, is elsewhere used in a good sense, Is. xxx. 23.

17. אֶפְרַיִם, *Ephraim*, as the most numerous and powerful of the tribes, and that in which the kingdom was established, is put for all the ten. חָבוּר, from חָבַר, *to be joined, closely united, adhere to*, to be allied to by voluntary choice, Gen. xiv. 3. In this last sense the term is here used. The Israelites had volun-

tarily addicted themselves to the service of idols, and thus identified themselves with their interests. While the word עֲצַבִּים, *idols*, suggests the idea of their being merely the fabrication of human labour, it also intimates the pain or sorrow resulting from idolatry. The root has both significations. הַנַּח־לּוֹ strongly implies the obstinacy and incorrigible character of the ten tribes, and indignantly abandons them to their fate. They are irreclaimably devoted to the gods of the heathen: let them take their own way, and reap the consequences of their perverse choice. Their case is desperate. Comp. Jer. vii. 16; Ezek. xx. 39. Thus, Tanchum, Jarchi, Kimchi, Calvin, Tarnovius, Zanchius, Coverdale, Drusius, Lively, Leo Juda, Pococke, Kuinoel, Michaelis, Tingstadius, Newcome, Stuck, and Ewald. Others, as the Targ., Jerome, Mercer, Diodati, Grotius, Rosenmüller, Maurer, &c., regard the words as simply containing a warning to the inhabitants of Judah to keep aloof from, and take no part in the idolatries of the Ephraimites. The LXX. ἔθηκεν ἑαυτῷ σκάνδαλα, reading הניח in the preterite, and supplying the idea of idols from the preceding part of the verse.

18. Before סָר, the particle אִם *when*, is to be supplied, which in poetry, for the sake of conciseness and energy, is frequently omitted. For the acceptation *past, passed away, over*, &c. comp. 1 Sam. xv. 32, סָר מַר־הַמָּוֶת. Horsley, Ewald, and some others, are of opinion that סָר means *rapid, degenerated, sour*, &c., but less aptly. The meaning is, that no sooner were their compotations over than they indulged in excessive lewdness. Instead of סׇבְאָם, *their drink, drinking bout*, one of De Rossi's MSS. has originally read סוֹבְאִים, *drunkards*; another צְבָאָם, *their host*; and one of Kennicott's סְבָאִים, *Sabæans*; but none of these variations suits the entire construction of the verse.

19 The wind hath'bound her up in its wings,
     That they may be ashamed of their sacrifices.

The LXX. strangely, ἠρέτισε Χαναναίους, which the Arab., as usual, follows. The impurity in which, when inflamed with liquor, they indulged, was most probably that connected with the worship of Venus. To express the excess to which it was carried, the verb is first put in the infinitive absolute, and then repeated in the finite form. הֵבִי is not separately expressed in the LXX., the Arab., or in either of the Syriac versions; though it cannot hence be inferred that it was not in the Hebrew text. It is wanting, however, in three of Kennicott's MSS. If it did not originate in some copyist having written the two last syllables of the preceding word over again, it must be regarded as having originally formed part of that word in the reduplicate form אֲהֵבוּהָבוּ; in which, not only is the second syllable of the verb repeated (אֲהֵבְהֵבוּ), but the pronominal sufformative is retained in the middle of the word, and the first radical (א) rejected on that account in the reduplication. Such form is of extremely rare occurrence: צְמִתָּתוּנִי, lit. *they destroy, destroy me,* Ps. lxxxviii. 17, being the only other instance of the kind with which I am acquainted. In this way the form is partly accounted for by the ancient Jewish grammarian Abuwalid Ibn Jannahi, as quoted by Pococke. What confirms this view of the reduplicate form is the use of הַבְּהָבִים, a gemination somewhat resembling it, by our prophet, chap. viii. 13. The rendering *give ye,* as if it were the imperative of יָהַב, proposed by Abenezra and Kimchi, and adopted by our translators, is not so suitable to the connexion.

Maurer; mirificè amant ignominiam: Ewald; es lieben lieben Schmach seine Schilde. Kuinoel very unjustifiably omits הֵבִי in his Heb. Text. קָלוֹן, *shame,* a collective abstract noun, expressive of the infamous acts connected with idolatrous worship. מָגִנִּים, *shields,* are tropically used for *princes,* as the natural protectors of their people, here and Ps. xlvii. 10. The feminine suffix ה, refers to אֶרֶץ, understood; the inhabitants being meant.

19. By an expressive figure, borrowed from the sudden force with which any thing is carried off by the wind, the prophet announces the suddenness and violence with which the ten tribes should be removed from their land. The combination כַּנְפֵי רוּחַ, *wings of the wind,* is too firmly established in Hebrew usage, see Ps. xviii. 11; civ. 3, to allow either of the acceptation *spirit* or *vanity* being given to רוּחַ, or that of *borders* to כְּנָפַיִם in this place. רוּחַ being of both genders, accounts for the masculine of the verb, and the feminine pron. affix. For אוֹתָהּ, two of De Rossi's MSS., and the Vat. and Alex. copies of the LXX. read אַתָּה, which gives no suitable sense. In the distant countries of the Medes by whom all image-worship was held in abomination, the exiles would be brought to a due sense of the wickedness and absurdity of their conduct. ﬩, in וְיֵבֹשׁוּ, is used τελικῶς. Jer. xlviii. 13. *Sacrifices* are here put by synecdoche for the whole system of idolatry in which they indulged. For the reading מִמִּנְבְּחֹתָם, *of their altars,* adopted by Newcome, there is no authority except the Targ. and Syr.

CHAPTER V

This chapter commences with an objurgation of the priests and the royal family, as the principal seducers of the nation to idolatry, 1, 2. Then follows a description of the unblushing wickedness of the people, interspersed with denunciations of impending punishment, 3—7. The approach of the divine judgments is ordered to be proclaimed, and their certainty declared, 8, 9. The prophet then abruptly turns to the two tribes and a half whose guilt and punishment he denounces; yet so as to show that his predictions were chiefly directed against the northern kingdom, the rulers of which, like those of Judah, instead of looking to Jehovah for deliverance from civil calamities, applied in vain for foreign assistance, 10—14. The 15th verse sets forth the certainty and the beneficial effects of the divine judgments.

---

1 HEAR this, O ye priests!
　And hearken, O house of Israel!
　Give ear, likewise, O house of the king!
　For the sentence is against you,
　Because ye are a snare at Mizpah,
　And a net spread upon Tabor.
2 The apostates slaughter to excess,
　But I will inflict chastisement on them all.

---

1. בֵּית יִשְׂרָאֵל, *house of Israel*, i.e. the ten tribes. בֵּית הַמֶּלֶךְ, *house of the king*, i.e. the king and his court. From the references made to the idolatry and punishment of Judah in this and the following chapter, it would appear that the king whom Hosea had specifically in view was Pekah, the son of Remaliah; since it was in the reign of Ahaz, who was cotemporary with him, that idol-worship was carried to such a height in that kingdom as to call for the calamities inflicted upon it by the confederate forces of Israel and Syria, as well as by the king of Assyria. By לָכֶם הַמִּשְׁפָּט is not meant, as the Targ. interprets, followed by Abenezra, Kimchi, Abarbanel, Pagninus, Junius, Tremellius, and others, that it belonged to them to know and execute justice, but that the judgment or punishment was directed against them. They had merited it, and it was now coming upon them. LXX. πρὸς ὑμᾶς ἐστὶ τὸ κρίμα. Thus most Christian expositors. מִצְפָּה, *Mizpah*. As there were several places of this name, some degree of uncertainty attaches to it as occurring here; but as the object of the prophet seems to be to set forth the means employed for seducing the whole of the ten tribes to idolatry, it is more probable that he had in his eye Mizpah of Gilead, on the east of the Jordan,

just as he specifies mount Tabor to the west of that river. See Judges x. 17; xi. 29. On both of these elevated positions false worship had been established for the purpose of ensnaring the inhabitants of the adjacent regions. The means employed to bring them over to it are compared to the snares and nets used for catching birds and wild beasts upon the mountains. By metonymy, the leaders of the people are spoken of as such nets and snares, because of their bad example, and the influence which they otherwise exerted for evil.

2. שַׁחֲטָה, *slaughtering*, the infinitive absolute, with ה paragogic, of שָׁחַט, *to kill*, for food or sacrifice. Here, from its close connexion with the preceding verse, it has the latter signification. Some think murder is meant; but this is less likely, though the verb is also used in this sense in other places. שַׁחֲטָה הֶעְמִיקוּ, lit. *they deepen to slaughter*, i.e. by a peculiar idiom, *they slaughter to excess*, kill an immense number of sacrificial victims. Comp. הֶעְמִיקוּ סָרָה; Is. xxxi. 6. שֵׂטִים, *apostates*, the Benoni participle of שׂוּט, *to turn aside, decline from the right way, apostatise;* as לֵצִים, *scoffers*, from לוּץ, *to scoff.* Comp. Ps. xl. 5, שָׂטֵי כָזָב, *those that turn aside to* falsehood; and עֹשֵׂי־סֶטֶים, Ps. ci. 3. Two or three MSS., the edit. of Soncin., and

3 I know Ephraim,
   Israel is not hid from me;
   Surely now thou committest lewdness, O Ephraim,
   Israel is defiled.
4 They frame not their deeds
   To return to their God;
   For a lewd spirit is within them,
   And they regard not Jehovah.
5   Yea, the pride of Israel testifieth to his face;
   Therefore Israel and Ephraim shall fall through their iniquity;
   Judah also shall fall with them.

a few others, have ס instead of שׁ, in our text. Syr. ܐܣܛܝ, *seduxit*, ܡܣܛܝܢܘܬܐ *declinatio, apostasia*. The idolatrous Israelites multiplied their sacrifices in order that they might enjoy prosperity under the protection of the deities to whom' they offered them; but Jehovah here declares that none of them should escape the punishment which he was about to inflict upon them. Before מוּסָר supply אֶהְיֶה. The ancient versions are here greatly at fault, from their authors having supposed that the reference to hunters is still continued in this verse.

3. *Ephraim*, as distinguished from *Israel*, means the tribe of Ephraim, from which most of the apostate kings sprang, and in which idolatry most abounded. By Israel, the other nine tribes are meant. As having incurred the more aggravated guilt, the former is here addressed in the second person. Two of Kennicott's MSS. indeed, and one of De Rossi's, originally read הִזְנֵיתָ; and one of Kennicott's has נִטְמֵאתָה for נִטְמָא, but both are, in all probability, from the hand of correctors. עַתָּה is here used figuratively. The polluting influence of the Ephraimites was felt through the whole nation. To express an assertion more strongly the Hebrews put it first in the form of an affirmative, and then in that of a negative. עַתָּה, *now*, is not without emphasis; pointing out the undeniable fact that they had been the cause of the spread of idolatry.

4. The language here changes to the plural, to express the character of the people generally. By some מַעַלְלֵיהֶם is construed as the nominative to יִתְּנוּ, and rendered, *their deeds do not permit them*, &c. Thus the Syr. Abenezra, Drusius, &c.; and among the moderns, Horsley, Tingstadius, Manger, Kuinoel, Stuck, Maurer, and Ewald. But in order to establish this construction, we should have to read יִתְּנוּם, or יִתְּנוּ אֹתָם, "permitted *them*," the accusative of the person always following the verb in such case. See Gen. xx. 6; Exod. iii. 19. In the present instance נָתַן is used in the sense of *placing, ordering, framing*, like שׂוּם and שִׁית, as it is given in the common version, and rendered by Tanchum, Leo Juda, Mercer, Tarnovius, Michaelis, Rosenmüller, Noyes, and Hitzig. The meaning is, that the Israelites did not reform, did not so regard their wicked practices as to abandon them and return to the pure worship of Jehovah.

5. That עָנָה בְּ means *to testify for* or *against* any person or thing, is obvious from its use, Gen. xxx. 33; Job xvi. 8. It is properly a judicial phrase, and refers to the testimony given by a witness, either *for* or *against* another, according to circumstances. The rendering *to be humbled*, which is that of the LXX., Syr., Targ., Jarchi, and recently of Michaelis, Newcome, Noyes, and Maurer, cannot be philologically sustained. The addition בְּפָנָיו, *to his face*, gives emphasis to the phrase, *openly, publicly*, in such a manner that he himself may see it, without the adduction of further evidence. That גְּאוֹן signifies *pride, insolence*, not-

6 With their flocks and their herds
　They may go to seek Jehovah,
　But they shall not find him :
　He hath withdrawn from them.
7 They have proved false to Jehovah ;
　For they have begotten strange children :
　Now shall a month destroy them and their portions.

withstanding what Horsley asserts to the contrary, is sufficiently apparent from Prov. xvi. 18, and Is. xvi. 6. I should rather think, however, that by the term as here used, we are to understand the objects of which the ten tribes were proud, their splendid or magnificent idols, &c. As Jehovah is spoken of as גְּאוֹן יַעֲקֹב, *the excellency* or *boast* of Jacob, Amos viii. 7, so the idols might be called גְּאוֹן יִשְׂרָאֵל, *the excellency*, or *proud boast* of Israel. They gloried in them as the objects of their confidence and attachment. These very gods, by their utter impotence, bare open witness that they could afford no help to those who trusted in them; so that their worshippers could not but have been convinced of their folly, if their hearts had not become morally obscured by the practice of iniquity. The religion itself (עֲוֹנָם, *their iniquity*,) from which they expected safety, would prove the cause of their ruin. The words are repeated with a similar reference, chap. vii. 10.

The concluding line of the verse contains an abrupt and unexpected application of the threatening to the Jews. As they had suffered themselves to be influenced by the example of the Israelites, they should also share in their punishment. The respective captivities of both are here threatened. On comparing this threatening with chap. iv. 15, it appears to have been delivered at a period considerably subsequent to that which is there spoken of, when the evils of idolatry had made some progress in the southern kingdom. To express more strongly the certainty of the event, the verb עָשָׂל is put in the preterite ; whereas it had simply been used in the future יַעֲשֹׂלוּ, in reference to the Israelites.

6. The idolaters are here told that though in the hour of calamity they might bring their flocks and herds as propitiatory sacrifices to Jehovah in order to avert the punishment, it would be altogether in vain. חָלַץ signifies *to draw* or *put off* any person or thing, to *withdraw one's self.* Comp. the Arab. خلص, *salvus evasit, progressus est,* and خلع, *extraxit, exuit.* Pococke's Arab. MS. has الله خلع معونته منهم, *God hath withdrawn his help from them.* The Israelites and Jews could no longer reckon on the divine presence, and the effectual aid which that presence implied.

7. The prophet seems here to allude to the mention made of יַלְדֵי זְנוּנִים, and בְּנֵי זְנוּנִים, *lewd children,* chap. i. 2; ii. 4. זָרִים, *strange, foreign,* is selected in order to show that the idolatry was the result of intercourse with foreigners. The verb בָּגַד, *to act unfaithfully,* is also used of the breach of the matrimonial covenant, Jer. iii. 20. This idea is expressed in the Arab. MS. of Pococke, بعد الله غدروا, *they have broken the covenant of God.* פִּי has here the signification of *itaque,* and marks the consequence of the conjugal infidelity just specified—the production of a race of idolaters. The relation of the words is well expressed by Stuck: "quoniam Deo infideles sunt, propterea liberos peregrinos habent." עַתָּה, *now,* is here to be taken, not as determining the exact point of present time, but the speedy and certain arrival of the event. The term חֹדֶשׁ, *month,* has greatly, and in my opinion, very unnecessarily perplexed interpreters. Houbigant at once cuts the knot by an arbitrary emendation : עַתָּה יֹאכְלֵם חָדָשׁ, omnino est legendum וְעַתָּה יֹאכַל הֶחָסִל, *nunc igitur absumet rubigo.* He appeals to

8 Blow ye the horn in Gibeah,
   The trumpet in Ramah ;
   Raise a shout at Beth-aven ;
   He is behind thee, O Benjamin !
9 Ephraim shall become desolate
   In the day of punishment ;
   Among the tribes of Israel
   I have made known that which is sure.

the ἐρυσίβη of the LXX. as his authority ; but ἐρυσίβη signifies *mildew*, with which חָסִיל, *a locust*, the word he proposes to substitute for חֹרֶשׁ, has no manner of affinity. That the same word which is now in the Hebrew text was found in it in the time of Aquila, is evident from his rendering it νεομηνία. Symm. and Theod. have. μήν. Michaelis, Dathe, Kuinoel, and Stäudlin, give to the word the signification of the Arab. حدث what is *new and unexpected*, and explain it of a sudden calamity. Most moderns take it in the sense of *new-moon*, i. e. either at the feast of the new moon, when the Israelites were assembled to worship ; or, at that time their calamities should commence. It seems most natural to abide by the usual meaning of the term, and consider the prophet as announcing, that within the space of one month they should be visited with merited punishment. The calamity predicted seems to have been that occasioned by the invasion of Tiglath-pileser, who ravaged the country, and carried into captivity the tribes of Reuben and Gad, the half-tribe of Manasseh, and that of Naphtali, besides the inhabitants of several cities in other parts of the country, 2 Kings xv. 29 ; 1 Chron. v. 26. That Judah also suffered on this occasion, see 2 Chron. xxviii. 19—21. חֶלְקֵיהֶם, *their portions*, are commonly interpreted to mean their possessions or property ; but I should rather think the prophet has in view their idols, whom they regarded as the authors of their possessions and enjoyments. See Is. lvii. 6, and my Comm. on that verse.

8. An alarm is ordered to be given to the southern kingdom of the approach of the enemy. The verse intimately coheres with the foregoing, and is not to

be taken for the commencement of a new prophecy, as Jerome, Abarbanel, Michaelis, Dathe, Manger, and others, suppose. The difference between the שׁוֹפָר and the חֲצֹצְרָה seems to be, that the former was the same as the קֶרֶן, *horn*, being made of the curved horn of animals, Josh. vi. 5, 6, 8. Arab. شبور, *lituus foraminibus instructus ;* whereas, the latter was made of metal, such as the two silver trumpets which were employed for convoking the congregation, Numb. x. 2 ; from חָצַר, Arab. حصر, *in angustiam redegit ; angusto pectore præditus fuit.* Gesenius considers the word to be an onomatopoetic, imitating the broken pulse-like sound of the trumpet, (*hâtzotzĕrâh*,) like the Latin *taratantara*, and the German *trarara*. Their shape and size may be seen in the representations of the arch of Titus. Comp. Jer. iv. 5 ; Joel ii. 1 ; Hos. viii. 1. The LXX. render גִּבְעָה, *Gibeah*, and רָמָה, *Ramah*, τοὺς βουνοὺς and τῶν ὑψηλῶν, as if heights or elevated places in general were meant ; but they are to be taken as proper names, just as Beth-aven and Benjamin are. They both lay in the tribe of Benjamin, see on Is. x. 29, as did also Bethel, here called *Beth-aven*. See on chap. iv. 15. Before אַחֲרֶיךָ, subaud. אוֹיֵב, *the enemy* " is behind thee," i. e. close upon thee. The fifth Greek version has κατὰ νότου σοῦ, *to the south of thee ;* but if the local signification were at all admissible, the *west* is the only sense in which the word could be understood.

9. Having apprised the Jews of the danger with which they were threatened, the prophet returns to describe the calamity which was to be inflicted upon

10 The rulers of Judah are like those who remove the boundary;
I will pour out my wrath upon them like water.

11 Ephraim is oppressed,
He is crushed in judgment;
Because he consented,
He followed the order.

12 I am as a moth to Ephraim,
And as rottenness to the house of Judah.

13 And Ephraim saw his sickness,
And Judah his wound;

the ten tribes; and in the course of the following verses directs his discourse to the two kingdoms alternately. The nominative to תִּהְיֶה is אֶרֶץ, implied in אֶפְרַיִם.—תּוֹכֵחָה, primarily means *proof* or *demonstration*, from יָכַח, *to be before one*, *be clear*, *obvious*; in Hiph. *to place before one* in the way of evidence, *convince*, *convict*, and then *rebuke*, *chastise*, *punish*. The word is synonymous with מוּסָר, ver. 2. The latter hemistich of the verse shows that the ten tribes were the scene of the prophet's ministry. נֶאֱמָנָה, the feminine used for the neuter.

10. By the "princes" or "rulers of Judah," king Ahaz and his courtiers are intended. For כְּמַסִּיגֵי גְבוּל, comp. Deut. xxvii. 17, אָרוּר מַסִּיג גְּבוּל רֵעֵהוּ; Prov. xxii. 28; xxiii. 10; Job xxiv. 2. It was reckoned a flagrant offence to remove the marks by which the divisions of property were defined. The language seems to have become proverbial to designate unprincipled conduct. What the prophet here reprobates appears to be the means adopted by Ahaz and his supporters to introduce idolatry into Judah. See 2 Kings xvi. 10—18. If the כְּ be regarded as the *Caph veritatis*, it will strongly express the fact, that these princes had actually removed the boundaries which separated the true religion from the false.—Divine judgments are frequently compared to the overflowing of water from a river. שָׁפַךְ, *to pour out*, expresses the fulness of their infliction. Comp. Zeph. iii. 8. עֶבְרָה, prop. *effervescence*, *flowing over*, also denotes the greatness of the punishment.

11. רְצוּץ מִשְׁפָּט, the genitive of cause; *broken in pieces* by the *judgment*, or punishment inflicted. צַו refers not to

any divine commandment, but to the order issued by Jeroboam to worship the golden calves, 1 Kings xii. 28—33. Such an order his subjects were bound by higher authority to have resisted; but they readily complied with it, and thus became prepared to indulge in all the gross idolatries to which this worship proved the introduction. From the circumstance that the LXX. have rendered the passage ὀπίσω τῶν ματαίων, *after vanities*, it has been conjectured that they read שָׁוְא instead of צַו; but it is more likely they intended to give the sense of the whole, rather than the signification of this particular word. They are followed by both the Syriac versions, and in part by the Targ.: Jerome, on the other hand, has read the same letters which now stand in the text; for he renders *sordes*, pointing the word צֹא, and regarding it as merely a contracted form of צוֹא or צוֹאָה, *filthiness*.

12. The reference in עָשׁ, Arab. عث, *moth*, is to the consumption of garments, Ps. xxxix. 12; Is. l. 9; in רָקָב, *rottenness*, to that of wood. See Job xiii. 28, where both words occur together as here. The LXX. freely render the former by ταραχή, the latter by κέντρον. The meaning is not that God was regarded as the moth and rottenness, *i. e.* with disgust; but that he was the author of those judgments by which the idolaters should be consumed.

13. רָאָה, *to see*, has here the sense of *feeling*, *experiencing*, as in the phrases *to see life, death, good, evil*, &c. מָזוֹר, lit. *a bandage*, from זוּר, *to compress*, *bind* as a wound, see Is. i. 6; hence, as here, *a bandaged wound*, corresponding to חֳלִי,

Then Ephraim went to Assyria ;
And [Judah] sent to the hostile king ;
But he could not cure you,
Nor remove your wound from you.

14 For I will be like a lion to Ephraim,
And like a young lion to the house of Judah ;
I, even I will tear the prey, and depart: .
I will carry it away, and there shall be none to rescue.

15 I will depart, I will return to my place,
Till they suffer punishment ;

sickness, disease, in the other member of the parallelism. For the use of such metaphors in application to the state of political affairs, comp. Is. i. 5, 6 ; iii. 7 ; Hos. vi. 1 ; vii. 1. After וַיִּשְׁלַח, supply as its nominative יְהוּדָה, Judah, from the preceding part of the verse, which forms an alternate quatrain ;· the third line connecting with the first, and the fourth with the second: יָרֵב, is not a proper name, but an appellative, signifying one who contends, is contentious, hostile ; from רִיב, to strive with, quarrel, contend. The form is the apocopated future, and is contracted for אֲשֶׁר יָרִיב, he that acts hostilely. Tanchum ملك يخاصم, the king that contended. Comp.יוֹיָרִיב, Joiarib, Neh. xi. 5. Aq. δικαζόμενον ; Symm. ἔκδικον, or ἐκδικητήν ; Theod. κρίτην. Jerome, ad regem ultorem. De Wette, Der könig der rächen soll. That the king of Assyria is meant there can be no doubt. See chap. x. 6. He was ever ready to mix himself up with the affairs of neighbouring states, in order to extend or consolidate his gigantic empire, and was justly regarded by the Hebrews as their most powerful adversary. The application made by the northern kingdom was that which took place in the reign of Menahem, when that monarch sent to Pul a thousand talents of silver for the purpose of engaging him on his behalf, 2 Kings xv. 19. But this alliance proved of no real value ; for the subsidy was raised by oppression, and, in the course of the following reign, Tiglath-pileser invaded and depopulated great part of the country, ver. 29. The embassy from

the kingdom of Judah was that sent by Ahaz to Tiglath-pileser, when attacked by the united kings of Syria and Israel, 2 Kings xvi. 7, 8 ; 2 Chron. xxviii. 20, 21. גֵּהָה, as a verb, occurs only in this place; but a noun derived from it is used Prov. xvii. 22, in the sense of healing. If we may judge from the Syr. ܐܬܓܗܪ recedere, fugere, Aph. liberare, it properly signifies to remove, relieve, and so with respect to a wound, to heal. LXX. οὐ μή διαπαύσῃ ; Syr. ܕܢܐܣܐ ܠܐ, neque sanabit.

14. No effort to recover a state of prosperity while the anger of Jehovah was excited against them, could possibly succeed. שַׁחַל, the black lion, and כְּפִיר, the young lion, are frequently employed to convey the ideas of strength and ferocity, Ps. xci. 13. The reduplication אֲנִי אֲנִי is, as usual, emphatic. Comp. Is. xliii. 25 ; xlviii. 15. טְרֵפָה, prey, is understood after טָרַף and נָשָׂא.

15. As God's coming to a people, and being with them, implies their experiencing efficient protection and aid, so his withdrawment of his presence implies the deprivation of these blessings. אָשֵׁם, like many other verbs, has a sensus pregnans ; conveying not only the idea of contracting guilt, but of suffering its consequences. The latter idea seems clearly to be conveyed in this passage. The Rabbins, indeed, and after them, Glassius, and many others, attempt to attach to the verb the superadded signification of acknowledging, which is that adopted by our translators ; but it is by

Then will they seek my face:
When they are in trouble, they will seek me early.

no means supported by Lev. iv. 22 ; v.
5 ; Zech. xi. 5 ; the passages usually
adduced in proof. פְּנֵי שׁ׳, *to seek the
face* of any one, means to strive to obtain
his favour. See 1 Kings x. 24; Prov.
xxix. 26. The phrase occurs very frequently in the Psalms, in reference to
application to Jehovah in prayer. Comp.
Dan. ix. 3. שָׁחַר is synonymous with
בִּקֵּשׁ, but is only used in poetic diction.

CHAPTER VI

The nation, in both its divisions, is here introduced as taking up language suitable
to the circumstances described in the concluding verses of the preceding
chapter, 1—3 ; but however appropriate it was to the condition of the people,
that it was not the result of sound and thorough conversion, appears from ver. 4,
in which they are expostulated with on the ground of their inconstancy. Notice
is then taken of the means, both of a moral and a punitive nature, that had
been employed for their recovery, 5, 6 ; their deceitful and wicked conduct,
especially that of the Israelites, is placed in a strong light, 7—10; and a
special denunciation of punishment is directed against the Jews, who flattered
themselves with the hope that whatever might befal the northern tribes, no
calamity would happen to them, 11.

---

1 COME, let us return to Jehovah,
   For he hath torn, but he will heal us ;
   He hath smitten, but he will bind us up.
2 He will restore us to life after two days ;

1, 2. It has been disputed whether
these words be those of the prophet exhorting his countrymen to repent and
turn to God, or whether they are to be
regarded as employed by themselves to
give expression to their feelings of peni-
tence, their confidence in God for deliverance from punishment, and their
resolutions of amendment for the future.
The latter appears, from the bearing of
ver. 4, to be the preferable interpretation.
The intimate connexion of the words
with the preceding context, and the repetition, in part, of its language, induces
to the conclusion that the same subject
is here continued, viz. the castigation of
the Hebrew kingdoms on account of
idolatry, and the effect produced by it.
This connexion the ancient versions have
endeavoured to establish by inserting a
word corresponding to לֵאמֹר; though it
is not found in any Heb. MSS. From
the apparent agreement of the language
of ver. 2, with the circumstances of
time connected with the death and resurrection of our Saviour, many interpreters, as Lactantius, Tertullian, Origen,
Jerome, Augustine, Luther, Œcolam-

On the third day he will raise us up,
And we shall live before him.

3 Then we shall know, we shall strive to know Jehovah :
Like the dawn, his going forth is fixed,
Yea, he will come to us like the rain,
Like the latter rain, which watereth the earth.

padius, Mercer, Ribera, Tarnovius, Hammond, &c., have maintained that it is to these respect is had in the prophecy. I fully concur, however, in the judicious remarks of Calvin on this interpretation, "Sed sensus ille videtur mihi nimium argutus. Et semper hoc spectandum est nobis, ne volitemus in aëre: placent argutæ speculationes primo intuitu, sed postea evanescunt. Ergo quisquis volet proficere in Scripturis, semper hanc regulam teneat, ut solidum sit quicquid colligit sive in Prophetis, sive in Apostolis." The exegesis of Grotius, Horsley, and many others, who regard the words as primarily applicable to the Jews, and secondarily, or allusively, to the resurrection of Christ, is equally unsatisfactory. The simple meaning of the passage is, that on their conversion from the service of idols to that of Jehovah, the Hebrews should experience the removal of the national calamities with which they had been visited; the nation which had been reduced to a state of political death would be resuscitated, and enjoy a renewal of its former prosperity. From the metaphor of disease, ver. 1, there is in ver. 2, an advance to that of actual death, and a consequent resurrection, in order to place their present and also their anticipated condition in a more striking light. For the use of the latter metaphor in application to the national affairs of the Jews, see Is. xxvi. 19; Ezek. xxxvii. 1—14. בַּיּוֹם הַשְּׁלִישִׁי, on the third day, is expletive of מִיָּמִים, after two days; LXX. μετὰ δύο ἡμέρας. That a short period is meant, appears from two, and two three being used to denote a few, or very few, 1 Kings xvii. 12 : Is. vii. 21; xvii. 6. Comp. Luke xiii. 32, 33. The afflicted Hebrews confidently hoped that their punishment would be of brief duration, and that God would assuredly restore them to the enjoyment of his favour. Such enjoyment is expressed by living, לְפָנָיו, before him, experiencing

his presence and blessing. The phrase contrasts with that employed chap. v. 15, and indicates the result of בַּקְשׁוּ פָנָי, there predicted.

3. In וְנֵדְעָה נִרְדְּפָה לָדַעַת, there is a rise from a resolution simply to acquire a true knowledge of Jehovah, to a determination to make such knowledge the object of earnest and unwearied pursuit. The ה of the elongated futures marks this bent or inclination of mind. To separate the verbs, and connect the former with the preceding verse, as Horsley does, would quite destroy the force of the prophet's language. At the same time the ו at the beginning of the verse is inferential, intimating that what follows would be the result of the divine interposition on behalf of the Hebrew people. Some few MSS. insert ו before נִרְדְּפָה. נָכוֹן, to be fixed, established, certain. As certain and delightful as the dawn of the morning would be the coming forth of the favour of Jehovah after the dark night of adversity. This beautiful metaphor is taken from the sunrise. See, for such application of מוֹצָא, Ps. xix. 7. The other images were peculiarly appropriate in Palestine, where rain falls seldom, except in spring and autumn. At these seasons it is heavy, and greatly contributes to the fertility of the soil, on which account its bestowment was regarded as among the most necessary of temporal blessings, and its absence a source of awful calamity. The former, commonly called יוֹרֶה or מוֹרֶה, the darting rain, from the root יָרָה, to dart, cast, &c. ; here הַגֶּשֶׁם, the rain, by way of eminence ; the heavy, violent rain, as the word properly signifies. It falls from the middle of October till about the middle of December, and is called the early or former rain. LXX. ὑετὸς πρώϊμος, because the Jews commenced their year at that time. It prepares the ground for the reception of the seed. מַלְקוֹשׁ, the latter rain, LXX.

4 What shall I do to thee, O Ephraim!
　What shall I do to thee, O Judah!
　For your goodness is like the morning cloud,
　And like the dew which early departeth.
5 For this cause I have hewed them by the prophets,
　I have slain them by the words of my mouth:
　Thy judgments went forth like the lightning.
6 For I desired mercy and not sacrifice;
　And the knowledge of God, rather than burnt offerings.

ὑετὸς ὄψιμος, falls in the latter half of February and during the months of March and April, just before the harvest; from which circumstance it receives its name,—לֶקֶשׁ, signifying to gather or collect, the late fruit. Comp. לֶקֶשׁ, to collect, Syr. ܚܡܣ, serotinus. Before יוֹרֶה supply אֲשֶׁר.

4. That the declarations contained in the preceding verses are not to be viewed as divine promises, but express the hopes and resolutions of the afflicted Hebrews, appears from the affecting expostulations here addressed to them, and the description of the temporary and evanescent character of their boasted reformation. Like a tender parent who is anxious, if possible, to reclaim a wayward child, Jehovah asks what other means could possibly be employed for the recovery of his rebellious people. They had been tried both with mercies and judgments, but without effect. Comp. Is. v. 4—7. חֶסֶד properly means kindness, benignity, mercy; here piety, religion, as Is. xl. 6. Syr. ܪܚܡܬܟܘܢ, your goodness; Pococke's Arab. MS. دينكم, your religion. Theodoret not inaptly gives the meaning thus: ἡ παρ' ὑμῶν γενομένη μεταμέλεια πρόσκαιρος ἐστι, καὶ οὐ διαρκής. In Palestine, and other countries of the same latitude, the dense clouds which cover the heavens during the morning are all gone by nine or ten o'clock; and the dews, however copious, early disappear. מַשְׁכִּים is here, as frequently, to be taken adverbially; early, in the morning. As the cognate Ethiop. ጾሐዐ : signifies to carry a burden, and beasts of burden are usually loaded in the morning, the Hebrew שָׁכַם came in Hiphil to signify the doing of any thing at an early hour. הֹלֵךְ is not to be construed with הַסְדְּכֶם, but with טַל.

5. The severity of the threatenings communicated through the instrumentality of the prophets is compared to the incisions made in stone or wood with the axe, and those made in the human body with the sword. Comp. Is. xi. 4; Heb. iv. 12. After חָצַבְתִּי supply ם or אֹתָם. To make the pronominal affixes agree, the LXX., Syr., and Targ. read מִשְׁפָּטַי, "my judgments," and so likewise Dathe, Kuinoel, Boeckel, Newcome, Boothroyd, and Ewald, instead of מִשְׁפָּטֶיךָ, "thy judgments." Vulg. judicia tua. Hexap. Syr. ܘܕܝܢܝ. There is no variety in the MSS., except that one of Kennicott's, and originally one of De Rossi's, have מִשְׁפָּטֶךָ, "thy judgment," in the singular. The reference of the affix is to ךְ, ver. 4; and the meaning is, the judgments which belong to thee, which thou deservedst, and which were inflicted upon thee. The genitive is that of object. Comp. מִשְׁפָּטֶךָ, 1 Kings xx. 40; מִשְׁפָּטָהּ, Jer. li. 9; and especially מִשְׁפָּטֶךָ, Zeph. iii. 15. Thus Lyranus: "poenæ tibi inferendæ." יֵצֵא, though future, is modified by the preceding preterite, and is to be rendered accordingly. אוֹר has here the sense of lightning, as in Job xxxvii. 3, 15. The LXX., Syr., Targ., and Arab., supply כְּ before אוֹר. Sudden and awful as the lightning were the inflictions of merited punishment upon the idolatrous Hebrews.

6. חֶסֶד means here true piety, of which mercy or charity is only a branch. דַּעַת אֱלֹהִים corresponding to it in the second member of the verse, likewise means a

7 But they are like men that break a covenant :
   There they proved false to me.

8 As for Gilead, it is a city of evil-doers ;
   Marked with footsteps of blood.

practical knowledge of God, in opposition
to that which is merely speculative.
Comp. Jer. xxii. 16. The present is one
of several passages in the Old Testament,
in which the comparative worthlessness
of ceremonial observances is taught.
See Is. i. 11—17 ; Ps. xl. 7—9 ; l. 8—
23 ; Mic. vi. 6—8. Comp. Matt. ix. 13 ;
xii. 7.

7. Translators and commentators have
been greatly divided respecting the pre-
cise meaning of אָדָם as occurring in this
passage. Some, as Jarchi, Jerome, Leo
Juda, Castalio, Grotius, Clarius, Manger,
Tingstadius, Newcome, Rosenmüller,
Boothroyd, and Stuck, regard it as a
proper name, and suppose the reference
to be to the conduct of Adam in trans-
gressing the divine commandment: while
Kimchi, Munster, Vatablus,· Tremellius,
Beza, Drusius, Liveley, Calvin, Rivetus,
Piscator, Zanchius, Œcolampadius,
Mercer, Lowth, De Wette, Maurer,
Hitzig, Ewald, &c., take it to be an
appellative, and interpret the passage of
the treacherous violation of contracts
among mankind. In favour of the former
view, it is alleged, that it places the
guilt of the Israelites in a much more
aggravated light ; and Job xxxi. 33,
Ps. lxxxii. 7, are appealed to in proof of
a similar allusion. It is, however, very
doubtful whether there be any such allusion in these passages ; and as to the
force of the comparison, it seems sufficiently supplied by supposing men in
general to be understood, who break the
engagements into which they have entered with each other. The Israelites
had treated God as if he had been one
of themselves, and as if the sanctions of
his covenant were as little to be regarded
as those of ordinary contracts were by
men of unprincipled character. If we
except the three passages in question, it
is universally admitted that there is no
other, after the first chapters of Genesis,
in which אָדָם is used as a proper name,
or in which any reference is made to
our first parent. The absolute and indefinite form too in which בְּרִית occurs,

(comp. on the other hand בְּרִיתִי, " *my*
covenant," chap. viii. 1,) shows, that
both this noun and the preceding verb
עָבְרוּ, stand in immediate relation to אָדָם,
which, as very frequently, is a collective,
and is thus used instead of a plural,
which it nowhere exhibits. It may
also be objected to the first mentioned
interpretation, that nowhere in Scripture
is God said to have entered into a בְּרִית,
or *covenant* with Adam. The obligations
under which he was placed are represented as those of a מִצְוָה, *command* or
interdict, rather than any of a fœderal
nature. כְּאָדָם, *like Edom*, the reading
proposed by Michaelis, has found no
supporters. Before עָבְרוּ, supply אֲשֶׁר, of
which there is frequently an ellipsis in
Hebrew poetry. See Noldius, p. 103.—
שָׁם, *there*, points graphically to the
northern or Israelitish kingdom as the
principal scene of idolatrous defection,
and anticipates the regions more specifically referred to in the two following
verses.

8. גִּלְעָד, *Gilead*, is the nominative absolute, and is here the designation of a
city, in all probability *Ramoth-Gilead*,
the metropolis of the mountainous region
beyond Jordan, and south of the river
Jabbok, known by the name of Gilead,
Josh. xxi. 38 ; 1 Kings iv. 13. It was
here that Jacob and Laban entered into
a solemn covenant with each other, Gen.
xxxi. 21, 23, 25. Burckhardt found
ruins of cities on two mountains in that
region, still known by the names of
Djebel Djelaâd, and Djelaûd, one or
other of which may have been that here
mentioned. It was one of the cities of
refuge, Deut. iv. 43 ; Josh. xx. 8 ; but
appears from the present passage to have
afterwards become notorious for idolatry
and bloodshed. Some would restrict
פֹּעֲלֵי אָוֶן to idolaters, in imitation of the
LXX. who render ἐργαζομένη μάταια ;
but it seems better to take the phrase in
its more enlarged meaning, as including
all manner of wickedness. Of this,
indeed, idolatry has ever been found to
be the fruitful parent. Various expla-

9　For as troops of robbers lie in wait for a man,
　　So is the association of priests:
　　They commit murder in the way to Shechem;
　　Yea, they practise deliberate crime.
10　In the house of Israel I have seen what is horrifying;
　　There is the lewdness of Ephraim;
　　Israel is polluted:
11　　Also for thee, O Judah! a harvest is appointed.

nations of עֲקֻבָּה have been advanced; but the simplest is that which regards it as signifying *traced*, from עָקֵב, *the heel, step, print of the foot*, and describing the marks or traces of blood left by the feet of the murderers who resided there.

Syr. ܒ݁ܰܕ݂ܡܳܐ ܨܶܒ݂ܥܳܐ, *stained with blood.* Jewish Span. *immunda de sangre.* To what historical facts the prophet refers we have no information, except perhaps that contained in 2 Kings xv. 25, from which it appears that fifty of the inhabitants of Gilead were implicated in the regicidal conspiracy against Pekahiah.

9. שְׁכֶם, *Shechem*, was another city of refuge, situated between Ebal and Gerizim. It still exists under the name of نابلس, *Naploos*, and has, from very ancient times, been the seat of the religious community of the Samaritans. Having been for a time the residence of Jeroboam, 1 Kings xii. 25, its inhabitants became so corrupted, that the priests resident there banded together, waylaid, and murdered with impunity the persons who were fleeing to the asylum for refuge. The ה in שֶׁכְמָה is that of direction, and connects in sense with דֶּרֶךְ. The interposition of the verb יְרַצְּחוּ between these two nouns occasions no difficulty, since we have instances of nouns in construction being separated. See Gen. vii. 6; Is. xix. 8; Hos. xiv. 3. Our common version, and many others, following the Targ. פְּתַף חַד, *one shoulder*, translate שְׁכְמָה, *with one consent*, which well suits the connexion; but is not borne out by Hebrew usage,— the term occurring but once, Zeph. iii. 9, in this metaphorical acceptation, and

then not שְׁכְמָה as here, but שְׁכֶם אֶחָד.— חַכֵּי is generally considered to be an imitation of the Chaldee form of the Infin. in Piel, from חָכָה, *to wait, lie in wait for;* but it seems more likely to be the abbreviated form of the Piel Participle מְחַכֵּי, the מ being dropped, as in שַׁבַּת, Eccles. iv. 2, and in several instances of the Pual Participles. See Gesen. Lehrgeb. p. 316. כְּחַכֵּי אִישׁ will thus form the genitive of object. Three MSS. substitute ה for י; and instead of the prepositive כְּ, three MSS. and three printed editions read כְּ. Before כֹּהֲנִים חֶבֶר there is an ellipsis of כְּ, corresponding to כְּ in כְּדֶרֶךְ.— זִמָּה is used to denote presumptuous or deliberate wickedness, from זָמַם; Arab. سم, *proposuit sibi, to form a purpose,* lay a deliberate plan of action; chiefly employed in a bad sense. LXX. ἀνομία. Hitzig, *Unthat.*

10. שַׁעֲרוּרִיָה, LXX. φρικώδη, occurs under the forms שַׁעֲרוּרִיָה and שַׁעֲרִרִת, Jer. v. 30; xxiii. 14; xviii. 13. It is explained immediately after of the atrocious idolatry which, through the influence of the tribe of Ephraim, had spread itself over the whole kingdom of Israel.

11. For the various interpretations which have been given of this verse see Tarnovius or Pococke. Ewald is the only modern that adopts *branch* as the rendering of קָצִיר, as Kimchi proposed, and explains it of the introduction of idolatry into Judah. How Horsley could assert that *harvest* is used in a good sense, as an image of the ingathering of the people of God, is inconceivable. See Jer. li. 33; Joel iii. 13; Rev. xiv. 15— 20. Nowhere in prophecy does it appear to be used in other than a bad sense. In all probability, the punishment predicted is that recorded, 2 Chron. xxviii. 6—8.

שׁיִת is here used impersonally. Instead of זְךָ, four MSS. originally two more, the Targ. and two old editions, read לֹה. The words בְּשׁוּבִי שְׁבוּת עַמִּי have no meaning, if connected with the preceding, which form a concise apostrophical warning to the Jewish kingdom. They must, therefore, be transferred to the following context, with which they will be found to be in harmony. Thus Moerlius, Michaelis, Jahn, Eichhorn, Kuinoel, Stuck, De Wette, and Boothroyd, divide.

CHAPTER VII

The prophet continues his description of the wickedness of the ten tribes. Regardless of Jehovah, they persevered in falsehood and violence, 1, 2 ; flattered their rulers, and thereby obtained their sanction to their nefarious conduct, 3, 5 ; and indulged to the utmost in licentiousness, 4—7. The murder of their kings successively is predicted, and their hardihood and folly are further set forth, 7—10. The prophet next adverts to their fruitless application for assistance to Egypt and Assyria, and their equally fruitless, because false professions of return to the service of God, 11—16.

---

1 WHEN I reversed the captivity of my people,
   When I healed Israel,
   Then was the iniquity of Ephraim revealed,
   And the wicked deeds of Samaria ;
   For they practised deceit;
   Yea, the thief entered,
   And the banditti plundered in the street.

---

1. Some would render בְּשׁוּבִי שְׁבוּת עַמִּי, "when I again lead my people into captivity;" but altogether contrary to the established usage of the language. See Deut. xxx. 3 ; Ps. xiv. 7 ; Jer. xxxi. 23 ; Zeph. iii. 20. The words are explained by the following כְּרָפְאִי לְיִשְׂרָאֵל, when I healed Israel. בְּ and כְּ frequently alternate with each other, when used of the time at which any thing is done. The restoration here mentioned is in all probability that of the two hundred thousand Jewish captives, to which reference is made, 2 Chron. xxviii. 8—15. The conduct of the Israelitish rulers upon that occasion held out some hope of improvement in the character of the nation, and a consequent change in the Divine conduct towards it; and this expectation was confirmed by a temporary cessation of the judgments of God, during which they might be said to have been healed ; but it was soon entirely frustrated by the open increase of wickedness among them. וְנִגְלָה has the force of then, on the contrary, became more manifest, &c. For Samaria, see on Is. xxviii. 1. Being the metropolis of the ten tribes, it was the head-spring of that corruption of manners which overspread the kingdom.

2 And they considered not in their heart,
　That I remembered all their wickedness :
　Now their deeds encompass them ;
　They are before my face.
3 With their wickedness they cheer the king,
　And with their falsehoods the princes.
4 They are all adulterers ;
　They are like an oven, heated by the baker ;
　Who resteth from heating it,
　From the time he kneadeth the dough,
　Until it be leavened.

יָבוֹא and פָּשָׁט בַּחוּץ describe the acts of violence that were committed by breaking into and plundering private houses, and those which were perpetrated on persons in the streets. The reference is not to foreign enemies, as Horsley and others expound, but to lawless Israelites.

2. For the phrase אָמַר לֵב, comp. the Arab. قال في نفسه, and قال في قلبه and our, *say to oneself*. Comp. דִּבֵּל, Ps. xiv. 1. *et freq.* Instead of לִלְבָבָם, the form exhibited in the printed text, "*to* their heart," ten MSS., originally seven more, now one, perhaps another, and the Complut. Bible, read בִּלְבָבָם, "*in* their heart." One of De Rossi's MSS. states in the margin that the latter reading is found in other copies. It is also supported by the Syr., Vulg., Targ., and Arab. versions. Both forms describe internal or mental conversation, only ל indicates an endeavour to persuade. So far were the persons spoken of from bringing themselves to act on the conviction that God was privy to their wicked deeds, that they evinced the contrary disposition. Still, however, the phrase may best be rendered by *think, consider*, or the like. To the words סְבָבוּם מַעַלְלֵיהֶם, two interpretations have been given. They either mean, that the evil practices of the Israelites crowded round them as so many causes of punishment, as enemies surround and shut up the object of their attack ; or, that they crowded about them as so many witnesses to reveal the wickedness of their character. The latter would

seem, from the following words, to be the true meaning.

3. Their rulers, instead of repressing, took delight in the immoral and irreligious conduct of the people.

4. In this connexion, מְנָאֲפִים is to be taken in its literal signification. Comp. Jer. ix. 1 ; xxiii. 10. For the conjecture of Stuck, that the word was originally מְאֻפִּים, *baked* or *cooked*, there is no foundation. To place the violent and incontinent character of their lust in the strongest light, the prophet compares it to a baker's oven, which he raises to such a degree of heat, that he only requires to omit feeding it during the short period of the fermentation of the bread. Such was the libidinous character of the Israelites, that their impure indulgences were subject to but slight interruptions. Comp. ἀκαταπαύστους ἁμαρτίας, 2 Pet. ii. 14. בֹּעֵרָה, in the feminine, agrees with תַּנּוּר, which is of common gender. The latter word Gesenius derives from the Aram., חנן, *to smoke*, and נור, *fire*. Comp. the Arab.

تنور, and Syr. ܬܰܢܽܘܪܳܐ, *fornax, clibanus*.

The oven here referred to is not the pitcher-oven of the Arabs, but the larger kind, pretty much like our own, which was, as it still is, used in public bake-houses. בֹּעֵרָה מֵאֹפֶה is elliptical for *burning*, having been kindled *by the baker*. Before יִשְׁבּוֹת supply אֲשֶׁר. The meaning is, who *only* ceaseth from heating, &c. Most interpreters take מֵעִיר in the sense of *stirring, rousing up*, &c., and apply it to the stirring of the fire in

5 On the day of our king,
  The princes are sick with the fever of wine;
  He stretcheth out his hand with the scoffers.

6 For though they approach with their heart [warm] as an oven,
  Yet it is in their plot;
  Their baker sleepeth all the night;
  In the morning it burneth like a blazing fire.

---

the oven; but it is preferable to regard it as the part. of עִיר, Arab. عَار, *to be hot, burning*; hence in Hiph. *to cause to burn, heat*, &c. Thus the LXX. ἀπὸ τῆς φλογὸς. The interpretation *from the city*, given in the Syr., Targ., and Vulg., is altogether inappropriate. For the feminine form of the Infin. חִמְצָתוֹ, comp. חִמְלָה, Ezek. xvi. 5.

5. By יוֹם is meant *a festal day*: either that of the king's birth, or, as the Targ., Jarchi, and Kimchi give it, that of his inauguration. The preposition בְּ is understood. Michaelis thinks the reference is to the accession of a new king to the throne. Instead of מַלְכֵּנוּ, *our king*, twenty-two MSS. and the Syr. read מְלָכֵינוּ, *our kings*; LXX. ἡμέραι τῶν βασιλέων ὑμῶν. הֶחֱלוּ is used intransitively. The LXX., Syr., Targ., Vulg., Abarbanel, Leo Juda, Newcome, Michaelis, and Boothroyd, refer this verb to the root חָלַל; but, not to insist on its requiring in such case to be read הֵחֵלּוּ, there is something so intolerably tame in the rendering, "The princes *began* to be heated with wine," that it cannot be admitted as the language of the prophet. Besides, חֲמַת would likewise require to be changed into חִמֹּת, which would produce an anomalous infinitive. חֵמָה, *bottle*, less agrees with מ following than חֵמָה, *heat*. Comp. the Arab. حَمِيَّة, حُمِيَّة. חֲמַת מִיִן is an instance of the construct state with a preposition intervening between the nouns. Comp. נְבִיאֵי מִלָּם, Ezek. xiii. 2; שִׁכְרַת וְלֹא מִיָּיִן, Is. li. 21, and see Gesen. Lehrgeb. p. 679. The words mean the heat or fever produced by intoxication. While the courtiers thus indulged to excess, the monarch, forgetting his dignity, participated in their cups, and joined in

their scoffs. Because לֹצְצִים occurs nowhere else, Houbigant would have it changed into the usual form לֵצִים, most uncritically. Comp. קִיץ and קָץ. Aq. χλευαστῶν; LXX. less properly, λοιμῶν. The reduplicate form is intensive, and expresses the awfully profligate character of the persons described.

6. I consider the prophet to be continuing in this verse his description of the abandoned courtiers, in imagery borrowed from that introduced, ver. 4. In their intercourse with the monarch, they approached him with the warmest professions of loyalty; but in private they were scheming how to get rid of him. The ringleader waited till he could conveniently carry the plot into execution; and speedily they effected the nefarious purpose. Were it not that all the ancient versions render קֵרְבוּ as a verb, I should have been inclined to point it קָרְבוּ, and translate, "For their inward part is like an oven; their heart is in their plot." Comp. וַיְּקָרְבוּ יָמִים אָרְבוּ, Jer. ix. 7. The rendering I have given, however, equally suits the connexion. Though there is no word in the text corresponding to "warm," its insertion in the translation is fully justified by the comparison in כְתַנּוּר, *like an oven*, and the intensive force of קָרֵב in Piel. That this verb ever signifies *to make ready* or *prepare*, I do not find. All attempts to justify the rendering of the LXX. and Syr. ἀνεκαύθησαν, ܥܡܠ, by the conjectural readings חָרְבוּ, צָרְבוּ, and קָרְדוּ, have proved abortive. According to the Hexapla, Symm. (عَمِلَ), Aq. and Theod. (عَمَلَ كِ وَسَمِ), read as we now do; as did likewise the Targ. אִתְקְרָבוּ.—אֹפֶהֶם, *their baker*, (many MSS.

7 They all glow as an oven,
 And they devour their judges;
 All their kings have fallen:
 None among them calleth unto me.
8 　Ephraim mixeth himself up with the nations;
 Ephraim is a cake unturned.
9 Strangers devour his strength,
 But he knoweth it not;
 Yea, grey hairs are sprinkled upon him,
 Yet he knoweth it not.

and various printed editions have אֲפֵיהֶם, which may also be regarded as a singular form, ' taking the place of the third radical ה, as in other nouns or participles derived from verbs in ‏לה,‏) the Targ. and Syr. render רוּגְזְהוֹן, ܐܘܦܗܘܢ as if the reading were אַפָּם, *their anger.* 'Εφραἵμ, found in the LXX. shows that the former must have been the reading of the MS. which they used, as the latter could not have so easily been mistaken for this proper name. אֲפֵיהֶם, which Dathe proposes, and Kuinoel adopts into his Heb. text, nowhere occurs in the sense, *ira, furor eorum.* By "their baker" seems to be meant the leader of the conspiracy, whom some suppose to be Menahem, others Shallum, 2 Kings xv. 10—15; but I should rather infer from what is stated ver. 7, that the prophet includes all the conspiracies which took place in Israel. Having prepared the rest of the conspirators, he, like the baker, abided his time, when on a sudden, the plot burst forth like a flame.

7. Comp. 2 Kings xv. כֻּלָּם, *all of them,* corresponds to כֻּלָּם, ver. 4. יֵחַמּוּ is the future in Kal of חָמַם, *to be warm, hot,* &c. The prophet still continues the comparison. As the fire in the oven devours the fuel, so the persons spoken of destroyed those who were in authority. נָפַל is not to be taken in the sense of *falling off* or apostatizing from God, as Jerome, Ribera, Menochius, Tirinius, and some others interpret, but in that of falling by the hands of murderers. This, אָכְלוּ, *they devour,* in the preceding hemistich, shows. The source of the evil, however, lay in apostasy from Jehovah,

which had reached such a height, that none implored the Divine aid even when in calamity.

8. Ewald renders יִתְבּוֹלָל, *veraltet,* "hath become old," which might seem to derive some support from the latter part of ver. 9; but the verb can, with no propriety, be referred to any other root than בָּלַל, Arab. بلبل, *madefecit, commistus fuit,* Syr. ܒܠܠ *confudit,* to *mix by pouring, mix, confound.* LXX. συνεμίγνυτο. Syr. ܐܬܒܠܠ. Targ. אִתְעָרַבוּ. Comp. Psalm cvi. 35, where יִתְעָרְבוּ בַגּוֹיִם is similarly used of promiscuous intercourse with idolaters. That such intercourse generally, including the adoption of their idolatrous practices, and not specifically the entering into leagues with them, is meant, appears from the following clause, in which, to express the worthlessness of the Ephraimitish character, the people are compared to a cake, which, from not having been turned, is burnt, and good for nothing. The Arabs bake their bread on the ground or hearth, covering it with hot embers, and turning it every ten minutes or quarter of an hour, to prevent its being burnt. When neglected it is unfit for food, and is thrown away. Such was the state of the apostate Israelites. They had corrupted themselves, and were only fit for rejection. LXX. ἐγκρυφίας, *bread baked in hot ashes.* Cyril, τῶν ἐπὶ λίθοις. ὀπτωμένων ἄρτων.

9. זָרִים, *strangers, foreigners,* i. e. the Syrians, Assyrians, &c. See 2 Kings xiii. 7; xv. 19, 20; xvii. 3—6. The state, drawing to its close, without the

10 And the pride of Israel testifieth to his face,
    Yet they turn not to Jehovah their God,
    Nor seek him for all this.

11 For Ephraim is like a silly dove, without understanding;
    They call in Egypt, they go to Assyria.

12 As they go, I will spread my net upon them,
    I will bring them down like the fowls of heaven;
    I will chastise them,
    As it hath been heard in their assembly.

13 Wo unto them! for they have wandered from me;
    Destruction unto them! for they have rebelled against me.
    Though it was I that redeemed them,
    Yet have they spoken lies against me.

fact being observed by its citizens, is compared to a person on whose head grey hairs begin to make their appearance, without his becoming sensible of the approach of age.

"Sparserit et nigras alba senecta comas."   *Propertius.*

10—12. A repetition of part of chap. v. 5, which see. Though the apostate Israelites had abundant proof of the inefficiency of their idols, yet they returned not in the exercise of true repentance to God, who alone could deliver them in the hour of trouble, but formed alliances with foreign powers in the delusive hope of protection. The simplicity of the dove is proverbial.

Thus the Arabs, ليس شي ابله من الحمام, there is nothing more simple than the dove. The word פּוֹתָה is here, however, used in a bad sense, as אֵין לֵב, without heart, i. e. without understanding, shows. The point of comparison is the inconsiderate flight of the dove from one danger into another, owing to the alarm which makes her leave her abode for the net of the fowler. Such would be the case with the Israelites. Jehovah had distinctly announced to them, that foreign alliances would prove their ruin; yet they heedlessly rushed into destruction. אַשּׁוּר stands either for אֲשׁוּרָה or לְאַשּׁוּר. The spreading of the net refers to the taking of birds that are on the ground; the bringing down, to those that are in the air, by the use of missile weapons. Instead of the Hiphil אֲיִסְרֵם, which occurs only here, the Soncin. edit. of the Prophets, and some few MSS. read אֲיַסְרֵם in Piel, which may also be interpreted causatively. כְּשֵׁמַע לַעֲדָתָם, lit. *according to the report to their assembly,* i. e. the public congregations, to which the Divine messages were delivered. God had given them sufficient warning by Moses and the prophets. The versions vary in rendering the last word, which has given rise to the conjectural readings לְעֵלָתָם, לְצָרָתָם, and לְמַצָּה. Aq., however, renders, κατὰ ἀκοῆς τῆς συναγωγῆς.

13. That אוֹי is denunciative, and not plaintive, the following שֹׁד plainly shows. נָדַד is often used of the flight of birds that wander from their nest, see Prov. xxvii. 8; Is. xvi. 2; Jer. iv. 25; and is here employed with reference to the silly dove, ver. 11. The redemption from Egypt, and that which, in numerous instances, they afterwards experienced, Jehovah adduces in aggravation of their guilt. Their preferring the service of idols to that of the true God, was not merely a practical denial of his all-sufficiency, but a violation of the solemn pledge which they had given of undivided obedience to his law, when, as stated, chap. vi. 1—3, they professed to return to him.

14. When pressed down by the calamities which their sins had brought upon

14 Yea, they cry not to me with their heart,
      But howl upon their beds :
      For the sake of corn and new wine they assemble ;
      They rebel against me.
15 Though I instructed them, and strengthened their arms,
      Yet they devised evil against me.
16 They may turn, but it is not to the Most High ;
      They are like a deceitful bow ;
      Their rulers shall fall by the sword,

them, they cried to God for deliverance, but without any genuine repentance or sincere resolution to obey him in future. עַל־מִשְׁכְּבוֹתָם, *upon their beds*, i. e. in the night-season, when their anxiety prevented them from sleeping. יִתְגּוֹרָרוּ, the LXX. reading יִתְגּוֹדָדוּ, render κατετέμνοντο, *they cut themselves*, supposing that in token of grief, or, like the maddened priests of Baal, 1 Kings xviii.l28, they inflicted wounds upon their bodies. This is also, in all probability, what the Syr. translator intended by ܥܶܓ̈ܠܳܐ.

But though יִתְגּוֹדָדוּ is found in six MSS., has been in eight more originally, and is the reading of two early editions, one of which is the Soncin. of 1486, it is not sufficiently supported to warrant its adoption into the text. The Targ., Abul-walid, Jarchi, Abenezra, Kimchi, Munster, Piscator, Leo Juda, Junius, Tremellius, Boothroyd, Rosenmüller, Maurer, and Gesenius, support the textual reading, and render *congregate*. This decidedly agrees better with the following בִּי. Instead of returning to Jehovah, the Israelites assembled before their idols to propitiate them by sacrifices, in order to obtain a fruitful harvest. Lee renders, *they become withdrawn, withdraw themselves*, i. e. for idolatrous purposes. To mark more strongly the atrociousness of their apostasy, בִּי, "*against* me," is employed, instead of מִמֶּנִּי, "*from* me," the preposition that otherwise follows סוּר, which is frequently used of apostasy from God to idolatrous practices. The whole phrase is in this case best rendered by *rebel against*, as in our common version.

15. יָסַר does not signify *to bind*, but *to chastise* or *instruct*. The LXX.

instead of rendering the last words of the preceding verse, or rather, perhaps, confounding both verbs, have ἐπαιδεύθησαν. Pococke's Arab. MSS. وانا ادبت Those whose character is here described, had been instructed not only by words, but also in a more severe manner, by the judgments which had been inflicted upon them ; but that the former kind of instruction is meant, seems clear from the phrase חִזַּק זְרוֹעַ, *to strengthen the arm*, i. e. to impart strength or power for the performance of any undertaking. Comp. Ezek. xxx. 24, 25, where both the impartation and the deprivation of such power are mentioned. What the רַע, *evil*, or *wickedness* was, which they cogitated, is not specified ; but it most likely consisted in some new idolatrous alliance, such as that with Egypt, referred to in the next verse. LXX. πονηρά ; Targ. בִּישָׁן, *evil things*.

16. עַל לֹא יָשׁוּבוּ, "*convertunt se ad non-summum*, i. e. ad non-deum, collect. nondeos, i. e. ad deos fictos, vanos." Maurer. Thus also Gesen. in voc. עַל. Comp. for the use of this idiom, Is. x. 15, note. Hosea, who is fond of brevity, uses here and chap. xi. 7, עַל, instead of the longer form עֶלְיוֹן, *Most High*. Kametz is used instead of Patach, on account of the accent. Arab. علم, *altus, excelsus fuit*, to be high in dignity. عال, *altus*. Pococke's Arab. MS. in chap. xi. 7, العالي ; Syr. ܐ̈ܠܳܗܳܐ, *God* ; one of De Rossi's MSS. אֵל. What the apostate

On account of the insolence of their language :
This shall be their derision in the land of Egypt.

Israelites worshipped so far from being the Most High, was the direct opposite, —wood or stone, the produce of the earth. The LXX. ἀπεστράφησαν εἰς οὐδὲν, and Syr. ܐܠ ܩܒܠ ܚܠ ܡܢ, ܡܒܙܚ, to the same effect, though giving the sense rather than an exact translation. The Latin translation of the Syr., *nulla de causa,* is quite erroneous. Most moderns, less aptly, take עַל in its adverbial acceptation, and render, *they return not upwards ;* which yields, however, nearly the same meaning. Thus Rosenmüller, Winer, Manger, Stuck, and others. Newcome's conjectural emendation, לֹא יוֹעִיל, *that which cannot profit,* has not been approved ; while the translation of Dathe, *Pœnitentiam agunt, sed non sinceram,* though approved by Kuinoel, Tingstadius, and others, is not borne out by Hebrew usage. קֶשֶׁת רְמִיָּה some render *a slack bow,* supposing that its inutility, owing to the absence of elasticity, is what is intended ; but *false* or *deceitful* better suits the connexion,

and Ps. lxxviii. 57 ; and the reference is to something faulty in the construction of the bow, which causes it to shoot or throw out the arrow wide of the mark. Root רָמָה, Arab. رمى, *jecit, projecit ; to throw, shoot,* &c. There seems no ground for the opinion of Gesenius, that the phrase is used poetically for treacherous bowmen, who feign fight in order to deceive. The Israelites hypocritically pretended to turn to Jehovah, but their actions took a different direction. Comp. לְשׁוֹן רְמִיָּה, *a deceitful tongue,* Ps. cxx. 2, 3. The *insolence* (Aq. and Symm. ἐμβρίμησιν) *of their language* doubtless consisted in their proud boast of Egypt as a source of protection from the Assyrian invasion, which God was about to bring upon them. לַעֲנָם, *their derision,* i. e. the subject of derision to the Egyptians, to whom they should in vain apply for help. Comp. 2 Kings xvii. 4 ; Is. xxx. 1—7, though the latter passage is immediately directed against a contemporaneous application on the part of the Jews.

CHAPTER VIII

The prophet announces the sudden irruption of the Assyrians, 1 ; by whom the Israelites were to be punished, on account of their hypocrisy and apostasy, 2, 3 ; their illegitimate government, and their idolatry, 4. He then exposes the folly of their idolatrous confidence, and predicts their captivity, 5—10 ; remonstrates with them for their devotion to the worship of idols, in opposition to the express and numerous prohibitions of the evil contained in the divine law, 11, 12 ; and insists that their pretended service of Jehovah, while in reality they forgot him, so far from being of any avail to them, would only bring destruction upon them, 13, 14.

1 PUT the trumpet to thy mouth :
 " Like an eagle against the house of Jehovah ; "
 For they have transgressed my covenant,
 And have rebelled against my law.
2 They may cry to me : " O my God;
 We—Israel—acknowledge thee."
3 Israel hath rejected what is good ;
 [Therefore] the enemy shall pursue him.
4 They made kings, but it was not from me ;

1. It is not unusual for the prophets, without naming the invading foe, to announce his approach. See Is. xiii. 2. The words אֶל־חִכְּךָ שֹׁפָר, *to thy palate the trumpet!* are singularly abrupt, and indicate the suddenness of the threatened invasion. חֵךְ, *palate*, is here, as Job xxxi. 30, Prov. viii. 7, put for the mouth. Comp. chap. v. 8. The LXX. (εἰς κόλπον αὐτῶν ὡς γῆ) appear to have read אֶל־חֵקָם כְּעָפָר, which makes no sense. The following words נֶּשֶׁר עַל־בֵּית יְהֹוָה, which contain the announcement, are equally abrupt. The point of comparison is the rapidity of flight for which the eagle is celebrated, and which is frequently employed to denote the speedy approach of an enemy. Comp. Deut. xxviii. 49 ; Jer. iv. 13, xlviii. 40 ; Lam. iv. 19. בֵּית יְהֹוָה, *the house of Jehovah,* cannot here mean the temple at Jerusalem, which is otherwise so designated, since the threatenings are specially denounced against the kingdom of the ten tribes. It must, therefore, be taken to denote the people of Israel, the whole nation viewed as the family or church of God. Comp. chap. ix. 15 ; Numb. xii. 7 ; Heb. iii. 2 ; just as the Christian church is called *the house of God*, 1 Tim. iii. 15, and of Christ, Heb. iii. 6. For עָבְרוּ בְרִיתִי, comp. chap. vi. 7. The nominative to עָבְרוּ. *they have transgressed*, is בֵּית יְהֹוָה, *the family*, i. e. the members of the church, *of Jehovah*. The Israelites had violated the obligations of the theocracy. בְּרִית and תּוֹרָה are synonymous.

2. יִזְעָקוּ is the future used potentially, and not without irony. אֱלֹהַי, " O *my* God," is construed as a distributive with the plural verb—each of the persons spoken of being regarded as using the language. Inattention to this has led

the Syrian translator to render [Syriac] *O our God.* יִשְׂרָאֵל, *Israel*, is in apposition with יְדַעֲנוּךָ, *we acknowledge thee*, and not the nominative to יִזְעָקוּ, from which it is too far removed. It is entirely omitted in the ¦LXX., Syr., and Arab., as it is in one of Kennicott's MSS., and originally in one of De Rossi's. אֱלֹהֵי יִשְׂרָאֵל, *O God of Israel*, the conjecture of Houbigant, is unnecessary. The present position of the word is more in keeping with the style of Hosea, and the use of it well agrees with the vain confidence which the unbelieving Israelites were ever prone to place in their relation to the patriarchs.

3. זָנַח, Arab. زنخ, *corruptum fuit et fœtuit*, to be corrupt, loathsome, and *to reject* as such. To treat as loathsome what was truly excellent, such as the worship of God and the practice of religion, argued an awfully depraved state of moral feeling. The use of יִשְׂרָאֵל, *Israel*, finely contrasts with that made of it in the preceding verse. טוֹב, *good*, is, by Jerome, Abenezra, Kimchi, and others, taken for God himself, who is described as טוֹב וּמֵטִיב, *good and doing good*, Ps. cxix. 68. *Deum summum bonum*. Œcolampadius. It seems, however, to be used in a more general acceptation. Before אֹיֵב there is an ellipsis of the illative לָכֵן. Forty-seven of De Rossi's MSS. and two more by correction ; eight of the most ancient, and sixty-two other editions ; the Syr., Vulg., and Targ. read יִרְדְּפוּ instead of יִרְדְּפוּ, exhibited in the Textus Receptus. See De Rossi's Scholia Critica.

4. Some think the kings and princes here referred to were Shallum, Menahem,

They set up princes, but I acknowledged them not :
Of their silver and their gold they have made for themselves idols,
In order that they may be cut off.

5   Thy calf, O Samaria! is abominable ;
Mine anger burneth against them :
How long shall they be incapable of purity?

6 For it came even from Israel,

Pekahiah, Pekah, Hoshea, and such of their partizans as were invested with authority ; but from the allusions made in the following verses to the origination of image-worship in Israel, it is more probable that the entire series of Israelitish kings and rulers is intended. Though in the providence of God, and agreeably to the declaration of Ahiah the prophet, the ten tribes revolted from the house of David, and set up a separate and independent kingdom, yet they were actuated merely by rebellious motives, and had no regard to a divine sanction, 1 Kings xi. 31—39, xii. 20. יָדַע signifies not only *to know*, but also *to approve* of that which is known, *regard, allow, own.* Job. ix. 21 ; xxxiv. 4 ; Ps. i. 6, *et freq.* LXX. καὶ οὐκ ἐγνώρισάν μοι. Syr. ܘܠܐ ܐܘܕܥܘܢܝ, *and did not acquaint me,* i. e. held no communications with me upon the subject. The Heb. however, will not bear this interpretation. ו in both cases before לֹא, has the force of a relative, which must either be adopted in translation, or the personal pronoun must be supplied. For their conversion of their silver and gold into idols, comp. chap. ii. 8. לְמַעַן does not appear ever to be taken in a retrospective sense, and so to be referred to what goes before, but is always used with direct reference to what follows. לְמַעַן יִכָּרֵת is, therefore, to be rendered, *in order that they may be cut off;* not *so that they shall,* &c. Comp. Jer. vii. 10 ; xliv. 8. In all such cases the preposition is employed to give peculiar emphasis to the subject. The Israelites could not seriously, or in reality, have intended their own destruction, but they acted as if they had; and it would assuredly overtake them. The nominative to יִכָּרֵת may either be Israel, understood ; or it may have respect to the people collectively.

5. The *calf of Samaria* was not any set up in that city, but the one set up at Bethel, with another at Dan, (or both, if we take the noun as a collective,) which its inhabitants, and those of the country generally, worshipped. The metropolis appears to be used here by synecdoche for the whole land occupied by the ten tribes ; but at the same time, there can be little doubt that its inhabitants were pre-eminent in their devotion to idolatry. זָנַח is used in its primary acceptation, *to be loathsome, abominable.* See on ver. 3. Such construction is preferable to that which would make עֶגְלֵךְ the accusative to זָנַח, assuming יְהֹוָה understood to be the nominative ; or that in our common version which makes it the nominative, and *Samaria* in its pronominal reference the accusative. The introduction of the worship of the golden calves by Jeroboam, in imitation of that of Apis, at Memphis, and of Mnevis, at Heliopolis, which he must have seen during his residence in Egypt, paved the way for the imitation and adoption of the gross idolatries practised by the Phœnicians, Syrians, and Chaldæans. חָרָה אַף יְהֹוָה, *the anger of Jehovah burneth,* is an anthropopathic mode of expression of frequent occurrence in the Hebrew Scriptures, denoting the unconquerable opposition of God to all moral evil, and the severity of the punishment with which it is visited. בָּם *against them,* i. e. the Israelites who worshipped the golden calves. עַד־מָתַי לֹא יוּכְלוּ נִקָּיוֹן, *how long shall they be incapable of purity ?* i. e. how long shall they be obstinately attached to the impure service of idols, and reject the means by which they might be recovered from its stain and punishment ?

6. The golden calf had its origin in Israel : it was not made by any of the surrounding idolaters. The ו in וְהוּא is emphatic. שְׁבָבִים יִהְיֶה, *shall be* or *become flames,* i. e. shall be burned. שְׁבָבִים is a

The carpenter made it;
It is not God:
Surely the calf of Samaria shall become flames.

7 Because they have sown wind,
They shall reap the whirlwind.
They shall have no stalk;
The growth shall produce no grain;
Should it peradventure produce it,
Strangers shall swallow it up.

8 Israel is swallowed up;
They are now among the nations,
Like a vessel in which is no delight.

9 For they went up to Assyria,
Like a solitary wild ass:
Ephraim hath given the hire of love.

ἅπαξ λεγ. and has no root in Heb.; but comp. the Arab. شب, *accendit ignem.* شيب, *ardor, flamma.* As the calf was made by man, so it should by man be converted into fuel for the flames. It consisted, in all probability, of wood, thickly overlaid with gold. When taken as a present to the king of Assyria, (see chap. x. 6,) instead of being worshipped or held in respect, it would be stripped of the gold, and consigned to the flames. The LXX. followed by the Arab., Horsley, and Newcome, improperly translate בִּ, מִיִשְׂרָאֵל, ἐν τῷ Ἰσραήλ, في اسرايل, *in Israel,* and join the words to those of the preceding verse.

7. סוּפָתָה is the emphatic form of סוּפָה, *a tornado, whirlwind.* Leo Juda, *magnum turbinem.* Comp. אֵימָה, Exod. xv. 16; יָשׁוּעָתָה, Ps. iii. 3. The nominative to לוֹ is יִשְׂרָאֵל understood; but it is best to take it collectively, in harmony with the plural of the preceding verbs. Observe the paronomasia in צֶמַח בְּלִי יַעֲשֶׂה קֶמַח. The Israelites should be unsuccessful in all their undertakings; and whatever partial gains they might acquire, would be eagerly seized by the Assyrians.

8. What Hosea had just foretold is here realized in prophetic vision. He sees them in a state of exile—the objects of contempt to their oppressors. Comp. Jer. xxii. 28.

9, 10. עָלָה, *to go up,* is elsewhere used of foreigners coming to the land of Israel; but it is here employed with singular propriety of the Israelites going to Assyria, to intimate their depressed condition, and their acknowledgment of the superiority of the Assyrian power. The reference is not to their going into captivity, but to the embassy which they sent for the purpose of obtaining aid from that quarter. אַשּׁוּר stands for אַשּׁוּרָה, the ה of direction being omitted. The point of comparison in the "wild ass" is his untractableness, and his disposition to take his own way, in consequence of which he forsakes the society of others, and loves the solitariness of the desert. See Job xxxix. 5—8. Thus it was with Israel. Despite of all the counsels and warnings given them by the prophets, they persisted in entering into foreign alliances. הָנָה, *to give presents, hire,* &c. is purposely chosen, to convey the idea of a violation of the marriage-contract by unlawful commerce with another party—the derivatives אֶתְנָן and אֶתְנָה, properly denoting a gift or reward given to a whore. See on chap. ii. 12. The aggravation of the evil is signified by representing the female as offering these

10 Yet though they have hired among the nations,
   I will now gather them ;
   And they shall suffer in a little
   By reason of the tribute of the king of princes.

rewards to her paramours to induce them to commit lewdness, instead of her being prevailed upon by presents made by them. Comp. Ezek. xvi. 33, 34. Though in Hiphil, the verb has here the same signification as in Kal. אֹהֲבִים, lit. *loves*, a plural not in use in English. Jerome, who renders, *munera dederunt amatoribus*, either read אֹהֲבִים, which is found in one of De Rossi's MSS., or he took אֲהָבִים in a concrete sense, as our translators appear to have done, for which there is no necessity. Instead of יִתְנוּ at the beginning of ver. 10, two of De Rossi's MSS., the LXX., Syr., Vulg., Targ., and Arab. read יִתְּנוּ, as if from נָתַן ; according to which the Israelites are represented as *delivered over to*, or placed in the power of the nations. The fifth Greek version, however, has ἀλλὰ καὶ ὅταν μισθώσηται ἔθνη, which is preferable, as it is most likely that the prophet repeated the verb he had just used, and as the other rendering is less suited to the connexion. עַתָּה, *now*, i.e. shortly. Comp. מְעַט immediately after. The suffix in אֲקַבְּצֵם, "I will collect *them*," belongs to הַגּוֹיִם, *the nations*, and not to the nominative to יִתְנוּ, or the Israelites. קָבַץ is used in Piel in a bad as well as in a good sense. Comp. Ezek. xvi. 37. Thus Kimchi and Abarbanel. Instead of affording any assistance, the Assyrians would be collected against the apostate Israelites, invade their land, and carry them into captivity. Into that state of suffering, imposed upon them by the king of Assyria, they were shortly to be brought, as a punishment for their idolatrous desertion of the true worship of God. וַיָּחֵלּוּ מְעָט מִמַּשָּׂא מֶלֶךְ שָׂרִים has been variously interpreted. Gesenius renders, " *and they* (the hostile nations,) *shall presently set* them *free from the burden of the king*, i.e. from his oppressive yoke ;" but without any suitable sense—the whole passage being of a comminatory nature, and not promissory of good. הָחֵל, the Hiph. of חָלַל, has nowhere the signification of *loosing*

or *setting free*. Nor is there any propriety in taking it in the usual sense of *beginning*, and so construing it with מְעָט, as if the latter word were the infinitive of the verb מָעַט, *to be diminished*. The ancient versions refer to חוּל, as the root, in the sense of *waiting, desisting from*, &c. LXX. κοπάσουσι. Symm. μενοῦσιν. Theod. διαλείψουσι. Syr. ܢܬܬܢܝܚܘܢ. Vulg. *quiescent*. And in this reference I concur, especially as ten MSS. and forty-four editions, read וְיֶחְדְּלוּ without the Dagesh in the Lamed: only I would abide by the signification, *to be in pain, affliction*, which is that given to the verb in our common version. Such construction alone suits the connexion. By some מֶלֶךְ שָׂרִים are considered to be an instance of asyndeton ; and twenty-one MSS. and originally ten more, the LXX., Aq., Syr., Vulg., Targ., and Talm. Babyl. supply the copulative ו before שָׂרִים. So Kimchi, Mercer, Grotius, Houbigant, Dathe, Michaelis, Kuinoel, Newcome, Tingstadius. It has been doubted, however, whether, according to this resolution of the word, they should be referred to the native king and princes, or to those of Assyria. Some, as Maurer, take them to be the nominative to וְיֶחְדְּלוּ, and make the sense end with מַשָּׂא, *the burden* or *tribute*, supposing the heavy taxes imposed by the Israelitish rulers to be intended. The best sense is brought out by reading מֶלֶךְ שָׂרִים in construction, *the king of princes*, and applying the phrase to the king of Assyria, who had many kings and princes subject to his sway. Comp. Is. x. 8. Thus Pococke's Arabic MS., Leo Juda, Drusius, Jun. and Tremel., Piscator, Eichhorn, Boeckel, Goldwitzer, Hitzig, and Ewald. The מַשָּׂא, *burden*, was the tribute exacted by Menahem, and paid to Pul, amounting to a thousand talents of silver, 2 Kings xv. 19—22. Comp. כֶּסֶף מַשָּׂא, *tribute money*, 2 Chron. xvii. 11.

11   When Ephraim multiplied altars to sin,
  They became to him altars to sin.
12   I may prescribe for him the numerous things of my law;
  They are treated as a strange thing.
13   As for my sacrificial offerings,
  They sacrifice flesh and eat it;
  Jehovah accepteth them not:
  He will speedily remember their iniquity,
  And will punish their sin:
  They shall return to Egypt.

11. By multiplying altars, in opposition to the express prohibition, Deut. xii. 13, 14, the Ephraimites not only contracted great guilt, but paved the way for the introduction of other sins.

Syr. إِذًا أَهْكَمَا, *ad crimen ingens.*

There is an easy but beautiful variation in the repetition of the words. As used the second time, חָטָא possesses considerable emphasis. Comp. for a similar instance of varied repetition, Is. xxvii. 5. It shows how much the mind of the prophet was affected by the wickedness of his people. Some suppose that there is a play upon the double meaning of חָטָא as signifying *to sin*, and *to be punished for sin*, just as our Lord uses νέκροι in two senses, Matt. viii. 22; but the second signification cannot attach to the verb in this connexion.

12. אֶכְתָּב, Keri אֶכְתָּב, is continuative and potential, and is equivalent to, I have prescribed, I still prescribe by my prophets, and I may go on prescribing; it will be of no avail. Keri רֻבֵּי, in many MSS. רֻבֵּי, the plural of רֹב, which is properly the infinitive of רָבַב, *to be great, numerous*, &c. Here the idea of number is evidently designed to express the abundant provisions God had made in his written law, and its enforcement by the prophets, against the commission of idolatry. According to the Chethiv רֻבֵּי, we should render, "I may prescribe to him my laws *by myriads;*" Ewald, *by thousands;* Hitzig, *by ten thousands.*

The Syr. ܣܰܓܺܝܐܘ ܢܳܡܘܣܐ. Targ. סַגִּיאַת אוֹרָיְתִי. Vulg. *multiplices leges meas.*

Pococke's Arab. MS. عِثْرَةَ شَرِيعَتِي.

Aq. πληθυμένους νόμους. Symm. πλῆθος νόμων μου. חֻקִּים, *statutes*, are understood. חָשַׁב signifies not only *to think, regard*, &c., but also to treat in a manner corresponding to the estimation in which a person or thing is held.

Tanchum, يطرحونها كالغريب الذي لا يوبه إليه, *they reject them like a strange thing to which no regard is paid.*

13. וּבְחֵי הַבְהָבַי form the nominative absolute. הַבְהָבַי, *my gifts* or *offerings*, i.e. such as they professedly offer to me. The word is contracted for יְהַבְהָבַי, and is derived from יָהַב, *to give.* It seems preferable to abide by this usual signification of the verb, which it has likewise in Aramaic, Arabic, and Ethiopic, than to follow Kimchi, who refers the noun to a root הָבְהַב, to which he assigns the signification *to burn, scorch, roast;* or Ewald, who, appealing to the Chald.

הַבְהֵב, and the Arab. هَبْ and هَبْهَبْ, renders, *raw offerings.* הַבְהָבַי is a more choice term for מִנְחוֹת, or מַתָּנוֹת. For the reduplicate form, comp. אֲהַבְהֵבוּ, chap. iv. 18; which word the LXX., Syr., and Targ. appear to have followed in this place; of which Hitzig seems to approve. Aq., observant of the gemination, renders, θυσίας φέρε φέρε θυσιάζουσιν. Symm. θυσίας ἐπαλλήλους. Theod. θυσίαν μεταφορῶν ἐθυσίασαν. Jehovah rejected the sacrifices that were offered, not

14 Because Israel hath forgotten his Maker, and built temples,
And Judah hath multiplied fortified cities;
Therefore will I send a fire into his cities,
And it shall consume the palaces of each.

according to his own appointment, but to gratify the carnal appetite of the worshippers. Reference is had to the sacrifices offered to him, as represented by the golden calf. In רָעֵם לֹא is a meiosis. עַתָּה, *now*, is here used in the sense of *speedily, shortly*. From the references made chap. ix. 3, 6, xi. 11, it is clear that the last clause of the verse predicts the actual return of a number of the Israelites to Egypt, whither, in all probability, they fled when the kingdom was broken up by the Assyrians. The threatening pointedly reminded them of the depressed condition in which their ancestors had been in that country. Comp. Deut. xxviii. 68. The LXX. add, καὶ ἐν Ἀσσυρίοις ἀκάθαρτα φάγονται; but the words are wanting in the Aldine edition, and in seven MSS. They have evidently found their way into the text from chap. ix. 3, where they stand in

accordance with the reading of all the Heb. MSS.

14. ו in וַיִּשְׁכַּח marks the protasis; in וְשִׁלַּחְתִּי the apodosis. The הֵיכָלוֹת were doubtless *idolatrous temples* erected after the models of those in use among the Syrians and Phœnicians. See, for the. word, my note on Is. vi. 1. Though idolatry had not made the same progress in Judah, the inhabitants nevertheless evinced a want of confidence in Jehovah by fortifying a number of cities, to which they trusted for defence. The masculine suffix in בְּעָרָיו refers to Judah; the feminine in אַרְמְנוֹתֶיהָ to each of the cities, taken singly. Ewald strangely asserts, that the words of this verse appear to have been inserted from some book of Amos no longer in existence! Compare, however, for the latter distich, Jer. xlix. 27; Amos i. 4, 7, 10, 12, 14; ii. 2, 5; and see note on Amos i. 4.

CHAPTER IX

The prophet checks the propensity of the Israelites to indulge in excessive joy on account of any partial relief from their troubles, 1; predicts the failure of the crops, &c. in consequence of the Assyrian invasion, 2; their removal to Egypt and Assyria, where they should have no opportunity, even if they were inclined, to serve Jehovah according to their ancient ritual, 3—5; and the hopelessness of their returning to enjoy the property they had left behind, 6. He then announces the certain infliction of the divine judgments, and points out the true character of the false prophets, by whom the people had been led astray to their ruin, 7, 8. Illustrative references are next made to the early history of the Hebrew nation, accompanied with appropriate comminations couched in varied forms, in order to render them more affecting, 9—17.

1 CARRY not thy joy, O Israel! to exultation, like the nations,
　For thou hast lewdly departed from thy God;
　Thou hast loved the hire,
　On all the corn floors.

2 Neither the floor nor the vat shall nourish them;
　And the new wine shall fail therein.

3 They shall not dwell in the land of Jehovah,
　But Ephraim shall return to Egypt,
　And in Assyria, they shall eat what is unclean.

1. אַל־תִּשְׂמַח—אֶל־גִּיל, lit. *rejoice not to exultation.* The LXX., Syr., Targ., and Vulg. read אַל גִּיל, *exult not;* but contrary to the *usus loquendi,* which requires the verb following אַל to be in the future tense, as Seeker properly observes. Some find in the comparison "like the nations," an imitation of their idolatrous festivities; but the language is rather predictive of the joyless condition to which the Israelites were to be reduced. While those by whom they were surrounded, and especially their Assyrian invaders, should indulge in unrestrained mirth, they should experience affliction and sorrow. There is most probably a reference to the joy occasioned by the league entered into with Pul, by which peace seemed to be secured. Their joy was to be of short duration, and therefore required to be moderate. Instead of בַּעֲמִּים, thirteen MSS., originally five more, one by correction, and five editions, read בְעַמִּים, "*among* the nations," of which Rosenmüller, following Abarbanel, approves. The prophet adds the reason why they should have no cause for exultation—their abounding idolatries, by which they incurred the judgments of God. These idolatries they carried to such a pitch, that they erected shrines at their threshing-floors, in order to offer at them the oblations of their grain. The crops were considered to have been bestowed by the idols in compensation for the worship rendered to them, (see chap. ii. 5, 12, 13;) and are therefore spoken of as אֶתְנַן, *a meretricious reward.*

2. For וְכִחֵשׁ, in reference to the failure of the productions of the earth, see Hab. iii. 17. The verb properly signifies *to lie, deceive,* &c.; figuratively, *to fail.* Twenty-six MSS., originally sixteen more, and perhaps two, three

editions, with the support of the LXX., Syr., Targ., and Vulg., read בָּם, *in them,* i. e. *them,* the Israelites, instead of בָּהּ, *in her,* the received reading. It is, however, too plainly an emendation to entitle it to adoption. Nothing is more common than for our prophet to use first a plural, and then a singular suffix of the same subject: according to the rule laid down by Tanchum, that when in a continued discourse a nation or people is spoken of, either the feminine affix agreeing with עדה, *congregation,* or the masculine agreeing with עם, *people,* may be used; as also, that the singular may be used of them, viewed as a body, and the plural, when they are regarded as consisting of distinct individuals. See in Pococke. At the same time it is better in a translation to render them alike, as in the ancient versions just quoted.

3. Canaan was called אֶרֶץ יְהוָה, *the land of Jehovah,* because he had appropriated it for an inheritance to those whom he had chosen to be his peculiar people. It was his gift to Abraham and his posterity, to be enjoyed by them on condition of their fidelity in his service. For this end he attached to it his special blessing, Deut. xi. 10—12. Comp. Jer. ii. 7; xvi. 18; Ezek. xxxvi. 20. The return to Egypt being here mentioned in connexion with an exile in Assyria, proves that it is to be taken literally, and that it is not designed to express a servitude similar to that of Egypt. See on chap. viii. 13. The fulfilment of this prediction in the history of the ten tribes, is nowhere mentioned in Scripture. No doubt the number that fled to Egypt was small, compared with the body of the nation carried into the Assyrian exile. By מִצְרָא is meant *pro-*

4 They shall not pour out wine to Jehovah,
Neither shall their sacrifices please him;
They shall be to them as the bread of mourners,
All that eat thereof shall be unclean:
For their bread shall be for themselves;
It shall not come unto the house of Jehovah.

5 What will ye do on the day of assembly?
On the day of Jehovah's festival?

6 For, behold! they go away from destruction,
But Egypt shall gather them, Memphis shall bury them;
As for their coveted treasuries of money, nettles shall possess them:
Thorns shall be in their tents.

---

hibited food, meats pronounced unclean by the Mosaic law. Comp. Ezek. iv. 13. To such necessity should they be reduced as captives.

4. נָסַךְ is used of the pouring out of wine for a libation, Gr. σπένδειν, Exod. xxx. 9. עָרַב, properly *to mix, mingle,* came to signify *sweet, agreeable, pleasing,* from the circumstance, that what was pleasant to the taste, often consisted of mixed ingredients. לֶחֶם אוֹנִים, *bread,* or *food of sorrows,* i. e. such as was eaten by mourners for the dead, and consequently regarded as unclean, on account of the contact in which they were supposed to come with the dead body. See Numb. xix. 14, 15, 22; Jer. xvi. 7, 8; Ezek. xxiv. 17; Hagg. ii. 12, 13. Instead of feasting upon the sacrifices as their fathers had been accustomed to do, when they slew them according to the law, which was always an occasion of joy, they should be placed in circumstances in which no such sacrifices could be offered, and no such feasts enjoyed. Their food should all be common,— לְנַפְשָׁם, *for their soul* or *life,* i. e. merely for their own sustenance; not fit to be presented to the Lord. Thus Schmidius, Grotius, and others.

5. In captivity they would find it impossible to observe their solemn feasts,— a great aggravation of their punishment. Comp. chap. ii. 11. The exposition of Jarchi, Abenezra, Kimchi, Mercer, Capito, and others, according to which, the day of punishment, represented under the idea of sacrifice, is meant, cannot be sustained.

6. The prophet here specially describes those Israelites who should take alarm at the invasion of the country by the Assyrians, and flee for safety into Egypt. They imagined that their stay there would only be temporary; but it is predicted that they should no more return to their possessions, and be buried in their fathers' sepulchres, but should die in the land, and have their interment among the mummies of Egypt. For *Memphis,* as the great necropolis of that country, see my note on Isaiah xix. 13. קָבַץ, *to gather,* is here used in reference to the removal of the soul at death into the world of spirits, and is equivalent to נֶאֱסַף. Numb. xx. 26, or the full phrases נֶאֱסַף אֶל־עַמּוֹ, and נֶאֱסַף אֶל־אֲבוֹתָיו, *to be gathered to one's people or fathers,* which is always spoken of as something different from death and burial. Comp. Jer. viii. 2; Ezek. xxix. 5, in which latter passage אָסַף, and קָבַץ, are used as synonymes. According to the signification of the cognate Arab. verb, قبض, *cepit, apprehendit manu rem,* it conveys the idea of God's taking away the soul. Hence the phrase قبض الله, *mortuus est,* literally, *God took him;* and قبض simply, *mortuus est* (ad Dei misericordiam delatus). Freytag. When it is said that Egypt should gather and Memphis bury the Israelitish fugitives, the meaning is that they should be removed out of this world, and that their bodies should be buried there. The

7 The days of punishment are come,
The days of retribution are come;
Israel shall know it :
The prophet is foolish,
The man of the spirit is frantic,
Because of the greatness of thy punishment,
And because the provocation is great.

personification is employed, as usual, for the sake of effect. מַחְמָד, *desire, covetousness;* that which is *the object of desire, what is covetable, coveted,* from חָמַד, *to desire, covet.* As the verb יְרָשֵׁם has a plural suffix, this noun is here to be taken as a collective, and rendered in the plural. The idea of treasury is supplied by the connexion. כֶּסֶף is used generally of *money,* as in most other places, when זָהָב, *gold,* is not combined with it. Targ. בֵּית חֶמְדַת בִּסְפְּהוֹן, *the house of their desirable money.* Symm. τὰ ἐπιθυμήματα τοῦ ἀργυρίου αὐτῶν. Others, less aptly, explain the words of houses, palaces, &c. adorned with silver. On leaving those treasures which they could not carry with them, the Israelites would naturally bury them in the earth, which accounts for the very significant phrase, "the nettles shall inherit them." For the combination קִמּוֹשׂ or קִמּוֹשׂ and חוֹחַ, comp. Is. xxxiv. 13. The whole verse is miserably translated by the LXX.

7. פְּקֻדָּה, *visitation, punishment.* Comp. Is. x. 3; 1 Pet. ii. 12. יֵדַע, *shall know experimentally.* By the נָבִיא is obviously to be understood in this place, the false *prophet* or prophets by whom the people of the ten tribes were seduced from the right worship of Jehovah, who taught them to worship the golden calves, and otherwise encouraged them in their idolatrous practices. Thus Pococke's Arab. MS. ‏البدعي نبوة‎, *he that pretends to prophecy;* and Kimchi, נביאי שקר, *lying prophets.* With this, the phrase אִישׁ הָרוּחַ, *the man of the Spirit,* is synonymous; one pretending to inspiration, or professing to deliver oracles under the influence of a divine efflatus. LXX. ἄνθρωπος ὁ πνευματοφόρος. Syr. ‏ܐܢܫܐ ܕܟܠܝܠܐ ܗܘ ܪܘܚܐ‎, *the man*

that is clothed, or *endued with the spirit,* only adding, by way of explanation, but erroneously, ‏ܕܣܟܠܘܬܐ‎, *of folly.* Comp. Mic. ii. 11, אִישׁ הֹלֵךְ רוּחַ ; 1 Cor. xiv. 37, εἴ τις δοκεῖ προφήτης εἶναι ἢ πνευματικός; 2 Pet. i. 21, ὑπὸ πνεύματος ἁγίου φερόμενοι; and see my Lectures on Divine Inspiration, p. 25. מְשֻׁגָּע, *insane, frantic;* Arab. ‏سجع‎, *locutus fuit rhythmicè,* to speak in an impassioned manner, like an inspired poet; hence, from the violence of the gesticulations, tones, &c., *to act like a madman, to be mad, insane.* Comp. Jer. xxix. 26, where אִישׁ מְשֻׁגָּע and מִתְנַבֵּא are synonymous. The meaning is, that the pretenders to inspiration, by whose false predictions of uninterrupted prosperity the people had been deluded, should be convicted of *folly,* and reduced to a state of absolute frenzy by the infliction of the divine judgments upon the nation. Hosea introduces this declaration respecting the Israelitish prophets parenthetically, thereby giving force to his own prediction of impending calamity. The affix in עֲוֹנְךָ refers to יִשְׂרָאֵל, to whom the prophet turns in the way of direct address. עָוֹן, means here, not the *crime,* but its punishment. Comp. for this signification of the term, Is. v. 18, and my note there. In וְרַבָּה subaud. כִּי, *because.* The adjective רַבָּה, is here placed before its substantive for the sake of emphasis. See on Is. liii. 11. From the use of שָׂטַם in the sense of *hating, evincing hostility,* &c., there can be little doubt that the derivative מַשְׂטֵמָה, which occurs only in this and the following verse, has the signification of *hostility, provoking conduct, provocation.* That of *snare* or *trap,* which Gesenius assigns to it, is not borne out, even by the

8 Ephraim expecteth help from my God ;
     The prophet is a fowler's snare in all his ways ;
     The cause of provocation in the house of his god.
9 They have deeply corrupted themselves,
     As in the days of Gibeah ;
     He will remember their iniquity,
     He will punish their sin.
10   I found Israel, like grapes in the desert ;
     Like the first early fruit of the fig tree, at its commencement,

---

Syriac ܡܚܠܦ, which signifies *vinxit,
compedivit*, but not to *ensnare*. Comp.
the Arab. ܣܠܛ, *acies gladii ; acutiores
et fervidiores hominum*. LXX. μανία;
Aq. ἐγκότησις; Αλλ. ἔκστασις; all of
which convey the idea of great excitement, and yield support to the interpretation I have given. The idolatrous
practices of the Israelites are meant, by
which they provoked the righteous indignation of Jehovah.

8. צֹפֶה אֶפְרַיִם, are not in construction,
and to be rendered as in most versions,
"the watchman of Ephraim," to justify
which construction various modes of
exegesis have been resorted to; among
others that of Horsley, who would have
the watchman to be Elijah. Nor can
the rendering of Ewald be sustained,
who gives the passage, *Ein Späher ist
Efraim gegen meinen Gott ;* "Ephraim
is a spy against my God." When עִם
signifies *against*, it follows verbs of
more active import. *E. schaut nach
Weissagungen aus neben meinem Gott ;*
"Ephraim looks for prophecies besides
my God,"—the rendering of Hitzig, is
equally objectionable. I quite agree
with Gesenius and Lee, in assigning to
צָפָה in this place the signification of
looking out, expecting, as in Ps. v. 4;
Lam. iv. 17, in Piel. עִם, *with*, is used
elliptically for מֵעִם, *from with*, i.e. *from.*
A similar ellipsis undeniably occurs, Job
xxvii. 13. זֶה חֵלֶק־אָדָם רָשָׁע עִם־אֵל, *this is
the portion of a wicked man from* (עִם,
with,) *God*, as appears, not only from
the synonymous phrase מִשַּׁדַּי, "FROM *the
Almighty*," in the corresponding hemistich, but from the actual use of מִן,
from, in the parallel passage, chap. xx.

29. What the prophet asserts is, that
the Ephraimites indulged in expectations
of good from Jehovah, notwithstanding
their dereliction of his worship in its
pure and legitimate forms, and their
adoption of the idolatrous practices of
the heathen around them. In this they
were encouraged by the false prophets,
who caught them by their ensnaring
doctrines, as is declared immediately
after. מַשְׂטֵמָה is here used in the same
acceptation as in the preceding verse,
only there is a metonymy of the effect
for the cause. By בֵּית אֱלֹהָיו, " the house
of his god," is not meant the temple or
people of the true God, but the temple
or temples in which the false worship
was performed, which the prophets here
reprobated were specially active in pro-
moting.

9. הֶעְמִיקוּ שִׁחֵתוּ, an instance of the constructio asyndeta. The former of the
two verbs is to be rendered adverbially.
For its use before infinitives, see on
chap. v. 2. Mercer, " Quam corruptis-
simi sunt." שִׁחֵתוּ may either be taken
intransitively, or עֲלִילוֹתֵיהֶם, דַּרְכֵּיהֶם, or the
like, must be supplied. So great was
the depravity evinced by those whose
conduct the prophet here describes, that
it could only be paralleled by the
atrocity of the inhabitants of Gibeah,
specified Judges xix. 22—30.

10. יִשְׂרָאֵל, *Israel*, here means the ancestors of the Hebrew nation. It has
been asked, " How could God be said to
find the Hebrews in the wilderness,
since he conducted them into it from
Egypt ?" To remove the difficulty, some
very unwarrantably explain the wilderness of Egypt itself; but others connect
כַּעֲנָבִים בַּמִּדְבָּר, *like grapes in the desert*,
and explain מָצָא of *finding by experience*,

I regarded your fathers;
But they came to Baal-peor,
And separated themselves to the object of shame;
They became abominable, like the object of their love.

11 As for Ephraim, their glory shall fly away, like a bird;
There shall be no birth, no womb, no conception.

12 Yea, though they should rear their children,
I would take them away from among men;
But wo to them! when I depart from them.

---

trial, &c. Such they were, proved themselves to be in my judgment. And this seems to be the proper division and interpretation of the words. At the same time מָצָא בְּאֶרֶץ מִדְבָּר occurs in reference to the same subject, Deut. xxxii. 10, where the verb must be taken in the sense of *reaching* with sufficient aid.

Comp. the Eth. ዐጸወ : *venit;* Arab.

قضى, *perduxit, tractavit negotium;* and chap. xiii. 5; Jer. xxxi. 2. The point of comparison in the verse is the delight with which a traveller enjoys grapes found in a desert, in which they were unexpected, and where they served most opportunely to quench his thirst; or the early fig, which is accounted a great delicacy in the East. When Jehovah entered into covenant with the people of Israel at Sinai, they were regarded by him with delight, being free from idolatry, and engaging to adhere to his service. Comp. chap. xi. 1; Jer. xxxi. 3. The scene, however, was soon changed. הֵמָּה, *illi, these* very persons. At Baal-peor, they proved faithless, and indulged in the very atrocities of which their posterity were guilty in the days of the prophet. For the transactions referred to, see Numb. xxv. 1—5. Priapism, which Hosea justly characterises as in the highest degree abominable, was the worship peculiarly acceptable to the god of Peor. See Calmet and Winer in voc.—נָזַר signifies *to separate oneself* from any person or thing, and also, followed by לְ, to separate or *devote oneself* to some religious object. Hence the substantive נָזִיר, *a Nazarite;* נֵזֶר *consecration.* בֹּשֶׁת is the abstract for the concrete, and denotes the obscene

or shameful idol which the Moabites worshipped. שִׁקּוּצִים, lit. *abominations,* but used here adjectively, *loathsome, abominable.* אֹהֲבָם is properly the substantive, אֹהֵב—the points being changed on account of the suffix. Vulg., facti sunt abominabiles sicut ea, quæ dilexerunt. The Hebrews became as abominable as the impure idol whose rites they celebrated. העובד שקוץ הוא שקוץ, *he that serveth an abomination, is himself an abomination.* Kimchi's MS. note in Pococke.

11, 12. אֶפְרַיִם, *Ephraim,* is of the nominative absolute, which gives prominence to the name, and its signification. As for *Ephraim,* (אֶפְרַיִם, from פָּרָה, *to be fruitful,* Gen. xli. 52,) such may be his name, but, &c. כָּבוֹד, *glory,* is in contrast with בֹּשֶׁת, *shame,* in the preceding verse. The lewd and idolatrous conduct of the Israelites should meet with a fit retribution. Instead of having an increase of children, that might grow up and become the *glory* of the land, those who might now be accounted such should speedily be removed into Assyria, and there would be nothing but sterility to characterise the nation. The preposition מ, prefixed to the three last substantives, is privative in signification. בֶּטֶן, *womb,* stands here for *pregnancy,* or for the *fœtus* in the womb. The order of the words presents an instance of the gradatio inversa. מֵאָדָם, *among men,* as תִּשְׁכַּל מִנָּשִׁים אִמֶּךָ "thy mother shall be childless *among* women," 1 Sam. xv. 33. Ewald and Hitzig translate בְּשׂוּרִי, *when I look away from them,* contending that we should read שׂ instead of שׁ; but no MS. is thus pointed, and the present punctuation is so far supported by the LXX. (σάρξ μου,

13 I see Ephraim, like Tyre, planted in a pleasant place ;
But Ephraim shall bring out his children to the murderer.

14   Give them, O Jehovah!—what wilt thou give?
Give them a miscarrying womb, and dry breasts.

15 All their wickedness is in Gilgal ;
Surely I have hated them there :
On account of the wickedness of their deeds,
I have driven them out of my house ;
I will love them no more :
All their princes are rebels.

16 Ephraim is smitten, their root is dried up :
They shall produce no fruit :

---

i.e. בְּשֹׂרִי), Aq., Vulg., and Targ. Three
MSS. and one edit. have בְּכוֹרִי, to which
בְּשׂוֹרִי is doubtless here equivalent. Many
instances occur of the substitution of שׂ
for ס, and *vice versâ*. The meaning is,
when I withdraw my protection from
them; no longer showing them any
favour, but delivering them over to their
enemies. For the abortive attempt of
Lyra to prove a corruption of the passage
by the Jews, and to palm upon the rendering of the LXX. σάρξ μου ἐξ αὐτῶν,
the doctrine of the incarnation of the
Messiah, see Pococke.

13. After אֶפְרַיִם supply רָאִיתִי, from the
following כַּאֲשֶׁר רָאִיתִי לְצֹר. Though רָאָה
commonly governs the accusative, yet,
in Ps. lxiv. 6, it is followed as here by
the dative, without any difference of
signification. LXX. εἰς θήραν, reading
צֵד, instead of צֹר. Aq., Symm. ἀκρό-
τομον ; Theod. πέτραν ; Arnoldi, and
after him Hitzig, would derive צוֹר from
the Arab. صور, as signifying the Palm ;
but it only signifies the root of that tree,
or describes it as small in size, an acceptation which would ill suit the present
connexion. Ewald renders, *Bild, image*
or *likeness*. The point of comparison is
the beautiful situation of Tyre. See
Ezek. xxvii. 3 ; xxviii. 12, 13. The
notion of planting seems to have been
suggested by the name of Ephraim.
See the preceding note. The territory
occupied by that tribe and several of
the other nine, was distinguished for
its beauty and fertility ; and the prosperity of its inhabitants, who traded

extensively with the Phœnician ports,
was only surpassed by that of Tyre herself. Yet the fruit of this lovely region
was only to be produced in order to its
being destroyed. The inhabitants were
to be slain in great numbers with the
sword. The ל before the infinitive in
לְהוֹצִיא, is future in signification, indicating what was about to be, or would be
done.

14. These words strongly mark the
effect produced upon the mind of the
prophet by the contemplation of the
wickedness of his people. In holy ardour of soul, he feels himself excited to
imprecate what he had predicted ver. 11.
Some, less appropriately, render מָה, not
as an interrogative, but as signifying *that
which*, i.e. give them whatever thou wilt.
Barrenness was accounted a great mis-
fortune among the Jews.

15. For *Gilgal*, see on chap. iv. 15.
Being one of the chief places of idolatrous worship, the wickedness of the
nation might be said to be concentrated
in it. When God is represented as
hating the wicked, it must be understood
in regard to the odiousness of their
moral character, and his infliction of
positive punishment upon them on account of it. Hitzig considers שָׂנֵא to be
here used inchoatively. For the sense
in which בֵּית, *house*, is to be taken, see
on chap. viii. 1. Hatred and love are
contrasted as here, Mal. i. 2, 3. In
שָׂרֵיהֶם סוֹרְרִים is a paronomasia.

16. The figurative language here employed is suggested by the meaning of
the name Ephraim, as in verses 11, 13.

Yea, though they should beget children,
I will kill the beloved of their womb.

17 My God will abhor them,
Because they have not listened to him :
And they shall be wanderers among the nations.

יְעֵשׂוּן is in the future, while הָפָּה and יָבֵשׁ are in the preterite, to mark the state of unfruitfulness as following upon the injury done to the tree. The resolution of the figure in the latter half of the verse possesses much force. Most of the MSS. and some few editions read, with the Keri, בְּ instead of בְּלִי, which occurs, however, before a verb, Job xli. 18. For מַחֲמַדִּים, comp. on מַחְמַד, ver. 6.

17. Though the pronominal affix in אֱלֹהַי is omitted by the LXX. and Arab. and one of Kennicott's MSS., it is, in such connexion, more in the style of Hosea than אֱלֹהִים. The dispersion of the ten tribes is here expressly predicted.

CHAPTER X

In this chapter the prophet continues to charge the Israelites with idolatry, anarchy, and want of fidelity, 1—4. He expatiates with great variety on the judgments that were to come upon them in punishment of these crimes, 5—11 ; and then abruptly turns to them in a direct hortatory address, couched in metaphorical language, borrowed from the mode of representation which he had just employed, 12. The section concludes with an appeal to the experience which they had already had of the disastrous consequences of their wicked conduct, 13—15.

---

1 ISRAEL is a luxuriant vine ;
   He putteth forth his fruit ;
   According to the increase of his fruit,
   He increased altars ;
   According to the excellence of his land,
   They prepared goodly statues.

1. The wickedness which manifested itself in idolatry, &c. is here traced to the abuse of the prosperity which God had conferred on the Israelites. Instead of spending the bounties of providence for the glory of God, they appropriated them to idolatrous uses, and that in proportion to the abundance of their bestowment. בָּקַק, Arab. بَقَّ, multum fudit, fœcundus fuit, multum pluviæ demisit, florere cœpit planta, is here used to express the luxuriance of the vine, and not, as in our common version

2 Their heart is divided, they shall now be punished :
   He will cut off their altars, he will destroy their statues.

3 Surely now shall they say : We have no king ;
   For we fear not Jehovah :
   As for the king then , what can he do for us ?

4   They utter empty speeches ;
   Swearing falsely, making covenants :
   Therefore judgment blossoms like the poppy
   On the ridges of the field.

and some others, its unfruitfulness. The
idea of emptying, which the verb also
has, derived from that of *pouring out
entirely* or *abundantly* the contents of a
vessel, does not suit the present connexion. LXX. εὐκληματοῦσα, or, as
in other copies, ἐγκληματοῦσα. Aq.
ἔνυδρος. Symm. ὑλομανοῦσα. Vulg.
frondosa. Comp. Gen. xlix. 22 ; Ps.
lxxx. 9—11 ; Ezek. xvii. 6. In every
other instance גֶּפֶן is construed as a feminine ; but here the masculine name
יִשְׂרָאֵל, *Israel*, required it to be taken as
of that gender. שָׁוָה, *to resemble, be
equal to, sufficient ;* in Piel, like the Eth.
ቀወመ, *to bring to maturity, produce
fruit.* לֹו, in the phrase יְשַׁוֶּה־לֹו, is pleonastic, as in הָלַךְ־לֹו, &c., but may here be
rendered as a possessive pronoun.

2. הָלַק is here to be taken intransitively,
as in our common version, and refers,
not to any differences of opinion among
the Israelites respecting the claims of
their numerous idols, but to their in-
sincerity in the service of Jehovah,—
professing to worship him, while they
likewise addicted themselves to the
worship of idols. Thus Tanchum :—

تفسم بالهم وعقلهم ورايهم اذ اشركوا

بالله غيره, " *their mind and their understanding, and their opinion are divided,
while they associate others with God.*"
The acceptation *to be smooth*, which
some propose, is to be rejected, on the
ground that, though the verb is used in
this signification of the *tongue*, it nowhere
is of the *heart*. For the meaning of
אֲשַׁם, see on chap. v. 15. The nominative to הוּא, *He*, is אֱלֹהִים, *God*, in אֱלֹהַי
chap. ix. 17. Jehovah is here said to
do, what he would effect by means of

the Assyrians. עָרַף is properly a sacrificial term, signifying *to cut off the head
of a victim, by striking it on the neck ;*
hence, *to drop as blood* from the place
thus struck ; and *to drop* generally. It
is here, with much force, used metonymically, in application to the destruction
of the altars on which the animals were
offered. Ewald renders, *Er wird ihre
Altäre enthaupten;* " he will decapitate
their altars." For the distinction between
מִזְבְּחוֹת and מַצֵּבוֹת, see on chap. iii. 4.
עַתָּה, *now*, in this and the following
verse, has the signification of *soon,
speedily.*

3. The language of desperation is
here put into the mouth of the apostate
Israelites, at the time of the infliction
of divine judgment. Their king, to
whom they had naturally looked for
protection, was removed ; they had forfeited the favour of God, who was now
become their enemy ; and, therefore, it
was vain to expect help from an earthly
monarch. Some think the prophet refers
to the time of anarchy during the interregnum, between the murder of Pekah
and the accession of Hoshea.

4. דַּבֵּר דָּבָר, lit. *to speak a word* or
speech, i. e. what is merely such ; empty,
false pretences. Comp. the Lat. *verba
dare.* The prophet begins with the
finite form of the verb, and then, for
the sake of more specific description,
changes it for the infinitive. Comp. Is.
lix. 13. For אָלוֹת, as an absolute infinitive, instead of אָלֹה, comp. שָׁתוֹת, Is.
xxii. 13 ; רָאֹה, chap. xlii. 20. בְּרִית, *covenant*, is here used as a collective noun,
and is to be rendered in the plural.
Whether the false swearing and the entering into covenants refer to the conduct
of the Israelites in regard to each other,
or whether they respect their conduct in

5 For the calves of Beth-aven,
 The inhabitants of Samaria shall be in fear;
 Surely the people thereof shall mourn on account of it;
 And the priests thereof shall leap about on account of it—
 On account of its glory,
 Because it hath departed from it.
6 It shall itself also be carried to Assyria,
 A present to the hostile king:
 Ephraim shall take disgrace,
 And Israel shall blush for his own counsel.

reference to foreign powers, has been disputed. The latter would seem to be the more probable, since it is the making of covenants and not the breaking of them, of which the prophet speaks as something criminal. He seems to have in his eye the historical circumstances narrated 2 Kings xvii. 4. By מִשְׁפָּט is meant the divine judgment which was to be inflicted upon the people of Israel. So Jarchi, משפטי יסורין ופורענות. This he compares to the rapid and luxuriant growth of the poppy, which overruns the fields, and is destructive as a poison. Celsius, in his Hierobot. supports the common rendering *hemlock*, as the signification of ראש; but that of *poppy*, proposed by Gesenius, is preferable, both to such construction of the term, and to that of *colocynth* advanced by Œdmann, or that of *lolium* or *darnel* suggested by Michaelis. The term is usually rendered *poison* in our common version; sometimes *gall*. LXX. ἄγρωστις. תְּלָמִים rather signify the ridges between the furrows than the furrows themselves. See Pococke.

5, 6. In these verses the object of idolatrous worship is spoken of, now in the plural, and now in the singular number, which Hitzig accounts for on the ground, that though the Israelites might have multiplied golden calves, that set up by Jeroboam would still be held in peculiar honour. Four MSS. have עֵגֶל, *calf*, in the singular, which is also the rendering of the LXX., Syr., and an anonymous Greek version in the Hexapla. This reading is very uncritically adopted by Kuinoel, Dathe, Newcome, and some other moderns. For בֵּית אָוֶן, *Beth-aven*, see on chap. iv. 15.

שָׁכֵן is a collective. The nominative to the pronominal affixes in כְּמָרָיו, עָלָיו, עַמּוֹ, &c. is the עֵגֶל, *calf* of Jeroboam, singled out from the rest. עַמּוֹ, *its people*, those devoted to its worship. Comp. Numb. xxi. 29. כְּמָרִים is only used in Hebrew to designate *idolatrous priests*, and occurs but twice besides, viz. 2 Kings xxiii. 5; Zeph. i. 4; but in the Syriac ܟܘܡܪܐ, *kumro*, signifies a priest of the true God, as well as one engaged in the service of idols. Gesenius derives the noun from כָּמַר, *to burn, be scorched, black*, supposing the reference to be to the black dress of monks or ecclesiastics; but this seems too modern to be entitled to adoption. The derivation of Iken, in his Dissert. de *Cemarim*, who refers the word to the Persic كمر, *sacrum magorum ignicolarum cingulum*, of which frequent mention is made in the Sadder of Zoroaster, is much more natural. Comp. the Chald. קְמוֹר, קְמִירָא, *a belt* or *girdle*. Some think the Lat. *camillus*, an inferior order of priest, who attended upon and assisted the flamens, is derived from this root. Ewald renders the word by *Pfaffen*, which is used of priests by way of contempt in German. Those who render יָגִילוּ, *they rejoiced*, which is the usual signification of the verb, supply אֲשֶׁר before it; but the Vau conversive connects it so closely with אֶגֶל, as to render such supplement inconsistent with the construction. It is, therefore, better to revert to the primary signification of גִּיל, *to move about, leap, dance*, or the like. Comp. the Arab. جال, *circumivit*. Such would be the excitement of the

7 As for Samaria, her king is cut off;
He is like a chip upon the surface of the water.

8 And the high places of Aven, the sin of Israel, are destroyed ;
Thorns and thistles shall grow upon their altars :
They shall also say to the mountains, Cover us ;
And to the hills, Fall upon us.

9 Since the days of Gibeah, thou hast sinned, O Israel!
There they remain :
Shall not the war against the unjust overtake them in Gibeah?

idolatrous priests at the capture of their god, that they would leap about in a state of desperation, like those of Baal, 1 Kings xviii. 26. The *glory* of the idol consisted in its ornaments, wealth, &c. גַּם אֹתוֹ is emphatic : *itself also*, i. e. the idol or golden calf. For the meaning of יָרֵב, *Jareb*, see on chap. v. 13. The worshippers of the golden calf would be ashamed of him, when they found that, instead of protecting them, he was himself carried into captivity. That בָּשְׁנָה is not to be changed into בְּשֵׁנָה, and rendered *in a sound sleep*, as Horsley does, nor into בְּשָׁנָה, *in this year*, with Michaelis, the parallelism sufficiently shows.

7. For the sake of emphasis, שֹׁמְרוֹן is put absolutely. The whole phrase is equivalent to *the king of Samaria*, &c. That נִדְמֶה agrees with מַלְכָּהּ, and not with שֹׁמְרוֹן, the gender shows. קֶצֶף has nowhere the signification of *foam*, or *scum*. It is derived from קָצַף, Arab. قَصَفَ, *fregit, to cut, cut off*, and signifies any *chip*, or small fragment of wood. Comp. קְצָפָה, *a fragment*, Joel i. 7. Arab. قَصِيف, *fractus arboris ramus*, قَصْفَة, *tenuitas arboris*. LXX. φρύγανον. Syr. ܦܝܣܐ *festucam*. The comparison of the king to a small chip of wood, which cannot resist the force of the current, is very beautiful and forcible. *Spuma*, which is the rendering of the Targ., Jerome, Symm., Abulwalid, Tanchum, and many moderns, is less apt, even if it could be philologically sustained.

8. אָוֶן, *Aven*, is an abbreviation of the full form בֵּית־אָוֶן, *Beth-aven*, or Bethel. חַטַּאת, *the occasion of sin* to Israel. See

ver. 10. In the midst of the calamities that should come upon the people, death would be preferable to life. Comp. Rev. vi. 15, 16.

9. That reference is here made to the transactions recorded Jud. xix. xx., there can be no doubt. The prophet declares that as a nation his people had all along, from the period referred to, evinced a disposition to act in the same rebellious and unjust manner as the Gibeonites had done. Comp. chap. ix. 9. The words שָׁם עָמָדוּ, *there they remain*, continue, persist, graphically expressed the character of the inhabitants in his day. The Gibeonites were still, what they had ever been, a wicked and abandoned people. They are here singled out as a fit specimen of the whole nation; and are called בְּנֵי־עַלְוָה, *sons of wickedness*, to mark the enormity of their conduct. Instead of עַלְוָה, the Brixian edition, thirty-nine MSS., originally seventeen, and perhaps a few more, have עַוְלָה, the common form, which is supposed to have been changed by a simple transposition of the letters. Albert Schultens, however, in his notes ad Harir. i. p. 15, justifies the present reading by deriving it from the Arab. غَلَا, *modum excessit, extulit se ;* and Michaelis, in his Supplem. by referring it to the Syriac, أَدْلَـ, and the Eth. ዐለወ: *fidem fefellit, perfidus fuit.* Comp. שׁוּעֲלִין : ዐለወ: *Rex tyrannus, scelestus.* ዐለወት : *transgressio æqui et boni, scelus, perversitas.* That the Targumist read the text as it now stands is clear

10　My desire is to punish them ;
　　The nations, therefore, shall be collected against them,
　　When they are bound for their two iniquities.

11　For Ephraim is a well-trained heifer, loving to thresh ;
　　But I will pass on beside her fair neck ;
　　I will place a rider on Ephraim :
　　Judah shall plough,
　　And Jacob shall break the clods.

from his rendering the word סָלִיקוּ, *they went up.* The words לֹא־תַשִׂיגֵם בַּגִּבְעָה מִלְחָמָה עַל־בְּנֵי עַלְוָה are somewhat involved, but the meaning is obvious. Destruction should assuredly overtake the wicked Israelites. ם, the verbal suffix in תַּשִׂיגֵם, is anticipative of בְּנֵי עַלְוָה. לֹא stands for הֲלֹא, the interrogatory negative.

10. גְּאַוָּתִי, the LXX. have read בָּאתִי; rendering it ἦλθε ; or, according to the Alexandrian MS. and the editions of Aldus and Breitinger, ἦλθεν. Of this Houbigant, Dimock, Newcome, Tingstadius, and Boothroyd, approve, and adopt it as an emendation; but contrary to all other authority, ancient or modern, and without necessity. בְּ prefixed is the *Beth Essentiæ,* indicating the substantive character of the affection. See my note on Is. xxvi. 4. אִוָּה, *to be strongly propense, desire greatly,* expresses the irresistible inclination of infinite purity to punish sin. אֶאֱסָרֵם is the future in Kal of יָסַר, *to chastise, punish,* compensation having been made for the first radical י, by inserting Dagesh in the ם. אֶאֱסָרֵם, the infinitive of אָסַר, *to bind, bind as a prisoner* or *captive,* which is the sense in which the word is here to be taken. עֲלֹנָתָם has occasioned great variety of interpretation. Michaelis translates it *plough-shares,* attempting to derive it from the Arabic. Jarchi, Liveley, and, among the moderns, Ewald, render *eyes,* " before their *two eyes,*" i. e. openly ; but the word is always written עֵינַיִם when applied to real eyes, and only עֲיָנוֹת when applied to fountains, or artificial eyes. Some translate *habitations ;* but most, *furrows,* which is the rendering adopted by Abenezra, Kimchi, Abulwalid, Tanchum, Munster, Vatablus, Zanchius, &c., after the Targum—some expounding the passage one way, and some another. The only satisfactory

exegesis is that founded on the Keri, לִשְׁתֵּי עֹונֹתָם, *for their two iniquities,* i. e. the two golden calves which Jeroboam had erected, and which proved the source of all the evils which they had afterwards committed. They had many other idols, but these were the principal ; and they are called *iniquities* by a metonymy of the cause for the effect. Comp. ver. 8, where הַטַּאת, *sin,* is similarly applied. This reading is in the text of a great many MSS. and is expressed in all the ancient versions.

11. The general meaning of this verse seems to be, that the Ephraimites had been accustomed in the plenitude of their power to crush and oppress others, especially their brethren of the two tribes; but they were now themselves to be brought into subjection to the king of Assyria, by whom they should be placed in circumstances of great hardship in foreign countries. The metaphors are agricultural. For דּוּשׁ, *to tread* or *beat out the corn,* partly by the feet of oxen, and partly by sledges with instruments adapted to the purpose, see on Is. xxviii. 27, 28. The י in אָהַבְתִּי, is paragogic, as יֹשַׁבְתִּי and מְקַנַּתִּי, Jer. xxii. 23 ; שֹׁכַנְתִּי, chap. li. 13, though in these passages it has been left unpointed by the Masoretes. See Ewald, § 406. The form is otherwise the participle אֹהֶבֶת. עָבַר עַל signifies here *to pass on beside* one, as the driver does beside an ox in the yoke. Thus Jehovah would, in his providence, lead forth the Israelites, from the midst of their prosperity, to the toils and hardships of captivity. אַרְכִּיב אֶפְרַיִם, lit. *I will cause to ride Ephraim,* meaning I will place a rider upon him—a conqueror, who shall lead him forth from his land. Thus Calvin, Zanchius, Lyra, Tarnovius, Rosenmüller, and Ewald. The judgments of God were not, how-

12   Sow to yourselves for righteousness;
      Reap according to piety;
      Break up for yourselves the fallow ground:
      For it is time to seek Jehovah,
      Till he come, and teach you righteousness.
13   Ye have ploughed wickedness, ye have reaped iniquity;
      Ye have eaten the fruit of falsehood:
      Because thou trustedst in thy way—
      In the multitude of thy mighty ones.

ever, to be confined to the northern kingdom: the southern should also be involved in them. In short, they should overtake the whole posterity of Jacob. The prediction was fulfilled during the two captivities. לוֹ, in יְשֻׁדֶּד לוֹ, is pleonastic.

12. Continuing his agricultural metaphors, the prophet here abruptly calls upon the nation to reform its manners. לָכֶם is the Dat. commodi. ל in לִצְדָקָה points out the end or object to be obtained by sowing. Sow what will produce the fruits of righteousness. The second imperative is here equivalent to the future: "Sow, and ye shall reap;" or the subjunctive, "Sow, so that ye may reap." That חֶסֶד, piety or goodness, is to be referred, not to God, but to man, its being parallel with צְדָקָה, righteousness, manifestly proves. To change וְעֵת into דַּעַת, and join this word with נִיר, preceding, as Newcome, following the LXX. and Arab., does, is unauthorized and inept. The Israelites had long neglected Jehovah: it was now high time to return to his fear; and though they might not meet with immediate tokens of his favour, they were to persevere in seeking him, in the assurance that he would be gracious to them. Such is the force of עַד, until. This favour was to be manifested by his coming and communicating to them instruction respecting the only righteousness which could avail the guilty at his bar. That the words וְיוֹרֶה צֶדֶק לָכֶם are not to be rendered he will grant you suitable rain, but, he will teach you righteousness, and that they contain a prophecy of the advent and prophetical office of the Messiah, has been maintained by Jerome, and many other in-

terpreters. In support of the rendering, He will teach you righteousness, may be adduced the Syr. ܗܘ ܐܬܐ ܕܟܐܢܘܬܐ, ܥܕܡܐ ܕܢܐܬܐ ܘܢܚܘܐ, till he come and show to you his righteousness; Pococke's Arab. MS. الي ان يجي ويرشدكم العدل, till he come and guide you to righteousness. The Targ. to the same effect, כְּעַן יִתְגְּלֵי וְיֵיתֵי זְכוּ לְכוֹן, now he shall be revealed, and shall bring righteousness to you; Vulg. cum venerit qui docebit vos justitiam. Thus also Dathe, Hitzig, Winer, and others. Kimchi remarks, וי״מ אם תדרשו את ה׳ לדעת תורתו ומצותיו הוא יבא ויורה אתכם צדק, there are those (of the Rabbins) who expound, If ye seek the Lord, to know his law and his commandments, he will come and teach you righteousness. And Abenezra asserts the same, in nearly the same words. Such construction of the passage seems, from the preceding use of צְדָקָה, to be more apt, than to take צֶדֶק absolutely for לִצְדָקָה, in due proportion, adequately, fully, according to the claims or necessities of your condition. See on Joel ii. 23.

13. Instead of following such a course as that to which they had just been exhorted, the Israelites had pursued one directly opposite, and now reaped the disastrous consequences. The same metaphors are here continued. פְּרִי־כַחַשׁ, fruit of falsehood, seems rather to mean the effects of their false and hypocritical conduct in professing attachment to the true God, while they addicted themselves to the worship of other deities, than fallacious and disappointing results.

14 Therefore a tumult shall arise among thy people,
   And all thy fortresses shall be destroyed,
   As Shalman destroyed Beth-arbel in the day of battle:
   When the mother was dashed in pieces with her children.

Secker would read בְּרִכְבְּךָ, *in thy chariots*, instead of בִּדְרָכֶיךָ, *in thy way*, on the authority of the LXX. ἐν ἅρμασί σου, which reading is found in Compl., Ald., Barb., Reg., Laud., Cyrill, Ital., Ambros., Arab., Slav., Hexap. Syr., and a Copt. MS.; and Kuinoel has actually adopted it into his Hebrew text. It is, however, unsupported by any Heb. MSS., or any of the ancient versions, and is justly to be rejected. Four MSS., originally two, the Syr., and Targ. read בִּדְרָכֶיךָ, *in thy ways*. The *way* of the Israelites was the wicked course of conduct which they had adopted in opposition to the will of God. Kimchi: דרך הרשע והאמונה הרעה, *the way of wickedness and bad religion*. The Vat. copy of the LXX. has ἐν τοῖς ἁμαρτήμασί σου. Comp. Is. lvii. 10; Jer. ii. 23.

14. The prophet now denounces a severe threatening against his rebellious countrymen, foreshowing that they should be involved in all the horrors of war. וְקָאם, with א epenthetic, after the manner of the Arab. قَائِم; or it may be regarded as merely a *mater lectionis*. Some few MSS., and some others in the margin, read וְקָם. Twenty-four MSS., one originally, four of the early editions, and all the ancient versions, read בְּעַמְּךָ, *thy people*, instead of בְּעַמֶּיךָ, *thy peoples*. For minor varieties in the readings, see Kennicott and De Rossi. The nominative to יוּשַּׁד is כֹּל, taken as a collective, comprehending the whole. That שַׁלְמַן, *Shalman*, and בֵּית אַרְבֵּאל, *Beth-Arbel*, are proper names, is now universally admitted. The best interpretation of them is that given by Tanchum: واما شلمن فهو اسم وقيل انه شلمنأصر ملك اشور فاختصر ولعل شلمنأصر مركب من اسمين فاسقط احدهما للعرف وبيت اربأل اسم بلد ويقول انها التي يقال لها اليوم اربأل. " As for *Shalman*, it is a

proper name, and is said to stand for *Shalmanassar*, king of Assyria, only it is abbreviated; and perhaps *Shalmanassar* is compounded of two names, one of which is omitted because it was well known : and *Beth-Arbel* is the name of a city, and is said to be that which is called *Arbel* at the present day." The abbreviation of proper names is not uncommon in Scripture, as כָּנְיָהוּ, *Coniah*, for יְהוֹיָכִין, *Jehoiachin*, &c. It was this Assyrian monarch that besieged Samaria for the space of three years, and took it in the ninth of Hoshea, B.C. 722, carrying the king and most of his subjects into exile. 2 Kings xvii. 1—6. To this interpretation it has been objected that our prophet wrote before the time of Shalmaneser, and therefore could not speak of his destroying Arbel as something that had already happened. It must, however, be recollected, that though Hosea prophesied before the time of that king, he continued to deliver his predictions as far down as the time of his successor Sennacherib, and must, therefore, have been well acquainted with the previous Assyrian invasions. With respect to בֵּית אַרְבֵּאל, or, as some MSS. read, אַרְבֵּל, *Beth-Arbel*, commentators are divided in opinion. Some think that the Assyrian city *Arbela*, situated between the Lycus and the Tigris, celebrated for the victory obtained there by Alexander the Great over Darius, is meant; but it is far more probable that the prophet refers to the Ἀρβήλα of 1 Macc. ix. 2, which Josephus places near Sephoris in Galilee; Eusebius, in the plain of Esdraelon. Of the battle here mentioned, no account indeed is given either in sacred or profane history; but as the contemporaries of Hosea are supposed to have been acquainted with it, there is reason to believe that it took place on the invasion of the kingdom of Israel by the Assyrian army. The ancient versions of this clause of the verse are more or less at fault; but have afforded abundant scope for the exercise of emendatorial

15 Thus shall he act towards you at Bethel,
      On account of your flagrant wickedness :
      In the morning shall the king of Israel be utterly cut off.

criticism. See Newcome, who renders, *Like the destruction of Zalmunna by the hand of Jerubbaal;* and supposes the reference to be to Jud. viii. עַל here signifies *with*, in the sense of being superadded. See Gen. xxviii. 9; xxxi. 50.

15. The nominative to עָשָׂה is Shalman in the preceding verse, or perhaps יְהֹוָה, *Jehovah*, understood, but not בֵּית אֵל, *Bethel*, as in our common version, since this does not so well agree with what follows. The words contain a special prediction against Bethel, where the wickedness of the Israelites had been most conspicuously exhibited. רָעַת רָעַתְכֶם, lit. *the wickedness of your wickedness*, i.e. your excessive, or most flagrant wickedness. A rare example of a noun put in construction with itself repeated *in the singular*, in order to form the superlative degree. There is no neces-

sity, with Newcome, to resort to emendation. Instead of בַּשַּׁחַר, " *in* the morning," fifteen MSS., and perhaps one more, six originally, the Proph. of Soncin. 1486, the Venet. edit. of 1518, in the margin, and the Vulg. read כַּשַּׁחַר, " *like* the morning." Were the following verb דָּמָה to be taken in the sense of *resembling, being like,* &c., the latter reading might possess some claim on our attention; but as the idea of *being destroyed* best comports with the connexion, that of the Textus Receptus is preferable. The difference of reading has arisen from the similarity of the letters ב and כ. The reference is to the suddenness with which Hoshea was to be seized by the king of Assyria, and an entire end put to the regal dignity. See 2 Kings xvii. 4. The doing of anything early or soon is frequently expressed by its being done in the morning.

CHAPTER XI

To aggravate his representations of the guilt of the Israelites, the prophet adduces the divine benefits conferred upon them from the earliest period of their history, 1—4. He then threatens them with unavoidable punishment on account of their obstinacy, 5, 6; but, all on a sudden, introduces Jehovah, compassionating his rebellious children, and promising them a restoration from their captivity in foreign lands, 7—11.

---

1 WHEN Israel was a child, I loved him,
      And called my son out of Egypt.

1. That these words relate to the nation of Israel—being a description of what Jehovah had done for it ages before the prophet wrote, and not a

prophecy of any future event, is so evident, that no person who impartially examines the preceding and following context, can for a moment call it in

2 According as they called them, they went from their presence,
　They sacrificed unto Baals,
　And burned incense to graven images.
3 Though I taught Ephraim to walk,
　Taking them by their arms,
　Yet they knew not that I healed them.

question. Nor but for their having been applied by the Evangelist Matthew (ch. ii. 15,) to our Lord's return from Egypt, would it ever have been imagined that they had or could have any other reference. It is only, therefore, with respect to such application, that any difficulty can exist respecting their exegesis; and, in my judgment, there appears to be nothing in the N. T. application beyond the mere appropriation of the language of the prophet, for the purpose of giving to Jewish readers a more vivid impression of the strikingly analogous circumstances of the sojourn of our Saviour in Egypt, and his return from it, to those of the ancient Israelites. The Evangelist does not affirm, that the words as used by Hosea were a prophecy of Christ; he only adduces them, to show how aptly they described the historical event which he was narrating, just as he does, Jer. xxxi. 15, in application to the murder of the infants at Bethlehem, and Ps. lxxviii. 2, in application to our Lord's teaching in parables. " He must be a stranger to the *Hebrew* writers, that does not know, that nothing is more common among *them* than such accommodations of the text upon all occasions. They *abound* in such applications; I may say their Midrashim do very much *exceed* in them." Kidder's Demon. of the Messiah, Pt. II. p. 216. "Parodiarum in N. T. omnia sunt plena, e. g. *Matt.* ii. 15 et 23, ubi *impletæ* dicuntur *Scripturæ* tum etiam, cum nulla historica aut *typica* est impletio, sed analogica tantum." Hottinger, Primit. Heidelberg., p. 80. See Surenhusii, βιβλος καταλλαγης, p. 338. Horne's Introd. vol. ii. pp. 341, 342. Robinson's Greek Lex. in ἵνα, C. 2, d. Instead of לְבָנִי, the LXX. appear to have read לְבָנָיו; but instead of τὰ τέκνα αὐτοῦ, *his children*, which is their reading, that of Aq., Symm., Theod., the Slavon., and Matthew, agree with the Hebrew text.

The Hebrew people are also called the son of God in the same figurative sense, Exod. iv. 22, 23. The early period of their existence is frequently represented as their youth. See Is. liv. 4; Jer. ii. 2; iii 24, 25; xxii. 21; Hos. ii. 15.

2. The use of the verb קָרָא, *to call*, in the preceding verse, suggested the idea of the subsequent messages which had been delivered to the Israelites by the prophets, to which Hosea now appeals, in order to contrast with the means which had been employed for their reformation, the obstinate character of their rebellion. Before קָרְאוּ, subaud. כַּאֲשֶׁר, to correspond to כֵּן. Thus the LXX. καθ' ὡς. See on Is. lv. 9. The nominative is the prophets, understood. The very presence of the prophets being an annoyance to them, they withdrew from it, that, unmolested, they might indulge in idolatry.

3. תִּרְגַּלְתִּי, an instance of the *Tiphil* conjugation, equivalent to Hiphil in signification, and, in all probability, formed by hardening the preformative ה into ת. Indeed, one of De Rossi's MSS. reads הִרְגַּלְתִּי, instead of תִּרְגַּלְתִּי. There exist only two other instances in the Hebrew Bible, viz. תְּחָרֶה, Jer. xii. 5, and מִתְחָרֶה, xxii. 15, if תְּפוֹצוֹתִיכֶם, xxv. 34, is not to be so taken. Compare the Shaphel Conjugation in Syriac, in which language this very verb occurs in the form ܓ݁ܺ݇ܪ. See Knös Chrest. Syr. p. 112. It is a denominative from רֶגֶל, *the foot*, and signifies to cause or *teach to use the feet*, or *walk*. Syr. and Targ. דַּבְּרִית, ܕ݁ܰܒ݁ܪܶܬ݂, *I led*, only the latter paraphrases, וַאֲנָא בְּמַלְאַךְ שְׁלִיחַ מִן קֳדָמַי דַּבְּרִית, *and I led*, &c. *by an angel sent from my presence.* The use of the personal pronoun אָנֹכִי before the verb gives additional force to the language. קָח in קָחָם is the infinitive used as a gerund, as in Ezek. xvii. 5. Both the suffixes ם and ו refer to

4 I drew them with the bands of man,
   With the cords of love ;
   I was also to them as those who lift up the yoke from their neck,
   I held out meat to them, I made them eat.

5   They shall not return to the land of Egypt;
   But Assyria shall be their king:
   Because they would not be converted.

6 The sword, also, shall be whirled in their cities,
   Yea, it shall destroy their barriers, and devour,
   Because of their devices.

Ephraim. See on chap. ix. 2. Four MSS. for וְרֹעֹתָיו, " *his* arms," read וְרֹעֹתַי, "*my* arms," which is also in another originally, and now in another, and in the Soncin. edition of 1486. It is also supported by the LXX., Syr., Vulg. Another MS. reads וְרֹעֹתָם ; but they are all corrections of the original, and are only to be tolerated in translation. The metaphor taken from teaching children to walk is continued, as those who do so take hold of their arms to keep them from falling while they move their feet. It beautifully expresses the condescension of God to the circumstances of his people, and the kind care which he exercised over them. Comp. Deut. i. 31; xxxii. 11. His *healing them*, refers to his recovering them from the calamities which they brought upon themselves by their sins.

4. חַבְלֵי אָדָם, *the bands of man*, are explained by the parallel phrase עֲבֹתוֹת אַהֲבָה, *cords of love*, i. e. *humane*, gentle, persuasive methods, such as men generally employ when they would induce to action. There seems to be still a reference to the case of children, who, when taught to walk, are not only held by the arms, but also, by soft cords or leading-strings, are led about, or drawn in a gentle manner by those who have the care of them. The terms, however, naturally suggesting the idea of the ropes by which oxen are bound and led about, the metaphor is immediately changed into one borrowed from agricultural life. כְּמְרִימֵי עֹל וגו' does not mean to *remove* the yoke entirely, but to raise it from the neck and cheeks of the animal, so as to allow it freely to eat its food. This better suits the following connexion than the idea of taking the yoke off any place that may have been galled by it, in order to afford relief. The עֹל, *yoke*, not only included the piece of wood upon the neck, by which the animal was fastened to the pole, but also the whole of the harness about the head, which was connected with it. The yokes used in the East are very heavy, and press so much upon the animals, that they are unable to bend their necks. וְאַט אֵלָיו, Ewald renders, *und sanft gegen ihn*, " and gently towards him," &c.; but it is preferable to take אַט as the apocopated future in Hiph. of נָטָה, to *stretch out, extend, reach any thing* to another. The verse sets forth the kind relief afforded to the Hebrew nation in Egypt, and the provision with which they were miraculously supplied in the wilderness.

5. שׁוּב, *to turn, return*, which is used at the beginning of the verse in its proper acceptation, is employed at the close metaphorically to express *conversion to God*. The Israelites seem to have been very generally inclined to migrate for a time to Egypt, in order to enjoy the protection of its monarch ; the prophet assures them that they should not carry their purpose into effect, but that they should be subject to the Assyrian rule, as a punishment for refusing to listen to the calls given them to repent and turn from their idolatries.

6. Most of the Rabbins take חוּל in the sense of *resting, remaining ;* but it seems preferable to adopt the signification *to turn, be turned*, or *whirled about*, as a sword when it is brandished, or when it is employed in cutting down

7 For my people are bent upon defection from me ;
   Though they call them to the Most High,
   Yet none of them will exalt him.

8   How shall I give thee up, O Ephraim ?
   How shall I deliver thee over, O Israel ?
   How shall I make thee as Admah ?
   How shall I set thee as Zeboim ?
   My heart is turned within me ;
   All my feelings of compassion are kindled.

9 I will not execute the fierceness of my anger ;
   I will no more destroy Ephraim ;

the enemy. Comp. the Arab. حال،
conversa fuit res. V. *se convertit ; versus
mutatusque fuit.* בַּדִּים, *barriers,* Gesenius and Lee take metaphorically, as
denoting *chiefs* or *princes.*

7. תְּלוּאִים = תְּלוּיִם, which one of De
Rossi's MSS. reads originally, the Pahul
Part. of תָּלָה, *to hang,* used here metaphorically in the sense of *bending,* or
being propense to any thing. The idea
of *doubt* or *suspense,* which some attach
to the word in this connexion, ill agrees
with the character of the Israelites as
otherwise depicted in this book. מְשׁוּבָה
is always used in a bad sense, *defection,
apostasy,* &c. Comp. chap. xiv. 4, (Hebr.
5). The suffix in מְשׁוּבָתִי is to be taken
passively ; defection which has me for its
object; and cannot with any propriety be
rendered as by Horsley, "my returning."
For אֶל־עַל, *ad summum,* see on chap. vii.
16 ; and for יִקְרָאֻ, on ver. 2. After
יְרוֹמֵם, supply אֹתוֹ, *him,* from עַל, *the
Supreme,* preceding. Jehovah had been
degraded by his being worshipped through
the medium of images, and having idols
associated with him ; yet none of his
apostate people were inclined to raise
him from this degradation, by rejecting
them and celebrating His praise, as the
sole and glorious object of adoration.
Pococke's Arab. MS. لم يكن احد
منهم يشرف اسم الله, *there was not
one of them that glorified the name of
God.* יַחַד with a negative is to be rendered *not one ;* without it, *all, altogether,
wholly,* as in the following verse.

8, 9. Now follows one of the most
affecting instances of the infinite tenderness of the divine compassion to be
found in Scripture ; the point of which
is enhanced by its being introduced
immediately after a description of the
odious conduct of the Israelites. It is,
as Bishop Lowth characterises it, exquisitely pathetic. The repetitions and
synonymous features of the parallelism
greatly add to the effect. The words
belong to the period after the subjugation of Samaria, and the carrying away
of the Israelites by Shalmaneser, 2 Kings
xvii. 5, 6; xviii. 9—12. They were designed to inspire the captives with hope
in the mercy of God, and thus lead
them to true repentance. אֲמַגֶּנְךָ, the
LXX. render ὑπερασπιῶ σου ; Aq.
ὅπλῳ κυκλώσα σε ; Vulg. *protegam te ;*
deriving the idea from the signification
of the substantive מָגֵן, *a shield ;* but it
is used of *delivering over enemies,* Gen.
xiv. 20. Symm. ἐκδώσω σε. Before
אֲשִׂימְךָ is an ellipsis of אֵיךְ, which had
already been twice repeated. The destruction of Admah and Zeboim is only
referred to as an example in one other
case, viz. Deut. xxix. 23, and then in
connexion with Sodom and Gomorrah.
To the awful catastrophe recorded Gen.
xix. the sacred writers frequently appeal,
in order to produce a sense of the evil
of sin, and the severity with which it
deserves to be punished ; or when they
would convey the idea of complete and
irretrievable ruin. Comp. Is. i. 9 ; xiii.
19 ; Jer. xlix. 18 ; Lam. iv. 6 ; Amos iv.
11; Matt. x. 15 ; 2 Pet. ii. 6 ; Jude 7.
Some would render נֶהְפַּךְ עָלַי לִבִּי, " my

For I am God and not man,
The Holy One in the midst of thee;
I will not come in wrath.

10 They shall follow Jehovah, when he roareth like a lion;
When he roareth, the children shall hasten from the sea.

heart is turned *against* me," i. e. my pity rises in overpowering opposition to the determination to which I had come to inflict punishments; but the phraseology will scarcely bear such construction, though it cannot be questioned, that it is designed to express a powerful inward revolution. Comp. עָלַי—נֶהֶמִי, Ps. xlii. 6, 12, xliii. 5; הִתְעַטֵּפָה עָלַי רוּחִי, cxlii. 4; עָלַי לִבִּי דַוָּי, Jer. viii. 18; in all which passages the preposition conveys the idea of mental *contiguity, nearness, in, within*, as נֶהְפַּךְ לִבִּי בְּקִרְבִּי, *my heart is turned* WITHIN *me*, Lam. i. 20, incontestably shows. From the connexion in which it occurs, in the last cited passage, it is obvious the phrase is there designed to express great mental distress. נִכְמְרוּ is used in Niphal, of *the stirrings of natural affection*, Gen. xliii. 30; 1 Kings iii. 26. The idea seems to be derived from the commotion produced by the kindling of a fire, and the heat or warmth in which it results. Tanchum explains the word by خمل, *concitatus fuit*. LXX. συνεταράχθη, or, as in the Complut. διεταράχθη. נְחוּמִים, the same in effect as רַחֲמִים, *compassion, feelings of tender pity and affection.* Targ. רַחֲמֵי, *my compassions.* It is derived from נָחַם, *to be inwardly affected*, whether with grief, pity, consolation, or anger. In the idea of displeasure with oneself, has originated the signification, *to repent*, which accounts for the renderings, μεταμέλεια, *pœnitudo, repentings*, &c. See my note on Is. i. 24. The language is in the highest degree anthropopathical. The 9th verse contains a declaration of the purpose of God founded upon his compassion, and quite in keeping with the manner in which expression had just been given to it. שׁוּב in לֹא אֶשּׁוֹב לְשַׁחֵת is, as frequently, to be taken adverbially. The captivity was the last judgment that was to come upon the ten tribes as a punishment for their idolatry. The rendering, " I will not enter into the city,"

affords no suitable sense, and would require the article בְּעִיר, as, indeed, one of De Rossi's MSS. reads. Bishop Lowth's translation, " though I inhabit not thy cities," (Lectures, vol. ii. p. 38,) is equally unsatisfactory with the interpretation of Jerome and Castalio: I am not like those who dwell in cities, living after human laws, and deeming cruelty to be justice. Such construction Maurer states to be in his opinion " artificiosior quam elegantior." I, therefore, adopt the interpretation hinted at by Jarchi, and since approved by Schroeder, Secker, Dathe, Manger, Tingstadius, Eichhorn, De Wette, Noyes, Boothroyd, Gesenius, Maurer, and Ewald, which takes עִיר not in the sense of *city*, but of *anger* or *wrath;* comparing the Arab. غار, *ferbuit æstu* dies. Comp. Jer. xv. 8; Hos. vii. 4; and עָר, *an enemy*, 1 Sam. xxviii. 16; Ps. cxxxix. 20. The words are thus strictly parallel, and synonymous to וְלֹא אִישׁ, *and not man.* The derivation from بعر, to which Michaelis assigns the signification *angry*, بعرة, *ira in Deo*, Orient. Bib. Pt. XIX. p. 9, is less appropriate, though the sense which he gives is the same.

10, 11. These verses contain gracious promises of the return of the Israelites to the true worship and service of God, and their restoration to their own land from the different places in which they had been scattered during the captivity. הָלַךְ אַחֲרֵי יְהוָֹה, *to walk after Jehovah*, is always used in the religious sense of addicting oneself to his worship, and keeping his commandments, and is not to be interpreted, as Hitzig does, of a mere following of providence by taking advantage of the opportunity that would be afforded of returning from Babylon. So the Targ. בָּתַר פֻּלְחָנָא דַיָי, *after the worship of Jehovah.* For the contrary, see ver. 2. As שָׁאַג, *to roar*, like the

11　They shall hasten, like a sparrow, from Egypt,
　　And, like a dove, from the land of Assyria :
　　And I will cause them to dwell in their own houses,
　　Saith Jehovah.

lion, always conveys the idea of terror or awe, it cannot be here applied either to any invitation to the Jews as a people, or to the preaching of the gospel gene- rally; but must be referred to the awful judgments which God executed upon Babylon, Egypt, &c. through the in- strumentality of Cyrus and his succes- sors; thereby opening the way for the liberation of the Israelites who were found in these countries. Comp. Is. xxxi. 4; Jer. xxv. 30; Joel iii. 16; Amos i. 2; iii. 8. By בָּנִים, *sons*, or *children*, are meant the Israelites, who had been for a time rejected, but were again acknowledged in that character, because they were to be reinstated in the privileges of adoption. Comp. chap. i. 10. חָרַד is here pregnant with mean- ing—signifying to come or hasten under the influence of great agitation. The idea of trepidation, though implied, and connecting well with that of the roaring previously mentioned, is not so promi- nent as that of quick or nimble motion. Excited to the utmost by the revolutions of empires, which allowed them to take possession of their native country, they would use all haste in repairing thither. LXX. ἐκστήσονται; but in the following verse ἐκπέτεσονται. Syr. נֶפֹּחֻ̈ם, *they shall move* or *be moved*. "Sic Lat. *tre- pidare* etiam sumitur pro *festinare*,

observantibus Bocharto in Hieroz. et Schultensio in Animadverss. philol. ad Is. xix. 17." Winer, *in voc.* The same idea of velocity is further carried out by comparing the return of the Israelites to the flight of birds remarkable for their swiftness. צִפּוֹר is here used not in its generic sense of *bird*, but specifically of the *sparrow*, as the use of יוֹנָה, *dove*, immediately after, shows. The יָם, *sea*, is the Mediterranean, or the islands and other maritime regions in the west. Kimchi, מערב, *the west*; Pococke's Arab.

MS, من جزاير البحر, *from the isles of the sea.* Comp. Is. xi. 11—16, a passage strictly parallel, only including the Jews as well as the Israelites. The three quarters of the globe here specified embrace all the countries mentioned by Isaiah; and as the ten tribes form the subject of Hosea's discourse, the present prophecy furnishes an additional proof of their return also, after the Babylonish captivity. To argue, therefore, from this passage, that they are still in ex- istence, and are yet to be restored in their tribal capacity, is hermeneutically unwarranted. עַל in the phrase עַל־בָּתֵּיהֶם, instead of בְּ, seems to have special re- ference to the custom of the Orientals, who enjoy their time *upon*, rather than *in* their houses.

CHAPTER XII

This chapter commences with renewed complaints against both Ephraim and Judah, more especially against the former, 1, 2. The conduct of their pro- genitor Jacob is then adduced, in order to excite them to apply, as he did, for the blessings which they required, 3, 4; to copy which they are further encouraged by the unchangeable character of Jehovah, 5, 6. The prophet next reverts to the deceitful and hypocritical character of the ten tribes, notwithstanding the numerous means that had been employed to promote true piety, 7—10; renews his castigation of their idolatrous practices, 11; again appeals to the kindness of God to the nation in its obscure origin in the person of Jacob, 12, 13; and denounces anew the judgments that were to be inflicted upon it, 14.

---

1 EPHRAIM hath encompassed me with falsehood,
  And the house of Israel with deceit;
  And as for Judah, he is still inconstant with God,
  Even with the faithful Holy Ones.

1. The LXX., Vulg., Targ., and our common version, join this verse to the preceding chapter; but improperly—there being no connexion whatever with the previous verses, whereas it is manifest from the renewed reference to Judah, ver. 3, that the three verses intimately cohere. The proper exegesis of this verse depends upon the signification assigned to רָד, and the consequent application of נֶאֱמָן. That the former cannot grammatically be referred either to רָדָ or רָדָה, to subdue, bear rule, or to יָרַד, to descend, as Jerome renders it, is now agreed on all hands; and there is no alternative left but to derive it from רוּד, which occurs only in three other passages, viz. once in Kal, Jer. ii. 31, and twice in Hiph. Gen. xxvii. 40, and Ps. lv. 3. In the two first, the ideas of becoming or being *unfaithful, rebelling, wandering at large*, are obviously conveyed. In the third, the verb is applied figuratively to an agitated or unsettled state of mind, to which the notion of *wandering* seems much more natural than that of mourning, which is that expressed by our translators. Thus also the derivative מָרוּד may best be rendered *circumvagatio, erratio*, Lam. i. 7; iii. 19. Compare the Arabic رَادَ, رَوَدَ, *quæsivit* pabulum; *ultro citroque ivit; mobile fuit; discurrit huc illuc* mulier *apud vicinas suas.* رَوْم, *locus, quo in pascuis cameli modo prodeunt modo retrocedunt.* Eth. ረደየ : *persequi, insurrexit*, &c. The signification *domi-*

natur, which has been given to רוּד, is altogether gratuitous. The meaning of the prophet will, therefore, be, that Judah or the inhabitants of the southern kingdom acted with vacillancy in regard to Jehovah. So far were they from adhering stedfastly to his covenant, and seeking their happiness in obedience to his will, that they resembled animals that are dissatisfied with their pasture, break loose, and run wildly up and down in search of what is more agreeable to their appetite; or like a female who, discontented at home, seeks for satisfaction by gadding about among her neighbours. The description applies to the state of things among the Jews towards the end of the reign of Jotham, and during that of Ahaz, who introduced a Syrian altar, and other idolatrous objects, by which the people were tempted to infidelity towards Jehovah, but had not yet altogether renounced his service. Hence the force of עֹד, *yet, still.* Though the idea of hostility implied in the verb would not justify the use of the preposition עִם, *with*, taken as in the phrases רִיב עָם, נִלְחַם עָם, *to fight with, contend with;* yet it well agrees with its use after verbs of acting *towards*, or *in reference to* any one, such as עָם רָצָה, עָשָׂה טוֹב עָם, &c. Thus Schroeder, Dathe, Eichhorn, De Wette, Boothroyd, Kuinoel, Gesenius, Noyes, Hitzig, Maurer, and Ewald. Such construction of the passage is fully borne out by ver. 3, which cannot be consistently interpreted, if Judah were here represented as faithfully maintaining the principles of the theocracy. But if the signification which has been

2 Ephraim feedeth upon wind,
　　Yea, he pursueth the east wind;
　　Every day he multiplieth falsehood and violence;
　　Yea, he maketh a covenant with Assyria,
　　And oil is carried into Egypt.

3 Jehovah hath also a controversy with Judah,
　　And He will punish Jacob, according to his ways;
　　According to his deeds, He will recompense him.

4 　　In the womb he took his brother by the heel,
　　And by his strength he strove with God;

given to רָד be alone justifiable, then it is evident וְאָמָן, *faithful*, cannot apply to Judah, but must be taken as qualifying קְדוֹשִׁים, the adjective noun immediately preceding. To this it cannot be objected, that the one is in the plural, while the other is in the singular; for we find a precisely similar combination in אֱלֹהִים צַדִּיק, *the righteous God*, Ps. vii. 10. That קְדוֹשִׁים, *the Holy Ones*, cannot here be applied either to human saints, or to angels, but must be interpreted of God himself, the law of parallelism clearly requires. Comp. Josh. xxiv. 19, אֱלֹהִים קְדֹשִׁים הוּא; Prov. ix. 10, דַּעַת קְדֹשִׁים בִּינָה; xxx. 3, וְדַעַת קְדֹשִׁים אֵדָע. Kimchi himself allows that קְדוֹשִׁים must be so understood in this place. Between the inconstancy of the Jews, and the faithfulness of God, the contrast is placed in a very striking point of view. They had never found him to fail in giving effect to any of his promises; while they, on the contrary, had all along shown more or less of a fickle and roving disposition. The ancient versions exhibit considerable diversity of rendering in this place; but none of them suggests a meaning preferable to that just given, or warrants any alteration in the reading of the Hebrew.

2. By "the wind," and "the east wind," are meant empty, unsatisfying and pernicious objects. Such were the idolatrous confidence and foreign alliances of the Israelites. קָדִים, the LXX. render καύσων, the Arab. السموم, the *Samoom*, or scorching wind, called the "east wind," because it blows from the desert to the east of Palestine. See on Is. xxvii. 8. In proportion to the in-

sincerity and faithless conduct of the nation was the destruction which it brought upon itself. Such conduct was specially exhibited in the leagues that were formed, and the friendships that were entered into with the two most powerful of the ancient monarchies. שֶׁמֶן, *oil*, was one of the most valuable productions of Canaan, and formed a profitable article of exportation. It is here spoken of as a present sent to the king of Egypt, doubtless among other costly articles, with a view to obtain a favourable hearing to the embassy which was despatched to secure his aid against the Assyrians.

3. "Judah" and "Jacob" stand for the two kingdoms respectively, the latter name denoting the ten tribes, as in Is. xvii. 4. The declaration here made manifestly shows, that in ver. 1, the conduct of Judah is to be viewed in an unfavourable light. At the same time the language of both verses in reference to that power is not so strong as that which is employed respecting Israel.

4, 5. Having introduced the name of Jacob in reference to his posterity, Hosea adverts to three interesting incidents in his personal history, with the view of encouraging his countrymen to apply themselves with all assiduity to the service of God, who alone could, and would extricate them from the calamitous circumstances into which their sins had brought them. Though יַעֲקֹב, from which the name יַעֲקֹב, *Jacob*, is derived, Arab. عقب, *e vestigio sequutus fuit, a calce venit*, &c. signifies *to come behind any one, take him by the heel, trip, circumvent*, &c., it is obviously used

5 Yea, he strove with the Angel, and prevailed ;
  He wept and made supplication to him ;
  He found him at Bethel, and there He spake with us ;

here in a good sense, to denote the supernatural indication which his taking his brother Esau by the heel afforded of the superiority, which, in the course of divine providence, he and his posterity were to obtain. Gen. xxv. 22, 23, 26. To this effect the Targ. הֲלָא יַעֲקֹב עַד דְּלָא אִתְיְלִיד אֲמִיר דִּיסְגֵּי מִן אֲחוּהִי, *was it not said of Jacob before he was born, that he should be greater than his brother ?* The Israelites were reminded of the promise, "The one people shall be stronger than the other people;" and had they acted on the faith of it, they would have found that, with Jehovah on their side, they were not only stronger than the Edomites, but even than the Assyrian power itself. The idea of *power* having thus been suggested to the mind of the prophet, he was reminded of the remarkable occurrence which took place at Peniel, when Jacob wrestled with the divine messenger of the covenant, and prevailed. שָׂרָה, *to put forth power, exercise rule as a prince,* or *commander,* the verb from which יִשְׂרָאֵל, *Israel,* the other name of Jacob, is derived, is that employed Gen. xxxii. 29, (Eng. version, 28,)where the language is nearly identical with that used in these two verses. In the resumption of the subject, ver. 5, יָשׁׂר is employed, which, though equivalent to שָׂרָה in signification, must be referred to the root שׂוּר. Comp. Jud. ix. 22, and Hos. viii. 4. אוׁן properly signifies *manly vigour.* Here מַלְאָךְ, *the Angel,* corresponds to אֱלֹהִים, *God,* ver. 4, and designates the UNCREATED ANGEL, of whom we read so frequently in the Old Testament, to whom, as here, names distinctive of Deity are ascribed, and who is represented as possessing the divine attributes. See on Is. lxiii. 9, and Dr. M'Caul's Observations appended to his translation of Kimchi on Zechariah, chap. i. אֵל specially points to the Angel as the object towards whom the conflicting efforts of the patriarch were directed. Of the circumstances of his weeping and making supplication, no particular mention is made in Genesis, but they may be regarded as implied in the words, "I will not let thee go, except thou bless me." The struggle was not merely corporeal, it was also mental. The outward conflict was only a sign of that which was internal and spiritual. The prophet, as in the former reference, leaves the Israelites to make the application. If they would only now redeem their character as descendants of Israel, and show that they were entitled to the name, by sincerely and earnestly engaging in supplication to the God of their ancestor, they too should prevail, and obtain every necessary blessing. The third reference is to the narrative, Gen. xxviii. 11—22, which contains an account of the scene at Bethel, and the promises which God then made, not to the patriarch only, but also to his posterity. The nominative to מָצָא, *he found,* is God, and not Jacob, as Abenezra, Tanchum, and several others have attempted to maintain. The meaning is, that Jehovah afforded to the solitary traveller the gracious aid which his exposed situation rendered desirable. בֵּית־אֵל, *Bethel,* is here the accusative of place, and is used with singular effect, in reference to the contrasted appropriation of it by the patriarch, and by his apostate posterity. The LXX., not perceiving this, have rendered it οἶκος Ὦν, *the house of On,* as elsewhere in this book. עִמָּנוּ, "*with us,*" Aq., Symm., Theod., Syr., Tanchum, Abulwalid, and several moderns, render as if it were עִמּוֹ, "with him ;" but there is no variety of reading in the MSS., and ־נוּ, is nowhere used of the third person singular. The LXX. have πρὸς αὐτοὺς, *to them,* as if they had read עִמָּם, which, so far as pronunciation is concerned, goes to confirm the Masoretic punctuation. That the prophet here speaks per κοινώσιν, identifying himself and his contemporaries with their progenitor, in whose loins they may be said to have been, when he received the gracious promises which related not to himself only, but also to his posterity, is the interpretation advocated by Manger, Horsley, Hitzig,

6 Even Jehovah, the God of hosts :
　Jehovah is his memorial.

Maurer, and Rosenmüller. Comp. Ps. lxvi. 6 ; Heb. vii. 9, 10. On the other hand, Ewald, following Jarchi and Joseph Kimchi, renders the words יְדַבֵּר עִמָּנוּ, *he will speak with us*, in the future, and considers the prophet to be announcing, that God would renew his communications at Bethel, provided the Israelites returned to obedience. But though this seems less entitled to adoption, it cannot be denied that his design in the adduction of this instance was to lead his people to repentance, in order that they might inherit the promised blessings.

6. ו in וַיהוָה is expletive. Ewald strangely gives to the combination the form of an oath : " bei Jahve," explaining it in his note, "wahr ist das bei Jahve," By Jehovah it is true ! The incommunicable name is here introduced for the express purpose of showing that He who had made promises respecting the posterity of Jacob, would not prove unfaithful to his word. While אֱלֹהֵי הַצְּבָאוֹת, *the God of hosts*, LXX. Παντοκράτωρ, conveys the idea of supreme and infinite power by which he is able to carry all his purposes into effect, his peculiarly distinctive name יְהוָה, conveys that of *immutable constancy*, and, by implication, fidelity to his promises. Some refer the word to the root הָוָה, *to exist, be ;* but that it is to be derived from the cognate and more ordinary verb הָיָה, appears evident from Exod. iii. 14, where, in the explanation of the name, the form of the future is not אֶהֱיֶה, but אֶהְיֶה. But as ו is nevertheless inserted in יְהוָה, which also retains י, the preformant of the third person singular, it is impossible not to acquiesce in the opinion, that the noun is made up of הָיָה, *He was*, הֹוֶה, *He is*, and יִהְיֶה, *He will be*. What confirms this hypothesis, is the peculiar designation of God, Rev. i. 4, 8. Ὁ ὢν καὶ ὁ ἦν καὶ ὁ ἐρχόμενος, *He that is, and that was, and that is to come*, which is merely a translation into Greek of these different forms of the verb. See Pococke on Joel i. 19. In this derivation Abenezra and other Rabbins concur; and, accordingly, the second article of the Jewish creed concludes with the words והוא לבדו אלהינו היה הוה והיה ויהיה, " And He alone is our God ; HE WAS, HE IS, and HE SHALL BE." It is a coincidence in no small degree remarkable, that this threefold description of the divine existence obtained both among the ancient Egyptians and Brahmins. On the Saïtic temple of Isis was the inscription, Ἐγώ εἰμι πᾶν τὸ γεγονὸς καὶ ὂν καὶ ἐσόμενον, καὶ τὸν ἐμὸν πέπλον οὐδείς πω θνητὸς ἀπεκάλυψε, " I am all THAT WAS, AND IS, AND SHALL BE, and no mortal hath ever uncovered my veil." Plutarch de Iside. In the Bhagavat the Supreme Being thus addresses Brahma :—" Even I WAS at first, not any other being ; THAT WHICH EXISTS unperceived ; Supreme : afterwards I AM THAT WHICH IS ; and HE WHO MUST REMAIN am I." Asiat. Researches, vol. i. p. 245. Comp. Ζεὺς ἦν Ζεὺς ἐστί· Ζεὺς ἔσσεται· ὦ μεγάλε Ζεῦ. "Zeus was ; Zeus is ; Zeus shall be ; O great Zeus ! " Pausan. Phoc. x. 12. Whether the name יְהוָה was in use before the time of Moses, has been, and still is matter of dispute. That the patriarchs were unacquainted with it, has been concluded from Exod. vi. 3, where God declares, that the name under which he revealed himself to them was אֵל שַׁדָּי, GOD ALMIGHTY, but that he was not known to them by his name יְהוָה, JEHOVAH. Since, however, we meet with this name not only in the history of the patriarchs, but also expressly employed by themselves, as in Gen. xv. 2 ; xvi. 2 ; xxii. 14 ; xxiv. 3 ; xxvii. 7 ; xxviii. 20, 21, &c., it seems undeniable that they were acquainted with it ; so that what is meant by the words וּשְׁמִי יְהוָה לֹא נוֹדַעְתִּי לָהֶם, is, that God had not caused them *to experience the import* of his name יְהוָה, JEHOVAH. For this signification of the phrase יָדַע שֵׁם, *to know a name*, or, *to know*, comp. Is. lii. 6 ; lxiv. 1 ; Jer. xvi. 21. It had special reference to something future—the fulfilment of the promises which he had given them ; and as these promises began to be fulfilled when he interposed for their deliverance from Egypt, there was singular propriety in its being selected as the name by which Moses was to announce him to

7 Thou, therefore, return to thy God;
　Observe mercy and judgment,
　And wait continually on thy God.

8　　As for Canaan, deceitful balances are in his hand;
　He loveth to oppress.

9 And Ephraim saith, Surely I am rich,
　I have acquired wealth;
　In none of·my labours am I chargeable with guilt.

---

his people, on opening his commission to them. The same futurity of reference may be said to have continued to attach to it all along till the advent of Messiah, in whom all the promises are yea and amen, 2 Cor. i. 20; just as it is still prominently exhibited in Ὁ ἐρχόμενος, THE COMING ONE, of the Apocalypse, which obviously respects the revelation of the Lord from heaven to fulfil the mystery of God. Such interpretation alone goes to fully justify the emphatic statement made in the text of our prophet, יְהֹוָה זִכְרוֹ, compared with Exod. iii. 15, זֶה זִכְרִי לְדֹר דֹּר. in which the Most High declares, that this name was to be employed for the purpose of perpetuating the knowledge of his character with respect to promised blessings. Comp. also Ps. cxxxv. 13. That it should have come into oral disuse among the Jews, can only have originated in a feeling of superstitious veneration, which led them to regard it as too sacred to be pronounced without profanation. The earliest trace of such superstition is thought to be found in the words, Ecclesiasticus xxiii. 9, ὀνομασία τοῦ ἁγίου μὴ συνεθισθῇς, "use not thyself to the naming of the Holy One;" but Philo de Nomin. mutat. makes express mention of it. Whenever the Jews meet with it in the text, they read אֲדֹנָי, LORD, instead of it, except when it follows אֲדֹנָי, in which case they point it יְהֹוִה,, and read אֱלֹהִים, GOD. Some are of opinion, that the present punctuation יְהֹוָה is merely that of יָּ, the simple Shevah taking the place of Hateph-Patach, which only occurs in connexion with gutturals; but the employment of the two first syllables with precisely the same points in the formation of compound proper names manifestly goes to show that our present pronunciation is correct. Compare

יְהוֹשֻׁעַ, יְהוֹנָתָן, יְהוֹיָדָע, &c. The change of the Segol into Kametz may be accounted for on the ground of the grave manner in which the final syllable required to be accented, if it was not intended to stand for the second vowel of the preterite הָיָה.

7. An exhortation to duty derived from what God had been, and would still, in accordance with the significant aspect of his name, in continuance be, to those who served him in sincerity.

8. כְּנַעַן, Canaan, is the nominative absolute, introduced abruptly for the purpose of graphically describing the real character of the Ephraimites. The word may, indeed, be rendered merchant, but then אִישׁ, man, must be supplied; אִישׁ כְּנַעַן, a man of Canaan, meaning a merchant—the inhabitants of that country being the celebrated merchants of antiquity. The prophet seems rather to place the names of Canaan and Israel in antithesis; in which there is great point, as the Israelites were accustomed to hold the Canaanites in the utmost contempt. Comp. Ezek. xvi. 3. Horsley renders a trafficker of Canaan, which weakens rather than strengthens the antithesis. The fraudulent practices of merchants were quite proverbial among the Jews. "As a nail sticketh fast in the joinings of the stones, so doth sin stick close between buying and selling." Ecclesiasticus xxvii. 2.

9. The character assumed in the preceding verse is here directly applied, only the ten tribes are represented as flattering themselves that they had employed no illegal means in acquiring their affluence. יִמְצָאוּ, they shall find, is used impersonally. עָוֹן is employed to denote the act of distortion or iniquity; חֵטְא its guilt or culpability. The words literally rendered are, with respect to all

10 Yet I, Jehovah, am thy God from the land of Egypt;
　　I will still cause thee to dwell in tents as on feast-days.

11 I have also spoken to the prophets,
　　And have multiplied visions;
　　And through the prophets I have used similitudes.

my efforts, they shall not find attaching to me iniquity which is sin; and the meaning is, any fraudulent transactions for which I might be punished. " The merchant imagines it is not possible to get through business without some deceit; but he takes care not to commit any gross or deadly act of delinquency, hoping that God will not be strict in regard to the rest."—*Michaelis.*

10. Commentators have been greatly divided in opinion as to whether these words are to be taken as a promise, or as a threatening. Those who take the latter view interpret the living in tabernacles of such a life as those lead who have no settled habitations, like the Israelites in the wilderness, or like those who assembled at the annual festivals, and who could only be accommodated in tents without the city. But, though such exegesis might at first sight seem to suit the connexion, yet there is something so forced in comparing a state of captivity to that of the Hebrew nation during the celebration of the most joyful of all their festivals, that I am compelled to regard the verse as containing a promise of what God would still do for the Israelites on their repentance and reformation. Those who are familiar with the sudden and abrupt transitions which abound in Hosea, and the frequency with which he intermingles promises with threatenings, will not be surprised at this unexpected assurance of the divine clemency. The argument is this: the Israelites have indeed acted a most wicked and deceitful part, and justly deserve to be for ever cast off from all participation in my favour; but I am still, what I have been from the beginning of their history, their covenant-God, and will yet cause them to renew their joy before me. That they were not to enjoy any such privilege in their apostate condition is taken for granted. The promise was fulfilled on the return from the captivity.

11. Jehovah adduces a further proof of the kindness of his disposition towards the nation—the abundant means of instruction which he had afforded them; while, at the same time, the language is so worded as to draw their attention to the messages which the prophets had delivered. These messages contained the most powerful dissuasives from idolatry, and the greatest encouragements to cleave unto the Lord. עַל in דִּבַּרְתִּי עַל־הַנְּבִיאִים, following a verb of announcement, is equivalent to אֶל, *to,* and is not to be pressed so as to make it signify the *coming down* or *resting* of inspiration upon the prophets. Comp. Job xxxvi. 33. LXX. πρὸς προφήτας. If Hosea was one of the earliest of the Hebrew prophets, whose books are now in our hands, reference must here be had to those who had flourished before his time, such as Ahijah the Shilonite, Shemaiah, Iddo, Azariah, Hanani, Jehu, Jahaziel, Eliezer, Elijah, Elisha, Micaiah, Joel, and Amos, not to include the hundred prophets of the Lord whom Obadiah hid in a cave, after Jezebel had put a number to death. Not only had Jehovah made numerous communications of his will through the instrumentality of these messengers, but he had employed such modes in making these communications as were calculated at once to gain and secure attention. For חָזוֹן, see on Is. i. 1. אֲדַמֶּה, from דָּמָה, *to be like, resemble;* in Piel, to *liken, compare, employ similes,* or *comparisons;* or, in general, to use figurative language. In such language, including metaphor, allegory, comparison, prosopopœia, apostrophe, hyperbole, &c. the prophets abound. They accommodated themselves to the capacity and understanding of their hearers by couching the high and important subjects of which they treated under the imagery of sensible objects, and invested them with a degree of life and energy which could only be resisted by an obstinate determination

12 Verily, Gilead is iniquitous,
   Surely they are false:
   In Gilgal they sacrifice oxen;
   Yea, their altars are like the heaps
   On the ridges of the field.

13 Jacob fled also to the country of Syria;
   Yea, Israel served for a wife;
   And for a wife he kept the flocks.

14 By a prophet also Jehovah brought Israel up from Egypt,
   And by a prophet he was kept.

not to listen to religious instruction. Though אֲרַמֶּה is in the future, it borrows its temporal signification from the two preceding verbs, דִּבַּרְתִּי and הִרְבֵּיתִי, which are in the preterite.

12. אִם is not used here as a particle expressing doubt; it rather expresses the certainty of what is affirmed, as אַךְ following, evidently shows. The two places here mentioned were celebrated in the history of the Hebrews:—*Gilead*, on account of the solemn agreement which Laban and Jacob entered into there with each other; and *Gilgal*, on account of the general circumcision of the people, and the solemn observance of the passover when they had passed over Jordan. They are adduced by the prophet to remind the Israelites of the sacred obligations under which they lay, and the sacred character which, as the peculiar people of God, they ought ever to sustain. Pointing, as it were, to the heap of stones which Jacob had erected in testimony of the transaction between him and Laban, Hosea asks, Is Gilead the scene of iniquity? Are its inhabitants actually worshippers of idols? And then he fearlessly charges them with idolatry. Both אָוֶן and שָׁוְא are specially used of idols, in order to express their nothingness and vanity. The abstract stands for the concrete. By גִּלְעָד, *Gilead*, is meant not merely the place, but its inhabitants. Comp. for the wickedness of the Gileadites, chap. vi. 8. גִּלְגָּל, *Gilgal*, had also become desecrated by idolatrous practices, chap iv. 15, ix. 15, which abounded to such an extent, that the number of the altars was like that of the heaps of stones which have been collected and left in various parts of the

ridges of a field. In גַּלִּים, *heaps*, comp. Josh. vii. 26, there is an obvious reference to the name גִּלְגָּל. Both are derived from גָּלַל, *to roll, roll stones*, &c. For תַּלְמֵי שָׂדָי, comp. chap. x. 4.

13, 14. The argument of both these verses is the same, though it is only in the latter that it is expressly stated, viz. the divine goodness in preserving Jacob and his posterity. God was with the patriarch, according to his promise, and protected and prospered him all the time he was in servitude in Padan-aram; and he likewise delivered his descendants from Egyptian bondage, and conducted them safely to the land of Canaan. אֲרָם, *Aramæa*, Syria, *the high country*, from רוּם, *to be high;* here specially the region between the Euphrates and the Tigris, called, on this account, אֲרַם נַהֲרַיִם, *Aram of the two rivers;* LXX. Μεσοποταμία, *Mesopotamia*. Being lower than the rest of Syria on the west, it is here called שָׂדֶה, *field*, which corresponds to פַדֶּן, *a level* or *plain*, Gen. xlviii. 7; hence *Padan-aram*. שָׁמַר, *to keep*, is used without צֹאן, *sheep*, in the sense of *keeping a flock*. See Gen. xxx. 31; 1 Sam. xvii. 20. To the verb as thus employed in its literal acceptation, ver. 13, the figurative use in נִשְׁמָר, ver. 14, corresponds. The church of God is frequently compared to a flock. The נָבִיא, *prophet*, here referred to was Moses, who was so κατ᾽ ἐξοχήν. See Exod. iv. 15, 16; Numb. xii. 6—8; Is. lxiii. 11, 12. The repeated reference to the Hebrew legislator in this character, was evidently intended to impress the minds of the Israelites with a conviction of the necessity of attending to the messages which the Lord sent to them by his prophets.

15 Ephraim hath given most bitter provocation ;
　Therefore will his Lord leave his blood upon him,
　And bring back upon him his reproach.

15. תַּמְרוּרִים, lit. *bitternesses,* i. e. *most bitter,* or *bitterly.* The object of provocation is not expressed, but that it is Jehovah is clear from the following clause. The blood of Ephraim was, in all probability, that of human victims which had been shed in the service of Moloch. אֲדֹנָיו, *his Lord,* is improperly applied by Horsley to the king of Assyria.

By חֶרְפָּתוֹ, *his reproach,* is meant the disgraceful conduct of the ten tribes in abandoning the true God as unworthy of their service, and transferring it to idols. אֲדֹנָיו is the nominative to יִטּוֹשׁ as well as to יָשִׁיב, and in our language the corresponding term *Lord* requires to be used before the former, and understood before the latter of the two verbs.

———◆———

CHAPTER XIII

After contrasting the prosperity of the tribe of Ephraim, during the period of its obedience to the divine laws, with the adversity which it had suffered in consequence of idolatry, 1, the prophet proceeds in the same manner, as in the preceding chapter, to intermingle brief descriptions of sin and guilt, 2, 6, 9, 12 ; denouncements of punishment, 3, 7, 8, 13, 15, 16 ; and intimations of mercy, 4, 5, 9, 14.

————————

1 WHEN Ephraim spake, there was tremour,
　He was exalted in Israel ;
　But he offended through Baal, and died.

1. *Ephraim* means here the tribe properly so called, in distinction from the other tribes of *Israel,* mentioned immediately after. Such was the power and influence which it originally exercised over the rest, that they showed it the utmost deference. רְתֵת, a ἅπαξ λεγ.; but obviously cognate with רְטֵט, Jer. xlix. 24, Syr. ܪܬܝܬܐ, Targ. רְתִיתָא, *fear, trembling.* In Pococke's Arab. MS. the words are rendered عند خطاب افرايم الرعدة تقع علي الناس, *when Ephraim spake, trembling fell upon men.* And so Tanchum, المعني ان الناس يهابوه ويرعدون من كلامه, *the meaning is, that men revered him, and trembled at his word.* The same construction is adopted by Jerome, Kimchi, Abarbanel, Munster, Vatablus, Clarius, Drusius, Liveley, Grotius, Rivetus, Tingstadius, Dathe, Kuinoel, Horsley, De Wette, Maurer, Noyes, and Hitzig. It is impossible to approve the translation of Ewald : "Wie Efraim redete Empörung, es Aufruhr machte in

2　And now they continue to sin,
　　And make for themselves molten images,
　　Idols of their silver, according to their skill;
　　All of them the work of artificers;
　　The men that sacrifice, say of them,
　　Let them kiss the calves.

Israel," *When Ephraim gave utterance to sedition, it produced rebellion in Israel.* Neither רָחַת nor נָשָׂא admits of being so translated. To take רְחַת adverbially, and render it *tremblingly,* or *trembling,* as in our common version, though it affords an apt sense in itself, is less suited to the connexion. נָשָׂא occurs in the sense of *elevating oneself,* Ps. lxxxix. 10; Nah. i. 5, or *being exalted.* Hence נָשִׂיא, *a prince.* בְּ in בְּבַעַל, has the force of, *in union with, in the matter of,* and marks the participation of the Ephraimites in the service of Baal. מוּת, *to die,* is here to be taken in a civil or political sense; to lose one's influence, become subject to misery, punishment, &c. It forms an antithesis to נָשָׂא, *to be exalted.* No sooner did the Ephraimites forsake the true God and take up with idols than he inflicted judgments upon them, by which their power was weakened, and at last became entirely extinct— " ex quo peccavit, nulla jam est autoritate in populo Dei." Œcolampadius.— " Vita ærumnosa et tristis pro morte censetur; idcirco exules mortui dicuntur, et exilium sepulchri nomine notatur, Ezech. cap. 37." Rivetus.

2. This verse sets forth their perseverance in idolatrous practices, notwithstanding the chastisements with which they had been visited. וְזֹבְחֵי אָדָם, the LXX., Vulg., Jarchi, Abenezra, Abarbanel, Tanchum, Calvin, Piscator, Leo Juda, and among the moderns, Schmid, J. H. Michaelis, Horsley, Hitzig, Stuck, and J. Fr. Schröder, render *sacrifice,* or *sacrificers of men,* on the principle, that the presentation of human sacrifices is meant. This, however, was called in question by Kimchi, who explains, בני אדם הבאים לזבח, *the men who come to sacrifice.* To the same effect Munster, Piscator, Junius and Tremellius, Rivetus, Mercer, Glassius, Liveley, Drusius, Bochart, our own and most of the authorized versions, Lowth, Newcome,

Boothroyd, Noyes, De Wette, Gesenius, Maurer, and Ewald. The rule of syntax laid down by Gesenius respecting this mode of construction, Lehrgeb. p. 678, is, that when a genitive following an adjective is a noun of multitude, or of the plural number, such adjective is particularly used in poetry for the purpose of designating those of the multitude to which the specified quality belongs. Instances are Is. xxix. 19, אֶבְיוֹנֵי אָדָם, *the poor of men,* i. e. those of men who are poor; Mic. v. 4, (Eng. version 5,) נְסִיכֵי אָדָם, *the anointed of men.* i.e. such of men as are anointed. So in the present case, וְזֹבְחֵי אָדָם, *sacrificers of men,* i.e. *those of* or *among men that sacrifice,* which is merely a periphrasis for *priests.* Although, therefore, it is a fact, that the ten tribes did sacrifice their children to Moloch, 2 Kings xvii. 17, it would be more than precarious to draw any such inference from the present passage, especially as the prophet mentions the *calves,* of whose worship human sacrifices, so far as we know, formed no part. עֲגָלִים יִשָּׁקוּן, *let them kiss the calves.* It was customary for idolaters to give the kiss of adoration to the objects of their worship. This was sometimes done by merely touching the lips with the hand, to which reference is made Job xxxi. 27. Comp. Lucian περὶ Ορχήσεως i. p. 918, edit. Bened.; Minutius Felix, cap. 2, *ad fin.*; Apuleius Apol. p. 496. At other times the idol itself was kissed by the worshippers. Comp. 1 Kings xix. 18. Thus Cicero tells us, that at Agrigentum in Sicily there was a brazen image of the Tyrian Hercules whose mouth and chin were worn by the kisses of his worshippers—"non solum id venerari, verum etiam *osculari* solebant." Act ii. in Verrem, lib. iv. cap. 43. Nothing is more common than in the Russian churches than for the devotees to kiss the picture of the Virgin, or of St. Nicholas. The construction of the words

3 Therefore shall they be like the morning cloud,
　　And like the dew which early departeth,
　　Like chaff blown by a whirlwind from the threshing-floor,
　　And like smoke from the window.

4 　Yet I, Jehovah, have been thy God from the land of Egypt,
　　And thou knewest no God besides me;
　　Nor besides me was there any Saviour.

5 I regarded thee in the wilderness,
　　In the land of burning thirst.

6 As they were fed, so were they satiated;
　　They were satiated, and their heart was lifted up;
　　Therefore they forgat me:

7 So that I became to them as a lion,
　　I watched for them as a leopard by the way.

8 I met them as a bear bereaved of her cubs,

לָהֶם הֵם אֹמְרִים זֹבְחֵי אָדָם עֲגָלִים יִשָּׁקוּן is somewhat difficult. As usually divided, they are interpreted thus: they, *i.e.* the Ephraimites, say of them, *i.e.* the images, let the sacrificers kiss the calves; but it is better to take זֹבְחֵי אָדָם, *the sacrificers,* as in apposition with, and exegetical of הֵם אֹמְרִים, *they say,* i.e. *they,* the men that sacrifice, *say* to the people, let them kiss the calves. While the priests presented the sacrifices, they encouraged the worshippers to come forward and kiss the objects of their adoration.

3. Comp. chap. vi. 4. גֹּרֶן, *the threshing floor,* being an open area, generally on an eminence, was peculiarly exposed to the wind, which carried off the chaff, on its being trodden out, or separated from the grain. אֲרֻבָּה, Aq. ἀπὸ καταρρ́άκτου, which Jerome explains, "foramen in pariete fabricatum, per quod fumus egreditur;" Symm. ὀπῆς, ὀπῇ, *an orifice;* Theod. καπνοδόχη, *a hole for the passage of smoke.* It is very common in the East for the light to be admitted, and the smoke to make its escape by the same passage or orifice in the wall. The idea of a speedy removal is that conveyed by all the images here employed.

4. Comp. chap. xii. 10. The long addition in the LXX. is totally unsupported, and was most probably inserted in that version by some scholiast.

5. Here יְדַעְתִּי, *I knew,* contrasts with תֵּדַע in the preceding verse, only it is to be taken in the sense of *knowing effectively, taking notice of, caring for.* Comp. Amos iii. 2. תַּלְאֻבֹת, lit. *thirstinesses, great thirst, extreme drought,* from לָאַב, Arab. لاب, *sitivit.* Comp. לָהַב, *to burn,* Arab. لهب, *arsit, sitivit, siti arsit.* Munster renders, "terra siti ardente." Comp. Deut. viii. 15.

6. כְּמַרְעִיתָם, *according to their feeding,* i.e. in proportion to their enjoyment of the provision which I made for them, feeding them with manna from heaven, and afterwards abundantly supplying their wants. It is equivalent to, "as they were fed." For the rest of the verse comp. Deut. xxxii. 13—15.

7. 8. ו in וָאֱהִי is inferential, showing that what follows was the result of what is stated in the preceding verse. The context requires the verb to be taken in the past time. The images here employed are of frequent occurrence. Comp. Job x. 16; Ps. vii. 2; Is. xxxviii. 13; Lam. iii. 10. נָמֵר, *the leopard,* so called from his *spots* or *streaks.* Arab. نمر, *maculosus fuit, maculis punctisve respersus fuit; pardus.* See Jer. xiii. 23, הֲיַהֲפֹךְ נָמֵר חֲבַרְבֻּרֹתָיו. The leopard is noted for his swiftness, ferocity, and especially

And rent the caul of their heart ;
Yea, I devoured them there, as a lioness ;
The wild beast rent them in pieces.

9   O Israel! Thou hast destroyed thyself,
Nevertheless in me truly is thine help.

10   Where is thy king now?
That he may save thee in all thy cities ;
And thy judges, of whom thou saidst,
Give me a king and princes.

11   I gave thee a king in mine anger,
And took him away in my wrath.

his cruelty to man. He lurks in the dense thicket of the wood, and springs with great velocity on his victim. With respect to the bear, Jerome remarks, "Aiunt, qui de bestiarum scripsere naturis, inter omnes feras nihil esse ursa sævius, quum perdiderit catulos vel indiguerit cibis." דֹב being of common gender, the participle שַׁכּוּל is put in the masculine, though the female bear is meant. Comp. אַלּוּפֵינוּ מְסֻבָּלִים, Ps. cxliv. 14. סְגוֹר is the pericardium, or membrane which contains the heart in its cavity, and is thus fitly called its enclosure. For אֲשׁוּר, I watched, sixteen of De Rossi's MSS. and one in the margin, three ancient editions, and twenty-four others, the LXX., Syr., Vulg., and Arab. read אַשּׁוּר, Assyria, which some prefer, on account of the number of lions, panthers, tigers, &c. with which the regions of southern Asia abound. The text would then read, as a leopard, in the way to Assyria; but the common reading is more in accordance with the spirit of the passage.

9. שִׁחֶתְךָ, I take to be a noun with the suffix, thy destruction! i.e. the destruction is thine own; thou hast brought it upon thyself by thy sins. It is, therefore, equivalent to "thou hast destroyed thyself," and cannot be better rendered. Thus the Vulg. Perditio tua, Israel. Dathe, Ipsi estis o Israelitæ! exitii vestri causa. Some, however, as Kimchi, supply הָעֵגֶל, the calf; others, מַלְכְּךָ, thy king, from the following verse ; others, some other noun ; and take שִׁחֵת to be the third person singular of Piel. Comp. for the form, שִׁלֵּם, Deut. xxxii. 35 ; דִּבֶּר, Jer. v. 13; Hos. i. 2; קִשֵּׁר, Jer.

xliv. 21. Newcome unwarrantably adopts the rendering of the Syriac, "I have destroyed thee." Most of the moderns give a hostile sense to the בְּ in the following בִּי בְעֶזְרֶךָ, against me, against thy help; but, considering how frequently declarations of kindness are mixed up with charges of evil, and that some verb denoting rebellion would be required to support such construction, it seems preferable to give to כִּי the common adversative signification of yet, nevertheless, and to regard the בְּ in בְעֶזְרֶךָ as the Beth Essentiæ, which renders the phrase much more emphatic than the pronoun, or the substantive verb would have done. It is equivalent to, In me is thy real help ; other sources may be applied to, and they may promise thee assistance ; but from me alone efficient aid is to be expected, and in me it is to be found. Thus our translators. See on Is. xxvi. 4. This exegesis is strongly supported, if not rendered absolutely necessary, by the pointed interrogations in the following verse. The LXX. τίς βοηθήσει; turning בְּ into מִי, and omitting the second בְּ altogether. Thus also the Syr.

10, 11. אֱהִי is in all probability a metathesis for אַיֵּה, where? It is thus rendered by the LXX., Syr., Vulg., Targ., Abulwalid, Tanchum, Luther, Drusius, Mercer, Osiander, Rivetus, Castalio, and by most modern expositors. It is also so taken by Gesenius, Lee, Winer, and Fürst ; and alone suits the connexion. Comp. in support of this interpretation, the combination אַיֵּה אֵפוֹא, Jud. ix. 38 ; Job xvii. 15 ; Is. xix. 12. One of Kennicott's MSS. and perhaps another, one of De Rossi's in the margin, read

12　　The guilt of Ephraim is bound up,
　　　　His punishment is laid up in store.

13　The pangs of a woman in labour shall come upon him;
　　　　He is an unwise son,
　　　　Otherwise he would not remain long
　　　　In the place of the breaking forth of children.

14　I will deliver them from the power of Sheol;
　　　　I will redeem them from death:

אַיֵּה instead of אֱהִי, though probably by correction. Another of De Rossi's has a note in the margin, stating that the word is so explained. The ו in וְאוֹשִׁיעֵךְ is pleonastic, except it be regarded as introducing the apodosis. אֱהִי is so intimately connected with the past transactions implied in אָמַרְתָּ תְּנָה־לִּי, *thou saidst, give me*, that, though future in form, it cannot with any propriety be rendered otherwise than in the preterite. Some refer the circumstances here mentioned to the selection and removal of Saul; but it is more in keeping with the speciality of the prophet's address to consider the king to be Jeroboam and his successors in the regal dignity; and that the removal regards the frequent changes which took place in the history of the Israelitish kings, which proved a source of great calamity to the nation. See 2 Kings xv.

12. The metaphors are here borrowed from the custom of tying up money in bags, and depositing it in some secret place, in order that it might be preserved. The certainty of punishment is the idea conveyed by them. Comp. for the former, Job xiv. 17; and for the latter Deut. xxxii. 34, Job. xxi. 19.

13. Another instance of two metaphors closely connected, the transition from the one to the other of which is; in the manner of the Orientals, rapid and unexpected. See Dathe's very judicious note. It is not unusual in Scripture to compare the calamities of a people to the sorrows of childbirth. In addition to this the danger and folly of Ephraim in protracting repentance, in the midst of the afflictive circumstances in which he was placed, is fitly compared to the extremely critical condition of a child on the point of being born, but, owing to the want of strength on the part of the mother, or other causes, detained in its passage from the womb. The LXX. οὗτος ὁ υἱός σου ὁ φρόνιμος has doubtless originally been οὗτος ὁ υἱός οὐ φρόνιμος. כִּי introduces the contrary of the preceding proposition, and is used elliptically for the sentence, "*For* if it were not so," &c. It may best be rendered into English by *otherwise, else*, or the like. עֵת, *time*, is here to be taken adverbially, in the sense of *for a time, long*, &c. Winer, *aliquod tempus, aliquamdiu*. Comp. the Arab. زمن, when used in opposition to وقت.—מִשְׁפַּר, the *os uteri*. Comp. 2 Kings xix. 3; Is. xxxvii. 3; lxvi. 9. Without a national παλιγγενεσία, no prosperity could be expected. It was for the Israelites by true repentance to accelerate and ensure their deliverance from threatened destruction, and their enjoyment of a new period of peace and happiness.

14. The ideas of Sheol and Death were naturally suggested by the perilous circumstances described in the preceding verse. Extinction as a people is there apprehended. Here it is viewed as having already taken place; and a gracious promise is given of the restoration of the Israelites, and the complete destruction of the enemies by whom they had been carried into captivity. מִיַּד, *from the hand*, a common Hebraism for *from the power*. פָּדָה properly signifies to *redeem*, or *buy loose*, by the payment of a price; גָּאַל, to *avenge* the murder of a relative, and also to *recover* or *redeem* property by repayment. Both verbs, however, are used in a more extended signification, and especially in reference to the deliverance of the Hebrews from Egypt, and from the captivity in Babylon. That שְׁאוֹל, *Sheol*,

Where is thy plague, O Death?
Where is thy destruction, O Sheol?
Repentance is hid from mine eyes.

and מָוֶת, *Death*, are here to be taken in a figurative sense, with application to the state of the Israelites in the Assyrian and Babylonish captivity, deprived as they were of all political existence, and subject to the most grievous calamities, the exigency of the passage imperatively demands. Comp. Is. xxvi. 19. Respecting אֱהִי, interpreters are far from being agreed. Symm., the Vulg., Coverdale, Drusius, Tingstadius, Horsley, Dathe, Kuinoel, De Wette, Noyes, Rosenmüller, Hesselberg, and Maurer, take it to be the first person future of the substantive verb הָיָה, *to be;* whereas the LXX., Aq., the fifth edition, Paul (1 Cor. xv. 55), Syr., Arab., Abulwalid, Tanchum, Junius and Tremellius, Mercer, Newcome, Boothroyd, Ewald, and Hitzig, consider it to be used as in ver. 10, for אַיֵּה, ποῦ, *where?* With the latter authorities I concur, partly on the ground that it is not likely the prophet would employ the same word in the same form in two different acceptations in verses 10 and 14; and partly because I find אֱהִי nowhere used absolutely as an apocopated future; but always with the Vau conversive prefixed. See for the full form אֶהְיֶה, chap. xiv. 6. To which add, that the interrogation is more in keeping with the animated style of the passage. Instead of the plural דְּבָרֶיךָ, *thy destructions,* one hundred and twenty-two MSS., originally five more, now two, and four of the early editions, read דְּבָרְךָ, *thy destruction,* in the singular. דֶּבֶר, Arab. بر, *death;* specially *the plague, pestilence;* the awful *destruction* of human life effected by it. Hence the LXX. mostly render it θάνατος; here δίκη, but in all probability originally νίκη, for which Paul reads νῖκος, only transposing νῖκος and κέντρον, by which latter term the LXX. render קֶטֶב, *excision, cutting off, destruction.* The cause of this transposition is obvious. The apostle had just quoted the passage in Isaiah, agreeably to the version of Theodotion, in which νῖκος occurs, whereby he was reminded of the same

words as occurring in Hosea, and, under the influence of strong emotion, he commences his quotation with νῖκος prominently in his mind. Olshausen thinks νῖκος is a later form for νίκη.

Root קָטַב, Arab. قطب, *to cut, cut off, destroy.* That דֶּבֶר is the genuine reading, and that דָּרְבָן, *a goad,* which some would substitute for it, in order to make the Hebrew correspond to κέντρον, is to be rejected, may very conclusively be gathered from the similar occurrence of the words דֶּבֶר and קֶטֶב together, Ps. xci. 6. Comp. Deut. xxxii. 24. The import of this animated apostrophe, as used both by Jehovah in the prophet, and by the apostle, is, Where are now the effects of the destructive influence which you have exerted? your victims are recovered‾ from your dominion: they are alive again, and shall no more be subject to your power. The speakers place themselves as it were in the period after the resurrection: the former in that after the restoration from Babylon; the other in that after the literal restoration of the dead to life at the last day. Both look back, and triumphantly exult over the conquerors. With respect to the appropriation of the words by the apostle in reference to the doctrine of the final resurrection, it appears to be made, not in the way of proof, but merely to give expression, in the triumphant language of the prophet, to the animated feelings which had taken possession of his breast. His direct quotation in the way of argument is made from Is. xxv. 8, and consists of the words, κατεπόθη ὁ θάνατος εἰς νῖκος. It would, therefore, be improper to identify the subject of which he treats with that treated of by our prophet. " Neque enim ex professo semper locos adducunt apostoli, qui toto contextu ad institutum quod tractant pertinent: sed interdum alludunt ad unum verbum duntaxat, aliquando aptant locum ad sententiam per similitudinem, aliquando adhibent testimonia.—Atqui satis constat, Paulum illo 15 cap. 1 ad Corinth.

15　　Though he be fruitful among his brethren,
　　　Yet an east wind, a wind of Jehovah,
　　　Shall come up from the desert,
　　　And dry up his fountain;
　　　And his spring shall become dry:
　　　He shall spoil the treasure of all pleasant vessels.

16　Samaria shall be punished,
　　　Because she hath rebelled against her God:
　　　They shall fall by the sword;
　　　Their infants shall be dashed in pieces,
　　　And their pregnant women shall be ripped up.

epist. non citasse prophetæ testimonium ad confirmandam illam doctrinam de qua disserit." Calvin *in loc.* See also Horsley's critical note. נֹחַם, LXX. παράκλησις, Syr. ܟܘܒܐ, Vulg. *consolatio;* but *repentance* better suits the connexion. It expresses the immutability of the divine purpose, which had the deliverance of his people for its object. Comp. Rom. xi. 29. Horsley strangely refers the repentance to man, and not to God.

15. This and the following verse set forth the devastation and destruction of the kingdom of the ten tribes, which was to precede the deliverance promised in that which precedes. While the promise was designed to afford consolation to the pious, and encouragement to the penitent, the threatening was equally necessary for the refractory and profane. הוּא, *he,* refers to Ephraim, ver. 12. יַפְרִיא, a ἅπαξ λεγ. but obviously equivalent to יַפְרִיה, the Hiphil of פָּרָה, *to be fruitful.* It is here used with special reference to the name of אֶפְרַיִם, being the root whence it is derived, and not improbably exhibits א instead of ה, because it forms the first letter of the noun. The tribe of Ephraim was the most numerous in regard to population, and was for a time in the most flourishing circumstances. That such is the signification of the verb, and that it is not to be rendered *divide* or *separate,* as in the ancient and several of the modern versions, nor *act like a wild ass,* which others exhibit, appears from the mention

of a *spring* and a *fountain,* which naturally suggest the idea of a tree, the roots of which are plentifully supplied by their water. For קָדִים, see on chap. xii. 2, and Is. xxvii. 8. רוּחַ יְהוָה, like אֵשׁ אֱלֹהִים, Job. i. 16, is the genitive of cause, a wind caused, sent by, or proceeding from Jehovah; not "a great wind," as some interpret. The Assyrian army is meant. הוּא יֵשְׁסֶה, *He,* i. e. *the Assyrian,* couched under the metaphor of the destructive wind, *shall plunder* every valuable article belonging to the Israelites.

16. [Chap. xiv. 1.] This verse begins the following chapter in the Hebrew Bible, but it more intimately coheres with the preceding context. תֶּאְשַׁם, LXX. ἀφανισθήσεται, Vulg. *pereat.* The word signifies *to be guilty of crime,* and *to be treated as guilty, to suffer punishment, be punished.* Samaria, as the metropolis, and the source of all the calamities which were coming upon the Israelites, is put as representing the whole nation; but not to the exclusion of the peculiarly severe punishment which the inhabitants of that city had to expect. מָרָה, some render *to embitter, provoke bitterly;* but *rebelling, resisting, striking against* any one, are the ideas more properly conveyed by the verb. Thus the LXX. ἀντέστη πρὸς τὸν θεὸν αὐτῆς. The addition of the affix in אֱלֹהֶיהָ, " her God," gives great emphasis in such connexion. Comp. chap. xii. 10; xiii. 4. The aggravations of sin are increased by the relations sustained by the sinner. For the concluding portion of the verse, comp. 2 Kings viii. 12; xv. 16;

Amos i. 13. That such cruelties were not unknown among other nations, see Iliad vi. 58 :—

  ——μηδ' ὅντινα γαστέρι μήτηρ
 Κοῦρον ἐόντα φέροι, μηδ' ὅς φύγοι ;—

and Horace, Carm. iv. Ode 6. The construction הָרִיּוֹתָיו יְבֻקָּעוּ is *ad sensum*, though not according to the strict rule of grammar, and may have been occasioned by the form of יְרַשֵּׁוּ immediately preceding.

———◆———

CHAPTER XIV

This chapter contains an urgent call to repentance, the supplication and confession expressive of which are put in a set form of words into the mouths of the penitents, 1—3. To encourage them thus to return to God, he makes the most gracious promises to them, 4—7 ; their entire abandonment of idolatry is then predicted, and the divine condescension and goodness are announced, 8 ; and the whole concludes with a solemn declaration, on the part of the prophet, respecting the opposite consequences that would result from attention or inattention to his message, 9.

———————

1 RETURN, O Israel ! to Jehovah thy God ;
 For thou hast fallen by thine iniquity.
2 Take with you words, and return to Jehovah ;
 Say to him,
 Forgive all iniquity, and graciously receive us,
 Then we will render to thee the calves of our lips.

1, 2. The ה of direction in the imperative שׁוּבָה is, as usual, intensive, marking a strong desire on the part of the speaker that the action expressed by the verb might take place. For the emphasis attaching to the affix in אֱלֹהֶיךָ, " *thy* God," see on chap. xiii. 16. נָשָׂא עָוֹן is a phrase of such frequent occurrence with the meaning *to pardon iniquity*, that it is surprising how Horsley could insist upon its meaning to "take away the sinful principle within us—the carnal heart of the old Adam." His construction of קַח טוֹב, " accept as good, what, so regenerate, we shall be enabled

to perform," though sound divinity, is equally indefensible on the ground of philology. טוֹב is used adverbially, *benignè, in bonam partem ;* and the meaning is, graciously receive us back into thy favour. With respect to the interposition of the verb תִּשָּׂא, between בֹּל and עָוֹן, it may be observed, that it is not a solitary instance of such construction. See on Is. xix. 8, and comp. Job xv. 10. פָּרִים, *calves* or *bullocks*, used here metaphorically for *victims, sacrifices*. The word occurring in the absolute form, some render פָּרִים שְׂפָתֵינוּ, *bullocks our lips*, as if the two nouns were in apposition ;

3 Assyria shall not save us;
  We will not ride upon horses;
  Neither will we say any more, " Our gods,"
  To the work of our hands:
  For by thee the destitute is pitied.

4   I will heal their apostasy;
  I will love them freely;
  For my anger is turned away from them.

5 I will be as the dew to Israel;

but there are instances of nouns thus put, which cannot be explained otherwise than in the construct, as to sense. Thus Deut. xxxiii. 11, מְתְנַיִם קָמָיו, *the loins of those who oppose him ;* Jud. v. 13, אַדִּירִים עָם, *the princes of the people;* Prov. xxii. 21, אֲמָרִים אֱמֶת, *words of truth.* Gesenius supposes the governing noun to be mentally repeated, and that the full form would be פָּרִים פְּרִי שְׂפָתֵינוּ, *bullocks, the bullocks of our lips.* Such construction in full he adduces in the instance Exod. xxxviii. 21, הַמִּשְׁכָּן מִשְׁכַּן הָעֵדֻת, *the tabernacle, the tabernacle of testimony.* Some would change פָרִים into פְּרִי, *fruit,* on the ground of the reading found in the LXX. ἀνταποδώσομεν καρπὸν χειλέων ἡμῶν, which is followed by the Syr. and Arab., and is supposed to have been borrowed by the apostle, Heb. xiii. 15. There is, however, no variety in the Hebrew MSS.; while the Targum and all the other authorities support the textual reading. The LXX. have committed a similar mistake in rendering פְּרִי, *her bullocks,* τους καρπους αὐτῆς, *her fruits,* Jer. l. 27. The conjecture of Pococke, that they used καρπὸς in the sense of κάρπωμα, which they employ to express SACRIFICE, *oblation,* &c., is less probable. See the important note of Horsley. The prophet's meaning is, We will render, in grateful return for thy forgiving and restoring mercy, the only sacrifices worthy of it—our tribute of thanksgiving and praise. For such use of שִׁלֵּם, *to requite, render back,* comp. Ps. lvi. 13, אֲשַׁלֵּם תּוֹדֹת לָךְ, *I will render thanks unto thee:* so that the construction proposed by some, "we will offer the sacrifices which our lips have vowed," cannot be regarded as unexceptionable, even if it were in keeping with the spirit of the passage. The only

parallels fully corresponding to it are Ps. li. 15—17; lxix. 30, 31.

3. Three of the sins to which the ten tribes were specially prone are here implied :—dependence upon the aid of the Assyrians;—application to Egypt for horses, in direct violation of the divine command, Deut. xvii. 16; (Comp. Is. xxxi. 1);—and idolatry. These they now for ever renounce, and avow their determination henceforth to trust in Jehovah alone; adding as the reason of such determination, the experience which they had had of the divine favour in time of need. אֲשֶׁר is here used in a causal sense, *because, for, forasmuch as.* Comp. Gen. xxxi. 49; Eccles. iv. 9. יָתוֹם, *orphan,* is applied in this place metaphorically to the unprotected and destitute circumstances in which the Israelites had been, while in a state of separation from the Lord.

4. מְשׁוּבָתָם is not, with Horsley, to be rendered *" their conversion,"* but *their apostasy.* See on chap. xi. 7. נְדָבָה, lit. *spontaneousness, willingness,* is used adverbially for *willingly, liberally, freely.* It is derived from נָדַב, Arab ندب, *instigavit, impulit* ad aliquid ; *agilis in conficienda re promptusque* vir ; *generosus ;* and is expressive of the free, unmerited, and abundant love of God towards repentant sinners. מִמֶּנּוּ, " from *him,*" i.e. Israel, the collective noun, ver. 2, resolved by the Syr., Lat., and other translators into a plural.

5, 6. The love of God to his people, and its effects in their happy experience, are here couched in similes borrowed from the vegetable kingdom. The dew is very copious in the East, and, by its refreshing and quickening virtue, supplies the place of more frequent rains in

He shall blossom as the lily,
And strike his roots like Lebanon.

6 His suckers shall spread forth,
And his beauty shall be as the olive tree,
And his fragrance as Lebanon.

7 They that dwell under his shade shall revive as the corn,
And shoot forth as the vine :
Their fame shall be as the wine of Lebanon.

8 Ephraim shall say,
What have I any more to do with idols?

other countries. Kimchi thinks that the constancy with which the dew falls is the point here more specially referred to, and to which the divine blessing is compared. שׁוֹשַׁנָּה, *lilies*, abound in Palestine, even apart from cultivation. There are two kinds : the common lily, which is perfectly white, consisting of six leaves, opening like bells ; and what the Syrians call ܫܘܫܢܬܐ, *the royal lily*, the stem of which is about the size of a finger in thickness, and which grows to the height of three and four feet, spreading its flowers in the most beautiful and engaging manner. Comp. Matt vi. 29. To these productions the moral beauty of regenerated Israel is very aptly compared. For *Lebanon*, see on Is. x. 34. The mountain stands here by metonymy for the trees which grow upon it, such as the celebrated cedars, whose roots striking far in depth and length into the ground, give them a firmness which no storms can shake. The ideas of strength and stability are those conveyed by the simile, whether we refer the roots to the trees, or, figuratively, to the mountain itself ; but the amplification in the following verse renders the former the preferable construction. הָלַךְ is often used, not merely of continued, but of increased action, and here denotes *to spread out*, as the suckers or small branches of trees. The olive is frequently referred to, on account of its beautiful green, and the pleasing ideas associated with its produce. Though the former only is expressed, yet the idea of fragrance is implied, only it is with the strictest propriety extended in the following clause to the whole of Lebanon, on account of the number of odoriferous trees and plants with which it abounds. In these verses, the rendering *frankincense*, which Newcome prefers to *Lebanon*, is not to be admitted. The stability, extension, glory, and loveliness of the church of God are forcibly set forth.

7. The Israelites are represented as again enjoying the protection of the Most High, and affording the most convincing proofs of prosperity. שׁוּב is used as auxiliary to חָיָה; both verbs, in such connexion, signifying nothing more than *revive, thrive again*, or the like. The pronominal affix in צִלּוֹ, *his shade*, refers to Jehovah ; but in זִכְרוֹ, *his celebrity, fame*, to Israel, understood as before, collectively, but best rendered in the plural. שֹׁבֵי בְצִלּוֹ, the construct with the preposition, as in חוֹסֵי בוֹ, Ps. ii. 12. Modern travellers concur in their high commendations of the excellence of the wines of Lebanon. Von Troil, in particular, says, " On this mountain are very valuable vineyards, in which the most excellent wine is produced ; such as I have never drunk in any country, though in the course of fourteen years I have travelled through many, and tasted many good wines."

8. Several interpreters take אֶפְרַיִם to be in the vocative case, but, as it seems harsh to refer the words immediately following to Jehovah, it is better to regard it as a nominative absolute, and to supply אָמַר, thus : As for Ephraim— the tribe distinguished above all the rest for its addictedness to idolatry, and the fit representative of the whole people— his language in future shall be, &c. For לִי, *to me*, the LXX. read לוֹ, *to him*,

I have answered him, and will regard him;
I am like a green cypress;
From me thy fruit is found.

9　　Who is wise, that he may understand these things?
Prudent, that he may know them?
For the ways of Jehovah are right;
The righteous, therefore, shall walk in them;
But the rebellious shall stumble in them.

which facilitates the construction, and is adopted by Ewald, but without sufficient authority. אֲנִי, *I*, is not without emphasis in this connexion, in which mention is made of idols. שׁוּר signifies to *view with regard and care, care for, watch over*. Every provision should henceforth be made for the protection and prosperity of restored Israel. בְּרוֹשׁ, *the cypress*, with all its tall and fair ever-green appearance, not being a fruit-bearing tree, it is added with singular effect, that in this respect there existed a difference between the object and the subject of the metaphor. The children of Israel should not only enjoy protection and refreshment as the result of the divine favour, but rich supplies of spiritual provision for their support. Such supplies were to be found in God alone. Manger thinks there is here a dialogistic parallelism, which he exhibits thus :—

EPHRAIM. What have I further to do with idols?
GOD. I have answered him, and will regard him.

EPHRAIM. I am like a green cypress.
GOD. From me is thy fruit found.

9. These words form an epilogue or conclusion to the whole book. The interrogation is employed for the purpose of excitement, and to give energy to the truths conveyed. It is worthy of remark that this is the only verse in which the prophet uses צַדִּקִים, *the righteous*, or any synonymous term, in the course of his recorded prophecies. So awfully depraved were the times in which he lived, that the very character had disappeared. The contrasted characters and states of the godly and the wicked are pointed and affecting. הָלַךְ, *to walk*, signifies here *to go forward prosperously;* כָּשַׁל, *to stumble*, so as to fall to one's injury and utter ruin.

"—— anfractu et libera ab omni
Hanc justus teret, hoc semper se in calle tenebit,
Felicique gradu ad requiem contendat amicam.
At defectores videas impingere in iisdem,
Exitiumque sibi factis properare scelestis."　　　　　*Rittershusius.*

J O E L

PREFACE

WE possess no further knowledge of Joel than what is furnished by the title of his book, or may be gathered from circumstances incidentally mentioned in it. That he lived in Judah, and, in all probability, at Jerusalem, we may infer from his not making the most distant reference to the kingdom of Israel; while, on the other hand, he speaks of Jerusalem, the temple, priests, ceremonies, &c. with a familiarity which proves them to have been before his eyes.

With respect to the age in which he flourished, opinions have differed. Bauer places him in the reign of Jehoshaphat; Credner, Winer, Krahmer, and Ewald, think he lived in that of Joash; Vitringa, Carpzov, Moldenhauer, Eichhorn, Holzhausen, Theiner, Rosenmüller, Knobel, Hengstenberg, Gesenius, and De Wette, in that of Uzziah; Steudel and Bertholdt in that of Hezekiah; Tarnovius and Eckermann assign the period of his activity to the days of Josiah; while the author of Sedar Olam, Jarchi, Drusius, Newcome, and Jahn, are of opinion that he prophesied in the reign of Manasseh. The most probable hypothesis is, that his predictions were delivered in the early days of Joash; that is, according to Credner, B.C. 870—865. No reference being made to the Babylonian, the Assyrian, or even the Syrian invasion, and the only enemies of whom mention is made being the Phœnicians, Philistines, Edomites, and Egyptians, it seems evident that Joel was unacquainted with any but the latter. Had he lived after the death of Joash, he could scarcely have omitted to notice the Syrians when speaking of hostile powers, since they not only invaded the land, but took Jerusalem, destroyed the princes, and carried away immense spoil to Damascus, 2 Chron. xxiv. 23, 24. The state of religious affairs as presented to view in the book is altogether in favour of this position. No mention is made of idolatrous practices; while, on the contrary, notwithstanding the guilt which attached to the Jews, on account of which Jehovah brought judgments upon the land, the principles of the theocracy are supposed to be maintained; the priests and people are re-presented as being harmoniously occupied with the services of religion; and Jerusalem, the temple and its worship, appear in a flourishing condition. Now this was precisely the state of things during the high-priesthood of Jehoiada, through whose influence Joash had been placed upon the throne. See 2 Kings xi. 17, 18; xii. 2—16; 2 Chron. xxiv. 4—14. It will follow that Joel is the oldest of all the Hebrew prophets whose predictions have come down to us.

The delivery of his prophecy was occasioned by the devastations produced by successive swarms of locusts, and by an excessive drought which pervaded the country, and threatened the inhabi-tants with utter destruction. This calamity, however, was merely symbolical of another, and a more dreadful scourge—the invasion of the land by foreign enemies, on which the prophet expatiates in the second chapter. In order that such calamity might be removed, he is commissioned to order an universal fast, and call all to repentance and humiliation before God; to announce as consequent upon such repentance and humiliation, a period of great temporal prosperity; to predict the effusion of the Holy Spirit at a future period of the history of his people; to denounce judgments against their enemies; and to foretel their restoration from the final dispersion.

In point of style Joel stands pre-eminent among the Hebrew prophets. He not only possesses a singular degree of purity, but is distinguished by his smoothness and fluency; the animated and rapid character of his rhythmus; the perfect regularity of his parallelisms; and the degree of roundness which he gives to his sentences. He has no abrupt transitions, is everywhere connected, and finishes whatever he takes up. In description he is graphic and perspicuous; in arrangement lucid; in imagery original, copious, and varied. In the judgment of Knobel, he most resembles Amos in regularity, Nahum in animation, and in both respects Habakkuk; but is surpassed by none of them. That what we now possess is all he ever wrote, is in the highest degree improbable: on the contrary, we should conclude from the cultivated character of his language, that he had been accustomed to composition long before he penned these discourses. Whatever degree of obscurity attaches to his book, is attributable to our ignorance of the subjects of which it treats, not to the language which he employs.

CHAPTER I

After summoning attention to the unexampled plague of locusts with which the country had been visited, 2—4, the prophet excites to repentance by a description of these insects, 5—7, and of the damage which they had done to the fields and trees, 8—12; calls the priests to institute a solemn season for fasting and prayer, 13, 14; and bewails, by anticipation, a more awful visitation from Jehovah, 15, while he further describes the tremendous effects of the calamity under which the country was suffering, 16—20.

---

1 The word of Jehovah which was communicated to Joel, the
    són of Pethuel:
2 Hear this, ye aged men!
    Yea, give ear, all ye inhabitants of the land!
    Did such as this happen in your days,
    Or in the days of your fathers?
3 Tell your children of it,
    And let your children tell their children,
    And their children another generation.

1. דְּבַר־יְהֹוָה הָיָה אֶל, the more usual introductory formula employed to express the communication of divine revelations to the prophets, or the divinely-inspired matter which they were commissioned to teach. Comp. Hos. i. 1; Mic. i. 1; Zeph. i. 1; Mal. i. 1. The name יוֹאֵל, Joel, Jerome interprets "ἀρχόμενος, id est, incipiens," referring it to the verb יָאַל, which signifies to *begin*; but, that he was not ignorant of another derivation is evident from his commentary, in which, after giving "*incipiens*," he adds, "vel, *est Deus*." It is, however, beyond all doubt compounded of יְהֹוָה, in one of its more contracted forms, and אֵל, and signifies, *Jehovah is God*. Who פְּתוּאֵל,

LXX. Βαθουήλ, *Pethuel*, the father of our prophet was, we are not informed. The introduction of his name was necessary in order to distinguish the present Joel from others of the same name, and cannot be admitted in proof of his having been a prophet or some person of eminence. It was common among the Hebrews, as it still is among the Orientals, to add the name of the father to that of the son.

2, 3. These verses contain an animated introduction to the following subject. זֹאת, properly *this*, the feminine according to the Hebrew idiom being used for the neuter, but it occurs here elliptically for כָּזֹאת, *like this*, *such*

4　That which the gnawing locust hath left,
　　The swarming locust hath devoured ;
　　And that which the swarming locust hath left,

the like, and refers to the astounding calamity of the locusts about to be described. שָׁמַע and הַאֲזִין frequently occur as parallel initiatives in Hebrew poetry. See Gen. iv. 23 ; Deut. xxxii. 1 ; Is. i. 2. For the latter verb, הַקְשִׁיב is sometimes used. See Is. xxviii. 23 ; Mic. i. 2. זְקֵנִים is here to be understood, not in the official sense of *elders*, but in that of *aged men*, as the connexion shows. Those who were most advanced in years, and might be expected to have their memories stored with ancient occurrences, are appealed to for a parallel to the case referred to. Comp. Deut. xxxii. 7 ; Job xxxii. 7. אָבוֹת is often used in the sense of *ancestors, forefathers*. ה in עֲלֵיהָ, like וֹאת, refers to the plague of locusts. בְּנֵי בָנִים, *children's children*, is not unfrequent, but the language here employed by Joel is cumulative beyond example.

　" Et nati natorum, et qui nascentur
　　　ab illis." 　　　　　　*Æneid* iii. 98.
　καὶ παῖδες παίδων, τοί κεν μετόπισθε
　　　γένωνται. 　　　　　　*Iliad* xx. 308.

4. The plague, which occasioned the following discourses of the prophet, is now described in terse, though repetitious terms. This verse may be considered as the text on which he afterwards expatiates. Interpreters have found great difficulty both in determining the precise signification of the several terms employed to describe the scourge, and the light in which it was designed to be understood. While some are of opinion that different kinds of insects are meant, most are agreed in considering locusts to be intended. Yet here again discordant views obtain : some insisting on different species of locusts, and others on different states of the same species. Credner, for instance, in a work on our prophet, full of erudition, considers גָּזָם to be the migratory locust; אַרְבֶּה the young brood; יֶלֶק the young locust in the last state of transformation; and חָסִיל the perfect locust. The locust belongs to the genus of insects known among entomologists by

the name of *grylli*, which includes the different species, from the common grasshopper to the devouring locust of the East. The largest of the latter is about three inches in length ; has two antennæ, or horns, about an inch long, and two wings, which, with their cases, are applied obliquely to the sides of the body when in repose. The feet have only three joints, but are six in number. The two hind ones are much larger than the rest, and are formed for leaping. The locusts are of different colours, brown, grey, and spotted. In all stages, from the larva to the perfect insect, the locusts are herbivorous, and do immense injury to vegetation. The subject, so far as it occurs in Scripture, may be said to have been almost exhausted by the learned Bochart, in his Hierozoicon, Pars Post. Lib. iv. cap. i.—viii. The fourth chapter he specially devotes to the explanation of the passages in Joel. See also Œdmann's Vermischte Sammlungen, and Credner's Joel. The first name, גָּזָם, occurs only here and Amos iv. 9, and is rendered by the LXX. κάμπη; and by the Vulg. *eruca, caterpillar*. This interpretation is supported by the Targ. זַחֲלָא, *the crawling insect*, by which, however, may be meant the locust in its wingless state. The Syr. renders the

word by ܩܡܨܐ, *locusta non alata*.

It is evidently derived from the same root with the Arab. جزم, *resecuit, amputavit,* جازم, *secans ;* Eth. ⶐሐⶈ : *excidit, abscidit ;* Syr. ܓܰܙ *incidit ;*

Talmud, גָּזַם, *amputavit ;* and expresses the gnawing or cutting action of the sharp teeth of the locusts on the leaves, and even the bark of trees. Comp. Plin. Nat. Hist. lib. xi. cap. 29 : omnia vero *morsu erodentes.*—אַרְבֶּה is the generic name of the locust, so called from the almost incredible numbers which breed in different parts of the East ; being

The licking locust hath devoured ;
And that which the licking locust hath left,
The consuming locust hath devoured.

derived from רָבָה, *to multiply, be numerous*, &c. Comp. Jer. xlvi. 23, רַבּוּ מֵאַרְבֶּה, *more numerous than the locusts*. From its migrating in swarms it is called by Forskål *gryllus gregarius*, and by Linnæus, *gryllus migratorius*. By the LXX. the word is rendered seventeen times by ἀκρὶς, *the common locust ;* thrice by βροῦχος, *the unwinged locust*, which browses on the grass ; once by ἐρυσιβη, *mildew ;* and once by ἀττέλαβος, *the young* or *small locust*. That אַרְבֶּה is generic, appears from Lev. xi. 22, where we read, הָאַרְבֶּה לְמִינוֹ, *the locust according to its species*.—The third name, יֶלֶק, from יָלַק, equivalent to לָקַק, *to lick*, designates the locust as *licking off* the leaves, and whatever is green on the trees, grass, &c. This derivation is preferable to that proposed by Michaelis, who refers the word to the Arab. ولق, *properavit, volubilis fuit*, or to يلق, *albus fuit*, and thinks that the chafer is meant. In Nah. iii. 16, it is represented as *winged*, and in Jer. li. 27, it is described as סָמָר, *rough, bristly, terrific*. LXX. βροῦχος four times ; ἀκρὶς thrice.—חָסִיל, the remaining term, comes from חָסַל, *to consume, devour*. LXX. βροῦχος, or βροῦκος. Vulg. *rubigo*, mildew. Syr. ܙܕܘܕܐ, which

Risius, the Archbishop of Damascus, describes as resembling the locust, only differing from it, inasmuch as it never migrates, and confines its ravages to the fruits and herbs, but leaves the trees untouched. It is also noted for the noise which it makes at night. A comparison of the different passages in which these names occur, renders it more than probable that they are here employed by the prophet, not with any reference to the species into which the locusts may be scientifically divided, but to designate four successive swarms, according to certain destructive qualities, by which, as a genus of insects, they are distinguished, and thereby to heighten the

terror which his description was intended to produce. Just as Job accumulates the terms אַרְיֵה, שַׁחַל, כְּפִירִים, לַיִשׁ and לָבִיא, chap. iv. 10, 11, with a similar view. They are rather poetical synonymes, than distinctive of different species. At all events, that locusts are meant, may be inferred from the facts, that wherever יֶלֶק occurs, with the exception of a single passage, it occurs along with אַרְבֶּה ; and that אַרְבֶּה, which Moses uses in describing one of the plagues of Egypt, Exod. x. 12—20, is not only employed by the Psalmist, lxxviii. 46, cv. 34, but also חָסִיל and יֶלֶק, as synonymous terms, for the sake of variety. Add to which that the verb חָסַל, from which חָסִיל is derived, is employed to express the action of the אַרְבֶּה, Deut. xxviii. 38 : יַחְסְלֶנּוּ הָאַרְבֶּה, "the locust shall consume it." In the translation I have given the meaning of the several names in terms expressive of the qualities suggested by each. The passage might otherwise be rendered with Noyes :

"That which one swarm of locusts left,
    a second swarm hath eaten ;
And that which the second left, a third
    swarm hath eaten ;
And that which the third left, a fourth
    swarm hath eaten."

It is a question of greater importance: Are the statements of Joel in the first and second chapters to be understood literally of these insects, or figuratively of enemies that were to invade and lay waste the Holy Land ? The latter is the more ancient opinion. It is that of the Targum, the Jews whom Jerome consulted, and Abarbanel ; and is, with various modifications, adopted by the following christian interpreters : Jerome, Ephraim Syrus, Theodoret, Cyril of Alexandria, Hugo de St. Victor, Ribera, Sanchez, a Lapide, Luther, Grotius, Marckius, Bertholdt, Theiner, Steudel, and Hengstenberg. On the other hand, Abenezra, Jarchi, Kimchi, Lyranus, Vatablus, Joh. Schmidius, Jahn, Eichhorn, Rosenmüller, von

5   Awake, ye drunkards! and weep ;
       Yea, howl, all ye drinkers of wine !
       On account of the sweet wine,
       For it is made to cease from your mouth.
6 For a nation hath come up upon my land,
       Mighty and innumerable ;
       Their teeth are the teeth of a lion ;
       Yea, they have the grinders of a lioness.

Coelln, Justi, Credner, and Hitzig, maintain that the language is to be understood literally of locusts. This interpretation has certainly much in its favour, and if it could without violence be applied throughout, might fairly be adopted. But the announcement of a second and more awful judgment, chap. i. 15 ; ii. 1, 2 ; the distinct recognition of a foreign rule, ii. 17 ; and the assignment of the *North* as the native country of the enemy, ii. 20 ; present insuperable obstacles to its adoption. See on these verses. There seems no possibility of effecting a consistent interpretation on any other principle than that laid down and defended by Cramer, Eckermann, and Holzhausen, *viz.* that in the first chapter, Joel describes a devastation of the country which had been effected by natural locusts ; but predicts in the second, its devastation by political enemies, in highly-wrought metaphorical language, borrowed from the scene which he had just depicted.

5. הָקִיצוּ, the Hiph. of קוּץ, is here used, like the cognate root יָקַץ, Gen. ix. 24, in the sense of awaking from a sleep occasioned by wine. Since, however, the persons addressed had been deprived of the means of intoxication, the prophet is rather to be understood as borrowing the term from the state in which they had too often been found. שִׁכּוֹרִים being parallel with שֹׁתֵי יָיִן, *drinkers of wine,* does not here mean persons actually *intoxicated,* but such as were in the habit of using intoxicating liquors; and by implication, to excess. Thus Kimchi: אתם הרגילים להשתכר ביין, *ye who are accustomed to make yourselves drunk with wine.* It is derived from שָׁכַר, *to drink to the full.* Arab. سكر, *implevit* vas, *ebrius fuit.* Hence שֵׁכָר, *strong,* or *intoxicating drink,*

whether wine itself, or, more commonly, liquor resembling wine, which is distilled from barley, honey, or dates, and sometimes mingled with spices. By עָסִיס, is meant the *fresh wine,* or juice of the grape, or other fruit, which has just been *pressed out,* and is remarkable for its sweet flavour, and its freedom from intoxicating qualities. R. עָסַס, *to tread, tread down,* or *out.* Targ. חֲמַר מְרַת, *pure wine.* It differs from תִּירוֹשׁ, inasmuch as the latter term is confined to the juice of the grape ; and being derived from יָרַשׁ, *to take possession of,* indicates that however new, it had already obtained an inebriating quality. The locusts are here represented as specially attacking and destroying the vines and other fruit-trees, from the produce of which these wines were prepared. To such they are known to be very destructive. Comp. Theocrit. Idyll. 5, 108, in which a shepherd beseeches them not to injure his vines :

'Ακρίδες, αἳ τὸν φραγμὸν ὑπερπαδῆτε τὸν
         ἀμόν,
Μή μευ λωβάσησθε τὰς ἀμπέλος· ἐντὶ
         γὰρ ἅβαι.

כָּרַת properly signifies to *cut, cut off,* but here, as wine is the subject spoken of, it must be taken in the sense of *destroying,* or *causing to cease.*

6. גּוֹי, *nation,* especially used of foreign, barbarous, and profane nations, and here selected on purpose to express the number and hostility of the locusts, and at the same time to prepare the minds of the Jews for the allegorical use made of these insects in chap. ii. If it had not been for some such end, the prophet might have adopted the term עַם, *people,* which Solomon applies to the ants, Prov. xxx. 25, 26, and which would equally have conveyed the idea of multitude. Comp. chap. ii. 2. This metaphorical

7 They have laid waste my vine,
 And broken down my fig-tree:
 They have completely stripped it, and thrown it dówn;
 Its branches they have left white.

use of the term is common in the classics.
See instances in Bochart and Gesen.
Heb. Lex. *in voc.* גוי. The Arabs employ أَكَل in a similar way. עָלָה עַל is
used in a hostile sense of an army,
Is. vii. 1; but here figuratively of the
locusts. In אַרְצִי, "*my* land," the pronominal affix belongs to Jehovah, not to the
prophet. Comp. Is. xiv. 25; Jer. xvi. 18;
Ezek. xxxvi. 5; xxxviii. 16; Joel ii. 18.
See on Hos. ix. 3. עָצוּם, *strong, powerful.* The strength of the locust consists
in the immense numbers, which, forming
themselves into compact bodies, darken
the air, and advance forward, one swarm
after another, attacking whatever comes
in their way. They may well be described as וְאֵין מִסְפָּר, *innumerable.* All
who refer to them, both in ancient and
modern times, speak of them in the
same language.

'Ακρίδων πλῆθος ἀμύθητον.
                              Agatharc. v. 27.

" Immensæ locustarum multitudines."
Orosius, v. 11. Shaw speaks of " infinite swarms following each other."
Barrow states that those which he saw
in South Africa, might literally be said
to cover the ground for an area of 2000
square miles. A later writer in the Cape
Town Gazette, describes a cloud of them
as passing before him in a train of many
millions thick, and about an hour in
length; and mentions further that, though
millions perished in consequence of attempts made to destroy them, their number appeared nothing decreased. And Dr.
Bowring states in his Report, that some
years ago the army of Ibrahim Pasha,
in the attempt to extirpate an immense
swarm, gathered up no less than 65,000
ardebs, equal to 325,000 bushels of English measure! How appropriate the
name אַרְבֶּה! What is innumerable is frequently compared to them by the sacred
writers. See Jud. vi. 5; vii. 12; Ps. cv.
34; Jer. xlvi. 23; Nah. iii. 15. מְתַלְּעוֹת,
teeth, Gesenius considers as standing by

transposition for מַלְתָּעוֹת, and derives the
noun from an obsolete root לָתַע, *to bite;*
but it may more properly be referred to
the Arab. لَثَّ, *longum fuit,* and denotes
the grinders or jaw-teeth of animals.
The metaphor, however, has no respect
to the size of the teeth of lions, but only
to the terrible and complete destruction
which they effect. Pliny, speaking of
the locust, says: "Omnia morsu erodentes
et fores quoque tectorum." According to
Fabricius, in his Genera Insectorum,
p. 96, the teeth of the locust are three-
forked and sharp. The same metaphor
is used Rev. ix. 8, ὀδόντες αὐτῶν ὡς
λεόντων ἦσαν.

7. For the pronominal reference in גַּפְנִי
and תְּאֵנָתִי, see on אַרְצִי in the preceding
verse. The vines and fig-trees might
be called Jehovah's, because, in a special
sense, the land on which they grew was
his. The *vine* has, from time immemorial, abounded in Palestine. It often
grows to a great size, and produces
grapes of corresponding bulk. Schulz
describes one at Beitshin, near Ptolemais,
the stem of which was about a foot and
a half in diameter, its height was about
thirty feet, and by its branches and
branchlets, which had to be supported,
it formed a hut upwards of thirty feet
broad and long. The clusters of these
vines are so large, that they weigh ten
or twelve pounds, and the berries may
be compared with our small plums.
When such a cluster is cut off, it is laid
upon a board about an ell and a half
broad, and three or four ells long, and
several persons seat themselves about it
to eat the grapes. Rosenmüller, in Bib.
Cab. vol. xxvii. p. 223. Comp. Numb.
xiii. 23, 24. Palestine was equally celebrated for its *fig-trees,* which are not
reared in gardens, as with us, but grow
spontaneously in the open country. The
figs were not only eaten fresh, but also
preserved for food. שׂוּם, *to put,* is often
used with nouns instead of the simple
forms of the verbs to which the nouns

8   Lament, as a virgin girded with sackcloth,
     On account of the husband of her youth.
9   The offering and the libation,
     Are cut off from the house of Jehovah :
     The priests howl, the ministers of Jehovah.

are related. קְצָפָה, *breakage,* Arab. قصف
fregit. قصيف, *a branch broken off* from
a tree. See on Hos. x. 7. LXX.
συγκλασμός, *Compl.* κλασμός. Syr.
ܩܘܨܐ, *concissio, divulsio.* The locusts
not only consume the fruit and leaves of
trees, but strip them of the very bark.
—"Nec culmus, nec gramen ullum re-
maneat, et arbores frondibus et cortice
tanquam vestibus nudatæ, instar trun-
corum alborum conspiciantur." Ludolf,
Comment. p. 178. הִשְׁלִיךְ is here taken
in its proper causative signification.
What they do not devour, they so injure
that it falls off the tree. שָׂרִיגִם, *branches,*
properly the *intertwining tendrils* of the
vine, from שָׂרַג, *to interweave.* The vine,
being the more valu'able of the two kinds
of trees, the suffix refers back to it ; and
the fig-tree is treated as subordinate.
הֶלְבִּינוּ, *they have made* or *left white.*

8. The land, under the metaphor of a
female, is here addressed. · אֱלִי is the
second person feminine of the Imperative in Kal of אָלָה, which usually means
to swear, call on God as witness ; but
here it takes the signification of the
Syriac ܐܠܝ, *ululavit, deploravit.* ܐܠܝ,
ܐܠܝܐ, *ululatus, lamentum.* The derivation from אֵל, *God,* in the sense *God have
mercy,* is less natural. One of Kennicott's MSS. reads אֲבְלִי. LXX. θρηνήσον.
A country is frequently said to mourn,
when it is subject to devastation. See
Is. xxiv. 4; Jer. iv. 28 ; xii. 4 ; Hos. iv. 3.
בְּתוּלָה, *a virgin,* a young woman, affianced
to a husband, and, in this sense, viewed
as married to him. The idea of the
strength of youthful affection, is that designed to be conveyed by the passage.
In proportion to the force of such affection, would be the excessive degree of

grief for his loss. Holzhausen thinks
that she would also grieve עַל־בְּתוּלֶיהָ, *on
account of her virginity,* and compares
Jud. xi. 38 ; but this the text does not
suggest. LXX. νύμφη. Compl. παρ-
θένος. Wrapping oneself in sackcloth was
a token of deep mourning. בַּעַל, properly
lord, master, possessor ; and secondarily
husband, because in the East, wives were,
and still are, considered as the property
rather than the companions of their husbands. Comp. the Greek κύριος γυναι-
κός ; and for the application of ἀνήρ to
one only betrothed, Matt. i. 19. According to the Roman law, *consensus
facit nuptias.*

9. To a pious mind the gloomiest
view of external calamities will be taken
from their influence upon the cause of
God. The cessation of the usual solemnities of the temple-worship, occasioned
by the destruction of the fruits of the
earth, must have occasioned great grief
to the religious Jew. Jerome and others
think that as the priests would be deprived of their regular support, by the
cessation of the offerings, they mourned
on that account ; but of this I should say
with Maurer, "Vates hic non videtur cogitasse." מִנְחָה, stands here for *offerings* in
general, whether bloody or unbloody,—
comp. Gen. iv. 4 ; LXX. θυσία,—even
when restricted in its signification to
meat-offering, such as consisted of meal,
salt, oil, and incense, the proper sacrifices. נְבָחִים, are understood, as they
were always connected with them, except
in the case of the sin and trespass-offer-
ings. The libation, or drink-offering,
was called נֶסֶךְ, on account of its being
poured out, from the root נָסַךְ, *to pour.*
From the circumstance that Joel pre-
fixes the article to כֹּהֲנִים, *priests,* but not
to אִכָּרִים, *husbandmen,* and כֹּרְמִים, *vine-
dressers,* (ver. 11,) Credner argues that he
must either have been personally related
to them, or that prophets and priests
must have been more closely united at the
time he wrote than afterwards. Comp.

10 The field is laid waste,
    The ground mourneth;
    For the corn is laid waste,
    The new wine is dried up,
    The oil languisheth.

11   Be ashamed, ye husbandmen!
    Howl, ye vine-dressers!
    On account of the wheat and the barley;
    For the harvest of the field hath perished.

12 The vine is dried up,
    And the fig-tree languisheth;
    The pomegranate, the palm-tree also, and the apple-tree,
    All the trees of the field are withered;
    Yea, joy is withered away from the children of men.

הַכֹּהֲנִים, ver. 13; ii. 17. מְשָׁרְתִים, *ministers*, is a more dignified official term than עֲבָדִים, *servants*, which is employed to denote common slaves, as well as persons in more elevated situations about a king.

10—12. The prophet enters here more minutely into a description of the devastation occasioned by the locusts. תִּירוֹשׁ, *new wine*, which is already in a state of fermentation, and so intoxicating; from יָרַשׁ, *to take possession* of any thing. See on ver. 5, where it is distinguished from עָסִיס. " Syr. محزأܐ,

sic dictum, quod *se possesserem* hominis *facit*, ejus cerebrum *occupando*, ut ille non amplius sui compos sit. Sic. Arab. *vinum* dicitur سبيّة, a *captivando*, et

عقار, a *tenendo* et *vinctum habendo*."

Winer *in voc.* שָׂדֶה, *field*, and אֲדָמָה, *ground*, are synonymes; but differ in this respect, that the former denotes the open, free, uninclosed part of a country, Arab. سلا, *extendit, dilatavit;* the latter, the rich red soil which is particularly fit for cultivation. Hence אִישׁ הַשָּׂדֶה, *a man of the field*, means a hunter, Gen. xxv. 27; אִישׁ הָאֲדָמָה, *a man of the ground*, an agriculturist. Root אָדַם, *to be red*. The land is here, as frequently in the Hebrew prophets, made the subject of personi-

fication. Some would render הוֹבִישׁ, as applied to the new wine, *to be ashamed :* but occurring as it does in parallelism with אָמַל, *to droop, languish* like plants, it is better to retain the primary notion of יָבֵשׁ, *to become dry, dry up.* Both יָבֵשׁ and יָצְהָר stand for the *vine* and the *olive tree*, from which the wine and oil are obtained. In the second instance הוֹבִישׁ takes the signification of בּוֹשׁ, *to be ashamed*, being another form of the Hiphil for הֵבִישׁ. Both are used intransitively. The LXX. retaining the signification of יָבֵשׁ, improperly render ἐξηράνθησαν γεωργοί.—רִמּוֹן, *the pomegranate tree*, is indigenous in Palestine and Syria, and is reckoned one of its noblest botanical productions. It grows to the height of twenty feet, has a straight stem, spreading branches, lancet-formed leaves, with large and beautiful red blossoms. The fruit is of the size of an orange, brown in colour, and affording a highly delicious and cooling juice. It is also planted in gardens, and in the courts of the houses; and its fruit is greatly improved by cultivation. It is still one of the trees most frequently seen in those countries. So celebrated were the dates of Palestine, that Pliny, speaking of the תָּמָר, *date*, or *palm-tree*, says, "Judæa vero inclyta est vel magis palmis." It was adopted as a symbol of the country in coins struck under Vespasian and Domitian; and is frequently referred to in the Old Testament.

13   Gird ye, and mourn, O ye priests !
      Howl, ye ministers of the altar !
      Enter, spend the night in sackcloth,
      Ye ministers of my God !
      For the offering and the libation
      Are withholden from the house of your God.
14 Appoint a sacred fast, proclaim a day of restraint ;

It sometimes reaches the height of an hundred feet, is remarkable for its straight upright growth, and forms one of the most beautiful trees in the vegetable kingdom. The fruit, which grows in clusters under the large leaves, is of an exceedingly sweet and agreeable taste, and, as an article both of sustenance and traffic, is of great value to the inhabitants. In Abyssinia, the natives extract a juice from it which théy manufacture into a spirituous liquor resembling champagne. Its importance is here significantly expressed by the particle בַּם being used intensively before it. תַּפּוּחַ, Arab. تفّاح, the *apple-tree*.

Rosenmüller derives the word from נָפַח, *to breathe*, and in this Gesenius concurs, supposing the fragrant *breath*, i. e. *smell* or *scent*, to have originated the name. The former of these writers adopts the opinion of Celsius, that the quince tree is specially intended ; but as the Arabs include under تفّاح, oranges, lemons, peaches, apricots, &c. the Hebrew term is likewise in all probability generic in its signification. To give to his description the utmost latitude, Joel adds, כָּל־עֲצֵי הַשָּׂדֶה, *all the trees of the field*, i. e. as Jerome explains, "omnia ligna, vel infructuosa, vel fructifera;" and, to bring it more home to the feelings of his countrymen, he represents the consequence to be the entire removal of their joy. Some improperly limit שָׂשׂוֹן to the joy of harvest. The construction הוֹבִישׁ מִן, *to dry away from*, is what is usually termed pregnant, and more forcibly expresses the removal of the object on which the verb terminates.

13. The prophet now addresses himself to the priests, and calls them first to personal mourning, and then, in the

following verse, to institute a sacred fast, in order that such mourning might be general. After חִגְרוּ supply with the Syr. שָׂק, as in one of Kennicott's MSS., or שַׂקִּים, as in one of De Rossi's. Both forms occur in connexion with the verb, which is not here to be restricted to *mere* girding, but rather signifies to *wrap round* one. Comp. Jer. iv. 8 ; Is. xxii. 12. סָפַד, primarily *to smite*, *strike*, then *to strike the breast*, in token of mourning. See on Is. xxxii. 12. The LXX. always render it by κόπτεσθαι, except in two instances, in which they give it by κλαίειν, *to weep*. For מְשָׁרְתֵי מִזְבֵּחַ, comp. οἱ τῷ θυσιαστηρίῳ παρεδρεύοντες, 1 Cor. ix. 13. Some think that בֹּא, *come*, is to be taken idiomatically as a particle of exhortation, like לְכוּ before another verb, and appeal to chap. iv. 13, (Eng. version, iii. 13,) for another instance in our prophet. As, however, the verb is, to say the least, not necessarily to be so understood in that passage, and as mention is made of the altar immediately before, it appears more proper to take it in the sense of *entering*, i. e. into the court of the temple, where, in the more immediate presence of Jehovah, the priests were to bewail their sins, and those of the people. Thus the LXX. εἰσέλθετε, and Kimchi, באו בית י״י ושם ספדו, *enter ye the house of God, and there mourn*. לִין or לוּן, signifies *to spend* or *remain over the night*, and retains this signification in the present passage, though, from the connexion, it is obvious not one night only, but many nights are meant. The priests were not only to wear the habit of mourning during the day, they were also to remain in it all night. Ahab is said to have lain in sackcloth, when he humbled himself before God, 1 Kings xxi. 27. LXX. ὑπνώσατε.

14. קַדֵּשׁ, *to hallow, consecrate ; to*

Assemble the elders—all ye inhabitants of the land,
To the house of Jehovah your God,
And cry unto Jehovah.
15   Alas for the day!
For the day of Jehovah is near,
And cometh as a mighty destruction
From the Almighty.
16 Is not the food cut off before our eyes?
Are not joy and gladness from the house of our God?
17 The seeds are become dry beneath their clods;
The granaries are desolate, the store-houses are destroyed,
Because the corn is withered.

---

keep holy; to appoint sacred or religious services; here, to institute a sacred fast, by fixing the time and circumstances, and preparing the people for its proper observance. The Pual participle is used even of warriors; see on Is. xiii. 3. The interpretations of the Rabbins, Jarchi and Kimchi, הוּמִינוּ, and Abenezra, הָכִינוּ, are defective, by leaving out the idea of sacredness, which the verb always conveys. עֲצָרָה, restraint, or being held back or prevented from labour: יוֹם, day, or period, understood. See on Is. i. 13. The Jews were to abstain from their worldly avocations, and spend the portion of their time thus consecrated to the immediate and solemn duties of humiliation, confession, and prayer. זְקֵנִים, elders, in this connexion, might be taken in an official sense, denoting those holding office among the people, who were expected to take the lead, and, by their example, to excite others to engage in the religious solemnities; but a comparison of this verse with chap. ii. 15, 16, in which "children" and "sucklings" are mentioned, would rather require us to understand the term as referring to age. The central point of convocation was the temple—the special theocratic residence of Him whose wrath was to be deprecated and his mercy implored. זָעַק, Arab. زعق, to cry out, cry earnestly for help. LXX. κεκράξετε ἐκτενῶς. "Ardentissimas fundite preces." Rosenmüller.

15. Joel now exclaims, אֲהָהּ לַיּוֹם, alas!

for the day! "O infaustum et tristissimum illum diem!" Rosenmüller. To give intensity to the exclamation, the LXX. have the triple οἴμοι, οἴμοι, οἴμοι. That the יוֹם יְהֹוָה, day of Jehovah, i. e. the period of punishment, does not mean that of the plague of the locusts, but a more awful period still future, the term קָרוֹב, near, at hand, which is never used to denote the actual presence of any thing, but its speedy approach, sufficiently proves. What the Jews were then suffering was only a prelude to still more dreadful calamities. For כְּשֹׁד מִשַּׁדַּי, which forms an elegant paronomasia, see on Is. xiii. 6, where the same form occurs. The כְּ is, as there, the Caph veritatis, and expresses the greatness of the evil.

16. The verb כָּרַת is understood in the latter hemistich. The annual festivals were occasions of great rejoicing. See Lev. xxiii. 40; Deut. xii. 12, 18.

17. This, and the three following verses, describe the drought which was simultaneous with the judgment of the locusts. It exhibits the singular phenomenon of four ἅπαξ λεγόμενα within the short space which it occupies. For the elucidation of עָבַשׁ, some compare the Chaldee בְּאֵשׁ, to rot, but it is with more propriety referred to the Arab. عبس, siccus fuit; and so is of the same signification with יָבֵשׁ, to be dry, dried up. Thus Abulwalid. By the desiccating influence of the heat, the seeds that had been sown in the ground

18   How the cattle mourn!
     How the herds of oxen are perplexed!
     Because they have no pasture;
     Yea, the flocks of sheep are destroyed.
19   To thee, O Jehovah! I cry,
     For fire hath consumed the pastures of the desert,
     And a flame hath burned all the trees of the field.

would lose all their moisture, and perish. That פְּרֻדוֹת mean *seeds* or *grains* of corn, &c. seems satisfactorily determined by the use of the Syr. ܓܪܰܢܽܘܡ, *granum,* Matt. xiii. 31; John xii. 24; 1 Cor. xv. 37, in the Peshito; and the signification of פָּרַד, *to separate,* an action which takes place when, in sowing, the husbandman scatters the seed in distinct grains. To the same effect Tanchum,

الحبوب المعدودة للزراعة لانها تفرق في الارض, *grains prepared for sowing,* so called because they are scattered in the ground.— מְגֻרָפוֹת, *clods,* or lumps of earth. Comp. the Arab. جرف, *gleba terræ;* ارض جرفة, *terra diversa varia.* Thus also مجروف, signifies a mark on the body, occasioned by the contracting or drying up of the skin, and resembling a round lump of earth or dung. מַמְּגֻרוֹת is synonymous with אֹצָרוֹת, *granaries;* and, according to the force of the local מ prefixed, signifies *places* or *houses containing store-rooms,* or granaries, in which grain was deposited. The Dagesh in the second מ is euphonic. The simpler form מְגוּרָה, occurs Hag. ii. 19; and both are to be referred to the root גּוּר, *to gather, collect.* For the diversified and unsatisfactory renderings of the ancient versions, see Pococke *in loc.* The verbs שָׁמֵם and חָרַס are here to be taken in the sense of being left or neglected like places that have been laid waste or destroyed.

18. נָדַף, in Niphal, expresses the *per-*

plexity to which any one is reduced who does not know how to extricate himself from difficulty. The brute creation are graphically represented as being in this condition from the total failure of pasturage. The גַם before עֶדְרֵי־הַצֹּאן is intensive; *even* the sheep, which subsist on herbage unsuitable for the oxen, are deprived of food. As the idea of *punishment* is conveyed by the verb אָשֵׁם, it was in all probability used by the prophet, in order to teach the Jews that innocent creatures are involved in the consequences of guilt incurred by transgressors. Comp. Exod. xii. 29; Jonah iii. 7.

19. It is not unusual for the Hebrew prophets to give expression to their own feelings, while describing the judgments that were brought upon their country. Comp. Is. xv. 5; xvi. 11; xxii. 4; Jer. xxiii. 9. It has been questioned whether the "fire" and "flame" are here to be taken literally of the actual burning of the grass, which often happens in extreme heat, or whether they are used figuratively of the heat itself. The former is more probably the meaning. נְאוֹת, Kimchi explains, מקומות הדשאים, *grassy places,* places of pasturage; hence pasturage itself. It is derived from נָוָה, *to be pleasant,* (comp. נָאָה,) *to dwell:* but signifying in this connexion the green, grassy spots, so eagerly desired by the cattle, and pleasant both to man and beast. From the circumstance that such places would naturally be selected for occupancy by tents, dwellings, &c. the word came also to signify *habitations.* Comp. the Arab. اوي, *diversatus fuit, hospitio excepit:* ماوي, *mansio, sedes commorationis.*

20 The very beasts of the field look up to thee,
      Because the streams of water are dried up,
      And fire hath devoured the pastures of the desert.

20. עָרַג, Arab. عرج, Eth. ዐርገ :
ascendit : to look up with panting or earnest desire. Arab. اِنْجِعَ, *inclinatio, propensio in rem.* The word beautifully expresses the natural action of animals parched with thirst, and deprived of all supply of water. They hold up their heads, as if their only expectation were from the God of heaven. LXX. ἀνέβλεψαν. Comp. Ps. xlii. 2, where the force of עַל־אֲפִיקֵי־מַיִם is lost by the rendering of our common version, "*after* the water-brooks." It should be *at* or *beside*, as the Psalmist evidently intended to represent the deer standing on the brink of the channels in which water usually flowed, but which had become dry. To their pitiable condition he compares his own circumstances when deprived of the usual means of spiritual refreshment. The idea of their crying to God, which the Syr. ܐ݂ܶ, and the Rabbins attach to the word, is derived from such passages as Job. xxxviii. 41, Ps. civ. 21, cxlvii. 9, rather than from anything expressed by the word itself.

———◆———

CHAPTER II

The prophet reiterates his announcement of the approach of a divine judgment more terrific in its nature than that of the locusts, but employs language borrowed from the appearance and movements of these insects, in order to make a deeper impression upon his hearers, whose minds were full of ideas derived from them as instruments of the calamity under which they were suffering, 1—11. He then summons anew to humiliation and repentance, 12—17; giving assurance that on these taking place, Jehovah would show them pity, destroy their enemy, and restore them to circumstances of great temporal and religious prosperity, 18—27; and the chapter concludes with a glorious promise of the abundant effusion of the influences of the Holy Spirit in the apostolic age, 28, 29, and a prediction of the Jewish war, and the final subversion of the Jewish state, 30, 31, in the midst of which such as embraced the worship and service of the Messiah should experience deliverance, 32.

———————

1   BLOW ye the trumpet in Zion!
      And sound the alarm in my holy mountain!

1. To give the greater effect to the alarm here commanded to be sounded, Jehovah himself is introduced as speaking. The persons addressed are the priests, on whom it devolved to blow with trumpets. ἡ σάλπιγξ ὄργανον

Let all the inhabitants of the land tremble;
For the day of Jehovah cometh; it is near.
2 A day of darkness and gloom,
   A day of clouds and dense obscurity;
   Like the dawn spread over the mountains,
   A numerous and mighty people:
   None such have ever been,
   Neither shall there ever be after them,
   During the years of successive generations.

ἔστι πολέμου.   Philo. de Septenario.
They were to warn all of the threatened
judgment. Comp. chap. i. 15, where
the prophet anticipates what is now
about to be the subject of special description.

2. Synonymes are here accumulated
to give intensity to the expression of the
thought.   The awful calamity which
was to come upon the Jews is set forth
under the metaphor of darkness, which
is of frequent occurrence in the Hebrew
Scriptures, when sufferings and misery
are the subjects of discourse. Comp.
Is. viii. 22; lx. 2; Jer. xiii. 16; Amos
v. 18; Zeph. i. 15. In the present
instance, however, there was a singular
propriety in adopting the language, since
the prophet was just going to introduce
an allegory founded upon the fact, that
swarms of locusts had come over the
land, and intercepting, by their density,
the light of the sun, had occasioned an
universal darkness. See on ver. 10.
Some interpreters have stumbled at the
apparent incongruity of comparing the
coming affliction with the שַׁחַר, aurora,
since the idea usually suggested by the
figurative use of that term is joy, or
prosperity; but as this idea is not exclusively conveyed by the use of it, as
it is also employed to express the certainty, Hos. vi. 3, and suddenness of
anything, Hos. x. 15, so here the obvious points of comparison are merely
the suddenness and extent of the change
produced by the diffusion of the rays
of light, without any reference to the
nature of the change itself.

Joel now proceeds to introduce and
describe the hostile army of the Assyrians in the same terms in which he had
metaphorically described the locusts,

chap. i. 6; only exchanging גּוֹי, nation,
for עַם, people, which is also used of
foreign and idolatrous nations, Numb.
xxi. 29; 1 Chron. xvi. 20; Jer. xlviii. 42.
In this description, he not only transfers
the metaphor back to the proper subject
from which it was taken, but converts it
into an allegory, and at considerable
length, and in the most minute manner,
exhibits the invasion, the formidable
character, and the ravages of the bar-
barian foe. So perfectly is the allegorical
veil woven throughout, that most commentators have been able to discover
nothing more than natural locusts in the
passage.   At the time in which the
prophet delivered his message, the locusts
covered the land; they were before his
eyes; the idea of them had so taken
possession of his mind, that, considering
the striking resemblance which they
bore to an invading army, nothing was
more natural than to exhibit the latter
in sensible images taken from the scene
by which both he and his hearers were
surrounded.   And, accustomed as they
had been to the parabolic style of prophecy, they could have been at no loss
to discover, that when in this part of
his discourse he appeared to speak of
locusts, it was not natural but political
locusts he had in view. While the decidedly future aspect of the calamity,
chap. i. 15, ii. 1, proves that it had not
taken place at the time the words were
delivered, a comparison of the language
in the concluding part of verse 2, with
that employed chap. i. 2, equally proves
that a plague of locusts could not have
been intended. We must, therefore,
with the alteration of a single word,
adopt the language of Jerome, "dum
locustas legimus, Assyrios cogitemus."

3 Before them fire devoureth,
   And behind them a flame burneth;
   Before them the land is like the garden of Eden,
   But behind them a desolate wilderness :
   And there is no escape from them.
4   Their appearance is like the appearance of horses,
   And they run like horsemen.
5 They bound like the rattle of chariots on the tops of the mountains;

That the Assyrian invasion under Sennacherib, and not that of the Chaldæans
under Nebuchadnezzar, is meant, appears from the immense number of the
army, its entire destruction in the land
of Palestine, and there being no reference whatever to the captivity in
Babylon, the omission of which is un-
imaginable, on the supposition that the
latter of the two invasions was intended.
The army of Sennacherib must have
been the largest that ever entered Palestine, since only that division of it
which invested Jerusalem, amounted to
nearly 200,000 men, Is. xxxvii. 36. It
was marching forward to the conquest
of Egypt, and, like a swarm of locusts,
covered the whole land. All the fortified
cities of Judah were taken, Is. xxxvi. 1;
the cultivated fields and vineyards were
trodden down or consumed, xxxvii. 30;
and nothing short of utter destruction
seemed to await the inhabitants. The
design of the Divine Spirit, to whose
infinite mind the future event was
present, in dictating the prediction in
the language here employed, appears to
have been, to deepen the impressions
produced by the plague of locusts, and
thereby to excite to that repentance and
amendment of life, which alone could
secure to the Jews the continuance of
their national blessings.
3. A description of the desolate state
to which Judæa was to be reduced, in
language borrowed from that given of
the drought, chap. i. 19. לְפָנָיו, before
him, and אַחֲרָיו, behind him, are used to
express universality; ubicunque. Comp.
1 Chron. xix. 10. This construction is
confirmed by what follows : גַּם פְּלֵיטָה
לֹא־הָיְתָה לּוֹ, and there is no escape from
them, or, more literally, in reference to
them. פְּלֵיטָה properly signifies those who
have escaped in war; who have not

been killed, or taken prisoners; but it
is also used of fruits of the earth which
have not been destroyed, Exod. x. 5.
The contrast between the beauty of
Paradise and the desolation of a desert,
is exquisitely forcible and affecting.
4. The allegory now becomes special
and minute in its features, which are
selected from the phenomena and operations of an invading army, the subject
concerning which it is to be understood;
but having the invasion by the locusts as
its basis, and therefore presenting these
prominently to view, and comparing
them to the army, which is thus stu-
diously concealed. On this principle
there is no difficulty in accounting for the
particle of comparison, so liberally used
in this and the following verses. So
strong is the resemblance of the head of
the locust to that of a horse, that they
are on this account called cavalette by
the Italians. This feature Theodoret
thus notices : εἴ τις ἀκριβῶς κατίδοι τὴν
κεφαλὴν τῆς ἀκρίδος, σφόδρα τῇ τοῦ
ἵππου ἐοικυῖαν εὑρήσει. In Rev. ix. 7,
the locusts are compared to horses har-
nessed for battle : τὰ ὁμοιώματα τῶν
ἀκρίδων ὅμοια ἵπποις ἡτοιμασμένοις εἰς
πόλεμον. Such comparison is very
common among the Arabs. The point
of comparison in the second member of
the parallelism, is the swiftness with
which cavalry advance to the attack.
5. יְרַקֵּד is used of the rapid and bounding course of chariots over a rough surface, Nah. iii. 2. See also Rev. ix. 9.

   "— per purum tonantes
Egit equos, volucremque currum."
                    Horace, Carm. i. 34. 7.

   "————vacuos dat in aëra saltus
Succutiturque alte, similisque est cur-
rus inani."
                    Ovid. Metam. ii. 165.

Like the crackling of the flame of fire devouring the stubble;
Like a mighty people arranged for battle.

6 Before them the people tremble;
All faces withdraw their colour.

7 They run like mighty men;
They scale the wall like warriors;
Yea, they all march in their courses,
And they break not their ranks.

8 They press not each other:
They march on, each in his path;
Though they fall among the missiles,
They break not up.

9 They run eagerly through the city;
They run upon the wall;

Speaking of the noise made by a swarm of locusts, Forskål says: "Transeuntes grylli super verticem nostrum sono magnæ cataractæ ferebant." To the same effect Morier: "On the 11th of June, while seated in our tents about noon, we heard a very unusual noise, that sounded like the rustling of a great wind at a distance. On looking up, we perceived an immense cloud, here and there transparent, in other parts quite black, that spread itself all over the sky, and at intervals shadowed the sun." It is, however, not improbable, that the sound here referred to is that produced by the large hind legs of the locust in leaping. The comparison at the end of the verse, is to the clashing of arms, and the shouting of an army on the point of engaging in battle.

6. יְחִילוּ, *they tremble*, from חוּל, *to turn round, twist oneself, writhe with pain;* then *to tremble.* Arab. حال, med. Wau, *to be turned.* פָּארוּר, *warmth, ruddiness of countenance.* Arab. فار, *æstuavit, efferbuit.* קָבַץ פָּארוּר, *to withdraw their ruddiness,* or *colour,* i.e. to change colour, grow pale with terror. Nah. ii. 11. Comp. כָּסַף, *to turn pale.* The ancient versions concur in rendering the words, *every face like the blackness of a pot;* deriving the last word from פּוּר; hence פָּרוּר, *pot,* without א. Of the terror inspired

by locusts, we cannot have a better proof than the Arabic proverb: اجرد من الجراد, *more terrible than the locusts.*

7—9. Here the description quite excels in the graphic. The comparison to warriors is admirably carried out. First, their rapid advance upon the city is specified; next, their scaling the walls in the most regular order; then their consentaneous encounter with the troops of defence, their invulnerability, their progress through the streets, their climbing the walls, and entering the windows of the houses, are set forth in terms of singular and appropriate beauty.

יְעַבֵּטוּן, Arab. عبط, *fidit, vulneravit,* عبيط, *fissus,* has here the signification of *breaking up* the order or regularity with which a body of troops proceed when marching to the attack. Abenezra and Kimchi compare עָוַת, *to pervert, turn aside,* which comes nearly to the same thing. LXX. ἐκκλίνωσι. Syr. ܢܫܚܠܦܘܢ. Gesenius thinks the verb is here used in a sense cognate with the significations in Kal and Hiphil, *to give* or *take a pledge;* but the idea of *exchange, change,* is not clearly brought out. The regular military order with which the locusts advance, has been frequently described. Ἀβασίλευτον γὰρ ἡ ἀκρὶς, ἐκστρατεύει μὲν γὰρ ἐξ ἑνὸς

They go up into the houses;
They enter the windows like a thief.

10 Before them the earth trembleth,
The heavens shake,
The sun and the moon are darkened,
And the stars withdraw their shine.

11 Jehovah also uttereth his voice before his army;
Surely his camp is very large;
Surely it is mighty, executing his order;

εὐτάκτως κελεύσματος· φασὶ δὲ αὐτὰς στοιχηδὸν ἰέναι, καὶ ὡς ἐν τάξει διίπτασθαι, καὶ ἥκιστα μὲν ἀπονοσφίζεσθαι, περιέπειν δὲ οὕτως ἀλλήλας, ὡσανεὶ καὶ ἀδελφαὶ, φύσεως αὐτῆς βραβενούσης τὸ φιλάλληλον. Cyril. The testimony of Jerome, as an eye-witness in Palestine, is peculiarly valuable: "Hoc nuper in hac provincia vidimus. Quum enim locustarum agmina venirent, et aerem, qui inter cœlum et terram est, occuparent, *tanto ordine* ex dispositione jubentis Dei volitant, ut instar tesserularum, quæ in pavimentis artificis figuntur manu, *suum locum teneant, et ne puncto quidem, ut ita dicam, ungueve transverso declinent ad alteram.*" Morier also remarks on those which he saw: "They seemed to be impelled by one common instinct, and moved in one body, which had the appearance of being organized by a leader." Comp. Prov. xxx. 27, מֶלֶךְ אֵין לָאַרְבֶּה וַיֵּצֵא חֹצֵץ כֻּלּוֹ, *there is no king to the locusts, yet they go forth, all of them dividing,* i. e. *themselves* into regular companies or swarms, with all the discipline of a well-ordered army. רָחַק, signifies so to *press upon* one as to compel him to move from his place. Notwithstanding the immense crowds of the locusts, not only does none of them break the ranks by deviating from the straight course which they pursue, but none forces his fellow from his rank. Their watchword may be said to be *onward;* for they never turn back. If they enter houses, they go straight through them, and out at the opposite side. Thus Abulpharagius relates in his Chron. Syr. p. 134: "postquam a latere meridionale domos intraverant, a latere septemtrionale egrediebantur." שֶׁלַח, properly means any missile weapon thrown at an

enemy, from שָׁלַח, *to send* or *cast forth;* but it is also frequently used of the sword. Comp. the Arab. سلم, *arma.* בְּעַד, is of somewhat difficult determination. The ground idea seems to be that of *mediation, a being* or *doing anything between two;* hence הִתְפַּלֵּל בְּעַד, *to make supplication* for any one, *i. e.* by interposing *between* him and the party to whom the supplication is addressed. To this the signification derived from the Arab. بعد, *post,* nearly approximates, as occurring in the Hebrew. *Between,* or *among,* will suit most of the passages in which the word occurs. See Winer and Credner. Taking שֶׁלַח as a collective noun, the meaning of נָפַל בְּעַד הַשֶּׁלַח, will be *to fall among the missiles,* i.e. *to light,* or *come down among them;* and referring יִבְצָעוּ to the whole swarm, what it expresses is, that they are not *broken up,* or *interrupted* in their course. Compare a similar use of שָׁבַר, *to break,* Dan. xi. 22. —בְּעִיר, *in the city,* i.e. *any city* or town that may lie in their way. Credner's appeal to chap. iv. [iii.] 17, in proof that Jerusalem is specifically meant, cannot be sustained, since that part of the prophecy relates to a totally different subject. The scene is rather the land of Judah, with its fortified cities, which were overrun and plundered by the Assyrian troops.

10, 11. Though the language here employed may in part admit of a literal application to the obscuration of the air by the locusts, yet it is, as a whole, to be regarded as a specimen of the highly-wrought hyperbolical, which forms one of the more distinguishing features of Hebrew poetry. קוֹל יְהוָה, *the voice of Jehovah,* is here, as frequently, *thunder,*

Surely the day of Jehovah is great, and very terrible:
Yea, who can endure it?

12　　Now, therefore, saith Jehovah,
Turn ye to me with all your heart,
And with fasting and weeping and mourning;

13　And rend your heart, and not your garments,
And turn to Jehovah your God;
For he is pitiful and compassionate,
Long-suffering, and of great mercy,
And repenteth of the evil.

14　Who knoweth? He may turn and repent,
And leave a blessing behind him—
An offering and a libation,
For Jehovah your God.

---

and not any word of command, as some have imagined. Comp. Exod. ix. 23, 29, 33; Ps. xviii. 14 [13]; Ps. lxxvii. 18, 19 [17, 18]. The locusts are called the חֵיל, *army* of Jehovah, with further reference to the numbers and power of an army. One of the laws of Mohammed is thus expressed:

لا تقتلوا الجراد فانها جند الله الاعظم

Ye shall not kill the locusts, for they are the army of God Almighty. Damir. And رب الجراد, *Lord of the locusts*, is one of the names of God among the Mohammedans. The entire description closes with the brief but pointed interrogation, מִי יְכִילֶנּוּ, *Who can endure it?* to which the implied answer is, None. Comp. Mal. iii. 2, וּמִי מְכַלְכֵּל אֶת־יוֹם בּוֹאוֹ, and Jer. x. 10. לֹא יָכִלוּ גוֹיִם זַעְמוֹ.

12. Jehovah himself is here introduced, urging the necessity of immediate humiliation. וְגַם־עַתָּה, is intensive. The ו is that of consequence, deducing an argument from what had preceded; גַם is augmentative and emphatic, as usually in Joel; and עַתָּה has special reference to the existing circumstances of the persons addressed, and the instant attention which the divine message required. The combination marks strong feeling in the speaker, and the urgent nature of the subject to which it is introductory. It is to be connected with שֻׁבוּ עָדַי, and not with נְאֻם יְהוָה.

13. The prophet resumes his address, and founds upon the call of Jehovah, contained in the preceding verse, an exhortation to sincere inward repentance, which he supports by encouragements deduced from the benignity of the divine character. Rending the garments was usual on occasions of great mourning, see Gen. xxxvii. 29, 34; 1 Sam. iv. 12; 1 Kings xxi. 27; Ezra ix. 3, 5; Is. xxxvii. 1. This custom obtained not only among the Hebrews, but also among the Babylonians, Persians, Egyptians, Greeks and Romans. הָרָעָה, is neither the plague of locusts, nor the invasion of the Assyrians, but the calamities in general which God brings upon mankind. This interpretation the preceding context requires.

14. The question מִי יוֹדֵעַ, *who knoweth,* while it suggests the idea of the greatness of the sin to be pardoned, also conveys that of the possibility of such pardon.

"———— ἀλλ' ἔτι καὶ νῦν,
Ταῦτ' εἴποις Ἀχιλῆϊ δαΐφρονι, αἴκε πίθηται.
Τίς δ' οἶδ', εἴ κέν οἱ, σὺν δαίμονι, θυμὸν ὀρίναις,
Παρειπών;"

Iliad xi. 789.

God's leaving a blessing behind him, pre-supposes his return to visit his people in mercy. The first-fruits of prosperity are due to Him through whose blessing it is conferred.

15   Blow ye the trumpet in Zion,
        Appoint a sacred fast ;
        Proclaim a day of restraint.
16   Assemble the people : convene a sacred assembly ;
        Collect the aged ; gather the children,
        And those that suck the breasts ;
        Let the bridegroom come forth from his chamber,
        And the bride from her nuptial bed.
17   Between the porch and the altar,
        Let the priests, the ministers of Jehovah, weep ;
        And let them say, Have pity, O Jehovah! upon thy people,
        And deliver not thine heritage to reproach,
        That the nations should rule over them.
        Why should they say among the people,
        Where is their God ?
18   Then Jehovah will be jealous for his land,

15, 16. Comp. ver. 1, and chap. i. 14. Here the distribution into classes is more minute than in the latter of these passages. The mourning was to be universal. The חֻפָּה, was the bridal couch, richly provided with a canopy, curtains, &c. Root חָפַף, to cover, protect. See for the force of the reference to the last class mentioned, Deut. xxiv. 5.

17. אֵלָם, Arab. اول, prior, anterior ; the προνάος, or porch, before the temple, more strictly taken. It was an hundred and twenty cubits high, twenty broad from north to south, and ten long from east to west. The מִזְבֵּחַ, altar, was that of burnt-offering in the court of the priests. Here, with their backs toward the altar, on which they had nothing to offer, and their faces directed towards the residence of the Shekinah, they were to weep, and make supplication on behalf of the people. לִמְשָׁל בָּם גּוֹיִם. Jarchi, Secker, Michaelis, Rosenmüller, Justi, Credner, Winer, Gesenius, Maurer, Noyes, Hitzig, and Ewald, render, that the nations should make a proverb of them ; but such construction is totally unauthorized by Hebrew usage. In upwards of fifty instances, in which בְּ מָשַׁל occurs in the Hebrew Bible, it is never once used in the sense of employing derisive, or satirical language, but uniformly in that of likening, or of exercising rule or dominion. In fact, the verb is nowhere used either with or without the preposition in the signification of deriding. It is the noun alone that is thus employed in the forms הִצִּיג, הָיָה, שׂוּם, נָתַן לְמָשָׁל, to be, set, give, &c. for a derision. Ezek. xvi. 44, forms no exception. The ancient versions all agree in the translation, that the heathen should rule over them. LXX. τοῦ κατάρξαι αὐτῶν ἔθνη. Targ. לְמִשְׁלַט בְּהוֹן עַמְמַיָא. Syr. ܠܡܫܠܛ ܒܗܘܢ ܥܡܡܐ. Vulg. ut dominentur eis nationes. Hexap. Syr. ܘܡܢܘ ܗܘܐ ܟܕ ܢܫܠܛ. Thus also Kimchi, Abenezra, Leo Juda, Junius and Tremellius, Jewish-Spanish, Lyranus, Drusius, Calvin, Newcome, Dathe, Boothroyd, and Hengstenberg ; and there does not appear to be any reason why it could ever have been rendered otherwise, but for the influence of the hypothesis, that the preceding part of the prophecy relates to locusts, and not to political enemies. "Ideo ridiculum est quod multi putant contexti sermonem de locustis : illud prorsus alienum est a Prophetæ mente." Calvin, in loc.

18. קָנָא, Arab. قني, valde rubuit ; in Piel קִנֵּא, to be jealous, from the redness or flush by which the face is suffused,

And take compassion upon his people;

19 Yea, Jehovah will answer, and say unto his people,
Behold! I will send you the corn,
And the new wine, and the oil,
And ye shall have abundance thereof;
And I will no more deliver you to reproach among the nations.

20 I will also remove the Northern from you,
And drive him into a dry and barren land;
His van towards the Eastern sea,
And his rear towards the Western sea;

when a person is under the influence of passion.

19, 20. In the former of these verses, respect is had to the removal of the calamity, from which the Jews were suffering at the time the prophecy was delivered; in the latter, that of the foreign enemy by whom the country was to be invaded. The article is placed before דָּגָן, תִּירוֹשׁ, and יִצְהָר, to give them prominence, as the principal objects which had suffered from the locusts, and which were now to be restored. The term הַצְּפוֹנִי, *the Northern, Northlander*, or, as Coverdale renders, *Him of the North*, is of prime importance in the interpretation of the prophecy. It has been urged against its having any reference to the locusts, that they visit Palestine from the south, and not from the north; but this objection can scarcely be regarded as valid, since, though they do not usually come from that quarter, yet they may be carried by a south wind across Arabia Deserta, and then, when to the north of Palestine, be driven south, or south-west into that country. That, however, which determines the question, is the addition of the patronymic י to צָפוֹן, indicating that the North was not merely the quarter whence the subject of discourse came, but that its *native country* lay to the north of Palestine: just as הַתֵּימָנִי, *the Temanite*, means *the Southern*, or him who dwells to the right of Palestine; מִצְרִי, *a native Egyptian;* in Arabic مَكّي, *a Meccite,* مَدِينِي, *a Medinite*, i.e. a native or inhabitant of Mecca and Medina. Now it is agreed on all hands, that the native country of the locusts is

the regions of Arabia, the Lybian deserts, and the Sahara of Egypt; so that according to the *usus loquendi*, they cannot be meant by the term here employed. Indeed, so much has this been felt by some of those who have advocated the hypothesis that locusts are intended, that they have been under the necessity of having recourse to far-fetched expedients, in order to support it. Justi, contrary to all analogy, proposes to render, "the locusts that march *northwards*," or to explain the term *north* of what is dark, hostile, or barbarous; which construction of the meaning is, in part, adopted by Hitzig. Maurer, on the other hand, setting aside these and other methods, has recourse to the Arab. ضفن, *deposuit excrementum,* and thence deduces for צְפוֹנִי, the signification of *stercoreus*, or, in case this derivation should not be approved, to سفن, *decorticare radendo,* and considers the reference to be either to the injurious influence of their dung on the trees, herbage, &c. or to their stripping them of their verdure.

On the supposition that by הַצְּפוֹנִי, *the Northern*, the Assyrians are meant, every difficulty vanishes. And that they may with the strictest propriety be so termed, is proved by Zeph. ii. 13: "And he will stretch out his hand עַל־צָפוֹן, upon *the North*, and destroy *Assyria*, and will make *Nineveh* a desolation, and dry as a wilderness." The Jews were accustomed to call Assyria and Babylonia *the North*, and the North country, because they lay in that direction from Palestine. "Quæres, quisnam hic Aquilonaris? S. Hieron., Theodor., Remigius, Albertus et Hugo

And his odour shall come up,
And his stench ascend,
Because he hath done great things.

21 Fear not, O land! rejoice and be glad,
    For Jehovah doeth great things.

22 Fear not, ye beasts of the field!
    For the pastures of the desert spring up,
    For the tree beareth its fruit;
    The fig-tree and the vine yield their strength.

23 Rejoice, ye sons of Zion! and be glad in Jehovah your God;

---

accipiunt Sennacherib, quem Dominus longè fecit à Jerusalem: quia dum eam obsideret, angelus Domini una nocte percussit centum octuaginta quinque millia militum, itaque eum fugere compulit. 4 Reg. xix. 35."—*A Lapide.*

The geographical specification which follows in the verse is designed to express the universality of the destruction of the Assyrians. They were to be dispersed in every other direction but that from which they had come. By הַיָּם הַקַּדְמֹנִי, *the Eastern Sea*, is meant the Asphaltic lake; by הַיָּם הָאַחֲרוֹן, *the Western Sea*, the Mediterranean; and by אֶרֶץ צִיָּה וּשְׁמָמָה, *a dry and desolate land*, the deserts of Arabia. Literally the words הַקַּדְמֹנִי, and הָאַחֲרוֹן, signify what is *before* and *behind*, and are applied geographically in reference to the Orientals who reckon the different quarters according to the positions of front and rear, right and left, while they face the east, which is with them the principal point of the compass. The language of the prophet is figurative, the metaphor being still borrowed from the locusts, which perish when blown by a storm into the sea, or the sandy desert. Jerome refers to a similar scene, which literally happened when he was in Palestine. "Etiam nostris temporibus," he says, "vidimus agmina locustarum terram texisse Judæam, quæ postea,...vento surgente, in mare primum et novissimum præcipitata sunt." And he immediately adds, what illustrates the statement of Joel relative to the ascending of the stench: "Cumque littora utriusque maris acervis mortuarum locustarum quas aquæ evomuerant, implerentur, putredo earum et fœtor in tantum noxius

fuit, ut aerem quoque corrumperet, et pestilentia tam jumentorum, quam hominum gigneretur." פָּנִים and סוֹף, *face* and *end* are here used in the military sense of *van* and *rear*, and cannot, without violence, be interpreted of the swarm of locusts, and a brood which succeeded them. צַחֲנָה, is a ἅπαξ λεγ. comp. זָנַח, *to be foul, putrid, to stink.* Arab. صَنِخَ, *sordes.* Giving an account of the locusts, Thevenot says, "They live not above six months, and, when dead, the stench of them so corrupts and infects the air, that it often occasions dreadful pestilences." The concluding words of the verse convey the idea of moral agency, and can with no propriety be interpreted of the locusts. הִגְדִּיל לַעֲשׂוֹת. LXX. ἐμεγάλυνε τὰ ἔργα αὐτοῦ. Syr. ‏ܐܪܒܝ ܠܡܥܒܕ‏,

he exalted himself in acting. The phrase is obviously used here in a bad sense, and indicates the pride of the Assyrians; comp. 2 Kings xxi. 6, where הִרְבָּה לַעֲשׂוֹת, a similar idiom, occurs. As employed in the following verse of our prophet, it is placed in antithesis with the sense in which it is here used, and is to be differently understood: *viz.* of the great things that God would do for his people, comp. Ps. cxxvi. 2, 3.

21—23. In these verses there is a beautiful gradation. First, the land, which had been destroyed by the enemy, is addressed in a prosopopœia; then the irrational animals which had suffered from the famine; and lastly, the inhabitants themselves. All are called upon to cast off their fears, and rejoice in the

For he giveth you the former rain in due measure;
Yea, he causeth the heavy rain to descend for you—
The former and the latter rain as before :

happy change which Jehovah would effect. Desolation, barrenness, and famine, would disappear, and times of prosperity and happiness return. בְּנֵי צִיּוֹן, *Sons of Zion*, properly the inhabitants of Jerusalem, but here evidently used to denote those of the land generally, of which Jerusalem was the metropolis, and Zion the centre of religious influence. מוֹרֶה לִצְדָקָה, is rendered in the Targ. כַּלְפְּכוֹן בְּזִכּוּ, *your teacher in righteousness ;* which Abarbanel explains, הוא מלך המשיח שיורה את הדרך ילכו בה ואת המעשה אשר יעשון. *And he is the king Messiah, who shall teach them the way in which they should walk, and the works that they should do.* The same, or a similar construction of the words is found in the Vulg., Rufinus, Jarchi, Pagninus, Munster, Leo Juda, Castalio, the Jewish-Spanish, Remigius, Rupertus, Vatablus, Ribera, Mercer, Œcolamp., Luther, and most of the early Lutheran interpreters ; and, among the moderns, Pick and Hengstenberg, the latter of whom contends for it at considerable length, and decidedly considers the passage to be one of the Messianic prophecies. That מוֹרֶה signifies *teacher*, is beyond all doubt, see 2 Chron. xv. 3; Job xxxvi. 22; Is. ix. 15 ; xxx. 20 ; and from the occurrence of the word in this place in connexion with צְדָקָה, *righteousness*, which is so frequently referred to the Messiah both in the Old and New Testaments, there is something very plausible in the application of the term to him who is specially callee by Malachi שֶׁמֶשׁ צְדָקָה, THE SUN OF RIGHTEOUSNESS, *i. e.* the author of that illumination or knowledge which has righteousness for its object. To such interpretation, however, there appear to me the following insuperable objections :—First, it is repugnant to the circumstances of the context; "non videtur tamen ferre hunc sensum circumstantia loci." Calvin ; who says of the reason adduced in support of it, that it would be out of place to give such prominence to merely temporal blessings, "sed ratio illa est nimis frigida;" and goes on to show that, in accordance with the custom of the prophets, Joel begins with these inferior blessings, and afterwards, in ver. 28, proceeds to treat of those which are spiritual. Secondly, the repetition of the same term, מוֹרֶה, immediately after, where, as all allow, it must be taken in the acceptation of *rain.* And thirdly, the peculiar force and coherence of the words, אֶת־הַמּוֹרֶה, and שָׁם מוֹרֶה וּמַלְקוֹשׁ. The emphasis given to מוֹרֶה, by prefixing not only the article ה, but also the determining particle אֶת, shows that the prophet had some immediate and definite object in view, which we cannot imagine to have been any other than the autumnal rain, which was indispensable any year, and more especially after such a season of drought, to prepare the ground for nourishing the seed. It must have been an object of universal and anxious desire, and has, in consequence, a high degree of importance and prominence allotted to it in the text. See on the force of אֶת the Lexicons of Lee and Gesenius. The same consideration will account for the form, and the particular signification of לִצְדָקָה in this place. The ל is to be taken adverbially, as pointing out the rule or measure according to which the rain was to be bestowed, which is declared to be צְדָקָה, so that the meaning will be, *in just quantity, adequately*, in the proportion suitable to the exigency of the case. צָדַק, the root from which this noun is derived, signifies to be *just, right ;* to come up to certain claims, *to be what a person or thing ought to be.* Comp. Lev. xix. 36, where צָדָק is used of weights and measures that were exact, or came up to the demands of the law. Some propose to render לִצְדָקָה, *bountifully*, but this would give the Chaldee rather than the Hebrew signification. Ewald translates, *the early rain for justification*, and explains it of the Jews being again accounted righteous by God. To the objection of Hengstenberg, that if מוֹרֶה in the first half of the verse does not designate a different divine benefit from מוֹרֶה in the second, an idle tautology will ensue, it is only necessary to reply, that the words occur in parallelism, and that in the second

24 So that the floors shall be full of grain,
   And the vats shall run over with new wine and oil.
25 Thus I will make good to you the years
   Which the swarming locust hath devoured,
   The licking locust, the consuming locust, and the gnawing locust,
   My great army which I sent against you.
26 And ye shall eat plentifully and be satisfied,
   And shall praise the name of Jehovah your God,
   Who hath dealt wondrously with you:
   And my people shall never be ashamed.
27 Then shall ye know, that I am in the midst of Israel,

instance מוֹרֶה is merely a resumption for the sake of dividing the גֶּשֶׁם mentioned immediately before into its two regular divisions, the *former* and the *latter*. The term elsewhere used for the *former* or autumnal *rain*, which falls from the middle of October until the middle of December, is יוֹרֶה, lit. *the waterer*, being the Benoni Participle of יָרָה, *to dart, cast*, or scatter, as drops of water. מוֹרֶה, however, which is the Hiph. Participle of the same verb, does occur in the same acceptation, Ps. lxxxiv. 7. Comp. my note on Hosea vi. 3, where מַלְקוֹשׁ, the *latter* or vernal rain is also explained.

The reading יוֹרֶה, which is found instead of the former מוֹרֶה, in twenty-three MSS., originally in eleven more, now in three, in the Jerusalem Talmud, and as Keri in the margin of two of De Rossi's Codices, is in favour of the rendering *rain*, which is that of all the early versions, but may possibly have originated in emendation. With respect to the latter occurrence of the word, there is no variety of reading. גֶּשֶׁם, Arab. جسم,

corpus, et omne id quod longum, largum, et profundum est ; Chald. *the body :* applied to such rain as is *heavy*, or violent, and pours down as it were in a body. The verbs נָתַן, and וַיּוֹרֶד, are prophetic futures. To render בָּרִאשׁוֹן, *in the first month*, would involve a contradiction, since only one of the two rains could happen in that month. It seems, therefore, necessary to suppose an ellipsis of כְּ, the particle of comparison, and read כְּבָרִאשׁוֹן, *as formerly*, or *as in former times*. Comp. Is. i. 26 ; Jer. xxxiii. 11, where

כְּבָרִאשׁוֹנָה is similarly used ; and for רִאשׁוֹן, in the sense of *former*, 1 Sam. xvii. 30 ; Hagg. ii. 3. Thus the LXX., Syr., Vulg., Arab. One of Kennicott's MSS., and perhaps another, reads כְּרִאשׁוֹן. The ellipsis of כְּ is not infrequent in the Hebrew Scriptures.

24. Here the happy results of the plentiful and seasonable rains are set forth. The ו in וּמָלְאוּ, is consequential. הֵשִׁיקוּ, comp. the Arab. شوق, *propulit,*

vii. Conj. *impulsus fuit, fluxit*, to *cause to flow*, or *run over*. For יֶקֶב, see on Is. v. 2.

25. That the prophet has here in view the plague of locusts described in chap. i. cannot well be doubted. The names, though placed in a different order, are identical with those there specified. They are called God's great *army*, a name still given to them by the Arabs. See on ver. 11. Though the scourge lasted only one year, yet as they not only destroyed the whole produce of that year, but also what was laid up in store for future years, there is no impropriety in the plural form of שָׁנִים, *years*. The term is used metonymically for the produce and supply of years. The loss of these Jehovah promises to recompense or make good, by not only furnishing the Jews with an abundance of temporal enjoyments, but affording them the delightful experience of his presence and favour as their covenant-God. This promise is amplified in verses—

26, 27, In which the future prosperity of the Jewish church is described in terms, which obviously characterise the

And that I, Jehovah, am your God, and none else ;
And my people shall never be ashamed.

28 [III. i.]—And it shall come to pass, afterwards,
That I will pour out my Spirit upon all flesh ;
And your sons and your daughters shall prophesy,
Your old men shall dream dreams,
Your young men shall see visions ;

29 And even upon the male and the female servants
I will pour out my Spirit in those days.

period which succeeded that of the Babylonish captivity. The divine recompense was not merely to cover the evils sustained by the ravages of the locusts ; it was to extend to those which both the Assyrians and the Chaldæans were to inflict upon the nation. This interpretation is confirmed by what immediately follows respecting the outpouring of the Holy Spirit. By God's being in the midst of his people, is meant the special manifestation of his presence in the communications of his favour. The resumption of אֲנִי in וַאֲנִי, forms a beautiful anadiplosis.

28, 29. The prophet now proceeds to predict the impartation of richer gifts in future times than those temporal blessings which had just been promised to the Jews. אַחֲרֵי־כֵן, *afterward*, LXX. μετὰ ταῦτα, Hengstenberg would place in antithesis with בְּרִאשׁוֹן, ver. 23, which he renders *first ;* but the latter phrase has reference to what had already taken place, and was not future to the time of the prophet. אַחֲרֵי־כֵן, though indefinite, is nearly equivalent in force to אַחֲרִית הַיָּמִים, Is. ii. 2, as appears from its having been rendered by the Apostle Peter ἐν ταῖς ἐσχάταις ἡμέραις, *in the last days.* Jarchi, לעתיד לבא, *in futurity :* Abenezra, אמר ר׳ ישוע כל ואת הנבואה היא לעתיד ור׳ משה הכהן אמר אם כן למה אמר אחרי כן רק והיה באחרית הימים. "Rabbi Jeshua saith, All this is a prophecy of the future ; and Rabbi Moses the priest saith, If so, why does he say *after this ?* but it is the same as, *and it shall come to pass in the latter days ;*" in which interpretation Kimchi concurs, adding, לפי שאמר וידעתם כי בקרב ישראל אני אמר עתה חדעו ולא ידיעה שלמה כי עוד תשובו ותחטאו לפני אבל אחרי זאת תידיעה יבא זמן שתדעו אותי ידיעה שלמה ולא תחטאו עוד והוא לימות המשיח שנאמר כי מלאה הארץ דעה את

יהוה, "Because it is said, And ye shall know that I am in the midst of you. What he says is, Now ye know, but not with a perfect knowledge, for ye will again commit sin before me ; but after this knowledge there shall come a time when ye shall know me with a perfect knowledge, and shall sin no more, namely, in the days of the Messiah," &c. That the two phrases are identical in meaning, clearly appears from a comparison of Jer. xlviii. 47, with xlix. 6. See on Is. ii. 2. שָׁפַךְ signifies to *pour out, to communicate in a plentiful and abundant manner,* and is here used with the greatest propriety to denote the larger and richer supplies of divine influence, which were to be afforded to the church under the gospel dispensation. רוּחַ, *spirit,* means here the *influences* and *gifts* of the Holy Spirit, as in numerous other passages, in which the Spirit is said to be *put, given,* &c. ; and these communications are described in language which shows that they were both to be more general and more special in their character. In a more general point of view, they were to be bestowed upon כָּל־בָּשָׂר, *all flesh,* i. e. mankind generally, without distinction of nation or country. To restrict this phrase to the Jews, as is done by Abenezra, Kimchi, Albo, Hitzig, and others, is irreconcilable with Scripture usage, according to which it constantly signifies mankind generally, or the whole human race ; just as in Arabic, بشر and ابشار signify *homo, humanum genus,* and Adam is called ابو البشر, *the father of flesh,* i. e. of mankind. Credner would have the phrase to include the animal creation,

30 And I will show prodigies in the heavens and in the earth,
       Blood and fire, and columns of smoke.

than which no construction could be more preposterous in such connexion, or more at variance with other passages in which the communication of the influences of the Spirit are limited to the human family. The influence, of which universality is here predicated, is the saving energy which is exerted by the Holy Spirit, in commencing, carrying on, and consummating the work of grace in the souls of men. It accompanies the presentation of divine truth to the mind, and removes the obstacles which the force of innate depravity opposes to the reception of the gospel. See my Lectures on Divine Inspiration, pp. 525—530. Besides the influence which was thus to be vouchsafed for the purposes of salvation, the prophet specifies that which should be more limited in its communication, consisting in the miraculous endowment of a certain number of Jews, of different classes and conditions, with the knowledge of divine things, and the ability infallibly to communicate them to others. The persons on whom these gifts were to be conferred are their "sons and daughters;" their "aged men," and their "youths;" their "male" and "female servants;" terms which are manifestly designed to teach that their bestowment was to embrace persons of different classes, ranks, and conditions of life. נָבָא, Arab. نبأ, *indicavit, annunciavit*, Eth. **ⵥⵐ** : *locutus est*, **ⵟⵣⵙ** : *vaticinatus est, prædixit*, is used not merely to denote the foretelling of future events, but to express the giving of utterance to divine truth under a miraculous impulse, or the pretending to such impulse, whether the utterance was made in the way of direct communication, as was the case when the prophets addressed their hearers, or by the rehearsal or singing of sacred hymns under extraordinary divine impulse, as when Miriam sung at the Red Sea, Exod. xv. 20, 21; or when the sons of the prophets and Saul prophesied, 1 Sam. x. 5, 6; xix. 20—24. Comp. Acts xix. 6; xxi. 9; 1 Cor. xi. 4, 5; xiv. 1, 5, 6, 22,

24, 31, 39; which passages furnish striking illustrative examples of the fulfilment of the prophecy of Joel. See also 1 Chron. xxv. 1—3; and Mede's works, Book I. Discourse xvi. That we are fully warranted to interpret it of the extraordinary supernatural gifts which were vouchsafed in the apostolic age, is placed beyond doubt by its allegation by Peter, in justification of the phenomenon which took place on the day of Pentecost; τοῦτό ἐστι, *this is the fact* predicted by Joel; Acts ii. 16. The quotation was the more apt, since the words of the prophet had just been read in the pentecostal service of the Synagogue. See my Biblical Researches and Travels in Russia, p. 326. חֲלֹמוֹת, *dreams*, and חֶזְיֹנוֹת, *visions*, belonged to the different modes in which God revealed his will to the prophets. Numb. xii. 6; 1 Sam. xxviii. 6, 15; Jer. xxiii. 25—28; Dan. vii. 1, 2. See my Lectures on Inspiration, pp. 147—165. Though no express mention is made of dreams in the apostolic writings, yet there is repeated reference to *visions*. See Acts ix. 10, 12; x. 3, 17; xi. 5; xvi. 9; xviii. 9; xxvi. 19; 2 Cor. xii. 1; Rev. ix. 17. וְגַם, *and even*, indicates a rise in the prophecy, which was intended to exclude none, not even the lowest and most despised "servants," from a participation in the large bestowment of divine influence. In beautiful harmony with this feature of the prophecy is the special recognition of οἱ πτωχοὶ, *the poor*, in the New Testament. The repetition אֶשְׁפֹּךְ אֶת רוּחִי, *I will pour out my Spirit*, shows, that the influence of which, in general, they were to be partakers, was not merely that which consisted in the miraculous gifts, but also that ordinary and saving influence which is experienced by all believers. What incontrovertibly proves that the prophecy includes both a more ordinary, and a more extraordinary or miraculous divine agency, is the extension given to it by the apostle Peter, Acts ii. 38, 39; where he teaches that it was to comprehend "all that are afar off," *i. e.* the Gentiles, "even as many as the Lord our God shall call."

30, 31. In connexion with this period of the rich enjoyment of divine influence,

31 The sun shall be turned into darkness,
　　And the moon into blood,
　　Before the great and terrible day of Jehovah come.

Joel introduces one of awful judgment, called as usual יוֹם יְהוָֹה, *the day of Jehovah*, the precursors of which he describes in very alarming language. That the destruction of Jerusalem and the Jewish polity is intended, most interpreters are agreed; but there exists a diversity of opinion respecting the character of the language, some taking it literally, as setting forth physical prodigies, such as those which Josephus relates to have taken place before the destruction of Jerusalem, and tremendous massacres and conflagrations in different parts of the country; while others maintain that it is symbolical, and consequently is to be figuratively explained. The latter position is more in accordance with the style of prophecy, in which we not only find a fixed set of symbols, but also, very frequently, an accumulation of images introduced for the purpose of producing a more powerful effect on the mind. See on Is. xiii. 10; xxxiv. 3—5. The heavens and the earth, therefore, mean the political world, with its civil and religious establishments; the sun and moon, the higher and superior ruling powers; while the other images are employed to denote the disastrous prognosticatory changes that were to happen in relation to both. Comp. Matt. xxiv. 29; Mark xiii. 24, 25; Luke xxi. 25—27, where the subject is the same as that exhibited by Joel, and the symbolical language in a great measure parallel. Similar images are used by pagan writers, when describing the forerunners of civil wars, as, for instance, Lucanus, Pharsal. lib. i. ver. 529 :—

"——— Superique minaces
Prodigiis terras implerunt, æthera, pontum.
Ignota obscuræ viderunt sidera noctes.
Ardentemque polum flammis, cœloque volantes,
Obliquas per inane faces, crinemque timendi
Sideris, et terris mutantem regna cometen.
Fulgura fallaci micuerunt crebra sereno,
Et varias ignis denso dedit acre formas."

מוֹפְתִים, *prodigies*, whatever objects are *unusual*, *portentous*, or *miraculous*, in their character. The word is most probably a derivative from יָפָה, Arab. Conj. iii.

وفي‎, *eminuit*, to be *conspicuous, admirable, wonderful*. LXX. τέρατα. It frequently occurs in combination with אוֹתוֹת, σημεῖα, *signs*. תִּימָרוֹת, only occurs once besides, and, as here, in construction with עָשָׁן, viz. Song iii. 6; where, however, nineteen MSS. and originally another read תִּמָרוֹת, without the Yod, which is doubtless the more correct orthography, the Yod having been inserted as a help to the pronunciation. There can be little doubt that it is derived from תָּמַר, *to be erect*, whence תָּמָר, the palm-tree, from its tall and erect growth. Comp. the Chaldee תִּמְרָה, *a column of smoke*; תִּימוֹר, Arab. تامور‎ and تَأْمُورَة‎, *turris*; and תִּמֵּר, *to rise like a column*. The phrase will, therefore, be equivalent to עַמּוּדֵי עָשָׁן, of which we have the singular עַמּוּד עָשָׁן, Jud. xx. 40. LXX. ἀτμίδα καπνοῦ; but in Song iii. 6, στελέχη καπνοῦ. Vulg. *vaporem fumi*. Targ. יְתוּרִין דִּתְנָן, *columns of smoke*, the singular of which is used Jud. xx. 40. Tanchum: اعمدة الدخان المرتفعة‎, *pillars of smoke ascending up*. Those who are familiar with the account given by Josephus of the disorders, convulsions, excesses, and rebellions, which preceded the subversion of the Jewish state, will readily admit, that the figurative language here employed most appropriately sets forth the awful circumstances of the inhabitants of Palestine at that period. To render more prominent the tremendous nature of the final judgment of the Jews, when their city and polity were destroyed, it is not merely called יוֹם יְהוָֹה, but יוֹם יְהוָֹה הַגָּדוֹל וְהַנּוֹרָא, *the great and fearful day of Jehovah*; terms which are employed by the prophet Malachi, iii. 23 (Eng. iv. 5.), in reference to the same event.

32   And it shall come to pass,
        That whosoever shall call upon the name of Jehovah shall be
            delivered :
        For in Mount Zion, and in Jerusalem shall be the escaped,
        According as Jehovah hath promised,
        Together with those who are left,
        Whom Jehovah shall call.

32. The phrase קְרָא בְשֵׁם יְהֹוָה, usually means *to invoke Jehovah according to his true character*, and designates such as he would regard in the light of acceptable worshippers ; but, on comparing the quotation of the words with direct reference to our Saviour, Rom. x. 13, with Acts ix. 14, 1 Cor. i. 2, it appears to be here employed as a periphrasis for those Jews who should embrace the faith of the Messiah, and render to him as יְהֹוָה, *Jehovah*, the same supreme worship which had been rendered to God by their pious ancestors. From the passage just quoted from the Acts, it is clear that the disciples of Christ were characterised as *invokers of his name*, i. e. as his worshippers, before they were called Christians. The prophecy contains a gracious promise, that, however terrible might be the final catastrophe in which the unbelievers should perish, provision would be made for the safety of those who believed in the Messiah. And church-history records its fulfilment ; for, on the approach of the Roman army, the Christian inhabitants of Jerusalem took to flight, in compliance with the Saviour's warning, and retiring to Pella, on the eastern side of the river Jordan, found there a safe asylum, while the devoted city was being besieged and destroyed. —οὐ μὲν ἀλλὰ καὶ τοῦ λαοῦ τῆς ἐν Ἱεροσολύμοις ἐκκλησίας, κατά τινα χρησμὸν τοῖς αὐτόθι δοκίμοις δι' ἀποκαλύψεως δοθέντα πρὸ τοῦ πολέμου, μεταναστῆναι τῆς πόλεως, καί τινα τῆς περαίας πόλιν οἰκεῖν κεκελευσμένον. πέλλαν αὐτὴν ὀνομάζουσιν· ἐν ᾗ τῶν εἰς Χριστὸν πεπιστευκότων ἀπὸ τῆς Ἱερουσαλὴμ μετῳκισμένων, κ. τ. λ. Euseb. lib. iii. cap. v. פְּלֵיטָה, is a collective noun, signifying *those who have escaped ;* in other words, ἡ ἐν Ἱεροσολύμοις ἐκκλησία, "the church *in Jerusalem*," as Eusebius phrases it in the above quotation, who not only made their escape from the impending calamity, but from the "untoward generation" to which they had belonged, Acts ii. 40 ; Is. iv. 3 ; so that the meaning is, not that there should continue to be deliverance for those who remained in Zion and Jerusalem during the infliction of the punishment, but that those who resided there should make their escape from it, having previously been delivered from the condition of those on whom it was inflicted. The words וּבַשְּׂרִידִים, *together with those that have been left*, from

שָׂרַד, Arab. شَرَد, *aufugit, vagatusque fuit,*

شَارِد, and شَرُود, *aufugiens,* to flee, make one's escape, survive a slaughter, or any other calamity. The reference seems not to be to converted Gentiles, as Schmidius, Michaelis, Holzhausen, and others interpret, but to those Jews who did not perish in the national judgments, but were called into the church of Christ. קְרָא, as employed in the last clause of the verse, signifies *to call*, in the sense of effectually prevailing upon any one to choose and participate in the blessings of the divine kingdom. Comp. Καλέω, as used by Paul, Rom. viii. 28, 30 ; ix. 24 ; 1 Thess. ii. 12. קֹרֵא, the Participle here denotes the future.

CHAPTER III [IV]

In this chapter the prophet returns from the parenthetic view which he had exhibited of the commencement of the Christian dispensation, and the overthrow
of the Jewish polity, to deliver predictions respecting events that were to transpire
subsequent to the Babylonish captivity, and were to fill up the space which should
intervene between the restoration of the Jews and the first advent of Christ. He
announces the judgment to be holden on their enemies after the return to Judæa,
1, 2; specifies the reasons why they were to be punished, and expressly mentions
by name the neighbouring nations of Tyre, Sidon, and Philistia, 3—6; promises
the restoration of those Jews whom these states had sold into slavery, while they
are threatened with slavery in return, 7, 8; summons the nations to engage in
the wars in which they were to be destroyed, 9—15; shows, that since these
convulsions were brought about by the providence of Jehovah, whose earthly
throne was at Jerusalem, his people had no ground for alarm, and would experience his protection, 16, 17; predicts times of great prosperity to them, 18;
and concludes with special denunciations against Egypt and Idumæa, with whose
fate is placed in striking contrast the protracted existence of the Jewish polity,
19—21.

1　FOR, behold! in those days, and at that time,
　　When I shall reverse the captivity of Judah and Jerusalem,
2　I will gather all the nations,
　　And bring them down into the valley of Jehoshaphat,
　　And will plead with them there,

1, 2. בַּיָּמִים הָהֵמָּה וּבָעֵת הַהִיא, is a double
mode of expression, employed to give
greater prominence to the period. That
the "days and time" here specified,
are not identical with the period spoken
of in the last five verses of the preceding
chapter, is evident from their being connected by the relative conjunction אֲשֶׁר,
with the following words, which relate
to the restoration of the Jewish state.
כִּי, at the beginning of the verse, is properly rendered for, and refers back to
chap. ii. 21—27, in which verses times
of great temporal prosperity are promised to the Jews. With this prosperity
was intimately connected the punishment
of the nations by which they had been
afflicted; and, accordingly, such punishment forms the subject of the present
chapter. Instead of אָשׁוּב, the Keri substitutes אָשִׁיב, in which it is supported by

twenty-five of Kennicott's MSS.; but
the frequent occurrence of שׁוּב שְׁבִית, in
which the Kal form is to be taken causatively, shows that there was no necessity
for the emendation. See Ps. xiv. 7;
liii. 7; cxxvi. 1; Is. lii. 8. Some interpret the phrase of a general restoration to circumstances of prosperity,
without any reference to previous circumstances of actual captivity, as in the case
of Job (xlii. 10); but considering its
common application to the return from
Babylon, and the express mention of the
scattering of the nation among the
heathen, ver. 2, it seems more natural to
refer it to the same event in this place.
That the restoration of the Jews from
their present dispersion is meant, and
that the judgments to be inflicted on the
nations are those which are predicted,
Rev. xvi. 14, 16, is rendered impossible

On account of my people, and Israel mine inheritance,
Whom they have scattered among the nations,
And have divided my land ;

3 And have cast lots for my people,
And given a boy for an harlot,
And sold a girl for wine,
That they might drink.

4 And truly, what are ye to me, O Tyre and Zidon,
And all the coasts of Philistia?
Will ye retaliate upon me?

by the introduction of the Tyrians, Sidonians, Philistines, &c. verses 4 and 19, since these states all received their punishment prior to the advent of Christ. By עֵמֶק יְהוֹשָׁפָט, *the valley of Jehoshaphat,* some understand the narrow valley through which the brook Kedron flows, between the city of Jerusalem and the mount of Olives. To this valley or glen, in which is the celebrated burying-place of the Jews, the Rabbins have appropriated the name, and maintain, that in it the final judgment of the world is to be held; —a conceit in which they have been followed by many Christian writers, as well as by the Mohammedans. Others suppose it to be a designation of the valley, otherwise called עֵמֶק בְּרָכָה, *the valley of blessing,* 2 Chron. xx. 26 ; but as neither of these localities at all comports with the magnitude of the subject treated of by the prophet, we have no alternative but that of considering the words, not as constituting a proper name, or the name of any specific locality, but as symbolical in their import, and designed to characterise the theatre of the bloody wars that took place after the Babylonish captivity, by which the hostile nations contiguous to Judæa had signal vengeance inflicted upon them. They literally signify, *the valley where Jehovah judgeth,* and mean the scene of divine judgments. The term *valley* appears to have been selected on account of such locality being mentioned in Scripture as the usual theatre of military conflict. This view of the subject is supported by the Targ., in which the words are not retained, but translated מֵישַׁר פְּלוֹג דִּינָא, *the plain of the distribution of judgment,* and by the translation of Theodot., τὴν

χώραν τῆς κρίσεως. The nations to be punished are restricted, ver. 2, to such as should have scattered the Jews, and occupied their land. Comp. chap. ii. 17.

3. The Jews were frequently treated in the most ignominious manner by their enemies. Such conduct is here affectingly set forth. That it was customary to cast lots for those who were taken captive, see Obad. ver. 11 ; Nah. iii. 10. The giving of a boy for a whore, does not mean the exchange of the one for the other, but the payment of the captive for an act of sensual indulgence ; just as the selling of a girl for wine, means giving her in compensation for a draught of it. Comp. Gen. xxxviii. 17 ; comp. also Deut. xxiii. 19 (Eng. 18), where אֶתְנַן זוֹנָה, *the hire of a whore,* is coupled with מְחִיר כֶּלֶב, *the price of a dog ;* and the Arabic proverb, ابن زانية بزيت

the son of a whore hired with oil. Meid. xciv. Charden mentions that when the Tartars came into Poland, they carried off all the children they could, and, finding at length that they were not redeemed, sold them at the low price of a crown. In Mingrelia, he adds, they sell them for provisions, and for wine.

4. Among the nations bordering on the country of the Jews, which had rendered themselves particularly obnoxious to the divine wrath, were those on the west, for which see on Is. xxiii. and xiv. 28. וְגַם מָה אַתֶּם לִי, *and truly what are ye to me?* Think ye that I make any account of you? or that ye can successfully oppose yourselves to me? The interrogation is altogether different in meaning, as it is in form, from the idiom

If, indeed, ye retaliate upon me,
Speedily and swiftly I will bring your retaliation
Back upon your own head.

5 Because ye have taken away my silver and my gold;
And my goodly objects of delight
Ye have carried into your temples;

6 And have sold the sons of Judah and the sons of Jerusalem
To the sons of the Javanites,
That they might be removed far from their own border.

7 Behold! I will rouse them from the place
Whither ye have sold them;
And bring back your retaliation
Upon your own head;

8 I will also sell your sons and your daughters
Into the hand of the sons of Judah,

מַה־לִּי וְלָכֶם, *what have we in common?* with which Kimchi compares it. גְּלִילוֹת, *circuits, districts.* Comp. Josh. xiii. 2, where the word is rendered *borders* in our version. They were properly provinces, of which there were five in number, each governed by a סֶרֶן, *prince,* or *lord.* כֹּל, *all,* before גְּלִילוֹת, expresses contempt. אִם, is not here correlate with הַ, in הֲגְמוּל, but puts a fresh case for the sake of argument. The case supposed, however, was true in fact. The interrogative ה assumes here the form of the article, as in several other places. See on Amos v. 25. גָּמַל, signifies to *do good* or *evil* to any one; then to *recompense* him, either with good or evil; to *reward, retaliate.* The meaning here seems to be, that if these bordering states, taking advantage of certain untoward circumstances in the history of the Jews, attempted to revenge the victories gained over them by the latter, they should be dealt with in the way of divine retaliation. Jehovah here speaks of what was done to his people as done to himself. Comp. Zech. ii. 8; Matt. xxv. 40. קַל מְהֵרָה, is an asyndeton. Comp. Is. v. 26, where the order of the words is reversed.

5. As in the preceding verse God had identified himself with his people, so here he speaks of their property as his. Some suppose the precious vessels belonging to the temple to be intended by מַחֲמַדֵּי הַטֹּבִים, but the articles of private property most highly esteemed by the Jews are more probably meant; since it does not appear that ever the enemies specified by Joel plundered the temple at Jerusalem, though express mention is made of the plunder of the royal palace by the Philistines, &c., 2 Chron. xxi. 17. Comp. Hos. xiii. 15; 2 Chron. xxxvi. 19. It was customary to hang up or deposit in the idolatrous temples, as presents dedicated to the gods, certain portions of the spoils taken in war. Arrian, ii. 24. Curtius, iv. 2.

6. בְּנֵי הַיְּוָנִים, *the sons of the Javanites,* i. e. the Grecians. Comp. υἷες Ἀχαιῶν, of Homer; and see on Is. lxvi. 19. Credner, Hitzig, and some others, think that the prophet refers to Javanites of Arabia Felix, mentioned Ezek. xxvii. 19; but the reasons they adduce in favour of their opinion are insufficient to establish the point. In Ezek. xxvii. 13, Javan is mentioned, along with Tubal and Meshech, as trading in the persons of men with the merchants of Tyre. Slavery formed an important article of Phœnician commerce, and equally so of that carried on by the Greeks, to whom the former might easily convey the Jewish captives. So famous did the island of Delos become as a slave mart, that sometimes 10,000 were bought and sold in a single day.

7, 8. שְׁבָאִים, *Sabæans;* Pococke's Arab. MSS. اهل اليمن, *the people of Jemen.*

> And they shall sell them to the Sabæans, to a distant nation;
> For Jehovah hath spoken it.
>
> 9   Proclaim ye this among the nations;
> Prepare war; rouse the mighty;
> Let all the warriors approach; let them come up.
>
> 10   Beat your coulters into swords,
> And your pruning-hooks into spears;
> Let the feeble say, I am mighty.
>
> 11   Hasten and come, all ye nations around,
> And gather yourselves together;
> Thither cause thy mighty ones to come down, O Jehovah!
>
> 12   Let the nations be roused, let them come up

See on Is. lx. 6. As the Sabæans traded with India, it is not improbable that רָחוֹק, *distant*, may be designed to include that part of the East; though it is said of the Queen of Sheba, that she came ἐκ τῶν περάτων τῆς γῆς, Matt. xii. 42. This prophecy was fulfilled before and during the rule of the Maccabees, when the Jewish affairs were in so flourishing a state, and the Phœnician and Philistine powers were reduced by the Persian arms under Artaxerxes Mnemon, Darius Ochus, and especially Alexander and his successors. On the capture of Tyre by the Grecian monarch, 13,000 of its inhabitants were sold into slavery. When he took Gaza also, he put 10,000 of the citizens to death, and sold the rest, with the women and children, for slaves. Favourable, on the other hand, as he was to the Jews, there can be no doubt that he ordered the liberation of such of them as were captives in Greece.

9. זאֹת, *this*, refers to what immediately follows: the assembling of the different nations, in order to engage in the wars in which, in succession, they were, as political states, to be subdued and perish. קַדְּשׁוּ, is not simply to *prepare*, as Kimchi explains it, but to prepare by the use of religious rites and ceremonies, such as the heathen employed when they undertook a military enterprise.

10. Here a state of things is presented to view, directly the opposite of what was to exist in the days of the Messiah, Is. ii. 4; Micah iv. 3. Such was to be the extent of the conflict, that, in the lack of a sufficient number of arms, the

ordinary implements of husbandry would be converted into weapons.

> "———— squalent abductis arva
> colonis,
> Et curvæ rigidum falces conflantur in
> ensem."
>
> *Virgil. Georg.* i. 507.

> "Sarcula cessabant, versique in pila
> ligones,
> Factaque de rastri pondere cassis erat."
> *Ovid. Fast.* i. 699.

11. עוּשׁ, a ἅπαξ λεγ. in all probability the same in signification with חוּשׁ, *to hasten*. The ancient versions follow the LXX. who render, συναθροίζεσθε.

Arab. عَاشَ, *vitam duxit, vixit;* hence

the idea of *liveliness, activity, agility,* &c. הַנְחַת, is the Imperative in Hiphil of נָחַת, *to descend,* go or come down. The place whither, is the scene of warfare, the valley of Jehoshaphat, implied in שָׁמָּה, which, with the ה, is frequently the same in signification with שָׁם. The abrupt transition to Jehovah has a powerful effect. Whatever might be the individual views of those engaged in the conflict, they were the instruments of Divine wrath, and are on this account called the "mighty ones" of Jehovah. Comp. Is. x. 5—7.

12. To give prominence to the interest which God had in what was to take place, the metaphor is here changed into that of a judicial process, in which

To the valley of Jehoshaphat;
For there I will sit to judge all the nations around.

13   Put ye in the sickle, for the harvest is ripe;
Come, descend, for the wine-press is full,
The vats run over;
For their wickedness is great.

14   Multitudes! multitudes,
In the valley of decision!
For the day of Jehovah is near,
In the valley of decision.

15   The sun and the moon shall be darkened,
And the stars shall withdraw their shine.

16   For Jehovah shall roar out of Zion,

he acts as judge, and gives a just decision against the enemies of his people. For עֵמֶק יְהוֹשָׁפָט, see on ver. 2. Here, as in that verse, the nations to be punished were those מִסָּבִיב, *circumjacent* to Judæa.

13. The prophet now employs metaphors taken from the harvest and the vintage which strikingly express the havoc and destruction effected by war; the one denoting the slaughter or cutting down of armies, and the other the effusion of their blood. The same images are similarly employed, Is. xvii. 5, 6; lxiii. 2; Lam. i. 15; and especially Rev. xiv. 14—20. מַגָּל, *a sickle*, Arab. منجل,

Syr. ܡܓܠܐ. In Arab. the root, نجل,

signifies *to cut*. The sickles of the East, as represented on Egyptian monuments, pretty much resembled ours, only some of them were smaller, and had more the appearance of a knife hooked at the end. רְדוּ, from יָרַד, *to descend*, some take to be used here in the acceptation of Arab. ردى, *calcavit*. Thus the LXX.

πατεῖτε. But as in order to tread the grapes it was necessary to *go down* into the wine-press, it seems better to abide by the ordinary signification of the Hebrew verb, and to consider the action of treading to be implied, rather than expressed. At the close of the verse the metaphor is dropped, and the cause of the thing signified is boldly presented to view.

14. הֲמוֹנִים הֲמוֹנִים, *multitudes, multitudes*, a Hebraism for *immense multitudes*. This rendering is preferable to that of *tumults*. In the preceding verses, the nations are called upon to assemble, and here the prophet, beholding them congregated in obedience to the summons, breaks out into an appropriate exclamation in regard to their number. חָרוּץ, Piscator, the Geneva English, Calvin, Leo Juda, Michaelis, Justi, Holzhausen, and Credner, take in the sense of *threshing*. Kimchi, Tanchum, Abulwalid, Newcome, and some others, render *excision;* but the LXX., Theodot., Syr., Targ., Theodoret, Dathe, Rosenmüller, Gesenius, Hitzig, Maurer, Ewald, and Fürst, translate the word by *decision* or *judgment*, which seems more in keeping with the name of the valley, and the idea of a judicial process, set forth ver. 12. Comp. for the acceptation *to determine, decide*, as attaching to the verb חָרַץ, 1 Kings xx. 40; Is. x. 22. The meaning is the decision or doom of the nations to which the prophecy refers. The repetition of עֵמֶק הֶחָרוּץ, heightens the effect.

15. A figurative mode of representing the removal of the political rulers of the world. Comp. chap. ii. 10, 31.

16. These words, as Chandler properly remarks, seem to intimate very plainly, that at least part of the judgments here threatened to be executed upon the neighbouring nations, should be executed by the Jews themselves. They doubtless refer to the victories obtained by Mattathias, and his sons the Maccabæans. As

And utter his voice from Jerusalem,
And the heavens and the earth shall shake;
But Jehovah is a refuge for his people,
Even a stronghold for the sons of Israel.

17 And ye shall know that I Jehovah am your God,
Dwelling in Zion, my holy mountain:
Then shall Jerusalem be holy;
And foreigners shall invade her no more.

18 And it shall come to pass in that day,
That the mountains shall drop new wine,
And the hills shall flow with milk,
And all the channels of Judah shall flow with water,
And a fountain shall go forth from the house of Jehovah,
And water the valley of Acacias.

king of the Jewish nation, Jehovah had his residence in Jerusalem, whence he caused his power to be exerted to the discomfiture of his enemies, and the deliverance and protection of his people. Comp. Ps. xviii. 13; Hab. iii. 10, 11. שָׁאַג, to roar, is properly used of the lion, but is metaphorically applied to God, to express the terrible majesty with which he encounters his foes. Comp. Jer. xxv. 30; Amos i. 2; iii. 8; Hos. xi. 10.

17. יָדַע, is here, as in Is. lii. 6; lx. 16; Hos. ii. 20, to be taken in the acceptation of *experiencing*, knowing by experimental proofs of the divine kindness. This the Jews did in the deliverances effected on their behalf, after the return from the captivity, especially on the death of Antiochus Epiphanes, and in the enjoyment of their national and religious privileges, till the termination of their polity. That the strong language at the close of the verse does not imply a state of immunity from invasion, to which there was absolutely to be an end, will appear on comparing Is. lii. 1, and Nah. i. 15. See my note on the former of these passages. From the death of Antiochus till the coming of the Messiah, no hostile power should take possession of the holy city. To express the perfect immunity from idolatry, by which Jerusalem should be characterised, קֹדֶשׁ, *holiness* in the abstract, is used. Comp. Obad. 17. By זָרִים, *strangers*, or *barbarians*, foreign enemies are meant.

18. A splendid figurative representation of the extraordinary prosperity to be accorded to the Jewish people after the destruction of their enemies. Thus Tanchum in Pococke, استعارة لكثرة الخصب والبركات, "metaphorical language, denoting abundance of plenty and blessings." Comp. Is. xxx. 23—25; xliv. 3; and especially Amos ix. 13.

"Flumina jam lactis, jam flumina nectaris ibant,
Flavaque de viridi stillabant ilice mella."
Ovid. Metam. i. 111.

Καὶ τοτε δὴ χαρὰν μεγάλην θεὸς ἀνδράσι δώσει.
Καὶ γὰρ γῆ καὶ δένδρα καὶ ἄσπετα θρέμματα γαίης
Δώσουσι καρπὸν τὸν ἀληθινὸν ἀνθρώποισιν
Οἴνου, καὶ μέλιτος γλυκέως, λευκοῦ τε γάλακτος,
Καὶ σίτου, ὅπερ ἔστι βροτοῖς κάλλιστον ἁπάντων.
Sibyl. Orac.

נַחַל הַשִּׁטִּים, *the valley of Shittim*, i.e. *Acacias*. There was a place of this name in the country of Moab, Num. xxv. 1; xxxiii. 49; Josh. ii. 1; but most interpreters think that the valley is meant through which the Kidron flows to the Dead Sea. Consistency of interpretation

19 Egypt shall become desolate,
And Edom a desolate wilderness,
For the violence done to the sons of Judah,
Because they shed innocent blood in their land.

20 But Judah shall be inhabited for ever,
And Jerusalem to successive generations.

21 And I will regard their blood as innocent,
Which I have not regarded as innocent;
And Jehovah shall dwell in Zion.

requires us to understand this part of the verse figuratively of the most desert and arid spots, such as the acacia is fond of. Fertility was to go forth from the presence of Jehovah into the whole land. Viewed in this light, there is no incongruity in representing the water as extending even across the Jordan, however impossible it might be as a physical phenomenon. Comp. Ezek. xlvii. 1—12; Zech. xiv. 8.

19. The wrongs done to the Jews by the Egyptians and Idumæans, which the prophet here declares were to be avenged, were those committed at different times after the captivity. Palestine suffered greatly during the wars between the Syrian and Egyptian kings, especially in the reign of Ptolemy Epiphanes, when the Jews exposed themselves to the indignation of that king by siding with Antiochus the Great. In the time of Cleopatra also, her son Lathyrus gained a victory over the army of Alexander Jannæus, in which the Jews lost upwards of thirty thousand men: and who, to increase the terror of his name, massacred the women and children, cut their bodies in pieces, and boiled the flesh. The Idumæans, though less formidable, never omitted any favourable opportunity that offered of showing their hostility to the Jews. The condition to which both these countries were speedily reduced, and in which they have remained to the present day, verifies the prediction here delivered. Instead of לִשְׁמָמָה, a number of MSS. exhibit the synonymous לִשְׁמָה.—חֲמַס בְּנֵי יְהוּדָה, *the violence of the sons of Judah*, is the Genitive of object, meaning the violence done *to* them. Comp. Obad. 10. נָקִי is spelt נָקִיא here and Jonah i. 14; but in the present text, nine of Kennicott's

MSS. and four of De Rossi's, with eight more originally, read נָקִי. Among these are four Spanish MSS., two of which De Rossi characterises as *accuratissimi.* The pronominal affix in אַרְצָם, refers to the Jews spoken of immediately before.

20. תֵּשֵׁב, is used passively, as in Is. xiii. 20. עוֹלָם and דּוֹר וָדוֹר, are to be limited by the subject of which they are predicated. Thus the state of desolation during the seventy years' captivity in Babylon, is said to be עוֹלָם, *for ever,* Jer. xviii. 16.

21. In the words וְנִקֵּיתִי דָּמָם לֹא נִקֵּיתִי, there is an ellipsis of אֲשֶׁר, after דָּמָם, the affix in which refers to the Jews, not to their enemies. Almost all the interpreters have stumbled at נִקֵּיתִי, the verb here employed, but they have generally got over the difficulty, by giving to it the signification of נָקַמְתִּי, *I have avenged*—a signification which nowhere attaches to it in the Hebrew Bible. For the different explanations, see Pococke. נָקָה,

Arab. نَقِيَ, *purus, mundus fuit,* ii. and iv. *mundavit.* Syr. in Pael, *sacrificavit, libavit.* In Niph. the Heb. verb signifies *to be morally pure, to be free from punishment;* in Piel, as here, *to regard, pronounce,* or *treat as innocent, to pardon.* The words were doubtless suggested by דָּם נָקִיא in the nineteenth verse, and are to be rendered, *I will regard their blood as innocent, which I have not regarded as innocent;* i. e. I will pardon those whom I have treated as guilty. My people, whom I have punished on account of their apostasies, I will henceforth regard with favour and love. The affix ם in דָּמָם, corresponds to the same in אַרְצָם, ver. 19.—שֹׁכֵן, the Participle used with futurity of signification.

AMOS

PREFACE

AMOS (Heb. עָמוֹס, *burden*, a word purely Hebrew, and not of Egyptian origin, and the same as Amasis or Amosis, as Gesenius conjectures) was, as we learn from the inscription, a native of Tekoah, a small town in the tribe of Judah, at the distance of about twelve miles south-east of Jerusalem. The country round being sandy and barren, was destitute of cultivation, and fit only to be occupied by those addicted to pastoral life. Among these our prophet was originally found; and, though it was counted no disgrace in ancient times, any more than it is at the present day in Arabia, to follow this occupation, kings themselves being found in it, (2 Kings iii. 4,) yet there is no reason to suppose that Amos belonged to a family of rank or influence, but the contrary. No mention is made of his father; but too much stress is not to be laid upon this circumstance. That he had been brought up in poverty, however, appears from the statement made chap. vii. 14; from which also it is incontrovertible, that no change of circumstances intervened which may be supposed to have been more favourable to mental culture, but that he was called at once to exchange the life of a shepherd for that of a prophet.

Though a native of the kingdom of Judah, he discharged the functions of his office in that of Israel—a fact which is to be accounted for, not, as Bertholdt conjectures, on the ground of some personal relations, but by an express Divine commission to occupy it as the scene of his labours. Eichhorn ingeniously supposes the reasons of his selection to have been, that the appearance of a foreign prophet was much more calculated to excite attention than that of a native, and that such a prophet was more likely to command respect than any belonging to a kingdom in which impostors and fanatics abounded.

The time at which he prophesied is stated in general terms, chap. i. 1, to have been in the reigns of Uzziah, king of Judah, and Jeroboam II., king of Israel, the former of whom reigned B. C. 811—759, and the latter B. C. 825—784, but in which of these years he was called to the office, and how long he continued to exercise it, we are not told. Even if any dependence could be placed upon the Jewish tradition, Joseph. Antiq. ix. 10, 4, and Jerome on Amos i. 1, that the earthquake mentioned here, and Zech. xiv. 5, took place when Uzziah attempted to usurp the sacerdotal functions, we should still be unable to fix the exact date, since it is uncertain in what year the attempt was made.

That he was contemporary with Hosea, appears not only from the dates assigned in both their books, but from the identical state of affairs in the kingdom of the ten tribes, which they so graphically describe. Whether he flourished also in the days of Isaiah and Micah cannot be determined.

As we have already found from the prophecy of Hosea, idolatry, with its concomitant evils, effeminacy, dissoluteness, and immoralities of every description, reigned with uncontrolled sway among the Israelites in the reign of Jeroboam the son of Joash. It is chiefly against these evils that the denunciations of Amos are directed.

The book may properly be divided into three parts: First, sentences pronounced against the Syrians, the Philistines, the Phœnicians, the Edomites, the Ammonites, the Moabites, the Jews, and the Israelites, chapters i. and ii. Second, special discourses delivered against Israel, chapters iii.—vi. Third, visions, partly of a consolatory, and partly of a comminatory nature, in which reference is had both to the times that were to pass over the ten tribes, previous to the coming of the Messiah, and to what was to take place under his reign, chapters vii.—ix.

In point of style, Amos holds no mean place among the prophets. The declaration of Jerome, that he was *imperitus sermone*, has not been justified by modern critics. On the contrary, it is universally allowed that, though destitute of sublimity, he is distinguished for perspicuity and regularity, embellishment and elegance, energy and fulness. His images are mostly original, and taken from the natural scenery with which he was familiar; his rhythmus is smooth and flowing; and his parallelisms are in a high degree natural and complete. In description, he is for the most part special and local; he excels in the minuteness of his groupings, while the general vividness of his manner imparts a more intense interest to all that he delivers. In some few instances, as in chapters iv. vi. and vii., the language approaches more to the prose style, or is entirely that of narrative.

From chap. vii. 10—13, it appears that the scene of his ministry was Bethel. Whether he left that place in consequence of the interdict of Amaziah, the priest, we know not. According to Pseudo-Epiphanius, he afterwards returned to his native place, where he died, and was buried with his fathers; but no dependence can be placed on the statement.

CHAPTER I

After a chronological and general introduction, ver. 1, 2, this chapter contains a heavy charge, accompanied with denunciations, against the Syrians of Damascus, 3—5; the Philistines, 6—8; the Phœnicians, 9, 10; the Idumæans, 11, 12; and the Ammonites, 13—15.

---

1 THE words of Amos, who was among the shepherds of Tekoah, which he saw concerning Israel, in the days of Uzziah, king of Judah, and in the days of Jeroboam, the son of Joash, king of Israel, two years before the earthquake.

1. With the exception of the book of Jeremiah, that of Amos is the only one of the prophets commencing with דִּבְרֵי, "The words of—." Comp., however, Hag. i. 12. The meaning is, the subjects or matters of oracular communication which he was employed by the prophetic Spirit to deliver, and which were now, under the influence of the same Spirit, committed to writing. Their divine origin is clearly determined by what is added, אֲשֶׁר חָזָה, "which he saw," i.e. which were supernaturally presented to his mental vision. See on Is. i. 1. The preposition בְּ in בַּנֹּקְדִים, does not denote distinction, intimating that Amos was greater in point of wealth or respectability than the rest of the shepherds, as Kimchi would have it, but simply that he was of their number; he belonged to their condition of life, and followed their occupation. The phrase הָיָה בַנֹּקְדִים expresses, in fact, nothing more than הָיָה נֹקֵד. Comp. for similar usage, 1 Sam. xix. 24; Ps. cxviii. 7; and the Arabic وما نحن بعالين.

נֹקֵד occurs only here, and 2 Kings iii. 4. By some it is supposed to denote the shepherd or keeper of a species of sheep and goats, distinguished by certain marks, and to be derived from נָקַד, to prick, or mark with punctures, and so to distinguish by such marks. By others, it is more properly referred for illustration to the Arab. نقد, genus ovium deforme et brevipes; and نقاد, ovium, نقد appellatarum, pastor. From the disesteem in which such animals were held, arose the proverb, لذل من النقد, more vile than the NIKAD. At the same time, as their wool was valuable, they were kept in great numbers. In both instances in which the term occurs, it seems to be used in a more general acceptation. Aq. ἐν ποιμνοτρόφοις; Symm. and the fifth edit. ἐν τοῖς ποιμέσιν. The explanation of Cyril is not inept: Ἀμὼς γέγονεν αἰπόλος ἀνὴρ καὶ ποιμενικοῖς ἔθεσί τε καὶ νόμοις ἐντεθραμμένος. The LXX. ἐν Ἀκκαρείμ, mistaking it for the name of a place where they supposed the prophet to have been when he received his Divine communications. The ruins of תְּקוֹעַ Arab. تقوع, Tekû'a, Dr. Robinson found

2   And he said:

Jehovah roareth from Zion,

And uttereth his voice from Jerusalem;

Therefore the pastures of the shepherds mourn,

And the summit of Carmel withereth.

3   Thus saith Jehovah:

For three transgressions of Damascus,

---

covering an extent of four or five acres on an elevated hill, not steep, but broad at the top, about two hours distant from Bethlehem. On approaching it, he describes the landscape as rocky and sterile, yet rich in pasturage, as was testified by the multitude of the flocks. (Palestine, ii. pp. 181, 182.) The surrounding region, especially that in the direction of the Dead Sea, is called מִדְבַּר תְּקוֹעַ, 2 Chron. xx. 20, and ἡ ἔρεμος Θεκωέ, 1 Macc. ix. 33. In this pasturing district, our prophet originally tended his flocks, and collected the sycamore figs. For the dates here specified, see the Introduction. The prophecy is specially directed against Israel, or the kingdom of the ten tribes, though that of Judah, and likewise several foreign states, are also expressly denounced. We possess no data by which to fix the year in which the earthquake, here mentioned, occurred. Zechariah, chap. xiv. 5, refers to it as having happened in the days of Uzziah, but he does not specify the year. According to Josephus, it took place on occasion of the invasion of the sacerdotal office by that monarch, Antiq. ix. 10, 4. As earthquakes are by no means uncommon in Palestine, it must have been unusually severe to entitle it to the speciality of reference here employed. Some interpret רַעַשׁ of a civil commotion, but without sufficient ground, as the connexion Zech. xiv. 4, 5, shows.

2. Zion, or Jerusalem, being the central point of the theocracy, was the special residence of Jehovah, to whom the judgments afterwards denounced, are, in highly figurative language, immediately referred. שָׁאַג, commonly employed to express the roaring of the lion, is here used to set forth the awful character of those judgments. Dathe, stumbling at the boldness of the figure, renders, *Jova e Zione dira pronunciat;* thereby destroying the poetical force of the language. Comp. Jer. xxv. 30; Job xxxvii. 4. ו in וְאָבְלוּ, marks the apodosis. For נְאוֹת הָרֹעִים, comp. נְאוֹת דֶּשֶׁא, Ps. xxiii. 2. כַּרְמֶל, Michaelis, Justi, and others, take to be the Carmel, now called by the Arabs كُرْمُل, *Kurmul,* which lies near Yutta, or Juttah, between two and three hours to the south of Hebron; but though the mountainous region about that place was more in the proximity of the prophet, yet the established scripture reference to the fertility of the celebrated Mount Carmel in the tribe of Asher seems to entitle the latter to the preference. In fact, there does not appear to be any mountain deserving the name in the hill country of Judah. The hill of Maon, which is close by, is not less than two hundred feet higher than the site of the ruins of the castle of Kurmul. See Robinson, *ut sup.* pp. 193—200. Besides the identical phrase, רֹאשׁ הַכַּרְמֶל, *the summit of Carmel,* which again occurs chap. ix. 3, in immediate connexion with the sea, is employed in application to the western Carmel, 1 Kings xviii. 42.

3. Here begins a series of minatory predictions against different states, which extends to chap. ii. 8, where it merges in a continued denunciation of judgments directed almost exclusively against the Israelites. Instead of proceeding at once to charge the ten tribes with the flagrant evils of which they had been guilty, Amos commences with the Syrians, and, after exposing their wickedness, and that of the Philistines, the Phœnicians, the Edomites, the Ammonites, the Moabites, and the Jews, he comes to his proper subject, on which he dwells throughout the rest of the book. Having roused the indignation of those among whom he prophesied, against sin as exhibited in others, he charges it

And for four, I will not reverse it ;
Because they threshed Gilead with threshing-sledges of iron.

4 But I will send a fire into the house of Hazael,
And it shall devour the palaces of Benhadad.

5 I will also break the barrier of Damascus,
And cut off the ruler from the valley of Aven,

home upon themselves. Each of the eight predictions is ushered in by the solemn כֹּה אָמַר יְהוָֹה, *thus saith Jehovah ;* and consists, in part, in a repetition of the same symmetrical stanzas, with an intermixture of matter, varying according to the nature of the subjects treated of. Interpreters differ in regard to the precise meaning of the use made by our prophet of the numerals *three* and *four.* Similar formulæ are frequent in Hebrew. See Exod. xx. 5 ; Job v. 19 ; xxxiii. 14, 29 ; Prov. xxx. 15, 18, 21, 29 ; Eccles. xi. 2 ; Is. xvii. 6 ; Mic. v. 5 (Heb. 4). Comp. the τρὶς καὶ τετράκις of Homer ; the *terque quaterque* of Virgil ; and the *ter et quater* of Horace. The notion, that the two numbers are to be added so as to bring out the perfect number *seven,* and thus to express the completeness or full measure of the iniquity, is not borne out by Hebrew usage. That the numbers are to be taken literally, as in Prov. xxx. where there is an enumeration of each of the particulars, is equally out of the question ; the specification of the prophet being, in each case, limited to a single act of wickedness. Nor can the construction be admitted, I have not punished Damascus, &c. on account of three transgressions, but on account of a fourth I will punish her ; since לֹא אֲשִׁיבֶנּוּ, obviously connects with both numerals. The only satisfactory mode of explication is, to regard the phrase as intensively proverbial, and designed to express multiplied or repeated delinquencies, of which the last, as the most atrocious, is uniformly described. The noun to which the suffix in אֲשִׁיבֶנּוּ relates, is not expressed, either before or after the verb, on the principle, that the subject referred to would naturally suggest itself to the mind of the reader. It is anticipative of the sentence of punishment delivered in the following verses. Comp. Num. xxiii. 20, in which is an ellipsis of the noun בְּרָכָה, the idea of which is expressed

by the verb. Bp. Lowth proposes to render, "I will not restore it ;" but without sufficient authority. שׁוּב שְׁבוּת, "to reverse the captivity," is the phrase employed in such case. In the phrase, "I will not reverse," is a litotes—the meaning being, "I will certainly execute." For Damascus, which, as the metropolis, is put for the kingdom of Syria, see on Is. xvii. 1. The cruel treatment of the inhabitants of Gilead here referred to, is that to which they were subjected by Hazael and Benhadad, 2 Kings x. 32, 33 ; xiii. 3—7 ; both of which princes Amos mentions by name, ver. 4. It consisted in their being thrown before the threshing-sledges, the sharp teeth of iron in the rollers of which tore and mangled their bodies. See on Is. xxviii. 27 ; and comp. 2 Sam. xii. 31, where we find the same punishment inflicted by David, by the law of retaliation. חֲרֻצוֹת, the LXX. render πρίοσι σιδηροῖς, and add unwarrantably, τὰς ἐν γαστρὶ ἐχούσας ; Symm. and Theod. τροχοῖς σιδηροῖς. דּוּשׁ, *to thresh,* is the very term used in the history of the transaction, 2 Kings xiii. 7. Gilead comprehended the whole of the territory beyond the Jordan, belonging to the tribes of Reuben and Gad, and the half tribe of Manasseh ; and as it bordered on the kingdom of the Syrians, was particularly exposed to their attacks.

4. The Benhadad here mentioned was the son and successor of Hazael, and not the king of that name whom Hazael succeeded. Comp. 2 Kings viii. 7, 15, with xiii. 3, 24. A similar prediction was afterwards delivered by Jeremiah, chap. xlix. 27, from which and from Hos. viii. 14, it is evident that the phraseology employed by Amos here, and verses 7, 10, 12, 14, chap. ii. 2, 5, is not peculiar to that prophet.

5. According to the testimony of a native, whom Michaelis consulted, there is a most delightful valley called *Oon,* about four hours distant from Damascus,

And the sceptre-holder from Beth-Eden ;
And the people of Syria shall go captive to Kir,
Saith Jehovah.

6　　Thus saith Jehovah :
For three transgressions of Gaza,
And for four, I will not reverse it ;
Because they effected a complete captivity,
To deliver it up to Edom.

towards the desert, which has given rise to a proverb, "Have you ever been in the valley of Oon ?" meaning, Have you ever been in a place of delight ? As, however, this has not been confirmed by any traveller, most expositors are inclined to refer the place to what is otherwise called בִּקְעַת הַלְּבָנוֹן, "the valley of Lebanon," or البقاع, *el Buká'a*, between the ridges of Lebanon and Anti-Lebanon. Here are the celebrated ruins of the temple of Baalbec, the Syrian Heliopolis, to which the LXX. have expressly referred אָוֶן, *Aven*, only pronouncing it אוֹן, *On*—ἐκ πεδίον Ὤν; just as they have rendered the latter word when it is employed to denote the city of the same name in Egypt, which was dedicated to the sun. The Hebrews in Palestine, to express their abhorrence of the idolatrous worship practised at both places, pronounced the word אָוֶן, *Aven*, which properly signifies *nothingness, vanity*, and hence an *idol*, on account of its inutility. Comp. with the present passage Ezek. xxx. 17. יוֹשֵׁב does not here denote inhabitant, or inhabitants generally, but as the parallel תוֹמֵךְ שֵׁבֶט, *sceptre-holder*, shows, one who *sits* upon, or occupies a throne—a judge, prince, or king—the person exercising authority in the district specified. For the latter phrase, the σκηπτοῦχος of Homer may be compared. בֵּית עֶדֶן, *Beth-Eden* was, in all probability, the locality in the mountains of Lebanon, which Ptolemy, v. 15, calls Παράδεισος ; where the royal family had a palace, and where one of its members usually resided. The name is still given to a delectable valley to the west of Damascus. The *Aram*, or Syria, here referred to, is that of which Damascus was the capital. By קִיר, *Kir*, is meant the river and region of the Cyrus in Iberia, now called *Kur*.

See on Is. xxii. 6 ; and for the accomplishment of the prediction in the successful expedition of Tiglathpileser, king of Assyria, 2 Kings xvi. 9. The version of the LXX. is here extremely faulty, as the slightest comparison with the original will show.

6. עַזָּה, Arab.غِزَّة, *Ghuzzeh, Gaza*, was the southernmost of the five principal cities of the Philistines, which formed the capitals of so many satrapies of the same names. It was situated at the distance of about an hour's journey from the south-east coast of the Mediterranean, from which it was separated by low hills, and tracts of sand. It was built upon a hill, and strongly fortified, as the name imports. The modern city is built partly on the hill, but mostly on the plain below ; and, according to Dr. Robinson, contains a population of about 15,000 souls. It must have been a place of high antiquity, for its name occurs in the genealogical table, Gen. x. ; and it occupied so commanding a position, that it formed the key to Palestine on the south. It stands here by synecdoche for the whole of Philistia. By גָּלוּת שְׁלֵמָה, we are neither to understand, with the LXX. αἰχμαλωσίαν τοῦ Σαλωμών; nor with Justi, "a holy or pious captivity ;" nor with Grotius and Michaelis, *captivitatem pacificam* ; but the *immense number* of captives who were carried away from Judæa in the reign of Ahaz, 2 Chron. xxviii. 18. The capture was indiscriminate and universal ; none escaped. Comp., for the phrase, Jer. xiii. 19. What aggravated the guilt of the Philistines was, that they did not treat the Jews as prisoners of war, but sold them as slaves to the Edomites, who were their bitterest enemies, and would treat them with the utmost cruelty. They were doubtless conveyed

7 But I will send a fire into the wall of Gaza,
  And it shall devour her palaces;
8 And I will cut off the ruler from Ashdod,
  And the sceptre-holder from Ashkelon;
  And will turn back my hand upon Ekron;
  And the residue of the Philistines shall perish,
  Saith the Lord Jehovah.
9   Thus saith Jehovah:
  For three transgressions of Tyre,
  And for four, I will not reverse it;
  Because they delivered up a complete captivity to Edom,
  And remembered not the covenant of the brethren.
10 But I will send a fire into the wall of Tyre,
  And it shall devour her palaces.

---

to Petra, the great emporium of commerce, and there sold to such as might purchase them. Comp. Joel iii. 4—6.

7. אֵשׁ, *fire*, is here metaphorically used for *war*, in carrying on which, however, it is often employed as one of the most destructive elements. Comp. Num. xxi. 28; Is. xxvi. 11.

8. For the meaning of יוֹשֵׁב, see on ver. 5. Three others of the principal cities of the Philistines are now threatened, אַשְׁדּוֹד, *Ashdod*, for which see on Is. xx. 1; אַשְׁקְלוֹן, Arab. عسقلان, *Askelon*, occupying a strong position on the top of a ridge of rock, which encircles it, and terminates at each end in the sea, and distant from Gaza about five hours, in the direction of NN.E.; and עֶקְרוֹן, *Ekron*, now called by the natives علقر, *Akir*, the most northerly of the five, and at some distance inland from the line of hills, which run along the coast of the Mediterranean. See Dr. Robinson's Palestine, iii. 21—25. The reason why *Gath*, the remaining city of the five, is not mentioned, is assigned by Kimchi to be its having been already subdued by David; but as it was afterwards occupied both by the Syrians, 2 Kings xii. 17, and the Philistines, 2 Chron. xxvi. 6, it seems more natural to refer its omission to the fact of its reduction by Uzziah, in the

days of our prophet, as narrated in the latter of the above passages. It is also omitted Zeph. ii. 4, 5. הֵשִׁיב יָד עַל, *to turn the hand upon*, means to exert one's power anew, whether in the way of favour or of hostility. Here it is obviously to be taken in the hostile sense. No part of Philistia was to remain unvisited by Divine judgments. Comp. Jer. xlvii. 4; Ezek. xxv. 16. In which of the reductions of the Philistines, the prediction received its fulfilment, we cannot determine. One of these took place during the reign of Uzziah, 2 Chron. xxvi. 6, 7; another in that of Hezekiah, 2 Kings xviii. 8. They were afterwards successively reduced by Psammeticus, king of Egypt, by Nebuchadnezzar, by the Persians, by Alexander, and ultimately by the Asmonæans.

9. A similar charge is here brought against the Phœnicians, with the superadded aggravation of a breach of ancient faith. Comp. Joel iii. 4—6. The בְּרִית אַחִים, *covenant of brethren*, includes the terms of friendship and mutual assistance which were agreed upon between David and Hiram, 2 Sam. v. 11; and afterwards between Solomon and the same monarch, 1 Kings v. See especially ver. 12, (Heb. ver. 26,) where it is expressly stated, that וַיִּכְרְתוּ בְרִית שְׁנֵיהֶם, "they two made a league," or *covenant*.

10. For *Tyre*, and the accomplishment of this prediction, see on Is. xxiii.

11   Thus saith Jehovah :
       For three transgressions of Edom,
       And for four, I will not reverse it ;
       Because he pursued his brother with the sword,
       And did violence to his pity,
       And his anger tore continually,
       And he retained his wrath for ever.

12   But I will send a fire into Teman,
       And it shall devour the palaces of Bozrah.

13   Thus saith Jehovah :
       For three transgressions of the sons of Ammon,
       And for four, I will not reverse it ;

11. For *Edom,* and the fulfilment of the prophecy here pronounced against it, see on Is. xxxiv. 5. The guilt of the cruelties exercised by the Idumæans upon the Jews was greatly aggravated by the circumstance of their original relationship, Obad. 10, and the unrelenting perpetual character of their hatred. שִׁחֵת רַחֲמִים, lit. *to spoil,* or *destroy compassions; i. e.* so to repress all the tender feelings of pity, as to become hardened against objects of distress. Compare the phrase, שִׁחֵת חָכְמָה, *to destroy wisdom,* Ezek. xxviii. 17. The LXX., Ital., Arab., Döderlein, Dathe, Vater, Justi, and some others, take רַחֲמִים, in the sense of רֶחֶם, *the womb,* and explain it either of pregnant females, or of the fruit of the womb, *i. e.* children; but the plural is never used in this acceptation. Aq. σπλάγχνα αὐτοῦ ; Symm. σπλάγχνα ἴδια. The

root רָחַם, Arab. رحم, Syr. ܪܚܡ, signifies

to love, in Piel, *to regard with tender affection, to cherish feelings of compassion* towards any one. The ה in שִׁמְרָה, is generally considered to be an instance of a paragogic in the third person, but it is preferable to construe it as the pronominal feminine affix, agreeing with עֶבְרָה in the nominative absolute. The absence of the Mappic forms no objection, as there are several instances of its omission where we might have expected it. The accent on the penultimate favours this construction, being occasioned solely by the absence of the Mappic. The verb, to be taken as a

feminine, must be pointed שָׁמְרָה, but this would require עֶבְרָה to be the subject instead of the object, which would be intolerably harsh. Comp. for the sentiment, and an elliptical form of the phraseology, Jer. iii. 5. The Hebrews speak of *keeping* a quality whether good or bad, when they would express its prolonged or continued exercise. See Neh. ix. 32 ; Dan. ix. 4.

12. That תֵּימָן, *Teman,* was a city, seems evident from its being mentioned along with בָּצְרָה, *Bozrah,* for which see on Is. xxxiv. 6. Though Jerome speaks of it as a region, he mentions, in his Onomasticon, a town of this name, at the distance of five miles from Petra. On the map of Burckhardt and Grimm, it is placed to the south of Wady Mûsa. It was doubtless the principal place in the district inhabited by the descendants of Teman, one of the grandsons of Esau, Gen. xxxvi. 11, 15, who were celebrated on account of their superior wisdom, Jer. xlix. 7. Comp. Obad. 8, 9, and Baruch iii. 22. Eliphaz, one of Job's friends, was a Temanite. The reason why no mention is made of Sela, or Petra, Credner thinks is to be found in the fact, that it had already been captured by Amaziah, 2 Kings xiv. 7, of whose conquests in that direction advantage was taken by his son Uzziah, ver. 22 ; 2 Chron. xxvi. 2.

13. בְּנֵי עַמּוֹן, *the Ammonites,* descendants of Lot, Gen. xix. 38, occupied the territory on the east of the Jordan, between the rivers Jabbok and Arnon, but more in the direction of the Arabian

Because they ripped up those who were pregnant in Gilead,
That they might enlarge their border.

14 But I will kindle a fire on the wall of Rabbah,
And it shall devour the palaces thereof,
With a shout in the day of battle,
With a tempest in the day of the storm.

15 Their king also shall go into captivity,
He and his princes together,
Saith Jehovah.

desert. That portion of country which lay along the Jordan, of which they had possessed themselves, originally belonged to the Amorites, which accounts for its being given to the tribe of Gad, Josh. xiii. 25. They frequently annoyed the Hebrews, but were repelled by David and several of his successors. For the sake of plunder, they joined the Chaldæans on their invasion of Judæa; and, even after the captivity, they evinced the same hostile disposition. They were severely chastised by Judas Maccabæus, 1 Macc. v. 6, 7. Justin Martyr speaks of them as still a numerous people in his day, Ἀμμανιτῶν ἔστι νῦν πολὺ πλῆθος. Dial. cum Tryph. p. 347. Ed. Paris, 1615. The atrocious cruelty here charged upon the Ammonites, appears to have formed no unusual part of the barbarities practised by the ancients in war. Comp. 2 Kings viii. 12; xv. 16; Hos. xiii. 16; and my note on the last passage. See also 1 Sam. xi. 2. The object of the Ammonites was to effect an utter extermination of the Israelites inhabiting the mountainous regions of Gilead, in order that they might extend their own territory in that direction.

14. רַבָּה, Rabbah, i. e. "the Great," was the metropolis of the country of the Ammonites, the extensive ruins of which have recently been discovered by Seetzen and Burckhardt on the banks of the river Moiet Amman, which empties itself into the Jabbok. The full form of the name was רַבַּת בְּנֵי עַמּוֹן, Deut. iii. 11, by which it was distinguished from Rabbah of Moab, and a city of the same name in the tribe of Judah. It is called Ῥαβαθάμμανα by Polybius and Stephen of Byzantium; but it otherwise went among the Greeks by the name of Φιλαδέλφεια, which it

derived from Ptolemy Philadelphus. It is now known by that of عمان, Amman, the same given to it by Abulfeda in his Tab. Syr. p. 91. By תְּרוּעָה, is meant the tremendous shouts which eastern armies give at the commencement of battle, partly to excite their courage, and partly to strike terror into the enemy. Comp. Exod. xxxii. 17; Josh. vi. 5, 20. Thus the Iliad, iii. 1, &c.—

Αὐτὰρ ἐπεὶ κόσμηθεν ἅμ' ἡγεμόνεσσιν
　ἕκαστοι,
Τρῶες μὲν κλαγγῇ τ', ἐνοπῇ τ' ἴσαν,
　ὄρνιθες ὥς·
Ἤΰτε περ κλαγγὴ γεράνων, κ. τ. λ.

סַעַר, hurricane, and סוּפָה, storm or tempest, mark the resistless force of the onset, and the utterly destructive consequences resulting from it. That they are poetically applied to the warlike operations against Rabbah, is clear from יוֹם סוּפָה, the day of storm, being parallel with יוֹם מִלְחָמָה, the day of battle.

15. מַלְכָּם, their king, the Syr. and Vulg. have understood of Malcam or Milcom, i. e. Moloch, an idol of the Ammonites and Moabites; but the LXX. and Targ. support the common rendering, which שָׂרָיו, his princes, following, would seem absolutely to require. It is true, this term might be taken figuratively to signify priests, as in Is. xliii. 28; and such interpretation might appear to be countenanced by the occurrence of כֹּהֲנָיו, his priests, in the parallel prophecy of Jeremiah, chap. xlix. 3; but the use of שָׂרָיו, his princes, immediately after by that prophet, shows that if the former term be not an interpolation, it denotes the idolatrous priests who were in attendance upon the king, just as the princes were

the chiefs and civil officers about the
court. Οἱ ἱερεῖς αὐτῶν, which the LXX.
have added in Amos, and which is copied
in the Syr. and Arab., was probably
borrowed from the passage in Jeremiah;
or it may have been inserted in the Greek
text by some copyist before these other
versions were made. The combination
of שָׂרִים, *princes*, with שֹׁפֵט, *judge*, chap.
ii. 3, confirms the above interpretation.

CHAPTER II.

In this chapter we have the continuation of charges and denunciations against
different nations, as the Moabites, 1—3; the Jews, 4, 5; and finally, the Israelites,
who were to form the principal objects of the prophet's ministry, 6—8. Amos
then proceeds to insist on their ungrateful conduct, notwithstanding the experience which they had had of distinguished favours at the hand of God, 9—13;
and the futility of all hopes of escape which they might be led to entertain,
14—16.

1　Thus saith Jehovah:
　　For three transgressions of Moab,
　　And for four, I will not reverse it;
　　Because they calcined the bones of the King of Edom.
2　But I will send a fire into Moab,
　　And it shall devour the palaces of Kerioth;
　　And Moab shall die in the tumult,
　　At the shout, at the sound of the trumpet;
3　I will also cut off the judge from the midst thereof,
　　And kill all the princes thereof with him,
　　Saith Jehovah.

1. For *Moab*, see on Is. xv. The
particular act here charged against the
Moabites is nowhere recorded. Michaelis
is of opinion, that reference is had to
2 Kings iii. 27; but the prince there
spoken of was the son of the king of
Moab, and not the future heir to
the Idumæan throne. The wickedness
appears to have consisted in a wanton
violation of the sanctity of the tomb, by
the disinterment and burning of the
royal remains. It was indicative of an
enmity which was not satisfied with
inflicting every possible injury upon its
victim while living, but pursued him even
into the regions of the dead. Comp. Is.
xxxiii. 12.

2. קְרִיּוֹת, *Kerioth*; LXX. τῶν πόλεων
αὐτῆς; Targ. כְּרַכָּא, *the fortress* or *citadel*;
in all probability, the chief city, elsewhere
called קִיר מוֹאָב, *Kir-Moab*, and here put
in the plural, to describe its size, or
appearance, as comprehending more than
one. Comp. Jer. xlviii. 24, and on Is.
xv. 1. שָׁאוֹן, here means the *tumult* of
battle. Is. xiii. 4; xvii. 12.

3. From the circumstance that שֹׁפֵט,
judge, and not מֶלֶךְ, *king*, is selected to

4　　Thus saith Jehovah :
　　For three transgressions of Judah,
　　And for four, I will not reverse it ;
　　Because they have despised the law of Jehovah,
　　And have not kept his statutes ;
　　And their false deities have caused them to err,
　　After which their fathers walked.

5　But I will send a fire into Judah,
　　And it shall devour the palaces of Jerusalem.

6　　Thus saith Jehovah :
　　For three transgressions of Israel,
　　And for four, I will not reverse it ;
　　Because they sold the righteous for money,
　　And the poor for a pair of sandals :

describe the chief magistrate of Moab, it has, not without reason, been supposed, that, at the time the prophet wrote, or, at least, at the time to which his prophecy refers, a change had taken place in the government of that country ; but whether it was occasioned by the extinction of the royal house, or the appointment of a ruler by a foreign power, it is impossible to decide. The reference which some have made to Ps. ii. 10, in proof that judge and king are identical, is not in point ; for, though the terms as there used are so far synonymous, that they both designate persons high in office, yet there is an obvious distinction both as it respects the degree of their rank, and the nature of the offices with which they were invested. The connecting of the princes with Moab (שָׂרֶיהָ) and not with the judge (שָׁפְטֶיהָ) as in chap. i. 15, goes to confirm the view just given.

4, 5. The charges brought against the Jews differ from any of the preceding, in the crimes which they involve having been committed directly against God, and not against man. They had become weary of his service, abandoned his worship, and addicted themselves to idolatrous practices. Between the synonymes here employed there is this difference of meaning : תּוֹרָה, *law*, stands for the institute of Moses generally, of which the moral code formed the basis ; חֻקִּים, *statutes*, for the ceremonial and judicial enactments. By כְּזָבִים, *lies*, idols

are meant, and the word is so rendered here in the Vulg. The LXX. have taken the same view of it, rendering it μάταια, *vanities*. Comp. for this acceptation, Ps. xl. 5 (Eng. 4). Idols were so called because their pretensions and oracles were founded on falsehood, and because they deluded with false hopes those who worshipped them. Instead of being weaned from their attachment to the gods which their ancestors had, at different times, served, the Jews became increasingly addicted to them, and thereby brought upon themselves the punishment inflicted by Nebuchadnezzar.

6. The prophet, having secured the attention of the Israelites by his predictions against those communities which they regarded with feelings of hostility, comes now to his proper subject, which was to charge upon themselves the guilt which, in various ways, they, as a people, had contracted. יִשְׂרָאֵל, *Israel,* i. e. *the Israelites*, consisted, after the revolt in the time of Rehoboam, of the ten tribes, whose capital was Samaria, and whose worship, originally that of Jehovah under the visible image of the golden calves, speedily merged in the basest and most licentious idolatry. מָכַר, *to sell,* has no reference, as some have thought, to the conduct of a corrupt judge, who for money gives a verdict against the innocent, the term never being used to express any such act ; but describes the selling of a person into slavery. They

7 Who pant for the dust of the earth on the head of the poor,
   And turn aside the way of the afflicted;
   A man and his father go in to the same damsel,
   In order to profane my holy name.
8 They stretch themselves also upon pledged garments,
   Close to every altar;
   And drink the wine of the amerced
   In the house of their gods.
9 Yet it was I that destroyed the Amorite before them,
   Whose height was as the height of the cedars,

even deprived the poor of their liberty for the most paltry consideration. Comp. chap. viii. 6. נְעָלִים, *sandals*, are greatly inferior in value to shoes, consisting merely of soles of leather or wood, fastened by two straps to the feet, one of which passes over the forepart of the foot, near the great toe, and the other round the ankle.

7. שָׁאַף, signifies to *breathe hard, to pant, eagerly to desire,* which well suits the connexion, so that there is no necessity, with Houbigant, Newcome, and others, to change the verb into שׁוּף, *to attack, bruise,* &c. The meaning of the prophet is, that the persons whom he describes were so avaricious, that, after having robbed others of their property, and reduced them to a state of poverty, they even begrudged them the small quantity of dust which they had cast on their heads in token of mourning. Comp. 2 Sam. i. 2; Job ii. 12. בְּ, as in בְּרֹאשׁ, is elsewhere used in the acceptation of *on* or *upon,* and is here the more appropriately adopted, on account of the more usual preposition עַל having just been employed. Comp. chap. viii. 4.—הִטָּה דֶרֶךְ, *to turn,* or *thrust aside* as to *the way;* i. e. *to turn any one out of his right course,* into a trackless region, where he can expect nothing but inconvenience, perplexity and danger; here, *to render the afflicted still more miserable.* From the reference made in the following verse to idolatrous deities and altars, it is most probable that הַנַּעֲרָה, *the damsel* here spoken of, was not an ordinary or common strumpet, but one who prostituted herself in honour of Astarte, at one of her shrines. LXX. τὴν αὐτὴν παιδίσκην. Such an act of daring pro-

fligacy was the more atrocious from its having been committed in a heathen temple, with the express design, as the prophet states, of doing indignity to Jehovah. See Gesenius, Lex. in מַעַן, A) 2.

8. To retain pledged raiment over night was expressly prohibited by the Mosaic law, Exod. xxii. 26, 27, as it deprived the owner of his covering: to stretch oneself upon it in an idol's temple was a great aggravation of the crime. חֲבֻלִים, *pledged,* lit. *bound,* held in bondage, from חָבַל, *to bind.* Arab. خبل Syr. ܚܘܒܬܐ, *debitum.* It was not unusual for the heathen to sleep near the altars of their gods, that they might obtain communications in dreams; but as it was customary to eat in a recumbent posture, the stretching here referred to would rather seem to have respect to participation in idolatrous feasts, especially as the drinking of wine in the temples is specified in the following line. יֵין עֲנוּשִׁים, *the wine of the amerced,* means wine purchased with money exacted by the imposition of fines. בֵּית, for בְּבֵית, as frequently. Regardless of the sufferings of those whom they oppressed, the apostate Israelites revelled in sensual indulgences.

9. ו in וְאָנֹכִי, is strongly adversative, and introduces the contrast between the Divine conduct and that of the Israelites. The signal benefits which, as a nation, they had received from Jehovah, ought to have attached them for ever to his service. The conjunction and pronoun are repeated for like effect, verse 10. הָאֱמֹרִי, *the Amorites,* are here taken in a wide sense, as including all the inhabitants

And who was strong as the oaks;
Yea, I destroyed his fruit above,
And his roots beneath.

10 It was I also that brought you up from the land of Egypt,
And led you in the desert forty years,
To inherit the land of the Amorite.

11 And I raised up of your sons to be prophets,
And of your young men to be Nazarites.
Is it not even so, O ye sons of Israel?
Saith Jehovah.

of Canaan, on account of their being the largest and most powerful of the nations which occupied that country. Comp. Gen. xv. 16; xlviii. 22. In a more special point of view, they inhabited both sides of the Jordan, and particularly the mountains afterwards possessed by the tribe of Judah. In consequence of their gigantic height and extraordinary strength, to which reference is frequently made in the history of the Hebrews, they are here beautifully compared to cedars and oaks, the most majestic and sturdy trees of the forest. The Hebrew as well as the profane poets, often compare men to trees. Comp. Ps. xxxvii. 35; xcii. 12 —15; Isa. x. 33, 34; Ezek. xvii. 3; xxxi. Sixteen MSS., originally twelve more, and now five; five of the oldest editions, and the Rabboth read מִפְּנֵיכֶם, "before *you*," instead of מִפְּנֵיהֶם, "before *them;*" but these authorities, under all the circumstances of the text, are insufficient to warrant an alteration.

10. Jehovah goes back to still earlier, but no less remarkable displays of his kindness to the nation, showing that from the commencement of its history he had been its benefactor. Comp. Jer. ii. 6. עָלָה, *to come,* or *go up,* is always used in Hebrew in reference to local or political elevation, and not, as Rosenmüller asserts, to the North. The circumstance that many of the regions or places to which persons are said to have gone up, lay to the north of those from which they came, is purely accidental; whereas the propriety of the use of the term lies in the fact of the mountainous character of the land of Canaan, while Egypt and the intervening regions were low and flat.

11. The prepositive מ in מִבְּנֵיכֶם, and

מִבַּחוּרֵיכֶם, is partitive, indicating that some or certain persons out of the number were selected. The Divine condescension in the selection of any of their race to fill the offices here specified, laid them under additional obligations to devote themselves to the service of the true God; and not only was thereby a distinguished honour conferred upon them, but such institutions furnished them with the means of religious instruction, and examples of holy living. For נְבִיאִים, the *prophets,* see on Hos. xii. 11. נְזִרִים, *Nazarites,* (LXX. ἡγιασμένος, εἰς ἁγιασμόν), from נָזַר, *to separate, set oneself apart, abstain,* were a class of persons among the Hebrews who ordinarily bound themselves by a voluntary vow to abstain either for a time, or for the whole period of life, from wine and all intoxicating liquors, and everything made of the produce of the vine; and not to shave their head nor touch any dead body. Sometimes persons were, before their birth, devoted by their parents to this abstinence; as in the cases of Samson, Samuel, and John the Baptist. For the law of the Nazarite, see Num. vi. and Winer's Realwörterb. The object of the institute appears to have been, to exhibit to the view of the nation the power of religious principle operating in the way of self-control, indifference to sensual gratification, and an entire consecration to the service of God. The importance which was attached to it in a moral point of view, is evident from those who thus exercised themselves in self-denial being classed along with the prophets. Respecting the undeniableness of the fact a pointed appeal is made at the close of the verse.

12 But ye made the Nazarites drink wine,
   And ye charged the prophets,
   Saying, Prophesy not.

13 Behold, I will press you down,
   As the cart presseth which is full of sheaves.

14 And refuge shall fail the swift,
   And the strong man shall not exert his strength,
   Neither shall the mighty deliver himself;

15 And he that handleth the bow shall not stand,
   Nor shall the swift-footed escape,
   Neither shall he that rideth the horse deliver himself.

16 And he that is courageous among the heroes,
   Shall flee away naked in that day,
   Saith Jehovah.

---

12. What could have been more flagrant than to tempt the pious to break their solemn vow, and attempt to induce the inspired ambassadors of Jehovah to withhold the communications of his will?

13. Here commence the denunciations against the apostate Israelites. The Participle מֵעִיק, after הִנֵּה, is future in signification. See on Is. vii. 14. עוק occurs only here as a verb; but that it signifies *to press*, *oppress*, &c., is clear from the signification of the derivatives עָקָה, Ps. lv. 4, and מוּצָקָה, Ps. lxvi. 11, as well as from the connexion in which it here occurs. Comp. צוּק, and the Syr.

ܐܣܬܩ, *angustiatus est:* ‫حَكْمٌ‬, *angustia, pressura.* Comp. also the Ar. ‫عَاق‬, *retinuit, impedivit;* ‫عَوَايِق‬, *accidentia fortunæ, quæ impediunt hominem.* The verb is used transitively in both instances, according to the ordinary signification of Hiphil. There is more force in speaking of a fully laden cart pressing the ground under it, than its being itself pressed by its contents. תַּחַת is to be taken in the sense of *down*, as in Job xl. 12. לָה is pleonastic. The renderings of the LXX.

and Vulg., ἐγὼ κυλίω ὑποκάτω ὑμῶν, *ego stridebo subter vos*, though advocated by some, are less appropriate. Newcome translates the latter hemistich thus: "As a loaded corn-wain presseth its sheaves;" but עָמִיר is the objective case to הַמְּלֵאָה, and not to תָּעִיק. As the object of the verb, supply אֶת־הָאָרֶץ.

14—16. Every attempt to resist or escape from the evils that were coming upon the nation, would prove utterly fruitless. This sentiment is expressed under various forms, which are obviously accumulated for the sake of effect. ו at the beginning of ver. 14, is not merely conjunctive, but marks the consequence or result. Verse 15th is wanting in some of Kennicott and De Rossi's MSS. and in the Arab.; but the omission is no doubt owing to the homoioteleuton of this and the preceding verse; just as, for the same reason, the words corresponding to וְלֹא־יְמַלֵּט נַפְשׁוֹ, at the end of ver. 14, are omitted in the Alexandrian copy of the LXX. The preposition בְּ in בַּגִּבּוֹרִים, gives to אַמִּיץ לִבּוֹ the force of the superlative. Comp. גִּבּוֹר בַּבְּהֵמָה, *the strongest of beasts*, Prov. xxx. 30; הַיָּפָה בַּנָּשִׁים, *the most beautiful of women*, Song i. 8; v. 9; vi. 1; εὐλογημένη ἐν γυναιξίν, Luke i. 28.

CHAPTER III

The prophet resumes the subject of the Divine goodness towards the Hebrew
people, and grounds upon their misimprovement of it, the certainty of their
punishment, 1, 2; he then, in a series of pointed and appropriate interrogations,
illustrates this certainty, 3—6; which he follows up by a vindication of his
commission, 7, 8. Foreign nations are then summoned to witness the execution
of judgment upon the kingdom of Israel, which would be signally severe, 9—15.

---

1 HEAR ye .this word, which Jehovah speaketh against you, O
    sons of Israel,
    Against all the family which I brought up out of the land of
      Egypt;
    Saying:
2 Only you have I known of all the families of the earth,
    Therefore I will punish you for all your iniquities.
3 Will two walk together
    Except they be agreed?

1. Instead of בְּנֵי יִשְׂרָאֵל, "*sons* of Israel,"
forty-three MSS., one in the margin,
originally seven, and five by correction,
read בֵּית יִשְׂרָאֵל, "*house* of Israel;" which
reading is supported by the LXX. and
Arab. versions. Both forms are employed
in the book of Amos, but the former is
the less frequent; which awakens the
suspicion that the latter has been introduced here by way of correction. That
the phrase is intended to include the
whole Hebrew people, is evident from
the words which follow in apposition, and
and describe the distinguished favour
conferred upon the entire race of Jacob.
מִשְׁפָּחָה, Eth. ብፈዐ, *to spread out*, a
tribe, or *clan ;* but here obviously used in
a national sense, as in Jer. viii. 3; xxv.
9; Micah ii. 3.

2. יָדַע, *to know*, is here employed in
the sense of knowing with the idea of
volition, or goodwill; to *acknowledge,*
regard, care for, and by implication, *to*
show favour to. Comp. Ps. i. 6; cxliv. 3;
and γινώσκω, John x. 14; xiv. 17; 2 Tim.

ii. 19. The Israelites alone were acknowledged by Jehovah as his people,
and as such treated with peculiar favour;
but in proportion to the distinction which
they enjoyed, was the degree of punishment which their ungrateful and rebellious
conduct merited.

3. In this and the three following
verses, a series of parabolic interrogations are employed, highly calculated to
produce conviction in the minds of those
to whom they were addressed. They
are familiar indeed, but so much the
more appropriate and forcible. Instead
of נוֹעָדוּ, the LXX., Arab., and Vulg. read
יָוֹדְעוּ, with apparent reference to the
signification of יָדַע in the preceding verse.
The primary signification of יָעַד, Syr.

ܝܣܕ, *condixit, constituit*, Arab. وعد,

significavit affuturum alicui *quid*, is *to*
point, point out, appoint a time or place;
hence in Niphal, *to meet by appointment ;*
to do anything by common consent ; to be
agreed. This last seems to be the accepta-

4　Will the lion roar in the forest
　　When he has no prey?
　　Will the young lion cry out from his den,
　　Except he have taken it?

5　Will the bird fall into an earth-snare,
　　And there is no gin for it?
　　Will the snare spring from the ground,
　　When nothing whatever is caught?

6　Shall the trumpet be blown in a city,
　　And the people not tremble?
　　Shall there be evil in a city,
　　And Jehovah hath not inflicted it?

tion in which the verb is to be taken in this place: for to render, How can two set out upon a journey, except they meet by appointment? would express that to be impossible, which is very often true in fact. Interpreters are divided in opinion respecting the persons to whom the number שְׁנַיִם, *two*, refers. Munster and some others think, that the prophets generally, or Joel and Amos in particular, are meant; Vatablus, Drusius, Liveley, Newcome, Bauer, Rosenmüller, Ackermann, and Maurer, explain it of God and the prophet; while Clarius, Grotius, Danæus, Marckius, Lowth, Harenberg, and Dahl, are of opinion that God and Israel are intended. The last construction of the passage best agrees with the bearing of the other interrogations. Between Jehovah and his apostate people there could no longer be any fellowship; and instead of the blessings which accrued to them from such fellowship, they had now nothing to expect but punishment. As they had walked contrary to him, so he would now walk contrary to them. They had broken his covenant, and must take the consequences.

4. The lion is quiet till he sees his prey, but roars at the sight of it, and thereby inspires it with such terror, that it is deprived of the power of escape. In like manner the young lion, which has been weaned, and is just beginning to hunt for prey, will be silent in his den, till it is brought near, when the smell of it will rouse him from his quiet. Poiret, in his Travels in Barbary, Strasb. 1789, vol. i. p. 283, states, that the lion has

two different modes of hunting his prey. When not very hungry, he contents himself with watching behind a bush for the animal which is the object of his attack, till it approaches, when, by a sudden leap, he attacks it, and seldom misses his aim; if, however, he is famished, he does not proceed so quietly, but, impatient and full of rage, he leaves his den, and fills, with his terrific roar, the echoing forest. His voice inspires all living beings with fear and dread; no creature deems itself safe in its retreat: all flee, they know not whither, and by this means fall into his fangs. אַרְיֵה, *the lion*, and not כְּפִיר *the young lion*, is the nominative to the verb יִלְכַּד. The certainty of destruction is the point at which the prophet aims in the similitude.

5. Between פַּח and מוֹקֵשׁ there is no essential difference. The sense would have been the same had the latter word been omitted, and we had simply read, וְאֵין לָהּ; but the insertion of the synonyme gives more force to the sentence. לָהּ connects with צִפּוֹר, as its antecedent. יַעֲלֶה is to be taken as the future of Kal, and regarded as expressing the sudden spring of an elastic snare, or net, which, on the bird's touching it, suddenly rises and incloses it. Instruments were prepared by the providence of God for the capture of the Israelites, which would certainly do their work: there would be no escape.

6. The prophet here closes his interrogatory appeals;—first, by a reference to the effect produced upon the inhabitants of a city by the sounding of the trumpet,

7 Surely the Lord Jehovah inflicteth nothing,
  Except he reveal his purpose
  To his servants the prophets.

8 The lion hath roared, who will not fear?
  The Lord Jehovah hath spoken, who will not prophesy?

9   Proclaim ye in the palaces of Ashdod,
  And in the palaces in the land of Egypt,
  And say:
  Assemble yourselves on the mountains of Samaria,
  And behold the great commotions within her,
  And the oppressions in the midst of her.

as a signal of war; and then, by directly ascribing the infliction of temporal calamities to Jehovah, as the punisher of sin. For רָעָה in the sense of temporal evil, or calamity, see Gen. xix. 19; xliv. 34; Exod. xxxii. 14; Ezek. vii. 5. Arab.

بلل, experimentum, *calamitas, afflictio.*

7. Though the infliction of punishment on his guilty people was determined in his holy and righteous counsel, yet Jehovah would not proceed to execute it until he had given them full warning, and afforded such of them an opportunity of escaping as should repent and return to his service. He thus mixed mercy with judgment. סוד, Theod. βουλὴ, *counsel, purpose, decree;* from יָסַד, Arab. وسد,

posuit, firmiter statuit; to found, lay a foundation, *establish a plan, ordain.* It is rather, I imagine, on this acceptation of the verb that the idea of *purpose* or *decree* is based, than upon that of a divan, or an assembly of persons, sitting and deliberating on couches: but see Gesenius in סוד. As the Divine plan or purpose is necessarily secret till it be revealed, hence the acceptation *secret* came to be attached to the word. In this verse a high honour is vindicated to the prophetical office. The holy men of God were, by inspiration, entrusted with a knowledge of the Divine purposes, in so far as it was necessary for them to divulge them to the world. יַעֲשֶׂה, is the frequentative future, indicating what God is accustomed to do, and it is best rendered by our present. For the sentiment, comp. Gen. xviii. 17.

8. With reference to what he had expressed ver. 4, and in keeping with the mode of representation which he had employed chap. i. 2, Amos formally announces the awful character of the message he had heard from the Lord, and the impossibility of withholding the communication. The roar of the lion is loud and terrific, especially in the solitary forests which form his proper domain. See on ver. 4.

9. הַשְׁמִיעוּ, *cause it to be heard, publish ye!* Those are addressed who had intercourse with the places here specified, and had thus an opportunity of conveying the message. Comp. ὁ ἀκούων εἰπάτω· Ἔρχου! Rev. xxii. 17. For *Ashdod,* see on chap. i. 8. It is here used synecdochically for the whole of Philistia. Instead of בְּאַשְׁדּוֹד, the LXX. have read בְּאַשּׁוּר, ἐν Ἀσσυρίοις, which Secker attempts to justify! For הַשְׁמִיעוּ עַל אַרְמְנוֹת, comp. κηρύξατε ἐπὶ τῶν δωμάτων, Matt. x. 27. It was, and is still, customary in the East to assemble on the flat roofs of the houses. To the princes and courtiers thus assembled on their palaces, as well as to all within hearing, the invitation was to be conveyed. There is something exceedingly forcible in these heathen rulers, &c. being called to witness the enormities that were practised in Samaria. If their judgment, pagans as they were, could not but be unfavourable, what must be the judgment of the holy and righteous God? What the punishment which he must inflict? Nothing can be more graphic than the description of the position which these foreigners were to occupy. They were

10 For they regard not the practice of rectitude,
   Saith Jehovah,
   That amass rapine and spoil in their palaces.
11 Therefore thus saith the Lord Jehovah:
   There shall be an enemy, and that around the land;
   And he shall bring down thy strength from thee,
   And thy palaces shall be plundered.
12 Thus saith Jehovah:
   As the shepherd rescueth from the mouth of the lion
   Two legs, or the portion of an ear,

to assemble עַל הָרֵי שֹׁמְרוֹן, *upon the mountains of Samaria.* שֹׁמְרוֹן, *Samaria,* the metropolis of the kingdom of Israel, was built on a round hill, near the middle of a large valley, surrounded by mountains on every side, by which it was completely overlooked. From these elevations persons might distinctly see what was done in the city. That מְהוּמֹת רַבּוֹת and עֲשׁוּקִים are intimately connected, and are both to be referred to the rich and powerful inhabitants of Samaria, appears evident from what is stated in the following verse. The latter term is properly the Pahul Participle, *oppressed,* but is here used as a noun, as in Job xxxv. 9; Eccles. iv. 1. Comp. the forms זְבוּל, *dwelling,* מְלוּכָה, *kingdom.*

10. לֹא יָדְעוּ, *they know not,* is not intended to express simple ignorance, but that state of mind which is hostile to the entertainment of knowledge. The magnates of Samaria had no regard for the practice of what was just and right, but the contrary. נְכֹחָה, *rectitude,* that which is straight, in opposition to what is crooked, distorted, or morally wrong. Comp. Is. xxvi. 10; xxx. 10; lix. 14. חָמָס וָשֹׁד, *violence and desolation,* mean by a metonymy of the cause for the effect, what has been obtained by violating the rights and desolating the property of others. Such spoils they accumulated in their palaces, but they should not enjoy them. On the contrary, as the prophet shows in the following verses, they should be plundered and carried away by the enemy. Dathe well expresses the meaning of the verse: "Recte factis nequaquam delectantur, inquit Jova, sed thesauros in ædes suas congerunt vi atque injuria partos."

11. צַר, the LXX., who are followed by Aq. and the Arab., preposterously render Τύρος, *Tyre;* one of De Rossi's MSS. reads צֹר, and one of Kennicott's, צוֹר. The Syr. Chald. *tribulation,* which has been adopted in many modern versions. Thus Dathe, Hesselberg, Dahl, Justi, and Hitzig. But Calvin, Newcome, Michaelis, Struensee, Bauer, Rosenmüller, Vater, and Noyes, translate *enemy,* which better suits the connexion, as it supplies a proper nominative to the verb הוֹרִיד, immediately following. Comp. as to derivation, the Arab. ضَرَّ, *nocuit, noxa affecit, læsit.* The words, צַר וּסְבִיב הָאָרֶץ, are abrupt and elliptical, but, for this very reason, possess more point. At צַר, supply יָבֹא, הִנֵּה, or the like. ו in וּסְבִיב has the force of *et quidem,* or *isque.* The reading יְסֹבֵב suggested by Houbigant, considered probable by Newcome, and adopted by Bauer, is altogether unsustained by any example of a similar case in verbs whose second and third radicals are the same. סְבִיב הָאָרֶץ is equivalent to בְּכָל הָאָרֶץ, 2 Kings xvii. 5, where the invasion by Shalmaneser is described. עֹז, *strength,* denotes whatever Samaria confided in, or made her boast of, such as her treasures, fortifications, warriors, &c. All was to be brought down into the valley, and what was capable of being removed, carried away by the enemy, *i.e.* Shalmaneser, the king of Assyria;—a just retribution for the spoliations which her inhabitants had committed.

12. A very appropriate image is here borrowed from a scene in pastoral life, such as the prophet himself may have witnessed. Nothing but a mere remnant of the Israelites should with difficulty

So shall the sons of Israel be rescued,
Who sit in Samaria on the corner of a bed,
And in Damascus on that of a couch.

13   Hear ye, and testify against the house of Jacob,
Saith the Lord, Jehovah, the God of hosts.

14   Surely in the day when I punish the transgressions of Israel,

escape from the enemy. Although a lion may not be induced to quit his prey, if he is hungry and has but just seized it, Is. xxxi. 4; yet if he has almost devoured it, leaving nothing but what is here specified, no difficulty would be found in effecting a rescue. For יַצִּיל מִפִּי הָאֲרִי, comp. ἐρρύσθην ἐκ στόματος λέοντος, 2 Tim. iv. 17; 1 Sam. xvii. 34, 35. בְּדַל occurs only this once, but signifies a *part* or *piece*; from בָּדַל, *to separate*. There is a species of goat in the East, the ears of which are often a foot in length, and broad in proportion; so that more importance would be attached to them by the shepherd, than would be the case with us in the West. The concluding words of the verse have greatly perplexed interpreters. Most of the moderns explain דַּמֶּשֶׂק of the silk stuff manufactured at Damascus, which, from the name of the place, is called *damask*, and render בִּדְמֶשֶׂק עֶרֶשׂ, *in damask couches*. What has been supposed to confirm this explanation of the term is the occurrence of the same word in Arabic, only with the letters, or similar letters, transposed, as دمقس, دمقاس,

دمقص, &c., all signifying *silk*. Gesenius has a long article on the word in his Thesaurus, p. 346; but fails in establishing the point of identity. Instead of דַּמֶּשֶׂק with *Shin*, upwards of twenty of De Rossi's MSS. read, or have read, דַּמֶּשֶׂק with *Sin*; which reading is also that of eighteen printed editions, and is the proper orthography of the name of Damascus. What appears to have originated the above view of the word was the idea, that as the wealthy and voluptuous inhabitants of Samaria are supposed to be intended, there was a special propriety in adverting to the sumptuousness of the couches or sofas on which they reclined. But this idea is totally alien from the bearing of the passage, which requires something to

correspond to what had been expressed in the comparison of the fragments left by the lion. Besides, פֵּאָה signifies the *outer* or *extreme* corner, and not the inner, which is regarded as the seat of honour, so that the observations of Harmer, chap. vi. Obs. xxx. are totally inapplicable, even if there were much point in them. The words are elliptical, and the parallelism, expressed in full, would stand thus:

הַיֹּשְׁבִים בְּשֹׁמְרוֹן בִּפְאַת מִטָּה
הַיֹּשְׁבִים בְּדַמֶּשֶׂק בִּפְאַת עָרֶשׂ׃

The persons referred to are the sick and infirm poor, who had nothing left but the side or part of a couch, and whom the king of Assyria would not think it worth his while to be at the trouble of removing. All the rest, the robust and active, the opulent and powerful, should be carried into captivity. For the fulfilment see 2 Kings xvii. 5, 6; xviii. 9—12. The reason why Damascus is mentioned along with Samaria, is, that, at the time of the Assyrian invasion, that city was in the power of the Israelites, having been conquered by Jeroboam II. See 2 Kings xiv. 28. On the conquest, no doubt many belonging to the ten tribes went there to reside.

13. The same persons are here addressed, who were summoned from Philistia and Egypt to witness the enormities practised in Samaria, ver. 9. They were now to testify to the facts of the case, that the punishment might be seen to have been inflicted upon the inhabitants might be seen to have been richly deserved. הֵעִיד בְּ, as frequently means to *testify against any one*. אֲדֹנָי יְהוָֹה אֱלֹהֵי הַצְּבָאוֹת, LXX. Κύριος ὁ Θεὸς ὁ Παντοκράτωρ: an accumulation of Divine appellatives for the purpose of striking awe into the minds of the guilty.

14. Signal vengeance was to be taken upon the place whence all the evils which spread through the ten tribes originated. For *Bethel*, see on Hos. iv. 15. From the term הַמִּזְבֵּחַ having the determinative

I will punish the altars of Bethel;
Yea, the horns of the altar shall be cut down,
And they shall fall to the ground.

15 I will also smite the winter-house with the summer-house,
And the ivory mansions shall perish,
And the great houses shall come to an end,
Saith Jehovah.

article, rendering it emphatic, while מִזְבְּחוֹת in the plural also occurs, it may be inferred that at Bethel, besides the great altar erected by Jeroboam, there were many lesser ones at which sacrifices were offered. Comp. Hos. viii. 11; x. 5. The קַרְנוֹת, *horns*, were four projecting points in the shape of horns at the corners of ancient altars. They may be seen in the representations of those dug up by Belzoni in Egypt. As they were ornamental, the action here described was designed to express the contempt in which the altar would be held by the Assyrians.

15. Eastern monarchs and princes, as well as others of the great, have summer as well as winter residences. The latter are in cities and sheltered situations; the former in forests, or upon mountains.

שֵׁן, properly *tooth*, but used specially of the tusk of the elephant; *ivory*. LXX. οἶκοι ἐλεφάντινοι. By ivory houses are not meant houses or palaces composed of that material, but richly ornamented with it. The ancients used it for decorating the ceilings, panels, doors, &c., of their rooms, by inlaying it with other costly articles. See 1 Kings xxii. 39; Ps. xlv. 9. Odys. iv. 73. Diod. Sic. iii. 47. Pausan. i. 12. 4. Horat. lib. ii. Od. 18. 1. All these sumptuous palaces in which the leaders of the people rioted, and indulged in all manner of profaneness, were to be completely destroyed. סוּף, *to come to an end, cease*. The rendering of בָּתִּים רַבִּים, by "*large* houses," is more agreeable to the connexion than that of "*many* houses," though this is equally expressed by the phrase.

CHAPTER IV

This chapter contains a continuation of the denunciation pronounced against the Israelites, at the close of the preceding, 1—3; an ironical call to them to persevere in their will-worship, which was the primary cause of their calamities, 4, 5; an enumeration of the different judgments with which they had been visited, but which had effected no reformation, 6—11; and a summons to them to prepare for the last and most awful judgment, which the omnipotent Jehovah was about to inflict upon them, 12, 13.

---

1 HEAR ye this word, ye kine of Bashan,
That are in the mountain of Samaria;

1. בָּשָׁן, *Bashan*, was celebrated for the richness of its pasturage, and its excellent breed both of large and small cattle.

Deut. xxxii. 14; Ps. xxii. 12; Ezek. xxxix. 18. It lay on the east of the Jordan, between Hermon and the mountains of

> That oppress the poor ; that crush the needy ;
> That say to their master,
> Bring now, that we may drink.

2   The Lord Jehovah hath sworn by his holiness :
> Behold, the days are coming upon you,
> When ye shall be taken away with hooks,
> And your posterity with fish-hooks.

Gilead, and extended eastward as far as the cities of Salchah and Edrei, which it included. Some are of opinion, that by פָּרוֹת הַבָּשָׁן, the kine, or cows of Bashan, the proud and luxurious females of Samaria are intended; and that they are introduced on account of the corrupting influence which, through their husbands, they exerted on the state of public affairs. Of these may be mentioned, most of the Rabbins, Theodoret, Liveley, Grotius, Michaelis, Vater, Dahl, Justi, Gesenius and Winer. Others, as the Targ., Jerome, Munster, Calvin, Vatablus, Clarius, Drusius, Danæus, Mercer, Marckius, Harenberg, Dathe, Rosenmüller, and Maurer, maintain that the prophet has the princes and rulers in view, whom he describes in this debasing language, in order to set forth the effeminacy, wantonness, and obstinacy of their character. At first view the former exposition might appear to recommend itself for adoption; but I am induced to give my adhesion to the latter, chiefly on the ground, that it is scarcely possible, otherwise, to account for the repeated intermixture of masculine forms with the feminine. Thus we have שִׁמְעוּ, הַבִּיאָה, אֲדֹנֵיהֶם, אֲלֵיכֶם, אֶתְכֶם, all occurring very closely together. Now, though it must be admitted that there are instances in which the gender is neglected, as in Ruth i., yet none of them will bear comparison with the present case. On the principle, that males are the real, and females the figurative subjects of discourse, it is easy to perceive how the genders would be used just as the one or the other were prominently in the mind of the prophet. Some translators suppress the figurative language altogether, as Dathe : *Audite hoc, vos divites et potentes Samariæ ;* but such practice is quite unwarrantable, as it destroys the effect of the prophetic mode of representation. צִנּוֹת, one of those onomatopoetic verbs, the very

sound of which strongly expresses the character of the action which they are intended to describe. It signifies to *break, crush, dash in pieces.* Comp. the Arab. رَضَّ *contudit, fregit.* אֲדֹן in אֲדֹנֵיהֶם, though plural in form, is singular in signification, and means the king of Israel, whom his courtiers and others, indulging in their compotations, importuned for fresh supplies of wine, reckless of the oppression and rapine by which it might be procured. Comp. Hos. vii. 5. ה suffixed in הַבִּיאָה, is the ה directive, or optative.

2, 3. כִּי is pleonastic. It is surprising that so judicious an interpreter as Calvin should attempt to vindicate the rendering of קֹדֶשׁ, *his sanctuary,* when that of *his holiness* is so natural and proper. Comp. Ps. lxxxix. 36, and lx. 8. Jehovah appeals to all that is involved in the infinite excellence of his moral character for the certainty of his punishing sin. The Nominative to נִשָּׂא is the enemy, understood; but as the verb is put in the impersonal form, it is best rendered passively. Döderlein and some others object to the adoption, in this place, of *hooks* and *fish-hooks,* as the signification of צִנּוֹת and דוּגָה סִירוֹת, as too violent a change of the figure; and propose that we should retain the primary acceptation of *thorns,* which they think is more in keeping with the idea of cows. They accordingly render the passage: "Ye shall be driven into thorny districts, and among the gloomy thorn-bushes." There is, however, no necessity for supposing that the prophet had the alleged idea in his mind when he delivered the words, but the contrary; and as *fishing* and *hooks* are elsewhere employed figuratively in reference to human beings, there can be no real ground for rejecting such tropical application of the disputed terms in this place. See 2 Chron. xxxiii. 11 ;

3 And ye shall go out through the breaches,
   Each one right before her;
   Ye shall even be thrown out of the palace,
   Saith Jehovah.

4   Come ye to Bethel, and transgress;
   At Gilgal, multiply transgression;
   Yea, bring your sacrifices every morning,
   Your tithes every third year;

5 Offer likewise incense of the leavened thank-offering;
   Proclaim also the voluntary offerings : publish them abroad ;
   For ye love to have it so, O ye sons of Israel,
   Saith Jehovah.

Is. xxxvii. 29; Jer. xvi. 16; Ezek. xxix.
4. אִשָּׁה נֶגְדָּהּ, *each one right before her,*
means, in a captive state, not being
permitted by the enemy to turn to the
right or the left. הִשְׁלַכְתֶּנָה is pointed
הָשְׁלַכְתֶּנָה in De Rossi's Spanish MS.
marked 23, which punctuation has been
adopted in Hahn's small printed edition.
Comp. הֻשְׁלַךְ, Dan. viii. 11. It is supported
by the LXX., Syr., Symm., Vulg., and
Arab., all of which versions exhibit the
passive. ה at the end of the verb is that
of the fuller form of the pronoun אַתֵּנָה,
the fragment of which is used as a suffix.
It occurs but seldom in the preterite. Of
הַהַרְמוֹנָה almost every possible interpretation has been given. LXX. τὸ ὄρος τὸ
Ῥεμμὰν; Cod. Vat. Ῥομμὰν; in many
of the MSS. of Flamin. Nob. Ἀρμανᾶ.

Syr. ܘܐܬܡܚܝ ܠܗܕ; Chald. טוּרֵי הַרְמִינֵי,
the mountains of Armenia. Vulg. *Armon.*
Arab. after the LXX. جبل الرامة. Aq.

Ἀρμανὰ ὄρος. Symm. Ἑρμηνίαν, doubtless for Ἀρμενίαν. Theod. ὄρος Μονά.
Edit. quint. ὑψηλὸν ὄρος. Luther and
Vater, *Hermon.* Michaelis, Struensee,
Dathe, Bauer, De Wette, *Armenia.*
Justi and Hezel, *Harem.* Volborth, *Net.*
Hitzig takes it to be a corruption of
הַהַרְמוֹנָה, *Hadadrimmon,* which he explains of a place near Samaria where
Adonis was worshipped. Newcome cuts
the knot, and renders "will utterly
destroy it." The only satisfactory solution of the difficulty presented by this
ἅπαξ λεγ. is that of Kimchi, which is
approved by Gesenius, Winer, and Lee,

viz. that הַהַרְמוֹן stands for אַרְמוֹן, *a palace,*
or *citadel.* Comp. the Arab. هرم, *a lofty
edifice, a pyramid.* Changes in letters of
the same organ are not infrequent in
Hebrew, as לָאָה, הָמוֹן, אָמוֹן; הֵיךְ, אֵיךְ;
הָדַר, אֶרֶז, לָהָה; &c. The ה at the end is not
the feminine termination, but simply
paragogic, as in אֶרְצָה, Job xxxiv. 13;
xxxvii. 12; Is. viii. 23; and הָחָרְסָה,
Judges xiv. 18. The noun will thus be
the accusative absolute, and the construction will be, " cast down *as to the
palace,*" i. e. *from it,* over its walls, or the
like. The place in which the princes
had rioted, and in the strength of which
they confided, should afford them no
safety.

4, 5. The language of these verses is
that of the keenest irony. The Israelites
were addicted to the worship of the
golden calf, and to that of idols, whereby
they contracted guilt before Jehovah,
and exposed themselves to his judgments ; at the same time they hypocritically professed to keep up the
observance of certain feasts which had
been appointed by Moses. For *Gilgal,*
as a place of idolatrous worship, see on
Hos. iv. 15. The opinion of Abenezra,
approved by Rosenmüller and Maurer,
that by שְׁלֹשֶׁת יָמִים, we are to understand
every third day, seems forced and
unnatural. That the words by themselves might have this meaning is un-
questionable ; but the idea of *tithes* being
brought every third day is inadmissible,
even in a passage so strongly ironical
as the present. I cannot doubt that the
prophet has in view the enactment

6　　And though I have given you cleanness of teeth in all your
　　　　cities,
　　And want of bread in all your places,
　　Yet ye have not returned unto me,
　　Saith Jehovah.

7　　And though I have withholden the rain,
　　Three months before the harvest;
　　And have caused it to rain upon one city,
　　But upon another city I have not caused it to rain;
　　One portion was rained upon,
　　And the portion upon which it rained not, withered:

8　And two or three cities wandered to one city,
　　To drink water, but have not been satisfied;
　　Yet ye returned not to me,
　　Saith Jehovah.

9　　I have smitten you with mildew and much blight;
　　Your gardens, and your vineyards, and your figs, and your olives,

recorded Deut. xiv. 29; xxvi. 12. יָמִים,
days, mean, here, as Lev. xxv. 29;
Judges xvii. 10, the fullest complement
of days, i. e. *a year*. קֶמַד is most probably
the infinitive, used for the second plural
of the imperative; or it may be the
second singular of the same. There is
no necessity for attaching to חֶמָם, the
meaning of *violence*, though Gesenius
would justify it, on the ground of חֹמֵץ
being used, Ps. lxxi. 4, to designate an
oppressor; and because the rendering of
the Chald. in this place is אוֹנֵס, *rapine* or
oppression. It is not impossible that
the translator mistook חֶמֶץ for חֹמֶס, which
has this signification. The point of
reference is doubtless the ordinance, Lev.
vii. 13, that, besides the unleavened cakes,
the Hebrews were to offer " *leavened*
bread" with the sacrifice of thanksgiving.
What the Israelites, therefore, are supposed to be in the habit of doing was, so
far as the material of the thing was concerned, not contrary to the law, but in
strict accordance with its requirement.
For בֵּן אֲהַבְתֶּם, comp. בֵּן אֲהָבוּ עַמִּי, Jer. v. 31.

6. From this verse to the 11th in-
clusive, Jehovah describes the different
corrective measures which he had employed for the purpose of effecting a
change in the Israelites; and at the close
of each mentioned in the series, the
obstinate impenitence, under the influence

of which they persisted in their wicked
courses, is emphatically marked by the
declaration, וְלֹא־שַׁבְתֶּם עָדַי נְאֻם יְהוָה : , *yet ye
returned not unto me, saith Jehovah.*
Such repetition gives great force to the
reprehension. נִקְיוֹן שִׁנַּיִם, *cleanness of teeth*,
and חֹסֶר לֶחֶם, *lack of bread*, are synonymous; both expressing the famine with
which the nation had been visited. עָדַי,
to me, the Chald. paraphrases, לְפָלְחָנִי, *to
my worship*, or *service*.

7, 8. The famine was followed by the
judgment of drought, which at once produced sterility, and cut off the necessary
supply of drink for man and beast. The
rain that had been withheld, was the
מַלְקוֹשׁ, *vernal*, or latter rain, which falls in
the latter half of February, the whole of
March and April, and thus precedes the
harvest, as here stated. See on Hos. vi.
3. Whatever rain fell was exceedingly
partial and insufficient. Instead of הִמְטִיר,
the reading אַמְטִיר is found in two MSS.,
and is supported by the renderings of the
LXX., Arab., and Vulg. The textual
reading must be taken impersonally.
עָרִים, *cities*, stands for their inhabitants.
Compare for a lengthened and graphic
description of the judgment here specified,
Jer. xiv. 1—6.

9. A bad harvest, arising from the
destruction of the corn by the *blighting*
influence of the east wind (שִׁדָּפוֹן, *scorching*,

The locust hath devoured;
Yet ye have not returned unto me,
Saith Jehovah.

10   I have sent among you the plague, such as that of Egypt;
I have slain your young men with the sword,
Together with your captive horses;
And I have even made the stench of your camps to come up
    into your nostrils;
Yet ye have not returned unto me,
Saith Jehovah.

11   I have overthrown some among you,
As God overthrew Sodom and Gomorrah;
And ye have been as a brand snatched from the burning;
Yet ye have not returned unto me,
Saith Jehovah.

---

blasting, from שָׁדַף, *to scorch;* Chald. שְׁדַף, *to burn;* Arab. اسدف, *niger*, LXX. πύρωσις. Arab. Ver. السموم, *the Simoom*,) and by the *mildew*, or smut, (יֵרָקוֹן, Arab. يرقان, *rubigo*). הַרְבּוֹת, the infinitive absolute of רָבָה in Hiphil, with the force of an adjective, or an adverb. This word some improperly connect, as a construct noun, with the following substantives. גֹּבַי, a name given to the *locust*. See on Joel i. 4.

10. Though the plague has from time immemorial been endemic in Egypt, and might so far be described as דֶּרֶךְ מִצְרַיִם, *the way of Egypt;* yet comparing Is. x. 26, in which the same phrase is used as here, it obviously means, *as the Egyptians were treated,* or as God punished them with the plague. See Exod. ix. 3, &c. שְׁבִי סוּסֵיכֶם, lit. *the captivity of your horses:* i.e. those taken and destroyed by the enemy. See 2 Kings xiii. 7. בְּאֵשׁ the LXX. render ἐν πυρί, having read בָּאֵשׁ, which is the pointing of three of De Rossi's MSS., and of three others originally; as also of the Brixian edition. Aq. σαπρίαν. The ו in וּבְאַפְּכֶם, Houbigant, Dahl, and some others would cancel, on the ground of its harshness, and its not having been expressed by the LXX.,

Arab., Syr., and Vulg. It is translated in the Targ., and is to be retained, as an intensive particle, adding force to the preceding verb. Comp. the somewhat similar use of the Greek καί.

11. בְּ in בָּכֶם is used partitively : *inter, among*, or the like; indicating that the subverting was not total. כְּמַהְפֵּכַת אֱלֹהִים, *like God's overthrowing :* properly the Hiphil participle, but construed as an infinitive. Comp. Deut. xxix. 22; Is. xiii. 19; Jer. l. 40; 2 Pet. ii. 6; Jude 7. אֱלֹהִים, which stands for the affix of the first personal pronoun, Newcome improperly converts into a superlative, and renders, "the great overthrow!" His remark on אֵת, as sometimes the sign of the genitive case, is likewise totally inapplicable, as in the present case it can only mark the accusative. To what physical phenomena reference is here specifically made, it is impossible to determine, owing to the absence of all historical data. Some think the earthquake, mentioned chap. i. 1, is intended; but this is altogether out of the question, since the prophecy was delivered two years before that event. From the allusion to fire, it has been deemed probable that some of the cities of the Israelites had been burned, either by lightning from heaven, or by the army of the king of Syria. At all events, that the language is not to be understood figuratively is evident from the close connexion of the

12   Therefore, thus will I deal with thee, O Israel!
Forasmuch as I will do this to thee,
Prepare to meet thy God, O Israel!
13 For, behold! it is He that formed the mountains;
And created the wind;
And declareth to man what is his thought;
That maketh the morning darkness,
And walketh upon the heights of the earth;
Jehovah, God of hosts, is his name.

verse with those preceding, each of which describes a separate physical calamity, and closes, as this one does, with a reprehension of the impenitence by which the nation continued to be characterised. אוּד מֻצָּל מִשְׂרֵפָה, *a brand snatched from* the *burning*, is proverbial, and expresses the narrow escape from utter extinction which had been experienced. Comp. Zech. iii. 2; and 1 Cor. iii. 15, αὐτὸς δὲ σωθήσεται, οὕτως δὲ ὡς διὰ πυρός.

12. All the means that had been employed to reform the Israelites having proved ineffectual, they are here summoned to prepare for the final judgment, which was to put an end to their national existence. To this judgment reference is emphatically made in the terms כֹּה, *thus*, and זֹאת, *this*. There is a brief resumption of the sentence delivered, verses 2 and 3. That by הָכוֹן any such *preparation* is intended as would involve genuine and universal repentance, by which the threatened judgment might have been averted, cannot be admitted in consistency with the bearing both of the preceding and the following context. The removal of the Israelites, as a nation, is denounced as certain, and inevitable. It is rather to be understood as הָכֶן לָךְ, *prepare thee*, Jer. xlvi. 14. God is now coming against you as the avenger of your wickedness. Consider how you shall meet, or endure the infliction. Comp. Ezek. xxii. 14; Heb. x. 31. Individuals might by repentance obtain the forgiveness of their personal transgressions, and thus have their minds brought into a state in which they would enjoy support and comfort in the midst of

national calamity; but this was all that could now be expected.

13. To give full effect to the preceding call, one of the most sublime and magnificent descriptions of Jehovah, to be met with in Scripture, is here introduced. The participial form of the five verbs employed by the prophet greatly enhances the beauty of the passage; but it cannot be successfully imitated in a translation. Some have doubted whether רוּחַ does not here signify *spirit*, rather than *wind*; but it seems more natural to take the term in the latter acceptation, on account of the close coherence of this clause of the verse with that immediately preceding. The rendering of the LXX. ἀπαγγέλλων εἰς ἀνθρώπους τὸν χριστὸν αὐτοῦ, *announcing to men his anointed*, has originated in their mistaking מַה־שֵּׂחוֹ for מְשִׁיחוֹ. Theodoret, in commenting upon the version, thinks Cyrus is intended, and not Christ, as we may otherwise imagine the fathers would expound it. By שֵׂחוֹ is not meant God's thought, or his purposes, as some have taken it, but the thoughts or meditations of man, of which alone the verb שִׂיחַ and its derivatives, when applied to intelligent beings, is used. עֹשֶׂה is followed by a double accusative: that of the material out of which the thing is made, and that of the matter into which it is converted. It must, however, be observed, that upwards of twenty of Kennicott's MSS. read, or have read, וְעֹשֶׂה, which is the reading of the LXX. and Arab. According to this construction, the passage must be translated thus: "He that maketh the aurora and the darkness."

CHAPTER V

After giving utterance to a brief elegy over the prostrate and helpless condition of the kingdom, which had just been predicted, 1—3, the prophet introduces Jehovah still addressing himself to the inhabitants, calling upon them to relinquish their superstitious and idolatrous practices, and return to his service, 4—9. He then adverts to the picture of wickedness which the nation exhibited, 10—13; repeats the call to cultivate habits of piety and righteousness, 14, 15; describes, in plaintive strains, the destruction that was coming upon the land, 16—20; exposes the inutility of ceremonial rites when substituted for moral rectitude, or combined with unauthorized worship, 21—26; and expressly threatens the Israelites with transportation into the East, 27.

---

1 HEAR ye this word, which I utter concerning you—
   A lamentation, O house of Israel!
2 The virgin of Israel is fallen;
   She shall rise no more;
   Prostrate upon her own land,
   There is none to raise her up.
3 For thus saith the Lord Jehovah;
   The city that went out by a thousand,

1. קִינָה is properly an *elegy*, or song of mourning and lamentation, from קִין, in Piel, to compose or chant such a song. It consisted of plaintive effusions poured forth by mourning relatives, or by persons hired for the purpose, at funerals; and was distinguished for the tender, pathetic, broken and exclamatory nature of the expressions of which it was composed, as well as the touching features of the subject which they were designed to embody. Of this mode of composition the Hebrew prophets frequently avail themselves, especially Jeremiah, who, besides introducing it into several of his prophecies, has left us a whole book of קִינוֹת, elegies, or lamentations. See Lowth, Lect. xxii. For the introduction of the present subject, comp. עַל שָׂא קִינָה אֶל, or עַל, Ezek. xix. 1; xxvii. 2; xxxii. 2; and the common oracular forms נָשָׂא מָשָׁל, &c. Some are of opinion that the elegy thus introduced extends to the end of the chapter, but it is far more likely that

it consists merely of the plaintive exclamations contained in verse 2. Compare the beautiful lament of David on the death of Jonathan, 2 Sam. i. 17—27.

2. The Israelitish state is called בְּתוּלָה, a virgin, because it had never been subdued by any foreign prince. See on Is. xxiii. 12. The passages, Jer. xviii. 13, and Lam. ii. 13, which Rosenmüller adduces against this interpretation of the term, are not in point, since both refer to the character which Jerusalem sustained previous to the deplorable condition to which she had been reduced by the violence of the enemy. It cannot, therefore, be regarded as merely synonymous with בַּת, *daughter*, as idiomatically applied to describe the inhabitants of a city or state. This brief, but touching elegy describes the utterly prostrate and helpless condition to which the Assyrians were to reduce the kingdom of the ten tribes.

3. The depopulated state of the country

Shall have an hundred left;
And she that went out by an hundred,
Shall have ten left
To the house of Israel.

4 For thus saith Jehovah to the house of Israel,
Seek ye me, and live.

5 And seek not Bethel;
And go not to Gilgal;
Neither pass through to Beersheba;
For Gilgal shall surely go into captivity,
And Bethel shall come to nought.

6 Seek ye Jehovah, and live,

is here affectingly depicted. עִיר, *the city*, stands by metonymy for its inhabitants. The LXX. ἡ. πόλις ἐξ ἧς ἐξεπορεύοντο χίλιοι, and so the other ancient versions. הַיֹּצֵאת, *that went out*, is used elliptically for הַיֹּצֵאת לַמִּלְחָמָה, *that went forth to war*. The population or size of a city was estimated according to the number of warriors it could furnish. Thus the Scholiast on Iliad ix. 383, 384: οὐ τὸ πλάτος τῶν πυλῶν θέλει σεμαίνειν, οὐδὲ γὰρ ἅμα πάντας ἐξιέναι φησίν· ἀλλὰ τὸ μέγεθος τῆς πόλεως, καὶ τὸ πλῆθος τῶν ἀνδρῶν.

4. While the divine judgments are not executed, there is still room for repentance and reformation. דָּרַשׁ, *to seek*, is very often used as a religious term, implying application to God, or to a false deity, for assistance, direction, &c. and then generally to worship him, and have respect to his will. Ps. xxiv. 6; Is. viii. 19; lv. 6. Comp. Heb. xi. 6, ἐκζητεῖν τὸν Θεόν. בִּקֵּשׁ is similarly used. חְיוּ, *live ye*, is employed as a second imperative, in order emphatically to express the certainty of the result that would ensue from compliance with the command given by the first.

5. A strong dissuasive from idolatry, derived from the predicted fall of the objects and places of false worship. בְּאֵר שֶׁבַע, *Beersheba*, lit. "the Well of the Oath;" LXX. τὸ φρέαρ τοῦ ὅρκου; see Gen. xxi. 22—31. It was situated about twenty-five geographical miles south of Hebron, on the frontier of the Holy Land towards Idumæa, and is still called by the Arabs بير السبع, *Bir-es-sebâ*.

Dr. Robinson fell in with its ruins on the north side of a Wady of the same name, but found nothing bearing the marks of high antiquity, except two wells, one of which he ascertained to be forty-four feet and a half in depth to the surface of the water, and the other forty-two feet. As it lay in the extreme south of Palestine, the verb עָבַר, *to pass over*, or *through*, is most appropriate. From this verse, and from chap. viii. 14, it appears to have been a place of idolatrous resort, but wherein the idolatry consisted we are not told. In הַגִּלְגָּל גָּלֹה יִגְלֶה is a forcible paronomasia, though the words are from different roots. "Gilgal gallando gallabitur, si posset fingi aliquod tale verbum; hoc est, vertetur volubili versione." Calvin, *in loc.* There is likewise a play upon the word אָוֶן, which is used to denote *wickedness, idolatry, idol, nothing*, &c. What had originally been בֵּית־אֵל, *Bethel, a house of God*, but had by the Israelites been converted into בֵּית־אָוֶן, *Beth-aven, a house of idolatry*, see Hos. iv. 15, and x. 5, should be reduced to אָוֶן, *aven, nothing*.

6. The prophet here repeats, for the sake of effect, the call which he had introduced, ver. 4. צָלַח, which more commonly has the significations attaching to the Arab. صلح, *rectè se habuit res, aptus fuit*, &c. has here that of the Syriac ܟ݁ܠܚ, *descendit, perrupit*. The general idea of motion, either forward or downward, seems to be conveyed by it, only,

Lest he rush down, like fire, upon the house of Joseph;
And it devour, and there be none in Bethel to quench it.

7 Ye who turn justice into wormwood,
And cast righteousness to the ground.

8 Seek Him that made the Pleiades and Orion;
That turneth deathshade into morning;
That maketh day dark as night;
That calleth the waters of the sea,

---

in certain cases, with the superadded notion of violence or force. Thus וַתִּצְלַח עָלָיו רוּחַ יְהוָה, Judg. xv. 14, is not improperly rendered in our common version, "And the Spirit of the Lord *came mightily* upon him." Dahl prefers the rendering *perdidit*, which he derives from the Arab.

صلوخ, *exitiale malum;* but the form

صلخم, مصلخم, *penetrans, vehemens,*

might rather be compared. Jehovah is often compared to *fire.* See Is. x. 17; Lam. ii. 3. אֵשׁ, being of common gender, is the nominative to אָכְלָה, so that the object of comparison takes the place of יְהֹוָה, who is the subject, and the proper nominative. בֵּית יוֹסֵף, *the house of Joseph,* is a less frequent designation of the ten tribes, the principal of which was that of Ephraim, the son of Joseph. It occurs several times in the historical books, but only twice besides in the prophets, *viz.* Obad. 18; Zech. x. 6. The name יוֹסֵף, *Joseph,* by itself, is similarly employed, Amos v. 15; vi. 6. Comp. Ezek. xxxvii. 16. For בֵּית־אֵל, *Bethel,* the LXX., Arab., and one of De Rossi's MSS., read בֵּית יִשְׂרָאֵל, *Beth Yisrael,* which reading is adopted by Newcome. One of Kennicott's MSS. has יִשְׂרָאֵל, *Israel,* which Houbigant, Dathe, and Bauer, approve. Jerome, Rosenmüller, Dahl, Justi, Struensee, and others, retain the received reading, which is supported by the Targ., Syr., and Vulg. Some would connect בֵּית־אֵל with מְכַבֶּה, and render, "there shall be none to quench Bethel;" but the verb כָּבָה is never construed with לְ, which marks here the Dative of possession. The true construction is, וְאֵין לְבֵית־אֵל מְכַבֶּה. The people of Israel put their trust in the idols which they worshipped at Bethel, but none of them

could remove the Divine judgments from the land.

7. הַהֹפְכִים, *ye that turn,* is to be referred to דֹּרְשׁוּ and בֵּית יוֹסֵף in the preceding verse. This construction is more natural than that which would take בֵּית יוֹסֵף alone as the nominative, in the third person. Such changes of person as that presented in דֹּרְשׁוּ, are too frequent to occasion any difficulty; nor is it always necessary to express them in a translation. Ewald takes an effectual method of removing the supposed difficulty, by striking out the verse, and inserting it at the beginning of verse 10. Of course, the whole will then read very smoothly; but the question still remains, Did Amos so connect the words?—לַעֲנָה, Arab. لعن, *abegit, execratus est,* is the Hebrew name of *wormwood,* and is given to it on account of its disgustingly bitter and injurious quality. The LXX. now read ὁ ποιῶν εἰς ὕψος κρίμα; but there can be little doubt that the original reading was ἄψινθος. The meaning is, that the persons spoken of so perverted their judicial proceedings, as to render them both obnoxious and injurious to those whom they affected. For הִנִּיחַ לָאָרֶץ, see on Is. xxviii. 2.

8. Another sublime description of the Most High, almost verbally identical with that furnished Job. ix. 9. The participles are to be referred to יְהֹוָה, *Jehovah,* ver. 6, as their antecedent. Newcome, following the Targ. and Syr., inserts "that have forsaken" at the commencement of the verse, but these authorities are not sufficient to warrant the addition, which, indeed, the text does not require. The article, used as a relative in הַקּוֹרֵא and הַמַּפְלִיג, is omitted before עֹשֵׂה and הֹפֵךְ, because they are in

And poureth them forth upon the surface of the earth ;
Jehovah is his name ;
9 That bringeth destruction suddenly upon the mighty,
And destruction cometh upon the fortress.

construction. Two of the principal constellations are selected from the heavenly
bodies as specimens of the effects of
Omnipotence. כִּימָה, *the Pleiades*, or
Seven Stars. This word occurs only here
and Job. ix. 9 ; xxxviii. 31. The derivation from a supposititious root כָּמָה, cognate with חוּם, חָמַם, חָמָה, *to be warm, hot*,
adopted by Castellus, Schultens, Parkhurst, and others, is to be rejected for
that preserved in the Arab. كرم, Conj.

II. *cumulum fecit ;* hence, كومة, *cumu-
lus ;* with which may be compared كيم
socius, according to which the name expresses what is brought or bound together,
especially *in abundance.* The name given
to this constellation by the Arabs is ثريا,
an abundance or *multitude*, from ثر, *multus
ac numerosus evasit, numerosus reddidit.*
For the same reason it was called by the
Greeks Πλειάδες, according to one of the
derivations of Eustathius on Homer,
Iliad. xviii. 486 : Αἱ δὲ πλειάδες ἤτοι
ἀπὸ τῆς μητρὸς αὐτῶν Πληϊόνης ἢ ὅτι
πλείους ὁμοῦ κατὰ μίαν συναγωγήν εἰσι,
κ. τ. λ. And most of the ancients express
the same idea ; as Seneca, *densi pleiadum
greges ;* Propertius, *pleiadum chorus,* &c.
According to the Greek mythology, the
Pleiades were seven daughters of Atlas,
who, being pursued by Orion, were
changed by Jupiter into doves, and,
having been transplanted to the heavens,
form the assemblage of the Seven Stars
in the neck of Taurus. In the passage
in the Iliad just referred to, they are por-
trayed on the shield of Achilles along
with Orion, in the same order as in our
prophet :

Πληϊάδας θ', Ὑάδας τε, τό τε σθένος
Ὠρίωνος.

In the mythology of the Sabians or
Mendaites, ‎ܠܡܚܐ‎, *the Seven*, and

‎ܟܘܟܒܐ‎ ‎ܫܒܥܐ‎, *the Seven Stars*, cut

no inconsiderable figure. See Norberg's
Liber Adami. For כְּסִיל, see on Is.
xiii. 10. Both terms have been entirely
mistaken by the LXX. who render ὁ
ποιῶν πάντα καὶ μετασκευάζων, which is
faithfully copied by the Arab. الصانع

צַלְמָוֶת.—‎ال ومهيعة‎, *the shadow of death*,
one of the very few Hebrew compounds.
See on Is. ix. 1. ל is to be supplied
before לַיְלָה, as, indeed, it is in fourteen
MSS., primarily in three more, and now
by correction in one; in both the Soncin. editions; in both of Bomberg,
1518 in the margin, and in the appendix
to Munster's, 1536. In וְהֶחְשִׁיךְ, there is
a transition from the participial to the
finite form of the verb. To render the
clause uniform, the construction would
be, מַחְשִׁיךְ יוֹם לְלָיְלָה. The passage quoted
from Pindar, by Clemens Alexandrinus,
is beautifully parallel :—

Θεῷ δὲ δυνατὸν ἐκ μελαίνας
Νυκτὸς ἀμίαντον ὦρσαι φῶς·
Κελαινῷ νέφει δὲ σκότος καλύψαι
Καθαρὸν ἀμέρας σέλας.

The following words are descriptive, not
of rain, as Jerome, Theodoret, Kimchi,
Drusius, Liveley, Marckius, Dahl, and
Rosenmüller maintain, but of a deluge
or inundation, the waters of which may
emphatically be said to be poured over
the earth. Thus Grotius, Clarius,
Bauer, and likewise Lowth, though he
admits the possibility of the other view
being right. The Alex. reading of the
LXX. ὁ θεὸς ὁ παντοκράτωρ is found in
the Arab., in a Copt. MS., and in the
Slavon. Bible, has the support of three
MSS., yet it is more likely an addition
from chap. iv. 13, than otherwise.

9. After the prophet had apparently
completed his magnificent description of
the Divine character, with the words
יְהוָה שְׁמוֹ, he appends in this verse an additional view of it, in order to make it
tell more practically on the fears of those
who boasted of the strength of Samaria.

בָּלַג, Arab. بلج, *nituit, fulgit* (aurora), not

10   They hate him that reproveth in the gate,
      And abhor him that speaketh uprightly.

11   Wherefore, because ye trample upon the poor,
      And take from him the tribute of corn:
      Though ye have built houses of hewn stone,
      Ye shall not dwell in them;
      Though ye have planted pleasant vineyards,
      Ye shall not drink of their wine.

12   For I know that your transgressions are many,
      And that your sins are great:
      Oppressing the righteous,
      Taking a bribe,
      And turning aside the poor in the gate.

13   Therefore the prudent shall be silent at that time;
      For it is an evil time.

---

only conveys the idea of *shining, being bright, cheerful,* &c. but also that of *suddenness,* suggested by the rapidity with which the dawning light is diffused over the horizon. The Hebrews applied such terms figuratively to the sudden production of misery, as well as to that of happiness. See on Joel ii. 2. Winer, *oriri faciens, inducens super potentes vastationem.* The ancient versions are all at fault here.

10. Ewald thinks that by בַּשַּׁעַר מוֹכִיחַ, *the reprover in the gate,* Amos himself is meant; but, from the recurrence of שָׂנֵא, and בַּשַּׁעַר, in connexion with מִשְׁפָּט, ver. 15, it is far more natural to interpret the phrase of a magistrate, senator, or judge. Comp. also ver. 12, and see on Is. xxix. 21. In תָּמִים, which is to be taken adverbially, as Judges ix. 19, is an ellipsis of בְּ.

11—13. בֹּשֵׁס is, in all probability, a faulty orthography of בֹּסֵס, the Polal. of בּוּס, Arab. باس, *vilipendit* rem, *to tread down, trample upon,* &c. De Rossi's codex 380, reads וּשִׁסְכֶם with *Sin.*—מַשְׂאַת, *what is raised,* as a *tax, tribute,* &c. from נָשָׂא, *to raise.* Instead of remitting to the poor the tax which they were unable to pay, the rulers and proprietors rigidly exacted it, that they might consume it upon their lusts. But in whatever state and luxury they might have lived, and whatever preparations they might be

making for further indulgences, Jehovah declares that they should not continue to enjoy them. The enemy would speedily remove them from all the objects on which they proudly doated, or from which they expected gratification. For the contrary of the threatening, see Is. lxv. 21, 22 ; Amos ix. 14. The adjectives רַבִּים and עֲצֻמִים are placed before their substantives, because they are predicatives, and not qualificatives. Before both, the conjunction כִּי is to be supplied. The ellipsis was probably occasioned by its having been used at the beginning of the verse. כֹּפֶר is most commonly used in the sense of λύτρον, ἀντίλυτρον, *ransom,* or *price of redemption,* on which account Ewald and some others render it so here; but the close connexion in which the whole phrase stands with the perversion of justice, specified in the last clause of the verse, decides in favour of the signification *bribe, bribery,* which the word unquestionably has, 1 Sam. xii. 3. Targ. מָמוֹן דִּשְׁקַר, *the mammon of falsehood.* Syr. ܐܘܚܕܐ, *a bribe.* LXX. ἀλλάγματα. The other Greek versions, ἐξίλασμα. If צֹרְרֵי צַדִּיק could be taken to mean, "*shutting up,* or *imprisoning* the righteous," then כֹּפֶר might mean *ransom;* but such usage does not obtain. The only course left for the pious to pursue in the midst of such atrocious

14   Seek good, and not evil, that ye may live ;
And it shall be so ; Jehovah, God of hosts, shall be with you,
According as ye say.

15   Hate evil, and love good,
And establish justice in the gate ;
Perhaps Jehovah, God of hosts, may pity
The residue of Joseph.

16   Therefore thus saith Jehovah, God of hosts, the Lord :
In all the broad places there shall be wailing ;
And in all the streets, they shall say, Oh ! Oh !
Yea, they shall call the husbandman to mourning ;
And all who are skilled in elegy to wailing.

perversion of order and justice, was that of quietly submitting to the hand of God, which they were taught to recognise in the permission of these evils, and patiently abiding the issue of events. Any attempt, under these circumstances, to stem the current, or effect a reformation, or even to plead for private or public rights, would only aggravate their calamities. הַמַּשְׂכִּיל, *the intelligent, prudent*, is to be understood, in the best sense, of one who acts upon the principles of enlightened piety.

14, 15. Reiterated calls to reformation, in order to ensure the return of Divine favour. Both the style and the sentiments have their parallel in Is. i. 16, 17. Notwithstanding the sad apostasies of the Israelitish people, they still had their profession of the religion of Jehovah to fall back upon, in case of necessity. They boasted that he was with them, but it was an empty pretence while their profession was insincere, being combined with the worship of idols. For the force of the conditional particle אוּלַי, *perhaps*, in such connexion, compare Gen. xvi. 2, and εἰ ἄρα, Acts viii. 22. Comp. also Joel ii. 14, where the same idea is expressed by מִי יוֹדֵעַ, *who knoweth ?*—שְׁאֵרִית יוֹסֵף, *the remainder of Joseph*. For this use of the patronymic, see on ver. 6. Numerous as the Israelites still were, they might well be called a *remainder*, in consideration of the havoc made by Hazael, who, when "the Lord began to cut" them "short," "smote them in all the coasts of Israel ; from Jordan eastward, all the land of Gilead, the Gadites, and

the Reubenites, and the Manassites, from Aroer, which is by the river Arnon, even Gilead and Bashan." 2 Kings x. 32, 33.

16. לָכֵן, *therefore*, refers not to the contents of verses 14, 15, but to verses 7, 10, and 12. We may suppose a considerable pause to intervene before ver. 16. Foreseeing that the people would not repent, Jehovah here declares that the threatened punishment was inevitable. The slaughter involved in this punishment would be general. Samaria, however, and its vicinity, seem specially intended. The position in which אָמַר יְיָ is here placed, is altogether unusual. Indeed, I am not aware that it is so found in any other passage. Yet I would not, with Newcome, cancel it, on the slender authority of seven MSS., the LXX., Arab., and Syr. It seems rather to have been purposely added, in order to give greater solemnity to the sentence which was to be pronounced. רְחֹבוֹת, *broad*, or *open places*, or *wide streets* in a city ; and distinguished from חוּצוֹת, which signify ordinary or narrow streets, such as are common in the East. Gr. πλατεῖα. מִסְפֵּד, strictly means *a smiting of the breast*, (LXX. κοπετὸς,) from סָפַד, *to beat, smite ;* see on Is. xxxii. 12. Here, however, it is used to denote wailing or mourning in general. הוֹ הוֹ, *Oh ! Oh !* This onomatopoetic I have rendered by the corresponding English interjection, which, when prolonged and swelled in the pronunciation, as it is by persons giving utterance to excessive grief, is much more appropriate than

17 And in all the vineyards there shall be wailing,
   For I will pass through the midst of thee,
   Saith Jehovah.

18 Wo unto you that desire the day of Jehovah!
   What is the day of Jehovah unto you?
   It shall be darkness, and not light.

19 As when one fleeth from a lion,
   And a bear meeteth him ;
   Or he entereth the house, and leaneth his hand on the wall,
   And a serpent biteth him.

20 Shall not the day of Jehovah be darkness and not light ;
   Even thick darkness, without any brightness ?

Alas! Alas! Syr. ܘܗܘ ܘܗܘ ; Chald.
וַי וַי ; Vulg. *væ ! væ !* in other Latin
versions, *eheu ! eheu !* The *husbandmen,*
(אִכָּר) were to be called to participate in the
mourning, not as Newcome, Rosenmüller,
and some others have thought, on account
of the desolation of the fields, but either
on account of the loudness of their rustic
voices, or because the slaughter of the
citizens of Samaria would be so great,
that a sufficient number would not be
left to perform the funeral rites. Such
construction of the meaning is required
by the following parallelism : וּמִסְפֵּד
אֶל־יוֹדְעֵי נֶהִי. There is no necessity for
supposing that the words of this sentence have been transposed, and that
they originally stood thus : וְיוֹדְעֵי נֶהִי
אֶל־מִסְפֵּד. The preposition אֶל is understood
before מִסְפֵּד ; and קָרָא, as repeated to
govern אֶל, which it often does, as well
as the accusative. נְהִי, *wailing, lamentation,* from נָהָה, Syr. ܢܓܐ, *to utter
lamentable cries.* The persons here
spoken of as " skilled in wailing," were
mourners by profession, who were hired
for the occasion, and sang doleful tunes
around the corpse of a deceased person,
which they preceded when it was carried
to the grave, giving utterance to dismal
cries and howlings, beating their breasts,
throwing ashes on their heads, and showing every artificial token of excessive
grief. These were the mourners whom
Solomon describes as going about the
streets, Eccles. xii. 5. That females were
especially employed on such occasions,

appears from Jer. ix. 17—19, where נֶהִי
is twice used as here by Amos. The
same custom obtained among the Greeks
and Romans. Thus Homer, speaking of
the funeral of Hector, says :

——————— τὸν μὲν ἔπειτα
Τρητοῖς ἐν λεχέεσσι θέσαν, παρὰ δ᾽ εἷσαν
   ἀοιδοὺς,
Θρήνων ἐξάρχους, οἵτε στονόεσσαν
   ἀοιδὴν
Οἱ μὲν ἄρ᾽ ἐθρήνεον, ἐπὶ δὲ στενάχοντο
   γυναῖκες.   *Iliad.* xxiv. 719, &c.

See also Horace de Arte Poet. ver. 431, &c.
In his edition of Harmer's Observations,
vol. iii. p. 42, Dr. A. Clarke gives a description of the ancient funeral solemnities of the Irish, and the translation of
a song of wailing prepared for the occasion, which bears a strong resemblance
to those used by the Orientals. Comp.
Wilkinson's Ancient Egyptians, second
series, vol. ii. pp. 402—407.

17. The vineyards, which usually exhibited scenes of rejoicing, should now
be frequented by disconsolate mourners.
For Jehovah's passing through the land,
comp. Exod. xii. 12, 23 ; only in the
latter case the punishment was miraculously inflicted ; in the former, by the
king of Assyria, as an instrument in the
hand of God.

18—20. These verses intimately cohere
with the preceding. *The day of Jehovah*
means the time when his judgments
should be inflicted. The Israelites could
only have given expression sarcastically
to the wish that this day might soon
reach them. It was an impious daring

21 I hate, I loathe your festivals;
   Neither do I delight in your days of restraint.
22 When ye offer to me holocausts and bloodless sacrifices,
   I will take no pleasure in them;
   Neither will I regard the thank-offerings of your fatlings.
23 Take away from me the noise of thy songs,
   For I will not hear the music of thy harps.
24 But let justice roll on like water,

of Jehovah to do his worst. Comp. Is. v. 19; Jer. xvii. 15. The prophet tells them plainly that it would be to them a day of unmitigated affliction. The fallacy of every hope of escape is illustrated by two simple, but forcible comparisons, borrowed from the pastoral life. Bochart regards the language as proverbial, and supports his opinion by two Arabic stories: the one beginning, اسد قصد انسانا

وهرب والتجا الي شجرة وانا علي "A lion, بعض اغصنها دب يقطف ثمرها, pursuing a man, he took refuge in a tree, in the branches of which a bear having fixed himself, was plucking its fruit," &c.; and the other, هرب رجل من الاسد فوقع في بير ووقع الاسد خلفه فانا في البير دب, "A man fled from a lion, and fell into a well, into which the lion went down after him. And there was a bear in the well," &c. Hierozo. lib. iii. cap. ix. pp. 810, 811. Kimchi tersely expresses the meaning thus, תצאו מצרה אל צרה, Ye shall go out of calamity into calamity. Comp. Job xx. 24; Is. xxiv. 18. The adjective אָפֵל is explained by the following words. It occurs only in this place; but the substantives אֲפֵלָה, אֹפֶל, dense obscurity, are used in several passages of Job, the Psalms, and the Prophets. אֲפֵלוֹת, however, in the sense of concealed, occurs Exod. ix. 32. Comp. the Arab. أفل, occidit sol, &c. Thus in Hariri, Consess. xv. the noun أفول is employed: انقراض العلم ودروسه وافول اقمارها وشمسه, "Extirpatio eruditionis et

obliteratio ejus: Lunarumque ac Solium ejusdem occasus." נָגַהּ, on the contrary, signifies to shine, be light; and its derivative נֹגַהּ is used of the rising of the sun, Prov. iv. 18, where it is contrasted with אֲפֵלָה, ver. 19.

21—23. The same aversion from the ceremonial observances of the insincere and rebellious Israelites which Jehovah here expresses, he afterwards employed Isaiah to declare to the Jews, chap. i. 10—15. The two passages are strikingly parallel; only the latter prophet amplifies what is set forth in a more condensed form by Amos. It is also to be observed, that where Amos introduces the musical accompaniments of the sacrifices, Isaiah substitutes the prayers; both concluding with the divine words, לֹא אֶשְׁמָע=אֵינֶנִּי שֹׁמֵעַ, I will not hear. The verbs שָׂנֵאתִי מָאַסְתִּי follow each other immediately, for the sake of more emphatically expressing the Divine abhorrence. Comp. הוֹעֵבָה הִיא לִי and שָׂנְאָה נַפְשִׁי in Isaiah.—לֹא אָרִיחַ, lit. I will not smell; but meaning here, I will take no delight in. עֲצָרוֹת, restraints, periods, days of restraint, or assemblies collected on such days. See on Is. i. 13. שָׁלֵם, used here collectively for the plural שְׁלָמִים.—הָסֵר מֵעָלַי, lit. remove from upon me; conveying the idea of a burden which vexes and annoys the bearer. Isaiah expresses it in full: הָיוּ עָלַי לָטֹרַח, "They are a burden upon me." Comp. further for the force of the compound preposition, Exod. x. 28. The music here referred to was that performed at the Hebrew festivals by the Levites, before and during the offering of the sacrifices, and on other public occasions.

24. While no direction is given respecting the regulation of the sacrifices, in order that they might be presented in an acceptable manner, a special injunction is imparted in regard to justice and

And righteousness like a mighty stream.

25 Did ye [not] present sacrifices and offerings to me,
During forty years in the desert, O house of Israel?

rectitude, on the principle that "to obey is better than sacrifice, and to hearken than the fat of rams," 1 Sam. xv. 22. "Nec in victimis, licet optimæ sint, auroque præfulgeant, Deorum est honos, sed pia ac recta mente venerantium." Seneca de Beneficiis, i. 6. That אֵיתָן, Arab. وَثُن, *perennis fuit*, is to be here rendered *perennial*, or *everflowing*, and not *mighty*, has been maintained by some interpreters; but a comparison of the several passages in which it occurs, goes to show that it is rather to be referred to اون, *validus fuit, multus fuit,* and is to be rendered *great* or *mighty.* It thus better corresponds with גָּלַל, *roll, to roll on,* used in the former hemistich. LXX. ὡς χειμάρρους ἄβατος. Syr. ܐܡܪ ܢܚܠܐ ܟܡܝܠܬܐ Vulg. *quasi torrens fortis.* Arab. مثل الوادي الذي لا يسلك *like a Wady that cannot be passed.* The ideas of abundance and moral power are those conveyed by the prophet. I must differ from Prof. Lee, who (Heb. Lex. in voc. אֵיתָן) renders, "for judgment rolleth (away) as the waters (roll away), and righteousness (disappears) like the mighty torrent." The verse as thus rendered ill suits the context, and is not in keeping with parallel passages, in which, after a reprehension of hypocritical observances, the moral qualities of truth and righteousness are required. The construction put upon it by Theodoret, Kimchi, Munster, Veil, and Hitzig, that the coming of the Divine judgments is intended, is, for the same reasons, to be rejected.

25—27. These verses have not a little perplexed expositors, both ancient and modern. The first difficulty lies in what is said respecting the presentation of sacrifices. Greve, Dahl, and Maurer, take the ה in הַזְּבָחִים to be the article, and not the particle of interrogation, and render, *the sacrifices and offerings ye presented to me,* &c., viz. those prescribed in the law: *but now ye bear the shrine,* &c. According to this mode of construction, the present idolatrous course of the Israelites is contrasted with their former obedience to the Divine will. In order, however, to justify this interpretation, the article must have been repeated before מִנְחָה, which it is not. The insertion of the compensative Dagesh in the letter *Zain* cannot be pleaded in its favour, since there are several instances in which the interrogative ה takes the form of the article, before words beginning with Sheva, as הַלְבֶן, Gen. xvii. 17; הַדְּרָכִי, Ezek. xviii. 29; הַנִּמְצָא, Joel iv. [Eng. iii.] 4, &c. The ancient translators have all read interrogatively. LXX. Μὴ σφάγια καὶ θυσίας προσηνέγκατέ μοι, κ. τ. λ.; Syr. ܠܡܐ ܕܒܚܐ ܘܩܘܪܒܢܐ ܩܪܒܬܘܢ ܠܝ. Vulg. *Numquid hostias et sacrificium obtulistis mihi,* &c. ? Targ. הַנִכְסַת קוּדְשִׁין וְקוּרְבָּנִין קָרֵבְתּוּן קֳדָמַי בְּמַדְבְּרָא. And so almost all the moderns, some of whom suppose the force of the question to lie in לִי, *to me,* taken emphatically, "Was it to ME," &c. ; while others think that an absolute denial of the presentation of sacrifices in the wilderness is implied in the words. In support of the latter opinion, it has been attempted to prove, that the Israelites could not have offered any sacrifices for want of cattle. Such a position, however, is contrary to the express declarations found in Exod. xii. 38; xvii. 3; xxxiv. 3; Lev. xvii. 1—9. Num. vii. *passim;* xx. 4, 19. The life which they led in the desert was that of Nomades, so that there could have been no lack of animals for sacrifice. The true construction of the passage is founded on the principle, that not unfrequently in Hebrew the interrogation implies, and calls for an emphatic affirmative, either expressed or understood; and is thus equivalent to a negative interrogation in our language, and indeed to הֲלֹא in Hebrew. See 1 Sam. ii. 27, 28; Job xx. 4; Jer. xxxi. 20; Ezek. xx. 4. In the present case, as in those just cited, the persons addressed are supposed to admit the fact couched in the appeal; but the question is so put in order the more forcibly to introduce the adversative

26 And yet ye bare the shrine of your king,

sentence which follows in the 26th verse. The connexion of the two verses is this : "Did ye not present sacrifices and offerings to me in the wilderness forty years, O house of Israel? Yes; and yet ye bare the shrine," &c. That the conjunction וֹ is frequently to be rendered *and yet, but yet*, or the like, see Gen. xvii. 21 ; Judges xvi. 15 ; Ps. l. 17 ; Is. liii. 7. What is here charged upon the ancient Israelites was their indulging in idolatrous practices while they professedly attended to the ritual observances of the Mosaic law—the very sin which Amos was commissioned to charge upon their descendants in his day, and on account of which they were to be carried into captivity. The opinion of Forsayeth (quoted by Newcome), Dahl, and others, that the sin reproved in ver. 26 was exclusively that of those who lived in the time of the prophet, is less admissible than that which refers it to their ancestors, yet so that the reproof was intended to be applied to their own case by those whom the prophet addressed.—The 26th verse has been very differently rendered, as well as variously interpreted. The translation of the LXX. is as follows: Καὶ ἀνελάβετε τὴν σκηνὴν τοῦ Μολὸχ, καὶ τὸ ἄστρον τοῦ θεοῦ ὑμῶν 'Ραιφὰν, τοὺς τύπους αὐτῶν, οὓς ἐποιήσατε ἑαυτοῖς ; as if the Hebrew had read, וּנְשָׂאתֶם אֵת סִכּוּת מֶלֶךְ וְאֵת כּוֹכַב אֱלֹהֵיכֶם כִּיּוּן צַלְמֵיכֶם אֲשֶׁר עֲשִׂיתֶם לָכֶם : No vestige, however, of any such order of the words is found in any Hebrew MS., or in any other monument of antiquity, except the speech of Stephen, as recorded by Luke, Acts vii. 43, which is an almost verbal quotation from the LXX. It is thus rendered by Theod.; Καὶ ἤρατε τὴν ὅρασιν τοῦ βασιλέως ὑμῶν, ἀμαύρωσιν εἰδώλων ὑμῶν, ἄστρον τοῦ θεοῦ ὑμῶν ; so that he must have read the words as they now stand in the Hebrew text. The same may be said of the Syr., Vulg., and Targ., though their renderings differ from each other in one or two minor particulars. The remark of Jerome on the discrepancies between the Hebrew text and the ancient Greek version deserves to be quoted here : "Observandum est, apostolos et apostolicos viros in ponendis testimoniis de Veteri Testamento, non verba considerare sed sensum, nec eadem sermonum calcare

vestigia, dummodo a sententiis non recedant." Comment. *in loc.* Most interpreters follow the LXX. in giving סִכּוּת by σκηνὴ, *a tent;* deriving it, like סֻכָּה, and סֹךְ, of the same signification, from סָכַךְ, *to intertwine*, as branches, so as to form a booth or hut. Others, such as Jarchi, Calvin, Mercer, and Rosenmüller, take it to mean an image or idol, and render, *Siccuth your king.* They explain it by referring to the Chald. סִכְּתָא, *a wooden post*, which they supposed formed the pedestal on which the idol stood, and so the word might be transferred to the idol itself. Ewald takes much the same view. The former derivation is alone admissible. The tent appears to have had something of the texture, as it had the design of the σκηνὴν ἱερὰν, *sacred tent*, in the Carthaginian camp, mentioned by Diodorus Siculus, lib. xx. cap. 65, and described as consisting ἐκ καλάμου καὶ χόρτου, of reeds and grass. Comp. Wilkinson's Ancient Egypt, second series, vol. ii. pp. 270—275. Only, as it is certain Moses would not have tolerated anything of the kind if its size had been such as to bring it to his cognizance, it may be inferred, that it was only a small temple or shrine, which might easily be concealed in the interior of a tent. Such diminutive temples were in use among the Egyptians, from whom no doubt the Hebrews took the idea. Herodotus, describing an idol worshipped at Papremis, says, (lib. ii. 63.) τὸ δὲ ἄγαλμα ἐὸν ἐν ΝΗΩι ΜΙΚΡΩι ξυλίνῳ κατακεχρυσωμένῳ προεκκομίζουσι τῇ προτεραίῃ ἐς ἄλλο οἴκημα ἱρόν, "The image, being in a *small temple* of gilt wood, they carry out on the previous day to another sacred habitation." Compare the ναοὶ ἀργυροῖ, shrines, or small temples of Diana, mentioned Acts xix. 24. That any connexion is to be traced between סִכּוּת, *Siccuth*, and סֻכּוֹת בְּנוֹת, *Succoth-benoth*, 2 Kings xvii. 30, the tents in which the daughters of the Babylonians prostituted themselves in worship of Venus, does not appear. מַלְכְּכֶם, *your king*, thus Symm., Theod., and Leo Juda, and most moderns ; but the LXX. Μολὸχ, Syr. ܡܰܠܟܽܘܡ, *Malcum*, Aq. Μέλχεμ, Vulg. *Moloch*, exhibit the word as the proper name of the god of the Ammonites, *i. e.* מֹלֶךְ,

And Chiun of your images, the star of your god,
Which ye made for yourselves.

also called מִלְכֹּם, *Milcom,* 1 Kings xi. 5, and מִלְכָּם, *Malcam,* by our translators, Zeph. i. 5; and this construction some moderns have adopted. As, however, מֶלֶךְ, *king,* is also employed by the Hebrews in application to idols, Is. xxxvii. 13, and may be so read in Zeph. i. 5, it seems better to retain its usual signification. The Phœnicians gave the title of מִלְךְ עֹלָם, *king of the world,* to the sun, and מִלְקַרְת=מִלְךְ קֶרֶת, *king of the city,* to Hercules. Comp. Ζεῦ ἄνα, Iliad. iii. 351; xvi. 233; and 'Ω 'ναξ ἦλθε παρ' ἡμέας ἱκέτης, Herod. I. 159. In Ethiopic **አምላክ**, *Amlak,* the proper name for God, is derived from **መለከ**, *imperavit, rexit,* and is applied in the plural to idols. The learned are generally agreed, that the Moloch of Scripture was the image of the planet *Saturn,* and thus identical with *Chiun,* mentioned by Amos in the following clause of the verse. The Phœnicians were in the habit of offering to him human sacrifices, especially children, to which horrible custom repeated reference is made in the historical books of the Old Testament. See Michaelis on the laws of Moses, Art. ccxlvii. Suppl. No. 1115; Selden de Diis Syris, cap. vi.; Spencer de Legibus Hebræor. lib. ii. cap. 10; Gesenius, in his Thesaurus, *sub. voc.;* Winer, Realwörter-buch. כִּיּוּן צַלְמֵיכֶם, *Chiun of your images,* i. e. represented by them; the model after which they were made. While the idol so called, which the Hebrews carried about in a sacred shrine, was itself a symbol or representative of one of the heavenly bodies, it was in its turn represented by a number of copies, or smaller images, which they used as penates or household-gods in the practice of astrolatry. Such appears to me to be the meaning of the words. To this construction, however, C. B. Michaelis, Vitringa, Rosenmüller, Hesselberg, Hengstenberg, and others object, that it makes כִּיּוּן a proper name, which, with the older grammarians, they allege cannot be put in regimen. But to this rule, it must be admitted, there are many exceptions, as בַּעַל גָּד, בַּעַל חֶרְמוֹן, מִשְׁפְּתוֹת צֹרְנַיִם,

יְהֹוָה צְבָאוֹת, כָּלֵב אֶפְרָתָה, אֲרַם נַהֲרַיִם, &c. Nor can it justly be objected that as סִכּוּת is an appellative, כִּיּוּן being parallel to it, must necessarily be the same. The necessity of the case is not obvious. Both are mentioned as objects which the Hebrews carried about for idolatrous purposes— the one, the portable temple of the idol; the other, the idol itself placed in this temple, of which numerous miniature resemblances were privately distributed throughout the camp. The LXX. unquestionably regarded the word as a prop r name, whatever they may thereby have intended to designate. And this view of the subject is confirmed by כּוֹכָב, *a star,* being put in apposition with כִּיּוּן, in order to explain it, an explanation which cannot apply, if by the latter term we understand merely the *pedestal* or *stand* on which the idol was placed. It is now almost a settled point, that by כִּיּוּן, *Chiun,* the planet *Saturn* is meant. If we except the Syr., which reads ܟܐܘܢ, *Kevon,* the earliest authorities which we have for this interpretation of the passage are the rabbins Abenezra and Kimchi; but their testimony as relating to a matter of fact is irrefragable, however slightingly Hengstenberg seems to treat it, Authen. des Pentat. p. 113. The former thus comments upon the passage: ומלה כיון ידוע בלשון ישמעאל גם פרס כי הוא כיואן והוא שבתי כי עשו לו צלם, "And as for the term *Chiun,* it is known in the Arabic and Persic languages by the name *Kivan,* which is Saturn, to which they made an image." And the latter, in nearly the same words: הוא כוכב שבתי וכן נקרא בלשון ישמעאל ופרס כיואן, "It is the star Saturn, and thus he is called *Kivan* in the Arabic and Persic."

كيوان, *Keiwan,* seems to have been adopted from the latter into the former of these languages, in the Lexicons of which, as a foreign word, it is explained by زحل, the usual name for Saturn in Arabic. It occurs in the Persian work entitled Dabistan, the author of which, describing the temples which the ancient Persians dedicated to the planets, says:

27 Therefore, I will carry you away captive beyond Damascus,
Saith Jehovah: God of hosts is his name.

بيكر شت كيوان را از سنک سياه

that "the image of *Keiwan* was of black
stone." (Lee's Hebrew Lex. *in voc.*

אֶשְׂרָה) He speaks, in fact, of the خانه,

shrine, and بيكر, *image*, of the planet, just
as Amos does of סִכּוּת and כִּיּוּן. According
to the Zendavesta the seven planets
are Tir, Behram, Achuma, Anahid,
Kewan, Gurtsher, and Dœdidom Mus-
hewer. Bundehesh V. In the codex
Nasaræus, containing the doctrines of
the Sabæans, which was published by
Norberg, we find a list of the demons
which rule these planets, among whom
ܣܡܟܡܠܐ ܟܡܘ, *the fifth is Kivan*, p. 54.

It is afterwards added in the same page:

ܘܡܐܘܕܚܡܠ ܟܡܘ ܢܘܥܟܬܐ ܘ܏ܟܚܡܘ
ܘ܏ܟܕܚܡܘ ܙܥܡܕܟܘ ܘܐܟܣܥܘܣܘ
ܘܟܚܕܟܘ "The demons of *Kivan* inject
lamentation, weeping, and mourning into
the hearts of men, and rob them of
happiness." And we farther read, p. 212,

ܠܟܡܘ ܟܕܪ܏ܟܬ ܟܘܣܟܠܐ ܘܥܟܕܘܚ
ܗܘܣ ܣܟܡ ܘ܏ܚܡܘܩ "To *Kivan* is
attributed malice, because from it come
diminution and want." Ascribing the
same evil influence to Saturn, the Arabs
likewise give to it the name of الكيس

الاكبر, *the great disaster;* and the idea
frequently occurs in the Latin classics.
See Lucan. i. 650; Juven. vi. 569;
Macrob. Saturn. i. 19. If the Hebrew
כיון be pointed כֵּיוָן, the exact pronunciation of the name of the planet in the other
Oriental dialects will be brought out, and

thus the evidence of identity be complete.
With respect to 'Ραιφὰν, the rendering
of the LXX., or 'Ρέφαν, as it is to be spelt
on the authority of the best MSS., (comp.
Acts vii. 43,) there is every reason to believe that they mistook ב for ר, as they
have done in other instances; and so
have given *Rephan*, instead of *Kephan*.
That PHΦAN should occur in the Arabico-
Coptic table of the planets exhibited by
Kircher in his Ling. Ægypt. Restit. p. 49,
by no means proves that this was the
ancient Egyptian name of Saturn; for
as that table is of no great antiquity, and
as the other names are chiefly derived
from the Greek, we may reasonably
infer that the one in question was copied
from the Coptic version of this very
passage of the LXX. At all events, no
such name of a deity has yet been found
in the Egyptian pantheon. כּוֹכָב, *the star*,
is expletive of כִּיּוּן, in so far as it informs
us that the figure of the idol was that of
a star, and thus proves the idolatrous
worship to have been the Sabæan, with
which the Hebrews became acquainted
during their stay in the Arabian desert.
27. Instead of מֵהָלְאָה לְדַמָּשֶׂק, LXX.
ἐπέκεινα Δαμασκοῦ, "beyond Damascus," with which all the other authorities
agree, Stephen has ἐπέκεινα Βαβυλῶνος,
"beyond *Babylon*," Acts vii. 43, obviously
by way of interpretation. הָלְאָה naturally
suggests the idea of *remoteness*, though
it is sometimes used in reference to what
is at no great distance. Root הָלָא, Arab.

هل, *recessit*, Syr. ܣܝܠܐܣ, *removit*,
elongavit. The ה added is paragogic.
While what Amos states is included in the
statement made by the proto-martyr, the
latter embraces what was known from
fact to be the fulfilment of the prophecy:
the Israelites having been carried, not
merely beyond Damascus, but beyond
Babylon, into the country of the Medes.
The chapter closes with a vindication of
the supremacy of Jehovah above all the
objects of Sabæan worship: אֱלֹהֵי צְבָאוֹת שְׁמוֹ,
God of Sabaoth is his name!

CHAPTER VI

This chapter embraces the character and punishment of the whole Hebrew nation. The inhabitants of the two capitals are directly addressed in the language of denunciation, and charged to take warning from the fate of other nations, 1, 2. Their carnal security, injustice, self-indulgence, sensuality, and total disregard of the divine threatenings, are next described, 3—6; after which the prophet announces the captivity, and the calamitous circumstances connected with the siege of Samaria, by which it was to be preceded, 7—11. He then exposes the absurdity of their conduct, and threatens them with the irruption of an enemy, that should pervade the whole country, 12—14.

---

1 Wo to them that are at ease in Zion,
  And to them that are secure in the mountain of Samaria;
  The distinguished men of the first of nations,
  To whom the house of Israel come!

1. Though chiefly directed against the northern of the two kingdoms, the language of this prophecy is so constructed as to apply to both; and in the present verse express mention is made of the inhabitants of Jerusalem, who resembled those of Samaria in carelessness and carnal security. שַׁאֲנָן and בָּטֵחַ are similarly connected and applied, Is. xxxii. 9, 11; so that the rendering of the LXX. τοῖς ἐξουθενοῦσι Σιὼν, adopted by Dathe, cannot be justified. For the primary meaning of שָׁאַן, compare the cognate שָׁעַן, in Niphal, to lean, lean upon, trust. The reduplicate Nun expresses intensity. נָקוּב has here the acceptation of the Arab. نقيب, rerum gentis administrator, princeps gentis: from نقب, perfodit, creatus est; creatus fuit dux. Whence also نقابة, prefectura. The Hebrew phrase נָקַב בְּשֵׁם, to be marked, distinguished by name, is always used in reference to persons who had been chosen or designated for some special service. Num.

i. 17; 1 Chron. xii. 31; xvi. 41; 2 Chron. xxviii. 15; xxxi. 19. The term is here employed for the purpose of specifying more particularly the leading men in the two kingdoms, whose profligacy and irreligion preeminently aggravated the national guilt. By רֵאשִׁית הַגּוֹיִם we are not, with Newcome, to understand "the chief of the idolatrous nations," and that the persons spoken of were called after them, but the Hebrew nation, which is so called because it was the principal, or most distinguished of all the nations of the earth: having been constituted the peculiar people of God, and possessing laws and privileges unknown to any other. It might well be said to occupy the first rank. Compare רֵאשִׁית גּוֹיִם עֲמָלֵק, Num. xxiv. 20, where the reference is to the distinguished place which the Amalekites held among the nations of Canaan. לָהֶם is to be construed with נְקֻבֵי, and not with גּוֹיִם, or with צִיּוֹן and שֹׁמְרוֹן. The people of Israel were in the habit of going up to their princes and leaders for the decision of differences, &c. The latter thus exerted an influence over the

2 Pass over to Calneh, and see;
And go thence to Hamath the great;
Go down also to Gath of the Philistines:
Were they better than these kingdoms?
Were their boundaries more ample than yours?

3 Wo to them that put off the day of evil,
And bring near the seat of oppression;

entire people. Both the LXX. and the Syr. are greatly at fault in the translation of this verse.

2. Three heathen cities are here selected as specimens of the greatness and prosperity of the nations to which they belonged, and the Israelites are challenged to institute a comparison of the circumstances of these nations and the extent of their territory, with those of their own, as also, to reflect on the present prostrate condition of the cities mentioned, in order that they might become sensible of the superiority with which Jehovah had distinguished them, and the greater punishment to which they had exposed themselves by their ungrateful returns. For כַּלְנֵה, *Calneh*, and חֲמָת, *Hamath*, see on Is. x. 9. Hitzig attempts to prove that by the latter name, אַחְמְתָא, *Ecbatana* or *Hamedan* is meant; but there is no reason to believe that the Hebrews had any knowledge of this city in the days of Amos. It is here called רַבָּה, *great*, not to distinguish it from other cities of the same name, but to express its size and magnificence. Comp. צִידוֹן רַבָּה, *Sidon the great*, Josh. xi. 8. גַּת, *Gath*, was the chief city of one of the five satrapies of the Philistines, with whose name it is here associated, to distinguish it from Gath-Hepher, and Gath-Rimmon. It had more than once been reduced before the time of Amos, and disappeared at an early period from the annals of geography. No trace of it has been discovered by any modern traveller. The ה in הַשֹּׁבִים has been regarded as the article by the LXX., Syr., and Vulg. translators, and is thus found in twelve of De Rossi's MSS.; but the more natural construction is that of the Targ. and most modern versions, which makes it interrogative. Before the מִן of comparison is an ellipsis of הֵנָּה; and הַמַּמְלָכוֹת הָאֵלֶּה, *these kingdoms*, must be understood

as designating those of Israel and Judah, with which the prophet had immediately to do, and to which he thus emphatically points. In this way only can an appropriate reference be found for the distinctive affixes in גְּבוּלָם and גְּבֻלְכֶם.

3. Supply הוֹי, *woo to*, from ver. 1. הַמְנַדִּים, the Targ. not inappropriately explains by מְרַחֲקִין, *remove to a distance*. The root is נָדָה, which in the other dialects signifies *to separate*, *remove* as an object of disgust. Aq. οἱ ἀποκεχωρισμένοι, Symm. ἀφωρισμένοι. The persons addressed could not bear the idea that the period of threatened punishment was impending; they endeavoured as much as possible to keep it out of view. Comp. Ezek. xii. 21—28. In striking antithesis to this, they are represented in the following hemistich, as acting in such a manner as speedily to bring it upon them. Thus Claudian;

"Sed quam cœcus inest vitiis amor!
    omne futurum
Despicitur, suadentque brevem præsentia
    fructum;
Et ruit in vetitum damni secura libido,
Dum mora supplicii lucro, serumque,
    quod instat,
Creditur."   *Eutrop.* lib. ii.

I cannot agree with Jerome, Grotius, Newcome, Justi, and some others, in referring שֶׁבֶת חָמָס, *the seat* or *throne of oppression*, to the rule of the king of Assyria: it is more natural to regard the prophet as describing the wickedness of the people themselves in yielding support to a system of flagrant injustice and oppression, on the part of their own rulers and judges. Thus most expositors. שֶׁבֶת occurs nowhere else in the sense of *throne*; but יָשַׁב, of which it is properly the infinitive, is used in application both to kings and judges, as is also the participle יוֹשֵׁב. The term is synonymous with כִּסֵּא, which is also used both of the

4 That lie upon beds of ivory,
  And are stretched upon their couches ;
  That eat lambs from the flock,
  And calves from the midst of the stall ;
5 That strike up songs to the sound of the lyre ;
  Like David, they invent for themselves instruments of music ;
6 That drink in bowls of wine,
  And anoint with the first of oils ;
  But are not grieved for the destruction of Joseph !
7 Therefore now they shall go captive at the head of the captives,
  And the shouting company of those that recline shall depart.

throne and the bench. הַגִּישׁ is here taken by most interpreters to have the same signification as in Kal, *to approach;* but as in every other instance in which the verb is used in Hiphil it vindicates to itself the causative acceptation, and in the present case is obviously intended to form a contrast to מִנַּדִּים, which conveys the idea of *removing to a distance,* I must retain the rendering of our common version. Thus Hitzig and Ewald. The meaning is, that instead of putting away from them all illegal and oppressive judgments, they encouraged those who were guilty of them, by assisting in carrying them into execution.

4. For מִפּוֹת שֵׁן, *beds of ivory,* see on chap. iii. 15; and comp. *lecti eburni* of Horace, and *lecti eborati* of Plautus.

סְרֻחִים, from סָרַח, Arab. سرح, *liberè dimisit,* to be thrown negligently along, is descriptive of the self-indulgent mode in which the Orientals recline upon their sofas or couches, being stretched upon them at full length. The whole verse sets forth in well-chosen expressions the luxurious habits of the opulent. LXX. κατασπαταλῶντες.

5, 6. פָּרַט is a ἅπαξ λεγ., and has been thought by Gesenius, Hitzig, and Ewald, to have been selected on purpose, instead of זַמֵּר, *to sing,* in order to express the contempt in which the music deserved to be held. Such interpretation, however, does not appear to be philologically sustained, and ill suits the corresponding hemistich. According to the LXX. ἐπικρατοῦντες, *presiding over,* or *at,* the verb is synonymous with נִצַּח, in Piel, to

superintend, lead in music. Hence מְנַצֵּחַ, the *chief musician.* Comp. the Arab. فرط, *prævertit, præcessit.* The persons reprobated were so passionately fond of song, that they could not be content to listen to the performances of professed musicians, but took the lead in striking up songs to the sound of the lyre. The reference to David, who was the sweet singer of Israel, and of whose musical instruments express mention is made Neh. xii. 36, is manifestly ironical; implying that, while that monarch devoted his musical talent to the glory of God, the dissipated grandees of Israel consulted only their personal gratification, and that of those who joined their giddy circle. מִזְרָקִים, were properly *basons,* or *bowls* of a larger size, used for sacrificial purposes, Exod. xxxviii. 3; Num. vii. 13, 19. The persons referred to, indulged to such excess, that ordinary cups were unsuited to their compotations. They likewise anointed themselves with the most precious oils, and evinced a total apathy in regard to the calamities to which their people had already been subject, or the still more serious evils which threatened them. For the meaning of יוֹסֵף, *Joseph,* see on chap. v. 6.

7. מִרְזַח, Arab. مرزيح, *vox,* the *shout* or *cry,* in which the merrymakers indulged over their cups. The persons giving the shout seem to be intended, and, as the term is also used in reference to a cry of lamentation, Jer. xvi. 5, it may be implied that their joy would be turned into sorrow. They are spoken of col-

8   The Lord Jehovah hath sworn by himself,
     Thus saith Jehovah, God of hosts,
     I abhor the splendour of Jacob,
     And I hate his palaces:
     Therefore will I deliver up the city, and all that is in it.

9   Yea, it shall be, that if ten men should be left in one house,
     They also shall die.

10 And one's relative, even he that burneth him, shall take him up,
     To remove his bones out of the house;

lectively. Symm. ἑταιρεία τρυφητῶν. Those who had taken the lead in revelry and all manner of wickedness, were to be first in the procession of captives. In such a position, their disgrace would be more conspicuous.

8. The double form of asseveration here employed is unusual, and is strongly emphatic. מְתָאֵב, the Piel participle of תָּאַב, a root of the same signification with תֵּעֵב. Compare for a similar interchange of these letters גָּמָא, גָּמַל and גָּאַל and גָּמַע. Though the phrase גְּאוֹן יַעֲקֹב, *the excellency of Jacob*, cannot be otherwise understood than of God himself, as the only legitimate object of glorying on the part of his people, chap. viii. 7, yet, in the present instance, it is to be taken in application to the country and peculiar privileges of the Hebrews. It was once a country piously celebrated in song as *the excellency of Jacob*, Ps. xlvii. 5 (Eng. 4), and the peculiar object of divine regard; but now, defiled by the wickedness of its inhabitants, it had become the object of his abhorrence. By עִיר, the *city*, Amos had most probably Samaria in his eye. Hitzig attaches to הִסְגַּרְתִּי, the signification of Kal, *to besiege, shut up*, but the usual Hiphil signification better agrees with the following connexion. מְלֹא, *fulness*, conveys the idea of multitude, or great abundance, and comprehends here both the numerous inhabitants themselves, and the wealth and means of gratification in which they abounded. Comp. Ps. xxiv. 1. For the accomplishment of the prediction, see 2 Kings xvii. 5, 6.

9, 10. The scene is not necessarily laid in the city; it might also have been realized in any of the towns or villages in the country that had been depopulated by the Assyrians. It depicts, in the most affecting manner, the deplorable condition of the few that had escaped the enemy, and had now been attacked by the plague—a usual attendant on war in the East. The prophet declares, that if as many as ten had been left in one house, which might be regarded as a rare instance, they should die, one after another, of this fatal disease. דּוֹד is not here to be taken in the special sense of *uncle*, but denotes any near relative on whom it devolved to attend to the funeral rites. Targ. קְרִיבֵהּ. Vulg. *propinquus*. In the present case, such would be the paucity of hands, that he would have to perform the whole himself. The copulative וְ, prefixed to מְסָרְפוֹ, is epexegetical, and is to be rendered *even*, as in Zech. ix. 9. Instead of מְסָרְף, many both of Kennicott's and De Rossi's MSS. read correctly מְשָׂרֵף. But compare the Syr. ‎ܣܪܦ‎. Some have attempted to prove from this, and some other passages, that it was the practice of the Hebrews to burn their dead. But what is said 2 Chron. xvi. 14; xxi. 19; and Jer. xxxiv. 5, obviously refers to the burning of spices, and not of dead bodies. 1 Sam. xxxi. 12, and our present text, exhibit special cases. In the former of these, the object was so to dispose of the corpses that it might not be in the power of the Philistines further to dishonour them; while in the latter, it was either, as Grotius supposes, to prevent contagion, or to dispose of the body in the only way which the circumstances of the time would allow. That by עֲצָמִים, not mere *bones* are meant, nor bodies so emaciated as to be nothing but skin and bone, which is Winer's opinion, but *dead bodies*, seems established beyond all doubt by a reference to Gen. l. 25; Exod. xiii. 19; 2 Kings xiii. 21; Jer.

And shall say to him that is in the innermost part of the house,
Is there yet any with thee?
And he shall say, None!
Then shall he say, Hush!
For we must not mention the name of Jehovah.

11　For behold! Jehovah hath commanded,
And he will smite the great house with breaches,
And the small house with fissures.

12　　Shall horses run upon a rock?
Will one plough there with oxen?
Yet ye have converted justice into poison,
And the fruit of righteousness into wormwood.

13　Ye that rejoice in a thing of nought,
That say,

viii. 1, 2. וְּירְפְּחֵי הַבַּיִת, is well rendered in the Vulg. *in penetralibus domus.* See on Is. xiv. 13. Having burned and removed one body after another, the relative, discovering a patient in one of the innermost rooms or corners of the house, inquires whether he is the only survivor? and on receiving for answer that he is, he suddenly enjoins silence upon him. There is some difficulty in determining what occasioned this injunction, and for what reason the Divine name was not to be mentioned. Most probably the patient had begun to give vent to his feelings in expressions of praise to Jehovah, for sparing his life in the midst of such prevailing mortality; when the other, from some superstitious notion, or from the supposed incongruity of praising God in such circumstances, interrupted his pious effusions. הִזְכִּיר בְּשֵׁם, means to *mention,* or *record with approbation,* as an object of trust. Comp. Josh. xxiii. 7; Ps. xx. 8. The phrase cannot, therefore, be construed into the language of despair—as if the person who gave utterance to the words besought God to take him away likewise, and thus terminate the melancholy scene. Nor, for the same reason, can it imply, as Michaelis interprets, that he had confirmed what he had stated with an oath.

11. Grotius, Dahl, Justi, and Ewald, adopt the interpretation of the Targ., Jerome, and Cyril, that by the "*great* house" is meant the kingdom of Israel, and by the "*small* house" that of Judah;

and comp. chap. ix. 8, 9, where the same participial form מְצַוֶּה is employed as here before another verb. רְסִיסִים, mean *atoms,* or the minute parts to which the materials of a building are reduced, when it is utterly destroyed. The word otherwise signifies the small drops of any liquid that is sprinkled, and is derived from רָסַס, *to sprinkle.* בְּקִיעִים, are *fissures,* or rents in an edifice, which threaten its fall. There was to be a marked difference in the treatment of the two kingdoms; the one was to be utterly destroyed, while the other, though greatly injured, was still to stand. Rosenmüller, however, regards this interpretation as "arguta magis, quam vera." Calvin, Vatablus, Marckius, Cocceius, Lowth, Michaelis, and Maurer, likewise take the words literally, as applying to the houses both of the rich and the poor. The destruction, more or less, was to be universal.

　　———"Pauperum tabernas,
Regumque turres."—*Horace.*

This construction of the verse is confirmed by a comparison with chap. iii. 15.

12. The folly of expecting real prosperity while committing acts of injustice, is forcibly represented by comparing it to the absurdity of attempting to run horses upon a rock, or to plough it with oxen. To add to the strength of the representation, it is put in the interrogative form. יְחֲרוֹשׁ is to be taken impersonally.

13. The participles, with the ה demon-

Have we not, by our own strength,
Taken to ourselves horns?

14 But behold! I will raise up against you, O house of Israel,
    A nation, saith Jehovah, God of hosts;
    And they shall oppress you,
    From the entrance of Hamath,
    To the river of the desert.

strative, are again employed as in verses 3, 4, 5, 6.—לֹא דָבָר, non-re, what is so perishable and evanescent, that it may well be said to have no existence.—*Horns* are the symbol of power and dominion.

14. Few instances will be found in Hebrew, in which the object of a verb is so far removed from it as גּוֹי here is from מָקִים. Some have referred נַחַל הָעֲרָבָה, *the river of the Desert*, to the Rhinocorura, otherwise called the river of Egypt; and others to "the brook of the willows," נַחַל הָעֲרָבִים, or the *Wady el-Ahsa*, which flows into the Dead Sea, near Zoar; but it

is obvious from 2 Kings xiv. 25, in which the limits here specified are described as constituting those of the kingdom of the ten tribes, that it must mean the brook Kidron, which falls into the Dead Sea to the south of Jericho. One of the names given to this sea is יָם הָעֲרָבָה, *the Sea of the Desert*; הָעֲרָבָה, *the desert*, forming what is now commonly called الغور, *El-Ghor*, or the low sterile region in which the valley of the Jordan terminates, and which extends as far as the Elanitic Gulf.

CHAPTER VII—VIII 3

This portion of the book contains four symbolical visions respecting successive judgments that were to be inflicted on the kingdom of Israel. They were delivered at Bethel, and in all probability at the commencement of the prophet's ministry. Each of them, as they follow in the series, is more severe than the preceding: The first presented to the mental eye of the prophet a swarm of young locusts, which threatened to cut off all hope of the harvest, 1—3; the second, a fire, which effected an universal conflagration, 4—6; the third, a plumbline, ready to be applied to mark out the edifices that were to be destroyed, 7—9; and the fourth, a basket of ripe fruit, denoting the near and certain destruction of the kingdom, viii. 1—3. The intervening eight verses, which conclude the seventh chapter, contain an account of the interruption of Amos by Amaziah, the priest of Bethel, whose punishment is specially predicted. In point of style, this portion differs from that of the rest of the book, being almost exclusively historical and dialogistic.

---

1   THUS the Lord Jehovah showed me, and, behold, he formed
     locusts at the beginning of the shooting up of the latter grass;
     and, behold, it was the latter grass after the king's mowings.

1. All the four visions are introduced in nearly the same language: פֹּה הִרְאַנִי אֲדֹנָי יְהֹוָה וְהִנֵּה. The repetition of הִנֵּה, *behold*, is peculiar to this verse. In the

2　And it came to pass, when they had entirely devoured the
grass of the land, I said:

O Lord Jehovah! forgive, I beseech thee!
Who is Jacob, that he should stand?
For he is small.

3　Jehovah repented of this:
It shall not be, saith Jehovah.

4　Thus the Lord Jehovah showed me, and, behold, the Lord
Jehovah called to contend by fire; and it consumed the great
abyss, and devoured the portion.

latter of the two instances, it is employed for the sake of emphasis, instead of the substantive verb. גֹּבַי, a name of the locust, occurring only here, and Nah. iii. 17, and synonymous with גֵּב, Is. xxxiii.

4. Comp. the Arab. جَابُ and جَايِي, *locusta*, from جَبَا *egressus fuit*, in reference to its coming forth out of the egg, which had been deposited in the earth to be hatched. The term is, therefore, strictly descriptive of the locust in its caterpillar state, and thus agrees with the use of יָצַר, *to form*, which is here used. Prof. Lee derives it from جُوب, *secuit*. Credner on Joel, pp. 299—302, elaborately attempts to set aside the above derivation of Bochart, yet allows that the word denotes the insect in the first stage of its existence. The plural termination בַ-, is found in several masculine nouns, as חַלּוֹנֵי, הָרֵי, חֲשׂוּפַי, &c.; but the anomaly has not yet been satisfactorily accounted for. See, however, Gesen. Lehrgeb. p. 523. Lee's Heb. Gram. Art. 139, 4; 2d edit. לֶקֶשׁ, an *after-math*, or second crop, which comes up immediately after the mowing of grass. לָקֵשׁ, cognate with לֶקֶשׁ, Arab. لَقَط, *legit, collegit*, signifies in Piel *to gather the late fruit*. Comp. the Syr. ܠܩܝܫܐ, *serotinus*, and מַלְקוֹשׁ, *the latter rain*. The phrase גִּזֵּי הַמֶּלֶךְ may either mean the mowings of the grass which grew on the royal domains, or the first mowings of that belonging to the people, to which the king tyrannically laid claim. Considering the character

of the times, there can be little doubt that the latter are meant.

2. That the locusts here referred to are not intended to represent a literal swarm of these insects, but are to be taken figuratively, as denoting a hostile army, just as the fire in the second vision is to be regarded as symbolical of war, may be inferred from the figurative character of the two visions, ver. 7, and chap. viii. 1. Most probably the army of Pul, king of Assyria, is meant. The Israelites had been greatly reduced by repeated invasions on the part of the Syrian kings, and were on the point of being attacked by the Assyrians, but purchased their retreat with the sum of one thousand talents of silver. See 2 Kings xv. 19, 20. מִי יָקוּם יַעֲקֹב, concisely for מִי יַעֲקֹב כִּי יָקוּם, *who is Jacob, that he should stand?* meaning, How can he possibly sustain the threatened attack, reduced and weak as he is in resources. קוּם signifies *to stand fast, continue, endure*, as well as *to rise*. One of De Rossi's MSS., and another originally, read יָקוּם, and another יָקֵם, and thus the LXX., Syr., Symm., and Vulg.; but less appropriately in such context.

3. נִחַם, Pick renders *gave consolation*, which is not so suitable here as the signification, *to repent*. Such repentance is to be understood θεοπρεπῶς, appearing, as Veil observes, "in effectu, citra mutationem in affectu." Comp. 1 Sam. xv. 11; Jer. xlii. 10. Targ. אֲתֵיב יְיָ רוּגְזֵהּ, *the Lord turned away his wrath*. זֹאת, the feminine pronoun, stands for the neuter of other languages.

4. קְרָא corresponds in form to יוֹצֵר, ver. 1.—לָרִב, an abbreviated form of the Hiphil infinitive, לְהָרִיב. Comp. Is. iii. 13.

5 Then I said:

 O Lord Jehovah! desist, I beseech thee!

 Who is Jacob, that he should stand?

 For he is small.

6 Jehovah repented of this:

 It also shall not be, saith the Lord Jehovah.

7 Thus he showed me, and behold the Lord stood upon a per-
8 pendicular wall; and in his hand was a plumb-line. And
Jehovah said to me, What seest thou, Amos? And I said, A
plumb-line. And the Lord said:

 Behold, I will set a plumb-line

 In the midst of my people Israel;

 I will pass by them no more.

The verb signifies to *contend judicially*, to treat according to one's deserts, to punish. By the fire here spoken of we are not to understand a great heat which produced a drought in the land, but *war*, of which it is an appropriate symbol. See Num. xxi. 28 ; Judges ix. 15, 20; Is. lxvi. 16. To express the extent of the threatened calamity, the fire, by a bold figure, is represented as drying up the *ocean* (תְּהוֹם רַבָּה), and consuming whatever was found on the *dry land*. This acceptation of חֵלֶק, a *division, portion*, or *allotment* of land, the antithesis requires; still, however, the term is chosen with special application to the land of Canaan, which was divided to the children of Israel as their portion. The definite form of the noun אֶת־הַחֵלֶק, indicates as much. The invasion of the land of Israel by Tiglath-Pileser, and the first captivity of that people, seem to be the subjects of the vision. See 2 Kings xv. 29 ; 1 Chron. v. 26. That in the former vision, the calamity had not been inflicted, the use of the verb סָלַח, *forgive*, intimates. In this, it had in part, as the use of חָדַל, *desist*, obviously implies.

5, 6. In these verses, as in vers. 2 and 3, we have a beautiful instance of the influence of prayer in averting or mitigating the judgments of God.

7, 8. This vision, and that described chap. viii. 1—3, differ from the two preceding, in the distinct and express application of the symbols to the punishment of the Israelites. The Divine patience is exhausted. Jehovah takes active measures for executing his threatenings, and at last inflicts the exterminating judgment on a people ripe for destruction. The prophet, in consequence, intercedes no more. חוֹמַת אֲנָךְ, *a perpendicular wall*, lit. *a wall of the plummet*, so called from the plumb-line being applied in order to secure its perpendicularity. אֲנָךְ, which occurs only in these verses, properly signifies *lead* or tin.

Arab. اَنُك, Syr. ܐܢܟܐ, *plumbum*. Aq.

γάνωσις, *stannatura*. The line and plummet were used not only when houses were building, but also when they were to be destroyed. See 2 Kings xxi. 13 ; Is. xxviii. 17 ; xxxiv. 11 ; Lam. ii. 8. The LXX. and Symm. ἀδάμας, which the Syr. also exhibits. In the explanation of the vision, it is expressly stated, that the plummet was to be applied to the people of Israel in order to mark them out for destruction; and its being placed in *the midst* of them denoted, that this destruction was not to be confined to a part only of the kingdom, as it had been in the case of Tiglath-Pileser's invasion, but that it should reach the very centre. This took place when Shalmaneser, the successor of that king, after a siege of three years, took Samaria, put an end to the kingdom of the ten tribes, and carried them away captive into Assyria, 2 Kings xvii. 3, 5, 6, 23. עָבַר, *to pass, pass on* or *away*, means, in

9   But the high-places of Isaac shall be desolated,
     And the sanctuaries of Israel laid waste ;
     And I will rise against the house of Jeroboam with the sword.
10   Then Amaziah, the priest of Bethel, sent to Jeroboam, the king
     of Israel, saying: Amos hath formed a conspiracy against thee,
     in the midst of the house of Israel: the land cannot contain
11   all his words.   For thus hath Amos said :
     Jeroboam shall die by the sword ;
     And Israel shall surely be led away captive from his land.
12   And Amaziah said to Amos : Seer ! Go, flee to the land of Judah,
13   and eat there bread, and prophesy there.   But prophesy no more

application to sin, *to pass it by,* to forgive, not to punish it. Prov. xix. 11 ; Micah vii. 18. See on this latter passage.

9. A definite prediction of the destruction which was to overtake the places of idolatrous worship, and the royal house by which that worship had been established and supported. These are specially mentioned, because to them, as the procuring causes, the destruction was to be traced. For the meaning of בָּמוֹת, *high places,* see on Is. lxv. 7. מִקְדָּשִׁים, the parallel term, denotes the temples, or structures, consecrated to the worship of idols. Comp. מִקְדָּשׁ, ver. 13.—יִשְׂחָק, instead of יִצְחָק, is not peculiar to our prophet ; the same orthography is found Ps. cv. 9; Jer. xxxiii. 26.   There is no reason whatever to suppose that the word was purposely so written, or that it was intended to be taken otherwise than as a proper name; yet the LXX. have βωμοὶ τοῦ γέλωτος ; so the Syr. likewise. Michaelis finds a paronomasia in it ; Dahl, an instance of irony ; and even Calvin thinks that the name was used by Amos μιμητικῶς. It is here, and ver. 16, parallel with יִשְׂרָאֵל, and denotes the ten tribes.

10, 11. Verses 10—17 contain an interesting historical episode. As there were doubtless many priests who conducted the idolatrous services at Bethel, כֹּהֵן must here be understood κατ᾽ ἐξοχὴν of the chief or high priest, attached to the royal temple. In the spirit which has characterised a false priesthood in every age, Amaziah brings against the prophet the groundless charge of treason.   That לְהָכִיל is to be rendered

contain, and refers to number and not to atrocity, appears from כֹּל, *all,* being employed before the following noun. Comp. for this signification of the verb in Hiphil, 1 Kings vii. 26, 37 ; Ezek. xxiii. 32. In the Syr. in which a verb signifying *to endure* is used, כֹּל is omitted, as not suiting the Oriental idiom.

12, 13. It does not appear that the king took any notice of the message that was sent him, so that Amaziah was left to try what the interposition of his own authority would effect. He addressed the prophet by the title חֹזֶה, *seer,* most probably with contemptuous reference to his visions ; though it was adopted in the later Hebrew, as equivalent to נָבִיא, and corresponds in signification to רֹאֶה, which was anciently used, 1 Sam. ix. 9. Not imagining that Amos could be actuated by any higher principle than that of selfishness, which reigned in his own heart, the priest advised him to consult his safety by fleeing across the frontier into the kingdom of Judah, where he might obtain his livelihood by the unrestrained exercise of his prophetical gifts. The words לְךָ בְּרַח־לְךָ, though pleonastic, are emphatic. At all events, he could not be permitted any longer to prophesy in the city of Bethel, which was distinguished not only as the principal seat of the king's religion, but also as being one of his royal residences. Though the ordinary residence of the Israelitish monarchs was at Samaria, yet as they went at certain stated seasons to Bethel to worship the golden calf, they had had a palace built there for their accommodation.

at Bethel, for it is the king's sanctuary, and a royal residence.
14 And Amos answered and said to Amaziah : I am no prophet ;
neither am I the son of a prophet ; but I am an herdsman, and
15 a cultivator of sycamores. And Jehovah took me from following the flock ; and Jehovah said to me : Go, prophesy to my
16 people Israel. And now, hear the word of Jehovah. Thou
sayest, Prophesy not against Israel ; and, Drop nothing against
17 the house of Isaac. Therefore thus saith Jehovah :
Thy wife shall commit lewdness in the city,

14. Amos modestly but firmly repels the charge of selfishness, by declaring, that he was not a prophet by profession ; that he had not been educated with a view to such profession ; that he was a person of rustic habits ; and that his Divine mission was altogether of an extraordinary character. אֶרְבָּנָא, *the son*, i. e. pupil or disciple *of a prophet*. In all probability some of the schools of the prophets, of which we read in the first book of Samuel, were still in existence, in which young men were educated, who devoted themselves to the service of the theocracy in the capacity of public instructors, and to these, or to more private studies, under the guidance of some prophet, Amos may be supposed to refer. בּוֹקֵר, strictly taken, means an *ox-herd ;* but as בָּקָר came, in a larger acceptation, to denote cattle in general, it might signify a keeper of any kind of cattle. There is, therefore, no occasion, with some, to suppose that the word was originally נֹקֵד, as in chap. i. 1. בּוֹלֵס occurs nowhere else in the Hebrew Scriptures ; but the Arab. بلس, signifies a *white fig*, and the Eth. በለሰ : both the *fig-tree* and its fruit. As, however, the participial form of the word is that which denotes agency, it must mean one who is occupied with, or cultivates figs. The particular mode in which the ancients cultivated fig-trees, the LXX. appear to have had in their eye, when they rendered it by κνίζων, a *nipper* or *scratcher ;* for we are informed by Theophrastus, that iron nails or prongs were employed to make incisions or scratches in the tree, that by letting out some of the sap, the fruit might be ripened : πέπτειν οὐ δύναται ἂν μὴ ἐπικνισθῇ· ἀλλ' ἔχοντες ὄνυχας σιδηροὺς ἐπικνίζουσιν· ἃ δ' ἂν ἐπι-

κνισθῇ, τεταρταῖα πέπτεται, iv. 2. See also Plin. Hist. Nat. xiii. 14 ; Forskål, Flor. Egypt. p. 182. שִׁקְמִים, *sycamores*, a species of tree, abounding in the East, pretty much resembling the mulberry tree, the fruit of which is similar to the fig. It is, however, very inferior in quality, and is only eaten by the poorest class of the people. From this circumstance it may be inferred that Amos occupied an humble station in life previous to his being called to prophesy in Israel.

15. נִבָּא אֶל is used both in a good and in a bad sense, and is here to be rendered indefinitely, *to prophesy to.* The pronominal suffix in עַמִּי, " *my people*," is not without emphasis. The Israelites were Jehovah's by right ; he still claimed his propriety in them ; and, by the ministry of his prophet, would have recovered them to his service.

16. Instead of listening to the prohibition of Amaziah, and retiring from his sphere of duty, Amos continued to discharge the duties of his office at Bethel ; but before proceeding to give an account of another vision which he had had, he directs a pointed prediction against the idolatrous priest by whom he had been interrupted. הִטִּיף, *to distil*, to cause to come down in pleasing and flowing discourse ; here parallel with נִבָּא, *to prophesy*. Comp. Ezek. xxi. 2, 7 (Eng. version, xx. 46, and xxi. 2) ; Micah ii. 6, 11. Syr. ܢܛܦ, Arab. نطف, Eth. ነጠበ : *stillavit*, ነጠበ : *percolavit*.

17. Between אָמַר יְהוָֹה in this verse, and אָמַר in ver. 16, is a marked antithesis. תִּזְנֶה is not to be understood of voluntary acts of infidelity on the part of the wife of Amaziah, but of the violence to which she would have to submit on the part of

And thy sons and thy daughters shall fall by the sword ;
Thy land, also, shall be divided by line,
And thou shalt die in a polluted land:
And Israel shall surely be taken away captive from his land.

the enemy. This being done בָּעִיר, *in the city,* i.e. openly and publicly, was a great aggravation of the evil.

Ὡδέ σφ' ἐγκέφαλος χαμμάδις ῥέοι, ὡς ὅδε οἶνος
Αὐτῶν, καὶ τεκέων· ἄλοχοι δ' ἄλλοισι μιγεῖεν.   Iliad. iii. 300, 301.

Every country, except Canaan, was regarded by the Hebrews as אֲדָמָה טְמֵאָה, *a polluted land,* though, at this time, their own land had become such. Is. xxiv. 5, where חָנֵף is similarly used; Jer. ii. 7. The land of Assyria is that to which Amos points.

---◆---

CHAPTER VIII

After giving an account of a fourth vision, in which was represented the ripeness for destruction at which the Israelites had arrived, and the certainty of such destruction, 1—3, the prophet resumes his denunciatory addresses to the avaricious oppressors of the people, 4—7; predicts the overthrow of the nation, 8—10; and concludes with threatening a destitution of the means of religious instruction, 11—14.

---

1 Thus the Lord Jehovah showed me, and, behold, a basket of
2 ripe fruit ! And he said, What seest thou, Amos? And I said,
A basket of ripe fruit.
Then said Jehovah to me:
The end is come to my people Israel ;
I will pass by them no more.

1. This vision may be regarded as a continuation of the subject with which the last concluded, in the development of which the prophet had been interrupted by Amaziah. כְּלוּב, Syr. ܟܚܕܐ, *a cage,* or *basket;* Arab. كلب, *inserto loro inter duas corii partes consuit;* كلبة, *lorum vel filamentum lignosum palmæ, quo consuitur:* what is braided from twigs, such as wicker-work. קַיִץ

is used both of *summer,* and of the *fruit* which is gathered in *summer.* It is to the *ripeness* of the fruit at this season that prominence is here designed to be given. The verb occurs but once in Heb., viz. Is. xviii. 6. Arab. قيظ, *media æstas:* قاظ, *admodum ferbuit, æstiva habuit.*

2. The paronomasia in קַיִץ and קֵץ is marked and forcible. Comp. Ezek. vii. 6: קֵץ בָּא בָּא הַקֵּץ הֵקִיץ אֵלָיִךְ הִנֵּה בָּאָה.

3 And the songs of the palace shall howl,
　In that day, saith the Lord Jehovah;
　The carcasses are many!
　Throw them out any where!
　Hush!

4 Hear this! ye that pant after the needy,
　That ye may destroy the poor of the land,

5 Saying, When will the new moon be over,
　That we may sell corn?
　And the sabbath,
　That we may open out grain?
　Making the ephah small,
　And the shekel great,
　And falsifying the balances for deceit.

6 That we may purchase the poor for money,

3. Instead of the pathetic elegies loudly and continuously poured forth at the princely funerals, nothing was to be heard but the frantic howl, announcing, but instantly checked in announcing, the greatness of the disaster. Into such howling the joyous songs of the palace were to be converted. Symm. ὀλολύξουσιν αἱ ᾠδαί. The dead bodies were to be cast forth indiscriminately, without any regard to the places where they might lie; and even this was not to be effected without exposing those who performed it to the attacks of the enemy. Hence silence was to be enjoined. Some improperly render הֵיכָל, *temple*. For הָס, comp. chap. vi. 10.

4. The prophet resumes his usual style of direct comminatory address. Comp. chapters iv., v., and vi. For שָׁאַף, see on chap. ii. 7. לְהַשְׁבִּית=לָשֶׁבֶת, *to cause to cease, bring to an end, annihilate, destroy*. The ו in וְלַשְׁבִּית is to be taken τελικῶς, as denoting the end or aim of the oppressions practised by the avaricious Israelites.

5. From this and other passages it is obvious that the Israelites, notwithstanding their idolatrous practices, still kept up the observance of the times and seasons appointed in the law of Moses. שֶׁבֶר and שֶׁבֶר הִשְׁבִּיר, lit. *to break a breaking*, but meaning *to sell grain*, is supposed to be so named from its being broken to pieces when ground at the

mill. Some, however, think the name is derived from its being broken up or separated by a measure into portions, with a view to sale; while others are of opinion that it is so called because it breaks or puts an end to hunger, comparing Ps. civ. 11. By פָּתַח בָּר, *opening the corn*, is meant opening the *sacks* or *granaries* in which it was kept, and bringing it out for sale. Thus the LXX., Syr., and Targ. The אֵיפָה, *ephah*, was a corn measure, containing three seahs, and, according to Josephus, equal to the Attic *medimnus*, or somewhat above three English pecks. It is uncertain whether the word be originally Hebrew, or whether it be Egyptian. שֶׁקֶל, from שָׁקַל, *to weigh*, Arab. ثَقَل, *ponderosus fuit*, *gravitatem et pondus exploravit*, is here used of weights in general. It was originally any piece of metal weighed as an equivalent for what was bought; but came afterwards to signify standard money, and differed in value, according as it was of silver or gold, and as it was estimated by the sacred or the royal standard, Exod. xxx. 13; 2 Sam. xiv. 26. For the sake of greater emphasis, instead of saying, *to make* or *to use* deceitful balances, the verb עָוַת, *to bend, twist, pervert*, is employed, which, in point of meaning, is pleonastic. LXX. ποιῆσαι ζυγὸν ἄδικον.

6. See chap. ii. 6. מַפַּל, from נָפַל, *to*

And the needy for a pair of sandals;
And sell the refuse of the grain?

7   Jehovah hath sworn by the excellency of Jacob :
I will never forget any of their deeds.

8   Shall not the land tremble for this,
And every one that dwelleth therein mourn?
Yea, shall not all of it rise like the river?
And shall it not be driven, and subside,
Like the river of Egypt?

9   It shall also come to pass in that day,
Saith the Lord Jehovah,
That I will cause the sun to go down at noon,
And will darken the land in the clear day.

---

fall; what has fallen off, *refuse,* chaff, &c.

7. The iniquitous conduct of the Israelites having been minutely described, the severe punishment which they had merited is now threatened. גְּאוֹן יַעֲקֹב, *the excellency of Jacob,* has been variously interpreted. The Targ., Grotius, Dahl, Newcome, and Bauer, understand the excellence conferred upon Jacob; Justi and Ewald, very preposterously, the pride or haughtiness of the people; the Rabbins and some others, the temple; but the only appropriate construction of the phrase, in this connexion, is that which refers it to Jehovah *himself,* in whom alone the Hebrews gloried while they adhered to the purity of his worship, and in whom they still ought to glory. Thus the Syr. ܡܳܪܝܳܐ ܥܰܫܺܝܢܳܐ ܘܰܬܩܺܝܦܳܐ, *the Lord, the Mighty One of Jacob;* Munster, Vatablus, Mercer, Drusius, Liveley, Gesenius, Hitzig, Maurer. Comp. chap. vi. 8, where נְשִׁבַּע בְּנַפְשׁוֹ occurs instead of the present phrase, which, however, is also there used in a bad sense. אִם אֶשְׁכַּח, *if I forget,* is the usual formula of swearing, implying that it should not take place. לֹא, in this connexion, implies both totality, and the single items of which that totality is made up. Comp. Ps. ciii. 2.

8. The guilt of the people was so enormous, that it was sufficient to induce an entire subversion of the existing state of things. To express this more strongly, the land is metaphorically represented as rising and swelling like the Nile, and again falling like the same river. Of course, the idea of the heaving and subsiding of the ground during an earthquake is what is intended, as the beginning of the verse shows. For the sake of energy and impression, the interrogative form is, as frequently, employed. That פָאר, by an elision of the letter Yod, is a defective form of יְאֹר, is evident from the parallel passage, chap. ix. 5. Fifteen MSS., originally two more, and perhaps other three, and one of the early editions, read כִּיאֹר in full. For the origin and meaning of the word, see on Is. xix. 6. נִגְרַשׁ is used in Niphal, to express the violent agitation of the sea when raised by the wind, Is. lvii. 20. It here denotes the rise of the Nile, which is generally above twenty feet. For נִשְׁקָה, the Keri and a great many MSS. in the text, read וְשִׁקְעָה, which is undoubtedly genuine. The root שָׁקַע occurs in a similar connexion, chap. ix. 5. It signifies to *sink down,* or *subside.*

9. Some think the prophet here predicts the total eclipse of the sun, which took place at one of the great festivals in the year that Jeroboam died, (see Usher's Annals, A.M. 3213); but whatever there may be in the language borrowed from such an event, consistency of interpretation requires it to be taken metaphorically, as descriptive of a change from circumstances of prosperity to those of adversity. Comp. Jer. xv. 9; Ezek. xxxii. 7—10.

10 I will turn also your festivals into mourning,
　　And all your songs into lamentation;
　　And I will bring sackcloth upon all loins,
　　And baldness upon every head;
　　Yea, I will make it as the mourning for an only son,
　　And the end of it a bitter day.

11　　Behold, the days come, saith the Lord Jehovah,
　　When I will send a famine into the land;
　　Not a famine of bread, nor a thirst for water,
　　But of hearing the words of Jehovah.

12 And men shall wander from sea to sea,
　　And shall run up and down, from the North even to the East,
　　Seeking the word of Jehovah,
　　But they shall not find it.

13 In that day the fair virgins shall faint,
　　And the young men also, for thirst;

14 That swear by the sin of Samaria,

10. The Hebrew festivals were occasions of great joy, and were no doubt on this very account kept up among the ten tribes after they had lost their religious importance. The calamitous result of the Assyrian invasion under Shalmaneser is here most graphically depicted. Comp. Is. xv. 2; Jer. xlviii. 37; Ezek. vii. 18. The death of an only son was regarded by the Hebrews as the most mournful of events. Comp. Jer. vi. 26; Zech. xii. 10. The pronominal reference in שָׂמְתִּיךָ and אַחֲרִיתָהּ is אֶרֶץ understood. כְּ in כְּיוֹם מָר, is the *Caph veritatis*.

"Nunc et amara dies, et noctis amarior
　　umbra est;
Omnia jam tristi tempora felle madent."
　　　　　　　　　Tibullus, lib. ii. Eleg. iv. 11.

11, 12. The Israelites now despised the messages of the prophets, and by a just retribution, in addition to all their other calamities, they should experience a total withdrawal of all prophetic communications. Comp. Ezek. vii. 26; Micah iii. 7. In whatever direction they might proceed, and whatever efforts they might make to obtain information relative to the issue of their trouble, they should meet with nothing but disappointment. מִזְרָח, *sun-rise*, is used, where

geographically we should have expected יָמִין, or נֶגֶב, *the south;* but the term may have been chosen in order to intimate the complete alienation of Israel from Judah, in consequence of which no one would think of repairing to Jerusalem for oracular information. That any transposition of the words has taken place, I cannot, with Houbigant and Newcome, suppose. It is, however, just as probable that the cardinal points were not intended to be strictly marked, but that the object was to indicate generally the hopelessness of the attempts mentioned. The Athnach is improperly placed under מִזְרָח, instead of under יְשׁוֹטְטוּ, as the Vau prefixed to צָפוֹן and the form of the verb show.

13. צָמָא in this verse, is to be understood of the natural *thirst* to be experienced by the inhabitants of Samaria during the siege predicted in the preceding verses. תִּתְעַלַּפְנָה, properly means, *they shall feel themselves involved in darkness*, which is physically true of those who are seized with syncope. The root עָלַף, Arab. غلف, signifies *to cover, envelope;* here, *with darkness*, understood. After הַבַּחוּרִים subaud. יִתְעַלָּפוּ.

14. אַשְׁמַת שֹׁמְרוֹן, *the sin* or *crime of Samaria;* i.e. the golden calf and other

And say, By the life of thy god, O Dan!
And, By the life of the way of Beersheba!
Yea, they shall fall, and rise no more.

objects of unlawful worship which were the occasion of sin and guilt to the Israelites. Hitzig thinks that Astarte is specifically meant; but the term was doubtless intended to comprehend the calf at Bethel, the religious veneration of which led to the grosser forms of idolatry. At the same time, אֲשֵׁרָה, *Astarte*, is spoken of, 2 Kings xiii. 6, in distinction from the worship specially instituted by Jeroboam. See on Is. xvii. 8. The *god of Dan* was the other golden calf, erected by Jeroboam in Dan, 1 Kings xii. 26—28. By דֶּרֶךְ בְּאֵר־שָׁבַע, Kimchi, Michaelis, and Bauer, understand lite-

rally the *way* or *pilgrimage* to Beersheba; but the phrase being parallel with the two former instances, in which objects of false worship are meant, it must here be taken in the same sense. Hence the LXX. render, ζῇ ὁ θεός σου. Strictly speaking, it denotes the *way* or *mode* of worship, or the *worship* itself, that was performed at Beersheba. Comp. Ps. cxxxix. 24; Acts ix. 2; xix. 9, 23. See on chap. v. 5. חַי is a formula of swearing: *By the life of*——, or, *As sure as such an one lives*, and was peculiarly absurd and sinful when applied to inanimate objects.

CHAPTER IX

This chapter commences with an account of the fifth and last vision of the prophet, in which the final ruin of the kingdom of Israel is represented. This ruin was to be complete and irreparable; and no quarter to which the inhabitants might flee for refuge, would afford them any shelter from the wrath of the Omnipresent and Almighty Jehovah, 1—6. As a sinful nation, it was to be treated as if it had never stood in any covenant-relation to him; yet, in their individual capacity, as the descendants of Abraham, how much soever they might be scattered and afflicted among the heathen, they should still be preserved, 7—10. The concluding part of the chapter contains a distinct prophecy of the restoration of the Jewish church after the Babylonish captivity, 11; the incorporation of the heathen, which was to be consequent upon that restoration, 12; and the final establishment of the Jews in their own land in the latter day, 13—15.

1　　I saw the Lord standing beside the altar, and he said:.
　　Smite the capital, that the thresholds may shake;
　　And break them in pieces, on the heads of them all;

1. By the Targ., Calvin, Drusius, Grotius, Justi, Rosenmüller, and Hengstenberg, the scene of this vision is laid in the temple at Jerusalem; by Cyril,

Munster, Tarnovius, Schmidius, Lowth, Michaelis, Dahl, Bauer, Hitzig, and Ewald, in the idolatrous temple at Bethel; and, in my opinion, rightly. Calvin

Their posterity I will also slay with the sword;
None of their fugitives shall make his escape,
Nor shall any that slip away be delivered.

2 Though they break through into Sheol,
Thence shall my hand take them;
Though they climb up to heaven,
Thence will I bring them down.

3 Though they hide themselves on the summit of Carmel,
There I will search them out and take them;
Though they conceal themselves from mine eyes in the bottom
of the sea,
There I will command the serpent, and he shall bite them.

4 Though they go into captivity before their enemies,
There I will command the sword, and it shall kill them:
Yea, I will set mine eyes upon them for evil,
And not for good.

does not show his usual tact in objecting to this interpretation, on the ground that it represents Jehovah as indirectly approving of superstition; for, though the true God was seen beside the idolatrous altar, it was not for the purpose of receiving homage, but of commanding that the whole of the erection and worship at Bethel should be destroyed. No argument in favour of Jerusalem can be built on the use of the article in הַמִּזְבֵּחַ, "*the* altar," but the contrary. The idolatrous objects to which sacrifices were offered at Bethel, having been mentioned in the preceding verse, nothing is more natural than a reference here to the altar on which they were presented. כַּפְתּוֹר, an ornamented *head* or *capital* of a column, in the shape of a sphere, or bowl surrounded by flowers. It is usually derived from כָּפַר, *to cover*, and פָּתַר, *to crown*. LXX. ἱλαστήριον, mistaking the word for כַּפֹּרֶת. When used of the ornamental part of the golden candlestick, they render it σφαιρωτήρ. For כַּפִּים, see on Is. vi. 4; the similarity, in some respects, between which passage and the present, appears to have suggested the idea that the temple at Jerusalem is here meant. The temple was to be smitten both above and below, to indicate its entire destruction. בְּצַעַם, *break them*, i. e. the capitals, &c., upon

the head of all the worshippers. It does not appear that רֹאשׁ and אַחֲרִית are here used antithetically. The latter denotes the *children* of those who perished in the attack upon the idolatrous temple. When threatened by the Assyrians, they would flock in crowds to Bethel, to implore protection from the golden calf, and, while thus assembled, they should perish, along with the vain object of their trust; they should, in fact, be buried in the ruins.

2—4. These verses exhibit a beautiful series of supposed cases of attempt at escape from the judgments of God, and the utter futility of every attempt of the kind. שְׁאוֹל and הַשָּׁמַיִם, are, as usual, employed as extreme points of opposition. Comp. Job xi. 8; Ps. cxxxix. 8; Is. xiv. 13—15; Matt. xi. 23.—רֹאשׁ הַכַּרְמֶל. Not only was Mount Carmel celebrated on account of its general fertility, but also on account of the dense forests and large caverns with which it abounded. These, together with its height, which is about twelve hundred feet, afforded the fittest possible places of concealment. Richter, in his pilgrimage, p. 65, says: "Mount Carmel is entirely covered with green; on its *summits* are pines and oaks, and further down, olive and laurel trees, &c. These forests would furnish safe hiding-places, equally with the caves,

5   For it is the Lord Jehovah of hosts,
     That toucheth the earth, and it melteth,
     And all that dwell in it mourn ;
     Yea, it riseth, all of it, like the river,
     And subsideth like the river of Egypt.
6   He that buildeth his upper chambers in the heavens,
     And foundeth his vaults upon the earth ;
     That calleth to the waters of the sea,
     And poureth them out on the surface of the earth ;
     Jehovah is his name.
7   Are ye not as the Cushites to me,
     O sons of Israel ? saith Jehovah.

which are chiefly on the west side facing the sea." קַרְקַע הַיָּם, *the bottom of the* Mediterranean *Sea,* forms a striking contrast to the summit of Carmel, which beetles above it. קַרְקַע, Arab. قُرْق, *terra æquabilis;* when spoken of a house, the *foundation* or *floor;* here the *bottom* or *basis,* on which the sea rests. For נָחָשׁ, *sea-serpent,* see on Is. xxvii. 1.

"———Immensis orbibus angues
Incumbunt pelago, pariterque ad littora
     tendunt."   *Æneid.* ii. 204.

The מ in מִשָּׁם, in verses 3 and 4, loses its proper prepositive signification, as in מִתַּחַת, מִבַּיִת, מִיָּמִין, &c. and merely denotes position or place.

5, 6. A sublime description of the almighty and uncontrollable power of Jehovah. For the reference to the Nile, see on chap. viii. 8. Instead of מַעֲלוֹתָו, the Keri and not a few MSS. read מַעֲלוֹתָיו in full. Comp. עֲלִיּוֹתָי, Ps. civ. 3, 13.

Αἰθέρος οἶκον ὑπέρτατον—ναιετάεις.
          Oppian. Halieut. i. 410.

Θεοῦ οἰκητήριον τοῦ κόσμου τὸ ἄνω.
                              Aristot.

אֲגֻדָּה, a body or mass, the parts of which are firmly compacted; Arab. اجال, *fornix firmæ compaginis et structuræ;* an *arch* or *vault;* obviously used of the רָקִיעַ, or hemispheric expanse or vault of heaven; which, from its appearing to the eye to rest upon the earth, is here

said to be founded upon it. To render it, with the Targ., *congregation,* and apply it to the Church, as a body of believers, firmly united together, is altogether unsuitable to the connexion. The rendering of the LXX., Syr., and Arab., would seem to indicate that יְהֹוָה צְבָאוֹת originally stood in the text, at the end of ver. 6 ; but only one of De Rossi's MSS. has this reading at first hand.

7. By appealing to the fact, that, in his providence, he had removed different nations from their original abodes, and settled them elsewhere, Jehovah repels the idea, which the Israelites were so prone to entertain, that, because he had brought them out of Egypt, and given them the land of Canaan, they were peculiarly the objects of his regard, and could never be subdued or destroyed. He now regarded, and would treat them as the Cushites, who had been transplanted from their primary location in Arabia, into the midst of the barbarous nations of Africa. כֻּשִׁיִּים, *Cushites,* are here the inhabitants of the African Cush, or Ethiopia. See on Is. xviii.

1, 2. Arab. بني الحبش, *Abyssinians.*

Αἰθίοπας, τοὶ διχθὰ δεδαίαται, ἔσχατοι
          ἀνδρῶν,
Οἱ μὲν δυσομένου ὑπερίονος, οἱ δ' ἀνι-
     όντος.   *Odyss.* i. 23, 24.

For פְּלִשְׁתִּיִּים, see on Is. xiv. 28. Gesenius hesitates between Crete and Cappadocia, as designated by the Hebrew *Caphtor,* but inclines to the former.

Did I not bring Israel from the land of Egypt?
The Philistines also from Caphtor?
And the Syrians from Kir?

8   Behold, the eyes of the Lord Jehovah are upon the sinful kingdom,
And I will destroy it from the face of the earth;
Yet I will not utterly destroy the house of Jacob,
Saith Jehovah.

9   For, behold, I will command,
And will sift the house of Israel among all the nations,
As one sifteth corn in a sieve,
And not a grain falleth to the ground.

10   [But] all the sinners of my people shall die by the sword,
That say, The evil shall not reach nor overtake us.

11   In that day I will raise up the booth of David that is falling,
And will close up its breaches;

Thesaurus, p. 709. LXX. Καππαδοκία. אֲרָם, *Aram*, or Syria, put for the *Syrians*, i. e. the inhabitants of the countries about Damascus. They are here represented as having migrated from קִיר, *Kir*, the country lying on the river *Kur*, or Cyrus. See on Is. xxii. 6.

8, 9. בְּ עֵינַים. The eyes of a person are said to be *in* any one, when he keeps him steadily in view, in order either to do him good, or to punish him. In the present instance, the phrase conveys the idea of hostility. Though the kingdom of the ten tribes was to be utterly and for ever destroyed, yet, as descendants of their patriarchal ancestors, they should not become extinct. In the midst of the wrath which their sinfulness should bring upon them, God would remember mercy. אֶפֶס כִּי is strongly adversative. כְּבָרָה, a *sieve*, which is used to separate the chaff and other refuse from the pure grain, is most probably derived from בָּבַר, *to be many*, from the number of small holes in it. LXX. λικμὸς. Aq. and Symm. Κόσκινον. צְרוֹר, *the smallest stone*, is used as a diminutive of צוּר, 2 Sam. xvii. 13; here it signifies the smallest *grain* or *particle* of corn. While the figurative language here employed expresses the violence of the sifting process to which the Israelites should be subjected in order that their idolatry and other sins might be removed from them, it

likewise sets forth the great care that would be exercised for their preservation. The universal character of their dispersion is likewise strongly marked.

10. Those are here specially intended, who scoffingly denied the possibility of the Assyrian conquest; namely, the dissipated magnates of Samaria. Such should perish in the war. הַקְדִּים בַּעַד is unusual. Perhaps the meaning is, Shall not come forward, nor advance in our rear, so as to cut off our retreat.

11. The Israelites now disappear from the scene, in order to give place to a brief but prominent exhibition of the restoration of the Jews from their depressed condition during the anticipated captivity in Babylon, and the great design of that restoration—the introduction of the Messianic dispensation, during which the blessings of the covenant of mercy were to be extended to the Gentile world. With this reference in view, the apostle James expressly quotes the prophecy, Acts xv. 15—17. The quotation is made from the version of the LXX.; but, as regards verbality, differs fully as much from it, as the latter does from the Hebrew text: his object being to give the general sense of the passage, and not the identical phraseology. It must further be observed that, though he quotes the entire passage, consisting of the 11th and 12th verses, his obvious

> And I will raise up its ruins,
> And build it, as in the days of old.
> 12 That the remnant of Edom may be possessed,
> And all the nations upon which my name shall be called,
> Saith Jehovah that doeth this.

design was to give prominence to what is contained in the latter, viz. the conversion of the Gentiles, the very point required by his argument ; so that all attempts to apply what is said respecting the booth of David to the Christian church, are unwarranted and futile. דָּוִד, *David,* is used by the prophet, not in its figurative, but in its proper meaning, as denoting the Hebrew monarch of that name. By יוֹם הַהוּא, *that day,* for which James has, quite indefinitely, μετὰ ταῦτα, we are to understand the period of the dispersion of the Israelites among the nations, subsequent to the fall of their kingdom. Though that kingdom would never be restored, yet the Jewish polity would be re-established at Jerusalem. This polity is here called סֻכַּת דָּוִד, *the booth,* or *hut of David,* to denote the reduced state of his family, and the affairs of the people. Comp. Is. xi. 1, and my note there. When the prosperity of that family is spoken of, the more dignified phrase, בֵּית דָּוִד, *the house of David,* is employed. See 2 Sam. iii. 1; 1 Kings xi. 38 ; Is. vii. 2, 13. אֹהֶל דָּוִד *the tent,* or *tabernacle of David,* Is. xvi. 5, would seem to express an intermediate state of things. That דָּוִד, *David,* is here to be understood of the Messiah, I cannot find. סֻכָּה, *tugurium, a hut,* or booth, so called from its being constructed by interweaving the boughs and branches of trees with each other, and its thus forming a rude shelter from the storm. It was in such booths the Hebrews were to dwell during the seven days of חַג הַסֻּכּוֹת, *the feast of booths,* commonly called "the feast of tabernacles." See Levit. xxiii. 40—43. Root סָכַךְ, *to weave, interweave, protect.* Still more definitely to mark the depressed condition of the Jewish kingdom, it is described as נֹפֶלֶת, *falling.* The present participle is here, as frequently, used to denote an action which was happening at the time of narration, and which would be continued. About the time of Amos the Jewish

affairs had begun to decline ; and, though they occasionally and partially revived, yet, taken as a whole, they continued to deteriorate till the Babylonish invasion, when they were reduced to the deplorably fallen state in which they continued till the return from the captivity, when the restoration here predicted took place. From the phraseology employed by the prophet, the Rabbins derived one of the names which they give to the Messiah : בַּר נִפְלִי, *the son of the fallen.* Thus in the Talmud, Sanhed. fol. 96, 2 : "R. Nachman said to R. Isaac, Hast thou heard when *Bar-naphli* comes ? To whom he said, Who is *Bar-naphli ?* He replied, The Messiah : you may call the Messiah *Bar-naphli ;* for is it not written, In that day I will raise up, &c. ?" quoting the present verse of Amos. For other passages to the same effect, see Schoetgenii Horæ Hebraicæ et Talmud. The feminine suffix in פִּרְצֵיהֶן is to be referred to the different parts or cities of the kingdom, understood. The masculine in דָּוִד, has הֲרִסֹתָיו for its antecedent, and the feminine in בְּנִיתִיהָ refers to סֻכָּה.

12. The grand end of the restoration from the captivity in Babylon is now stated, viz. the introduction of the universal economy of the gospel. The church of God had formerly consisted of persons belonging to a particular nation ; henceforth it was to comprehend those of all nations, even such as had been most hostile to its interests, whom God would call to be his people. יָרַשׁ, *to take possession of, inherit,* is here used figuratively of the influence for good which the church should exert over the Gentiles, bringing them within her pale, and using them for her holy and benevolent purposes. In the words, וְזַרְעֲךָ גּוֹיִם יִירָשׁ, "thy seed shall possess," or inherit "the nations," Is. liv. 3, we have a strictly parallel prophecy, couched in the same language. Comp. also Is. xlix. 8, and Rom. iv. 13, where, in reference to the blessing of the Gentiles with faithful

13   Behold, the days are coming, saith Jehovah,
      That the ploughman shall overtake the reaper,
      And the treader of grapes him that soweth the seed ;
      And the mountains shall drop with new wine,
      And all the hills shall melt.

Abraham, that patriarch is called "*the heir* of the world." Among the first of the foreign nations that were to experience this beneficent influence, the Idumæans are expressly mentioned. Owing to the enmity which had existed between them and the Jews, they had mutually harassed and wasted each other, in consequence of which, and of invasions and wars on the part of other powers, nothing but שְׁאֵרִית, *a remnant*, of the former was left. Of this remnant, a portion was proselytized to the Jewish faith in the time of John Hyrcanus, and the remainder amalgamated with the tribes of Arabia, which embraced the Christian faith. It is to these last that specific reference is here made. יִרְשׁוּ is to be taken impersonally, and rendered passively; and the power of its future must be carried forward to נִקְרָא. The calling of a name upon any person or thing, denotes the assertion of the claims of the individual whose name is mentioned upon the person or thing specified. כָּל־הַגּוֹיִם is the accusative, אֶת being understood as repeated. לְמַעַן יִרְשׁוּ אֶת־שְׁאֵרִית אֱדוֹם the LXX. have rendered, ὅπως ἐκζητήσωσιν οἱ κατάλοιποι τῶν ἀνθρώπων, or, as some MSS. read, ἐκζητήσωσι με, as if their Hebrew text had been לְמַעַן יִרְשׁוּ אֹתִי שְׁאֵרִית אָדָם, *that the residue of men may seek me.* Newcome supposes that the reading אֹתִי is a contraction for אֶת־יְהֹוָה ; but though τὸν Κύριον, which we find in the quotation, Acts xv. 17, might seem to favour this supposition, there is no evidence to prove that the contraction אֶת־י, so common in Rabbinical writings, is of such antiquity. Τὸν Κύριον I consider to be merely an interpretation of με. No Hebrew MSS. afford any countenance to the Greek translation, nor do any of the versions, except the Arabic, which, as usual, follows the LXX. For this reason, and regarding the latitude used by the writers of the New Testament when quoting from the Old, I cannot perceive how the passage can justly be

charged with corruption. To which add, that the words as they stand in the Hebrew text, admirably suit the connexion, as they equally do the argument of the apostle; though quoting, according to custom, from the Greek version, he adopted in the main the construction which it exhibits, as sufficiently expressive of the fact which he had in view.

13. Comp. Levit. xxvi. 5. The language imports the greatest abundance ; and this verse, with the two following, refers to a period subsequent to that of the calling of the Gentiles. This the introductory phrase הִנֵּה יָמִים בָּאִים, *Behold, the days are coming,* distinguished as it is from בַּיּוֹם הַהוּא, *In that day,* ver. 11, the position of the prophecy, and other features which characterise it, sufficiently show. The verses are parallel with Is. lxi. 4 ; lxii. 8, 9 ; lxv. 21—23; and are to be interpreted of the future restoration of the Jews to their own land, and their abundant prosperity in the latter day. For מֹשֵׁךְ הַזָּרַע, *to draw out the seed,* comp. מֶשֶׁךְ הַזָּרַע, Ps. cxxvi. 6. The idea seems to be that of conveying the seed with the hand from the sack or vessel in which it was carried, yet not to the exclusion of the act of sowing. Comp. the Eth. ዐዐሰአ : *jaculatus est sagittas.* For עָסִיס, *fresh* or *sweet wine,* see on Joel i. 5. The metaphorical language here employed is at once, in the highest degree, bold and pleasing. The Hebrews were accustomed to construct terraces on the sides of the mountains and other elevations, on which they planted vines. Of this fact the prophet avails himself, and represents the immense abundance of the produce to be such, that the eminences themselves would appear to be converted into the juice of the grape.

"——Subitis messor gaudebit aristis:
Rorabunt querceta favis, stagnantia passim
Vina fluent, oleique lacus."
          Claudian, in Rufin. lib. i. 382.

14 And I will reverse the captivity of my people Israel,
  And they shall build the desolate cities, and inhabit them :
  And they shall plant vineyards, and drink the wine of them ;
  They shall also make gardens, and eat the fruit of them.
15 For I will plant them in their own land,
  And they shall no more be plucked up from their land
  Which I have given them,
  Saith Jehovah thy God.

How striking the contrast between the scene here depicted, and that which the face of Palestine has presented during the long period of the dispersion !

14, 15. It is impossible to conceive of prophecy more distinctly or positively asserting the future and final restoration of the Jews to Canaan than that contained in these verses. Once and again they have been removed from that favoured land, on account of their wickedness; but still it is theirs by Divine donation to their great progenitor. And when they return to the faith of Abraham, beholding in retrospection the day of the Messiah, which he saw and was glad, but deeply bewailing their guilt in having crucified him, and persevered for so many centuries in the rejection of his gospel, they shall regain possession of it, and remain its happy occupants till the end of time.

OBADIAH

PREFACE

THE prophecy of Obadiah, consisting only of twenty-one verses, is the shortest book of the Old Testament. Jerome calls him, *parvus propheta, versuum supputatione, non sensuum.* Of his origin, life, and circumstances, we know nothing; but, as usual, various conjectures have been broached by the Rabbins and Fathers :— some identifying him with the pious Obadiah who lived at the court of Ahab; some, with the overseer of the workmen, mentioned 2 Chron. xxxiv. 12; and some, with others of the same name; while there is no lack of legendary notices respecting the place of his birth, sepulchre, &c. See Carpzovii Introd. tom. iii. pp. 332, 333.

That he flourished after the capture of Jerusalem by the Chaldæans, may be inferred from his obvious reference to that event, verses 11—14; for it is more natural to regard these verses as descriptive of the past, than as prophetical anticipations of the future. He must, therefore, have lived after, or been contemporary with Jeremiah, and not with Hosea, Joel, and Amos, as Grotius, Huet, and Lightfoot, maintain. Sufficient proof of his having lived in or after the time of that prophet, has been supposed to be found in the almost verbal agreement between verses 1—8, and certain verses inserted in the parallel prophecy, Jeremiah xlix., it being assumed that he must have borrowed from him. This opinion, however, though held by Luther, Bertholdt, Von Coelln, Credner, Hitzig, and Von Knobel, is less probable than the contrary hypothesis, which has been advocated by Tarnovius, Schmidius, Du Veil, Drusius, Newcome, Eichhorn, Jahn, Schnurrer, Rosenmüller, Holzapfel, Hendewerk, Hävernick, and Maurer. Indeed, a comparison of the structure of the parallel prophecies goes satisfactorily to show the priority of our prophet, as has been ably done by Schnurrer, in his Dissertatio Philologica in Obadiam, Tübing. 1787, 4to. Add to which, that Jeremiah appears to have been in the habit of partially quoting from preceding prophets. Comp. Is. xv., xvi., with Jerem. xlviii. This view is confirmed by the opinion of Ewald, that both these writers copied from some earlier prophet, since he admits that Obadiah has preserved, in a less altered condition, the more energetic and unusual manner of the original than Jeremiah. In brief, the portion in question is so entirely in keeping with the remainder of the book, that both must be considered as having been originally delivered by the same individual; whereas Jeremiah presents it in the form of *disjecta membra poetæ.*

In all probability the prophecy was delivered between the year B. C. 588, when Jerusalem was taken by the Chaldæans, and the termination of the siege of Tyre by Nebuchadnezzar. During this interval, that monarch subdued the Idumæans, and other neighbouring nations.

Of the composition of Obadiah, little, as Bishop Lowth observes, can be said, owing to its extreme brevity. Its principal features are animation, regularity, and perspicuity.

The subjects of the prophecy are the judgments to be inflicted upon the Idumæans on account of their wanton and cruel conduct towards the Jews at the time of the Chaldæan invasion; and the restoration of the latter from captivity. The book may, therefore, be fitly divided into two parts: the first comprising verses 1—16, which contain a reprehension of the pride, self-confidence, and unfeeling cruelty of the former people, and definite predictions of their destruction; the latter, verses 17—21, in which it is promised that the Jews should not only be restored to their own land, but possess the territories of the surrounding nations, especially Idumæa.

The reason why the book occupies its present unchronological position in the Hebrew Bible, is supposed to be the connexion between the subject of which it treats, and the mention made of "the residue of Edom," at the conclusion of the preceding book of Amos.

OBADIAH

The prophecy commences by announcing the message sent in the providence of God to the Chaldæans, to come and attack the Idumæans, ver. 1; and describes the humiliation of their pride, 2, 3; the impossibility of their escape by means of their boasted fastnesses, 4; and the completeness of their devastation, 5. It then proceeds with a sarcastic plaint over their deserted and fallen condition, 6—9; specifies its cause—their unnatural cruelty towards the Jews, 10—14; and denounces a righteous retribution, 15, 16. The remaining portion foretels the restoration of the Jews, their peaceful settlement in their own land, and the establishment of the kingdom of Messiah, 17—21.

---

1   THE Vision of Obadiah.
Thus saith the Lord Jehovah concerning Edom:
We have heard a report from Jehovah,
And a messenger is sent among the nations:
" Up! let us rise against her to battle!"

1. Eichhorn, Rosenmüller, Jaeger, and Hendewerk, have raised unnecessary doubt respecting the genuineness of the title and introduction contained in this verse, which have been fully obviated by Schnurrer, Maurer, and Hitzig. For חֲזוֹן, see on Is. i. 1. עֹבַדְיָה, Obadiah, "the servant of Jehovah," equivalent to עֲבְדְּאֵל, Abdeel, Jer. xxxvi. 26; Arab. عبد الله, Abd-allah; Ger. Gottesschalck. For אֱדוֹם, Edom, see on Is. xxxiv. 5. The words שְׁמוּעָה שָׁמַעְנוּ מֵאֵת יְהֹוָה, we have heard a report from Jehovah, are not to be regarded as designed to describe the reception of the Divine message by the prophet, but express the communication made to the nations by the ambassador sent to summon them to the attack upon Idumæa, as the following clause shows. The שְׁמוּעָה, report, or communication itself, is con-

tained in the last line of the verse. The plural form שָׁמַעְנוּ, "we have heard," for which Jeremiah has שָׁמַעְתִּי, "I have heard," is so qualified by the passive verb שֻׁלָּח in the second member of the parallelism, that it is equivalent to the passive form נִשְׁמְעָה, hath been heard. There is, therefore, no necessity to inquire whether Obadiah meant himself and other prophets, or whether he identified himself with his countrymen. All that is intended is the circulation of the hostile message in regard to Idumæa; and the tracing of the movement to the overruling providence of God, by which Nebuchadnezzar and his allies were led to turn their arms against that country. See Calvin, in loc. צִיר, a messenger, or ambassador; Arab. صار, صير, ivit, profectus est. LXX. περιοχὴν, but in Jer. ἀγγέλους; Symm. here ἀγγελίαν. Comp.

2 Behold, I have made thee small among the nations;
Thou art exceedingly despised.
3 The pride of thine heart hath deceived thee,
Thou that dwellest in the clefts of the rock,
Whose habitation is high;
That saith in his heart,
Who shall bring me down to the ground?
4 Though thou shouldest soar like the eagle,
And shouldest set thy nest among the stars,
Thence I will bring thee down, saith Jehovah.

Is. xviii. 2, and my note there. קוּמוּ, *arise! up!* like לְכִי, *come! go!* &c., is frequently used as a term of excitement. With it the address of the herald commences; who, identifying himself with the nations which he summons, proceeds to employ the plural of the same verb in its strictly hostile sense, followed by the preposition עַל. אֱדוֹם, though properly masculine, is here viewed as אֶרֶץ, *a country;* hence the feminine suffix in כֻּלָּהּ.

2. Here the masculine gender is adopted, which is continued throughout the prophecy—עָם, *people,* being understood. The past time of the verbs expresses the certainty of the events; and קָטֹן, *small,* and בָּזוּי, *despised,* are not designed to mark the comparatively limited and despicable character of Idumæa, geographically considered, as Newcome interprets, but describe the miserable condition to which it was to be reduced by its enemies.

3. The Idumæans are taunted with the proud confidence which they placed in their lofty and precipitous mountain-fastnesses, and the insolence with which they scouted every attempt to subdue them. These positions, strong by nature, and many of them rendered still more so by art, they deemed absolutely impregnable. Such inaccessible places are appropriately called חַגְוֵי־סֶלַע, *cliffs of the rock,* Syr. ⟨⟩, *rupes;* the Arab.

⟨⟩, *confugit;* and hence the idea of *refuge,* which is secondary, and less proper to be adopted here. LXX. ἐν ταῖς ὀπαῖς τῶν πετρῶν. Syr. ⟨⟩

⟨⟩, *in fortissima rupe.* Some interpreters are of opinion that by סֶלַע, *Sela,* we are to understand the city of that name, otherwise called *Petra,* situated in Wady Mûsa, and celebrated as the capital of Idumæa. See on Is. xvi. 1. The חֲגָוִים, *cliffs,* would, on this interpretation, be the high and inaccessible rocks which beetled over that metropolis. I prefer taking the word in its literal acceptation, and view it as a collective, equivalent to the plural of the LXX. and other ancient versions, and thus describing the rocky character of the country generally, as well as that about Petra in particular. Instead of הִשִּׁיאֶךָ, *hath deceived thee,* four of De Rossi's MSS. and originally two more, read הִשִּׂיאֶךָ; but though this reading is supported by the LXX., Arab., Vulg., and Hexaplar Syr., it is inferior to that of the Textus Receptus, which has the suffrages of the Syr. and the Targ., especially as there are no other instances in which הִשִּׂיא is used in the sense of *raising,* or *elevating.* The י in שֹׁכְנִי is simply a poetic paragogic, of which several examples occur in the Benoni participle. See Gen. xlix. 11; Deut. xxxiii. 16; Is. xxii. 16; Micah vii. 14. In שִׁבְתּוֹ there is a transition from the second person to the third, for the sake of more graphically pointing out the proud position of Edom. Comp. Is. xxii. 16.

4. By a bold but beautiful hyperbole, the Idumæans are told, that, to what height soever they might remove, and how entirely they might imagine themselves to be beyond the reach of their enemies, Jehovah would dislodge them, and deliver them into their power. For

5 If thieves had come to thee,
  Or robbers by night (how art thou destroyed!)
  Would they not have stolen what was sufficient for them?
  If vintagers had come to thee,
  Would they not have left some gleanings?

the soaring of the eagle, and his building his nest on the inaccessible crags of the rock, comp. Job xxxix. 27, 28:

אִם־עַל־פִּיךָ יַגְבִּיהַ נָשֶׁר
וְכִי יָרִים קִנּוֹ:
סֶלַע יִשְׁכֹּן וְיִתְלֹנָן
עַל־שֶׁן־סֶלַע וּמְצוּדָה:

"Is it at thy command the eagle soars,
And erects his nest on high?
The rock he inhabits, and makes his abode
On the point of the rock, and the fastness."

שִׂים, Ewald and Hitzig take to be a passive participle; but that it is the infinitive construct, is rendered certain by its having the preposition מִן before it, Job xx. 4. In the present instance, and in Num. xxiv. 21, in which, as here, it is followed by קֵן, it stands elliptically for שִׂים תָּשִׂים; which sufficiently accounts for the rendering of the LXX., Syr., Targ., and Vulg., which exhibit the second person singular of the verb. The term כּוֹכָבִים is to be understood literally of the *stars*, as the highest objects which present themselves to the eye, and not of the tops of the highest rocks, or even heaven itself, as some have maintained. אוֹרִידְךָ is a direct reply to the vaunting question, מִי יוֹרִדֵנִי, ver. 3. Theodoret well expresses the sense thus: Ἐπειδὴ τοίνυν, φησὶ ταύταις θαῤῥῶν ἀλαζονείᾳ καὶ μέγα φρονεῖς ὡς ἀχείρωτος, εὐάλωτόν σε καταστήσω καὶ εὐχείρωτον τοῖς ἐχθροῖς, καὶ τῶν πολεμίων οὐ διαφεύξῃ τὰς χεῖρας, οὐδὲ εἰ δίκην ἀετοῦ μετέωρος ἀρθείης, κ. τ. λ.

5. The Idumæans are here taught, that their devastation would be complete. This prophetic intelligence is communicated in the form of interrogative illustrations, derived from customs with which they were familiar. The manner in which they should be treated would be very different from that adopted by private thieves, or by a party of marauding nomades, who usually seize as much

as they can, and especially what they have set their minds on, in the hurry of the moment, leaving the rest of the property to its possessors. They should even fare worse than the vines, on which the vintagers, though they cut down the bunches generally, still left some that might be gleaned afterwards. In Jeremiah, the order of the illustrations is reversed, the vintagers being taken first. שֹׁדְדֵי לַיְלָה, *night-robbers*. In such a country as Idumæa, a predatory attack could only have been attempted in the night, especially on such places as were most strongly fortified by nature, and commanded a view of the immediately surrounding regions. Hitzig thinks the prophet has Petra specially in his eye, on account of its having been the great emporium of that part of the world. Instead of אִם גַּנָּבִים בָּאוּ לְךָ אִם שֹׁדְדֵי לַיְלָה, Jeremiah has only אִם גַּנָּבִים בַּלַּיְלָה, which is less forcible. He also substitutes הִשְׁחִיתוּ for יִגְנֹבוּ. The position of the words אֵיךְ נִדְמֵיתָה, *How thou art destroyed*, has offended fastidious critics, some of whom would remove them to the beginning of the verse, and others to the commencement of the following. What might be accounted their natural place would be the end of the present verse; but the prophet, struggling to give expression to the feeling which agitated his mind, breaks in upon his illustrations with the interjected exclamation, and then carries them on to a close. The words are omitted by Jeremiah. דָּמָה has two leading significations: *to be like*; and, according with the Arab. دمى, *vulneravit, perdidit*, it further means *to cause to cease, destroy*, &c. LXX. ποῦ ἂν ἀπεῤῥίφης; having read נִדְמֵיתָה, a verb, which nowhere occurs in Niphal. דַּיָּם, *their sufficiency*, i. e. what was requisite for supplying their present wants, or such a quantity as they had sufficient strength to remove. LXX. τὰ ἱκανὰ ἑαυτοῖς. Syr. ܣܦܩ ܠܗܘܢ,

6   How is Esau explored!
    And his hidden places searched!
7   All thine allies have driven thee to the frontier;
    Those who were at peace with thee have deceived thee;
    They have prevailed against thee:
    They that ate thy bread have laid a snare under thee;
    There is no understanding in him!

---

sufficientia eorum. The apodosis is omitted; but there is a beautiful propriety in leaving it to be supplied by those to whom the appeal was made.

6. The prophet here resumes his strain of sarcastic plaint over the fall of Idumæa, which he had abruptly adopted in the preceding verse, repeating the אֵיךְ there employed, which is again understood before נִבְעוּ. The patronymic עֵשָׂו is construed as a collective noun with the plural of the verb, and, at the same time, with the singular pronominal affix. In the translation I have been obliged to employ the singular in both cases. מַצְפֻּנָיו, like מַטְמֹנִים, may either signify places where treasures are *hidden*, or the treasures themselves; or the term may be explained of *hiding-places*, to which men resort in order to elude an enemy. I prefer the last of these significations, as better agreeing with the persons of the Edomites, mentioned in the former hemistich; though the hiding of their treasures is also naturally implied. The form is that of the Arabic passive مقطول. Such places abound in Idumæa. "Revera," says Jerome, "ut dicamus aliquid de natura loci, omnis australis regio Idumæorum de Eleutheropoli usque Petram et Ailam (hæc est enim possessio Esau) in specubus habitatiunculas habet. Et propter nimios calores solis, quia meridiana provincia est, subterraneis tuguriis utitur." Instead of the exclamatory form here employed, Jeremiah adopts that of direct personal assertion: כִּי־אֲנִי חָשַׂפְתִּי אֶת־עֵשָׂו גִּלֵּיתִי אֶת־מִסְתָּרָיו; changing, at the same time, חָשַׂף into חֲשֹׂף, and מַצְפֻּנָיו into מִסְתָּרָיו.

7. שָׁלַח, which in Kal has the signification *to send, send away*, signifies in Piel, *to dismiss, eject, expel*, conveying the superadded idea of compulsion or violence. Connected, as here, with עַד,

the verb implies expulsion beyond the frontier specified; and the whole sentence is descriptive of transportation into a state of captivity. Thus the Targ. מִן תְּחוּמָא אַגְלִיךְ, *they shall lead thee captive from the border.* By אַנְשֵׁי בְרִיתָךְ, *the men of thy covenant*, are meant those who had formally pledged assistance to the Edomites, *confederates, allies;* by אַנְשֵׁי שְׁלֹמְךָ, *the men of thy peace*, neighbouring states, which were on terms of peace and friendship with them. LXX. ἄνδρες εἰρηνικοί, those who were peaceably inclined towards them. Before לַחְמְךָ supply אַנְשֵׁי from the preceding—*the men of thy bread;* or אֹכְלֵי, may be understood,—*those who eat thy bread;* and thus the phrase will be descriptive of dependents; some of the poorer tribes of the desert, who subsisted on the bounty of the Edomites, and whose aid they might reasonably expect in case of any emergency. Comp. Ps. xli. 10, where a similar combination of אִישׁ לַחְמִי with אִישׁ שְׁלוֹמִי occurs; though there the idea of familiarity, rather than that of dependence, seems intended to be expressed. Five of De Rossi's MSS. and originally two more, read הַשִּׁיאוּךְ, instead of הִשִּׁיאוּךְ, as also one of the early editions, the LXX., and Arab.; but the common reading is to be preferred. To יָכְלוּ, thirty MSS., originally eleven more, four by emendation, the Soncin. and Complut. editions, the Soncin. Prophets, and the Syr., prefix the copulative, which the difference of sense in the two verbs requires. There is some difficulty in determining the meaning of מָזוֹר. LXX. ἔνεδρα; Syr. ܟܡܐܢܐ, *insidiæ;* Vulg. *insidiæ;* Targ. תַּקְלָא, *offendiculum*—all agreeing in the idea of treachery, or the employment of means by which one might be subverted or ensnared. This seems to be the only suitable meaning

8   Shall I not in that day, saith Jehovah,
       Cause the wise men to perish from Edom?
       And the men of understanding from the mountains of Esau?

in this place, as the signification of *wound*, which more or less attaches to the word, Jer. xxx. 13, Hos. v. 13, the other passages in which it occurs, will not, with any tolerable degree of propriety, apply. Two derivations have been proposed, the Arab. مزر, *distendit, equaliter distendit*, to which Tingstadius appeals in Supplement. ad Lexx. Hebrr. p. 23; but which is far-fetched, as there is no proof that the verb is used in the sense of spreading out a net, or the like; and زور, *mentitus fuit*, زور, *fallum, mendacium*, with which the Hebrew זוּר, *to decline* from the way of truth, has been compared. The use of יָשִׂימוּ תַחְתֶּיךָ, *they place under thee*, most naturally suggests the idea of a *gin* or *trap*, which may be said to deceive or act falsely by those who tread upon it; so that the notions of *treachery, plot, net, snare*, may be combined in furnishing the true signification. Fürst, who derives the word from זוּר, gives the significations thus: "circumligatio; obligatio vulneris; fascia; hinc, medicina ; moraliter, *laqueorum connexio, perfidia fallax, insidiosa, fraudulenta*." To no quarter could the Idumæans look for aid. Their allies, their neighbours, their very dependents, so far from assisting them, would act treacherously towards them, and employ every means, both of an open and covert nature, to effect their ruin. At the close of the verse, the prophet turns off again from the direct mode of address, and employs the third person, for the purpose of more emphatically exposing their folly in placing confidence in those who were totally unworthy of it. It would be highly uncritical, with the Targ., Houbigant, and Newcome, to change בּוֹ, *in him*, into בָּךְ, *in thee*.

8. The Idumæans confided, not only in the natural strength of their country, but in the superiority of their intellectual talent. That they excelled in the arts and sciences, is abundantly proved by the numerous traces of them in the book of Job, which was undoubtedly written in their country. They were, indeed, proverbial for their חָכְמָה, *philosophy*, for the cultivation of which, their intercourse with Babylon and Egypt was exceedingly favourable, as were likewise their means of acquiring information from the numerous caravans whose route lay through their country, thus forming a chain of communication between Europe and India. Speaking of wisdom, the author of the book of Baruch says, in reference to their celebrity as sages of antiquity, chap. iii. 22, 23 :—

" It hath not been heard of in Canaan,
Neither hath it been seen in Teman.
The Hagarenes that seek wisdom upon earth,
The merchants of Meran and of Teman,
The mythologists, and investigators of intelligence,
None of these have known the ways of wisdom,
Nor remembered her paths."

These sages are here called חֲכָמִים, and their accumulated stores of wisdom are expressed by תְּבוּנָה, *intelligence*, the term which had just been employed at the close of the preceding verse. The interrogative הֲלֹא is here strongly affirmative; and ו in וְהַאֲבַדְתִּי is merely conversive. הַר עֵשָׂו, *the mount of Esau*, is the mountainous region of Seir, to the south of Palestine, now called جبل شراه,

Jebel Sherah, and الشراه, *esh-Sherah*, extending as far south as Akabah. It was originally inhabited by the Horites, or Troglodytæ, (so called because they dwelt in the caves of the mountains,) whom the posterity of Esau expelled, and then taking possession of the country, spread themselves as far towards the north as the borders of Moab. It was particularly to the more northerly portion of this region that the name of جبل, *Jebel*, or Gebalene, was given. הַר, *mountain*, being here, and verse 9th, obviously used

9 Thy mighty men, O Teman! shall be dismayed,
  That every one may be cut off from the mountains of Esau.
10 For the slaughter, for the injury of thy brother Jacob,
  Shame shall cover thee, and thou shalt be cut off for ever.
11 In the day when thou didst take a hostile position,
  In the day when foreigners took captive his forces,
  And strangers entered his gates, and cast lots upon Jerusalem,
  Even thou wast as one of them.

in a collective sense, I have translated it in the plural.

9. For תֵּימָן, *Teman*, see on Amos i. 12. מִקָּטֶל has been variously construed. Ewald unnaturally renders it, *without battle*. Schnurrer treats it as a participle in Pael or Poel, pointing it מְקַטֵּל or מִקַּטֵּל, and regarding it as equivalent to the Arab. مقاتل, *vir prælio aptus*. He would thus make it parallel with גִּבּוֹרִים, *mighty men*, in the preceding hemistich. Rosenmüller, De Wette, and some others, translate, *by slaughter*. Leo Juda, most of the older modern translators, followed by Jaeger, Hesselberg, Hendewerk, and Maurer, render, *propter cædem*, and suppose the prophet to be here assigning the cause of the destruction of the Idumæans which he had just predicted, intending more fully to dilate on the subject in the following verse. To this construction, however, it must be objected, that it clogs the parallelism, which properly ends with הַר עֵשָׂו, as in the verse preceding; and also that the words מִקָּטֶל מֵחֲמַס are too closely allied, both in form and reference, to admit of such a pause as that which is introduced by the Soph-Pasuk. I, therefore, do not hesitate to follow the division of the verses adopted by the LXX., Syr., Hexaplar Syr., Vulg., Dathe, Liveley, Newcome, and Boothroyd, by which מִקָּטֶל is removed from verse 9th, and placed at the beginning of verse 10th.

10. מִקָּטֶל מֵחֲמַס אָחִיךָ. Both nouns are in construction with אָחִיךָ, and the genitive thus formed is that of object: *the slaughter of, and the violence done to, thy brother*. The Edomites had not only slain the Hebrews, but injured them in every possible way; and their cruelties were highly aggravated by the considera-

tion, that those who were the objects of them were descended from the same common parent. Comp. Amos i. 11. *Jacob* is used as a patronymic to denote the Jews. Two distinct periods in the future history of the Idumæans are here pointed out: that during which they should be the subjects of ignominy as a conquered people; and that during which they were to be entirely extinct. From the former they recovered about a century before the Christian era; but they were reduced by John Hyrcanus, and afterwards lost every vestige of their separate existence.

11. This and the three following verses contain a series of pointed expostulations, which, while they inculpate the Idumæans, describe the various modes in which they had manifested their malice towards the Jews. Some have thought that עֲמָד מִנֶּגֶד means here to stand aloof, to assume a neutral position, whence one may observe the movements of two opposing parties; but the declaration at the end of the verse, as well as what is stated in verses 13th and 14th, clearly shows that the phrase is to be taken in a hostile sense, as in 2 Sam. xviii. 13; Dan. x. 13. That חַיִל is not to be rendered *wealth* or *riches* in this passage, but *forces, army*, or the like, may be inferred from reference being made to the division of the substance of the citizens of Jerusalem by lot in the following hemistich. זָרִים and נָכְרִים describe the Chaldæans by whom Jerusalem was taken. יַדּוּ is in Piel, contracted for יַיְדּוּ. Comp. וַיִּדּוּ, Lam. iii. 53. Instead of שְׁעָרָו, the reading of the text, many MSS., four of the earliest printed editions, and some more recent ones, exhibit שְׁעָרָיו, the full form, as proposed by the Keri. That the word may originally have been read as the singular, is clear from its

12   Thou shouldest not have looked on in the day of thy brother,
In the day of his being treated as an alien;
Nor shouldest thou have rejoiced over the sons of Judah,
In the day of their destruction :
Neither shouldest thou have spoken insolently
In the day of ·distress.

13 Thou shouldest not have entered the gate of my people,
In the day of their calamity ;
Thou, even thou, shouldest not have looked on their affliction,
In the day of their calamity ;
Nor stretched forth thy hand to their wealth,
In the day of their calamity.

14 Neither shouldest thou have stood at the pass,
To cut off those of his that escaped ;

occurrence in this number, ver. 13 ; but then, in both cases, it is to be taken as a collective.

12. The future forms אַל־תִּשְׂמַח, אַל־תֵּרֶא, אַל־תַּמַד, אַל־תִּשְׁלַחְנָה, אַל־תָּבוֹא, אַל־תַּגְדֵּל, אַל־תַּסְגֵּר, are all qualified in signification, by the circumstance, that the speaker has a past event prominently in view, in reference to which he places himself and those whom he addresses in the time of its passing, and points out what was their duty in reference to it. They are properly subjunctives of negation, expressive of what *should not* have been done, and therefore have the usual force of the imperative. "Verba Hebræorum sæpe non actum, sed debitum vel officium significant." Glassii Philolog. Sacr. lib.iii. tract. 3, can. 6. Nicholson's Ewald, § 264. רָאָה בְּ, means here *to look upon with malignant pleasure*, to feast one's eyes with the calamity of another. יוֹם אָחִיךָ, *the day of thy brother*, is afterwards explained by אֵידָם, צָרָה, אָבְדָם, נִכְרוֹ which describe the calamitous circumstances in which the Jews were placed. יוֹם, *day*, is often used to express a *disastrous* or *calamitous period*. נֵכֶר, which is taken actively to denote *severe treatment, punishment*, Job. xxxi. 3, is here used passively of the experience of such treatment. Comp. the Arab. نَكِرَ,

difficilis ac durus fuit; gravis ac difficilis; improbavit. The idea radically inherent in the term is that of treating any one

as a stranger, *i. e.* as an alien or enemy. הִגְדִיל פֶּה, *to enlarge*, or *make great the mouth*, Ger. *den Mund voll nehmen :* to use insolent or contumelious language, such as those employ who exult over a fallen foe. Comp. Ezek. xxxv. 13.

13. נַם in נַם־אַתָּה is emphatic. תִּשְׁלַחְנָה, some take to be the third plural feminine, having for its object יָדַיִם ; but the entire construction of the passage requires the second person singular masculine, תִּשְׁלַח. The syllable נָה is added with a view to give intensity to the verb, as in Jud. v. 26 ; thus expressing the eagerness with which the Idumæans seized upon the spoil. Rosenmüller is of opinion that the ה is paragogic, and the נ epenthetic ; but Gesenius is rather inclined to compare it with the energetic Future of the Arabs. Lehrgeb. p. 801. LXX.

μὴ συνεπιθῇ; Syr. ܘܠܐ ܬܘܣܦ ;

Vulg. *non emitteris;* Targ. יְאוֹשִׁיטְתָּא. See for more instances of this intensive form, Job xvii. 16 ; Is. xxviii. 3 ; Exod. i. 10. For the omission of יָד, *hand*, see 2 Sam. vi. 6 ; Ps. xviii. 17.

14. פֶּרֶק is commonly rendered *biviam*, a parting of a way, or a place where a road breaks off into two. I should rather think, from the idea of violence implied in פָּרַק, that it signifies a *break* or *disruption* in a rock or mountain, through which a passage might be effected into the region beyond. Comp. מְפָרֵק הָרִים, 1 Kings xix. 11. LXX. διεκβολαί. Syr.

Neither shouldest thou have delivered up those of his
That were left in the day of distress.

15 For the day of Jehovah is near against all the nations:
As thou hast done, it shall be done unto thee;
Thy deed shall come back upon thine own head.

16 For as ye have drunk upon my holy mountain,
So shall all the nations drink continually;
Yea, they shall drink and swallow greedily,
And shall be as though they had not been.

ܡܟܬܐ, a narrow passage between two mountains. In all probability, the reference is to the means employed to cut off the retreat of those Jews who attempted to pass through Idumæa on their way to Egypt, whither they fled from the Chaldæans. עָמַד עַל הַפֶּרֶק, to *stand at the ravine* or *pass*, graphically describes the attitude of those who are watching in order to intercept a caravan, or a body of travellers, especially in the rugged mountainous regions to the south of Judæa. The Idumæans not only in this way prevented the escape of the fugitives; they carried them back as prisoners, and delivered them up to the enemy.

15. In this verse, the conquest of Idumæa and all the neighbouring nations by Nebuchadnezzar is declared to be at hand. In the war which he was to carry on against them, due retribution would be rendered to the Edomites. Comp. Ps. cxxxvii. 7, 8. For the phrase יוֹם יְהוָֹה, *the day of Jehovah*, see on Is. ii. 12.

16. The Targ., Kimchi, Munster, Vatablus, Calvin, Michaelis, Hendewerk, and Hitzig, consider the Idumæans to be still addressed, and most of them explain their drinking on Mount Zion of the festivities with which they celebrated the victory gained over the Jews. Grotius refers the words to the same people, only he takes the verb שָׁתָה in the bad sense, as denoting the drinking of the cup of divine wrath, and renders עַל־הַר קָדְשִׁי, *on account of my holy mountain*, which he explains thus: "propter Judæam a vobis lacessitam." But it seems more natural to regard the words as directed, by a sudden apostrophe, to the Jews,

assuring them, that, though the sufferings to which they had been subjected were great, still greater punishment would be inflicted upon the hostile nations by which they had been attacked. The punishment which they suffered was only temporary: that of their enemies would be perpetual. The structure of the passage requires the verb to be taken in the same sense in both parts of the verse. Such, in effect, is the construction put upon the words, Jer. xlix. 12. Compare also chap. xxv. 15—29. In this manner the verse is interpreted by Abenezra, Mercer,. Tremellius, Drusius, Liveley, Rosenmüller, Schnurrer, De Wette, Hesselberg, and Maurer. Instead of תָּמִיד, *continually*, the reading סָבִיב, *around*, is exhibited in not fewer than seventy-eight MSS.; in seventeen more originally; in three others in the margin; in seven of the earliest printed editions; and a few other authorities; but all the ancient versions support that of the Textus Receptus, which, according to De Rossi, is found in all the most accurate and best MSS., both Spanish and German. In all probability סָבִיב was substituted by some copyist from Jer. xxv. 9. What proves that the LXX. had the word תמיד in their Hebrew text, is their having mistaken it for חמר, rendering it οἶνον, *wine*. לוּעַ, *to swallow* or *suck down with greediness*. Arab.

لعو and لعي, *avidus*; لغا لغي, *multum*

aquæ *bibit*. Comp. לֹעַ, *the throat*; בָּלַע, *to swallow*, &c. The idea intended to be conveyed by the use of the verb here is that of drinking *completely off* the cup of wrath, as a thirsty person would a vessel of water.

17   But in Mount Zion shall be the escaped,
      And it shall be holy ;
      And the house of Jacob shall enjoy their possessions.
18   And the house of Jacob shall be a fire,
      And the house of Joseph a flame ;
      And the house of Esau shall become stubble,
      And they shall set them on fire, and devour them ;
      So that there shall not be a relic of the house of Esau ;
      For Jehovah hath spoken it.
19   And they of the south shall possess Mount Esau,
      And they of the plain, the Philistines ;
      They shall also possess the country of Ephraim,
      And the country of Samaria ;
      And Benjamin, Gilead.
20   And the captives of this host of the sons of Israel,

17. Obadiah here commences his predictions respecting the restoration of the Jews from the Babylonish captivity; their re-occupancy of Canaan ; and the reign of the Messiah. While the surrounding nations were to disappear, the Jews should regain possession of their holy city, and the land of their fathers. פְּלֵיטָה means such as had survived the captivity. קֹדֶשׁ, *holiness,* i. e. *holy,* refers to Mount Zion, which had been polluted by the idolatrous Chaldæans. See on Joel iii. 17. Jaeger and Hesselberg refer the suffix in מוֹרָשֵׁיהֶם, *their possessions,* to the hostile nations spoken of in the preceding verse ; but less naturally.

18. Though the houses of Jacob and Joseph are here spoken of separately, it was not the intention of the prophet to teach that the two kingdoms of Judah and Israel would be re-established ; yet the special mention of Joseph clearly shows that the ten tribes were to return at the same time, and, jointly with Judah and Benjamin, to possess the land of Palestine and the neighbouring regions. See Is. xi. 12—14; Hos. i. 11. The restored Hebrews would unitedly subdue the Idumæans, which they did in the time of John Hyrcanus, who compelled them to be re-circumcised, and so incorporated them with the Jews, that they henceforward formed part of the nation. See Joseph. Antiquities, book xiii. chap. ix. 1. For the metaphorical language, comp. Num. xxi. 28; Is. x. 17 ; and, for the ground of it, Is. v. 24.

19. By נֶגֶב, *the south,* or southern part of Palestine, is meant those who should occupy it ; and by הַשְּׁפֵלָה, *the plain,* those who should occupy the low country along the shore of the Mediterranean. LXX. Οἱ ἐν Ναγέβ ; οἱ ἐν τῇ Σεφηλά. According to the relative positions of those who should take possession of the different parts of the holy land, was to be the enlargement of their territory by the annexation of the adjoining regions, which had formerly been occupied by alien or hostile powers. As there is no subject specified before אֵת שְׂדֵה אֶפְרַיִם וְאֵת שְׂדֵה שֹׁמְרוֹן, it would seem to be intimated that the regions of Ephraim and Samaria were to be occupied by the Jews and Israelites jointly, without any regard to tribal distinctions : and the reason why the tribe of Benjamin is mentioned, is merely on account of the proximity of Gilead to the territory which it originally possessed. That שָׂדֶה is here employed to denote, not a plain or level country, but a region or district in general, is obvious from the nature of the territory to which reference is made. The mountainous country of Idumæa is called שְׂדֵה אֱדוֹם, Gen. xxxii. 4 (Eng. version, 3).

20. חֵל, i. e. חַיִל, *an army, host,* &c., is

That are among the Canaanites,
As far as Zarephath,
And the captives of Jerusalem,
That are in Sepharad,
Shall possess the cities of the south.

21 And deliverers shall come up in Mount Zion,

here used to express the number of Israelitish captives who were found in Phœnicia, into which they had been sold at different times as slaves, and thence into Greece. See Joel iii. 6, 7. כְּנַעֲנִים is elliptical for בִּכְנַעֲנִים, which is the reading of three MSS. Before עַד צָרְפַת, supply יְשׁוּ from the following. צָרְפַת, *Zarephath*, or Sarepta, now called صرفند, *Surafend*, a town belonging to Sidon, and situated between that city and Tyre, close to the shore of the Mediterranean. According to the etymology of its name, it must have been a place for smelting metals. In the rocks along the foot of the hills, Dr. Robinson found many excavated tombs, which he makes no doubt once belonged to this ancient city. Palestine, vol. iii. p. 414. The name is still given to a large village on a hill at some little distance. What city or country is meant by סְפָרַד, it has been hitherto found impossible to determine. The LXX. Ἐφραθά, which in all probability is a corruption of Σεφραθά. Aq., Symm., and Theod., σαφαράδ. Hexap. Syr. ܣܦܪܕ; but the Peshito ܐܣܦܢܝܐ, *Spain*, with which agrees אַסְפַּמְיָא of the Targ.: an interpretation unanimously adopted by the Rabbins, who in like manner concur in interpreting צָרְפַת of *France*. Jerome, as instructed by his Jewish teacher, renders it the *Bosphorus*. Some refer it to Sipphara in Mesopotamia, some to Sparta, in support of which hypothesis they appeal to 1 Macc. xii. 21; while others propose סְפָרָה, *Sephara*, Gen. x. 30, or the town of Σαπφὰρ, mentioned by Ptolemy, as lying between the territory of the Homerites and Sabæans. To judge from the other geographical relations stated in this and the preceding verse, we should conjecture, that some place to the south or east of Judæa is

intended. The following list of cities and places in the possession of the Jews in the time of Alexander Jannæus is given by Josephus : κατὰ τοῦτον τὸν καιρὸν ἤδη τῶν Σύρων καὶ Ἰδουμαίων καὶ Φοινίκων πόλεις εἶχον οἱ Ἰουδαῖοι· πρὸς θαλάσσῃ μὲν Στράτωνος πύργον, Ἀπολλωνίαν, Ἰόππην, Ἰάμνειαν, Ἄζωτον, Γάζαν, Ἀνθηδόνα, Ῥαφίαν, Ῥινοκούρουραν· ἐν δὲ τῇ μεσογείᾳ κατὰ τὴν Ἰδουμαίαν, Ἄδωρα, καὶ Μάρισσαν, καὶ Σαμάρειαν, Καρμήλιον ὄρος, καὶ τὸ Ἰταβύριον ὄρος, Σκυθόπολιν, Γάδαρα, Γαυλανίτιδα, Σελεύκειαν, Γάβαλα, Μωαβίτιδας, Ἐσσεβὼν, Μήδαβα, Λεμβᾶ, Ὀρώνας, Γελίθωνα, Ζᾶρα, Κιλίκιον αὐλῶνα, Πέλλαν—ἄλλας τε πόλεις πρωτευούσας τῆς Συρίας, αἱ ἦσαν κατεστραμμέναι.—*Antiq.* book xiii. ch. xv. 4.

21. Though forty-four MSS., besides several others at second hand, and eight printed editions, read מושיעים instead of מוֹשִׁיעִים, there is no difference in the meaning, the former reading being merely defective in orthography. The LXX., Aq., Theod., Syr., and Arab., appear to have read נושָׁעים or מושָׁעים in the passive, which is unsuitable to the connexion. Jerome observes that the word is active. Such *saviours* or *deliverers* are meant, as those who were raised up in the time of the Judges. There can be little doubt that the celebrated family of the Maccabees are intended, whose valiant princes governed the Jews for the period of an hundred and twenty-six years, during which time signal victories were gained over the Idumæans, as narrated 2 Macc. x. 15—23; Joseph. Antiq. book xiii. chap. ix. 1. שָׁפַט is here used in the sense of *punishing*, as in 1 Sam. iii. 13 ; and שפט in the phrase בְּ עָשָׂה שְׁפָטִים, Exod. xii. 12; Num. xxxiii. 4. Comp. κρίνω, Acts vii. 7. The concluding words of the prophecy, וְהָיְתָה לַיהֹוָה הַמְּלוּכָה, refer to the reign of the Messiah, called so

To judge mount Esau;
And the kingdom shall be Jehovah's.

frequently in the N. T. ἡ Βασιλεία τοῦ Θεοῦ. Comp. Dan. ii. 44; vii. 27. But for the introduction of this kingdom, no restoration of the Jews would have taken place; the temple would have remained in ruins, and the land a scene of desolation.

JONAH

PREFACE

Against no book of Scripture have the shafts of infidelity and the sapping arts of anti-supernaturalism been more strenuously directed than against that of the Prophet Jonah. As early as the days of Julian and Porphyry it was made the subject of banter and ridicule by the pagans, who accused the Christians of credulity for believing the story of the deliverance by means of a fish; and, in modern times, while the enemies of revelation have evinced the same spirit, many of its pretended friends have had recourse to methods of interpretation, which would not only remove the book from the category of inspired writings, but, if applied to these writings generally, would annihilate much that is strictly historical in its import, and leave us to wander in the regions of conjecture and fable. Blasche, Grimm, and some others, suppose the whole to have been transacted in a dream; but, as Eichhorn justly observes,[*] there is not a single circumstance in the narrative that would suggest such an idea; and, besides, whenever any account is given of a dream in Scripture, the fact that such is the case, is always intimated by the writer. The manner in which the book commences and closes, is also objected to this hypothesis, which J. G. A. Müller[†] scruples not to assert we are on no ground

---

* Einleit. Band iv. § 575.   † Paulus Memorabilien. Stück vi. p. 154.

whatever (durch gar nichts,) warranted to adopt. The theory of an historical allegory was advanced and maintained with great learning, but, at the same time, with the most extravagant license of imagination, by the eccentric Hermann von der Hardt, Professor of the Oriental languages at the university of Helmstedt.* According to this author, Jonah was an historical person, but is here symbolical, partly of Manasseh, and partly of Josiah, kings of Judah ; the ship was the Jewish state ; the storm, the political convulsions which threatened its safety ; the master of the ship, Zadok the high-priest ; the great fish, the city of Lybon on the Orontes, where Manasseh was detained as a prisoner, &c. Semler, Michaelis, Herder, Hezel, Stäudlin, Paulus, Meyer, Eichhorn, Niemeyer, &c. have attempted to vindicate to the book the character of a parable, a fable, an apologue, or a moral fiction ; while Dereser, Nachtigal, Ammon, Bauer, Goldhorn, Knobel, and others, consider it to have had an historical basis, and that it has been invested with its present costume in order that it might answer didactic purposes. On the other hand, Rosenmüller, Gesenius, De Wette, Maurer, and Winer, derive it from popular tradition : some tracing it to the fable of the deliverance of Andromeda from a sea monster, by Perseus, Apollod. ii. 4, 3 ; Ovid, Metamorph. iv. 662, &c. ; and some, to that of Hercules, who sprang into the jaws of an immense fish, and was three days in its belly, when he undertook to save Hesione, Iliad, xx. 145 ; xxi. 442 ; Diod. Sic. iv. 42 ; Tzetz. ad Lycophr. Cassand. 33 ; Cyrill Alex. in Jon. ii.

Much as some of these writers may have in common with each other, there are some essential points on which they are totally at variance ; while all frankly acknowledge the difficulties which clog the subject.

The opinion which has been most generally entertained, is that which accords to the book a strictly historical character ; in other words, which affirms that it is a relation of facts which actually took place in the life and experience of the prophet. Nor can I view it in any other light, while I hold fast an enlightened belief in the divine authority of the books composing the canon of the Old

* Ænigmata prisci Orbis. Jonas in Luce, &c. Helmstedt. 1723, fol. For the full title of this remarkable book, see Rosenmüller's Prolegom.

Testament, and place implicit reliance on the authority of the Son of God. Into the fixed and definite character of the canon, I need not here enter, having fully discussed the subject elsewhere;* but assuming that all the books contained in it possess the Divine sanction, the test to which I would bring the question, and by which, in my opinion, our decision must mainly be formed, is the unqualified manner in which the personal existence, miraculous fate, and public ministry of Jonah, are spoken of by our Lord. He not only explicitly recognises the prophetical office of the son of Amittai (Ἰωνᾶ τοῦ προφήτου), just as he does that of Elisha, Isaiah, and Daniel, but represents his being in the belly of the fish as a real miracle (τὸ σημεῖον); grounds upon it, as a fact, the certainty of the future analogous fact in his own history; assumes the actual execution of the commission of the prophet at Nineveh; positively asserts that the inhabitants of that city repented at his preaching; and concludes by declaring respecting himself, " Behold! a greater than Jonah is here." Matt. xii. 39—41; xvi. 4. Now, is it conceivable, that all these historical circumstances would have been placed in this prominent light, if the person of the prophet, and the brief details of his narrative, had been purely fictitious? On the same principle on which the historical bearing of the reference in this case is rejected, may not that to the Queen of Sheba, which follows in the connexion, be set aside, and the portion of the first book of Kings, in which the circumstances of her visit to Solomon are recorded, be converted into an allegory, a moral fiction, or a popular tradition? The two cases, as adduced by our Lord, are altogether parallel; and the same may be affirmed of the allusion to Tyre and Sidon, and that to Sodom in the preceding chapter.

It may be said, indeed, that a fictitious narrative of the moral kind would answer the purpose of our Saviour equally well with one which contained a statement of real transactions; just as it has been maintained, that the reference made by the Apostle James to the patience of Job, suited his purpose, irrespective of the actual existence of that patriarch; but, as in the one case, a fictitious example of patience would prove only a tame and frigid motive to

---

* Divine Inspiration, Lect. IX. pp. 450—488.

induce to the endurance of actual suffering, so, in the other, a merely imaginary repentance must be regarded as little calculated to enforce the duties of genuine contrition and amendment of life.

Certainly in no other instance in which our Saviour adduces passages out of the Old Testament for the purpose of illustrating or confirming his doctrines, can it be shown, that any point or circumstance is thus employed which is not historically true. He uniformly quotes and reasons upon them as containing accounts of universally admitted facts; stamps them as such with the high sanction of his divine authority; and transmits them for the confident belief of mankind in all future ages.

It is only necessary further to add, that if the book had contained a parable, the name of some unknown person would have been selected, and not that of a prophet to whom a definite historical existence is assigned in the Old Testament. On perusing the first sentence, every unprejudiced reader must conclude that there had existed such a prophet, and that what follows is a simple narrative of facts. The formula לֵאמֹר—וַיְהִי דְבַר־יְהוָה is so appropriated, as the usual introduction to real prophetical communication, that to put any other construction upon it would be a gross violation of one of the first principles of interpretation. Comp. 2 Chron. xi. 2; Is. xxxviii. 4; Jer. i. 4, 11; ii. 1; xiv. 1; xvi. 1; xxviii. 12; xxix. 30; Ezek. iii. 16; Hag. i. 1, 3; ii. 20; Zech. iv. 8.

Against the plenary historical character of the book, the miraculous nature of some of the transactions has been objected; but, referring for an investigation of these transactions to the commentary, and taking for granted an interposition of miraculous agency in the deliverance of the prophet, when cast into the sea, may it not be fairly asked, whether there is nothing in the circumstances of the case to justify such interposition? The commission was most important in its own nature, but likewise most unusual, and confessedly most hazardous in its execution; one from which it was extremely natural for Jonah to shrink, and which required the most confirmatory evidence of its divine origin to induce him to act upon it. The miracle selected for the purpose of furnishing him with this evidence, however extraordinary in itself, was in exact keeping with the circumstances in which he was placed; and, in so far, was

parallel with those wrought in connexion with the mission of Moses,
Exod. iii., iv. ; of Elijah, 1 Kings xvii. ; and of Christ and his
apostles. And it is undeniable, that most of the writers who have
called it in question, have either flatly denied the existence of all
scripture-miracles, or attempted, in some way or other, to account
for them on mere natural principles. The same mode of reasoning
which goes to set aside one, will, if fully carried out, go to set
aside all.

That our prophet is the same who predicted the restoration of
the ancient boundaries of the kingdom of the ten tribes, 2 Kings
xiv. 25, is rendered certain by identity of name, parentage, and
office; and as that prediction received its accomplishment in the
reign of Jeroboam II., it is obvious he must at least have been
contemporary with that monarch, if he did not flourish at a still
more early period. He is justly considered to have been, with the
exception of Joel, the most ancient of all the Hebrew prophets
whose writings are contained in the canon.

Whether Jonah composed the book himself, or whether it was
written at a more recent period, has been matter of dispute. Of
the circumstance, that he is spoken of in the third person, no
account is to be made, since it is a style of writing frequently
adopted by the sacred penman, as it also is by profane authors.
Nor can the occurrence of two or three Chaldee words, as סְפִינָה,
a ship, עָשַׁת, to think, טַעַם, command, be justly objected against
the early authorship; for the prophet must have had considerable
intercourse with persons who spoke foreign languages, which could
not but exert some influence on his style. With respect to סְפִינָה,
as it is also the Syriac ܣܦܝܢܬܐ, and Arabic سفينة, there is every
reason to conclude that it was a nautical term in use among the
Phœnicians, and so might have been adopted at an early period into
all the cognate dialects, though they had other words by which to
express the same thing. The use of the compound particles שֶׁלְמִי
and בְּשֶׁלִי does not necessarily argue a late date, since there was
nothing to prevent their being appropriated under the circumstances
of the prophet, just as they came to be adopted, under somewhat
similar circumstances, by other writers. The employment of שֶׁ, the

abbreviated form of אֲשֶׁר, in Judges v. 7, is an undeniable example of its adoption at an early period; and it is indeed very doubtful whether it be proper to regard it as a Chaldaism at all, though it is found in some portions of the Hebrew Scriptures and not in others.* It has also been alleged against the antiquity of the book, that the writer uses the substantive verb in the past tense, when describing the size of Nineveh, וְנִינְוֵה הָיְתָה עִיר־גְּדוֹלָה, chap. iii. 3; as if the city had been destroyed before his time; but the past tense is evidently employed for the simple purpose of preserving uniformity in the style of the narrative, and, as De Wette acknowledges, *bedeutet nichts.*†

In point of style, the book is remarkable for the simplicity of its prose: the only portion of poetry is chap. ii. 3—10 (Eng. version, 2—9), which possesses considerable spirit and force, though some parts of it are evidently a repetition of certain sentences in the Psalms of David, with which the prophet appears to have been familiar.

Of the numerous traditions, both Jewish and Christian, which profess to give us information respecting Jonah, I would say with Luther, *Das glaube wer da will, ich glaube es nicht.* All that we learn from Scripture is, that his father's name was Amittai, and that his birth-place was Gath-hepher (גַּת הַחֵפֶר, 2 Kings xiv. 25; גִּתָּה חֵפֶר, Josh. xix. 13), a city in the tribe of Zebulon, from which latter circumstance it appears that he was an Israelite, and not a Jew.

In this book the patience and clemency of God are strikingly contrasted with the selfishness and unbelief of man; and, as inserted in the canon of Scripture, it was no doubt primarily designed to teach the Jews the moral lessons, that the Divine regard was not confined to them alone, but was extended to other subjects of the general government of God; that wickedness, if persisted in, will meet with condign punishment; that God has no pleasure in inflicting such punishment, but delights in the repentance of the guilty; and that if pagans yielded so prompt a compliance with a single prophetic message, it behoved those who were continually

---

* See Holden on Ecclesiastes, Introd. Dissert. pp. 10—13.

† Lehrbuch, § 237.

instructed by the servants of Jehovah, seriously to reflect on the guilt which they contracted by refusing to listen to their admonitions. It has been usual to speak of Jonah as a type of our Saviour, and numerous points of resemblance have been attempted to be established between them, to the no small injury of the blessed character of the latter : whereas, there is nothing more in the passage of our Lord's discourse (Matt. xii.), from which the notion has been borrowed, than a comparison of his own consignment to the tomb for *the same space of time* which the prophet spent in the belly of the fish.* The record of the event in the Jewish Scriptures could never have suggested to its readers, before Christ made the reference, the subject in the anticipative illustration of which he applies it.

* See the excellent remarks of the Rev. W. Lindsay Alexander, M.A. on types, in his Congregational Lectures, Lect. VIII.

CHAPTER I

We have here an account of the prophet's commission to preach at Nineveh, and his attempt to evade it by embarking for Spain, 1—3; an extraordinary storm by which he was baffled in his purpose; the alarm of the sailors, and the means which they adopted for their safety; the detection of Jonah; and his being thrown into the sea, 4—16.

---

1 THE word of Jehovah was communicated to Jonah, the son of
2 Amittai, saying: Arise, go to Nineveh, that great city, and proclaim against it; for their wickedness is come up before me.

1. From the circumstance that the book commences with the conjunction ו, commonly rendered *and*, some have inferred that it is merely the fragment of a larger work, written by the same hand; but though this particle is most commonly used to connect the following sentence with something which precedes it, and is placed at the beginning of historical books to mark their connexion with a foregoing narrative, as Exod. i. 1; 1 Kings i. 1; Ezra i. 1; yet it is also employed inchoatively where there is no connexion whatever, as Ruth i. 1; Esth. i. 1; and, as specially parallel, Ezek. i. 1. It serves no other purpose in such cases than merely to qualify the apocopated future, so as to make it represent the historical past tense. The proper names יוֹנָה, *Jonah*, and אֲמִתַּי, *Amittai*, signify *a dove*, and *veracious* or *truthful*, but why they were given to the prophet and his father we are not informed.

2. By an emphatic idiom, קוּם, *arise*, is used before another verb, as a term of excitement. נִינְוֵה, NINEVEH, the ancient capital of the Assyrian empire, was situated on the eastern bank of the Tigris, opposite to the modern town of Mosul. The name of *Nunieh* or *Ninevouh* is still given to a village on the spot where there have recently been discovered walls of brick and earth, ex-

tending over a surface of about 30,000 feet, and enclosing an irregular quadrangle, which appears to have formed the chief part of the ancient city. The whole area is covered with bricks, tiles, and terra-cottas with cuneiform inscriptions. The name is generally allowed to signify "the residence of Ninus," from נִין, *Ninus*, and נָוֶה, *a dwelling;* but, according to Hebrew usage, the words should be reversed in order to bring out this meaning. By the Greek and Roman writers, it is called Νίνος, *Ninus*, after its founder, who must have been identical with Nimrod, to whom the foundation of the city is ascribed, Gen. x. 11. For, that אַשּׁוּר, *Asshur*, is there to be understood of the country so called, or Assyria, and not of a person of that name, is evident from ver. 22, where Asshur is mentioned as a descendant of Shem, and not of Ham. The omission of the local ה, which might have been expected to form אַשּׁוּרָה, cannot be brought as an objection, since it is frequently omitted. See Numb. xxxiv. 4; Deut. iii. 1. In point of size, it might well be designated הָעִיר הַגְּדוֹלָה, *that great city*, having been, as stated chap. iii. 3, "three days' journey" in circumference. If we reckon a day's journey at about twenty miles, which is the average rate of travelling in the East, it will give us sixty miles;

3 But Jonah rose up to flee unto Tarshish, from the presence of Jehovah; and he went down to Joppa, and found a ship going to Tarshish, and paid the fare thereof, and went down into her, to go with them unto Tarshish from the presence of Jehovah.

which, how immense soever it may appear, quite agrees with the estimate stated by Diodorus Siculus, ii. 3 : viz. 480 stadia in circuit, 150 stadia in length, and 90 stadia in breadth. He further calls it Νῖνος μεγάλη, and adds, τηλικαύτην δὲ πόλιν οὐδεὶς ὕστερον ἔκτισε κατά τε τὸ μέγεθος τοῦ περιβολοῦ, καὶ τὴν περὶ τὸ τεῖχος μεγαλοπρέπειαν. Making every allowance for the large spaces occupied by gardens, &c., it must, according to the computation specified, chap. iv. 11, have contained a population of upwards of six hundred thousand souls, which is nearly equal to that of Paris. As it had long been the mistress of the East, and its situation was favourable for commerce, it possessed immense wealth, but was, at the same time, notorious for the most flagrant corruption of manners. After a siege of three years, it was taken by Arbaces the Mede, about the seventh year of Uzziah; and a second time by the united forces of Cyaxares the Mede, and Nabopolassar, viceroy of Babylon, B.C. 626. קְרָא עָלֶיהָ, *make a proclamation against it.* This proclamation consisted in the announcement, that, within the space of forty days, the city should be destroyed. עַל the LXX. and Vulg. render *in ;* and some would assign to the word the signification *to,* which אֶל has, chap. iii. 3; but it better agrees with the flight of Jonah to retain that of *against.* The idea of his going to so great a city for the purpose of denouncing punishment against its wicked population so appalled him, that he shrunk from the task. It is also more in keeping with the reason assigned in the following clause of the verse. The phrase עָלָה לְפְנֵי יְהוָה, *to go,* or *come up before Jehovah,* is expressive of whatever is supposed specially to attract his notice, and require his interference. Comp. בָּא לְפְנַי, Gen. vi. 13 ; בָּאָה אֵלַי, xviii. 21. Βαβυλὼν ἡ μεγάλη ἐμνήσθη ἐνώπιον τοῦ Θεοῦ, Rev. xvi. 19. Αἱ ἐλεημοσύναι σου ἀνέβησαν εἰς μνημόσυνον ἐνώπιον τοῦ Θεοῦ, Acts x. 4.

3. For תַּרְשִׁישׁ, *Tarshish,* see on Is. xxiii. 10. The Rabbins vacillate between Tarsus and Tunis. Jonathan has יַמָּא, *the sea.* Jonah resolved to make his escape into the most distant regions of the West. Comp. Ps. cxxxix. 7. פְּנֵי יְהוָה, which strictly means the *face, person,* or *presence of Jehovah,* is sometimes employed to denote the special manifestation of his presence, or certain outward and visible tokens by which he made himself locally known. Thus God promised that *his presence* (פָּנַי), *i.e.* the sensible tokens of his presence, should accompany the Hebrews on their march to Canaan. Exod. xxxiii. 14. Comp. Ps. ix. 3; lxviii. 2, 8. It is also employed in reference to the *place* or *region* where such manifestations were vouchsafed, as Gen. iv. 14 ; where it obviously signifies the spot in which the primitive worship was celebrated, and sensible proofs of the Divine favour were manifested to the worshippers. 1 Sam. i. 22 ; ii. 18 ; Ps. xlii. 3. In like manner, the place where Jacob had intimate communion with God, was called by that patriarch פְּנִיאֵל, *the face,* or *manifestation of God,* Gen. xxxii. 31 (Eng., 30). The interpretation, therefore, of David Kimchi, כי חשב שאם יצא מארץ ישראל לחוצה לארץ לא תשרה עליו רוח נבואה, *he imagined that if he went out of the land of Israel, the spirit of prophecy would not rest upon him,* is perhaps not wide of the mark. Jarchi to the same effect, שאין שכינה שורה בחוצה לארץ, *The Shekinah does not dwell out of the land.* Though, as Theodoret observes, he well knew that the Lord of the universe was everywhere present, yet he supposed that it was only at Jerusalem he became apparent to men ; ὑπολαμβάνων δὲ ὅμως ἐν μόνῃ τῇ Ἱερουσαλὴμ αὐτὸν ποιεῖσθαι τὴν ἐπιφάνειαν. For the reason of Jonah's flight, see on chap. iv. 2. יָרַד is used of *going down* to the sea-coast from any inland place, so that it cannot be inferred from the use of the term that it was at Jerusalem Jonah received his commission. כִּי שְׁפַת

4   But Jehovah caused a great wind to come down úpon the sea,
and there was a great tempest in the sea, and it was apprehended
5 the ship would be wrecked. Then the mariners were afraid, and
cried, each to his god, and threw out the wares that were in the
ship into the sea, to lighten her of them; but as for Jonah, he
had gone down into the innermost part of the vessel, and lay
fast asleep.

הים הוא מקום נמוך כנגד שאר היבשה, Kimchi.
יָפוֹ, *Iapho*, LXX. Ἰόππη, Arab. يافا,
Yapha, Jaffa, Joppa, a celebrated harbour
on the east coast of the Mediterranean,
at the distance of ten hours from Jerusalem, of which it is properly the sea-
port. However insecure, it was used
as a harbour as early as the days of
Solomon, 2 Chron. ii. 16. It was likewise thus appropriated in the Persian
period, Ezra iii. 7; and was deemed so
important in the time of the Maccabees,
that, when recovered from the Syrians,
it was fortified, and afterwards underwent
various fates. Its present population
amounts to about 7000 souls. בּוֹא, which
usually signifies to *come, come into, enter,*
is obviously here used in the acceptation
go, go out. Comp. Numb. xxxii. 6. שָׂכָרָהּ,
her hire, i.e. of the vessel, the fare which
Jonah had to pay for a passage in her;
not, that he engaged the vessel, as
Benjoin, after Jarchi, would have it.
רק מה שהוא חייב ליתן בחלקו, *only what he was
obliged to pay as his share;* Abenezra.
This fare, it has been thought, he paid
beforehand, that he might secure his
flight from the land of Judæa; but it
may have been owing to a prudential
condition on the part of the captain.
The affix in צְמָרֶהָ refers to the ship's
crew, understood.

4. The force of הֵטִיל, *to cause to come
down at full length,* in application to the
storm, will appear on consulting Josephus,
who, speaking of the dangerous naviga-
tion of Joppa, says: κατὰ τοῦτον σαλεύ-
ουσι τοῖς ἀπὸ τῆς Ἰόππης ὑπὸ τὴν ἕω
πνεῦμα βίαιον ἐπιπίπτει· μελαμβόρειον
ὑπὸ τῶν ταύτῃ πλωϊζομένων καλεῖται.
"As they were driven about here, a
violent wind . . . fell upon them, which is
called by those that sail there, the *black
north wind.*" De Bello Jud. iii. ix. 3.
The whole section deserves to be read.
Coverdale renders, "But the Lord hurled
a greate wynde into the see." חִשְׁבָה, *the*

ship, i.e., by metonymy, the persons on
board, thought she would founder. Thus
Kimchi; but Jarchi, נדמית כאילו היא נשברת,
she appeared as if she would be broken.

Syr. ܡܣܬܒܪܐ ܗܘܬ ܕܡܬܬܒܪܐ,
was going to be broken, or was tossed, &c.
LXX. ἐκινδύνευε. It is best to render
the verb impersonally.

5. מַלָּחִים, *mariners,* from מֶלַח, *salt,* the
quality of the water which they navigate.
Syr. and Arab. the same. Comp. Ezek.
xxvii. 9, 27, 29. Kimchi, תופשי המשוטים,
those who handle the oars, with reference
to the ancient mode of propelling vessels
at sea. Being in all probability Phœnicians, they had each his tutelary deity,
whose interposition he invoked in the
hour of danger. From the circumstance
that כֵּלִים signifies *vessels,* Benjoin infers,
that the ship had not taken in a regular
cargo, Jonah having paid the entire
freight; but כְּלִי is used with such latitude
of signification in the Hebrew Scriptures,
that it may be understood of any kind
of manufactured articles, such as those
enumerated Ezek. xxvii. which formed
the merchandise of Tyre. These the
Phœnicians conveyed to Spain, whence
they brought back cargoes of silver,
iron, tin, and lead. That something
more ponderous than a few vessels on
the deck is meant, is evident from what
follows in the verse, ἐκβολὴν ἐποιήσαντο;
the words, employed by the LXX. in
translating which, are the same used by
Luke, Acts xxvii. 18. The dual form
in יַרְכְּתֵי הַסְּפִינָה, the *sides* or *two sides* of
the vessel, is not to be pressed; the word
in this number being adopted in Hebrew
usage to express a recess or remote part
of any place. Comp. Ps. cxxviii. 3;
1 Sam. xxiv. 4 (Eng., 3); Is. xiv. 15;
the innermost part best expresses the
meaning. Kimchi otherwise explains it,
אל אחד מן הירכתים, *to one of the sides,* and
appeals to Judges xii. 7, and Zech. ix. 9,

6　　And the captain went close up to him, and said to him: How
　　　is it, thou art fast asleep? Arise, call upon thy God, perhaps
　　　GOD will think upon us, that we perish not.

7　　And they said to each other: Come, and let us cast lots, that
　　　we may know on whose account this calamity hath happened to

8　　us: and they cast lots, and the lot fell upon Jonah. And they
　　　said to him: Tell us now on what account this calamity hath
　　　happened to us? What is thine occupation? And whence comest

9　　thou? What is thy country? And of what people art thou? And

---

in proof of the plural being used instead
of the singular. See Gesenius, Lehrgeb.
p. 665. It has been objected to the historical character of the book, that it is
not to be supposed that the prophet could
possibly have composed himself to sleep
in the circumstances here described; but
nothing was more natural than for a
person after the fatigues of a journey,
with a mind worn out by excessive
anxiety, to be thrown, in spite of himself, into such a condition. וַיֵּרָדַם, which
the LXX. render καὶ ἔρεγχε, is designed
to qualify the preceding verb, by expressing the profound stupor into which
Jonah had sunk. There is a singular
beauty in putting יוֹנָה, the name of the
prophet, in the nominative absolute.
"But *as for Jonah*"—while all were full
of consternation, expecting every moment
to become a prey to the raging elements,
he lay perfectly unconscious of what was
transpiring. For סְפִינָה, *ship*, which
occurs only in this place, see the Preface.

6. רַב הַחֹבֵל, lit. *the master of the rope-
men*—חֹבֵל being used as a collective.
Comp. רַב טַבָּחִים, *chief of the body-guard*,
2 Kings xxv. 8; רַב סָרִיסִים, *chief of the
eunuchs*, Dan. i. 3. Kimchi explains
thus: הסְפָּנִים נִקְרָאִים חוֹבְלִים לְפִי שמושכין ומתירין
חבלי התורן כפי הכמתם, "*the ship-men are
called rope-men, because they draw and
loosen the ropes of the mast, according
to their skill.*" LXX. Πρωρεύς. Vulg.
gubernator. הִתְעַשֵּׁת, *to show oneself con-
siderate, to think of, set one's mind upon;*
in Kal, *to invent, fabricate, produce
splendid work;* hence the noun עֶשֶׁת,
artificial work, Song v. 14. The idea
of *shining* seems to be a secondary meaning; see Jer. v. 28. Comp. עֶשְׁתֹּנוֹת,
thoughts, Ps. cxlvi. 4. The verb has
the signification of *thinking, purposing,*

&c. both in Chaldee and Syriac. LXX.
διασώσῃ. Targ. יִתְרַחֵים, Syr. ܦܫܐ,
to deliver. Hitzig prefers the idea of
shining, being friendly, gracious, and the
like. Having found that their heathen
deities rendered them no assistance, the
crew were anxious to try the effect of
supplication on the part of Jonah to the
God of the Hebrews, either from the
supposition that he was stronger than
their own gods, or that he might be displeased with the prophet, and required
to be placated. It deserves to be noticed,
that the word for God is here used with
the article הָאֱלֹהִים, which is certainly designed to give emphasis to it; GOD—the
true God. Comp. Deut. iv. 35, יְהוָה הוּא
הָאֱלֹהִים, and 1 Kings xviii. 39, יְהוָה הוּא
הָאֱלֹהִים יְהוָה הוּא הָאֱלֹהִים. Are we to infer
from this circumstance, that the captain
was a worshipper of Jehovah?

7—9. The casting of lots was common among the nations of antiquity,
not only when they wished to know
some future event, but also when they
would determine cases of difficulty, and
especially criminal causes, in which no
witnesses could be obtained. The mode
of using them is not described in Scripture, but from the verb נָפַל, הִפִּיל, *to fall,
cause to fall,* being commonly employed,
it is probable it was by shaking the lots
in some box or vase, and then causing
them to fall on the ground. Comp.
Prov. xvi. 33, where הֵטִיל, *to throw down,*
is used, in connexion with חֵיק, *the bosom,*
or large fold of the garment in front of
the body; intimating, that lots were also
mixed there for the sake of secrecy.
בְּשֶׁלְּמִי, lit. *for that which is to whom,* i. e.
בִּגְּוֹן מִי, *for whose guilt.* The words in
ver. 8, בַּאֲשֶׁר לְמִי הָרָעָה הַזֹּאת לָנוּ, are omitted

he said to them: I am an Hebrew, and I fear Jehovah, the God
10 of heaven, who made the sea, and the dry land. And the men
were greatly afraid, and said to him: What is this thou hast
done? For the men knew that he was fleeing from the presence
11 of Jehovah, because he had told them. They further said to him:
What shall we do to thee, that the sea may cease from raging
against us? for the sea groweth more and more tempestuous.
12 And he said to them: Take me up, and throw me into the sea,
and the sea shall cease from raging against you; for I know it
is on my account this great tempest is upon you.
13　　　And the men rowed hard to regain the land; but they could
not, for the sea grew more and more tempestuous against them.
14 And they cried to Jehovah, and said: O now, Jehovah! let us

in two of Kennicott's MSS., in the Soncin. edition of the Prophets, and in the
Vatican copy of the LXX.; and Kennicott's MS. 154, omits לְמִי; most probably
both by emendation, in order to avoid
the repetition of what had been said in
ver. 7. We should rather have expected
בַּאֲשֶׁר לְמָה, "on account of *what;*" but מִי
may be taken in a neuter sense, like the

corresponding **OY**: in Ethiopic, as,
indeed, it is in the phrase מִי שְׁמֶךָ, "*What
is thy name?*" Jud. xiii. 17. Comp.
also 1 Sam. xviii. 18, מִי חַיַּי, "*What* is my
life?" Micah i. 5, מִי־פֶשַׁע יַעֲקֹב and מִי בָּמוֹת
יְהוּדָה, "*What* is the sin of Jacob?"—
"*What* are the high places of Judah?"

Hexaplar Syr. [Syriac text], *on account
of what.* Leo Juda: "*unde* sit nobis
hoc malum." The seamen were anxious
to learn every particular connected with
the history of Jonah, in order that they
might discover the real cause of the
storm. יָרֵא, *to fear,* followed by the
accusative, signifies to cherish feelings
of reverence, to *reverence, honour,* &c.,
and is not here to be interpreted in the
sense of being afraid, which would have
required the preposition מִן before the
object in such a case as the present.
10. מַה־זֹּאת עָשִׂיתָ, *what is this thou hast
done?* is not put for the purpose of obtaining information respecting his flight,
for it is immediately added, that he had
previously informed them of it, but is a

formula which is intended to produce a
strong feeling of disapprobation in the
breast of him to whom it is addressed,
conveying, at the same time, the idea of
surprise that he could have been guilty
of such conduct. Comp. Gen. iii. 13;
xii. 18; xx. 9. The question shows that
what Jonah had said respecting the
character of the true God, had made a
deep impression upon the minds of the
sailors.
11. They had clearly the conviction,
that as the prophet was the cause of the
storm, some step must be taken in order
to get rid of him; but how to dispose of
him they knew not. That they wished,
if possible, to save his life, is clear from
the sequel. שָׁתַק מֵעַל conveys the idea of
subsiding, so as no longer to bear down
upon with violence, and graphically describes the threatening attitude of a
tempestuous sea, rising above the ships
that are exposed to it. שָׁתַק properly signifies *to settle down, be still, cease from
raging.* הוֹלֵךְ וְסֹעֵר, lit. *going and storming,*
meaning, to go on, increase, become more
and more tempestuous; a common idiom
in Hebrew. Comp. Exod. xix. 19;
1 Sam. ii. 26; xvii. 41; Esth. ix. 4; Prov.
iv. 18.
13. חָתַר, *to dig,* or *break forcibly through
anything,* is strongly expressive of the
great effort made by the seamen to avoid
sacrificing the life of Jonah. LXX.
παρεβιάζοντο. At לְהָשִׁיב supply אֶת־הָאֳנִיָּה.
14. An affecting prayer for pagans
to present to the true God! The

not perish, we beseech thee, for this man's life; and lay not innocent blood to our charge: for thou, O Jehovah ! hast done as
15 it pleased thee. And they took up Jonah, and threw him into
16 the sea, and the sea ceased from its raging. Then the men
feared Jehovah greatly, and offered a sacrifice to Jehovah, and
made vows.

words, אָנָּה יְהֹוָה אַל־נָא נֹאבְדָה, are peculiarly
earnest and tender. אָנָּה, the same as
אָנָּא, which Gesenius takes to be compounded of אָהּ, *oh!* and נָא, the usual
particle of entreaty. Comp. the Arab.
اون, *obsecro.* The Keri marks א in נָקִיא as
redundant, and a great number of MSS.
read נָקִי. נֶפֶשׁ, *life,* means here life that
is taken away, having דָּם נָקִי, *innocent
blood,* corresponding to it in the following clause. Comp. Deut. xix. 21;
2 Sam. xiv. 7. Coverdale, well as to the
sense, "this man's *death.*" The reference is not to anything that Jonah had
done, but to what they were about to do
to him. נָתַן דָּם עַל, *to give blood upon,*
means to charge with murder. Syr.
لَا تَسُمْ, *impute not.* The sense is,
Let us not be found guilty of killing an
innocent person. In the concluding
words of the verse, they refer the whole
affair to the mysterious providence of
God. They had not been brought into
their present circumstances by any conduct of their own; nor could they
account for the guilt of Jonah, since
he was chargeable with no act of immo-
rality. Yet he was the object of Divine
displeasure.

15, 16. They now proceed calmly,
though with great reluctance, to act in
accordance with what they had been led
to regard as the will of the Most High.
The calm appears to have taken place
instantaneously. According to the
Rabbins, Grotius, and some others, they
did not actually offer a sacrifice, but
only purposed to do it before Jehovah,
i. e. at Jerusalem; but it is more natural
to conclude that they sacrificed some
animal that was on board, and vowed
that they would present greater proofs
of their gratitude when they returned
from their voyage. Michaelis thinks
they intended to perform their vows
when they reached Spain.

"Quin, ubi transmissæ steterint trans
    æquora classes,
Et positis aris jam vota in litore solves."
             Æneid. iii. 403.

CHAPTER II

With the exception of the first and last verses, which give an historical account of
the fate of Jonah as preserved by a great fish, this chapter contains a brief but
beautiful hymn of deliverance. It was in all probability composed immediately
after his reaching the dry land, but embodies some of the leading topics
in reference to which he called upon Jehovah during his stay in the deep.

---

1   (CHAP. I. 17.) Now Jehovah had appointed a great fish to
swallow Jonah. And Jonah was in the bowels of the fish three
days and three nights.

1. (Chap. i. 17, in our common version.)
It has been supposed by some that the
fish here spoken of was created at the
moment for the purpose of swallowing
the prophet, though, according to Rabbi
Tarphon, it was ממונה משׁשׁת ימי בראשׁית,
prepared for the purpose at the creation
of the world; but there is nothing in the

2 And Jonah prayed to Jehovah his God from the bowels of the
3 fish; and said,

original word מָנָה which at all suggests
the idea of creation or production. Like
the Arab. ﻲﻨ, *certa quantitate certoque
modo definivit* alicui rem ; *decretus fuit ;*
it properly signifies to *appoint, order,
arrange,* and the like, so that all that can
be legitimately inferred from its use in
this place, is, that, in the providence of
God, the animal was brought to the
spot at the precise time when Jonah was
thrown into the sea and its instrumentality was wanted for his deliverance.
In other words, it was the result of a
special pre-arrangement in the Divine
plan, according to which the movements of all creatures are regulated, and
rendered subservient to the purposes
of God's universal government. LXX.
προσέταξε. Comp. chap. iv. 6—8. On
the subject of the fish itself, various
opinions have been broached. Mutianus,
and after him Hermann von der Hardt,
would have it to be nothing more than
an inn, with the sign of "The Whale,"
into which Jonah was received after
having been cast on shore ! Less, proposed the theory of a ship with this
name, which happened to be close by,
and rescued the prophet; while Thaddæus
supposed that, on being thrown out of
the vessel, he lighted upon a large fish,
on which he rode for the time specified,
and was at last cast on shore ! Till the
time of Bochart it was commonly supposed to have been the *balæna,* or whale
properly so called, owing to a mis-
interpretation of κῆτος, Matt. xii. 40,
which signifies any great fish in general.
With much ingenuity that learned author
endeavours to prove, that it must have
been the *carcharias,* or dog-fish, which,
though not the size of a whale, yet has
so large a gullet, and so capacious a
stomach, that one of them has been found
to contain a warrior, clad in all his
armour. Bochart, Hierozo. p. ii. lib. v.
cap. xii. Others have supposed that it
was a shark, a species of fish abounding
in the Mediterranean, exceedingly voracious, and in the belly of which whole
men have been found. See Parkhurst's
Greek Lexicon, *sub. voc.* Κῆτος. But
we may well acquiesce in the decision of

Rosenmüller: "Tota hæc de pisce Jonæ
disquisitio vana videtur atque inutilis."
The Scriptures leave it entirely undecided
to what species of marine animals the
fish belonged; merely stating that it was
דָּג גָּדוֹל, *a great fish,* one sufficiently large
for the occasion. Much has been written
to relieve the transaction of the miraculous; but that it is physically possible
for a human subject, which has been
accustomed for years to breathe the vital
air, to exist without respiration, or upon
the foul air in a fish, for the length of
time here specified, has never been
proved. The position of Abenezra is
the only one that can, with any consistency, be maintained: אין כח באדם לחיות
במעי הדנה כפי שעה ואף כי זה המספר רק במעשה נס,
" No man has the power of living in the
bowels of a fish for a single hour : how
much less for such a number of hours,
except by the operation of a miracle."
The transaction was, as Kimchi observes,
אחד מן הנסים, *one of the miracles.* As
such it is unequivocally recognised by
our Lord, when he calls it a σημείον, a
sign or *token* of divine interposition, a
supernatural event, manifestive of the
power of God, Matt. xii. 39 ; and it
behoves all his disciples implicitly and
cordially to receive his decision. For
the period of " three days and three
nights," see Whitby on Matt. xii. 40.

2. For וַיִּתְפַּלֵּל, comp. וַתִּתְפַּלֵּל, 1 Sam.
ii. 1. Some of the Rabbins, Hezel, and
others, would argue from the use of מִן,
from, out of, and not בְּ, *in,* before מְּעֵי,
that the prayer of Jonah was not presented while he was in the belly of the
fish, but after his deliverance ; but this
interpretation is justly rejected both by
Abenezra and Kimchi. The preposition
marks the place from which he directed
his thoughts to the Most High. Comp.
מִבֶּטֶן שְׁאוֹל, ver. 3 ; מִמַּעֲמַקִּים, Ps. cxxx. 1 ;
מִן הַמֵּצַר, Ps. cxviii. 5. The final ה in
הַדָּגָה is not feminine, as has been supposed, and upon which assumption
certain Rabbins have built the theory,
that a still larger female fish swallowed
that in which Jonah was preserved ;
but the ה paragogic, which corresponds
to the status emphaticus of the Aramaic,
and is designed to strengthen the termi-

I cried because of my distress to Jehovah,
And he answered me ;
From the interior of Sheol I cried out :
Thou heardest my voice.

4 Thou didst cast me into the deep,
Into the midst of the seas ;
So that the current surrounded me ;
All thy breakers and thy billows passed over me.

5 Then I said :
I am cast out from before thine eyes,
Yet I will look again towards thy holy temple.

nation. For other instances in which it is added, at the same time that the noun takes the article, comp. הֶחָרָה, Judges xiv. 18; הַפּוּחָה, Ps. cxvi. 15. The position of the accent is of no account.

3, 4. The hymn which commences here is partly descriptive, partly precatory, and partly eucharistical. These two verses are introductory, as is clear from the use of וָאֲנִי אָמַרְתִּי, ver. 5, and give expression to the feelings and pious exercise of the prophet in the awful circumstances into which he had been brought. That the language, not only of the prayer, but also of the introduction, is in part borrowed from the Psalms, appears from the following comparison :

Psalm cxx. 1.	Jonah ii. 3.
אֶל־יְהֹוָה בַּצָּרָתָה לִי קָרָאתִי וַיַּעֲנֵנִי:	קָרָאתִי מִצָּרָה לִי אֶל יְהֹוָה וַיַּעֲנֵנִי:
xlii. 8.	ver. 4.
כָּל־מִשְׁבָּרֶיךָ וְגַלֶּיךָ עָלַי עָבָרוּ:	כָּל־מִשְׁבָּרֶיךָ וְגַלֶּיךָ עָלַי עָבָרוּ:
xxxi. 23.	ver. 5.
וַאֲנִי אָמַרְתִּי נִגְרַשְׁתִּי מִנֶּגֶד עֵינֶיךָ:	וַאֲנִי אָמַרְתִּי נִגְרַשְׁתִּי מִנֶּגֶד עֵינֶיךָ:
lxix. 2.	ver. 6.
בָּאוּ מַיִם עַד־נָפֶשׁ:	אֲפָפוּנִי מַיִם עַד־נָפֶשׁ:
cxlii. 4.	ver. 8.
בְּהִתְעַטֵּף עָלַי רוּחִי:	בְּהִתְעַטֵּף עָלַי נַפְשִׁי:
xxxi. 7.	ver. 9.
הַשֹּׁמְרִים הַבְלֵי־שָׁוְא:	מְשַׁמְּרִים הַבְלֵי־שָׁוְא:
iii. 9.	ver. 10.
לַיהֹוָה הַיְשׁוּעָה:	יְשׁוּעָתָה לַיהֹוָה:

On the supposition that Jonah was familiar with the Psalms, it was very natural for him to incorporate sentences taken from them with his own language, just as we frequently do in extempore prayer, without thinking of the portion of Scripture from which they are derived. בֶּטֶן שְׁאוֹל, lit. *the belly of Sheol*, i.e. the vast and hidden receptacle of the departed. Targ. מֵאַרְעִית תְּהוֹמָא, *from the lowest part of the abyss*, but less properly. The remark of Jerome is : " Ventrem inferi alvum ceti intelligamus, quæ tantæ fuit magnitudinis, ut instar obtineret inferni." Before מְצוּלָה, ver. 4, supply בְּ. נָהָר is commonly used of a *river*, but here it is to be understood of the strong *current* or *stream* of the sea, which flows like a river. There is no foundation for the opinion of Abenezra and Kimchi, that it was intended to describe the confluence of the waters of a river with those of the sea.

———καὶ ἂν ποταμοῖο ῥέεθρα
Ὠκεανοῦ, ὅσπερ γένεσις πάντεσσι τέτυκ-
ται.   *Iliad.* xiv. 245.

Μέσσῳ γὰρ μεγάλοι ποταμοὶ καὶ δεινὰ
ῥέεθρα,
Ὠκεανὸς μὲν πρῶτα.   *Odyss.* xi. 156.

Τὴν δὲ κατ' Ὠκεανὸν ποταμὸν φέρε
κῦμα ῥόοιο.   *Ibid.* 638.

5. Having described his condition, the prophet now proceeds to give the words of his prayer. נֶגֶד עֵינֵי יְהֹוָה, to be *before the eyes of Jehovah*, means to be the object of his special notice and care. Jonah had fled from the Divine presence

6 The waters press around me to the very life;
   The abyss encompasseth me;
   The weed is bound to my head.

7 I go down to the clefts of the mountains;
   As for the earth, her bars are shut upon me for ever.
   But thou wilt bring up my life from destruction,
   O Jehovah my God!

8 When my soul was overwhelmed within me,
   I remembered Jehovah;
   And my prayer came in unto thee,
   Into thy holy temple.

in Canaan, but now he feels that he is expelled even from the abodes of life, and cut off, as it were, from the regard of that Providence which watches over the children of men. Still he does not abandon himself to despair. He confidently expects to be restored to the enjoyment of his privileges in the temple at Jerusalem, and there to render thanks to God for his deliverance. Green would supply the negative לֹא before אוֹסִיף, and Hitzig would point אֶךְ, אֶךְ, for אֵיךְ, *how;* but both without any authority. Such sudden transitions from fear to hope are frequently expressed in Scripture.

6. עַד־נֶפֶשׁ, *even to,* or *to the very soul,* i.e. the animal life; meaning, to the extinction of life. סוּף, is the *alga,* or *weed,* which abounds at the bottom of the sea, and from which the Arabian Gulf takes the name of יַם־סוּף, *the sea of weeds.* Kimchi explains it by גומא, the papyrus, or bulrush. Gesenius refines too much, when he attaches to חָבוּשׁ in this place the idea of binding round the head like a turban. Assuredly Jonah had no such idea in his mind. He rather describes how he felt, as if entangled by the sedge or weeds through which he was dragged.

7. קִצְבֵי, *sections, cuttings, clefts,* from קָצַב, *to cut;* Arab. قضب, *abscidit, resecuit.* Thus the LXX. σχισμὰς ὀρέων. Vulg. *extrema montium.* Targ. מְקָרֵי טוּרַיָא, *the roots of the mountains.* The word describes the deep indentations or clefts made in the roots of mountains which project into the sea, or those divisions which are found in the rocks at its bottom. הָאָרֶץ, *the earth,* is emphatically put in the nominative absolute, as the object to which the affections of the prophet still clung. He was expelled from it, as from a habitation, and its bars had been shut upon him, so that he could not return. Gesenius takes the bars to be those of Sheol; but as we have שַׁעֲרֵי־שְׁאוֹל, *the gates of Sheol,* Is. xxxviii. 10, the phrase here must have been שְׁאוֹל בְּרִחֶיהָ, and not הָאָרֶץ בְּרִחֶיהָ, if such had been the meaning. בְּעַד is put elliptically for סְגֻרִים בְּעַד, the verb סָגַר being obviously implied. Jonah adds, לְעוֹלָם, *for ever,* to express the impossibility of his ever again reaching the dry land, by any effort of his own. Yet, exposed as he momentarily was to death in the region of corruption (שַׁחַת, *the pit,* or *grave*), he confidently expresses his hope that God would restore him. He asserts his interest in Jehovah by calling him " *his* God."

8. The prophet here resumes his description of the circumstances of distress to which he was reduced, his application to Jehovah, and the answer which he received to his prayer. The composition of this and the following verses, like that of verses 3 and 4, belongs to a period subsequent to his deliverance; yet while describing his condition, he occasionally directs his language to Jehovah, towards whom, as his deliverer, his thoughts naturally rose. הִתְעַטֵּף, to be in a state of *faintness, swoon,* from עָטַף, to *cover,* to involve in darkness, *overwhelm.* LXX. well, as it respects the sense: Ἐν τῷ ἐκλείπειν ἀπ᾽ ἐμοῦ τὴν ψυχήν μου.

9　They that regard lying vanities
　　Forsake their Benefactor.

10　But as for me, I will sacrifice to thee with the voice of thanksgiving;
　　What I have vowed I will perform:
　　Salvation belongeth to Jehovah.

11　　And Jehovah commanded the fish, and it vomited forth Jonah
　　upon the dry land.

9. A striking description of idolaters, but which may also be extended to all who prefer created objects, in any shape, to God. חַסְדָּם, lit. *their mercy* or *goodness ;* by metonymy for their Benefactor: i.e. *God,* the author and source of all goodness: the Supreme Good. Comp. Ps. cxliv. 2, where David calls God his חֶסֶד. The word properly signifies *kindness* or *benignity,* and most appropriately designates Him who is good to all, and whose tender mercies are over all his works. The Syriac reads, ﺣﻨﺎﻧﮏ, *thy mercy,* which Green, on this authority alone, admits the text!

10. Deeply sensible of the merciful interposition of Jehovah on his behalf, Jonah now solemnly engages to give expression to his feelings of gratitude by accompanying his presentation of sacrifice with a song of praise, and faithfully performing his vows, of which we may conclude, the execution of his commission to go to Nineveh formed none of the least. The paragogic ה in יְשׁוּעָתָה is intensive. Comp. Ps. iii. 3. In both passages, the deliverance is ascribed to Jehovah as its author, as the ל in לַיהוָה imports.

On reviewing this prayer, and weighing the import of its several terms, it is obvious, that though Jonah was in a state of consciousness while in the belly of the fish, he had no idea that such was his situation. On the contrary, he appears to have been under the impression that he was engulfed in the sea, now forcibly carried along by its current, now entangled among its weeds, and now sinking into the profound ravines of its rocks.

11. Green and Boothroyd, on mere conjecture, remove this verse from its present position, and insert it before the hymn. Such a transposition Hitzig pronounces to be violent, unnecessary, and, in short, a perversion of the passage. It is not stated where the prophet was cast on shore, but in all probability it was somewhere on the coast of Palestine. According to some, the fish carried him, during the three days and three nights, down the Mediterranean, and through the Archipelago, and the Propontis, into the Euxine sea, and deposited him on the south coast, at the nearest point to Nineveh! Not to mention how the Rabbins make him reach that city by the Tigris!!

CHAPTER III

This chapter contains an account of the renewal of the prophet's commission, 1, 2 ; his preaching to the Ninevites, 3, 4 ; the universal humiliation and reformation effected by it, 5—9 ; and the reversal of the Divine sentence by which the city had been doomed to destruction, 10.

1　　AND the word of Jehovah was communicated to Jonah a
2　second time, saying : Arise, go to Nineveh, that great city, and

3 make the proclamation to it which I order thee. And Jonah arose, and went to Nineveh, according to the word of Jehovah. Now Nineveh was a great city even to God, of three days'
4 journey. And Jonah began to enter the city, a journey of one day; and he proclaimed, and said: Yet forty days, and Nineveh shall be overthrown.

5   And the men of Nineveh believed in God, and proclaimed a fast, and put on sackcloth, from the greatest of them, even to
6 the least of them. And the subject reached the king of Nineveh, and he rose from his throne, and put off his robe, and covered
7 himself with sackcloth, and sat in the ashes. And a proclamation was made through Nineveh, by order of the king and his grandees, saying, Let neither man nor beast, ox nor sheep, taste
8 anything; let them not feed, neither let them drink water. But let man and beast be covered with sackcloth, and cry mightily

---

3. עִיר גְּדוֹלָה לֵאלֹהִים, *a city great to God.* This phrase has been variously explained. Some, with Kimchi, deem it merely a superlative form; Gesenius construes the ל instrumentally, *great through God, i.e.* through his favour. Others consider it to be equivalent to לִפְנֵי אֱלֹהִים, *before God;* as, Gen. x. 9. Thus the Targ. יְיָ קֳדָם. Of this last interpretation I approve, as it was most natural to refer the size of a city, of which the Hebrews could form no adequate conception, to the Divine estimation. I have accordingly rendered the words literally, as our preposition *to* is often used to note opinion or estimate. For the dimensions of Nineveh, as here given, see on chap. i. 2. The opinion of Abarbanel, that the diameter of the city is intended, is justly exploded.

4. It is impossible to determine how far Jonah penetrated into Nineveh, since it is probable that in making his announcement he would stop at different places, as the crowds might collect around him. The LXX. here read Ἔτι τρεῖς ἡμέραι, καὶ Νινευὴ καταστραφήσεται, which Theodoret considers to have arisen from an error of transcription. Jerome says, "Miror cur ita translatum sit, quum in Hebræo nec literarum, nec syllabarum, nec accentuum, nec verbi, sit ulla communitas." For further authorities on the subject of this discrepancy, consult Dr. Burgess's Introd. to the metrical homily of Ephraem Syrus

on "the Repentance of Nineveh," p. xxiv.; Lond. 1853.

5. When הֶאֱמִין בֵּאלֹהִים, *believing in God,* is spoken of in reference to such as had previously been ignorant of him, it must be taken as involving the recognition of his being and character as the true God, and not simply their giving credit to the announcements of his messengers. To express the latter, הֶאֱמִין ל is employed. See Gen. xlv. 26; Is. liii. 1. All, without distinction of age or rank, put on sackcloth, the usual attire of deep mourning.

6—8. Who the king of Assyria was at the time, is not certain. Pul, the first monarch of that empire mentioned by name in Scripture, did not begin to reign till B. C. 769. Some are of opinion that it was Sardanapalus; if so, his repentance was the more remarkable, for according to the ancients he was proverbially notorious on account of his profligacy.

"Et venere, et cœnis, et plumis Sarda-
    napali."   *Juvenal. Sat.* x. 362.

It is said that he composed for his epitaph, "*Eat, drink, play; after death there is no pleasure.*" The description of the mourning here given is very affecting. That the irrational animals should be represented as partaking in it, is far from unnatural.

unto God; and let them turn every one from his wicked way,
9 and from the violence which is in their hands. Who knoweth
but that God may turn and repent, and turn away from the
10 fierceness of his anger, that we perish not. And God saw their
works; that they turned from their wicked way, and God repented of the evil which he had said he would inflict upon them,
and he inflicted it not.

" Non ulli pastos illis egere diebus
Frigida, Daphni, boves ad flumina : nulla
   neque amnem
Libavit quadrupes, nec graminis attigit
   herbam."   *Virg. Ecl.* v. 24.
" Post bellator equus, positis insignibus,
   Æthon
It lacrymans, guttisque humectat gran-
   dibus ora."   *Æneid.* xi. 89.
Plutarch informs us that when Masistias,
a Persian general, was slain, the horses
and mules were shorn, as well as the
Persians themselves.

9. The Jewish interpreters follow the
construction put upon the words מִי יוֹדֵעַ,
who knoweth, in the Targum: מַן יָדַע
דְּאִית בְּיָדֵיהּ חוֹבִין, *whoever is conscious that
there are crimes in his hands;* only
Kimchi proposes another, מִי שֶׁיּוֹדֵעַ דרכי
הַתְּשׁוּבָה, *He who knoweth the ways of
repentance;* but it is obviously a formula
expressive of great guilt, yet involving
the hope of pardon. Comp. Joel ii. 14.

10. God is anthropopathically said to
repent, when he changes his mode of
procedure, or acts differently from what
his promises or threatenings had given
reason to expect. The threatening in
the present case having been conditional,
was repealed on the performance of the
implied condition. To what extent the
repentance of the Ninevites was genuine
in its character, and how long the reformation of manners here specified lasted,
we are not informed; but there is reason
to fear it was of short continuance, for
after their city had been besieged for
three years by Arbaces the Mede, it was
taken and destroyed. Diod. Sic. ii. 26,
&c. Thus fell the ancient Assyrian
dynasty, and gave place to that of the
Medes, which continued till the time of
Cyaxares, when Nineveh, which had
been rebuilt, was again destroyed, and
finally ceased to be an imperial residence.
See Preface to the Book of Nahum.

CHAPTER IV

The selfish and repining spirit of the prophet, and the means employed by Jehovah
to reprove and instruct him, are here set forth.

1, 2 BUT Jonah was exceedingly displeased and vexed. And he
prayed to Jehovah, and said: Ah! now, Jehovah! was not this

1. Unwarrantable attempts have been
made to soften down the character of
Jonah, as exhibited in this chapter. The
utmost that can be advanced in extenua-
tion of his conduct, is, the strong tincture
of national prejudice with which his
spirit appears to have been imbued.
Comp. Luke ix. 54. וַיֵּרַע לְ, however, seems
to be here used, not in the sense of being

enraged or *angry*, but in that of being
the subject of *grief* or *sorrow*. Comp.
1 Sam. xv. 11 ; 2 Sam. vi. 8. Grief and
anger are passions nearly related; and
in illustration of this application of חרה,
to burn, the following instances may be
adduced :—
Τίς σκανδαλίζεται, καὶ οὐκ ἐγὼ πυ-
ροῦμαι;—2 *Cor.* xi. 29.

my word while I was yet in my own country? Wherefore I
anticipated it by fleeing to Tarshish; for I knew that thou art
a gracious and merciful God, long-suffering, and of great kind-
3 ness, and repentant of the evil. And now, O Jehovah! take,
I pray thee, my life from me; for my death were better than
4 my life. And Jehovah said to him : Art thou much vexed?
5   And Jonah went out of the city, and sat to the east of the city,
and there made a booth for himself, and sat under it in the
6 shade, till he should see what would happen in the city. And
Jehovah God had appointed a ricinus plant, and he caused it to
rise up over Jonah, to be a shade over his head, to deliver
him from his affliction: and Jonah rejoiced exceedingly on
account of the ricinus.

'Αλλ' ὦ Καλονίκη κάομαι τὴν καρδίαν,
Καὶ πολλ' ὑπὲρ ἡμῶν τῶν γυναικῶν,
ἄχθομαι.   *Aristoph. Lysist.* v. 9.

"Eheu disperii! voltus neutiquam hujus
    placet.
Tristis incedit, pectus *ardet.*"
    Plaut. Mercat. Act iii. Sc. 4, v. 24.

"Tum vero *exarsit* juveni *dolor* ossibus
    ingens."   *Æneid.* v. 172.

And the declaration of Cicero : " Non
angor, sed *ardeo dolore.*"—*Epist. ad
Attic.* vi. 9.
    2. דְּבָרִי, *my word*, i. e. what I spake
within myself, my cogitation. קֶדֶם is
here taken in the sense of doing anything
in order to anticipate another. Jonah
acknowledges that he used all despatch
in his attempt to leave Palestine. The
description of the Divine goodness here
given agrees verbally with that exhibited
Joel ii. 13. He recollected the numerous
instances in which, instead of executing
his threatenings, Jehovah had, in the
exercise of his patience, borne with the
guilty, and even interposed with illustrious acts of pardon ; and he was afraid
of compromising his character by announcing what he had reason to expect
might never take place.
    4. הַהֵיטֵב חָרָה לָךְ, most modern versions
improperly render, " dost thou well," or,
" is it right in thee to be angry?" their
authors not adverting to the fact that the
Hiph. Infinitive of יָטַב is often used
adverbially in the acceptation, *greatly,
exceedingly, thoroughly,* or the like. See

Deut. ix. 21 ; . xiii. 15 ; 2 Kings xi. 18.
In like manner the finite form הֵיטִבְתָּ לִרְאוֹת,
Jer. i. 12. Thus the LXX. εἰ σφόδρα
λελύπησαι σύ; the Syr. ‎ܒ ܟ‎
‎ܟ‎; and the Targ. הֲלָחֲדָא תְקִיף לָךְ. Kimchi
explains, אם חרה לך מאד, Art thou *much*
grieved? and adds, היטב עניני חזוק הענין,
As for היטב, *it imports the strengthening
of a subject.* The renderings, " Will
grieving do thee any good?" and, "Does
beneficence offend thee ?" are totally to
be rejected.
    5. We cannot determine on what day
Jonah abandoned his labours among the
Ninevites ; but it is evident from the
conclusion of this verse, that it must have
been before the lapse of the forty days
specified in his announcements.
    6. וַיְמַן I take to be the apocopated
Future of Hiphil, having יְהוָה אֱלֹהִים for
its nominative. קִיקָיוֹן, *the kikaion* or
ricinus plant (Ricinus communis, Linn.),
commonly known by the name of *Palma
Christi.* The word is the same as the
Egyptian KIKI, and the Talmudic *Kik,*
with the Hebrew termination. In Arabic
it is called الخروع, *El-Kheroa,* which is
not to be confounded with القرع, *El-
Karra,* the *cucurbita,* LXX. Κολοκύνθη.
Our English rendering *gourd* is equally
inappropriate. This plant is indigenous
in India, Palestine, Arabia, Africa, and
the east of Europe, and on account of
its singular beauty is cultivated in

7 But God appointed a worm, at the rising of the dawn, on the
8 morrow, and it injured the ricinus, so that it withered.   And it
   came to pass at the sun-rise, that God appointed a sultry east
   wind, and the sun beat upon the head of Jonah, and he fainted,
   and requested that he might die; for he said, My death were
9 better than my life.   And God said unto Jonah: Art thou
   much vexed on account of the ricinus? And he said: I am
10 much vexed, even to death.   And Jehovah said: Thou art
   affected on account of the ricinus, with which thou hadst no

gardens. It is a biannual, and usually grows to the height of from eight to ten feet. It is chiefly remarkable on account of its leaves, which are broad, palmate, and serrated, and divided into six or seven lobes. Only one leaf grows on a branch, but being large, sometimes measuring more than a foot, and spread out in the shape of an open hand with the fingers extended, their collective shade affords an excellent shelter from the heat of the sun. It is of exceedingly quick growth, and has been known in America to reach the height even of thirteen feet in less than three months. When injured it fades with great rapidity. See on ver. 10, Celsii Hierobot. pt. ii. p. 273 ; Michaelis, Supplem. No. 2263; Rosenmüller, in the Biblical Cabinet, vol. xxvii. p. 125 ; Michaelis, Bibel Uebersetz., note on the passage, where there is a plate with an excellent representation of a ricinus. How much such a shrub, throwing its palmy branches over the small hut which the prophet had erected, must have contributed to his relief in the sultry environs of Nineveh, may easily be imagined. His joy is emphatically described in the last clause of the verse.

8. The רוּחַ קָדִים, or *east wind*, is the sultry and oppressive wind which blows in the summer months across the vast Arabian desert, and produces universal languor and relaxation. It resembles the Sirocco, only is free from its dampness, and consequently more destructive to vegetation. Superadded, as in the present instance, to the heat of the morning sun, it is exceedingly oppressive. According to the versions, חֲרִישִׁית signifies *withering ;* otherwise, as derived

from חָרַשׁ, it signifies to be *quiet, silent,* &c., which better agrees with the idea of sultriness.

9. The words הֵיטֵב חָרָה־לִי עַד־מָוֶת, the LXX. translate, Σφόδρα λελύπημαι ἐγὼ ἕως θανάτου, which nearly agree with those of our Lord, Mark xiv. 34.

10. חוּס, properly signifies *to be affected* by the sight of anything ; hence to *feel concern* on account of it, to take pity or compassion. I have employed the passive form of our verb *to affect,* in order to present in the translation a word equivalent to that which is here used in the original. There seems no necessity for taking the Hebrew verb in two acceptations. The formula, שֶׁבִּן־לַיְלָה הָיָה וּבִן־לַיְלָה אָבָד, lit. *which was the son of a night, and perished the son of a night,* is obviously intended to express the extraordinary rapidity with which the ricinus put forth its leaves and afterwards withered. That the tree itself was instantaneously produced, cannot be proved from this mode of speech, any more than from the use of the verb מָנָה, ver. 6 ; otherwise we should be obliged, for the sake of consistency, to maintain, that the whole tree was miraculously destroyed, and had entirely disappeared during the night. הָיָה and אָבַד are strictly antithetical. But, as all that was required in the one case, was that the broad spreading leaves should wither, so as no longer to afford protection to Jonah, though the trunk remained ; so all that was necessary in the other was to give to the tree which had been previously produced, such an extraordinarily accelerated power of germination, that the leaves, which would otherwise have required some longer time to come to

trouble, and which thou didst not rear, which came in a night,
11 and perished in a night: and I, should not I be affected
on account of Nineveh, that great city, in which are
more than twelve times ten thousand human beings who cannot
distinguish between their right hand and their left, and much
cattle?

maturity, were brought to perfection in the course of a night. בֵּן, *a son*, is used idiomatically to express what is produced, or exists, during the time predicated of it. Thus it is resolved in the Targ. דִּי בְלֵילְיָא הֲוָה וּבְלֵילְיָא אֹחֲרָנָא אֲבַד, *which this night was, and in another night perished*.

11. The peculiar force of the appeal lies in the immense number of rational creatures which must have perished had Nineveh been destroyed. Estimating the age of the children at about three years, and assuming them to have formed a fifth part of the population, which is the allowance generally made, we shall have six hundred thousand as the number of inhabitants. In order to enhance this number, and render it more affecting, that of the irresponsible children is estimated; and if this did not produce a suitable impression upon the mind of the prophet, the number even of irrational animals is adverted to, the latter being far superior in point of mechanism and utility to the shrub for which he was so much concerned.

There is something in the abrupt manner in which the book closes which is highly calculated to produce its effect on the mind of a reflecting reader.

MICAH

PREFACE

ACCORDING to the introductory statement, chap. i. 1, Micah was a native of Moresheth, which some take to be the same as Mareshah, ver. 15; but it is rather the town called Moresheth-Gath, ver. 14, which, according to Jerome, lay in the vicinity of the city of Eleutheropolis, to the west of Jerusalem, and not far from the border of the country of the Philistines.

His name, מִיכָה, *Micah,* or, as it is given in full in the Chethib, Jer. xxvi. 18, מִיכָיָה, *Micaiah,* signifies, *who is like Jehovah ?*

The time at which he flourished is stated in the introduction to have been that of the reigns of Jotham, Ahaz, and Hezekiah; *i. e.* somewhere between B. C. 757 and B. C. 699; in addition to which statement, we have a positive testimony to his having prophesied in the days of Hezekiah, Jer. xxvi. 18, where chap. iii. 12 is verbally quoted. He must, therefore, have been a contemporary of Isaiah and Hosea, and is not to be confounded with Micaiah the son of Imlah, 1 Kings xxii. 8, who flourished upwards of a hundred years before the reign of Jotham.

Hartmann and Eichhorn would refer the period of his ministry to the reign of Manasseh; but their hypothesis is justly rejected by Jahn, Rosenmüller, De Wette, and Knobel, on the ground, that all the circumstances brought to view in his prophecies, perfectly harmonize with the state of things in the days of the kings whose names are here specified. The unrestrained licence given to idolatry in the reign of Ahaz, will sufficiently account for the numerous gross and crying evils for which Micah reproves the Jews, without our having recourse to the atrocities perpetrated in that of Manasseh. It is true, Hezekiah issued orders, that idolatry should be put down, and the worship of the true God re-established; but there is no reason to believe that the reformation was carried out to the full extent of his wishes. The relations also of the Hebrews to the powerful empires of Assyria and Egypt, are in exact accordance with the history of the same times.

The prophecies of Micah are directed partly against Judah, and partly against Israel; but by far the greater number are of the former description. He predicts the destruction of the kingdom of Israel, and of Samaria its capital; the desolation of Jerusalem by the Chaldæans, and the consequent captivity of the Jews; the restoration of the Jewish state; the successes of the Maccabees; and the advent and reign of the Messiah. He also administers reproof to different ranks and conditions of men, and furnishes some striking representations of the Divine character.

His style is concise, yet perspicuous, nervous, vehement, and energetic; and, in many cases, equals that of Isaiah in boldness and sublimity. He is rich and beautiful in the varied use of tropical language; indulges in paronomasias; preserves a pure and classical diction; is regular in the formation of his parallelisms; and exhibits a roundness in the construction of his periods which is not surpassed by his more celebrated contemporary. Both in administering threatenings and communicating promises, he evinces great tenderness, and shows that his mind was deeply affected by the subjects of which he treats. In his appeals he is lofty and energetic. His description of the character of Jehovah, chap. vii. 18—20, is unrivalled by any contained elsewhere in Scripture.

Several prophecies in Micah and Isaiah are remarkably parallel with each other; and there is frequently an identity of expression, which can only be fairly accounted for on the ground of their having been contemporaneous writers, who were not strangers to each other's prophecies, and their having, in a great measure, had the same subjects for the themes of their ministry. See on Isaiah ii. 2—4.

The book may be divided into two parts: the first consisting of chapters i.—v.; and the second, the two remaining chapters, which are more general and didactic in their character.

———————

CHAPTER I

The prophet commences by summoning universal attention, while, in sublime language, he describes the descent of Jehovah to punish the nation, 1—5; he predicts the destruction of Samaria by the Assyrians, which he pathetically laments, 6—8; and then the advance of Sennacherib against Jerusalem, 9—12; concluding with an enumeration of certain towns of Judah, the inhabitants of which had more especially enjoyed his ministry, but were to share in the desolating effects of the Assyrian invasion, and ultimately, with the whole land, those of the Babylonian captivity, 13—16.

1　THE word of Jehovah which was communicated to Micah the Morashthite, in the days of Jotham, Ahaz, and Hezekiah, kings of Judah, which he saw concerning Samaria and Jerusalem.

2　Hear, all ye people!
　　Attend, O earth! and its fulness!
　　And let the Lord Jehovah testify to you,
　　The Lord from his holy temple.

1. מוֹרַשְׁתִּי, contracted מֵרֵשְׁתִּי, a gentilic, and not a patronymic, as some have imagined. See the introduction, and on ver. 14.

2. It is not a little remarkable, that Micah should adopt as the first sentence of his prophecy, that with which his namesake concluded his denouncement against Ahab, 1 Kings xxii. 28. Hengstenberg is of opinion that he quoted the words designedly, in order to show that his prophetic agency was to be considered as a continuation of that of his predecessor, who was so zealous for God, and that he had more in common with him than the bare name. The words עַמִּים, peoples, and אֶרֶץ, earth, are by many, and recently by Hitzig, confined to the tribes and land of the Hebrews; but the sublimity of the style, and the parallel passages, Deut. xxxi. 28, xxxii. 1, and Is. i. 2, induce to the conclusion, that the prophet had all the inhabitants of the globe in his eye. Thus Justi, Maurer, and Ewald. כֻּלָּם, all of them, is an instance of irregular construction, in which the third person is put for the second, כֻּלְּכֶם, all of you. The same construction is repeated in מְלֹאָהּ, which the LXX. render according to the sense,

3 For, behold! Jehovah is coming forth from his place ;
   Yea, he will descend, and tread upon the heights of the earth.

4 And the mountains shall be molten under him,
   And the valleys shall cleave asunder,
   Like wax before the fire,
   Like water poured down a precipice.

5 By the transgression of Jacob is all this,
   And by the sin of the house of Israel.
   What is the transgression of Jacob?
   Is it not Samaria?
   And what are the high places of Judah?
   Are they not Jerusalem?

καὶ πάντες οἱ ἐν αὐτῇ. Comp. Amos vi. 8; Is. xlii. 10. Instead of אֲדֹנָי יְהֹוָה, four of Kennicott's MSS. read יְהֹוָה אֱלֹהִים; and, instead of אֲדֹנָי repeated, upwards of fifty of his and De Rossi's read יְהֹוָה; but as the former cannot be altered on the slight authority by which it is supported, so it would be unwarrantable to adopt the latter reading, since the second אֲדֹנָי is manifestly a repetition of the first. LXX. Κύριος κύριος. Syr. ܡܪܐ ܡܪܘܬܐ, the Lord of lords. It has been doubted whether by הֵיכַל קָדְשׁוֹ, his holy temple, in this place, the temple at Jerusalem or heaven be meant; but the language expressive of descent, which is employed in the following verse, would seem to determine the correctness of the latter interpretation. Comp. 1 Kings viii. 30; Ps. xi. 4. Jehovah would bear testimony against the Hebrews, not any longer by his prophets, as he now did, but by the judgments which he would inflict upon them.

3, 4. These verses are explanatory of that which precedes them, and set forth, in highly figurative language, the course of the Divine judgment, and the tremendous consequences that would follow. The terrible majesty and resistless power of Jehovah are expressed in images chiefly borrowed from earthquakes and volcanic eruptions. Comp. Amos iv. 13; Ps. l. 3; xcvii. 5; Is. lxiv. 1, 2; Hab. iii. 5. For a striking image of the same nature, see Jer. l. 25, 26, which cannot properly be explained, except on the principle of reference to a volcano. That of wax occurs Ps. lxviii. 3; xcvii. 5. Comp.,

> " Quasi igni
> Cera super calido tabescens multa liques-
> cat."   *Lucr.* vi. 515.

Some MSS. read הַגְּבָעוֹת, *the hills*, instead of הָעֲמָקִים, *the valleys*, but obviously as an emendation, the latter being the more difficult reading. מוֹרָד, a *descent* or *precipice*, from יָרַד, *to go*, or *come down*. The events referred to were the destruction of the kingdom of Israel by Shalmaneser, and the invasion of Judah by the armies of Sennacherib and Nebuchadnezzar, by the latter of whom the Jews were carried away captive. The form הִנֵּה יֹצֵא marks the futurity of the event, and transmits a future significance to the following verbs.

5. *Jacob* and *Israel* are applied to both kingdoms in common, and are merely used as synonymes for the sake of variety. After explicitly declaring, that the awful punishment which was about to be inflicted was on account of the sins of the people generally, the prophet, by the forcible employment of double interrogatives, the latter of which, being in the negative, greatly strengthens the appeal, traces these sins to their respective sources—metropolitan corruption. By metonymy, the effect is put for the cause. For מִי used as a neuter, see on Jonah i. 8. For חַטֹּאות the LXX., Targ., a considerable number of MSS., and four of the earliest printed editions, have the singular. The

6 Therefore I will make Samaria a heap in the field,
  The plantations of a vineyard ;
  I will moreover hurl her stones into the valley,
  And lay bare her foundations.
7 All her images also shall be broken to pieces,
  All her rewards shall be burned with fire,
  And all her idols will I lay waste ;
  For with the reward of a harlot she collected them,
  And to the reward of a harlot they shall return.

Syr. and Vulg. agree with the Textus Receptus. בָּמוֹת יְהוּדָה, *the high places of Judah,* were the elevated spots on mountains and hills on which the Jews erected chapels and altars for unlawful, and very often for idolatrous sacrifice, &c. 2 Kings xii. 3 ; xiv. 4 ; Ezek. vi. 6. That these existed at Jerusalem, see Jer. xxxii. 35 ; and for the length to which the practice was carried in the time of Ahaz, see 2 Kings xvi. 4. Instead of בָּמוֹת, the LXX., Syr., and Targ. translate, as if חַטָּאת, *sin,* were the true reading : *What is the sin of Judah?* but though the latter word is found in one of Kennicott's MSS., and in the margin of another, it most probably originated in a desire to render the parallelism complete, and cannot be allowed to encroach upon the present text.

6. Both in this and the preceding verse Samaria is taken up first, because its destruction was to precede that of Jerusalem, and also, perhaps, to afford the prophet an opportunity of afterwards expatiating more at large on the state of things in Judah during the approaching invasion. So complete should be the overthrow of the northern capital, that its site would resemble a heap of stones or rubbish that had been gathered out of a field ; it would even be reduced to what we may suppose it originally to have been, a place for the cultivation of the vine. Vineyards were most commonly planted on the south sides of hills or mountains, on account of their exposure to the sun ; and in all probability that of Samaria had been appropriated to this purpose before it was purchased by Omri, 1 Kings xvi. 24. The stones of the city are graphically said to be hurled down into the deep

valley below; and that such was actually the case, the present phenomena of the ruins strongly attest. "The whole face of this part of the hill suggests the idea that the buildings of the ancient city had been thrown down from the brow of the hill. Ascending to the top, we went round the whole summit, and found marks of the same process everywhere." —*Narrative of the Scottish Mission of Inquiry,* pp. 293, 294. הִגַּרְתִּי, (like מַעְיָן, ver. 4,) is from the root נָגַר, *to flow, pour,* or *hurl down.* For יְסֹדֶיהָ אֲגַלֶּה, comp. Ezek. xiii. 14. The very foundations of the edifices were to be laid bare, great and ponderous as the stones might be.

7. The prophet now delivers a special prediction against the objects and accompaniments of the idolatrous worship, which drew down the judgment of God upon the devoted city. The פְּסִילִים were the *images* or *idols,* whether carved, graven or molten, which were erected in the temples, for the purpose of receiving religious adoration. LXX. τὰ γλυπτά. אֶתְנָן, properly means the *wages* or *reward of prostitution;* from תָּנָה, *to give a present* or *reward.* The word is here, as elsewhere, employed in application to idolatry, viewed as spiritual adultery or fornication. Comp. Is. xxiii. 17, 18 ; Ezek. xvi. 31, 34 ; Hos. ix. 1. Kimchi, Abarbanel, Michaelis, Maurer, and others, are of opinion that the riches, &c., of Samaria are thus spoken of, because her idolatrous inhabitants imagined that they were rewards bestowed upon them by their gods for their zeal and devotedness to their service. It is more likely, however, that the rich gifts or presents are meant, which the apostate Israelites dedicated to their idols, and with which they adorned their temples. Comp.

8   Therefore will I wail and howl ;
I will go stripped and naked ;
I will set up a wailing like the wolves,
And a mourning like the ostriches.
9 For her wounds are desperate ;
Surely it hath come to Judah ;
He reacheth to the gate of my people,
Even to Jerusalem.

Ezek. xvi. 33, 34. Newcome seems to
incline to the idea, that the rewards of
harlotry, literally taken, are intended,
because these were appropriated to the
support of idolatry. מַצֵּבָה is synonymous
with פְּסִילִים ; only Hitzig thinks, that a
more costly kind of idols is meant by the
term, such as were made of silver, and
were of sufficient value to be carried
away as spoil. The entire establishment
of idolatry was to be broken up; the idols
were to be cut in pieces; such as were of
wood, to be burned in the fire; and whatever was costly was to be removed by
the enemy to Assyria, there to be again
devoted to idols.   Instead of קְבָּצָה, three
of De Rossi's MSS., three more originally,
and perhaps one more, the Brixian and
another ancient edition without place
or date, read קֻבְּצָה in Pual, which two of
Kennicott's exhibit with Vau Shurek
instead of the Kibbutz. The Syr., Targ.,
and Vulg., likewise have the passive, but
in the plural.   The LXX. render συνή-
γαγε ; which agrees with the common
punctuation.
8. So terrible should be the destruction with which the northern kingdom
would be visited, that it called for the
most marked tones and signs of sorrow.
In these the prophet declares he would
indulge, that he might thereby affect the
minds of his countrymen. אֵילְכָה, with
Yod, may have been occasioned by the
preceding form אֵילִילָה ; but there are
other verbs which do not reject it in the
future, as יֵיטַב, Ps. lxxii. 14. שֵׁילָל, or, as
the Keri has it, שׁוֹלָל, some interpret of
mental bereavement, a state in which the
mind is despoiled of its reasoning powers;
but, combined as it here is with עָרוֹם,
naked, it must be referred to the body,
and was in all probability designed to
describe the feet as stripped of shoes.

Thus the LXX. ἀνυπόδετος.   The Syr.
ܡܣܚܦ, for which compare יָחֵף, Is. xx. 2.
For תַּנִּים, wolves, and בְּנוֹת יַעֲנָה, ostriches,
see on Is. xiii. 21, 22, and Pococke's very
elaborate note on the present verse. The
Arab. has here, مثل التنانين, like the
wolves, and مثل بنات اوي, like the
jackals. The former Michaelis renders
crocodiles, but less properly, on account
of the combination. The ancient rendering, dragons, is altogether to be rejected.
Both kinds are selected on account of
the piteously howling noise which they
make, especially in the night.
9. אֲנוּשָׁה. the Pahul Participle of אָנַשׁ,
to be desperately sick ; spoken of a wound,
to be incurable. There is no necessity,
with Michaelis, to have recourse to נוּשׁ,
and so to regard the form as the elongated
future of the first person singular. The
following noun, מַכּוֹתֶיהָ, being in the plural,
the same number might be expected in
the Participle; but it is a rule of Hebrew
syntax, that when, as in this instance,
the predicate precedes the noun, the
number of feminine plurals is frequently
neglected. Comp. Jer. iv. 14. What
the prophet has in view is the irretrievable ruin in which the Israelites as a
nation would be involved. But he not
only beholds, in prophetic vision, the
devastation of Samaria and its depend-
encies by the Assyrians ; he sees their
invasion of Judah under Sennacherib,
and their investment of Jerusalem. Comp.
Is. x. 28—32. The nominative to בָּאָה
is the calamity implied in מַכּוֹתֶיהָ: that to
נָגַע is אוֹיֵב, the enemy, understood. There
is the utmost propriety in the distinctive
use of the genders in this place ; for

10 Tell it not in Gath ;
　　Weep not in Acco :
　　At Beth-aphrah roll thyself in the dust.
11 Pass on, thou inhabitant of Shaphir, naked and ashamed ;

though the inhabitants of Judah suffered from the Assyrian invasion, the calamity did not reach those of the capital : it was merely invested by the troops of Rab-shakeh, and was relieved by their miraculous destruction. See Is. xxxvi., xxxvii.

10. Comp. 2 Sam. i. 20, where the words בְּנַת אַל־תַּגִּידוּ occur, though not in the same order of arrangement. The Philistines would hail with joy tidings of any disaster that might befal the Hebrews, and especially that occasioned by the Assyrian attack. Deeply, therefore, as the Jews might be afflicted, they are cautioned by Micah not to give such public expression to their grief as would reach the ears of their natural enemies, but to repair to Beth-Aphrah, a city in the tribe of Benjamin, and there deplore in secret the calamity which had overtaken the land. Reland, Harenberg, Hitzig, Maurer, and Ewald, take בְּכוֹ to be a contraction of בְּעַכּוֹ, which Gesenius (Lex. *sub voc.* עַכּוֹ) is inclined to adopt. According to this construction, the rendering will be, *weep not in Acco*, i. e. Ptolemais, a maritime city in the tribe of Asher. Other instances of ע being dropped, we have in בִּי for בְּעִי, בֵּל for בְּעֵל, &c. ; and certainly the parallelism with בְּנַת, the continued list of the names of cities, and the regularity of the paronomasias בְּבֵית לְעָפְרָה ; בָּכוֹ—תִּבְכּוּ ; בְּנַת—תַּגִּידוּ עָפָר, are all in favour of this interpretation. Though Acco was allotted to the Asherites, they never took possession of it, Jud. i. 31, and its inhabitants are, therefore, appositely classed along with those of Gath, as taking pleasure in the reverses of the Israelites. The reading of the LXX. οἱ Ἐνακεὶμ μή, is in all probability a corruption of οἱ ἐν Ἄκει μή, which quite accords with the preceding οἱ ἐν Γὲθ μή. The Arab. has والذين في اكيم, *And those who are in Akim.* The name Ἄκη occurs in Strabo, xvi. 2, 25.

The town is still called عكّ, *Akka*, by the

Arabs, and is known to Europeans by the name of *St. Jean d'Acre*, which it obtained in the time of the Crusades, and is celebrated in later times by its holding out a siege of sixty-one days by the French army, and its destruction by the explosion of a magazine during the bombardment in 1840. It is situated on the north angle of a bay of the same name near the foot of Mount Carmel. בֵּית לְעָפְרָה, lit. *the House of Aphrah*, or simply עָפְרָה, *Ophrah*, Josh. xviii. 23 ; 1 Sam. xiii. 17 ; a city in the tribe of Benjamin. The ל is here merely the sign of the genitive. The verb פָּלַשׁ, which occurs only in Hithpael, signifies to *wallow* or *roll*, as in dust, ashes, or the like. See Jer. vi. 26 ; xxv. 34 ; Ezek. xxvii. 30. While the Hebrews were not to expose the wretchedness of their condition to the contempt of foreigners, it became them to bewail it within their own borders. הִתְפַּלָּשִׁי, *roll thyself*, is to be preferred to הִתְפַּלָּשְׁתִּי, *I roll myself.* It is the reading of the Keri, and many MSS. have it in the text. The Syr., Targ., and Vulg., have the third person plural, which is more easily traceable to הִתְפַּלָּשִׁי than to הִתְפַּלָּשְׁתִּי. Besides, it seems more natural to connect this verb with עָבְרִי in the following verse, than to suppose that the prophet resumes his lamentation ver. 8. Some take the verb to be the second feminine of the preterite, with the Yod paragogic ; but every difficulty is removed by adopting the imperative.

11. In עָבְרִי לָכֶם, the second singular feminine of the verb is followed by the second plural masculine of the pronoun, on the principle that though the collective participial noun יֹשֶׁבֶת is feminine, it was designed to include the inhabitants of both sexes. לָכֶם is not redundant, as Justi asserts, but emphatic, as the *Dativus incommodi*.—שָׁפִיר, *Shaphir*, means *fair* or *beautiful.* Dr. Robinson states that there are still three villages of the name of *Sawâfir*, which are noted on the map as lying nearly half way between Ashdod and Eleutheropolis, a position not much

The inhabitant of Zaanan goeth not forth;
The wailing of Beth-ezel will take away continuance from you.
12 Surely the inhabitant of Maroth pineth for her goods,
Because evil hath come down from Jehovah,
To the gate of Jerusalem.

differing from that assigned by Eusebius and Jerome to *Saphir*. Palestine, vol. ii. p. 370. Hitzig and Ewald think that שָׁמִיר, *Shamir*, is meant, which is enumerated among the cities of Judah, Josh. xv. 48, which Eusebius calls Σαφείρ. The Chald. of the Targ. עֲבַרוּ לְכוֹן דְּיַתְבִין בְּשַׁפִּיר is very improperly rendered in the Latin, "Transite vobis qui habitatis *in pulchritudine*," though the LXX. had translated the word by καλῶς. The Syr. has ܟܳܣܕܳܝܳܬ̈ܐ ܘܡܰܦܩ, *inhabitress of Shaphir*.

To Samaria there seems no good reason to refer it, since all the other places specified in the connexion were in Judah. עֶרְיָה־בֹשֶׁת, lit. *nakedness, shame*, for shamefully naked, *i.e.* entirely so. Comp. as to form, עֶבְנֵה־צֶדֶק, Ps. xlv. 5. What is here predicted is, that the inhabitants of Shaphir were to be led away as captives by the Assyrians; only for the sake of effect the Imperative is used. See on Is. vi. 10. For the naked condition in which captives were removed, see on Is. xx. 4. צַאֲנָן, *Zaanan*, in all probability the same as צְנָן, *Zenan*, a city in the tribe of Judah, Josh. xv. 37. It properly signifies *the place of flocks*; but to form a paronomasia with it, the prophet employs the verb יָצָא; or the peculiar orthography of the noun may have been adopted in order to make it correspond in appearance and sound with the verb. Comp. צֹנֶא, צֹאן, and צֹנֶה, which are only different modes of expressing *sheep* or *flocks*. The inhabitants of this city, under the influence of fear, did not venture forth from their retirement to condole with their neighbours who had been taken prisoners by the enemy; or, they did not come forth to their rescue. LXX. Σενναάρ. Aq. Σεναάν. בֵּית הָאֵצֶל, *Beth-ezel*, in all probability the same as אָצֵל, *Azel*, Zech. xiv. 5; but where the town so called was situated, we are not informed. To judge from the connexion, it must have been in the vicinity of Shaphir and Zaanan, and not near

Samaria, as Ephraim Syrus conjectured. The words מִסְפַּד בֵּית הָאֵצֶל יִקַּח מִכֶּם עֶמְדָּתוֹ have greatly perplexed interpreters. Some regard מִסְפַּד as the Aramaic Infinitive, and connect it with the preceding יָצְאָה; and, supposing אֹיֵב, *the enemy*, understood, to be the nominative to יִקַּח, explain עֶמְדָּה of a military post. But this construction affords no tolerable sense. Others render עֶמְדָּה, *measure*, *conjecture*, and the like, contrary to all usage. For other interpretations, see Pococke, *in loc.* It seems best to abide by the idea suggested by the root עָמַד, to *remain, continue, endure*, and interpret, *As for the wailing of Beth-ezel, it taketh away its continuance from you;* i.e. the inhabitants of that city cease to mourn on your account. The Shaphirites are addressed, as having gone at once into captivity and oblivion. Most likely their city was larger and more populous, and on this account was attacked by the Assyrians, while the smaller towns in the neighbourhood escaped. Gesenius thinks that in אֵצֶל there is an allusion to the Arabic etymology اصيل, *firmly*, or *deeply rooted* in the earth, as what was so might be expected to *continue;* but this is very doubtful.

12. Of מָרוֹת, *Maroth*, (bitternesses,) we have nowhere any account. מַעֲרָת, *Maarath*, Josh. xv. 59, to which Newcome refers, appears to have been a different place. From the relation in which it is here put to Jerusalem, it probably lay between the afore-mentioned towns and the capital, against which a great army under Rabshakeh proceeded from Lachish, and doubtless plundered all that came in their way. חָלָה לְטוֹב, Newcome, after Houbigant, changes into חָלָה לְמָוֶת, and renders, *is sick unto death;* but altogether without authority. The meaning is, that the inhabitants were pained or grieved on account of the property of which they had been robbed by the enemy. Thus

13 Bind the chariot to the swift steed, O inhabitant of Lachish!
   (She was the beginning of sin to the daughter of Zion)
   Surely in thee were found the transgressions of Israel.

14 Therefore thou shalt give a divorce to Moresheth-Gath;
   The houses of Achzib shall prove false to the kings of Israel.

15 Farther, I will bring the possessor to thee, O inhabitant of
   Mareshah!

Rosenmüller, Gesenius, De Wette, and Hesselberg. The former כִּי is not causative, but is used, as frequently at the beginning of a verse, to express certainty. For the last clause, compare ver. 9.

13. For *Lachish*, see on Is. xxxvi. 2. רֶכֶשׁ and לָכִישׁ, form a paronomasia. רֶכֶשׁ signifies a *fleet courser*. Arab. ركض *cucurrit*. רְתֹם is in the masculine, though connecting with יוֹשֶׁבֶת in the feminine, because placed first in the order of the words. The word occurs only here, but obviously has the signification of the Arab. رتم, *ligavit*. As a noun רֹתֶם signifies *broom*, because this shrub was used for binding. In the middle clause of the verse there is a change of person from the second to the third, but in the last clause the second is resumed. For a similar instance, in which, for the sake of graphic effect, the third person is thus abruptly introduced, see Is. xxii. 16. Lachish appears to have formed the link of idolatry between Israel and Judah. Lying on the frontier of the former kingdom, she was the first city in Judah that was led away by the sin of Jeroboam, and from her the infection spread, till at length it reached Jerusalem itself. In the prospect of a sudden attack, it behoved the inhabitants to use all despatch in removing their families, and what property they could take with them, to a distance. Lachish was besieged by Sennacherib before the threatened attack on Jerusalem, 2 Kings xviii. 14.

14. שִׁלּוּחִים is used of the presents or dowry *sent* with a wife, 1 Kings ix. 16, and of letters of divorce *sent* with her when she is dismissed by her husband. In the acceptation ἐξαποστελλομένους, *messengers*, as given by the LXX., it nowhere occurs. The term appears to be here employed metaphorically to denote the breaking up, or dissolution of

all connexion between Lachish and Moresheth-Gath; the former city, having been taken by the Assyrians, was no longer able to afford protection or support to the latter. The nominative to תִּתְּנִי is יוֹשֶׁבֶת in the preceding verse. עַל is equivalent, in this connexion, to אֶל. מוֹרֶשֶׁת, *Moresheth*, the birth-place of Micah, (see Preface) is here said to belong to *Gath*, most probably because it was in its vicinity, and under its jurisdiction, when in possession of the Philistines. אַכְזִיב, *Achzib*. There were two cities of this name, one on the sea-coast, between Acco and Tyre, now called by the Arabs الزيب, *Ez-Zib*, Josh. xix. 29; Jud. i. 31; and the other in the tribe of Judah, between Keilah and Mareshah, Josh. xv. 44. That the latter is here intended, is evident from the connexion; for though, at first view, the mention of *the kings of Israel* might lead us to suppose that a city bordering on the northern kingdom is meant, yet the fact that Israel is sometimes put for the whole people of the Hebrews, and sometimes even for the kingdom of Judah, as in 2 Chron. xxviii. 19, proves, that the mere use of the term can form no objection to this construction of the passage. It was most probably the same place that is called כְּזִיב, *Chezib*, Gen. xxxviii. 5. By an elegant paronomasia, בָּתֵּי אַכְזִיב, *the houses of Achzib*, are said to become אַכְזָב, *deceitful*. Comp. נַחַל אַכְזָב, *a deceitful torrent*, i. e. one which having dried up, disappoints the hope of the traveller. Job vi. 15—19;

Jer. xv. 18. Arab. كذب, *fefellit, irritus vanusque fuit*. The expectations of further aid from the families, or inhabitants of that place, should prove fruitless.

15. אֲנִי is a defective reading of אָבִיא, which many MSS. have in the text. In יֹרֵשׁ and מָרֵשָׁה is another paronomasia. *Mareshah* lay in the plains of Judah,

He shall come to Adullam, the glory of Israel.

16 Make bald thy head, and shave it because of thy darling children;
Enlarge thy baldness like that of the eagle;
For they are gone into captivity from thee.

Josh. xv. 44. It was fortified by Rehoboam, 2 Chron. xi. 8, and was famous for the victory obtained over the Ethiopians by Asa, 2 Chron. xiv. 9, 10. According to Josephus, Antiq. xii. 8, 6, it had been in the power of the Idumæans, but was retaken by Alexander the son of Aristobulus, Antiq. xiii. 15, 4; xiv. 1, 4. The *possessor* or *occupier* here predicted is Sennacherib, who took Mareshah and the other fortified cities of Judah, 2 Kings xviii. 13. To point him out with greater emphasis the article is used : הַיּוֹרֵשׁ, "*The* possessor." עֲדֻלָּם, *Adullam*, was another city of Judah in the same direction, and near the former, Josh. xv. 35. It was a royal residence in the time of the Canaanites, Josh. xii. 15; was fortified by Rehoboam, 2 Chron. xi. 7; and had villages dependent upon it, Neh. xi. 30. Of כְּבוֹד יִשְׂרָאֵל various interpretations have been given; such as the wealth or riches of Israel, their multitude, their nobility, their *weight* of calamity, &c. Some take the words to be in the nominative, some in the accusative, and some in the vocative case. The most natural construction is that of our common version, according to which they are in apposition with עֲדֻלָּם, *Adullam*, and express the superior situation of the place and its neighbourhood. Thus also Schmidius, Rosenmüller, and Hesselberg.

16. The prophet concludes this geographical part of his denunciations by addressing himself to the land of Judah, and calling upon her to put on signs of deep-felt grief on account of the removal of her inhabitants. אֶרֶץ, *land*, is to be supplied, rather than בַּת צִיּוֹן, *daughter of Zion*. Baldness, and cutting off the beard, are tokens of mourning in the East, as they were among the nations of antiquity. Ezra ix. 3; Job i. 20; Jer. vii. 29; xvi. 6; xlviii. 37. "Regulos quosdam barbam posuisse, et uxorum capita rasisse, *ad indicium maximi luctus*." Suetonius, in his Life of Caligula, chap. v. "When Khaled ben Walid ben Mogaïrah died, there was not a female of the house of Mogaïrah, either matron or maiden, who caused not her hair to be cut off at his funeral." Harmer's Observ. iii. p. 5. One species of eagle is called the bald eagle, from the circumstance of its having its head almost entirely bald; but they all more or less exhibit baldness during the moulting season. תַּעֲנוּגִים, *delights*, from עָנַג, Arab. غَلِج, *amatorius fœminæ gestus*, to *delight, be delighted, live delicately*. It is in the former of these acceptations that the noun is here used.

As but few of the inhabitants of Judah could have been carried away by Sennacherib, it is obvious the prophet must have a much more desolating calamity in view in this verse, viz. the Babylonish captivity.

CHAPTER II

Having announced the punishments which were to be inflicted upon his people for the evils in which they indulged, Micah now proceeds to specify some of these evils, 1, 2; and renews his denunciations, 3—5. He then censures those who could not endure to hear the truth, but wished for predictions of good, and shows that no such predictions could reasonably be expected by them, 6—11; concluding, however, with gracious promises of restoration after the captivity, 12, 13.

1   Wo to those who devise wickedness,
     And fabricate evil upon their beds;
     In the morning light they effect it,
     Because it is in the power of their hand.

2   They also covet fields, and take them by force,
     And houses, and take them away:
     They also oppress a man and his house,
     A man and his possession.

3   Wherefore thus saith Jehovah:
     Behold! I devise an evil against this family,
     From which ye shall not withdraw your necks,
     Neither shall ye walk haughtily;
     For it shall be an evil time.

1. Comp. Is. x. 1, 2. In the verbs חָשַׁב, פָּעַל, and עָשָׂה, is evidently a gradation. The first describes the conception of the evil purpose in the mind; the second, the preparation or maturing of the scheme; and the third, the carrying of it into effect. Comp. Ps. lviii. 2; Hos. xi. 9. The ה in יְעַשֹׁיהָ is the feminine used as a neuter, to agree with the nouns אֶרֶץ and רַע, as forming a neuter plural accusative. The phrase אֶל יַד פּ occurs also Gen. xxxi. 29; Prov. iii. 27; and with the negative, Deut. xxviii. 32; Neh. v. 5. It is rendered by the LXX. οὐκ ἦραν πρὸς τὸν θεὸν χεῖρας αὐτῶν, which the Syr. gives without the negative:

‪ܘܡܚܝܠܝܢ ܐܢܘܢ ܕܠܐ ܠܐܠܗܐ‬, and

lift up their hands to God. Vulg. *quoniam contra Deum est manus eorum.* Some consider the words to be equivalent to the *Dextra mihi Deus* of Virgil, and appeal to Job xii. 6, and Hab. i. 11, where, however, the phraseology is different; while others take אֵל to be the shorter form of the demonstrative pronoun אֵלֶּה. But the true meaning seems to be that given in our common version, according to which אֵל is to be taken in its literal signification of *power, strength,* &c. Thus Pococke, Rosenmüller, Bauer, Dathe, De Wette, Gesenius, Hitzig, and Ewald, after the Targ. אֲרֵי אִית חֵילָא בִּידֵיהוֹן, and Kimchi, כִּי יֵשׁ כֹּחַ בִּידָם לַעֲשׁוֹק הָעֲנִיִּים, *because there is power in their hand to oppress the poor.* Just as the LXX.

render, ἰσχύει ἡ χείρ, Gen. xxxi. 29, and Deut. xxviii. 32. That כִּי is to be taken causatively, and not conditionally, is evident from the connexion.

2. Before בָּתִּים repeat חָמְדוּ. Fifty-two MSS., six by correction, two originally; four ancient and nineteen other printed editions; the Alex. MS. of the LXX., the Targ., Vulg., and Arab., omit ו before אִישׁ. The parallelisms in this verse are very elegant.

3. חֹשֵׁב and רָעָה correspond here to חֹשְׁבֵי and רַע in ver. 1. מִשְׁפָּחָה Rosenmüller and Maurer understand to signify " certum genus hominum nequam et perversum;" as if the prophet intended to single out such of the people as committed the atrocious acts specified ver. 2; but it is more likely that the whole people, viewed as rebellious and corrupt, is meant. See on Amos iii. 1. The figure of a yoke is here employed for the purpose of expressing the heavy and oppressive nature of the bondage to which the Hebrews were to be subjected. מִשָּׁם, *thence,* has the force of a pronoun in this place. LXX. ἐξ ὧν. Syr. ܡܟܐ. Comp. Gen. iii. 23; 1 Kings xvii. 13; Ezek. v. 3. So oppressive should be the yoke, that it would be impossible for them to hold themselves erect. LXX. ὀρθοί. Targ. בְּקוֹמָה זְקוּפָה. The term רוֹמָה is selected with special reference to the elated and haughty manner in which they had conducted themselves. It is properly a substantive, from רוּם, *to be high,* but is here used adverbially.

4 In that day shall one sing a ditty respecting you,
And employ a doleful lamentation,
And say: We are utterly destroyed.
He hath changed the portion of my people,
How hath he withdrawn it from me!
To an apostate he hath divided our fields!

5 Therefore thou shalt not have one to cast the line by lot,
In the congregation of Jehovah.

6　　Prophesy not; those shall prophesy
Who will not prophesy of these things:
Reproaches are incessant.

4. For נָשָׂא מָשָׁל, see on Is. xiv. 4. The verb is here used impersonally. That this Mashal was to be employed by the Jews themselves, and not by their enemies, is evident from its tenor, as it follows in the verse. עֲלֵיכֶם, therefore, is not to be rendered *against you*, but *on your account*. נָהָה נְהִי נִהְיָה, *nâhâ, nĕhi, nihyâh*, form an elegant paronomasia. There can be no doubt that נְהִי, *lamentation*, is derived from נָהָה, *to lament;* but whether נִהְיָה be likewise derived from it, and consequently merely the feminine of נְהִי, or whether it be the Niphal of the substantive verb הָיָה, *to be*, is disputed. The harshness that would arise from rendering the words, *One shall lament with a lamentation, it is done!* militates against the latter derivation; whereas, by taking all the three words as cognates, having the same signification, the sentence is at once easy and forcible. The relative position of the verbs נָשָׂא, נָהָה, and אָמַר, confirms this construction. Thus the LXX. and Vulg. καὶ θρηνηθήσεται θρῆνος ἐν μέλει, *et cantabitur canticum cum suavitate*. And the Arab., employing for the two first words terms cognate with the Hebrew, نِهْيَه وَيَنُوحُ نَوْحٌ بِتَلْحِينِ is the feminine of נְהִי, just as שִׁבְיָה is of שְׁבִי, and צִבְיָה of צְבִי. The feminine is added to the masculine for the sake of emphasis; comp. Is. iii. 1, only there the nouns are joined by the copulative ו. The three verbs above specified are used impersonally. The nominative to the following verbs, יָמִיר, יְחַלֵּק and יָמִישׁ, is Jehovah, understood. מוּר

Syr. ܙܒܢ, *to buy;* in Aphel ܐܙܒܢ, *to sell*, or *deliver* an article into the hand of the purchaser; Arab. مَسَّ, *huc illuc commota fuit res, transivit*. The verb is here employed to convey the idea of a change of masters, or the passing of the land of the Hebrews into the power of their enemies. שׁוֹבֵב is a verbal noun, from the Pilel of שׁוּב, *to turn, turn back;* here used in a bad sense, one who has turned back, or away from God; *apostate, rebel, idolater*. Comp. Is. xlvii. 10; lvii. 17; Jer. xlix. 4. The idolatrous king of Babylon is meant.

5. לָכֵן is a repetition of that used at the beginning of ver. 3, and for the same purpose. The nominative to לְךָ, *thee*, is עָם, *people*, occurring in the preceding verse; and the denunciation relates to their being completely at the disposal of their enemies: none of themselves being permitted to allot any portions of the land for inheritance. According to Hitzig, the words are addressed by the ungodly Jews to Micah himself, and intimate that they would put him and his family to death for prophesying against them.

6. The words אַל־תַּטִּפוּ יַטִּיפוּן לֹא־יַטִּפוּ לָאֵלֶּה, which contain a smooth and elegant paronomasia, are very enigmatical, but must either be rendered, "Prophesy not, they say to those who should prophesy: they shall not prophesy to such." Or: "Prophesy not; they shall prophesy who will not prophesy of such things." In the former case the interdicting

7   What language, O house of Jacob!
Is the Spirit of Jehovah shortened?
Are these his operations?
Do not my words benefit him that walketh uprightly?

language of the rebellious to the prophets is simply given, and then we have the Divine declaration, that it should be as they desired. They should be judicially abandoned to their own ways; and, as they would not hearken to the prophets when they predicted evil, they should be deprived of their ministry altogether, and not receive from them any predictions of good. In the latter, the language is entirely that of the people, by which they not merely stop the mouths of the true prophets, but declare that those only should be permitted to prophesy to them who abstained from denunciations of evil. The former requires לַאֲשֶׁר to be supplied before יַפֵּיפוּן; the latter, אֲשֶׁר before לֹא־יַטִּיפוּ. The formula הַטִּיף לְ is used ver. 11, both in reference to the persons to whom the prediction is addressed, and to that which is the subject of the prophecy: אַטִּיף לְךָ לַיִן, "I will prophesy to thee of wine." Though contrary to the Masoretic division of the words, I prefer the second of the above modes of construction, as being the easier of the two. The use of the paragogic ן in יַפֵּיפוּן forms no objection; for though it is most commonly found at the end of a sentence, yet there are many instances in which it occurs at the beginning, or in the middle. See Gen. xviii. 28—31; Exod. xviii. 20; Deut. viii. 3; 1 Sam. ii. 22; Ps. xi. 2; lxviii. 13; Is. viii. 12. For הַטִּיף, see on Amos vii. 16. In the concluding words of the verse, לֹא יִסַּג כְּלִמּוֹת, literally, calumnies depart not, the Jews indignantly tax the prophets with exposing them to contempt by incessant castigation and reproof. Of this interpretation Maurer observes, "ut facillima et simplicissima per se est, ita ad nexum est aptissima." The verb occurring first, is in the masculine singular, though the noun is a feminine plural. See Gesen, § 144. Ward's edit.

7. The prophet boldly meets the charge expressed in the concluding clause of the preceding verse by asking, Whether the absence of auspicious predictions could possibly be ascribed to

any deficiency on the part of the Spirit of prophecy? whether the judgments denounced were operations in which Jehovah delighted, and were not rather procured by the wickedness of those on whom they were to be inflicted? and whether it was not a fact which experience had ever verified, that the Divine communications were productive of good to men of sincere and consistent piety? In הֶאָמוּר the ה is used as a qualifying demonstrative with all the force of an indignant exclamation, in order to point out the flagrant character of the language employed by the Israelites. Ewald: "O des Wortes!" אָמוּר is the Pahul Part. signifying what is said or spoken, and with the ה prefixed, O dictum! Almost all the versions and Lexicons assign to this participle the signification of being called or named; but this notion attaches to the verb only in Niphal, which, in such case, is uniformly followed by the preposition לְ. See Is. iv. 3; xix. 18; Hos. ii. 1 (Eng. i. 10). The LXX., Aq., Vulg., and Targ., have read הָאָמַר, which is found in four of Kennicott's MSS.—As קְצַר רוּחַ, short of breath or spirit, is contrasted with אֶרֶךְ אַפַּיִם, long-suffering, Prov. xiv. 29, and is obviously equivalent to קְצַר אַפַּיִם, ibid. ver. 17, (comp. קֹצֶר רוּחַ, Exod. vi. 9,) most of the moderns render in the present instance, Is Jehovah prone to anger? but prophecy being the subject to which reference had just been made, it is more natural to understand רוּחַ יְהֹוָה, the Spirit of Jehovah, in its appropriated meaning, as designating the Divine Author of prophetic communications; and to take the verb in the sense of weakness or inability. Comp. קְצַר יָד, short of hand, Is. xxxvii. 27.—אֵלֶּה, these, like אֵלֶּה, ver. 6, refers to the judgments which the Lord had threatened to inflict. The interrogative form, as frequently, requires a decided negative; such judgments are not Jehovah's usual operations. Comp. Is. xxviii. 21; Lam. iii. 33; Mic. vii. 18. In הַיָּשָׁר הוֹלֵךְ, the substantive, which is used adverbially, is placed first, for the sake of emphasis,

8 But of old my people hath risen up as an enemy;
  Ye strip off the vestment as well as the robe
  From those who walk along securely,
  From those who are returning from battle.

9 The women of my people ye thrust out from their darling home;
  From their children ye take away my glory for ever.

10 Arise! depart! for this is not the place of your rest;
  Because of pollution it will destroy,
  And the destruction shall be grievous.

and on this account also it takes the article, which properly belongs to הוֹלֵךְ. A similar instance of transposition occurs in יָקָר הָלַךְ, Job xxxi. 26, where the substantive is likewise used adverbially. For the meaning of the phrase, comp. הֹלְכֵי תֹם, Prov. ii. 7; הֹלֵךְ נְכֹחוֹ, Is. lvii. 2.

8. וְ at the beginning of this verse is strongly adversative. Very different was the character of those whom the prophet was now reproving. אֶתְמוּל, properly *yesterday*, is taken by some to signify *lately;* but it is more in keeping with the spirit of the passage to render it *anciently, of old,* or the like. See on Is. xxx. 33. The rebellious conduct of the Hebrew nation was no new thing. It had characterised every period of its history. LXX. ἔμπροσθεν. Abulwalid, contrary to the usage of the language, divides the word into אֵת and מוּל, and renders, *on the contrary.* Thus also the Vulg.— The לְ in לְאוֹיֵב is expressive of manner; comp. לְצֶדֶק, Is. xxxii. 1. מִמּוּל is selected to correspond in alliteration with אֶתְמוּל, and is here equivalent to מִלִּפְנֵי, or מֵעַל. It refers, not to אֲרֶר immediately following, but to the persons of those who were plundered. Though divided by the accent, שַׂלְמָה and אֶרֶר are to be regarded as asyndeta; the former signifying the large loose garment which was worn immediately over the tunic, and which being indispensable to the Orientals, is placed first, for the sake of emphasis; the latter, the costly robe of fur, or other rich stuff, the robbery of which, under the circumstances described, was a matter of course. So great was the rapacity of the lawless characters spoken of, that they were not satisfied with the more valuable part of the dress, but likewise possessed themselves of what was less costly. Comp. Matt. v. 40. For שַׂלְמָה

(by transposition of the first two letters of שִׂמְלָה, which is much more frequently in use,) comp. the Arab. شَمْلَة, *vestimentum,* pec. *totum corpus involvens,* from شَمَل, *circumdedit.* Before שׁוּבֵי repeat the preposition מ. The passive participle is here used intransitively to describe those who were returning after having defeated their enemy in battle, and who might therefore be considered perfectly secure. Even they were waylaid by their countrymen and neighbours, and robbed of the spoils which they had taken in war.

9. In תְּגָרְשׁוּן and עֹלָלֶיהָ, there is, as frequently, a transition from the plural to the singular pronoun. As the prophet refers to war, it is most likely he intended by the "women," the widows of those who had fallen in battle, and who ought to have been objects of special sympathy and care. Instead of which, both they and their fatherless children were expelled from their homes, and robbed of their property. הֲדָרִי, *my ornament,* collectively for the ornamental clothes which they wore, and with which they had been provided by Jehovah. The Holy Land, and everything connected with it, was his, so that whatever was enjoyed by its inhabitants, was to be regarded as peculiarly a Divine gift. Comp. Hos. ii. 8. לְעוֹלָם, *for ever,* i. e. never to make restitution. Some think there is reference to the command to restore the pledge before sun-set, Exod. xxii. 26, but this is doubtful.

10. As the Imperative is frequently used by the prophets to express more strongly the certainty of a prediction than a simple future would have done, קוּמוּ לְכוּ are to be so understood here,

11 If any one, conversant with wind and falsehood, lie, saying:
    I will prophesy to thee of wine and strong drink,
    Even he shall be the prophet of this people.
12   I will surely gather thee entirely, O Jacob!
    I will surely collect the remainder of Israel;
    I will put them together like the sheep of Bozrah,
    Like a flock in the midst of their pasture;

See on Is. vi. 10. Hitzig preposterously considers the words to be addressed by the pitiless Jews to the persons whom they oppressed by expelling them from their homes. They are obviously to be viewed as the language of Jehovah, threatening them with a removal from their own country, which they had polluted by their crimes, to a foreign and heathen land. Canaan was conferred upon the Hebrews as a *rest*, or place of quiet enjoyment, after their fatigues and troubles in the wilderness, Num. x. 33; Deut. xii. 9; Ps. xcv. 11. Before וְאֵת supply אֶרֶץ. The definite article in הַמְּנוּחָה is equivalent to the pronominal affix כֶם, and is to be rendered accordingly. A land may be said to destroy its inhabitants, when it withholds from them the means of subsistence, and forces them to leave it. With such reference it is described as devouring them and spewing them out of it, Lev. xviii. 28; xx. 22; xxvi. 38; Ezek. xxxvi. 12—14. The comparison of these passages shows the propriety of the Piel תְּחַבֵּל, and renders unnecessary the passive forms יְחֻבַּל and תֻּחְבַּל, which some have proposed. For נִמְרָץ, comp. the Arab. مُرِض *morbidus fuit;* only its significations would seem to be taken from the idea of a violent or deadly disease. Thus קְלָלָה נִמְרֶצֶת, *a grievous curse*, 1 Kings ii. 8. Gesenius, in his Thesaurus, renders חֶבֶל נִמְרָץ, *perditio gravissima.*

11. Micah reverts to the subject of smooth and flattering predictions, which he had spoken of ver. 6, and shows that so corrupt had the people become, that no prophet might expect to be acceptable to them who did not sanction their sinful indulgences. To those who did, they would give a ready ear. As רוּחַ signifies both *wind* and *spirit*, there is great force in representing those who pretended to inspiration as walking or being familiar with the wind: so utterly worthless was the instruction which they communicated. הֹלֵךְ רוּחַ is otherwise equivalent to אִישׁ רוּחַ, Hos. ix. 7, and הֹלֵךְ שֶׁקֶר to נִבָּא בַשֶּׁקֶר, Jer. v. 31. Dathe thinks this verse would better fit in after ver. 6, but there is no authority for the transposition; and, besides, there is a singular propriety in bringing forward the crowning sin of the Jews, viz. their preferring false prophets to the faithful messengers of Jehovah, just before introducing the glorious prediction of their restoration in the following verse.

12, 13. Theodoret, Kimchi, Calvin, Drusius, De Dieu, Grotius, Tarnovius, and others, consider these verses to be a denunciation of punishment, and not a promise of deliverance; while Struensee, Hezel, Michaelis, and Forsayeth (in Newcome) regard them as the language of the false prophets, continued from ver. 11. Ewald, who takes the same view, thinks they were originally written by Micah on the margin of his manuscript, and has printed them in italics, within brackets. Most modern interpreters, however, and among them Rosenmüller, Dathe, Justi, Hartmann, Maurer, and even Hitzig, are unanimous in viewing them as predictive of the restoration of the Jews after their dispersion. The manner in which the prophet concludes the preceding verse, proves that he had finished what he had to deliver respecting the favour shown to false prophets; and his sudden and abrupt transition to better times is so entirely in accordance with the manner of the prophets, that the last-mentioned interpretation at once recommends itself as the true. The point most difficult to determine is the period to which the prophecy has respect. Most Christian expositors explain it of the appearance of Christ, and his collecting of believers

They shall be in commotion,
Because of the multitude of men.
13 The Breaker is gone up before them;
They break through and pass to the gate;
They go out at it;
Yea, their King passeth on before them,
Even Jehovah, at their head.

into his church; but this construction is altogether arbitrary, resting on no other foundation than the principle of giving a spiritual interpretation to whatever may, by possibility, be so interpreted. So far is there from being anything in the phraseology of the text to warrant such appropriation of it, that the very terms compel to an adoption of the literal sense. Kimchi, Jarchi, and the Jews generally, as also several modern Christian writers, maintain, that the prophecy relates to the future literal restoration of the Jews under the Messiah. For my part, I cannot but regard the more immediate restoration from the literal Babylon as the theme of the inspired announcement. The deliverance predicted is the same to which reference is made chap. iv. 10, the scene of which is there expressly declared to be Babylon. "Jacob" stands here for the ten tribes, as in Is. xvii. 4; Hos. xii. 2; and "Israel" for the kingdom of Judah, as in Obad. 18; 2 Chron. xii. 1; xix. 8; xxi. 2, 4. The two tribes and a half being few compared with the ten, might well be described as שְׁאֵרִית, the remainder, which had been left in the land at the time of the Assyrian invasion. To express the great extent of the population after the return, it is compared to the large collections of sheep in the folds of Bozrah; a region celebrated for the abundance of its flocks. The Targ., Vulg., Gesenius, Winer, Hitzig, and Ewald, render בָּצְרָה, sheep-fold, but this signification of the word is totally unsupported by usage, and is not allowed by Lee. The LXX., mistaking מ for the preposition, translate, ἐν θλίψει. It

is seldom we meet with the article prefixed to a noun taking the pronominal affix, as in הַדִּבְרוֹ; yet see Josh. vii. 21; viii. 33. By הַפֹּרֵץ, the Breaker, some understand Cyrus; but the identity of structure between this sentence and the two with which the verse closes, compels us to interpret the term of Jehovah himself, who, through the instrumentality of that monarch, removed every obstacle which prevented the return of the Hebrews to their own land. When his providence so visibly interposed, it was easy for them to break down the minor barriers which had confined them in Babylonia, and triumphantly to march out through the gates of the hostile city. To intimate that they should suffer molestation from no enemy by the way, God is represented as going before them, like a monarch at the head of his army; just as he was said to go before his people when they went up from Egypt, Deut. i. 30. In the illustrious Deliverer here exhibited, Rosenmüller recognises the Messiah: "Perruptor, δεικτικῶς, est enim cum ה demonstrativo. Loquitur ergo de certa quadam persona, et antonomastice sic dicta, quæ mox vocabitur מַלְכָּם, rex illorum et יְהֹוָה, ut non sit dubium, Nostrum de Messia cogitasse, seu divino illo heroe, quo auspice, devictis omnibus Judæorum hostibus, aureum seculum orbem beabit." And to his interpretation I accede, only restricting the work of the Messiah, as here predicted, to his leading forth the Jews from Babylon. Comp. Exod. xxxiii. 14; Is. lxiii. 9, in which we are taught that the Divine Logos delivered, and conducted the Israelites through the wilderness.

CHAPTER III

Having inserted in the two preceding verses a gracious prediction for the comfort
of the few pious who might be living in the midst of the ungodly, the prophet
proceeds to expatiate at greater length against the latter, directing his discourse
especially to the civil and ecclesiastical officers, who, by their example, exerted
so baneful an influence upon the nation. The chapter may be divided into three
parts. Ver. 1—4, an objurgation of the princes; 5—7, that of the prophets;
and 8—11, that of princes, prophets, and priests together. The chapter closes
with a prophecy of the destruction of Jerusalem by the Babylonians, 12.

---

1 AND I said: Hear, I pray you, O heads of Jacob!
   And ye judges of the house of Israel!
   Is it not yours to know justice?
2 Who hate good and love evil;
   Who strip their skin from off them,
   And their flesh from off their bones.
3 Yea, who devour the flesh of my people,
   And flay their skin from off them;
   Who break also their bones in pieces,
   And separate them as in the pot,
   And as flesh in the midst of the cauldron.

1—3. The ל in לָכֶם is expressive of
duty or obligation; what the persons
spoken of were bound to do, and what
might naturally be expected from them
in the station which they filled. יָדַע is
here used, not of merely speculative
knowledge, but of that which is practical.
It was the province of the magistrates to
exercise their judicial authority for the
protection of the innocent, and the
punishment of evil-doers. But instead
of thus discharging the duties of their
office, they were themselves perpetrators
of the most flagrant acts of oppression
and cruelty. Their inhuman conduct is
very forcibly described by the prophet, in
language borrowed from the process of
slaying and preparing animals for food,
and the feasting consequent thereon.
Comp. Ps. xiv. 4; Prov. xxx. 14. The
pronominal affixes in ver. 2, refer to the
people, understood, and not to טוֹב and
רָעָה, immediately preceding, which are
obviously employed as abstract neuters.

4 Then they may cry to Jehovah,
  But he will not answer them,
  But will hide his face from them at that time ;
  Because they have corrupted their doings.

5   Thus saith Jehovah respecting the prophets,
  Who cause my people to err ;
  Who bite with their teeth, and cry, Peace ;
  But against him that putteth not into their mouth
  They prepare war.

6 Surely ye shall have night without vision ;
  Ye shall have darkness without divination ;
  Yea, the sun shall go down upon the prophets,
  And the day shall become black over them.

7 Then shall the seers be ashamed,
  And the diviners confounded ;
  Yea, they shall all cover their beard ;
  For there shall be no response from God.

Though many MSS. read רָע with the Keri, yet there are others which exhibit רָעָה, the proper pointing of the Chethib. No codex supports the emendation כְּאֲשֶׁר instead of כַּאֲשֶׁר. The LXX. may, or may not have so read. The etymology of קַלַּחַת is uncertain, but that it signifies a vessel for boiling in is clear from its being here parallel with סִיר, and in 1 Sam. ii. 14 with דּוּד, פִּיּוֹר and פָּרוּר.

4. אָז, *then*, and בָּעֵת הַהִיא, *at that time*, are anticipative of the period of divine judgment. The infliction of such judgment is implied, not expressed. The more emphatically to convey an impression of its certainty, the prophet takes it for granted. God is said to hear or answer prayer, when he grants what is supplicated ; and to hide his face, when he disregards or affords no relief to the suppliant. כַּאֲשֶׁר, with the LXX., Syr., Justi, Dathe, and others, I take to be causal, as in Num. xxvii. 14 ; 1 Sam. xxviii. 18 ; 2 Kings xvii. 26.

5. הַנּשְׁכִים בְּשִׁנֵּיהֶם, *who bite with their teeth*, the antithesis requires to be understood in the sense of eating the food supplied by the people. While such supplies were granted, the false prophets predicted prosperity ; but if they withheld them, measures of a hostile nature,

under a religious pretext, were adopted against them. Thus the Targ. דְּמַן מוֹכִיל לְהוֹן שַׂדְּוָן דִּבְסַר מִתְנַבָּן עֲלוֹהִי שְׁלָמָא, *They prophesy peace to him who feeds them with dinners of flesh.* The phrase is purposely selected in order satirically to expose the selfishness of the deceivers. For the meaning of קַדֵּשׁ, *to sanctify*, as here used, see on Is. xiii. 3 ; Joel i. 14 ; and comp. Jer. vi. 4.

6, 7. So completely should the predictions of the false prophets be disproved by the judgments that were to be brought on the nation, and so painfully should they themselves experience these judgments, that they could no longer have the effrontery to practise their deceptions. Under such circumstances they could not pretend to deliver any divine oracle to the people. The words do not imply that they ever had really received any such oracles : they merely professed to have received them. מ is here to be taken privatively, and not in the signification of *ob*, *propter*, &c., as interpreted by some. The obscuration of the heavenly bodies, or of the light of day, is frequently employed by the prophets, as it is by oriental writers generally, to denote affliction or calamity. Amos viii. 9. שָׂפָם, LXX., in 2 Sam.

8   But truly I am full of power by the Spirit of Jehovah,
    And of judgment and might;
    To declare unto Jacob his transgression,
    And to Israel his sin.

9   Hear this, I beseech you, ye heads of the house of Jacob!
    And judges of the house of Israel!
    Who abhor justice,
    And pervert all equity;

10 Building Zion with blood,
    And Jerusalem with wickedness.

11 Her heads judge for reward,
    And her priests teach for hire;
    Her prophets also divine for money;
    Yet they lean upon Jehovah, saying:

xix. 24 (Hebr. 25), μύσταξ, the *mustache* or *beard*, which is held in high estimation in the East, and in exhibiting which, properly grown and trimmed, the Orientals greatly pride themselves. To hide it, therefore, by covering it, was regarded as a striking mark of shame or sorrow. See Lev. xiii. 45; 2 Sam. xix. 24 (25); Ezek. xxiv. 17, 22.

8. Full of conscious sincerity, and of his divine commission, in the execution of which he was sustained by the supernatural influence of the Holy Spirit, and zealous for the glory of God, and the recovery of his people, Micah avows his readiness, with all boldness, to announce to them his inspired message respecting their sins. His character and conduct formed a perfect contrast to those of the false prophets. The compound particle וְאוּלָם, and the pronoun אָנֹכִי, are here emphatic. כֹּחַ, means the *supernatural power* necessary for the general discharge of the prophetic office; comp. δύναμις, Luke i. 17; xxiv. 49; Acts i. 8; מִשְׁפָּט, *a sense of moral rectitude*, distinguishing clearly between right and wrong, and impelling to the advocacy and maintenance of such actions, as are conformable to the Divine law; and גְּבוּרָה, *moral courage*, or a bold and intrepid spirit, inciting its possessor to throw aside all timidity in defending the cause of God and truth. Comp. 2 Tim. i. 7.

9. The prophet now proceeds to deliver in full, the message which he had commenced, ver. 1, employing the same formula, שִׁמְעוּ־נָא, as he also does chap. vi. 1. The remaining verses of the chapter furnish a noble specimen of that bold and uncompromising fidelity which characterised his ministry.

10. בָּנֶה, the LXX., Syr., Targ., and Vulg., render in the plural, but no Hebrew codex exhibits the variation. The authors of these versions doubtless regarded the participle as a collective, which mode of construction we must adopt, or, with Michaelis, we must suppose that the prophet had Shebna, Is. xxii. 15—18, Jehoiakim, or some other particular prince in his eye; the former interpretation is preferable. דָּמִים, *blood*, used for the *wealth* obtained by shedding the blood of its owners. Comp. Jer. xxii. 13; Ezek. xxii. 27; Hab. ii. 12, in the latter of which passages דָּמִים and עַוְלָה are used as parallels, with the same participle, בֹּנֶה.

11. שֹׁחַד, is a gift or bribe given to a judge to obtain freedom from punishment. Receiving bribes was strictly prohibited by the Mosaic law, Exod. xxiii. 8; Deut. xvi. 19. That the כֹּהֲנִים, *priests*, were authorized by that law to act in the capacity of ordinary religious teachers, does not appear. Their being thus employed by Jehoshaphat is narrated as something altogether extraordinary, 2 Chron. xvii. 7—9. Besides attending to the ceremonial observances, they had devolved upon them the decision of con-

Is not Jehovah in the midst of us?

No calamity shall come upon us.

12 Surely on your account

Zion shall be ploughed as a field,

Jerusalem shall become heaps,

And the mountain of the house woody heights.

---

troversies, Deut. xvii. 8—11; xxi. 5; Ezek. xliv. 24; cases of leprosy, divorce, &c. Lev. x. 11. They were to lay down the law in such cases, and pronounce the final sentence. Comp. Mal. ii. 7; Deut. xxxiii. 10; and see Michaelis on the Laws of Moses, Art. lii. They are here associated with the judges, because in certain cases they gave a joint verdict; and in the time of the prophet were equally avaricious and corruptible. The verb םסק, *to divine*, being only used of false prophets, shows that those reproved by Micah were of that description. Comp. Jude 11. With all their wicked perversion of right, they hypocritically claimed an interest in the favour of God, and scouted the idea that the calamities denounced by his true prophets could ever overtake them. Comp. Jer. vii. 4, 8—11, where the same presumptuous confidence in the Divine presence in the temple, is exposed and condemned.

12. We have here at last an awful epiphonema, in which the destruction of the metropolis is expressly and particularly predicted. The wicked leaders of the people were now building and beautifying it, by expending upon it their unrighteous gains, ver. 10; but the time was coming when it should be completely desolated. "Zion" designates the site of the city of David on the south; "Jerusalem," the houses occupied by the inhabitants generally in the centre and the north; and "the mountain of the house," Moriah on the east. Instead of ציין, the Chaldee termination, five MSS., five others originally, and the Babylonian Talmud, read םיע. הבית, *the house*, i. e. κατ᾽ ἐξοχήν, the

temple. That which was their boast and confidence, was to be converted into a wilderness. יער signifies not only a forest, but also a thicket of shrubs, a rough or rugged locality, from the Arab.

وعر, *asper, salebrosus fuit; difficilis incessu, asper* locus. The whole verse contains a description of utter ruin and desolation. The enunciation of such a prophecy evinced the greatest intrepidity on the part of Micah, and is quoted as an instance of prophetic boldness, Jer. xxvi. 18, 19. The ploughing of the city by the enemy, which has its parallel in Horace, lib. i. Od. 16,

"——— imprimeretque muris

Hostile aratrum exercitus insolens,"

has by some interpreters been referred to what is recorded in the Talmud, noticed by Jerome, and repeated by Maimonides, that Titus Annius Rufus, an officer in the Roman army, tore up with a ploughshare the foundations of the temple; but little or no credit is to be given to the story. See Deylingii Observationes Sacr. pt. v. pp. 448, 450. Robinson's Palestine, vol. ii. pp. 2, 8. The circumstance, however, that what Micah predicts relates to the city as distinguished from the temple, clearly militates against this application of his language. Equally inapposite as to the fulfilment of the prophecy are the appeals to the present partially cultivated state of Mount Zion, since the destruction to which it points was not either of the more distant devastations under Titus and Adrian, but the more proximate one under Nebuchadnezzar. For the accomplishment, see Neh. ii. 17; iv. 2; Lam. v. 18.

CHAPTER IV

By a sudden transition, as at chap. ii. 12, the prophet passes from his denunciation
of punishment to a description of the glorious state of the church subsequent
to the restoration from the captivity in Babylon. He predicts the establishment
of the kingdom of Christ upon the ruins of idolatry, and the accession of the
Gentiles, 1, 2 ; the peaceful nature of his reign, 3, and the security of his subjects, 4. He then abruptly introduces his captive countrymen, who, having been
recovered to the worship of the true God, declare, that, however the idolaters
around them might adhere to their several systems of creature-worship, they
would never renounce the service of Jehovah, 5. The Most High promises to
gather even the weakest of them from their dispersions, restore their national
existence, and reign over them for ever, 6—8. The intermediate invasion of
Judæa, the captivity in Babylon, and the liberation of the Jews, are next depicted, 9—11. Upon which follows a prediction of the victories which they
should gain over their enemies in the times of the Maccabees, and of the reverse
which took place on the establishment of Herod by the Roman power, 12—14.

---

1 AND it shall come to pass in the last of the days,
    That the mountain of Jehovah's house
    Shall be established on the summit of the mountains,
    And be elevated above the hills,
    And the people shall flow to it.
2 Yea, many nations shall go, and say :
    Come, let us go up to the mountain of Jehovah,
    To the house of the God of Jacob,
    That he may teach us his ways,
    And that we may walk in his paths ;

1—3. On the general identity of this prophecy with Is. ii. 2—4, see the note on that passage, to which the reader is also referred for the interpretation. The verbal discrepancies, which are few and trivial, will be best seen on consulting Newcome, who exhibits the Hebrew text of both prophets in parallel columns.

For out of Zion shall go forth the law,
And the word of Jehovah from Jerusalem.

3 And he shall arbitrate among many people,
And give decision to many distant nations,
So that they shall beat their swords into coulters,
And their spears into pruning-knives;
Nation shall not raise a sword against nation,
Neither shall they learn war any more.

4 And they shall sit, each under his vine, and under his fig-tree,
And none shall make him afraid;
For the mouth of Jehovah of hosts hath spoken it.

5 Though all the people should walk
Each in the name of his god,
Yet we will walk in the name of Jehovah our God,
For ever and ever.

6 In that day, saith Jehovah,
I will gather the halting,
And collect the outcasts,
And those whom I have afflicted.

The sense is the same throughout. Twenty MSS., originally ten more, one by correction, and the Complut. edition, read אֵלָיו instead of עָלָיו. For לֹא יִשָּׂא, thirty-six MSS., probably another, seven originally, and six by correction, together with four of the early editions, read וְלֹא; and for יִשָּׂא, five MSS., four originally, and now one, read יִשָּׂא.

4. This beautiful addition, which is not in Isaiah, appears to have been a common adage among the Hebrews to express a state of complete outward security. 1 Kings iv. 25; Zech. iii. 10. For a state of things precisely the reverse, see my Biblical Researches and Travels in Russia, &c. p. 436.

5. Many interpreters have been puzzled how to reconcile the statement made in the beginning of this verse with the prediction contained in verse 2; and Hartmann goes so far as to assert, that it was originally a marginal gloss, written by a different pen, and afterwards inserted in the text. The difficulty will be removed, if we consider the words to be those of the Jews during their dispersion. "Hic spectanda est diversitas temporis."

Calvin, in loc. They witnessed the eagerness with which the idolaters around them devoted themselves to the service of their gods—an eagerness which led them to despair of their ever being reclaimed; and they nobly resolved that nothing should ever again move them to abandon the service of Jehovah; but that, with equal earnestness, they would addict themselves to his worship, and the observance of his laws. כִּי is here a formula of concession: be it so that, although, or the like. Comp. for this use of the particle, Gen. viii. 21; Exod. xiii. 17; Josh. xvii. 18; Deut. xxix. 18. הָלַךְ בְּשֵׁם פ, to walk in the name of any one, means to frame one's conduct according to his will, to act by his authority, and in accordance with his character. שֵׁם, name, is often used for the person himself. Comp. the phrases הָלַךְ בְּדֶרֶךְ יְהֹוָה; הָלַךְ אַחֲרֵי יְהֹוָה, to walk in the way of, to follow Jehovah. It seems here to be specially employed in reference to religious worship. Comp. Zech. x. 12.

6—8. That the subject of these verses is the restoration from Babylon, and the re-establishment of the Jewish state,

7 And I will make the halting a remnant,
   And those that had been far removed a strŏng nation ;
   And Jehovah shall reign over them in Mount Zion,
   From henceforth, and for ever.
8 And thou, O tower of the flock!
   O hill of the daughter of Zion !
   To thee it shall come,
   Even the former rule shall come,
   The kingdom of the daughter of Jerusalem.

and not any spiritual gathering of men generally to the church of God, is placed beyond dispute by the prediction that the scattered and afflicted remnant of Israel was again to become a *strong nation*, ver. 7, and by the use of the phrase הַמֶּמְשָׁלָה הָרִאשֹׁנָה, *the former rule*, ver. 8, which can only be interpreted of the theocratic government at Jerusalem. When the Hebrews first returned to their own land, they were few in number, amounting only to 42,360 ; but they rapidly increased, and in the time of the Maccabees not only became an independent state, but acquired such power that they vanquished the formidable Syro-Grecian armies. The Asmonæan family possessed supreme authority from Mattathias to Herod the Great. To the above interpretation no valid objection can be taken on the ground that Jehovah is said, ver. 7, to reign *for ever* over those who were to be assembled. עוֹלָם, *eternity*, or long indefinite duration, whether applied to the past or the future, must always be determined by the nature of the subject. It is very often used of the Mosaic institutes, Exod. xii. 14, 17 ; xxvii. 21 ; xxviii. 43 ; Lev. iii. 17. It is even employed to denote the period of the seventy years' captivity, Jer. xviii. 16. For הַנַּדָחָה and הַצֹּלֵעָה, comp. Zeph. iii. 19 ; Ezek. xxxiv. 16. הַנַּהֲלָאָה is the Niphal participle of הָלָא, *to be removed.* Syr.

ܠܚܰܕ, *elongavit, removit.* Arab.

هل II., *recessit, abscessit.* Having employed metaphors taken from the treatment of sheep, Micah calls the Jewish people in their collective capacity, עֵדֶר, *a flock.* Comp. עֵדֶר יְהֹוָה, *the flock of Jehovah*, Jer. xiii. 17 ; and in refer-

ence to the strength of Jerusalem, and the watchful care exercised by the government, he characterises her as מִגְדַּל עֵדֶר, *the tower of the flock.* Some, indeed, think with Jerome, that a place of this name, to which reference is made Gen. xxxv. 21, and which that father says lay about a mile distant from Bethlehem, is intended ; but, from its being in apposition with עֹפֶל בַּת־צִיּוֹן, *mound of the daughter of Zion*, a fortified hill or elevation on the eastern part of Mount Zion, and here put for the whole, such interpretation is inadmissible. For עֹפֶל, comp. Is. xxxii. 14 ; 2 Chron. xxvii. 3 ; xxxiii. 14 ; Neh. iii. 26, 27, in which last passage הַמִּגְדָּל, *the tower*, is mentioned along with it, which is doubtless identical with בַּחַן, Is. xxxii. 14. The word is derived from עָפַל, *to swell, become tumid.* Arab. عفل, *tumore laboravit, pinguedo circa perinæum capri*, &c. Tὸν Ὀφλᾶν καλούμενον ὑψηλάν. Joseph. de Bell. Jud. lib. vi. cap. 6, § 3. The LXX., Aq., Symm., Syr., and Vulg., confound the word with אֹפֶל, *thick darkness.* The Targum applies the passage to the Messiah : וְאַתְּ מְשִׁיחָא דְיִשְׂרָאֵל דִּטְמִיר מִן קֳדָם חוֹבֵי כְּנִשְׁתָּא דְצִיּוֹן לָךְ עֲתִידָא מַלְכוּתָא לְמֵיתֵי : " *And thou, O Messiah of Israel, who art hid on account of the sins of the congregation of Zion, to thee the kingdom will come ;*" but there is no more foundation for this interpretation, than for that of Jonathan on מִגְדַּל־עֵדֶר, Gen. xxxv. 21 : אַתְרָא דְמַחְמָן עֲתִיד דְּאִתְגְּלִי מַלְכָּא מְשִׁיחָא בְּסוֹף יוֹמַיָּא, " *the place from which King Messiah is to be revealed at the end of the days*," whatever use may be made of it in the way of *argumentum ad hominem* in reasoning with the Jews. ל in לְבַת is a periphrasis of the genitive.

9   Why, now, dost thou cry aloud?
     Is there no king in thee?
     Have thy counsellors perished?
     That pains should have seized thee
     Like a woman in travail?

10   Be in pain, and bring forth, O daughter of Zion,
     Like a woman in travail;
     For now thou shalt go forth from the city,
     And shalt dwell in the field,
     Thou shalt even go to Babylon;
     There thou shalt be delivered,
     There Jehovah shall redeem thee,
     From the hand of thine enemies.

11   And now many nations are gathered against thee,
     That say: Let her be profaned!
     And: Let our eyes look upon Zion.

12   But, as for them, they know not the designs of Jehovah,

9. עַתָּה is not here used in its temporal signification, but merely as a particle designed emphatically to draw attention to what follows. Five MSS., and another originally, supported by the LXX. and Targ., read וְעַתָּה, which is the usual form. The prophet plunges at once into the circumstances of consternation in which the inhabitants of Jerusalem would be placed on the approach of the Chaldæan army. The questions relative to a king and his council are put ironically, and provoke the answer, "Yes, we have, but they are nothing worth: they cannot protect us, nor contrive any means of escape." יֹעֵץ the LXX. treat as a collective: ἡ βουλή σου.

10. גֹּחִי, instead of גִּיחִי, for the sake of euphony. Comp. in reference to childbirth, Job xxxviii. 8; Ps. xxii. 10. Having employed the metaphor of a parturient female, the prophet carries it on in this verse, strikingly depicting the condition of anguish and distress which the Jews had to anticipate before they should enjoy deliverance. The Babylonish captivity, and its happy termination, are predicted in express terms. Both were likewise expressly foretold by Isaiah, the contemporary of Micah, chap. xxxix. 7; xliii. 14; xlviii. 20. The repetition of שָׁם, there, is emphatic. The inhabitants of Jerusalem, when removed from the city, should be located in the open country, till the whole were collected, and then they should all be conveyed to Babylon.

11. The nations here referred to were those which composed the army of Nebuchadnezzar, or which joined that army in its attack upon Jerusalem. The more immediate neighbours of the Jews are no doubt specially intended. Comp. Lam. ii. 16; Ezek. xxxv; Obad. 12, 13. These defiled Jerusalem, when they shed the blood of her citizens and profaned her sacred places. חָנָה בְּ is used, like רָאָה בְּ, Obad. 12, in an emphatic sense, to denote the malignant delight with which the enemies of the Jews feasted on their calamities. For the use of the feminine singular תֶּחַז with the dual masculine, comp. 2 Sam. x. 9; Job xx. 10. Nothing is more common in Arabic than to employ the feminine form of the verb when the agent is any thing irrational or inanimate. The singular number is employed as the simpler form of the verb. It may be observed, however, that, instead of עֵינֵינוּ in the plural, four MSS., two of the most ancient editions, the Syr., Targ., and Vulg., read עֵינֵנוּ in the singular. The LXX. have the plural. Both תֶּחֱזַק and תֶּחַז are optative in force.

12. הֵמָּה is a nominative absolute, used

Neither do they understand his purpose;
For he shall collect them as sheaves into the threshing-floor.

13 Arise! thresh, O daughter of Zion!
For I will make thy horn iron,
And thy hoofs copper,
And thou shalt beat in pieces many nations;
And thou shalt devote their gain to Jehovah,
Even their substance to the Lord of all the earth.

14 Assemble yourselves now, O daughter of troops!
We are besieged!

for the sake of emphasis. The enemies of the Jews had not the most distant idea, that the object of Jehovah in permitting his people to be so treated was to recover them from idolatry, and thus prepare them for a triumphant restoration. The metaphor taken from the process of threshing out grain is frequently used by the prophets to denote the complete destruction of a people. Comp. Jer. li. 33. For the manner in which this process is carried on, see on Is. xxviii. 27, 28.

13. A continuation of the metaphor. Comp. for a real parallel, Is. xli. 15, 16. There is, however, a very natural instance of mixed metaphor, derived from the destructive power lodged in the horn of the ox, though it is not employed in threshing, which greatly adds to the force of the passage. That קֶרֶן, *horn*, should here be employed to signify the *horny* substance forming the hoof of the ox, cannot be admitted. Comp. 1 Kings xxii. 11. The horn was a symbol of power exercised in subduing and punishing enemies. The Orientals give to Alexander the Great the epithet of ذو القرنين, *bicornis;* and the kings of Macedon were actually in the habit of wearing the horns of a ram in their casques. הֲרִקֹמְתִּי I take to be the second person feminine, the Yod being a fragment of the old form of the personal pronoun אַתִּי, regularly preserved in the Syriac. Compare, for other instances, שָׁכֵמְתִּי, Ruth iii. 3; הָלַכְתִּי, Jer. xxxi. 21, though they are pointed with a Sheva, and the Keri directs that they should be read שָׁכַמְתְּ and הָלָכְתְּ. The LXX., Aquila,

Symm., Theodot., the Syr., and Vulg., all have the second person. חָרַם, Arab. حرم, *prohibuit; sacrum, quod non est promiscui usus; to make sacred, devote,* whether in a good or a bad sense. As conquerors used to consecrate a portion of their spoils to their deities by hanging them up in their temples, so the triumphant Hebrews would employ the riches which they acquired by their victories in beautifying the temple of Jehovah, and supporting his worship. The Maccabæan times are specially referred to.

14. I consider גְּדוּד, *troop*, to be a collective. Jerusalem is called *a daughter of troops*, on account of the great body of military quartered within her walls, and in the surrounding districts. That it is Jerusalem, and not the enemy, that is addressed, the close coherence of the forms with those of the preceding context sufficiently shows. For the paronomasia in תִּתְגֹּדֲדִי בַת־גְּדוּד, comp. Gen. xlix. 19. The common acceptation of גָּדַד, is *to cut* or *make incisions;* but that it also signifies *to assemble as troops*, see Jer. v. 7. Syr. ܓܘܕܐ *a portion* or *detachment of an army*. Though at שָׂם the enemy is understood, it is better to construe it impersonally, and give it in our language in the passive. In שָׂם and שֹׁפֵט is another paronomasia. Most understand by the שֹׁפֵט, *judge*, Zedekiah, who was treated contumeliously by the Babylonians; but it seems preferable to refer it to some of the chief rulers of the Jews at the time of the siege of Jerusalem described by the prophet; or the term may be used collectively. The position

With a rod they have smitten on the cheek
The judge of Israel!

of Hengstenberg and some others, that it is selected on purpose to mark a period during which no king of the house of David reigned, might be allowed, were it not for the influence of the foregoing שֵׁבֶט, with which it forms the paronomasia. Though the LXX. have rendered the term by φυλάς, Aq., Symm., and Theod., have κριτήν. The siege in question Michaelis thinks was that by Sosius, the Roman general, B.C. 37, when Antigonus, the last of the Asmonæan dynasty, was obliged to submit to the superior power. Whether this prince be specifically intended I shall not determine. So much is certain, that he was most contemptuously treated by Sosius; see Josephus, Bell. Jud. lib. i. cap. xviii. 2.

———◆———

CHAPTER V

Having just adverted to the calamitous circumstances in which the Jews should be placed at the commencement of the reign of Herod, the prophet foretels, in a very explicit manner, the birth of the Messiah, which was to take place during the lifetime of that king, 1. A prediction is then introduced respecting the final dealings of God towards the nation previous to that illustrious event, 2, on which the permanent and universal nature of the new dispensation is announced, 3. The subject of the victories of the Jews over the Syro-Grecian armies is again taken up, 4—8; and the chapter concludes with threatenings both against the Jews in the time of Micah, and the enemies by whom they were to be punished, 9—14.

———————

1   AND thou, Bethlehem Ephratha!
      Art small to be among the thousands of Judah,

1. Michaelis remarks, "If not even a word were found in Matt. ii. 5, 6, explanatory of our text, I should believe the subject to be Christ, who was born in the reign of Herod. The whole thread of the prophecy in the preceding chapter leads me to him, and the time of his birth." The Messianic application of the prophecy was formerly made by the Jewish Sanhedrim, in their official reply to Herod, Matt. ii. 5, 6; and is admitted both by the Rabbinical and the rationalistic interpreters, though, as might be expected, they differ as to the person of the Messiah. The Targum has, מִנָּךְ קֳדָמַי יִפּוֹק מְשִׁיחָא לְמֶהֱוֵי עֲבֵיד שׁוּלְטָן עַל יִשְׂרָאֵל דִּי שְׁמֵיהּ אֲמִיר מִלְּקַדְמִין מִיּוֹמֵי עָלְמָא, "From thee the Messiah shall come forth before me, to exercise dominion over Israel, whose name was announced long ago, from the days of old." The position of Theodore of Mopsuesta, Grotius, Dathe, and some others, that Zerubbabel was intended, is now given up by all; and most interpreters of the German school find their notion of an *ideal* Messiah

Yet from thee shall He come forth to me
To be Ruler in Israel,

sufficiently convenient in explaining this and other passages, as it relieves them from all investigation in regard to positive historical personality. בֵּית־לֶחֶם, *Beth-lehem*, literally, *the house of Bread.* Arab. بيت لحم, *Beit Lahm, the House of Flesh.* It was a small town in the tribe of Judah, built on the slope of a ridge, about six Roman miles to the west by south of Jerusalem, and originally celebrated as the birth-place of David, the first of the line of Jewish kings. אֶפְרָה, *Ephrath*, Gen. xlviii. 7, or, as it is commonly written, with the ה paragogic, אֶפְרָתָה, *Ephratha*, appears from the passage just cited to have been the original name of the place. This word has much the same signification as *Beth-lehem*, being derived from פָּרָה, *to be fruitful*; and no doubt the place received both names from the fertility of the region. Dr. Robinson observes respecting the present aspect of the town: "The many olive and fig-orchards and vine-yards round about are marks of industry and thrift; and the adjacent fields, though stony and rough, produce nevertheless good crops of grain." Biblical Researches in Palestine, vol. ii. p. 161. The names occur as parallels in the stanza, Ruth iv. 11 :—

וַעֲשֵׂה־חַיִל בְּאֶפְרָתָה
וּקְרָא־שֵׁם בְּבֵית לָחֶם :

It was likewise called *Bethlehem Judah*, Judges xvii. 7; xix. 1; Ruth i. 1; Matt. ii. 5; in order, it is thought, to distinguish it from another place of the same name in the tribe of Zabulon, Josh. xix. 15. צָעִיר, as well as אֶפָּה, is of the masculine gender, contrary to rule in Hebrew, but in accordance with Arabic usage, in which the names of cities are sometimes put in the masculine. In the present instance, however, the change was doubtless occasioned by בַּיִת, which is of that gender, being strongly prominent to the view of the prophet. Pococke, in the notes to his Porta Mosis, chap. ii., and in his commentary on the passage, labours hard to support the opinion of Tanchum and Abulwalid, that צָעִיר has the two contrary significations of *little* and *great*;

but the opinion rests upon nothing beyond the construction which these writers have put upon the term as occurring in Jer. xlviii. 4, and Zech. xiii. 7, which passages, when closely examined, admit of no other signification being attached to the word but that of *little*, of *small note*, or *esteem*, though it may seem to be supported by the Targumic rendering שִׁלְמוֹנִיהוֹן in the former of these passages, and by ποιμένας, the reading of the Alexandrian MS. of the LXX., and بتصير, that of the Syriac, in the latter.

In none of the cognate dialects has the word the signification of greatness or dignity. צָעִיר לִהְיוֹת is literally *little in respect of being, little to exist,* or *be reckoned.* There is no occasion to resort to the hypothesis that לְ here forms a comparative, and is equivalent to מִן. What the prophet asserts is, that Beth-lehem was positively little in point of size or population, to rank with the other subdivisions of the tribe of Judah. Comp. 1 Sam. xxiii. 23. The tribes were subdivided into מִשְׁפָּחוֹת, *families*, or *clans*, the chiliads or thousands of which had heads or princes, to whom, from this circumstance, was given the name of רָאשֵׁי אֲלָפִים, שָׂרֵי אֲלָפִים, *princes* and *heads of thousands.* It is highly probable that at the time to which the prophecy refers, if not in that of the prophet, the place might not have been able to muster a thousand men. No mention is made of it among the cities of Judah enumerated Josh. xv., though, with many others, it is found in the text of the LXX. Nor does it occur in the list, Neh. xi. 25, &c. It is spoken of in the New Testament as Κώμη, *a village,* or *hamlet,* John vii. 42. In the present day its inhabitants are rated at eight hundred taxable men. See Dr. Robinson, *ut sup.* Yet, small and inconsiderable as Bethlehem was, it was to have the distinguished honour of giving birth to the Messiah.

"O sola magnarum urbium
Major Bethlem, cui contigit
Ducem salutis coelitus
Incorporatum gignere."
Prudentius, Hymn. Epiph. 77.

Whose comings forth have been of old,
From the ancient days.

Between the former and the latter half of the verse is a marked antithesis. In this respect, יֵצֵא and מוֹצָאֹתָיו, correspond; the former, designating the future *coming forth* of the Illustrious Ruler here predicted, when he should actually assume human nature; the latter, his ancient *comings forth*, when he created the world, and appeared to Moses and the patriarchs, and revealed to them the Divine will. The idea conveyed by the noun must be identical with that expressed by the verb. Abenezra, Abarbanel, Grotius, Hartmann, Rosenmüller, Gesenius, Hitzig, Maurer, and Ewald, give *origines* as the signification of מוֹצָאוֹת, and regard the term as referring to the Davidic extraction of the Messiah. This signification is likewise strenuously maintained by Hengstenberg; but, instead of finding any reference to the ancient family of David, he adopts the opinion that the object of the prophet is to teach the eternal existence of the Messiah. His position, however, is perfectly untenable, since nothing can be more incongruous than the ascription of locality to eternity, which he expressly does in the translation, " his 'goings forth (in the sense of places of going forth) are the ancient times, the days of eternity, *i. e.* the very ancient times." None of the passages which he alleges, proves the local signification; they all describe the act, not the place or time of egress. מִן before קֶדֶם and in מִימֵי עוֹלָם, is used in its temporal acceptation, marking the *terminus a quo.* The LXX. ἔξοδοι αὐτοῦ ἀπ' ἀρχῆς ἐξ ἡμερῶν αἰῶνος.

Syr. ܘܡܦܩܗ ܡܢ ܪܫܝܬ ܡܢ ܝܘܡܝ ܥܠܡܐ " *Whose going forth is from the beginning, from the days of the ages.*" Vulg. "*Et egressus ejus ab initio, a diebus æternitatis.*" The Arab. though unwarrantably free as a version, gives pretty much the true sense : ومخارجه

في اسرائيل منذ ايام الدهر " *Whose goings forth in Israel are from the days of the age.*" It is, however, not unlikely,

that the words في اسرائيل, have crept into the text from the preceding clause. Though קֶדֶם is used of past duration absolutely in reference to God, Deut. xxxiii. 27, yet it is most frequently employed to denote past, especially *ancient time,* and is synonymous with עוֹלָם, with which it occurs in poetic parallelisms. Comp. the Arab. قدم , *præcessit ; tempus antiquum.* Syr. ܩܕܡ , *ante, coram.* In Ps. xliv. 2, יְמֵי קֶדֶם occurs, just as יְמֵי עוֹלָם does in the present verse; and in Ps. lxxvii. 6 we have יָמִים מִקֶּדֶם and שְׁנוֹת עוֹלָמִים corresponding to each other. Comp. also Micah vii. 14, 20 ; Mal. iii. 4. That the dogma of eternal generation or emanation is taught by our prophet, does not appear; but the actual preexistence of our Saviour, and his active comings forth, in the most ancient times, for the accomplishment of the Divine purposes, he not obscurely teaches. Thus Piscator : " Verto egressiones, nempe egressiones a Deo Patre ad sanctos Patres Adamum, Noachum, Abrahamum, Isaacum, Jacobum, quibus apparuit seseque familiari sermone patefecit." For the interpretation of Calvin, that the eternal decree respecting the future birth of the Messiah is intended, there is no foundation whatever. The term מוֹשֵׁל, *Ruler,* here employed, is that used by David in his Messianic Ode, 2 Sam. xxiii. 3 :—

מוֹשֵׁל בָּאָדָם צַדִּיק
מוֹשֵׁל יִרְאַת אֱלֹהִים :

Comp. Jer. xxx. 21:—

וְהָיָה אַדִּירוֹ מִמֶּנּוּ
וּמֹשְׁלוֹ מִקִּרְבּוֹ יֵצֵא
וְהִקְרַבְתִּיו וְנִגַּשׁ אֵלָי
כִּי מִי הוּא־זֶה עָרַב אֶת־לִבּוֹ
לָגֶשֶׁת אֵלַי נְאֻם־יְהֹוָה :

Comp. also Is. xi. 1—4. לִי, *to me,* is not without emphasis. The Messiah was to come for the express purpose of carrying into effect the will of his Father in the salvation of men ; and though Israel is specially mentioned as the sphere of his rule, it is not to the exclusion of the

2 Nevertheless he will give them up
  Till the time when she who is to bear hath brought forth,
  And the rest of his brethren
  Shall return to the sons of Israel.
3 And he shall stand, and feed in the strength of Jehovah,
  In the majesty of the name of Jehovah his God.

Gentile world, as ver. 3, and numerous passages in other prophets clearly show.

For the verbal discrepancies between the Hebrew text of Micah, and the quotation Matt. ii. 6, the reader is referred to the commentators on the latter passage. It may suffice to remark here, that the Hebrew words cannot with any propriety be rendered interrogatively, as some have proposed, and that the quotation in question, made by the Sanhedrim, and not by the evangelist, is obviously given from memory, and not with any view to verbal accuracy.

2. Notwithstanding the glorious prospect afforded by the promise of the Messiah, it was not to supersede the state of suffering to which the nation was to be previously reduced on account of its sins. Into that state it was to be brought by the Chaldæans, and was not to be fully restored till about the time of his birth. The return from Babylon was only partial at first; but, encouraged by the prosperity which attended the re-establishment of the theocracy, others who resided in the East were induced to follow, and multitudes returned from Egypt and other parts, before the Christian era. The words יֹלֵדָה יָלָדָה are susceptible of two interpretations. They may either be referred to the Jewish church, and regarded as descriptive of her deliverance from suffering, set forth under the metaphor of a travailing woman; or, they strictly and literally apply to the mother of the Messiah. The former interpretation is adopted by Lipman, Munster, Vatablus, Grotius, Drusius, Dathe, Justi, and others; the latter by the greater number of expositors—among other moderns, by Secker, Michaelis, Hartmann, Rosenmüller, Hitzig, Maurer, and Ewald. This construction of the passage alone suits the entire connexion. It would appear altogether incongruous to introduce a tropical designation of the church, in a verse in which the Jewish

people are more than once spoken of in language strictly literal. The birth of the Messiah, in so far as regards its place, and the preexistence of his person, had been predicted, ver. 1: the prophet, who, as already noticed, was contemporary with Isaiah, and in all probability was acquainted with his celebrated prophecy respecting the עַלְמָה, Is. vii. 14, now further adverts to the interesting fact by a somewhat indefinite, but by no means obscure reference to his virgin mother. This view is further confirmed by the use of the pronominal affix in אֶחָיו, which unquestionably belongs to the Messiah, the immediate antecedent, and not, as a collective, to Israel, as given in the LXX. and Targ. By his "brethren" cannot be meant the Gentile believers, which some interpreters have alleged, referring in proof to Ps. xxii. 22; Heb. ii. 11; but his brethren according to the flesh, those who still remained in foreign parts, but who were to be brought back to Judæa, in order that they might be there to receive him, when he should come forth to be ruler in Israel. The preposition עַל conveys here the idea of superaddition. The foreign Jews were to be gathered in addition to those who had already been collected. It is thus more expressive than אֶל. That the phrase בְּנֵי יִשְׂרָאֵל, the children of Israel, is not here to be taken in its distinctive application to the ten tribes, but denotes the descendants of Jacob generally, may be inferred from the fact, that it is thus appropriated after the Babylonish captivity, the period to which the prophecy refers. It is well known that the Maccabæan coins bear the inscription, שקל ישראל, the Shekel of Israel. Comp. for this use of the term יִשְׂרָאֵל, ver. 1 of the present chapter.

3. The verb עָמַד signifies not simply to stand, but also to stand firm, to endure, continue. This latter acceptation is

And they shall continue ;
For now shall He be great unto the ends of the earth.
4 And This Same shall be the peace.
When the Assyrian shall invade our land,
And tread our palaces,
We will raise against him seven shepherds,
And eight anointed men.
5 And they shall afflict the land of Assyria with the sword,
And the land of Nimrod at the entrances thereof ;

adopted here by many, who think it better suits the character of the predicted king, who is otherwise represented as *sitting* upon his throne, and not standing. But, as the following verb רָעָה, signifies *to feed* a flock, there is the greatest propriety in presenting him to view in the attitude of the good shepherd, who stands, that he may survey the whole of his sheep, and be in readiness to defend them against all attacks. Comp. Is. lxi. 5. The pastoral metaphor is beautifully expressive of royal care and protection. Comp. Iliad i. 263 :

Οἷον Πειρίθοόν τε, Δρύαντά τε, ποιμένα λαῶν,

where the scholiast has, βασιλέα ὄχλων. See for this use of the Hebrew verb רָעָה, 2 Sam. v. 2; vii. 7. The power and glory of the Messiah here predicted are those with which, as Mediator, he is invested. Comp. Is. xi. 2 ; Matt. xxviii. 18 ; Heb. ii. 7—9. Jehovah being called " his God," intimates his subordinate official relation. Comp. John xx. 17. If שֵׁם יְהֹוָה, *the name of Jehovah*, be not here a periphrasis for Jehovah himself, it may be regarded as descriptive of his attributes, or the character in which he hath revealed himself to mankind. The nominative to וְיָשְׁבוּ must be the subjects over whom Messiah reigns, understood. These were to consist not of believing Jews only, but likewise of believing Gentiles in the remotest regions of the globe, as it follows in the verse. Comp. for אַפְסֵי אָרֶץ, " the ends of the earth," in reference to the amplitude of the kingdom of Christ, Ps. ii. 8 ; xxii. 28 ; lxxii. 8. The verb conveys the idea of security and permanence. Such was to be the character of the new dispensation. It

remains to add on this verse, that instead of רָעָה, *to feed*, two MSS. and some printed editions read רָאָה, *to see*, while the LXX. and Arab. exhibit both readings ; and that three MSS. and another originally, the Syr., Targ., and Vulg., read וְיָשׁוּבוּ or וְיָשֻׁבוּ, *they shall return*, or *be converted*, instead of the current reading וְיָשְׁבוּ, *they shall remain*. The LXX. have ὑπάρξουσι.

4, 5. The words וְהָיָה זֶה שָׁלוֹם, *And This Same shall be the peace*, are intimately connected with the preceding words, but have no relation to those which follow, except in so far as the victories there assumed were to pave the way for that state of the Jewish affairs during which the Messiah was to appear in the world. זֶה, *This, This Same*, is used emphatically, with reference to the Messiah, who had just been spoken of. Comp. for a similar use of the pronoun, Gen. v. 29 ; Exod. xv. 2. שָׁלוֹם, *peace*, is put, by metonymy, for the author and introducer of reconciliation. Comp. Gen. xlix. 10 ; Is. ix. 5 (Eng. version, 6) ; Zech. ix. 10; Eph. ii. 14, 17; Col. i. 20. שָׁלֵם, signifies *to restore things to their former state, to make restitution ;* in Hiph. *to restore*, or *cause to be at peace*. Comp. the Arab. سلم,

reintegrare, sanare. The substantive is without the article, as frequently in the prophetic writings, when the object is to impart energy to the language, by condensing the mode of expression. If אַשּׁוּר be taken to signify the ancient Assyrian empire, the reference will be to the threatened invasion in the time of the prophet; but this construction ill suits the connexion, in which respect is had to the more distant future; and

And there shall be deliverance from the Assyrian,
When he shall invade our land,
And when he shall tread our borders.

what follows, relative to the resistance of the Jews, does not agree with any successful events in the history of that people during the Assyrian rule. I cannot, therefore, but think, that the term is employed by our prophet to denote the empire of the Seleucidæ, founded by Seleucus, one of the generals of Alexander the Great, by whom he was invested with the government of Babylonia and Media, and who, under the title of King of Syria, subjugated all the countries from the Hellespont to India and the Jaxartes. On the same principle that Darius is called מֶלֶךְ אַשּׁוּר, *the king of Assyria*, Ezra vi. 22, though that empire had long ceased to exist, the title might be applied to Seleucus and his successors. To them, during the period of their reign, belonged "the land of Assyria," which is also here called "the land of *Nimrod*," because, according to the proper rendering of Gen. x. 11, that monarch went forth from Babylon into the country of Assyria, where he built Nineveh and other cities there named. According to this interpretation, the prophecy in these two verses relates to the noble and successful opposition which the Maccabees offered to Antiochus Epiphanes, when he marched against Jerusalem, pillaged the temple, and desecrated every object sacred in the estimation of the Jews. By rousing a spirit of patriotic piety in the breasts of their countrymen, they not only recovered their sacred city from the enemy, but, after a series of the most brilliant victories, drove him to the gates of his own fortified cities, and finally succeeded in securing the national independence. It is to this protracted, but triumphant struggle, that reference is made, Dan. xi. 32. The assertion of Hartmann, that אַשּׁוּר כִּי־יָבֹא is not Hebrew in its construction, and that, consequently, אַשּׁוּר is to be connected with שָׁלוֹם, is without foundation; for we meet with the very same construction in אִישׁ אוֹ אִשָּׁה כִּי יַפְלִא, Numb. vi. 2. Thus also in Arab.

مدينتين اذا اتفقوا علي راي واحد

اهلها, "*two cities, when their inhabitants are of one accord*," Locman, Fable I. The numbers *seven* and *eight* appear to be used to denote indefinitely a full and sufficient number, as in Eccles. xi. 2; "Give a portion to seven, and also to eight." Comp. also Job v. 19 ; Prov. vi. 16; xxx. 15, 18, 21; Amos i. 3, 6, 9, &c. So the Greek τρὶς καὶ τετράκις, and the Latin *ter quaterque*. Were they to be taken literally, there would be no great difficulty in selecting the number from the Maccabæan period; but the comparison of the above passages shows that such a process would be unwarranted. רֹעִים, *shepherds*, and נְסִיכֵי אָדָם, *princely men*, are synonymous, signifying those who took the lead in opposing the enemy, and who administered the affairs of the Jews at the time. Because נָסַךְ also signifies *to pour out a libation*, Michaelis is inclined to render the phrase נְסִיכֵי אָדָם, *sacrifices of men*, and to interpret it of such as sacrificed their life in defence of their country. Not only, however, is the parallelism opposed to this construction of the meaning, but also the use of נְסִיכִים in other passages. Thus Josh. xiii. 21, נְסִיכֵי סִיחוֹן, *princes* (Com. Ver. *dukes*) *of Sihon ;* and Ezek. xxxii. 30, שָׁמָּה נְסִיכֵי צָפוֹן, *there are the princes of the north*. The title properly signifies *anointed*, those who had been consecrated to their office by anointing with oil ; and thus is equivalent to מְשִׁיחִים. In the present instance it is used tropically, without any reference to the ceremony. Syr. ܘܐܢܝܢ ܢܣܟ̈ܝ·

Targ. רַבְרְבֵי אֲנָשָׁא; Arab. عظماء من الناس, *great men*. רָעָה, *to feed*, being here used in connexion with "the sword," must be taken metaphorically, and means to *consume, devastate*, or the like. To refer רָעוּ to רָעַע as its root, is altogether inadmissible. The repetition in these two verses possesses peculiar elegance. הִצִּיל is used impersonally. Instead of גְּבוּלֵנוּ in the singular, גְּבוּלֵינוּ in the plural, is the reading of thirty-four MSS., originally

6 And the remnant of Jacob shall be in the midst of many people,
  Like the dew from Jehovah;
  Like the small rain upon herbs,
  Which waiteth not for man,
  And tarrieth not for the sons of man.

7 Yea, the remnant of Jacob shall be among the nations,
  In the midst of many people,
  Like a lion among the beasts of the forest,
  Like a young lion among flocks of sheep,
  Which, if he pass through, treadeth down and rendeth,
  And there is none to deliver.

8 Thy hand shall be high against thine adversaries,
  And all thine enemies shall be cut off.

9   And it shall be in that day, saith Jehovah,
  That I will cut off thy horses from the midst of thee;
  And I will destroy thy chariots.

four more; the Soncin., Brixian, and Complut. editions; the Soncin. Prophets, and all the ancient versions.

6, 7. The former of these verses depicts the beneficial influence which the remainder of the nation, after its restoration, should exert, by spreading the knowledge of the true God among the nations in the midst of which they were situated; their signal victories against such formidable armies, attracting attention to Him whom they worshipped, and to whom they ascribed their success. During the existence of the new Jewish state, the members of the theocracy had much intercourse with foreigners, multitudes of whom became proselytes to the faith of Jehovah, and were thus prepared to receive the gospel, when preached by the apostles. The idea of number lies both in טַל, *the dew*, and רְבִיבִים, *the rain;* and the sudden raising up of the Jews was to be as entirely a work of Divine providence, and independent of human aid, as the production of these material elements. The seventh verse describes the formidable character of the Jews in reference to the hostile nations by which they were attacked. For the accumulation and the rise in the meaning of the verbs עָבַר וְרָמַס וְטָרָף, comp. Exod. xv. 9: אָרְדֹּף אַשִּׂיג אֲחַלֵּק שָׁלָל.

8. Here the prosperous aspect of the

prophecy closes. The words are addressed optatively to Jehovah, and may be considered as those either of the prophet, or as designed to be adopted by the Jewish church. Comp. Is. xxvi. 11. Her enemies were the enemies of Jehovah.

9—14. The prophet now returns to times nearer his own, and predicts the beneficial moral changes that were to be effected in the condition of his countrymen by the Babylonish conquest and captivity. They had, contrary to the express command of the Lord, Deut. xvii. 16, kept up a formidable body of cavalry, and war-chariots; trusted in their fortified cities; encouraged sorcery, and indulged in abominable idolatry. These were all to be removed, when the Jewish state was broken up; and after God had employed the heathen in punishing his apostate people, they in their turn should be punished for their obstinate adherence to idol-worship, notwithstanding the testimony borne against their conduct by the Jews who lived among them. This portion of the chapter is strikingly parallel with Is. ii. 6—22. For פְּסָלִים, see on Is. xlvii. 9; for מִעוֹנְנִים, comp. עֹנְנִים, Is. ii. 6; and for אֲשֵׁירִים, see on Is. xvii. 8. As עָרִים had already occurred in the acceptation of *cities*, ver. 10, we should scarcely expect it to

10　I will cut off the cities of thy land,
　　And rase all thy fortresses.
11　I will cut off the sorceries from thy hand,
　　And thou shalt have no diviners.
12　I will cut off thy graven images and thy statues from the midst
　　　of thee,
　　And thou shalt no more worship the work of thine hands.
13　I will break down thine images of Astarte from the midst of thee,
　　And destroy thy cities.
14　And I will execute vengeance in anger and in wrath,
　　Upon the nations which have not been obedient.

be again used, ver. 13. To remove the difficulty Michaelis compares the word with the Arab. عرو, *arbor semper virens;* Arnold, with the Arab. غار, *spelunca;* others propose to read יְעָרִים, *woods,* i.e. groves, supposing the initial Yod to have been absorbed by that with which the preceding word terminates; while others would change the word into עֵדִים, *witnesses,* understanding thereby the statues &c. belonging to idol-worship. There seems, however, to be no absolute necessity for departing from the signification *cities,* only we thereby understand such as were specially appropriated to idolatrous uses, as Jerome suggests. Comp. עִיר בֵּית־הַבַּעַל, *the city of the house,* or *temple of Baal,* 2 Kings x. 25, by which is meant a separate part of Samaria, where the temple was situated. This construction is required in order to form a parallelism with אֲשֵׁירִים, *images of*

Astarte, occurring immediately before in the verse. In all the ancient versions the word is rendered by *cities,* except the Targum, in which it is translated *enemies.* Some refer the relative אֲשֶׁר, at the end of ver. 14, to נָקָם, and interpret, *unheard of vengeance,* but it is more natural to connect it with גּוֹיִם, *nations,* the immediate antecedent, and to regard the prophet as describing the refusal of the pagans, who had enjoyed opportunities of learning the true religion from the Jews, to listen to the instructions which had been tendered to them. Thus the Targ. עַמְמַיָּא דְּלָא קַבִּילוּ אוֹלְפָן אוֹרַיְתָא, " *the peoples that have not received the doctrine of the law.*" LXX. ἐν τοῖς ἔθνεσιν, ἀνθ᾽ ὧν οὐκ εἰσήκουσαν. Syr. ܟܣ̈ܡܐ ܘܠ ܐܠܟܡ, *the peoples who have not hearkened.* In the same way Michaelis, Hartmann, Justi, Dathe, Hitzig, Maurer, Ewald.

CHAPTER VI

It was not sufficient for the prophet to predict the punishments that were to be inflicted on the Jews; he was required to press the subject upon their attention, which he does in a very affecting manner, by calling a public court, in which the inanimate creation is summoned to supply evidence, 1, 2. An appeal is then made by Jehovah to the accused party, respecting his kindness to the nation from the earliest period of its history, 3—5. Convicted of guilt, the people are represented as deeply anxious to obtain, at any cost, reconciliation with God, 6, 7 ; and are pointed by the prophet to the only source whence it was to be obtained ; while, at the same time, they are reminded of the high properties and obligations of true piety, 8. He next demands attention to the threatened judgments, 9 ; specifies some of the crimes on account of which they were to be brought upon them, 10—12 ; repeats the threatening, 13 ; shows the blasting effects of the Divine wrath upon all their undertakings, 14, 15 ; and traces the evil to its true source—the idolatries of the kingdom of Israel, 16.

---

1   HEAR ye now what Jehovah saith :
    Arise ! plead in the presence of the mountains,
    And let the hills hear thy voice.

2   Hear, O ye mountains ! Jehovah's controversy,
    And ye rocks, the foundations of the earth ;
    For Jehovah hath a controversy with his people,
    And will contend with Israel.

3   O my people ! What have I done to thee ?
    And with what have I wearied thee ?
    Testify against me.

4   Nay, I brought thee up from the land of Egypt,

1, 2. It is not unusual with the prophets [to make appeals respecting the enormity of human guilt to the inanimate parts of creation, as if it were impossible for it not to inspire them with life, and call them forth as intelligent witnesses of what hath taken place in their presence. See Deut. xxxii. 1; Is. i. 2; Jer. ii. 12, 13. By a similar personification the mountains and durable foundations of the earth are here summoned to appear in the court of heaven. Jehovah, however, instead of bringing forward the charge, abdicates, as it were, his right, and leaves it to the guilty party to state the case. Comp. Is. xliii. 26. In the appeal to the lofty and ever-during mountains, in which the puny affairs of man could excite no prejudice, and which might therefore be regarded as quite impartial judges, there is something inexpressibly sublime. רִיב אֶת הֶהָרִים, does not mean, contend *with* the mountains, as if they were the party to be accused, but to carry on the cause in their presence.

אֶת is here to be taken in the signification of *apud*, *coram*, and is equivalent to לִפְנֵי, *before,* just as the forms הִתְהַלֵּךְ אֶת אֱלֹהִים, Gen. v. 24, and הִתְהַלֵּךְ לִפְנֵי אֱלֹהִים, xlviii. 15, are identical in meaning. אֵתָנִים, or as it is spelt אֵיתָנִים in a great many MSS., and in four early editions, standing absolutely, must be taken as a substantive, and not as an adjective qualifying מוֹסְדֵי אֶרֶץ. Arab.

وَاتِن, *stetit, constitit ;* اتَن, *petra.* اتِن,

est omne id, quod durat, et permanet sua in sede. Schultens, Origg. Hebr. p. 112. Instead of מוֹסְדֵי אֶרֶץ, *the foundations of the earth,* the Arabs call the mountains

اوتاد الارض, *the stakes,* or *posts of the earth.*

3, 4. The Israelites are asked, in the kindest and most affecting style, what ground of complaint they had against Jehovah, which could have induced them to act the part they did. Comp. Jer. ii. 5, 31. He had demanded of them

And redeemed thee from the house of slaves;
And sent before thee Moses, Aaron and Miriam.
5 O my people! remember now how Balak the king of Moab
    consulted,
And how Balaam the son of Beor answered him;
[Remember what happened]
From Shittim to Gilgal,
That ye may know the benefits of Jehovah.
6 With what shall I come before Jehovah?
With what shall I bow to the high God?
Shall I come before him with burnt offerings?
With calves of a year old?

nothing that was unreasonable. כִּי at the beginning of ver. 4, is very expressive, and is equivalent to *nay, on the contrary*, or the like. Instead of having done any thing to alienate them, God had shown the utmost kindness to them from the beginning; not only rescuing them from Egyptian bondage, but providing them with inspired leaders. Miriam is mentioned, on account of the prominent part she took in celebrating the Divine interposition for their deliverance. She is called הַנְּבִיאָה, *the prophetess*, Exod. xv. 20, because she led the female chorus which rehearsed the inspired song of Moses. The Targ. on Micah adds: לְאוֹרָאָה לִנְשַׁיָּא, *to instruct the women*. Comp. Numb. xii. 2.

5. The kindness of Jehovah to his people was manifested, not only in furnishing them with inspired teachers, but also in counteracting the designs of Balak, who wished to engage the prophetic influence of Balaam against them; for that avaricious prophet was compelled, contrary to the cherished desire of his heart, to pronounce blessings upon them instead of curses. See Numb. xxii., xxiii., xxiv. The words מִן הַשִּׁטִּים עַד הַגִּלְגָּל, *from Shittim to Gilgal*, are not to be construed with those immediately preceding; for Balaam did not cross over Jordan to Gilgal, but was slain in the land of Midian, as we read Numb. xxxi. 8. Nor are we, with Ewald, to suppose them to be a marginal gloss; but have merely to supply the ellipsis מֶה הָיָה, *what happened*, and repeat זְכֹר, *remember*, from the first clause of the verse. To this effect the Targ.

הֲלָא גְבוּרָן אִתְעֲבִידָא לְכוֹן מֵישַׁר שִׁטִּין עַד בֵּית גִּלְגָּלָא, "*Were not mighty deeds performed for you from the plain of Shittim to the house of Gilgal?*" Thus also Munster, Vatablus, Grotius, Calvin, Dathe, De Wette, Michaelis, Hartmann, and others. There was a peculiar propriety in specifying these two places. *Shittim* was the name of a valley in the country of Moab, where, on account of the impurities committed with the Midianitish women, twenty-four thousand Israelites were destroyed. The evil was so great that it might have caused the Lord to abandon them entirely; but he mercifully spared them as a people, miraculously divided the Jordan to afford them a passage, and gave them actual possession of Canaan, the land promised to their fathers. In proof of this last act of the Divine goodness, *Gilgal* is singled out from other places, because it was there they made their first encampment in the promised land. It was situated between Jericho and the Jordan, but no trace of its site now remains. צִדְקוֹת יְהֹוָה, *the benefits of Jehovah*. Comp. Jud. v. 11; 1 Sam. xii. 7; Ps. xxiv. 5. In this way the phrase is interpreted by Tanchum, Grotius, Drusius, and by most of the moderns. Calvin observes: "Per Justitias intelligit beneficia quemadmodum multis aliis locis;" and paraphrases thus: "Ut ipsa experientia tibi demonstret quam verax, quam beneficus, quam misericors semper fuerit Deus erga genus vestrum."

6, 7. The Jews, convicted of guilt, are represented as most anxious to propitiate the Divine favour. They could

7 Will Jehovah be satisfied with thousands of rams?
    With ten thousand rivers of oil?
    Shall I give my first-born for my transgression?
    The fruit of my body for the sin of my soul?
8 He hath showed thee, O man! what is good:
    And what doth Jehovah require of thee,

not deny the charges that had been brought against them; nor could they put in any plea of justification. They stood condemned before God and the universe. The language which they employ is not such as the prophet would have taught them, but such as well accorded with the notions which were prevalent among them, some of which had been learned from their heathen neighbours. How much soever they might formerly have grudged the expense of prescribed offerings, they are now willing to bring the most costly and abundant, rams by thousands, and oil sufficient to fill myriads of rivers; nay, what is more, human victims, and of these the most endeared, their own offspring. In רִבְבוֹת נַחֲלֵי־שָׁמֶן, *myriads of torrents of oil*, is a double hyperbole, quite in the style of the Orientals. For רְבָבוֹת, as thus used, comp. 1 Sam. xviii. 7; and for נַחֲלֵי־שָׁמֶן, Job xx. 17; xxix. 6. The fact of the presentation of human sacrifices is fully established in the ancient history of all nations. This barbarous custom was especially prevalent among the Phœnicians, and was by them introduced into the north of Africa, where it continued till the proconsulate of Tiberius. According to Porphyry, the book of Sanchoniathon was full of examples of such sacrifices. That they obtained among the idolatrous Israelites is clear from Jer. xix. 5, xxxii. 35, who offered their children to Moloch or Saturn, after the example of their Phœnician neighbours. Eusebius, in his Præpar. Evangel. lib. iv. 16, enters at length into the subject; and adduces a passage from Philo Byblius which has a special bearing upon the present text: Ἔθος ἦν τοῖς παλαιοῖς, ἐν ταῖς μεγάλαις συμφοραῖς τῶν κινδύνων, ἀντὶ τῆς πάντων φθορᾶς ΤΟ ΗΓΑΠΗΜΕΝΟΝ ΤΩΝ ΤΕΚΝΩΝ τοὺς κρατοῦντας ἢ πόλεως ἢ ἔθνους, εἰς σφαγὴν ἐπιδιδόναι, λύτρον τοῖς τιμωροῖς δαίμοσι. "It was customary among the

ancients, on calamitous or dangerous emergencies, for the rulers of the city or the state, to prevent the destruction of all, to offer up the *most dearly beloved of their children*, as a ransom to divine vengeance." אֶפֵּן is the future in Niphal of the root כָּפַף, *to bend, bow oneself down.* Comp. Ps. lvii. 7; cxlv. 14. Instead of נַחֲלֵי־שָׁמֶן, *rivers of oil*, the LXX. who have χιμάρων πιόνων, or, as the Alex. MS. reads, ἀρνῶν, have read וַחֲלֵי־שָׁמֶן, *fat sheep;* which rendering is followed by the Vulg. and Arab., but is unsupported by any other authority. The translator was evidently misled by an improper view of the parallelism.

8. The questions put in the preceding verses do not involve anything like irony, as Rosenmüller and Maurer imagine, but manifestly argue a deep anxiety about an atonement, and at the same time the grossest ignorance of what was necessary to constitute that atonement. In replying to them, the prophet first of all shows, that the ignorance of the people was culpable. They had been furnished with revelations of the mind of God upon the subject. הִגִּיד לְךָ, *He* (i. e. Jehovah) *hath shown* or *manifested it to thee;* or, the verb may be taken impersonally, and rendered in the passive: *It hath been shown thee.* No MS. supports אַגִּיד, *I will show*, the reading of the Syr., Vulg., and Arab. Had they searched the Divine records they could not have failed to discover, that, whatever prescriptions relative to sacrifices had been delivered to them, they had never been taught to attach to them any moral efficacy, but the contrary. Both reason and revelation combined to invest them with an ulterior reference. What that reference really was, the Apostle plainly teaches us, Heb. x. 1: Σκιὰν γὰρ ἔχων ὁ νόμος τῶν μελλόντων ΑΓΑΘΩΝ:— the מַה־טּוֹב of the prophet. Comp. Heb. ix. 23, where the sacrifice of Christ is, by way of eminence and dis-

> But to do justice, and love mercy,
> And be diligent in walking with thy God?
>
> 9   The voice of Jehovah crieth to the city,

tinction, called κρείττονες θυσίαι. Of this, the only intrinsically valuable atonement, the Levitical sacrifices, were ὑποδείγματα, *instructive examples*, or types, which were intended to suggest and foreshadow it; and, connected as they were with the progressive developments, which, from time to time, were made of the sacerdotal character and the personal oblation of the Great Deliverer promised from the beginning, the worshippers were without excuse if they did not, like Abraham, rejoice in the anticipation of his day. Having referred the inquirer to the revealed method of reconciliation, with a tacit intimation of the importance of availing himself of it, Micah proceeds to describe the conduct which alone could meet with the Divine approval. The piety required by Jehovah, he sums up under three heads: strict equity in all our transactions with our fellow-men; a heart set on doing them good, according to the claims which they have upon us; and diligent attention to every thing belonging to converse with God. Comp. Deut. x. 12, 13. See also, as contrasting a right state of the heart and life with ceremonial services, 1 Sam. xv. 22; Is. i. 11—20; Jer. vii. 21—23; Amos v. 22—24; Hos. vi. 6. A still more compendious description of genuine religion is given by our Lord, under the threefold division of κρίσις, ἔλεος and πίστις, Matt. xxiii. 23; or, as Luke has for the last, ἡ ἀγάπη τοῦ Θεοῦ, chap. xi. 42, which shows how completely mistaken Campbell is in referring it to the social virtues, and rendering it *fidelity*. There can be little doubt that Christ had the passage of Micah in his eye. צָנַע, Arab. صنع, *fecit, elaboravit in re aliqua; paravit*; also, *industrius et solers*; Syr. ܚܟܝܡܐ, *astutus, callidus*; Eth. ጸንዐ, *validus, constans fuit*; to be apt, ready, diligent, to bend the mind

to anything; here, to apply it carefully and sedulously to devotional and other spiritual exercises, which are essential to communion with God. Thus the LXX. ἕτοιμον εἶναι; Theod. ἀσφαλίζου: the fifth Greek version, φροντίζειν; the Syr. ܡܛܝܒ, *paratus;* Vulg. *solicitum.* The idea of *humility*, which is that adopted in our common version, seems to have been derived from the Arab. صنع فرس, *to train* one's horse, *i. e.* by rendering him *submissive* and patient of restraint; hence صنيع فرس, *equus bene exercitatus.* See A. Schultens on Prov. xi. 2. While this grace is an indispensable attribute of true religion, and lies indeed at its very foundation, it is only one of the several important qualities of which it is composed. The term employed by the prophet comprehends them all. Michaelis renders, *mit gewissenhafter Sorgfalt*, "with conscientious solicitude." The comment of Jerome is not unworthy of notice:—"Ita praecipitur ut praeparati simus ambulare cum Domino Deo nostro, nulla hora dormire, nullo tempore securi esse debemus, sed semper expectare patremfamilias venientem, et diem formidare judicii, et in nocte hujus seculi dicere: ego dormio, et cor meum vigilat." הַצְנֵעַ is the Hiphil Infinitive, used adverbially. Bps. Butler and Lowth, Mr. Peters, and some others, are of opinion that the sixth, seventh, and eighth verses contain a dialogue between Balak and Balaam; but there does not appear to be sufficient ground for it. The connexion of these verses with verse fifth is not so close as they suppose.

9. On the ground of the foreseen determination of the Jews, notwithstanding their present professions of repentance, to persevere in a line of conduct diametrically opposite to that required by the Most High, the prophet proceeds to summon their attention to the certainty of the judgments that were to be inflicted.

(And he who is wise will regard thy name)
Hear ye the rod, and Him who hath appointed it.

לָעִיר for לְהָעִיר, *to the city*, i. e. Jerusalem, by way of eminence. As she was pre-eminent in privilege, so she was also in regard to wickedness and guilt. תּוּשִׁיָּה Gesenius refers to an obsolete root יָשָׁה, which he thinks may probably have meant to *stand, stand out*, and so *to be*. From such a root both this noun, and יֵשׁ, *being, subsistence, substance*, may most naturally be derived. The signi-fications will then be, *that which really is, something solid or substantial, real wisdom, wealth, power, security, deliver-ance*, or whatever else best agrees with the context. Comp. the Arab. وشي, in the acceptations *juvit restituitque ægrotum medicina; abundavit opibus vir;* وشيَة, *opulentia, abundantia opum;* وسي, *largitus est.* The noun is used in parallelisms with חָכְמָה, *wisdom*, עֵצָה, *coun-sel*, עֶזְרָה, *assistance*, עֹז, *strength*, מָגֵן, *a shield*, &c. The LXX., who render it by ἀληθές, βοήθεια, ἰσχὺς, σωτηρία, ἀσφά-λεια, βουλή, give in the present text the verb σώσει, as if they had read תּוֹשִׁיעַ, from יָשַׁע; but they may, after all, have attached the same signification to יָשָׁה. The Syr. has ܡܘܠܦܢܐ, *doctrine;* the Targ. מַלְפָנָא, *teachers.* The construction of the word here will depend upon the reading of the following verb. If, with seven MSS., originally one more, and apparently another, one corrected, and one in the margin, the LXX., Syr., Targ., Vulg., and Arab., we read יִרְאֵי שְׁמֶךָ *those who fear thy name*, the passage will best be rendered, *there will be safety* or *deliverance*, i. e. for such. In this case we have to supply the substantive verb, and the ellipsis of לְ, *to* or *for*. On the other hand, if we retain the current reading יִרְאֶה שְׁמֶךָ, *he shall see thy name*, we must, with our own, and other translators and interpreters, understand אִישׁ before תּוּשִׁיָּה, and take the noun in the signification *solid*, or *sound wisdom.* That אִישׁ is frequently to be thus under-stood before abstract nouns, comp. Ps. cix. 4, אֲנִי תְפִלָּה, *I am prayer*, for אֲנִי אִישׁ

תְּפִלָּה, *I am a man of prayer;* Prov. xiii. 6, חַטָּאת, *sin*, for אִישׁ חַטָּאת, *the man of sin*, i. e. the *sinner;* xix. 15, עַצְלָה, *indolence*, for אִישׁ עַצְלָה, *the man of indolence*, &c. What greatly favours the reading יִרְאֶה שְׁמֶךָ is its occurring only in this place, whereas יִרְאֵי שְׁמֶךָ, and other forms of יָרֵא with שֵׁם, are of frequent occurrence. It was quite natural for copyists and punctators to substitute the common for the uncom-mon, but not the latter for the former. As to the ancient versions, the LXX. may, as frequently, have translated from hearing, and thus have mistaken the pronunciation of יִרְאֶה for that of יִרְאֵי, which it so nearly resembled. The com-mon reading bests suits the connexion. Before announcing his message, the prophet parenthetically declares, that, whatever might be the treatment it would receive from the bulk of the people, the truly wise would regard it as God's message, and having special respect to his revealed character as thereby disclosed, would find in it security and consolation in the approach-ing calamities. The *name* of the Lord is frequently used to express the sum total of the Divine attributes, and often stands for God himself. רָאָה, signifies not merely *to see*, but to *recognise practically, to experience;* 1 Sam. xxiv. 12; Ps. xxxiv. 13; lxxxix. 49; Lam. iii. 1. Contrasted with יִרְאָה שְׁמֶךָ, see Is. xxvi. 10, מַטֶּה, the LXX., Syr., Vulg., and, among the moderns, New-come and Ewald, take to signify *tribe*, or collectively *tribes*, and render in the vocative. The Targ. adopts a metaphor-ical signification, corresponding to that which attaches to שֵׁבֶט—rendering, מַלְכָּא וְשַׁלִּיטוֹנָא, *O King and Prince!* The accepta-tion *rod*, as emblematical of punishment, is best suited to the connexion. Comp. Is. ix. 3 (English version 4); x. 5, 24. יָעַד is also variously translated and ex-plained: some deriving it from the root עָדָה, *to adorn;* some from עוּד, *to testify;* some adopt the signification of the Arab. وعد, *minatus fuit;* while others would read עֵדָה, *congregation.* There is no necessity for departing from the ordinary

10 Are there still, in the house of the wicked, treasures of wickedness,
    And the accursed scanty ephah ?
11 Can I be innocent with wicked balances,
    And with a bag of deceitful weights ?
12 Whose rich men are full of violence,
    And her inhabitants speak falsehood ;
    Yea, their tongue in their mouth is deceitful.
13 I will surely smite thee incurably,
    Rendering thee desolate on account of thy sins.
14 Thou mayest eat, but thou shalt not be satisfied,

signification of יָעַד, *to fix*, *appoint*. The only real difficulty lies in the feminine suffix ה, which does not grammatically agree with מַטֶּה; but even this may be removed by taking the suffix as a neuter, or as referring to רָעָה, *the calamity*, understood. Comp. Jer. ix. 11. Ewald, *höre Gemeine und wer sie bestellt !* "let the community hear, and he that appoints it," understanding thereby the king as principal ruler. Hitzig and Maurer, as in our common version, both make Jehovah the nominative to the verb. Comp. Jer. xlvii. 7.

10—12. Several crimes are here specified as a sample of those which abounded, and on account of which the Divine judgments were to be brought upon the land. For עוֹד at the beginning of a sentence, comp. Gen. xix. 12. Forty-nine MSS., thirteen more originally, and perhaps one other, with one in the margin, read הָאִישׁ, *the man*, instead of הָאֵשׁ ; and this is also the reading of the Soncin., the Brixian, and five other printed editions, and has the approval of Jarchi, Abenezra, and Abarbanel, but it affords no suitable sense ; and, with הָאֵשׁ in Kennicott's MS. 201, must be regarded as the result of interpretation. Owing to the same cause, numerous MSS. and editions have הָאֵשׁ. The LXX., Syr., and Vulg., have read הָאֵשׁ, *the fire* ; but there cannot be any doubt, that it is only another form of הֲיֵשׁ, there being merely an omission of the *Yod*, as there clearly is, 2 Sam. xiv. 19 ; and the *Aleph* corresponds to the same letter in the cognate forms : Chald. אִית, Syr. ܐܺܝܬ, Arab. ايس, *est, exsistit.* The ellipsis of וְ before בֵּית is not un-

frequent. The Hebrews were much given to the falsification of their weights and measures, though such conduct was repeatedly prohibited by the law, Lev. xix. 35, 36 ; Deut. xxv. 13—16 ; and elsewhere severely condemned in their sacred writings. See Prov. xi. 1 ; xx. 10 ; and, for the practice, comp. Ezek. xlv. 9, 10 ; Hos. xii. 7 ; Amos viii. 5. וְזוּעָמָה, *accursed*, from זָעַם, to *be angry, indignant.* This participial form presents the object as suffering the effects of anger, or as marked with the Divine displeasure. אֶזְכֶּה, ver. 11, the LXX., Syr., and Targ., have read in the third person יִזְכֶּה, though the two last render it in the plural. As the MSS. show no variation, the present reading must be retained ; but as this verb is never used transitively in Kal, we cannot refer the nominative to God, and interpret it of his inquiring whether he could treat the persons in question as innocent, but must regard the prophet as putting the question, for the sake of effect, into the mouth of one of themselves, and making him ask, how he could possibly lay claim to the character, while he had none but instruments of fraud in his possession ? The antecedent to אֲשֶׁר, *whose*, ver. 12, is עִיר, *city*, ver. 9.

13. In this, and the following verses, severe judgments are threatened against the people on account of their iniquitous practices. The LXX., Syr., Vulg., and Arab., render הֶחֱלֵיתִי, *I have begun*, or, *I will begin*, as if it were the Hiphil of חָלַל, but it is that of חָלָה, *to be in pain, sick*, &c. As here used with the infinitive of הַכֵּה, *to smite, inflict punishment*, it gives intensity to the threatening, and expresses the incurable nature of the punishment.

14. יָשַׁח is not to be referred, with

For thou shalt be inwardly depressed ;
Thou mayest remove, but thou shalt not rescue,
Or what thou rescuest I will give to the sword ;
15 Thou mayest sow, but thou shalt not reap ;
Thou mayest tread the olive, but thou shalt not pour out the oil ;
And the grape of the new wine, but the wine thou shalt not drink.
16 The statutes of Omri are strictly kept,
And all the work of the house of Ahab,
And ye walk in their counsels ;
That I may make thee desolate,
And the inhabitants thereof an object of hissing ;
Therefore ye shall bear the reproach of my people.

Simonis and Gesenius, to the Arab. وحش, *fame exinanitus fuit*, but to شنع, *sequior*, et *imbecillis, infirmus ;* and was most likely intended to express what we find in the Syr. ܡܥܣܐܐ, "*the diarrhœa* shall be within thee." The LXX. taking יֶשְׁחֲךָ for יְחֻשֵׁךְ, renders, καὶ συσκοτάσει ἐν σοί. תַּסֵּג is the apocopated Hiphil of נָסַג, *to remove*, and expresses the attempt to save goods by removing them out of the way of the enemy. All the ancient versions have adopted the signification of הִשִּׂיג with שׂ, *to seize, lay hold on*, but that conjugation of נָשִׂיג has also the signification, *to remove* any thing. See Job xxiv. 2.

15. תִּדְרֹךְ וַיִת. Oil was expressed from the olive, by stamping or treading it out with the foot, in the same way as grapes were trodden. Hence the name גַּת שֶׁמֶן, *Gethsemane*, or the *oil-press*, Matt. xxvi. 36. Oil is indispensable to oriental comfort, being used for anointing the body, and perfuming the garments. It is also a very common ingredient in food.

16. Hartmann stumbles at the introduction of this verse ; but it is quite in the manner of the prophet, to recur to the wicked character of his people. יִשְׁתַּמֵּר is best rendered impersonally, though it refers to עַם, *people*, understood. Hithpael is here intensive of Piel. Omri is specially mentioned, because he was the founder of Samaria and the wicked house of Ahab, and a supporter of the superstitions of Jeroboam, 1 Kings xvi. 16—28. לְמַעַן, *in order that*. The Hebrews did not, indeed, commit the wickedness described with the intention of bringing upon themselves divine punishment ; but the punishment was as certainly connected with the sin, in the purpose of God, as if its infliction had been the end at which they aimed. חֶרְפַּת עַמִּי תִּשָּׂאוּ, *ye shall bear the reproach of my people*, i. e. your own reproach, that which you have deserved ; only the meaning is so expressed, in order to derive a high aggravation of their guilt from the relation in which they stood to Jehovah. The LXX. have λαῶν, which intimates that they either read עַמִּים, or עַמִּי as a defective masculine plural.

────◆────

CHAPTER VII

Before concluding, the prophet once more reverts to the wickedness of his people, which he depicts with the darkest colours, 1—6. He then represents them in their state of captivity, brought to repentance, and confidently expecting the

Divine interposition, which would be rendered the more conspicuous by the complete destruction of their enemies, 7—10. The restoration of Jerusalem, and the conversion of the hostile nations, are next predicted, 11, 12; while the previous desolation of Judæa is traced to the sins of the inhabitants, 13. Turning to Jehovah, he prays for the undisturbed and prosperous condition of the restored nation, 14; to which a gracious response is given, 15. The overthrow of the nations hostile to the Jews, and their reverence for Jehovah, are then pointed out, 16, 17; and the prophecy closes with a sublime and exulting appeal to his gracious character, 18, and an assurance that the covenant-people should experience the full accomplishment of the sacred engagements into which he had entered with their progenitors, 19, 20.

———————

1 ALAS for me!
   For I am as when they gather the summer-fruit,
   As when the vintage is gleaned:
   There is no cluster to eat,
   No early fig which my soul desireth.
2 The pious hath perished from the land,
   And there is none upright among men;
   They all lie in wait for blood;
   They hunt each other into the net.
3 For evil their hands are well prepared;
   The prince asketh,

1. In no part of his prophecy does Micah so fearfully describe the universal corruption of manners which prevailed among the Jews as in the first six verses of this chapter. The picture is peculiarly applicable to their character in the wicked reign of Ahaz, during which the prophet flourished, and was awfully anticipative of that which they again exhibited during the reigns immediately preceding the captivity. The preposition כְּ in כְּאָסְפֵּי־קַיִץ כְּעֹלְלֹת בָּצִיר denoting time as well as comparison, the two nouns in construction must be rendered as if they were verbs, though a literal translation would be, *the gatherings of the summer-fruit*, and *the gleanings of the vintage*. For בִּכּוּרָה, *the early fig*, see on Is. xxviii. 4. The prophet compares the strong desire which he felt to meet with a single pious man, to that eagerness with which the traveller looks in vain for one of those delicious figs after the summer has advanced.

2. Comp. Ps. xii. 1; xiv. 2; Is. lvii. 1. חֵרֶם, rendered in most of the versions *destruction*, signifies also a *net*, which is so called from its *enclosing* or *shutting up* whatever it catches. Occurring, as it here does, in connexion with the verb צוּד, *to hunt*, it is preferable to take it in this acceptation. The Orientals employed the net for hunting, as well as for fishing. The word is here in the accusative case.

3. This verse is very differently rendered by translators. The version of it which I have given appears to express as literally as possible the ideas, which, it is generally admitted, the prophet intended to convey. הֵימִיב is frequently used to express the doing of any thing *well, skilfully, aptly*, and the like. Here it is intransitive. Ewald, with Michaelis, Vogel and Döderlein, mistakes the meaning of the clause altogether, when he explains it of endeavouring by bribery to prevail upon the magistrates to pronounce that to be good which in itself is

And the judge also, for a reward;
And the great man gives utterance to the desire of his soul;
They combine to act perversely.

4 The best of them is like a prickly thorn ;
The most upright is worse than a thorn hedge ;
The day of thy watchmen, thy visitation cometh ;
Now shall be their perplexity.

5 Place no faith in a companion ;
Trust not a familiar friend ;
From her that lieth in thy bosom
Guard the doors of thy mouth.

6 For the son despiseth his father ;

---

evil. שֹׁאֵל, which he is obliged to convert into שִׁאֵל, a Pual form, of which no example occurs in the Hebrew language, can only refer to the avaricious passion of the ruler. It is, therefore, the wickedness of their governors and judges, and not that of the people themselves, which the latter clauses of the verse describe. After שֹׁאֵל supply שֹׁחַד; and after שֹׁפֵט, שֹׁפֵט. The substantive הַיָּה, like the Arab. هوي, *desideravit, voluit,* has here the signification, *wish, desire, will.* 'See Schultens on Prov. x. 3; and the Korân ii. 81: افكلما جآءكم رسول بما لا تهوى انفسكم, "*and whenever a messenger cometh to you with that which your souls desire not.*" Comp. Ps. lii. 9 ; Prov. xi. 6 ; and for the cognate אַוַּת נֶפֶשׁ, Deut. xii. 15, 20. —עָבַת, signifies *to intertwine, bind together,* as the branches of trees, ropes, &c.; here, metaphorically, *to effect by united effort.* Comp. the Arab. عبث, *miscuit, commiscuit,* Syr. خَבَל, *concordavit.* Dathe : *conjunctis viribus exsequuntur.* The princes, judges, and great men, conspired to set aside all law and right in their treatment of the poor of the land. The suffix ה is to be taken as a neuter, and refers to the injustice practised by the rulers. Thus Calvin : " Deinde complicant ipsam pravitatem : hoc est, hinc fit ut grassetur furiosa crudelitas, quoniam conspirant inter se et gubernatores et qui

volunt sibi acquirere peccandi licentiam: quasi contexerent inter se funes, confirmant hoc modo pravitatem."

4. Both טוֹב, *good,* and יָשָׁר, *upright,* are here used superlatively. Comp. for this use, Gen. xlv. 23 ; Is. i. 19 ; Exod. xv. 4. It frequently occurs in Arabic. חֵדֶק is now allowed to designate a species of *thorn,* and not a brier. As the מ now stands before מְסוּכָה, it must be taken as an emphatic comparative, which derives its force, not from any adjective expressed, but from the noun to which it is prefixed, as in Ps. lxii. 10 ; Is. xli. 24 ; or it may have originally belonged as a suffix to the preceding noun יָשָׁר, in which case טוֹבָם and יָשָׁרָם must have corresponded to each other, leaving an ellipsis of the כְּ which had just been used in כְּחֵדֶק. By " the day of thy watchmen," the period of calamity predicted by the prophets is meant. With this, the following פְּקֻדָּה, *visitation,* is explicatively parallel. For יוֹם מְבוּכָה, *a day of perplexity,* see on Is. xxii. 5. The reference in מ is not to the watchmen, improperly interpreted by some of false prophets; nor is it to be confined to the persons of rank and office described ver. 3 ; but to the people generally.

5, 6. אַלּוּף, Arab. اليف, *familiaris socius,* from الف, *conjunxit, sociavit,* &c., *a familiar,* and, by implication, a confidential, *friend.* מְיֻבָּל, LXX, ἀτιμάζει. Comp. Deut. xxxii. 15. The root נָבֵל, primarily signifies *to wither, fall off* as leaves, and tropically *to act wickedly,*

The daughter riseth up against her mother ;
The daughter-in-law against her mother-in-law :
A man's enemies are the members of his own family.

7 But I will look for Jehovah ;
　　I will wait for the God of my salvation ;
　　My God will hear me.

8　　Rejoice not over me, O mine enemy !
　　Though I have fallen, I shall rise again ;
　　Though I sit in darkness, Jehovah is my light.

9　I will bear the indignation of Jehovah,
　　Because I have sinned against him ;
　　Till he plead my cause, and give effect to my sentence ;
　　He will bring me forth to the light ;
　　I shall behold his righteousness.

irreligiously, as one that has fallen off from God. Comp. נָבֵל, Ps. xiv. 1. נְבָלָה, *an atrocious deed*, Gen. xxxiv. 7 ; Jud. xix. 23, 24. The state of things here described is that of the most wretched perfidiousness, anarchy, and confusion, in which the most intimate could have no confidence in each other, and the closest ties of relationship were violated and contemned. Comp. Jer. ix. 2—6. —ἀλλοτρίους ἀλλήλων εἶναι πάντας τοὺς μὴ σπουδαίους, καὶ γονεῖς τέκνων, καὶ ἀδελφοὺς ἀδελφῶν, οἰκείους οἰκείων. Diog. Laert. vii. 32. In language strikingly similar, Ovid describes the iron age :

" Vivitur ex rapto ; non hospes ab hospite tutus,
Non soror a genero ; fratrum quoque gratia rara est.
Imminet exitio vir conjugis, illa mariti ;
Lurida terribiles miscent aconita novercæ,
Filius ante diem patrios inquirit in annos."

　　　　　　　　　Metamorph. i. 144.

Our Saviour appropriates the words to the treacherous and cruel treatment which he taught his disciples to expect from their nearest relatives, Matt. x. 35, 36 ; Luke xii. 53.

7. Having described the wickedness of the Jews, the prophet abruptly changes the scene, and introduces them to view in that state of captivity in Babylon in which it was to issue. There,

at a distance from the land of their fathers, they are brought to repentance, and the exercise of true piety ; and seeking again to their covenant God, they express the fullest confidence that he would in due time deliver them from banishment. צָפָה, here used in Piel, signifies to *look out* for an answer to prayer, divine aid, &c. Comp. Ps. v. 4.

8, 9. Who is the enemy intended by the prophet, cannot be positively decided. Some interpreters think Babylon ; others, Edom. For the former, see Jer. l. 11 ; for the latter, Obad. 12 ; for both, Ps. cxxxvii. 7, 8. בַּת־בָּבֶל, *daughter of Babylon*, or בַּת־אֱדֹם, *daughter of Edom*, for Babylon and Edom themselves, is understood in the feminine participle אֹיַבְתִּ, *mine enemy*. For the idiom, see on Is. i. 8. The Jews understand Rome as professing Christianity to be meant by the enemy. See Pococke on verses 9th and 10th. " Light " and " darkness " are used, as frequently, for prosperity and adversity. The 9th verse contains a beautiful specimen of submissiveness and patient endurance of suffering, from an humbling conviction of the demerit of sin ; accompanied by the firm persuasion, that when the chastisement had answered its end, Jehovah would graciously afford deliverance. צְדָקָה, *righteousness*, is here to be understood with reference to the *kindness* or *favour* which God was to show to his people, in strict accordance with the tenour of his promises, rather than to the punishment of their enemies.

10 Mine enemy also shall see it,
And shame shall cover her.
She that said to me, Where is Jehovah thy God?
Mine eyes shall behold her ;
She shall now be trodden upon as the mire of the streets.
11   In the day when thy walls shall be rebuilt,
In that day the decree shall be extended ;
12 In that day they shall come to thee
From Assyria to Egypt,
Even from Egypt to the river,
From sea to sea, and from mountain to mountain.

10. The deliverance of the Jews was to be the occasion of the destruction of their foes, who, because the former had no visible object of worship, and had been delivered into their power, tauntingly asked: אַיּוֹ יְהֹוָה אֱלֹהָיִךְ, *where is Jehovah thy God?* The feminine suffix refers to בַּת־צִיּוֹן, *daughter of Zion,* understood.

11, 12. Micah resumes the language of prophecy, and, addressing Jerusalem, announces her restoration, and the way that would be paved for the conversion of the surrounding hostile nations to the true religion. Such appears to me to be the meaning of these verses, which have been very variously interpreted. חֹק, *statute, decree, order, appointment* (LXX. νόμιμα, Symm. ἐπιταγή, Theod. πρόσταγμα), some refer to the tyrannical enactments of the Babylonians ; some to the order of Artaxerxes, Ezra iv. 21; some to the punishment decreed upon the enemies of the Jews; some to the idolatrous statutes, with which the Jews complied ; some to the boundary of the Holy Land; and some to the preaching of the gospel among all nations, of which last interpretation Calvin says : " Sed locus hic non patitur se ita violenter torqueri." Secker, Newcome, Vogel, Döderlein, and others, join חֹק to יִרְחַק, and form a reduplicate verb רִחֲקְחָק of the whole ; with whom, as to meaning, Gesenius agrees, who rejects חֹק altogether, and renders, *dies ille procul abest.* Thesaur. p. 1284. What would seem to determine the meaning of the term, as here used, is the light thrown upon רָחַק, *to be distant, remove to a distance,* &c., by the geographical specifications contained in verse 12th. The subject of both verses is sufficiently proved to be identical, by

the repetition of יוֹם הוּא, *that day,* which indisputably is the יוֹם, *day,* spoken of at the beginning of verse 11th. Whatever the decree or command was, the effect of its promulgation was to be the coming of foreigners from different regions to the Jewish people, reassembling at Jerusalem, עָדֶיךָ יָבוֹא. The most natural construction is, that the decree of God respecting the political changes that were to take place, was not to be confined to Babylon, but was to be extended to all the countries round about Judæa, in consequence of which great numbers would become proselytes to the Jewish faith. There is an ellipsis of the preposition בְּ, *in,* before יוֹם, *day,* in all the three instances in which it here occurs. וְ before עָדֶיךָ is not pleonastic, but is used, as in several other instances, after words which imply condition or time. See Exod. xvi. 6 ; 1 Sam. xxv. 27. יָבוֹא is used impersonally : " *one, they* shall come ; " it is rendered in the plural in the LXX., Targ., and Arab., and one of Kennicott's MSS. reads יבואו. That וְעָרֶי has originally been וְעָרֵי, the parallelism, compared with other instances of its occurrence, sufficiently shows. The change of ד into ר, and *vice versâ,* by transcribers, owing to their great resemblance to each other, is very common. For example in רִיפַח and רִיפָה, 1 Chron. i. 6 ; and רוֹדְנִים and דּוֹדָנִים, ver. 7 ; עָרִים and דָרִים, Ps. liv. 5 ; מָדוּד and מָדוּר, lxxxi. 7 ; יַעֲרִין and יְרֵעִין, Prov. x. 32; and especially as corresponding to the present case, עָרֶיךָ and עָדֶיךָ, Ps. cxxxix. 20, where the latter reading is found in fifteen MSS., has been originally in eleven more, and is in one printed edition. No objection can be taken from the preposition

13 Nevertheless the land shall be desolate
　　On account of her inhabitants,
　　Because of the fruit of her doings.
14　　Feed thy people with thy crook,
　　The flock of thine heritage ;
　　That dwell alone in the wood, in the midst of Carmel ;
　　Let them feed in Bashan and Gilead, as in ancient days.

assuming the poetic form עָרַי, while in the following sentence we have עִד ; the same variety appears in אַחֲרֵי and אַחַר, 1 Sam. xi. 7. It is also worthy of notice, that the LXX. have read עָרֶיךָ at the beginning of the verse, as if it had been עָרַיִךְ, having rendered it αἱ πόλεις σου. By מָצוֹר, I understand *Egypt*, and not *fortification*. Comp. 2 Kings xix. 24, Is. xix. 6, on which see my note. Upon this construction, Assyria and Egypt are contrasted, just as they are Is. xix. 23, where the same subject is treated of in almost the same language. נָהָר, the *river*, κατ᾽ ἐξοχήν, *i. e.* the Euphrates, corresponding in the parallelism to אַשּׁוּר, *Assyria.* The Syr. and Targ. have mistaken צוֹר in מָצוֹר, for *Tyre ;* as the latter has מִנִּי, for *Armenia.* The concluding words of the verse, וְיָם מִיָּם וְהַר הָהָר, stand irregularly for וּמִיָּם וְעַד־יָם וּמֵהַר וְעַד־הַר. It does not appear that any specific mountains are intended ; the prophet describes in general terms the natural boundaries of the countries from which the persons spoken of were to come. For a prophetic illustration of these verses, see on Is. xix. 23—25.

13. The conjunctive ו in וְהָיְתָה is used antithetically to introduce a sentence predictive of what should take place previous to the arrival of the events mentioned in the verses immediately preceding. It has the force of *but yet, nevertheless,* or the like. However bright the prospects which opened upon the Jews in futurity, they were not to forget the punishment that was to intervene, but ought to repent of their sins, to which it was to be traced as its cause. Some interpret הָאָרֶץ, *the land,* of Babylonia ; but this construction seems less apt.

14. In the believing anticipation of the fulfilment of the Divine promises made to the covenant-people, Micah

addresses a prayer to Jehovah, which, though brief, is distinguished for the poetical elevation of its style, and the appropriateness of its petition. Like many other prayers in the Old Testament, it is prophetic in its aspect. The Jewish people are frequently spoken of under the metaphor of a flock, and Jehovah as their shepherd. See Ps. lxxx. 1 ; xcv. 7 ; c. 3. They are also often represented as his special heritage, Deut. iv. 20 ; vii. 6 ; xxxii. 9. Some understand שֹׁכְנִי לְבָדָד, *dwelling alone* or *solitarily,* as descriptive of the condition of the Jews in captivity, and יַעַר, *forest,* of the dangers and annoyances to which they were exposed while in that state. That it rather refers to the security and prosperity of their restored condition may fairly be concluded from the meaning of similar language in other passages. Thus, in the celebrated prophecy of Balaam, Numb. xxiii. 9, which, in all probability, Micah had in view, we read, הֶן־עָם לְבָדָד יִשְׁכֹּן וּבַגּוֹיִם לֹא יִתְחַשָּׁב, *Behold! the people shall dwell alone, and shall not be reckoned among the nations.* Comp. Deut. xxxiii. 28 ; Jer. xlix. 31 ; and for יַעַר, as used figuratively for a place of safety and cool repose, see Ezek. xxxiv. 25. The meaning of the prophet is, that on being brought back to their own land, they should no longer be mixed with, and exposed to enemies, but live by themselves in a state of undisturbed tranquillity. For instances of the paragogic Yod affixed to participles, see Gen. xlix. 11 ; Deut. xxxiii. 16 ; Obad. 3 ; Zech. xi. 17. That the Carmel here mentioned must be the celebrated mountain on the coast of the Mediterranean, see on Amos i. 2. The regions of *Bashan* and *Gilead,* on the east of the Jordan, were likewise celebrated for their rich pasturage, and were, on this account, chosen by the tribes of Reuben

15   As in the days of thy coming forth from Egypt,
      I will show them marvellous things.

16 The nations shall see it, and be ashamed of all their power ;
      They shall lay their hands upon their mouth ;
      Their ears shall become deaf.

17 They shall lick dust like the serpent ;
      Like reptiles of the earth they shall tremble from their hiding-
          places ;
      They shall turn with fear towards Jehovah our God ;
      Yea, they shall be afraid of thee.

18   Who is a God like thee,
      Pardoning iniquity, and passing by transgression,
      In regard to the remnant of his heritage ?
      He retaineth not his anger for ever,
      Because he delighteth in mercy.

19 He will again have compassion upon us,

---

and Gad, and the half tribe of Manasseh, Numb. xxxii. ; Deut. iii. 12—17. Comp. as strictly parallel, Jer. l. 19.

15. The answer of Jehovah to the prophet's prayer, assuring the nation, that the same Almighty power which had interposed in so remarkable a manner for their deliverance from Egypt, would again wonderfully appear on their behalf. Comp. Jer. xvi. 14, 15. Such changes of person as in ד, *thy*, and נו, *him*, are common. The reference in both is to the people of the Jews.

16. The גְּבוּרָה, *power*, spoken of, is that of the hostile nations, of which they were so proud, and which they regarded as invincible, and not that of the Jews when restored, as Junius and Tremellius, Tarnovius, Stokes, and some others, have imagined. The latter half of the verse most graphically describes the silence, astonishment, and utter consternation, with which they should be seized. Comp. Jud. xviii. 19 ; Job. xxi. 5 ; Ps. cvii. 42 ; Is. lii. 15.

17. An equally graphic description of the state of degradation and terror to which the enemies were to be reduced. Comp. Ps. lxxii. 9 ; Is. xlix. 23 ; lxv. 25. For זֹחֲלִים, *crawlers*, or *reptiles*, comp. Deut. xxxii. 24. The distinctive use of אֶל, *to*, and מִן, *from* or *of*, as here used, shows that there is not a change of person in

מִפָּךְ, and that the affix ך refers, not to Jehovah, but to the people of the Jews. The fear ultimately produced in the minds of their enemies was to be a religious fear or veneration which should attract them *towards* Jehovah as its object. Comp. for this construction of אֶל פָּחַד, *to exercise reverential regard towards* God, Hos. iii. 5. Combined with the circumstances under which the nations were to acknowledge the supremacy of Jehovah, was their standing in awe of the political power of the Jews. See on Is. xix. 17.

18. Impelled by strong feelings of gratitude at the anticipated deliverance of his people, the prophet breaks out into a strain of the sublimest praise and admiration, and gives a description of the gracious character of God, unrivalled by any contained in the Scriptures. The phrase עֹבֵר עַל־פֶּשַׁע, *passing by transgression*, is a metaphor, taken from the conduct of a traveller who passes on without noticing an object to which he does not wish to give his attention. The idea which it communicates is not, that God is unobservant of sin, or that it is regarded by him as a matter of little or no importance, but that he does not mark it in particular cases with a view to punishment ; that he does not punish, but forgive. Comp. Prov. xix. 11, Amos vii. 8, in which latter passage the verb alone is

> He will subdue our iniquities;
> Yea, thou wilt cast all their sins into the depths of the sea.
> 20 Thou wilt grant the truth to Jacob,
> The kindness to Abraham,
> Which thou didst swear to our fathers
> From the days of old.

used. The opposite is expressed by שָׁמַר עָוֹן, to watch iniquity, Ps. cxxx. 3, i. e. to keep it in view in order to punish it. שְׁאֵרִית, remnant, does not necessarily imply a small or inconsiderable number, but merely conveys the general notion of a surviving body of men : here it means those of the Jewish nation who should be alive at the termination of the captivity. חָפֵץ, to delight, according to the Arab. حفض, flexit, inflexit lignum, projecit, properly expresses the bent or propension of the mind, or what we commonly call its inclination towards an object; hence desire, affection, delight. The combined force of חָפֵץ חֶסֶד, bent on kindness, is inimitable, the primary idea of חֶסֶד being that of eager desire or love towards an object. It is the term which is so often rendered loving-kindness in our common version.

19. This verse may be regarded as containing a beautiful epiphonema, in which the people of the Jews exultingly avow their full confidence in the forgiving mercy and subduing power of their God. שׁוּב, to turn, in יָשׁוּב יְרַחֲמֵנוּ, is, as usual before another verb, employed adverbially to signify again. God had often pitied and delivered his people. It is here intimated that his compassion was not exhausted, but should be exercised towards them anew. All the meaning found by Rosenmüller, Gesenius and Maurer, in יִכְבֹּשׁ עֲוֹנֹתֵינוּ, is that of disregarding or not avenging; but there is no ground for rejecting the radical idea of trampling under foot as enemies. Sin must ever be regarded as hostile to man.

It is not only contrary to his interests, but it powerfully opposes and combats the moral principles of his nature, and the higher principles implanted by grace ; and but for the counteracting energy of divine influence, must prove victorious. Without the subjugation of evil propensities, pardon would not be a blessing. If the idolatrous and rebellious disposition of the Jews had not been subdued during their stay in Babylon, they would not have been restored. The total and irrevocable forgiveness of sins is forcibly expressed by casting them into the depths of the sea. What is deposited there is completely hid from the view, and cannot in any way affect us. Instead of חַטֹּאתָם, their sins, five MSS. read חַטֹּאתֵינוּ, our sins, which is the reading of the LXX., Syr., Vulg., and Arab. It may, however, only be a correction ; the change of person we have frequently had occasion to notice.

20. The return from captivity, while it furnished a striking specimen of the covenanted fidelity and kindness of Jehovah, was only preliminary to the infinitely greater display of these attributes in the mission of the Messiah, the Seed of Abraham in whom all the families of the earth were to be blessed. The words of this verse are quoted, with scarcely any variation, in the inspired song of Zacharias, with direct application to Him of whom his son had just been born to be the forerunner, Luke i. 72, 73. Before the names of the patriarchs, a verb signifying to declare, promise, or the like, is understood.

NAHUM

―――

PREFACE

OWING to the paucity of information respecting the prophet Nahum, little can be said in regard to his life and times. All that we know of him personally is, that he was the native of a town or village called Elkosh, chap. i. 1.

The only historical data furnished by the book itself with respect to the period at which he flourished, are the following: the humiliation of the kingdoms of Israel and Judah, by the Assyrian power, chap. ii. 3 (Eng. version, ii. 2); the final invasion of Judah by that power, i. 9, 11; and the conquest of Thebes in Upper Egypt, iii. 8—10. But the removal of the glory of the Hebrew kingdoms, to which reference is made, could only be that which was effected by Tiglath-pileser and Shalmaneser, by whom the Israelites were carried into captivity; when the Jews also were harassed and spoiled by the Syrians, as well as impoverished by the large sum of money paid by Ahaz to the former of these monarchs. See Is. vii.—ix.; 2 Chron. xxviii. Sargon, who appears to have succeeded Shalmaneser, not satisfied with the reduction of Phœnicia by that king, and fearing lest Egypt should prevail upon the conquered provinces of the west to join her in a confederacy against him, undertook an expedition into Africa; and, though history is silent as to the event, it would appear from chap. iii. 8—10, that the expedition proved so far successful, that

he took Thebes, the celebrated metropolis of Upper Egypt. It was
by his successor, Sennacherib, that the last attempt was made by
the Assyrians to crush the Jewish people, which issued in the total
defeat of their army.

Now, since the last of these events took place in the fourteenth
year of Hezekiah, and the circumstances connected with it are
clearly referred to by Nahum, partly prophetically, and partly as
matter of historical notoriety, chap. i. 9—13, it follows that he
must have lived in, or about the year B.C. 714. Jarchi, Abarbanel,
Grotius, Junius and Tremellius, and Justi, place him in the reign
of Manasseh, and some, as Ewald, would make him contemporary
with Josiah; but Bp. Newton, Eichhorn, Bertholdt, Rosenmüller,
Newcome, Horne, Gesenius, de Wette, Jahn, Gramberg, Winer,
Maurer, and Knobel, unanimously agree with Jerome in referring
his ministry to the latter half of the reign of Hezekiah. Neither
the opinion of Josephus, that he foretold the destruction of Nineveh
in the reign of Jotham, nor that of Clement of Alexandria, that he
lived between Daniel and Ezekiel, has met with any supporters.
But if, as is highly probable, he flourished in one of the latter years
of Hezekiah, his prophecy must have been delivered nearly one
hundred years before its accomplishment; for Nineveh was overthrown, and the Assyrian power destroyed, by the joint forces of
Cyaxares and Nabopolassar, in the reign of Chyniladanus, B.C. 625.

Considerable difference of opinion obtains with respect to the
birth-place of the prophet. That הָאֶלְקֹשִׁי, the Elkoshite, was
designed to point out the place of his nativity, and not his paternity,
as the Targumist interprets, is evident from a comparison of the
form with similar instances of the Yod affixed, 1 Kings xvii. 1;
Jer. xxix. 27; Micah i. 1. There are two cities of the name of
Elkosh, each of which has had its advocates, as that which may lay
claim to the honour of having given birth to Nahum. The one,
القوش, Elkosh, is situated in Koordistan, on the east side of the
Tigris, about three hours' journey to the North of Mosul, which
lies on the same side of the river, opposite to Nunia, supposed
to be the site of ancient Nineveh. It is inhabited by Chaldæan
or Nestorian Christians, and is a place of great resort by Jewish

pilgrims, who firmly believe it to be the birth-place and the burial-place of the prophet, to whose tomb they pay special respect. It is, however, generally thought that the tradition which connects this place with his name is of later date; and that it owes its origin to the Jews or the Nestorians, who imagined that he must have lived near the principal scene of his prophecy; and that the name had been transferred to the place from a town so called in Palestine, just as our colonists have given the names of towns in Britain to those which they have erected in America and Australia. The other place is *Elcesi*, or *Elkesi*, a village in Galilee, which was pointed out to Jerome as a place of note among the Jews, and which, though small, still exhibited some slight vestiges of more ancient buildings.* Eusebius mentions it in his account of Hebrew places; and Cyrill (ad cap. i. 1) is positive as to its situation being in Palestine.† It has been thought, and not without reason, by some, that Capernaum, Heb. כְּפַר נָחוּם, most properly rendered *the village of Nahum*, derived its name from our prophet having resided in it, though he may have been born elsewhere in the vicinity, just as it is said to have been ἡ ἰδία πόλις of our Lord, though he was born at Bethlehem.

Where the prophet was when he delivered his predictions, is not specified; but, from his familiar reference to Lebanon, Carmel, and Bashan, it may be inferred that he prophesied in Palestine; while the very graphic manner in which he describes the appearance of Sennacherib and his army, chap. i. 9—12, would seem to indicate that he was either in, or very near to Jerusalem at the time. What goes to confirm this supposition, is the number of terms, phrases, &c., which he evidently borrowed from the lips of Isaiah. Comp. שֹׁטֵף עֹבֵר כָּלָה יַעֲשֶׂה, i. 8, and כָּלָה הוּא עֹשֶׂה, ver. 9, with בּוּקָה וּמְבוּקָה, Is viii. 8, and כָּלָה עֹשָׂה, Is. x. 23; שֹׁטֵף וְעֹבֵר, וּמְבֻלָּקָה, ii. 11, with בּוּקֵק הָאָרֶץ וּבוֹלְקָה, Is. xxiv. 1;

---

* "Porro quod additur, *Naum Elcesæi*, quidam putant Elcesæum patrem esse Naum, et secundum Hebræam traditionem etiam ipsum prophetam fuisse; quum Elcesi usque hodie in Galilæa viculus sit, parvus quidem et vix ruinis veterum ædificiorum indicans vestigia, sed tamen notus Judæis, et mihi quoque a circumducente monstratus."— *Hieron. Præf. in Naum.*

† —τοῦ ἀπὸ τῆς Ἐλκεσέ· κώμη δὲ αὕτη πάντως που τῆς Ἰουδαίων χώρας.

מֶלְאוּ מָתְנֵי חַלְחָלָה, Is. xxi. ‏,‏וְחַלְחָלָה בְּכָל־מָתְנַיִם, ii. 11, with
3 ; הִנֵּה עַל־הֶהָרִים רַגְלֵי מְבַשֵּׂר מַשְׁמִיעַ שָׁלוֹם, ii. 1, with
מַה־נָּאווּ עַל־הֶהָרִים רַגְלֵי מְבַשֵּׂר מַשְׁמִיעַ שָׁלוֹם, Is. lii. 7, &c.

The subject of the prophecy is the destruction of Nineveh, which
Nahum introduces, after having in the first chapter, and at the
beginning of the second, depicted the desolate condition to which,
in the righteous providence of God, the country of the ten tribes
had been reduced by the Assyrian power; the invasion of Judah
by Sennacherib, whose destruction, and that of his army, he predicts; and the joyful restoration of both the captivities to their
own land, and the enjoyment of their former privileges. His
object obviously was, to inspire his countrymen with the assurance,
that, however alarming their circumstances might appear, exposed
as they were to the formidable army of the great Eastern conqueror,
not only should his attempt fail, and his forces be entirely destroyed, but his capital itself should be taken, and his empire
overturned. The book is not to be divided into three separate
parts, or prophecies, composed at different times, as some have
imagined, but is to be regarded as one entire poem, the unity of
which is plainly discoverable throughout.

The style of Nahum is of a very high order. He is inferior to
none of the minor prophets, and scarcely to Isaiah himself, in
animation, boldness, and sublimity; or, to the extent and proportion of his book, in the variety, freshness, richness, elegance,
and force of his imagery. The rhythm is regular and singularly
beautiful; and with the exception of a few foreign or provincial
words, his language possesses the highest degree of classical purity.
His description of the Divine character at the commencement is
truly majestic; that of the siege and fall of Nineveh inimitably
graphic, vivid, and impressive.

CHAPTER I

The prophet opens with a sublime description of the attributes and operations of Jehovah, with a view to inspire his people with confidence in his protection, 2—8. The Assyrians are then unexpectedly addressed and described, 9—11; and their destruction, together with the deliverance of the Jews connected with that event, are set forth in the language of triumph and exultation, 12—14.

1   THE SENTENCE OF NINEVEH:
     The Book of the Vision of Nahum the Elkoshite.
2   Jehovah is a jealous and avenging God;
     Jehovah is an avenger and furious;
     Jehovah is an avenger with respect to his adversaries;
     Yea, he keepeth his anger for his enemies.

1. For the meaning of מַשָּׂא, see on Is. xiii. 1; and for the historical circumstances connected with *Nineveh*, see on Jonah i. 2. Between the time of the prophet just referred to and that of Nahum, there must have elapsed a period of above one hundred years.—The inscription consists of two parts; the former of which is supposed by some to be from a later hand. If genuine, we should rather have expected the order to be reversed.

2. The exordium, which begins here and reaches to ver. 8, is highly magnificent. The repeated use of the Incommunicable Name, and of the participle נֹקֵם, *avenging* or *avenger*, gives great force to the commencement. Nothing can exceed in grandeur and sublimity the description which the prophet furnishes of the Divine character. The attributes of infinite purity, inflexible

rectitude, irresistible power, and boundless goodness, set forth and illustrated by images borrowed from the history of the Hebrews, the scenery of Palestine, and the more astounding phenomena of nature, present to view a God worthy of the profoundest reverence, the most unbounded confidence, and the most intensive love. How inferior the otherwise sublime description given of the anger of Jove by Æschylus:

χθὼν σεσάλευται·
βρυχία δ'ἠχὼ παραμυκᾶται
βροντῆς, ἕλικες δ' ἐκλάμπουσι
στεροπῆς ζάπυροι, στρόμβοι δὲ κόνιν
εἱλίσσουσι· σκιρτᾷ δ' ἀνέμων
πνεύματα πάντων, εἰς ἄλληλα
στάσιν ἀντίπνουν ἀποδεικνύμενα.
            Prom. vinctus, 1089.

קַנּוֹא, *jealous*, from קָנָא, *to be warm*, ζηλόω, *burn with zeal, anger, jealousy.* The

3 Jehovah is long-suffering, but great in power,
  And he will by no means treat them as innocent:
  Jehovah hath his way in the whirlwind and in the storm,
  And the clouds are the dust of his feet.

4 He rebuketh the sea, and maketh it dry,
  And he parcheth up all the rivers:
  Bashan languisheth, and Carmel,
  And the bloom of Lebanon languisheth.

5 The mountains quake at him,
  And the hills are melted;
  The earth also heaves at his presence,
  Even the world and all that inhabit it.

6 Before his indignation who can stand?
  And who can subsist in the heat of his anger?

term is here used ἀνθρωποπαθῶς, principally in the last of these acceptations, though not to the entire exclusion of the others. The term describes a keen feeling of injured right, coupled with a strong inclination to see justice done to the parties concerned. בַּעַל חֵמָה, lit. *a lord*, or *master of fury*, an idiom by which the possession of an attribute or quality is frequently expressed. Comp. בַּעַל הַחֲלֹמֹות, *a master of dreams*, i.e. a dreamer; בַּעַל הַלָּשׁוֹן, *a master of the tongue*, i.e. eloquent. In these verses the prophet appears to have an eye specially to the judgments which God had brought upon his country by means of the Assyrians, both when they carried away the ten tribes, and now when they had again rushed into the land, and taken the fortified cities of Judah. נָטַר, properly signifies to *watch*, *observe*, in a bad sense, *to mark* for punishment. Arab. نظر, *oculos convertit ad rem*; نظر, *custodem et observatorem egit*. Comp. Ps. ciii. 9; Jer. iii. 5, 12; and שָׁמַר, Ps. cxxx. 3.

3. נַקֵּה לֹא יְנַקֶּה, *holding pure will not hold pure*, i.e. will not treat as innocent those who are guilty, but, on the contrary, punish them according to their demerit. LXX., ἀθῷον οὐκ ἀθῳώσει. Comp. Exod. xx. 7; xxxiv. 7. The idea conveyed by the metaphor, *the clouds are the dust of his feet*, is exceedingly

sublime. Large and majestic as the clouds may be, in reference to God they are but as the most minute particles of dust raised by the feet in walking. אָבָק, signifies *light dust* or powder, what is easily raised.

4. What is here predicated of Jehovah is attributed to our Saviour, Luke viii. 24: ἐπετίμησε—τῷ κλύδωνι τοῦ ὕδατος. The action involves omnipotence. וַיַּבְּשֵׁהוּ is a contracted form of the Piel, for וַיְיַבְּשֵׁהוּ, as וַיְמֵה for וַיְיֵמֵה, Lam. iii. 33, in both of which the radical Yod gives its vowel to the preformative letter.

5. There is no authority for rendering וַתִּשָּׂא, *to be burnt up:* none of the MSS. or ancient versions directing us to any root signifying *to burn*. The verb is likewise thus rendered in our common version, 2 Sam. v. 21, but the marginal reading is, *took them away*. The Targ. indeed has חֲרוֹבַת, *vastata est*, but the LXX. render ἀνεστάλη. Symm. ἐκινήθη. The Syr. ܐܬܬܙܝܥ, *shaketh*. Vulg. *contremuit*. The root is נָשָׂא, *to raise, lift up;* intransitively, *to lift up oneself;* and appropriately expresses here the raising or heaving of the ground by an earthquake.

6. The *pouring out* of wrath, *like fire*, would seem to be a comparison taken from volcanoes, which pour out furiously their streams of liquid fire over the

His fury is poured out like fire,
And the rocks are overthrown by him.

7 Jehovah is good, a fortress in the day of distress;
And knoweth those that trust in him.

8 But with an overflowing inundation
He will effect a consummation of her place,
And darkness shall pursue his enemies.

9 What devise ye against Jehovah?
He will effect a consummation;
Distress shall not twice arise.

circumjacent regions. The breaking in pieces of the rocks, in the following hemistich, confirms this idea. Comp. Jer. li. 25, 26.

7, 8. There is a marked antithesis in these two verses, in the course of which the prophet arrives at his main topic, the destruction of Nineveh. Ver. 7 beautifully depicts the safety and happiness of those who make God their refuge, how severe soever may be the calamity which threatens or may have overtaken them; and was primarily intended to administer comfort to the pious Jews in the prospect of the Assyrian attack by Sennacherib. יָדַע, *to know*, is here, as frequently, taken in the sense of *knowing* with *regard*, *kindness*, or *love*. Comp. Ps. i. 6; cxliv. 3; Amos. iii. 2. In וּבְשֶׁטֶף עֹבֵר, the metaphor of a river impetuously overflowing its banks, rushing into the adjacent country, and passing through, carrying all before it, is employed to denote the ruthless invasion of a country by a hostile and powerful army. It is used by Isaiah, chap. viii. 8, to describe the resistless entrance of the Assyrian army into Palestine; and here Nahum appropriates the language for the purpose of describing the triumphant progress of the Medo-Babylonian troops when advancing towards Nineveh. He not only beholds, in prophetic vision, their approach to the devoted city, but announces its complete destruction. It is usual with the prophets, as it is with the Oriental poets, when powerfully affected, to introduce into their discourse persons or objects as acting, without having previously named them. See on Is. xiii. 2; and comp. מְקֹמָהּ, ver. 11 of the present chapter. See Nord-

heimer's Heb. Gram., § 867. They, as it were, take it for granted, that every one must, like themselves, clearly perceive the reference. On this principle there can be no difficulty in accounting for the feminine pronominal affix in מְקֹמָהּ, " *her* place," *i. e.* the place of Nineveh, the עִיר, *city*, or metropolis of Assyria, the overthrow of which the prophet was afterwards to describe, and which he here merely touches upon by way of anticipation. The use of מָקוֹם, *place*, is not without emphasis. Comp. chap. iii. 17. Those who desire to see the difference of opinion existing both among ancient and modern writers respecting the actual site of Nineveh, may consult Bochart, Phaleg. lib. iv. cap. xx. Lucian, speaking of it, says, ἡ Νίνος μὲν ἀπόλωλεν ἤδη, καὶ οὐδὲν ἴχνος ἔτι λοιπὸν αὐτῆς, οὐδ᾽ ἂν εἴπῃς ὅπου ποτ᾽ ἦν. Dialog. entitled Ἐπισκοποῦντες. Bochart, referring to the city of the name mentioned by Ammianus, expresses himself thus: "Merito dubitatur an restaurata fuerit *eo in loco*, in quo prius condita." In the Hebrew MSS., there is no various reading of מְקֹמָהּ; but the rendering of the LXX., τοὺς ἐπεγειρομένους, and of Aq., ἀντισταμένων, supported by Theod. and the fifth Greek version, would indicate, that their authors read מְקִימֶיהָ or מְתְקוֹמְמֶיהָ, in favour of which אֹיְבָיו in the following hemistich might be adduced. The Syriac, however, Vulg., and Symm., read with the received text.

9. By a sudden apostrophe Nahum here turns to the invaders, and boldly challenges them to account for their temerity in daring to oppose themselves to Jehovah. On which he repeats what he had declared in the preceding verse

10 For though they are closely interwoven as thorns,
    And thoroughly soaked with their wine,
    They shall be consumed like stubble fully dry.
11 From thee he came forth,
    The deviser of mischief against Jehovah,
    The wicked counsellor.
12 Thus saith Jehovah:
    Though they are complete and so very numerous,
    Yet in this state they shall be cut down,
    And he shall pass away :

respecting the total destruction of the
Assyrian power, and adds, for the special
encouragement of the Jews, that it should
never annoy them again. The parallel
to this brief apostrophe we have more
at length, Is. xxxvii. 23—29. For the
force of פַּעֲמַיִם, *twice*, comp. וְלֹא אַחַת פַּעַם
אֶשְׁנֶה לּוֹ, 1 Sam. xxvi. 8. That the renewal
of the affliction does not refer to any
supposable future overthrow of the
Assyrians, as Michaelis, Rosenmüller,
Hitzig, Ewald, and others maintain,
but to any further calamity to be apprehended from them by the Jews, appears
from ver. 12 to be the true construction
of the meaning.

10. However strong and vigorous the
Assyrian army might be, its complete
destruction would easily be effected by
Jehovah. עַי, *to, even to*, is here used as
a comparative particle of degree : *to the
same degree as*, or *like* thorns. Comp.
1 Chron. iv. 27. Briers and thorns are
employed by the prophets to denote
the soldiers composing a hostile army.
See Is. x. 17; xxvii. 4. The metaphor
is here taken from a thicket of thorns,
the prickly branches of which are so
closely intertwined as to present an
impenetrable front to those who would
enter it. Such were the celebrated
military phalanxes of antiquity, consisting of bodies of troops armed with
long spears, and arranged in the form
of a square. The other metaphor is
taken from drunkards who drench or
saturate themselves with wine, and
denotes the degree of moisture which
those thorny warriors possessed, and
by which they were prepared to resist
the action of fire.—No account is to
be made of the reading שָׂרֵי, *princes*,

which Newcome adopts from the Targ.
and Syr. It is found in no Heb. MS.—
אָכַל, *to eat*, is often used to express
consumption by fire. The application
of the language in this and the preceding
verse to the literal inundation of the
Tigris, the drunkenness of the Assyrian
camp, and the burning of the palace,
&c., at Nineveh by Sardanapalus, as
related by Diodorus Siculus, lib. ii., is
not justified either by the import and
usage of the terms, or by chronology,
the catastrophe described by Nahum not
having taken place till long after the
time of that monarch.

11. מִמֵּךְ, *from thee*, O Nineveh ! in the
feminine. Sennacherib, whose machinations against Jehovah had been adverted
to ver. 9, is here intended. The Heb.
בְּלִיַּעַל, frequently rendered in our common
version *Belial*, properly signifies *worthlessness, inutility*, and by implication,
badness in a moral sense, *wickedness*.
Hence the idiomatic combinations, אָדָם
בְּלִיַּעַל, *a man of Belial*, a wicked man ;
בֶּן־בְּלִיַּעַל, *a son of Belial*, a bad man ;
בַּת־בְּלִיַּעַל, *a daughter of Belial*, a wicked
woman. The word is compounded of
בְּלִי, *without*, and יַעַל, *profit*.

12. Another description of the formidable appearance of the hostile army,
accompanied with a prediction of its
sudden and complete annihilation, the
flight of Sennacherib, and the future
immunity of the Jews from an invasion
on the part of the Assyrians. שְׁלֵמִים,
complete, expresses the unbroken condition of the army of the enemy, and
their being fully provided with every
thing requisite for the successful siege
of Jerusalem. The word may also be
designed to convey the idea of mental

Though I have afflicted thee,

I will afflict thee no more.

13 For now I will break his yoke from off thee,

And burst thy bands asunder.

14　　And with respect to thee, Jehovah hath commanded:

There shall no more be sown any of thy name;

From the house of thy gods I will cut off the graven and the

molten image;

completeness, *i.e.* in this connexion, *security, martial courage*. Thus Kimchi, לא יפחדו מאדם כי כל הארצות כבשו, *they are not afraid of man, for they have subdued all the countries.* כן, as used the second time, signifies *thus, so, in this state, as thus constituted.* The change of number from the plural נָגֹזּוּ, " *they* are, or shall be cut down," to עָבָר, " *he* passeth away," is obviously intended to distinguish between the overthrow of the Assyrian army, and the immediate departure of Sennacherib to his own land. The nominative to עָבָר is יוֹעֵץ בְּלִיַּעַל in the preceding verse. גּזז, *to cut*, or *mow down*, is a metaphor derived from the hay-harvest, and forcibly sets forth the sudden and entire destruction of an army. See for the historical facts, 2 Kings xix. 35, 36; Is. xxxvii. 36, 37. At the close of the verse, Jehovah directs the discourse to his people, graciously assuring them that, though he had employed the Assyrian power to punish them, he would do so no more. New-come, almost entirely on the authority of the LXX., improperly changes אִם שְׁלֵמִים into אִם מֹשֵׁל מַיִם רַבִּים כֵּן וְכֵן רַבִּים נָגֹזּוּ וְעָבָר כֵּן וְכֵן עָבָר, " Though the Ruler of many waters has thus ravaged, and thus passed through." That these ancient translators did, from hearing אִם שְׁלֵמִים read as מֹשֵׁל מַיִם, render, κατάρχων ὑδάτων πολλῶν, there can be no doubt; but then, they place the words in apposition with τάδε λέγει κύριος; and make the Lord, and not the king of Assyria, to be " the ruler of many waters." The Syr., following the LXX., only changing the singular into the plural, has

" respecting the heads of many waters." עִנִּיתֵךְ is merely

a defective reading of עֲנִּיתִיךְ, which is found in a number of MSS., and in some editions. The object of the verb is *Judah*, understood, which Jehovah here kindly addresses, and not Nineveh, as Michaelis and Hitzig suppose. The Jews are addressed as a female, as they are in the words חַגִּי יְהוּדָה חַגַּיִךְ שַׁלְּמִי נְדָרָיִךְ, *Celebrate thy festivals, O Judah! perform thy vows*, chap. ii. 1. On the introduction of a predicate without previous mention of the subject, see on ver. 8. The meaning is, that the Jews were to be no more afflicted by the Assyrians, and not that Divine judgments were never afterwards to be inflicted upon them by others.

13. The suffix ךְ has here the same reference as in the preceding verse, and הוּ in מֹטֵהוּ, " *his* yoke," to the king of Assyria. Comp. Is. x. 27; Jer. ii. 20. For מֹטֵהוּ, some think the LXX. and Vulg. read מַטֵּהוּ, which is the reading of several MSS.; but they both signify *a staff* or pole; only the former denotes what is placed on the neck, in order to bear a burden.

14. We have here another apostrophe to the Assyrian monarch, announcing to him, that his dynasty should not be perpetuated, that his favourite idols should be destroyed, and that the very temple in which he worshipped them should become his grave. When it is said, that " no more of thy name shall be sown," the meaning is not, that none of his sons should succeed him in the government, but that his dynasty should cease on the arrival of the event predicted by Nahum, the destruction of Nineveh. The Medes being great enemies to idolatry, those of them who composed the army of Cyaxares would take singular pleasure in destroying the idols which they found in the chief temple at Nineveh. No mention is made

I will make it thy grave,
Because thou art worthless.

in history of the sepulture of Sennacherib, but we are expressly told,
2 Kings xix. 37, Is. xxxvii. 38, that he
was slain by two of his sons while in the
act of worship in the temple of Nisroch
his god; and there can be no doubt that
it is to this event reference is here made.
אֵשִׂים stands elliptically for אֲשִׂימֶנּוּ, *I will
make it*, i.e. the temple of thy gods, *thy
grave.* Some take קַלּוֹתָ, *thou art light*,

in the same sense in which the Chaldee
תְּקַל is used Dan. v. 27, but without
sufficient ground in Hebrew usage.
In application to persons it always signifies to be the object of shame or disgrace. Though to be buried in a temple
naturally conveys to our minds the idea
of honourable interment, it is otherwise
here, owing to the peculiar circumstances
of the case.

CHAPTER II

After prophetically describing the joyful announcement of the overthrow of the
Assyrian power, 1; and calling upon the Jews manfully to defend Jerusalem
against the attack of Sennacherib, in the assurance that there would be a glorious
restoration of the whole Hebrew people, 2, 3; the prophet arrives at his main
subject, the destruction of Nineveh, the siege and capture of which he portrays
with graphic minuteness, and in the most sublime and vivid manner, 4—11. In
a beautiful allegory he then, with triumphant sarcasm, asks where was now the
residence of the once conquering and rapacious monarch? 12, 13; after which,
Jehovah is introduced, expressly declaring that he would assuredly perform what
he had inspired his servant to predict, 14.

---

1 BEHOLD! upon the mountains are the feet of him that an-
     nounceth good,
   That publisheth peace:
   Celebrate thy feasts, O Judah! perform thy vows,
   For the wicked shall no more pass through thee;
   He is entirely cut off.

1. Some interpreters refer these words
to the messengers who should arrive
from the East, announcing to the inhabitants of Judah the joyful intelligence
of the destruction of Nineveh, which had
been briefly hinted at in the course of
the preceding chapter; but it better
accords with the spirit and bearing of
the immediate connexion to apply them

to what took place on the miraculous
deliverance of Jerusalem, recorded Is.
xxxvii. 36. They are almost identical,
so far as they go, with the language of
Isaiah, chap. lii. 7, relative to the return
from Babylon. During the Assyrian
invasion, the inhabitants of Judah were
cut off from all access to the metropolis;
now, they would be at liberty to proceed

2 The disperser hath come up before thee ;
   Keep the fortress, watch the way,
   Make fast the loins,
   Strengthen thee with power to the utmost.
3 For Jehovah will restore the excellency of Jacob,
   As he will the excellency of Israel ;
   Though the emptiers have emptied them,
   And destroyed their branches.
4 The shield of his heroes is dyed red,
   The warriors are clothed with scarlet ;

thither as usual, in order to observe their religious rites. בְּלִיַּעַל, *Belial*, doubtless means the same as יֹעֵץ בְּלִיַּעַל, *wicked counsellor*, chap. i. 11; *i.e.* as there explained, Sennacherib. Restricted as the declaration here made must necessarily be to this monarch, the passage is nowise at variance with the fact, that Manasseh was for a time in the power of the Assyrians, 2 Chron. xxxiii. 11.

2. Most moderns adopt the interpretation of Jerome, who is of opinion, that the prophet here turns to Nineveh, and directs the attention of her monarch to the approach of the Medo-Babylonish army. I rather think with Abarbanel, Kimchi, Jarchi, Hezel, Dathe, and others, that the words are addressed to Hezekiah, and the inhabitants of Jerusalem, for the purpose of inspiring them with courage to hold out during the Assyrian attack. מֵפִיץ, (from פּוּץ, Arab. فيض, *abiit, peregrinatus fuit, to scatter, disperse,*) properly signifies *the Disperser*, and is appropriately applied to the king of Assyria, by whose army the inhabitants of the different countries which it invaded were scattered from their abodes. Some prefer rendering the word by *hammer*, and compare Prov. xxv. 18, and Jer. li. 20, in the latter of which passages we have מַפֵּץ from פָּצַץ, *to break in pieces, disperse*, &c., rendered in our common version *battle-axe*. The address is beautifully abrupt, and derives great force from the use of the Infinitive instead of the Imperative of all the four verbs which here occur. The fuller forms would be נָצוֹר נְצוֹר, צַפֵּה תְּצַפֶּה, &c. נָצוֹר מְצוּרָה form a paronomasia.

3. Further to encourage the inhabitants of Jerusalem, a promise is here given of the restoration of the Hebrew people to their former independence and glory. גְּאוֹן יַעֲקֹב, &c., is not to be interpreted of the pride of the Hebrews, nor of the proud and insulting conduct of their enemies towards them; but, as in Ps. xlvii. 5, and Amos vi. 8, it means the land of Canaan, as distinguished above all other countries. This land, as the prophet immediately adds, had been spoiled by the Assyrians, who had not only carried away the ten tribes into captivity, but taken the fortified cities of Judah; but it was again to be restored, partly on the destruction of the Assyrians, and completely on the return from Babylon. שָׁב, *to return*, has here the force of the Hiphil הֵשִׁיב, *to restore*, as in Numb. x. 36; Ps. lxxxv. 5. Connected as this verb is with the future, implied in the abbreviated form בְּצוֹר, &c., in the preceding verse, it is to be rendered in this tense. *Jacob* and *Israel* are, as frequently, put for the people of the two kingdoms. The devastation effected by the Assyrians is described by a metaphor taken from the pruning of vines, or the cutting off of the young twigs or shoots. Parallel to the promise made in this verse is that given by Isaiah, chap. xxxvii. 31, 32.

4. The prophet now proceeds to describe the siege and capture of Nineveh, which involved the downfal of the Assyrian empire. The formidable, terrific, and invincible appearance of the Medo-Babylonish army is first noticed. גִּבּוֹרֵיהוּ, *his heroes*, i.e. the mighty men of Cyaxares. The suffix is the less fre-

The chariots are furnished with fiery scythes,
In the day of his preparation ;
And the cypresses are brandished.

quent form, instead of יֶ־, but represents more of the primitive pronoun הוּא, of which both are fragments. מְאָדָּם is the Pual participle of אָדַם, *to be red ;* and is applied to the shields, to intimate that they were dyed red. The bull's hide with which they were commonly covered was easily susceptible of this process ; and, on being anointed with oil, would shine brightly. See on Is. xxi. 5. This interpretation of the word, which is confirmed by the meaning of the corresponding participle, in the following hemistich, is preferable to that which would make it express the idea of *fiery, sparkling,* or the like. " Bloodstained " is altogether to be rejected. The LXX. mistaking מְאָדָּם for מֵאָדָם, preposterously render ὅπλα δυναστείας αὐτῶν ἐξ ἀνθρώπων. מְתֻלָּעִים, lit. *are crimsoned,* is a ἅπαξ λεγ., but is the Pual participial form, and is evidently derived from תּוֹלָע, the name specially used to denote the *coccus,* or *worm* which was used in dyeing, to give to cloth a deep scarlet colour. The manufacture of such stuffs was chiefly carried on by the Tyrians and Lydians. The LXX. have also mistaken this word for מִתְהוֹלְלִים, ἐμπαίζοντας, in which they are followed by the Syriac. Pollux describes the Medes as wearing a cloth called *Sarages,* which was of scarlet colour, striped with white ; Σαράγης, Μήδων τὶ φόρημα, πορφυροῦς, μεσόλευκος χιτών. Lib. vii. cap. 13. —בְּאֵשׁ פְּלָדת, *with fiery scythes.* That פְּלָדת stands here by transposition of the two first letters for לְפִדֹת, cannot be admitted ; the plural of לַפִּיד, *a lamp,* or *torch,* being always לַפִּידִים, in the masculine, so that the Syr., Targ., &c., give an erroneous interpretation. פְּלָדָה, *iron, steel.* Syr.

ܦܠܕܐ the same. Comp. the Arab.

فَلَاذ, *secuit, in partes concidit.*

ferrum durum, chalybs. مَفلُون, *e chalybe*

confectus (de gladio). For the manufacture of swords of the finest steel, not only Damascus but certain towns on the

east of the Caucasus have long been celebrated ; and that this compound metal is of high antiquity, is universally allowed. Its name, *Chalybs,* is derived from the Chalybes, a people bordering on the Euxine sea. It is doubtless what the prophet Jeremiah means by בַּרְזֶל מִצָּפוֹן, *iron from the North,* and which he distinguishes from בַּרְזֶל, *common iron,* chap. xv. 12. Now there appears to be no part of the war-chariots entitled to the character of irons flashing with fire, but the falces or scythes, which were " fixed at right angles to the axle, and turned downwards ; or inserted parallel to the axle into the felly of the wheel, so as to revolve, when the chariot was put in motion, with more than thrice the velocity of the chariot itself ; and sometimes also projecting from the extremities of the axle." Dr. William Smith's Dict. of Greek and Roman Antiquities, art. *Falx.* The ἅρματα δρεπανηφόρα were justly reckoned among the most terrific implements of ancient warfare, as they mowed down all that came in their way. In the אֵשׁ, *fire,* of these scythes is a reference to the coruscations produced by their excessive brightness and the rapidity of their motion. Instead of בְּאֵשׁ, " *with* fire," seven MSS., originally one more, and the Soncin. edition of the Prophets, read כְּאֵשׁ, " *like* fire." The suffix in הֲכִינוֹ may either form an accusative to הֵכִין, or the genitive of an agent not mentioned—the hostile commander. The latter construction is preferable, as it refers *the day of his preparation* to the period fixed upon by the general for commencing the attack. It would only be then that the scythes would be fixed in the chariots : it being not only useless but dangerous to have them attached at other times. By בְּרוֹשִׁים, *cypresses,* are meant *spears* or *lances,* the staves of which were made of the branches of the cypress. The LXX., followed by the Syr. and Arab., have taken the word for פָּרָשִׁים, *horsemen,* rendering it οἱ ἱππεῖς, which Michaelis is inclined to prefer, and Newcome has actually adopted. There is, however,

5 The chariots dash madly on the commons,
   They run furiously in the open places;
   Their appearance is like that of torches,
   They flash like lightnings.
6   He remembers his nobles;
   They stumble in their march;

no just cause for stumbling at the boldness of the figure. Homer, describing
the spear of Achilles, calls it an *ash*:

Ἐκ δ' ἄρα σύριγγος πατρώϊον ἐσπάσατ'
   ἔγχος,
Βριθὺ, μέγα, στιβαρόν· τὸ μὲν οὐ δύνατ'
   ἄλλος Ἀχαιῶν
Πάλλειν, ἀλλά μιν οἶος ἐπίστατο πῆλαι
   Ἀχιλλεύς,
Πηλιάδα ΜΕΛΙΗΝ, κ. τ. λ.
                    Iliad. xix. 387—390.

Hesiod also designates the lance ἐλάτη,
a pine, Scut. Herc. 188; and Virgil
uses the *fir* for the spear of Camilla:

——————"cujus apertum
Adversi longâ transverberat *abiete* pectus."   *Æneid.* xi. 667.

הָרְעָלוּ, a *ἅπαξ* λεγ., from the root רָעַל,
Syr. ܪܥܠ, *tremuit, to move tremulously,
wave, shake;* hence רַעַל and תַּרְעֵלָה, *trembling,* Zech. xii. 2; Ps. lx. 5. The reference seems to be to the custom of the
spear-men to wave their lances before
engaging in battle, for the purpose of
evincing their eagerness for the contest.
5. This verse Ewald explains of the
preparations made by the Ninevites for
the defence of the city; but the war-
chariots could not be used within the
walls: they could only be effective in
the open field. חוּצוֹת signifies not merely
streets, as being *without* the houses of a
city, but also the *out-fields* or *commons*
without the city itself. Comp. Job. v. 10;
Ps. cxliv. 13; Prov. viii. 26. In like
manner רְחֹבוֹת, as its parallel, denotes
any wide or open spaces in the suburbs
without the gates. Comp. 2 Chron.
xxxii. 6; Ps. cxliv. 14. הִתְהוֹלָל signifies
*to act the part of a madman, to show
oneself violent, to rage,* and the like. The
reduplicate form יִשְׁתַּקְשְׁקוּן is obviously
intended to give great force to the
expression; on which account, to render

it *run up and down* is too weak. I have
added *furiously,* which makes this hemistich better agree with the preceding.
Nor is the reduplication of the third radical of רוּץ, *to run,* in Piel, יְרוֹצְצוּ, without
a corresponding degree of energy. It
expresses the rapid zig-zag course of the
chariots, resembling the quick flashing
of lightning. As רֶכֶב is masculine, the
feminine suffix in מַרְאֵיהֶן must be taken
for a neuter, or regarded as an instance
of neglected gender.
6. The king of Nineveh is here represented as roused from a profound stupor;
and, contriving the necessary means of
defence, as first of all turning his attention to his principal officers, whom he
summons to their posts. Michaelis,
Maurer, and others think that by these
officers, the generals commanding in
the provinces are intended; but it is more
likely the prophet means the military
leaders within the city, since it is represented in the preceding verses as already
invested by the enemy; and they are
spoken of as hastening to the wall, and
not to the city, which the former interpretation would require. זָכַר is here used,
not in the sense of simply recollecting,
or calling to mind, but with the acces-
sory idea of carrying out or giving effect
to the recollection, in regard to the object
of remembrance. It therefore implies,
that the monarch ordered them to occupy
each his place in the defence of Nineveh.
On receiving the orders, they make such
haste, that they and their troops stumble
while marching to the walls. Instead
of ה in הֲלִיכָתָם, eight of De Rossi's MSS.,
another originally, the Brixian, and
another ancient edition, exhibit the local
ה, which is supported by the Targ., Syr.,
and Arab. By the סֹכֵךְ, *protector,* or
protection, here mentioned, some understand the *vinea,* or the *testudo,* military
coverings used by the besiegers of a city,
under the shelter of which they might
safely carry on their operations in under-

> They hasten to her wall,
> And the defence is prepared.
>
> 7 The flood-gates are opened,
> And the palace is dissolved,
> Though firmly established.
>
> 8 She is made bare; she is carried up,
> While her handmaids moan like doves,
> And smite upon their hearts.

mining, or otherwise destroying the walls. As, however, the term is here applied to something employed by those who acted on the defensive, it cannot be so interpreted. In all probability, some kind of breastwork, composed of the interwoven boughs and branches of trees, erected between the towers upon the walls, is intended. According to Diodorus Siculus, Nineveh had fifteen hundred towers, each of which was two hundred feet high. סָכַךְ signifies *to weave, intertwine, fence,* and the like, and so to *protect, shelter.* LXX. καὶ ἑτοιμάσουσι

τὰς προφυλακὰς αὐτῶν. Syr. ܚܣܝܢܐ,

fortifications. Targ. מִגְדְלַיָּא, *towers.*

7, 8. Though it is not unusual in Hebrew to represent invading armies or multitudes of people under the image of floods or waters, an interpretation adopted here by Rosenmüller, De Wette, and others, there does not appear to be sufficient ground to depart from the literal meaning. By נְהָרוֹת, *rivers* or *streams,* are meant the canals dug from the Tigris, which intersected the city, and more especially those which afforded a supply of water for the defence of the palace. The gates or sluices of these canals were doubtless strongly constructed, to prevent a greater influx of water than what was required; but having upon the present occasion been burst open by the besiegers, the waters of the Tigris rushed in, and, completely inundating the royal residence, dissolved and ruined it. The verb נָמוֹג describes the physical effects of the inundation, not metaphorically those produced by the event upon the minds of the inhabitants. הֻצַּב, ver. 8, has occasioned a great diversity of interpretations. Gesenius, dissatisfied with all those derived from its being the

Hophal of נָצַב, *to place, settle, fix,* has recourse to a new root, צָבַב, which he borrows from the Arab. ضَبَّ, *fluxit, stillavit* aqua, ضَبَّ, *fudit, effudit;* and then removing the word to the end of the preceding verse, reads thus, הַהֵיכָל נָמוֹג וְהֻצַּב, *the palace is dissolved and made to flow away.* That the verb is to be connected with the preceding נָמוֹג, the gender at once shows; but there is no necessity for departing from the usual signification of נָצַב, *to place, fix, stand firmly;* in Hiph. *to cause to stand, establish.* However strongly the palace might have been constructed, it would not be able to resist the fury of the water. וּ has here the force of *though, and though.* Comp. וְהִיא חֲרוּפָה, Mal. ii. 14. The nominative to the feminines גֻּלְּתָה and הֹעֲלָתָה is Nineveh understood. The first of these verbs some render, *is carried into captivity;* but this signification is confined to the Kal and Hiphil conjugations. It here describes the ignominy with which the Ninevites were treated, when, stripped of everything, they were forced from their capital. Comp. Is. xlvii. 3. Nineveh is represented as a queen degraded from her dignity, and led away captive by the enemy; her female slaves following and deploring her fate. That the queen of Nineveh herself, supposed to be here called *Huzzab,* is intended, is a position which cannot be sustained, though adopted by several interpreters, and recently by Ewald. Persons are never introduced by name into prophecy, except for some important purpose, as in the case of Cyrus. For נָהַג, *to pant, sigh, moan,* comp. the Arab.

نَهَجَ, *graviter, continuo anhelavit, vix*

9 Though Nineveh hath been like a pool of water,
   From the most ancient time,
   Yet they are fleeing :
   " Stop ! stop ! " but none looketh back.
10 Plunder the silver, plunder the gold ;
   There is no end to the store ;
   There is abundance of all covetable vessels.
11 Emptiness and emptiedness and void,
   Heart-melting and tottering of knees ;
   There is intense pain in all loins,
   And all faces withdraw their colour.
12   Where is the den of the lionesses ?
   And the feeding-place of the young lions ?
   Where the lion and the lioness walked,
   The lion's cub also, and none disturbed them.

interrupto spiritu ; Syr. ܓܥܐ, *clamavit, rugiit.*

9. The comparison of the population of Nineveh to a collection of water is here appropriate. מִימֵי הִיא is an antiquated mode of expressing the feminine pronominal affix—the absolute form of the pronoun being retained instead of the fragmental הָ being attached to the noun, מִימֶיהָ=מִימֵי הִיא; lit. *from her days,* i. e. during the whole period of her existence, or, from the most ancient time. The prophet compares the royal city to a reservoir of water, on account of the confluence of people from the surrounding provinces. All who could make their escape, now took to flight, and no entreaties could induce them to remain.

10. Nahum here apostrophizes the victorious enemy. They had now only to possess themselves of the immense riches which had been abandoned by the inhabitants, or which they might plunder at pleasure. The repetition of the verb בֹּזּוּ gives force to the diction. תְּכוּנָה, from כּוּן, in Hiphil, *to set up, prepare ;* anything *laid up, prepared,* and *ready for use,* as costly garments, ornaments, &c. Comp. Job. xxvii. 16. LXX. τοῦ κόσμου αὐτῆς. Vulg. *divitiarum.* Targ. אוֹצָרַיָּא, *treasures.* בָּבֹד, followed by מִן, is here a nominative absolute : *as for the abundance, it consists of,* &c.

11. The three synonymes, מְבֻקָה, בּוּקָה, מְבֻלָּקָה, all from roots signifying *to empty, empty out,* are exquisitely chosen, and from their increase in length, as well as from their similarity both in sound and meaning, give great force to the expression of total desolation—the idea here intended to be conveyed. Gesenius considers them to be onomatopoetic, imitating the sound of emptying out a bottle. Comp. Is. xxiv. 1, for the etymology of the verbs בּוּק=בָּקַק and בָּלַק ; and for a similar use of words varied in form, but nearly alike in sound, Is. xxiv. 3, 4 ; xxix. 2 ; Ezek. xxxiii. 29 ; xxxv. 3 ; Zeph. i. 15. הַלְחָלָה, an intensive form, from חוּל, *to be in pain.* For פָּארוּר see on Joel ii. 6.

12—14. A beautiful allegory, setting forth the rapacious, irresistible, and luxurious character of the king of Assyria, and the destruction of Nineveh, the seat of his empire, with all his armies and their means of supply. In the last verse the literal is intermixed with the figurative. Comp. for the metaphor, Is. v. 29 ; Jer. ii. 15. הוּא, in ver. 12, has the force of *that which ;* דְּ, ver. 13, *a sufficiency, supply,* &c. טֶרֶף and מִרְעֶה are employed idiomatically in the two genders to express different kinds of prey. Comp. Is. iii. 1. For בְּעָשָׁן the Targ. has בְּאֶשָּׁתָא, *with fire.* The meaning is, that such should be the number of chariots

13 The lion tore for the supply of his cubs,
   And strangled for his lionesses ;
   He filled his dens with prey,
   And his habitations with rapine.

14   Behold ! I am against thee, saith Jehovah of hosts ;
   And I will burn her chariots into smoke ;
   The sword also shall devour thy young lions,
   I will likewise cut off thy prey from the land :
   And the voice of thy messengers shall be heard no more.

consumed, that the smoke arising from the fire in which they were to be burned, should be visible to all. Comp. Ps. xxxvii. 20. The MSS. and editions differ in their punctuation of מלאככה, but there can be little doubt that it is a defective reading, מַלְאָכְבָה, for מַלְאֲכֵיכָה. Comp. פְּפֶּךָ, Ps. cxxxix. 5. The Syr. and LXX. have read מַלְאכְתֵךָ, "thy works."

CHAPTER III

The prophet, resuming his description of the siege of Nineveh, 1—3, traces it to her idolatry as its cause, 4, and the divine denunciations which he had introduced chap. ii. 14, he repeats, ver. 5—7. He then, to aggravate her misery, points her to the once formidable and celebrated, but now conquered and desolate Thebes, 8—10, declaring that such should likewise be her fate, 11—13; calls upon her sarcastically to make every preparation for her defence, but assures her that it would be of no avail, 14, 15; and concludes by contrasting with the number of merchants, princes, and generals, which she once possessed, the miserable, remediless state of ruin to which she was to be reduced, 16—19.

---

1 Wo to the city of blood !
   She is wholly filled with deceit and violence ;
   The prey is not removed.

2 The sound of the whip, and the sound of the rattling of the wheels,
   The horses prancing, and the chariots bounding ;

1. A portraiture of the atrocious character of the Ninevites. כַּחַשׁ פֶּרֶק form an asyndeton. The non-removal of the prey refers to the fact, that the Assyrians had not restored the ten tribes.

2, 3. The description which the prophet here gives of the approach of the enemy, his attack on the city, and the slaughter of the besieged, is exquisitely graphic. Every translator must acknow-

3   The mounting of horsemen, the gleaming of swords,
    And the lightning of spears ;
    The multitude of slain,
    And the mass of corpses ;
    There is no end to the carcasses ;
    They stumble over their carcasses :
4   Because of the multitude of the whoredoms of the harlot,
    The very graceful mistress of enchantments ;
    Who sold nations through her fornications,
    And tribes through her enchantments.
5   Behold ! I am against thee, saith Jehovah of hosts ;
    And I will throw up thy skirts upon thy face,
    And show the nations thy nakedness,
    And the kingdoms thy shame.
6   Yea, I will cast abominable things upon thee,
    And disgrace thee ;
    And will make thee a gazing-stock.

---

ledge with Jerome : "Tam pulchra juxta Hebraicum et picturæ similis ad prœlium se præparantis exercitus descriptio est, ut omnis meus sermo sit vilior." The passage is unrivalled by any other, either in sacred or profane literature. Comp. however Jer. xlvii. 3. דֹּהַר occurs only here, but in Judges v. 22, we find דַּהֲרוֹת אַבִּירָיו, *the charges of his mighty* warriors, in connexion with סוּס, *the war-horse.* It would seem to have some affinity to the Arab. دَهَّرَ, *celeriter incessit,* and expresses the *coursing* or *prancing* of the cavalry, when rapidly advancing to the attack. Their eagerness the LXX. expresses by rendering it διώκοντος. Syr. ܢܒܥ, *ebullivit, anhelavit.* D. Kimchi : דריסת הסוס בכח והליכתו, *the powerful trampling or prancing of the horse and his course.* The collectives require to be rendered in the plural. קוֹל is not to be understood as repeated before סוּס and the following substantives. Instead of יִכָּשְׁלִי or יְכַשְׁלִי, as it is read in some of the old editions, the Keri, many MSS., and the Soncin., Brix., and Complut. editions, read וְכָשְׁלוּ,

which is favoured by the renderings of the LXX. and Vulg.

4. The idolatrous practices of the Ninevites, and the means which they employed to seduce others to worship their gods, are here represented as the principal cause of their destruction. At the same time, the commerce, luxury, &c. which they carried to the greatest height, are not to be excluded ; for in making contracts and treaties with the more powerful of their neighbours, they not only employed these as inducements, but did not scruple to deliver into their power, nations and tribes that were unable to defend themselves. Comp. Joel iii. 3, 6—8 ; Amos i. 6. The metaphor of an unchaste female, and the seductive arts which she employs, is not unfrequent in the prophets.

5, 6. The language of commination here used, is suggested by the metaphor of an harlot, employed in the preceding verse. It would seem to refer to an ancient mode of punishing strumpets, by stripping them of all their gaudy attire, and exposing them, covered with mud and filth, to the gaze of insulting spectators. The abhorrent character of the figure constitutes the very reason of its selection. Comp. Ezek. xvi. 37—41. The כְּ in כִּרְאִי is the Caph veritatis. LXX., εἰς παράδειγμα.

7 And every one that seeth thee shall flee from thee,
And shall say, Nineveh is destroyed!
Who will commiserate her?
Whence shall I seek comforters for thee?
8 Art thou better than No-Ammon,
That dwelt in the rivers,
That had water around her;

7. יְאֶךְ carries out the idea implied in
יֹּאר, ver. 6. It is in the plural, but is followed by a singular verb, to agree with
כֹּל. Comp. for the sentiment Is. li. 19.

8. נֹא אָמוֹן, No Amon, Egyp. ⲚⲞⳞ
ⲀⲘⲞⲨⲚ, the line, or portion of Amon;
thus etymologically the LXX. μερίδα
Ἀμμών, though in Ezek. xxx. 15, they
render Διόσπολις, i. e. the residence or
possession of the Egyptian deity known
by the name of Jupiter Ammon. The
statement of Macrobius, that he was the
representative of the sun, is confirmed
by the name of Amon-Re, i. e. "Amon,
the Sun," being given to him in Egyptian inscriptions. On Egyptian monuments this god is represented by the
figure of a man sitting upon a chair,
with a ram's head, or by that of an
entire ram. In Jer. xlvi. 25, we have
אָמוֹן מִנֹּא, Amon of No, where, as well as in
the present passage in Nahum, our translators have regarded אָמוֹן as equivalent to
הָמוֹן, a multitude. Bochart, Schroeder,
and some others, have contended that
Διόσπολις, near Mendes, in Lower Egypt,
is intended, but all the later commentators are in favour of Thebes. The
Targum preposterously renders, אַלְכְּסַנְדְּרִיָא
רַבְּתָא, Alexandria the Great, which Jerome, deferring to his Rabbi, has adopted
in the Vulg. The city, which, from its
being the principal seat of his worship,
was called by the Greeks Διόσπολις, is
the celebrated Thebes, the ancient capital
of Upper Egypt, situated on both sides
of the Nile, about two hundred and sixty
miles south of Cairo. It was renowned
for its hundred gates, and was of such
extent, that its remaining ruins still describe a circuit of twenty-seven miles:

———— οὐδ' ὅσα Θήβας
Αἰγυπτίας ὅθι πλεῖστα δόμοις ἐν κτήματα
κεῖται,

Αἵ θ' ἑκατόμπυλοί εἰσι, διηκόσιοι δ' ἀν'
ἑκάστην
Ἀνέρες ἐξοιχνεῦσι σὺν ἵπποισιν καὶ
ὄχεσφιν·
Iliad. ix. 381.

Of the magnificent ruins, the most remarkable are the temples of Luxor and
Karnac, on the eastern side of the river.
The architecture is of the most gigantic
and superior description. Fragments of
colossal obelisks and statues are found
in every direction. The stupendous
colonnade at Luxor is in the highest
degree imposing; but the grand hall of
the temple at Karnac is of surpassing
interest. Wilkinson, in his Thebes,
p. 174, describes it as "one hundred and
seventy feet by three hundred and twenty-
nine, supported by a central avenue of
twelve massive columns, sixty-six feet
high, (without the pedestal and abacus,)
and twelve in diameter, besides one
hundred and twenty-two of smaller or
rather less gigantic dimensions, forty-
one feet nine inches in height, and
twenty-seven feet six inches in circumference, distributed in seven lines on
either side of the former." The walls
of the temples are covered with hiero-
glyphics, chiefly representing the victories gained by the Egyptian kings over
their enemies. One of the walls exhibits
the result of the expedition of Shishak
against Jerusalem, 1 Kings xiv. 25, &c.;
2 Chron. xii. 2—9, in the leading away
of the Jewish captives.

Of the conquest of this famous city,
here referred to by Nahum, no mention
is made in profane history, but it not
improbably took place on the advance
of the Assyrian army under Sargon, in
the year B.C. 714. See on Is. xx. It was
afterwards taken by Cambyses, B.C. 525,
and its ruin completed by Ptolemy
Lathyrus, B.C. 81. According to the

Whose strength was in the sea?
Her wall was on the sea.

9 Cush strengthened her, and Egypt,
With countless hosts;
Put and the Lybians were thine auxiliaries.

10 Yet she became an exile,
She went into captivity;
Her young children also were dashed in pieces,
At the top of all the streets;
They cast lots for her honourable men,
And all her great men were bound with chains.

11　　Thou also shalt be drunken,

---

representation of our prophet, Nineveh could not vie with it either in point of grandeur or of strength. They both possessed the advantage of mighty rivers for their defence—a circumstance to which he gives a special prominence, as it was that on which the inhabitants placed great dependence. By יָם, *sea*, is meant the Nile; see on Is. xix. 5; by יְאֹרִים, *streams*, the same as מְזָרוֹת, Nah. ii. 7, viz. the canals by which the water of the river was carried round or through the principal parts of the city. Ewald proposes to connect יָם with מִיָּם, thus, מִיָּם יָם, and renders *from sea to sea*, which he attempts to justify by appealing to Micah vii. 12, but the cases are not parallel. חֵיל stands elliptically for חֵילָה. The preposition מִ in מִיָּם expresses the material out of which the defence was made; and the triple reference to the Nile as a sea, in this verse, indicates the great importance which attached to it as a means of protecting the city.

9. Not only was Thebes strong by nature and art, and in the number of her native troops; she also possessed immense military resources in her African auxiliaries. For פּוּשׁ, *Cush*, see on Is. xi. 11. פּוּט, *Put*, Egyp.

ⲫⲀⲓⲀⲧ, the region immediately to the west of Lower Egypt, and conterminous with Lybia Proper, with the inhabitants of which, לוּבִים, it is here mentioned. Gesenius derives the name from ⲡⲓⲧ or ⲫⲓⲧ, *a bow*, and thinks the people were so called from their

being expert as archers. That they were descended from Ham, see Gen. x. 6. Josephus speaks of them as Mauritanians, Antiqq. i. 6, 2; and the river of the same name, which he describes as flowing through their country, is called *Fut* by Pliny, v. 1, and *Phtuth* by Ptolemy, iv. 1. They are spoken of as forming part of the Egyptian army, Jer. xlvi. 9, and as being in the Syrian marine, Ezek. xxvii. 10. Winer's Real W. B. *in voc.* לוּבִים, *Lybians*, the inhabitants of Africa to the south and west of the former country, stretching as far as Numidia. Hitzig, on Is. lxvi. 19, has endeavoured in vain to establish the hypothesis that the people of Nubia are meant. Comp. 2 Chron. xii. 3; xvi. 8. מִצְרַיִם, *Egypt*, is here taken for Lower Egypt, as distinguished from the Upper, of which Thebes was itself the capital. There is no reason, with some, to change the ך in בְּעֶזְרָתֵךְ into ה, though the LXX. and Syr. have the third person. The prophet concludes his description by apostrophizing Thebes. בְּ is the *Beth essentiæ*.

10, 11. If the celebrated metropolis of Egypt, with all its means of defence, was captured, and its inhabitants subjected to all the cruelties and indignities usually inflicted by the victors, what was there in Nineveh to claim exemption? Instead of שָׁבַר, *to drink, be intoxicated*, a mode of speech not uncommon in the prophets, denoting participation in severe punishment, Newcome, without authority, reads שָׂבַר, *to hire*, and renders, *thou*

Thou shalt hide thyself,
Thou also shalt seek a refuge from the enemy.

12 All thy fortresses are like fig-trees with early figs ;
     If they shake them, they fall into the mouth of the eater.

13 Behold ! thy people are as women in the midst of thee ;
     The gates of thy land shall be thrown wide open to thine enemies;
     Fire shall consume thy barriers.

14   Draw water for the siege ;
     Strengthen thy fortifications ;
     Enter the mire, and tread the clay ;
     Repair the brick-kiln.

15 There shall the fire consume thee,
     The sword shall cut thee off ;
     It shall consume thee like the licking locust,
     Be thou numerous as the licking locusts,
     Be thou numerous as the swarming locusts.

16 Thou hast increased thy merchants more than the stars of heaven;
     The licking locusts spread themselves out,
     And took their flight.

17 Thy princes were as the swarming locusts,
     And thy satraps as the largest locusts ;
     That encamp in the hedges in the cold day :

---

shalt become an hireling. In 1 Sam. ii. 5, to which he refers, the latter, and not the former verb, occurs.

12, 13. Two figures strikingly expressive of the extreme ease with which the Assyrians should be subdued. For the former, see on Is. xxviii. 4; and comp. Rev. vi. 13; for the latter, Is. xix. 16 ; Jer. l. 37. עִם, *with*, in the phrase תְּאֵנִים עִם בִּכּוּרִים, denotes *accompaniment*, &c.; the phrase itself is equivalent to תְּאֵנִים אֲשֶׁר לָהֶם בִּכּוּרִים. Thus the LXX.; συκαῖ σκοποὺς ἔχοντες. Comp. for this rare use of the preposition, 1 Sam. xvii. 42. בְּרִיחָיִךְ, Michaelis translates *thy fugitives;* but as fugitives are always represented as perishing by the sword, and never by fire, the signification *barriers* must be retained.

14. The prophet ironically summons the Ninevites to make every effort in the way of preparing for a long and vigorous defence of the metropolis itself. As water is one of the first necessaries, it behoved them to see to it, that the

cisterns, &c., were well filled. They were also to put the fortifications in a perfect state.

15—17. שָׁם, *there*, points emphatically to the fortified city. The nominative to הִתְכַּבֵּד is the masculine noun עַם, *people*, *i. e.* the inhabitants ; that to הִתְכַּבְּדִי, the feminine עִיר, *city*, understood. Instead, however, of הִתְכַּבֵּד, six MSS., originally four more, and one by correction, read הִתְכַּבְּדִי. For the names of the locusts which here occur, see on Joel i. 4, and Amos vii. 1. The reduplication גּוֹב גּוֹבַי, *locust of locusts*, is designed to express the largest or most formidable of that kind of insect. For the plural form גּוֹבַי, see on Amos vii. 1. מִנְּזָרִים is a ἅπαξ λεγ., derived from נָזַר, *to consecrate, separate* and *devote* to a high or noble office ; hence נָזִיר, *prince*, נֵזֶר, *consecration, diadem.* It denotes here the princes, crowned with diadems, who formed the glory of the Assyrian court. Thus Kimchi : שרים אשר נזר ועטרה על ראשיהם, " Princes with diadems and crowns on

The sun ariseth, then they flee,
And the place where they are is unknown.
18 Thy shepherds slumber, O king of Assyria !
Thy nobles have lain down ;
Thy people are dispersed upon the mountains,
And there is none that collecteth them.
19 There is no alleviation of thy ruin ;
Thy wound is grievous ;
All that hear the report of thee
Shall clap their hands at thee,
For upon whom did not thy wickedness unceasingly pass ?

their heads." The Arab. منذر, *monitor,* i. e. *counsellor,* is less apt, as the comparison to the locusts shows. Six of De Rossi's MSS. and three ancient editions omit the Dagesh in the Nun. The parallel term מִנְּזָרַיִם occurs only here, and in Jer. li. 27, in the singular מִנְזָר. It is obviously a foreign word, and is in all probability compounded of what we still find in the Persic, تاو, or ناب, *strength, power,* and سر, *chief, captain, prince.* It occurs in the Targum of Jonathan, Deut. xxviii. 12, as the name of a superior angel. For other derivations, see Gesen. Thesaur. *in voc.* Dr. Lee prefers deriving it from the Chald. שַׂב, *egregius,* and שׂר, *dux.* Whatever might be the power of these princes and generals, and whatever number of troops they might have at their command, they would, on the approach of the enemy, betake themselves to flight, and leave Nineveh to her own defence. No trace of them would be found.

18. The masculine suffixes in this and the following verse, refer to the king of Assyria. The רֹעִים, *shepherds,* were the satraps or *viceroys* appointed to govern the provinces under the king of Assyria; the אַדִּירִים were the *nobles,* who, as parallel with the רֹעִים, are to be regarded under the same image. See Jer. xxv. 34, where *principals* would have been better than *principal* in our common version. שָׁכְנוּ, corresponding to נָמוּ, *they slumber,* is a *vox pregnans,* implying, not only that they had lain down, but that they were taking rest or were asleep. פּוֹשׁ is cognate with פּוּץ, to *scatter, disperse;* Arab. فشّ, *propagata et multiplicata sunt* pecora; but is not to be substituted for it, as some propose. Comp. the Arab. نفش, *pastum noctu incesserunt* cameli aut oves *sine pastore.* The figure is carried on throughout the verse.

19. אֵין־כֵּהָה, lit. *nothing* of *infirmity,* by litotes, for *powerful, great* is thy breach. The deliverance of the king of Nineveh was utterly hopeless. Nothing remained but for the prophet to announce his end, and the joy which the surrounding states would express at the irretrievable ruin of an empire, whose iron sway had been so extended, and whose cruel oppressions had been unintermitting.

HABAKKUK

PREFACE

Of the prophet Habakkuk, we possess no information but what is purely apocryphal. The position of Delitzsch, founded upon the subscription, chap. iii. 19, that he was of the tribe of Levi, and engaged in the temple service, is too precarious to warrant its adoption. The statement made in the inscription to Bel and the Dragon in the LXX., which has been preserved from the Tetrapla of Origen, in the Codex Chisianus, ἐκ προφητείας Ἀμβακοὺμ υἱοῦ Ἰησοῦ ἐκ τῆς φυλῆς Λευί, may be nothing more than conjecture. Considerable difference of opinion obtains respecting the time at which he flourished—the Rabbins, Grotius, Kalinsky, Kofod, Jahn, and Wahl, placing him in the first years of Manasseh; Friedrich, De Wette, Bertholdt, Justi, and Wolf, in the period of the exile; while Usher, Newcome, Eichhorn, Horne, Winer, Maurer, and Ewald, are of opinion that he prophesied in the reign of Jehoiachin, about 608—604 before Christ. This last hypothesis seems best supported, since the Chaldæans are spoken of chap. i. 5, 6, as being upon the point of invading Judah, but not as having actually entered it. The position of Rosenmüller, that chap. i. was composed under Jehoiakim, chap. ii. under Jehoiachin, and chap. iii. under Zedekiah, is altogether gratuitous. The whole forms one prophecy, and does not admit of being thus dissected.

The book embraces the wickedness of the Jews which demanded the infliction of punishment, the infliction of this punishment by the Chaldæans, the destruction of the latter in their turn, and an ode composed by the prophet in anticipation of the consequent deliverance of his people. Its position immediately after Nahum is most appropriate, setting forth the judgments of God inflicted by and upon the Chaldæans, just as the latter treated of those to be inflicted upon the Assyrians. The two prophets take up separately what Isaiah had expatiated upon at large.

In point of general style, Habakkuk is universally allowed to occupy a very distinguished place among the Hebrew prophets, and is surpassed by none of them in dignity and sublimity. Whatever he may occasionally have in common with previous writers, he works up in his own peculiar manner, and is evidently no servile copyist or imitator. His figures are well chosen, and fully carried out. His expressions are bold and animated; his descriptions graphic and pointed. The parallelisms are for the most part regular and complete. The lyric ode contained in chap. iii. is justly esteemed one of the most splendid and magnificent within the whole compass of Hebrew poetry. See the introduction to that chapter.

The words מְנַמָּה, i. 9, עַבְטִיט, ii. 6, and קִיקָלוֹן, ii. 16, are peculiar to this prophet.

CHAPTER I

The prophet commences by briefly, yet emphatically and pathetically, setting forth the cause of the Chaldæan invasion, which was to form the burden of his prophecy,—the great wickedness which abounded in the Jewish nation at the time he flourished, 2—4. He then introduces Jehovah summoning attention to that invasion as the awful punishment of such wickedness, 5; describes, in a very graphic manner, the appearance, character, and operations of the invaders, 6—11; and then, by a sudden transition, expostulates with God, on account of the severity of the judgment, which threatened the annihilation of the Jewish people, 12—17.

---

1 THE SENTENCE, which Habakkuk the prophet saw.

2 How long shall I cry, O Jehovah, and thou hearest not?
How long shall I cry to thee of violence, and thou savest not?

1. For the signification of מַשָּׂא, see on Is. xiii. 1; and for the form חֲבַקּוּק, compare שַׁעֲרוּר, Jer. v. 30; xxiii. 14.

2. The evils complained of in this and the two following verses, are, by many interpreters, considered to be those consequent upon the invasion of Judæa by the Chaldæans. Such a construction, however, breaks up the symmetry of the connexion, as marked by ver. 5, and leaves out of view the wickedness of the Jews as the cause of the calamity, contrary to the universal custom of the Hebrew prophets. They were the intestine broils, litigations, and acts of oppression, which sprang up in the kingdom of Judah, after the death of the pious reformer Josiah, and had been long the subject of complaint on the part of Habakkuk. That such was the state of things at that time is evident from Jer. xxii. 3, 13. The argument

in favour of the contrary hypothesis, derived from the recurrence of the words עָמָל, חָמָס, &c., and the phrase יֵצֵא מִשְׁפָּט, &c., in the following part of the chapter, with undoubted application to the Chaldæans, is of no weight, since they are rather to be regarded as modes of expression familiar to the prophet, than indicative of identity of subject. The influence of עַד־אָנָה, how long, upon the Preterite and Future tenses in this verse, so modifies them as to give them the force of a present time, though the one includes what had taken place down to such time, and the other, the possibility of its being still carried forward into the future. Because חָמָס, violence, occurs without a preposition, Hitzig thinks it was what was done to the prophet himself; but it is better, with Kimchi, to suppose an ellipsis of בִּגְבֻּר, or, to supply עַל, on account of, because of, with the

3 Why dost thou permit me to see wickedness,
　　And beholdest misery ?
　　Destruction and violence are before me,
　　Contention and strife exalt themselves.
4 On this account the law faileth,
　　And true judgment goeth not forth ;
　　Because the wicked circumvent the righteous,

Targum. Comp. Job xix. 7; Jer. xx. 8. שׁיַעָ and זָעָק are synonymous, but the latter is the more expressive of the two.

3. Some, regarding תַּבִּיט and תֻּרְאֵנִי as strictly parallel, understand the suffix נִי to be omitted in the latter verb, and render : *Why dost thou cause me to see wickedness, and make me look upon wrong ?* but תַּבִּיט, though the Hiphil conjugation, is never used in a causative sense. Besides, לְנֶגְדִּי, and not תַּבִּיט, is the proper synonyme, corresponding to תֻּרְאֵנִי. Between the two clauses, the prophet introduces Jehovah, with whom he expostulates, as an inactive spectator of the evil, because his providence did not interfere for its removal, and it was allowed, unavenged, to take its course. The expostulation thus gains in force, and scope is afforded for the striking contrast, ver. 5, in which the Most High is represented as interposing for the punishment of the wicked. מָדוֹן יִשָּׂא has been variously explained. The LXX., taking מָדוֹן for מֵדִין, render it ὁ κριτής λαμβάνει; which the Syr. explains,

ܘܡܶܢ ܟܺܐܒܳܐ ܡܰܣܒ ܡܶܢܘܰ, *the judge taketh a bribe.* Abenezra translates thus : וַיְהִי אַנְשֵׁי רִיב וּמָדוֹן אֲשֶׁר יִשְׂאוּ רֹאשָׁם, *and there are men of strife and contention who lift up their head.* The structure of the sentence, however, obliges us to regard יִשָּׂא as parallel to וַיְהִי, so that it stands in the same relation to מָדוֹן, that the substantive verb does to רִיב. The nouns in both cases are nominatives to the verbs, and נָשָׂא is here to be taken intransitively in the sense of *exalting* or *raising oneself up.* Comp. Ps. lxxxix. 10; Hos. xiii. 1; Nah. i. 5. Thus Dahl, combining the two nouns, *Und Hader, und Gezank erheben sich ;* and Perschke, *Es gibt Streit, und Zwist erhebet sich.* The language is descriptive of the prevalence of a litigious spirit, in consequence of which no one was permitted quietly to possess or enjoy

his rights. What was not seized upon by main force, was obtained by perversion of law.

4. עַל־כֵּן, *therefore, on this account,* refers not to the state of things set forth in the verse immediately preceding, but to Jehovah's forbearing to punish, spoken of in ver. 2. Of the law, which ought to have been maintained in all its vital energy, it is said תָּפוּג, *it chilleth, groweth frigid, languisheth, faileth ;* by which is meant, that it was not enforced, but left, as it were, to grow stiff and torpid from want of use. The words, וְלֹא־יֵצֵא לָנֶצַח מִשְׁפָּט, may either be rendered, *judgment, i.e.* what is strictly and properly such, *righteous judgment, never goeth forth ;* or, *judgment goeth not forth according to truth ;* לָנֶצַח, signifying *to perpetuity, for ever,* (and, with a negative, *never,* like לֹא לְעוֹלָם,) and also *truly, according to truth.* Comp. the Arab. نصح, *sincerus, fidelis fuit ;* and the Eth. ንጹሕ : *purus, mundus fuit.* The latter signification of the word is that adopted by the Syr.

ܘܠܳܐ ܢܦܶܩ ܡܶܢ ܕܰܟܝܳܐ, and *judgment goeth not forth in purity ;* and is approved by Scheltinga, Hesselberg, Wolf, Rosenmüller, De Wette, Winer, Gesenius, Lee, and Ewald, chiefly on the ground of מִשְׁפָּט מְעֻקָּל, *wrong* or *perverted judgment,* occurring, as a contrasted formula, at the close of the verse. By the going forth of judgment is meant the publication of legal decisions delivered by a judge. In the time of the prophet, justice was utterly corrupted, in consequence of which there was no security either for person or property. יַכְתִּיר, from כָּתַר, *to surround,* is here used in a bad sense, to express the ensnaring of a person by fraud and artifice ; it depicts the windings of intrigue, and is best rendered by *circumvent.* Thus Dathe : *cum impius pium circumvenit.* מְעֻקָּל, *dis-*

Therefore perverted judgment goeth forth.

5　Look among the nations, and behold!
And be ye greatly astonished;
For I will perform a work in your days,
Which ye will not believe, though it should be told you.

6　For, behold! I will raise up the Chaldæans,
That bitter and impetuous nation;
Which traverseth the wide regions of the earth,
To seize upon habitations belonging not to it.

---

torted, perverse, wrong, from the root עָקַל.
Comp. the Syr. ܚܣܰܠ, pervertit, Arab.
عَقَلَ, constrinxit, distortos habuit pedes;
عَقَلَة, distortio linguæ in loquendo. LXX.
κρίμα διεστραμμένον.

5. By a sudden apostrophe Jehovah
calls upon the Jews, in anticipation of the
punishment which their sins deserved,
and which should assuredly be inflicted
upon them, to direct their attention to
the events that were taking place among
the surrounding nations. Nabopolassar
had already destroyed the mighty empire
of Assyria and founded the Chaldæo-
Babylonian rule; he had made himself
so formidable, that Necho found it
necessary to march an army against
him, in order to check his progress;
and, though defeated at Megiddo, he had,
in conjunction with his son Nebuchadnezzar, gained a complete victory over
the Egyptians at Carchemish. These
events were calculated to alarm the Jews,
whose country lay between the dominions
of the two contending powers; but,
accustomed as they were to confide in
Egypt, and in the sacred localities of
their own capital, Is. xxxi. 1, Jer. vii. 4,
and being in alliance with the Chaldæans,
they were indisposed to listen to, and
treated with the utmost incredulity, any
predictions which described their overthrow by that people. Such overthrow
God claims as his work, though he might
employ men as his instruments in effecting it. רָאָה and הִבִּיט are frequently
combined as here for the sake of effect.
The phrase בַגּוֹיִם, among the nations, is
translated by the LXX., οἱ καταφρονηταί,
ye despisers, in which they are followed
by the Syr. and Arab.; and this rendering
is adopted by Paul in his quotation of

the verse, Acts xiii. 41. On the other
hand, the Targ. חֲזוֹ בְעַמְמַיָא, Aq., Symm.,
Theod., and the Vulg. aspicite in gentibus;
which is sustained by all the Heb. MSS.
that have been collated, except five of
Kennicott's, which have גּוֹיִם, nations,
without the preposition. To account for
the rendering of the LXX., some are of
opinion that instead of בַגּוֹיִם, they must
have read בֹּגְדִים, בּוֹגְדִים, or בֹּזִים; others,
with Pococke, in his Porta Mosis, chap. iii.,
suggest a supposititious root, גָּבָא, the corresponding Arab. بغى, signifying, injustus
fuit; superbe, insolenter se gessit : most
unjustifiably insisting on the preference
of some such reading to that of the
Hebrew text. With respect to the quotation, Acts xiii. 41, it was obviously made
by the apostle on account of the exact
similarity of the case of the Jews in his
day, both as regards the destruction of
Jerusalem by the Romans, and the
incredulity of the nation in reference to
that event. "Paulus fideliter accommodat
in usum suum Prophetæ verba, quia
sicuti semel minatus fuerat Deus per
prophetam suam Habacuc, ita etiam
semper fuit sui similis." Calvin, in loc. The
double form, הִתַּמְּהוּ תְמָהוּ, is used for intensity. הִתַּמְּהוּ is the Hithpael for הִתְתַּמְּהוּ.
Comp. הִתְמַהְמְהוּ וּתְמָהוּ, Is. xxix. 9, and my
note on that verse. Before פֹּעַל subaud. אֲנִי.

6. Now follows a lengthened and
fearful description of the character and
operations of the instrument which Jehovah would employ in executing his
work. הִנְנִי מֵקִים, which has unquestionably the force of the future, must be
referred to the special raising up of the
Chaldæans to undertake the expedition
against Judæa, and not to their orga-
nization as a political power, since they
had already been upwards of twenty

7　It is terrible and dreadful ;
　　Its judgment and its dignity are from itself.

8　Swifter than leopards are its horses,
　　And lighter than evening wolves ;
　　Its horse also spread proudly along ;
　　Yea, its horse that come from afar :
　　They fly like an eagle hastening to devour.

9　It cometh entirely for violence ;
　　The aspect of their faces is like the east wind ;
　　And it collecteth the captives as sand.

10　For it maketh a mockery of kings,
　　And princes are a laughter to it ;

years in possession of such power under Nabopolassar. On this account, some prefer rendering the phrase, *Behold ! I will excite*. For an account of this people, see on Is. xxiii. 13. In הַמֵּר וְהַנִּמְהָר is a paronomasia. By מַר, *bitter*, the fierce and cruel disposition of the Chaldæans is expressed, comp. Jer. l. 42 ; by נִמְהָר, *rash, hasty*, the rapidity or impetuosity of their operations. In the latter part of the verse, their widely extended conquests under Nebuchadnezzar are clearly predicted.

7. שְׂאֵת, the LXX. render λῆμμα,

Symm. δόγμα, Vulg. *onus*, Syr. ‏ܡܛܠ‎

vision, Targ. גְּזֵרָה, *decree* or *sentence*, all deriving it from נָשָׂא, in the sense of נָשָׂא קוֹל, *to lift up*, or utter anything with *the voice*, and regarding it as equivalent to מַשָּׂא, from the same root. The signification *decree*, though approved by Hesselberg, De Wette, Winer, and Gesenius, is less appropriate than that of *dignity*, which is that of our common version, and which is adopted by Hitzig, Maurer, and Ewald. Comp. Gen. xlix. 3 ; Job xiii. 11 ; Ps. lxii. 5. שְׂאֵת nowhere occurs in reference to a judicial decree. What the prophet has in view appears to be the self-assumed political superiority of the Chaldæans in the Babylonian empire. As they had raised themselves to this dignity, so they would permit none to share in their counsels and determinations, but would act in the most arbitrary manner.

8. Frequent reference is made in Scripture to the " evening wolves," on account of the sudden ravages which, in the keenness of their hunger, they commit on the flocks at that time of the day. See Gen. xlix. 27 ; Jer. v. 6 ; Zeph. iii. 3 ; and comp. Virgil's Georg. iii. 537 ; iv. 433 ; and the Æneid, ii. 355 ; ix. 59. The LXX. render improperly, λύκους τῆς Ἀραβίας. פָּשׁ, from the root פּוּשׁ, having here the signification of the Arab. ‏فاش‎; *superbivit*, *gloriatus fuit*, describes the proud and spirited mien of the horses composing the Chaldæan cavalry. Comp. the inimitable description of the Arabian war-horse, Job xxxix. 19—24. The meaning of the two last lines of the verse is, that the eagerness of the cavalry to plunder the Jews should be so great, that they would make no account of the fatigue occasioned by the length of their march.

9, 10. כֻּלֹּה is the less correct orthography of כֻּלּוֹ, which occurs several times in the course of the Hebrew Bible. The affix refers to גּוֹי, ver. 6. So great was to be the invading army, that it would seem as if it were composed of the entire nation. Considerable difficulty has been experienced in the interpretation of the words, מְגַמַּת פְּנֵיהֶם קָדִימָה. By the LXX., the ἅπαξ λεγ. מְגַמָּה is rendered ἀνθεστηκότας ; by Symm. πρόσοψις ; by the Syr. ‏ܚܙܘܐ‎, *aspect* ; by the Targ. מְקַבֵּל, *front*, what is opposite to anything. The Vulg. omits the word altogether, obviously on the principle of its being sufficiently expressed by *facies*

It smileth at every fortress ;
Yea, it heapeth up earth, and taketh it.
11 Then it gaineth fresh spirit ;
　　It passeth onward, and contracteth guilt, [saying,]
　　Is this his power through his God ?

immediately following. With these Abenezra and Kimchi agree ; and thus also generally, Munster, Vatablus, Pagninus, Castalio, Calvin, and others. On the other hand, Gesenius derives the word from the supposititious root נֶמֶם, Arab. جمع, *to congregate, heap up,* and renders it *host, troop ;* but, as Lee observes, *the host of their faces* is anything but Hebrew phraseology. Rosenmüller, Lee, Maurer, Hitzig, and Ewald, derive it from the same root in the significations, *impetus, desire,* a *striving after ;* Ger. *streben :* while our own, and some other modern translators, adopt the idea of *absorption, supping up,* &c., from the signification of גְּמָא, גְּמָא. Considering the marked and independent coincidence of the ancient versions above quoted, borne out, as they are, by the Arab.

جمع, *adparuit, quod* de re quavis extrinsecus *apparet, corpus rei,* seu *res individua exstans et conspicua,* I cannot but regard *aspect* or *appearance* as the term best adapted to convey the meaning of the prophet. קְדִימָה, in every other passage in which it occurs, has the signification of *eastward,* and it is taken in this acceptation by Abarbanel, Parkhurst, Dahl, Wolff, and Hitzig, who explain it either of the direction in which the Chaldæans would return home with their booty, or of their first coming down along the coast of the Mediterranean, and then turning direct east upon the Jews. Both constructions are forced. Gesenius renders *forwards,* and gives the whole sentence thus : *the host of their faces is forwards.* Here again I prefer the rendering of Symm. ἄνεμος καύσων ; the Targ. פְרוּחַ קָדִים קָדוּמָא, the Vulg. *ventus urens,* which, or *east wind,* its equivalent, is the rendering of many of the moderns. It is true, that the east wind is elsewhere uniformly expressed by קָדִים, without the ה ; but this letter seems clearly to be here used paragogically, just as it is in

לַיְלָה, נֶגְבָּה, צָפוֹנָה, the primitive forms of which are לֵיל, נֶגֶב, צָפוֹן. In some instances, indeed, it is the ה directive, indicating motion towards the quarter specified, but in others it has lost all such power. For the east wind, or samoom, see on Is. xxvii. 8. Nothing could more appropriately describe the terrific appearance of the destructive Chaldæan army, than this phenomenon, which occasions awful devastation in the regions over which it passes. The collecting of the captives *like sand,* which the prophet immediately adds, corroborates the opinion that the samoom is intended, as it is frequently accompanied with whirlwinds of sand collected and carried with great rapidity across the desert. The 10th verse sets forth the haughty, fearless, and irresistible character of the Chaldæans. The last clause of the verse describes the throwing up of walls or batteries before fortified cities, from which to attack them. עָפָר seldom signifies fine dust ; it is more commonly used of *earth* generally, including clay, mire, &c.

11. אָז, τότε, usually rendered *then,* has here the force of *thereupon,* marking the transition from what had just been described to what immediately follows, and their intimate connexion with each other. רוּחַ is the accusative to חָלַף, which denoting *to succeed, exchange, change, renew,* &c., the phrase means, to assume, or gain a fresh accession of courage or military spirit. For this signification of רוּחַ, comp. Josh. ii. 11 ; v. 1. Elated by the fortresses they had taken, and the victories they had won in heathen countries, the Chaldæans are represented as passing onwards into Judæa ; and treating with contempt the puny resistance made to them by the Jews, asking sarcastically, "Is this all your boasted power conceded to you by the God in whom you confide ?" Comp. Is. x. 10, 11 ; xxxvi. 19, 20 ; Ps. lxxix. 10 ; cxv. 2. The aggravated guilt which they contracted (אָשֵׁם) lay in their vilifying

12   Art not Thou from eternity,
        O Jehovah ! my God, my Holy One ?
        We shall not die :
        O Jehovah ! thou hast appointed it for judgment,
        O Rock ! thou hast ordained it for correction.
13   Thou art of purer eyes than to regard evil ;
        And thou canst not behold injustice.
        Why dost thou behold the plunderers ?
        Why art thou silent when the wicked destroyeth
        Him that is more righteous than he ?
14   And makest men as the fishes of the sea,
        As the reptiles which have no ruler ?
15   It bringeth up all with its hook,
        It gathereth them into its net,
        Yea, it collecteth them into its drag ;
        Therefore it rejoiceth and exulteth.

Jehovah, by speaking of him as incapable of protecting his people. This
simple construction of the verse at once
frees it from the numerous difficulties
with which it has been clogged by interpreters, and gives peculiar force to
the interrogatory appeal in that which
follows. The ellipsis of לֵאמֹר is of frequent
occurrence in Hebrew. The absence of
the interrogative ה is more seldom ; but
comp. Gen. xxvii. 24, אַתָּה זֶה for הַאַתָּה זֶה ;
2 Sam. vii. 19, וְזֹאת, and this is, for הֲזֹאת ת,
and is this ; and xvi. 17, זֶה חַסְדְּךָ אֶת־רֵעֶךָ,
" This is thy kindness to thy friend,"
for, Is this, &c.
    12. The contemptuous manner in
which the enemy had treated the Most
High calls forth an impassioned appeal
from the prophet, in which he vindicates
the eternal existence and purity of
Jehovah, as that God who had formerly
wrought deliverance for his people, and
who was now employing the Chaldæans,
not for their annihilation, but only for
their punishment and correction. Since
צוּר, Rock, is elsewhere used metaphorically of God, I have retained it in the
translation. See on Is. xxvi. 4. It is here
parallel to יְהוָֹה. The Tikkun Sopherim
לֹא תָמוּת is unsupported by any authority.
    13. Habakkuk resumes the expostu-
latory mode of address which he had

employed, verses 2, 3. The בֹּגְדִים, plun-
derers, were the Chaldæans who had been
the allies of the Jews, but now treated
them with violence. Comp. Is. xxi. 2,
and xxiv. 16. The LXX., Syr., and
Arab., have nothing corresponding to
כְּמֹנוּ, but it is expressed in Aq., Symm.,
Theod., the Targ., and Vulg. Wicked
as the Jews were, they were righteous
in comparison of the Babylonians. Comp.
for the sentiment, Ezek. xvi. 51, 52.
    14. God is often said to do what he
permits to be done by others. רֶמֶשׂ is
used of aquatic animals, such as crabs
and other shell-fish, Ps. civ. 25, a sense
which the parallelism and connexion
here require.
    15—17. כֻּלֹּה is allowed by all to be
here the accusative, though it was, in
the same position, the nominative, ver. 9.
Converting the simile employed in the
preceding verse into a metaphor, the
prophet describes the rapacity of the
Chaldæans, the indiscriminate and universal havoc which they would effect,
and their proud confidence in their own
prowess. הֵעֲלָה, an unusual punctuation
for הֶעֱלָה. The hook, the net, and the
drag, are separately mentioned, to indicate that every means would be
employed in taking captives, and whatever else came in their way. To their

16 Therefore it sacrificeth to its net,
 And burneth incense to its drag;
 Because through them its portion is fat,
 And its food fattened meat.
17 Is it for this it emptieth its net,
 And spareth not to slay the nations continually?

arms, signified by these implements of fishers, they rendered divine honours, ascribing to them solely the success which they had in war. Comp. Justin. 43. 3. "Ab origine rerum pro diis immortalibus veteres hastas coluere." Lucian in Trag. Σκύθαι μὲν ἀκινάκῃ θύουσι. By the emptying of the net, ver. 17, is meant the depositing of the captives, &c., in Babylon, in order to go forth to fresh conquest and plunder. It is strongly implied in the questions with which the chapter concludes, that God would not permit the Chaldæans to proceed in their selfish conquests without a check, but the answer is reserved for the sequel.

CHAPTER II

This chapter contains an introductory statement respecting the waiting posture in which the prophet placed himself, in order to obtain a divine revelation in reference to the fate of his people and of the Chaldæans, their oppressors, 1; a command which he received to commit legibly to writing the revelation which was about to be made to him, 2; an assurance, that though the prophecy should not be fulfilled immediately, yet it would certainly be at length accomplished, 3; and a contrasted description of the two different classes of the Jews to whom it was to be communicated, 4. The insolence of the Chaldæans, and their insatiable lust of conquest, are next set forth, 5; on which the proper מַשָּׂא, sentence, or prophetical denunciation, commences, in the form of a taunt on the part of the nations, in which they anticipate the downfal of that hostile power, 6—8; and the punishment of its rapacity, 9—11; of its cruelty and injustice, with a special view to the universal spread of true religion, 12—14; of its wanton and sanguinary wars, 15—17, and of its absurd and fruitless idolatry, 18, 19. The last verse of the chapter beautifully contrasts with the two preceding, by representing Jehovah as the only God, entitled to universal submission and homage, 20.

---

1 I WILL stand upon my watch-post,
 And station myself upon the fortress,

1. מִשְׁמֶרֶת properly signifies observance, guard, watch, from שָׁמַר, to watch, observe, preserve, &c., but here, as a concrete, the place, or post of observation. Comp. Is. xxi. 8, where it is similarly used, with מִצְפֶּה for its parallel. Thus the

And will look out to see what he will say to me,
And what I shall reply in regard to my argument.

2 And Jehovah answered me, and said :
Write the vision, and make it plain on tablets,
That he who readeth it may run.

Syr. ܡܛܪܬܐ, *my place.* From the use
of מָצוֹר in the corresponding hemistich,
it is obvious that the post of a sentinel,
or watchman, appointed to keep an eye
upon what may transpire without a fortified city, is that from which the idea
is here borrowed. It has been questioned whether our prophet has any real
locality in view, or whether the words
are to be understood metaphorically.
The former is advocated by Hitzig, who
after describing it as a high and steep
point, such as a tower, and comparing
2 Kings ix. 17, 2 Sam. xviii. 24, says,
"Here, in a solitary position, far from
the bustle and noise of men, with his
eye directed towards heaven, and his collected spirit fixed upon God, he looks
out for revelations." With the exception, however, of Wolff, who preceded
him, the hypothesis has met with no
approbation. All that the passage seems
to teach is, that Habakkuk, anxious
to ascertain the Divine purpose relative
to the enemies of his people, brought
his mind into such a state of holy ex-
pectancy as was favourable to the reception of supernatural communications.
צָפָה, *to look about,* from which צוֹפֶה, a
speculator, watchman, is derived, (as likewise מִצְפֶּה, *a watch-tower,*) is employed,
as here in Piel, to express the looking
out for an answer to prayer, Ps. v. 4.
The paragogic ה of the Futures, marks
the intensity of his desire. The formula דִּבֶּר בְּ, which the Syr. and Targ.
render ܡܡܠܠ ܥܡܝ, יְחַמֵּל עִמִּי, in
the sense of speaking or conversing *with*
a person, the LXX. give by λαλήσει ἐν
ἐμοί, "will speak *in* me." That the
preposition בְּ is here purposely used, in
preference to אֶל, לְ, עִם, or אֵת, to denote
the *internal* mode of the Divine communication which the prophet received,
has been maintained by some who com-
pare רוּחַ יְהוָה דִּבֶּר בִּי, "the Spirit of Jeho-

vah spake *in* me," 2 Sam. xxiii. 2; Num.
xii. 6, 8; and particularly Zech. i. 9, 13,
14; ii. 2, 7; iv. 1, 4, 5; v. 5, 10; vi. 4,
where the interpreting angel that addressed him in vision is uniformly styled
הַמַּלְאָךְ הַדֹּבֵר בִּי, *the Angel that spake in me,*
which the LXX. as uniformly render
ὁ λαλῶν ἐν ἐμοί. This view was anciently expressed by Jerome, who says,
"Sed et hoc notandum, ex eo quod dix-
erat, Ut videam quid loquatur in me,
propheticam visionem et eloquium Dei
non extrinsecus ad Prophetas fieri, sed
intrinsecus et interiori homini respon-
dere." The same construction is put
upon the phrase by Delitzsch, in his
able commentary on our prophet. But
it seems after all more than doubtful
whether any such construction can fairly
be put upon the phrase in most of
the passages in which it occurs. In
2 Sam. xxiii. 2 it may be admitted, though
through or *by* will equally well suit. The
other declarations made Num. xii. 6,
show that it cannot there be so understood; while what is thus stated concerning Moses, taken in connexion with
1 Sam. xxv. 39, and the passages in
Zechariah, goes to prove that if any
stress at all is to be laid upon the preposition, it must be regarded as conveying the idea of *familiar* or *intimate*
communication. In תּוֹכַחְתִּי, the suffix is
not to be taken passively, but actively;
i.e. the תּוֹכַחַת, *argument, complaint, reproof,* or in what way soever the word
may be rendered, was not any employed
by others, but that which the prophet
himself had employed in the preceding
chapter. What he was desirous of obtaining, was an answer to the statement
which he had there made respecting the
Divine conduct in permitting the Chaldæans to multiply their conquests without end. Maurer: "causa querimoniæ
meæ."

2. חָזוֹן, the *vision,* or prophetic matter
which was about to be communicated to
the prophet. That the idea of *digging,
boring,* or *graving,* is to be attached to

3 For the vision is still for an appointed time,
But it shall speak at the end, and not lie;
Though it should delay, wait for it,
For it will surely come, and not tarry.

בָּאֵר, the position of the verb in such con-nexion clearly forbids. Had the cha-racter of the writing been durability, such an idea might fitly have been ex-pressed by a word signifying to *grave* or *dig deep*, into a hard substance; but as it is unquestionably legibility that is in-tended, we are compelled to understand the verb as relative to כְּתֹב, and that either as a new Imperative, or as an adverbial Infinitive qualifying it. In the latter case the clause should be rendered, *Write the vision, and that clearly.* Thus the LXX.: Γράψον ὅρασιν, καὶ σαφῶς. The Targ. has פְּתִיבָא נְבִיאֲתָא וּמְפָרְשָׁא, with which the Syr. so far agrees, rendering the verb by ܒ݁ܰܝ, *to explain.* Comp.

פְּתַבְתָּ — בַּאֵר הֵיטֵב, *write — very plainly,* Deut. xxvii. 8. The command, there-fore, has respect to the size, and not to the depth of the writing. הַלֻּחוֹת, *tables,* having the article, Ewald thinks the prophet refers to the tables which were openly exhibited in the market-place, on which public announcements were graven in large and clear characters, in common use among the people. The article, however, may only designate the tables which were to be employed for the purpose. It may merely indicate these as definite in the mind of the speaker. This is often the case in Hebrew, when it cannot be rendered by the definite article in other languages. For the writing tablets of the ancients, see on Is. viii. 1. The LXX. have πυξίον, *boxwood.* The reason why the prophecy should be easily legible, is stated to be, that whosoever read it might run and publish it to all within his reach. It was a joyful message to the Jews, involving as it did the de-struction of their oppressor, and their own consequent deliverance. Compare Dan. xii. 4, יְשֹׁטְטוּ רַבִּים וְתִרְבֶּה הַדָּעַת, "Many shall run to and fro," viz. with the ex-planation of the prophecy when unsealed, "and knowledge shall be increased." The two passages are remarkably pa-rallel as to their general meaning, though

the times and events to which they refer are totally different. Comp. also Rev. xxii. 17, Καὶ ὁ ἀκούων εἰπάτω· Ἔρχου! רוּץ, *to run,* is equivalent to נָבָא, *to prophesy,* Jer. xxiii. 21, obviously on the principle that those who were charged with a divine message were to use all despatch in making it known. The common interpretation, indeed, re-presents the meaning to consist in the writing being so large as to be easily read even by persons who were hasting past it. But in order to bear this con-struction, the words must read thus: לְמַעַן יִקְרָא בּוֹ הָרָץ, *that the runner,* or, *he that runneth, may read it.* Besides, such an addition would scarcely be requisite after בָּאֵר, and certainly would not corre-spond to the force of לְמַעַן, *in order that,* with which the hemistich commences.

3. The particles כִּי, and וְ in וְיָפֵחַ, are correlative. מוֹעֵד, from יָעַד, *to fix, appoint,* denotes, in such connexion, a season or period of time definitely fixed in the purpose of God for the occurrence of the predicted events. It is frequently employed by Daniel in this acceptation, along with קֵץ, *the end,* or termination of the state of the things comprehended in the prophecy. Comp. Dan. viii. 17, 19; xi. 27, 35; and somewhat similar phraseology, chap. viii. 26; x. 14. The term obviously implies that the period was still future, which is also expressed by the use of עוֹד, *still, yet.* This adverb is too closely connected in sense with מוֹעֵד, to admit of the rendering of Mi-chaelis: "There will still come a vision, which shall determine the time;" which he refers to Jeremiah's prophecy of the seventy years. יָפֵחַ has been variously translated. LXX. ἀνατελεῖ; Syr. ܢܐܕ, *to come;* Vulg. *apparebit;* Targ. מְתָקַן, *prepared.* As, like its cognates יָפַח and נָפַח, the root פּוּחַ, of which יָפֵחַ is the future in Hiphil, signifies *to breathe, blow, puff,* Michaelis, Bauer, Stäudlin, De Wette, Hesselberg, Maurer, Winer, Hitzig, Ewald, and Hengstenberg, in his Psalms, vol. i. p. 255, contend, that it is

4　Behold the proud! his soul is not right within him;

here to be taken in the acceptation of *panting, hasting, eagerly moving forward* to an object, and that the meaning is, that the prophecy hastened to its accomplishment. Such construction, however, requires us to attach to קֵץ the idea of the object or objects on which a prophecy terminates,—the end or extreme point, beyond which its import does not extend. But the word nowhere occurs in this acceptation, but, as Delitzsch has shown, it always designates, in a prophetico-chronological sense, *the time of the end,* whatever may be the compass of events to which reference may be had. Besides, לַקֵּץ and לַמּוֹעֵד are so obviously parallel, that they do not admit of being differently construed. לַקֵּץ here, is only an abbreviation of the phrase לְעֵת־קֵץ, Dan. viii. 17, of which we have again a varied form in לַמּוֹעֵד קֵץ, ver. 19. I therefore agree with Abarbanel, Jarchi, Kimchi, Vatablus, Calvin, Cocceius, Rosenmüller, Wolff, and Delitzsch, in assigning to יָפֵחַ in this place the acceptation of *speaking, breathing out words,* in which acceptation the verb is used Prov. xii. 17; xiv. 5, 25; xix. 5, 9. This interpretation derives support from the antithetical וְלֹא יְכַזֵּב, in which the idea of speaking is obviously implied. The meaning of the verse will accordingly be, that though the destruction of the Chaldæan power, about to be predicted, was not to take place immediately, yet it was definitely fixed in the Divine counsel, and would infallibly happen at the termination of the period appointed for the exercise of its oppression, and for the deliverance of the captive Hebrews; it was to be an object of confident expectation, though its arrival might be somewhat protracted. For יִתְמַהְמָהּ, see on Is. xxix. 9. בֹּא יָבֹא is emphatic, denoting the certainty of the event. אֵחַר, signifies *to stay long,* and intimates that the predicted event would not be protracted to any great length. Instead of לֹא יְאַחֵר, upwards of forty of Kennicott and De Rossi's MSS., four ancient editions, the LXX., Aq., Syr., Targ., and Vulg., read וְלֹא יְאַחֵר.

4. Most interpreters apply the former hemistich of this verse to the Chaldæans, supposing the denunciation against them to begin here; but its coherence with

the preceding verse is too close to admit of this construction, while the latter hemistich, were such application admitted, would awkwardly interrupt the prophecy at its very commencement. On the other hand, the whole verse most naturally and appropriately applies to the Jewish people, and contains a description of those who would proudly reject the prophetic vision, and of those who would give it a cordial reception: the two members forming a marked and striking antithesis. עֻפְּלָה, of which עֻפְּלָה may either be the third feminine singular of Pual, or a noun formed from that part of the verb, occurs elsewhere only in Hiphil, Num. xiv. 44; but it is evident, from the use of the derivative עֹפֶל, as denoting a *swelling, tumour, mount, hill,* &c., and the comparison of the context of both passages, that it is employed metaphorically to express the idea of *mental inflation, elation, pride, presumption,* or the like. Such Hebrew usage supports the relation of the verb to the Arab.

عَفِلَ, *tumore laboravit,* rather than to غَفَلَ, *neglexit* vel *omisit* rem, *per socordiam non curavit,* for which Pococke contends at great length in his Porta Mosis; though the rendering of the LXX. ὑποστείληται, and that of Aquila, νωχελευόμενον, may both be referred to the radical notion conveyed by this root. Its reference to אָפֵל, *to set, become dark,* as proposed by Abarbanel, and approved by Deutsch and Wolff, cannot be sustained. Nor must it be overlooked, that though the following words, לֹא יָשְׁרָה נַפְשׁוֹ בּוֹ, are not to be regarded as epexegetical of the term in question, they nevertheless appear to have been suggested by it. יָשַׁר signifies not only to be *straight* or *right,* in opposition to being *crooked,* but also, *even, level, plain, smooth,* in opposition to what is *rough, rugged,* and *difficult.* See 1 Kings vi. 35; Ezra viii. 21; Ps. v. 9; Prov. xxiii. 31, where יִתְהַלֵּךְ בְּמֵישָׁרִים means, *goeth sweetly* or *pleasantly down,* or as Jerome gives it, *ingreditur blande;* De Dieu, *subit facillime.* Comp. the Arab. يَسَرَ, *facilis fuit*

But the righteous shall live by his faith.

res; *facilitas, lenitas*. Of the reading עולפה, found in one of Kennicott's MSS., or עלפה, as it is written in another, no account is to be made, though in his Dissert. Gen. § 72, that author prefers it to that which is attested by all the other codices. The Syr. ܥܘܠܐ, *wickedness*, is founded upon a mistake of עָפְלָה for עֻלָּה. עָפְלָה I consider to be an abstract noun, used elliptically for אִישׁ עָפְלָה, *a man of arrogance* or *presumption*, and so to be rendered adjectively, the *proud, presumptuous*, &c. For instances of similar ellipsis, comp. אֲנִי תְפִלָּה, *I am prayer*, for אֲנִי אִישׁ תְפִלָּה, *I am a man of prayer*, Ps. cix. 4; זָדוֹן, *arrogance*, for אִישׁ זָדוֹן, *man of arrogance*, i. e. *arrogant*, Jer. l. 31, 32; חֲמֻדוֹת אַתָּה, *thou art delights*, Dan. ix. 23, for אִישׁ חֲמֻדוֹת אַתָּה, *thou art a man of delights*, i. e. *greatly beloved*, as it is expressed in full, chap. x. 11, 19. See on Micah vi. 9. The term is thus strictly antithetical to צַדִּיק, *the just*, in the following hemistich, precisely as the predicate לֹא־יָשְׁרָה נַפְשׁוֹ בּוֹ, *his soul is not right within him*, is to בֶּאֱמוּנָתוֹ יִחְיֶה, *by his faith he shall live*. With respect to this latter point of antithesis, it must be evident, that, as חָיָה, the latter predicate, signifies not merely *to live*, but *to live well, be happy*, the former must convey the idea of its opposite. This was clearly perceived by Luther, who often discovers a wonderful sagacity in seizing upon the meaning of a passage, though in his translation he may not adhere to the strict significations of single words. He renders the words thus: *Siehe, wer halsstarrig ist, der wird keine Ruhe in seinem Herzen haben.* "Behold, he who is stubborn shall have no tranquillity in his heart." So also Gesenius: "Lo, the lofty-minded, his soul is not tranquil within him." Maurer: "Non planus, complanatus, compositus, tranquillus, &c., est animus ejus." To this interpretation I adhere, as best meeting the exigency of the passage. While those Jews who, elated by false views of security, refused to listen to the Divine message, should have their security disturbed, and their minds agitated by the calamities with which they would be visited, such as lived righteously before God and men, should experience true happiness in the exercise of faith in that message, and others which God might communicate to them by his prophets. Thus a Lapide: "Incredulus habet animam, id est vitam, non rectam, sed distortam, anxiam, miseram, et infelicem; justus autem in fide et spe sua agit vitam rectam, puta lætam, quietam, sanctam et felicem." בּוֹ, *in*, or *within him*, is added to show that the verb יָשַׁר is not to be taken here as referring to any thing of an objective character, such as the Divine estimation, agreeably to the meaning of the phrase יָשַׁר בְּעֵינֵי יְהֹוָה, *to be right in the sight of Jehovah*, but must be understood as marking the subjective sphere of the predicate. For the fullest view of the various constructions, both logical and philological, that have been put upon this verse, I refer the more curious reader to Delitzsch. From the discrepancy existing between the Hebrew, and the version of the LXX., some have argued a corruption of the former, and have proposed emendations, but the difference has arisen either from a desire on the part of these translators to render the sense plainer, or from their mistaking one letter for another that is similar. They render, ἐὰν ὑποστείληται, οὐκ εὐδοκεῖ ἡ ψυχή μου ἐν αὐτῷ. ὁ δὲ δίκαιος ἐκ πίστεώς μου ζήσεται. To such rendering, its quotation by Paul in Heb. x. 38 gives no sanction, since he not unfrequently quotes passages from that version, containing renderings to which there never could have been anything corresponding in the Hebrew text. In the present instance he takes a liberty with the version itself, placing the latter part of the verse first, and the former last, and omitting μου after πίστις. Nor, it must further be observed, is it his intention either here, or in Rom. i. 17, and Gal. iii. 11, in employing the words, ὁ δίκαιος ἐκ πίστεως ζήσεται, to maintain, that the doctrine of justification by faith in Christ is taught by Habakkuk; he merely applies the principle laid down by the prophet, respecting the instrumentality of faith in securing the safety and happiness of the pious portion of the Jewish people, to the subject of which he is treating—the influence of faith in the gospel scheme of salvation. As צַדִּיק is

5 Moreover wine is treacherous;
    The haughty man stayeth not at home,
    Because he enlargeth his desire as Sheol;
    He is even as death, and cannot be satisfied;
    He gathereth for himself all the nations,
    And collecteth for himself all the people.

6 Shall not all these utter an ode against him,

the nominative absolute, בֶּאֱמוּנָתוֹ cannot be connected with it, except in regard to the pronominal reference, but must be joined with יִחְיֶה, *as for the righteous, he shall live by his faith.* From the circumstance, however, that the two former words are, in most MSS. and editions, joined by the accents Merca and Tiphca, while the latter, as a disjunctive, separates the second from the third, it might seem that the Rabbins construed the clause thus: *but the just by his faith, shall live.* And this construction would seem to confirm the hypothesis that in his quotation, Rom. i. 17, Gal. iii. 11, the Apostle connects ἐκ πίστεως with ὁ δίκαιος, and not with ζήσεται; but as quoted by him, Heb. x. 38, the former division of the words alone suits the connexion, in which his object evidently is to show the necessity of faith as a means of perseverance under all the afflictions and persecutions of the Christian life. See Owen on the passage.

5. The two first lines of this verse partake of the nature of a proverb, being expressed in a short and pithy manner, and admitting of general application. It is, however, obvious from the connexion with what follows, that they are introduced with special reference to the Chaldæan power, the nefarious conduct of which the prophet immediately proceeds to describe. The phrase הַיַּיִן בּוֹגֵד, *wine is a deceiver*, has its parallel, Prov. xx. 1, לֵץ הַיַּיִן, *wine is a mocker.* יָהִיר occurs only here, and Prov. xxi. 24, where, from its connexion with זֵד, *proud*, as its synonyme, it clearly signifies *elated, haughty.* LXX. ἀλαζών. Chald. יָהִיר, as used by the Rabbins, *superbivit.* See Buxt. *in voc.* Thus also in the Nazaræan Syr. ܣܘܳܚ, Ethpa. *superivit.* There is, therefore, no necessity for recurring to the Arab., the attempted derivations from

which are very precarious. The introductory particles כִּי אַף are designed to connect the proper prophecy with what had just been developed of the vision, as that which formed the most important part of it. אַף is expressive of addition, and כִּי of certainty. That the prophet had his eye upon the intemperance to which the Babylonians were greatly addicted, there can be little doubt. Comp. Dan. v., with Herod. i. 191; Xenoph. Cyrop. vii. 5, 15. "Babylonii maxime in vinum et quæ ebrietatem sequuntur effusi sunt;" Curtius, v. 1. How strikingly was the deceptive character of wine exemplified in the case of Belshazzar! נָוֶה, primarily signifies to *dwell, remain at rest*, which signification better suits the present passage than the secondary one of *being decorous, proper*, &c., adopted by the Vulg., Ewald, and some others. Still it is a question, whether the not remaining tranquil is to be viewed as a voluntary or as an involuntary act. The Targ., Rashi, Kimchi, Ben-Melec, De Wette, Justi, Maurer, and Delitzsch, refer it to the forcible ejection of the Babylonians: Abenezra, Abarbanel, Rosenmüller, Wolff, Wahl, Gesenius, and Hitzig, to their restless disposition, by which they were continually impelled to go forth upon new expeditions for conquest. The latter seems, from what follows, to be the preferable interpretation. For הִרְחִיב כִּשְׁאוֹל נַפְשׁוֹ, see on Is. v. 14, and comp. Prov. xxvii. 20; xxx. 15,16. The insatiable desire of conquest, which specially showed itself in the reign of Nebuchadnezzar, is here forcibly predicted. כָּל־הַגּוֹיִם and כָּל־הָעַמִּים must be restricted to all the nations with which the Jews were familiar.

6. Comp. Is. xiv. 4, and see my notes on מָשָׁל as there occurring. מְלִיצָה occurs only here, and Prov. i. 6, in which verse also all the three synonymes מְלִיצָה, מָשָׁל,

Even a song of derisive taunt against him, and say :
Wo to him that increaseth that which is not his !
How long?
And ladeth himself with many pledges !

7　Shall not they rise up suddenly that have lent thee on usury ?
　And awake that shall shake thee violently ?
　And thou shalt become their prey.

and חִידָה are found. It properly signifies *derision, taunt, scorn,* from לוּץ, *to stammer, speak barbarously* or *unintelligibly ;* hence *to mock, deride ;* and thus the substantive obtained the acceptation, *taunt, taunting song.* LXX., (in Prov.) σκοτεινὸν λόγον, here πρόβλημα. In later Hebrew, the word is used to denote poetry in general. חִידָה means *oratio inflexa, perplexa ; an enigma;* highly figurative and difficult language, requiring acuteness and ingenuity fully to understand it. Comp. the Arab.

حُونَ, حَانَ *superavit negotii difficultatem.*

Delitzsch not unaptly instances the words עַבְטִים, ver. 6, נֹשְׁכֶיךָ, ver. 7, and תִּקָלוֹן, ver. 16, as enigmata of this description. The derisive ode or song commences immediately, and occupies the rest of the chapter. It consists of five stanzas, composed of three verses each. Every stanza has its distinct and appropriate subject ; and, with the exception of the last, they all commence with הוֹי, *wo,* the denunciative interjection; and have each a verse at the close, beginning with כִּי ; thus forming an organic whole of singular force and beauty. וַיֹּאמַר is to be taken impersonally or collectively. עַבְטִים has been variously interpreted. Several of the Rabbins, the Syr., Vulg., and after them Luther, and other translators, take it to be compounded of עָב, *dense,* and טִיט, *clay,* which ten of Kennicott's MSS. read as two words, and most commentators who follow them suppose *riches* or *earthly goods* to be meant; but it is more in accordance with the grammatical form of the word to regard it as a quadriliteral noun, from the root עָבַט, *to exchange, give a pledge ;* in Hiph., *to lend on a pledge.* The signification of the noun is thus correctly given by Lee: "*an accumulation of pledges* in the hand of an unfeeling usurer." The form is that

of קָטִיל as in חֲלִיל from חָל ; פְּמָרִיר or כַּמְרִיר from כָּמַר ; סַגְרִיר from סָגַר ; שַׁפְרִיר from שָׁפַר. The reduplication expresses intensity or augmentation. Maurer, "*copia pignorum* captorum," an interpretation already given by Nic. Fuller in his Miscell. Sac. lib. v. cap. viii. The Chaldæan power is thus represented as a rapacious and cruel usurer, who had accumulated the property of others, and from whom it would again be taken. Comp. Deut. xxiv. 10—13, for the use of עָבַט, and the law against cruelty in usurers. The hypothesis of Delitzsch, that עַבְטִים is, as an enigmatical term, to be understood both as a compound, and as a quadriliteral, is not in keeping with his usual good sense.

7. פֶּתַע, *suddenly,* corresponds to עַד־מָתַי, *how long?* in the preceding verse, and not improbably refers to the unexpectedness of the attack made upon Babylon by the Medes and Persians. See on Is. xxi. 3, 4. נָשַׁךְ properly signifies *to bite,* and thus it is rendered in most versions. Some translate, *oppress ;* but, since it likewise signifies *to lend on usury,* there can be little doubt the prophet intended it to be understood in this acceptation, as a striking antithesis to עַבְטִים at the close of the preceding verse. Comp. the Aram.

נְכַב ,נְ֫כַב, *momordit, usuras exegit.* Arab.

قرض, the same. The like mode of speech was not unknown both to the Greeks and Romans. Aristoph. Nub. l. 12, δακνόμενος ὑπὸ—τῶν χρεῶν. Lucan. i. 171, *usura vorax.* The meaning is, that as the Babylonians had cruelly amassed the property of others, so other nations, like devouring usurers, would unmercifully deprive them of all they had acquired. וְיִקְצוּ, defective for וְיִיקְצוּ, as in Jud. xvi. 20, comp. 14. מְזַעְזְעֶיךָ, the Pil. participle of זוּעַ, *to shake, agitate.* The

8   Because thou hast plundered many nations,
      All the remainder of the people shall plunder thee;
      Because of the blood of men, and of the violence done to the earth,
      To the city, and all that dwell in it.

9   Wo to him that procureth wicked gain for his house,
      That he may establish his nest on high,
      To be preserved from the power of calamity.

10 Thou hast devised what is a disgrace to thy house,
      Cutting off many people, and sinning against thyself.

11 For the stone crieth out from the wall,
      And the brick from the timber answereth it:

reduplicate form conveys the idea of violent or excessive agitation. The allusion is to the violent seizure of a debtor by his creditor. See Matt. xviii. 28.

8. The remainder of the nations consisted of those who had escaped the devastation of the Chaldæans. The terms *man, earth,* and *city,* are to be understood generally, and are not to be restricted to the Jews, with their country and its metropolis. חֲמַס־אֶרֶץ is the genitive of object.

9. In the stanza, comprising this and the two following verses, the avarice and selfishness of the Chaldæans are denounced. The phrase בֹּצֵעַ בֶּצַע is very common in Hebrew. The verb denotes *to cut,* or *break off,* as the Orientals, especially the Chinese do, pieces of silver and other metals in their money transactions with each other. Hence it came to be applied, in a bad sense, to such as were greedily occupied with such transactions, and its derivative בֶּצַע, to signify *wicked gain, lucre.* To mark it, in the present instance, as specially atrocious, רָע, *wicked,* is added. בַּיִת, *house,* stands here for the royal family; קֵן, *nest,* for the *arx regia,* to express its inaccessible height, the allusion being taken from the nest of the eagle, which is built on high rocks, difficult of access. See Job xxxix. 27, and comp. Numb. xxiv. 21; Jer. xlix. 16.

10. "Thou hast devised disgrace to thy house," means, Thy schemes and projects shall issue in the infamy of thy family. Instead of קָצוֹת, the infinitive of קָצָה, the ancient versions have read קְצוֹת, the preterite of קָצָה. The infinitive may

either follow in construction יָעַץ preceding, or the following חוֹטֵא. I have adopted the latter, and rendered it participially. It properly denotes the direct aim of the action predicated by the preceding finite verb. For the last clause, comp. Prov. viii. 36; xx. 2.

11. An exquisite instance of bold and daring personification, by which the materials, used in the construction of the royal palace and other sumptuous buildings at Babylon, are introduced as responsively complaining of the injustice which they had suffered, either in their having been taken from their original owners, or in their being made subservient to the scenes of wickedness that were enacted in their presence. Comp. Luke xix. 40. The Targ. adds to the first line, עַל דְּאָנַס לַהּ, *because violence has been done to it.* כָּפִיס occurs only here, but from the signification of the cognate Syr. ܟܦܣ, *connexuit,* it has been supposed to mean the *cross beam* by which the walls of a building are held together. Thus Symm., Theod., and the 5th version, σύνδεσμος; LXX. κάνθαρος, *scarabæus;* but which some think was originally κανθήριον, which Vitruvius explains as signifying a cross beam. Arab. الوَتَد، مِن الشَّجَرَة، *the pin from the wood.* According to the Mishnah, the word signifies *a half brick,* which Parchon also gives as the meaning. He thus describes it: כפיס פי לבנים קטנים עשויין בכבשן, *small bricks prepared in the kiln, like pottery, and used* כלי חרס ובונים בהם הבניינים

12　Wo to him that buildeth a town through bloodshed,
　　And establisheth a city through injustice.
13　Behold! is it not from Jehovah of hosts?
　　So that the people shall labour for the very fire;
　　Yea, the nations shall weary themselves for mere vanity.
14　For the earth shall be filled
　　With the knowledge of the glory of Jehovah,
　　As the waters cover the sea.
15　Wo to him that giveth drink to his neighbour,
　　Pouring out thy wrath, and making him drunk;
　　In order to look upon their nakedness.

in building edifices. This interpretation is confirmed by the rendering of Aquila, μάζα, *what is baked,* and by the abundant use of bricks by the Babylonians, which are still visible in the ruins of their city. Citing this passage in the Taanith, Rashi explains it to be "half a brick which is usually laid between two layers of wood," Delitzsch. That it was not the wood itself is evident from the following מֵעֵץ, *from* or *out of the wood,* except we take the preposition as indicating the material of which the beam consisted. In this latter case, the words should be rendered, *And the wooden beam answereth it;* but against such construction the parallel מִקִּיר, *out of the wall,* is an insuperable objection.

12, 13. The subject of the third stanza, which begins here, was naturally suggested by the concluding verse of the preceding. The riches which enabled the king of Babylon to rebuild and enlarge the royal city, were procured in the bloody wars in which he had engaged; and the works themselves were carried up by people from different parts of the empire, and by captives from other nations. The preposition מִן prefixed in מֵאֵת יְהֹוָה, points out the ultimate cause of the destruction of the Babylonian empire—the overruling providence of God, who, in order to give prominence to his resistless omnipotence, is designated יְהֹוָה צְבָאוֹת, *Jehovah of hosts.* For this epithet, see on Is. i. 9. דַּי is not a poetic form for בְּ, but is intensive, דַּי, signifying *sufficiency, abundance.* The preposition here points out the final issue or result of the labour and fatigue connected with the erections in question, the conflagration and depopulation of the city of Babylon. The last two lines of ver. 13 are found in Jer. li. 58; only אֵשׁ and רִיק have exchanged places, וְיָעֵפוּ stands for יָעֵפוּ, and the defective form וְיִגְעוּ for וְיִיגְעוּ. For the destruction by fire, comp. Jer. li. 30, 58; for her desolation, ver. 43. Hitzig, from the mere circumstance of the use of the same terms Micah iii. 10, applies the prophecy to Jehoiakim!

14. This verse is clearly predictive of the gospel dispensation, to the introduction of which the destruction of the Babylonian power was indispensable, inasmuch as it involved the deliverance of the Jews from captivity, and their re-occupation of their own land before the advent of the Messiah. See on Is. xi. 9, 11, the former of which verses contains a similar prediction of the same event. יָם, *sea,* is used for *the bed of the sea.*

15. The commencement of the fourth stanza. Though the idea of the shameless conduct of drunkards, here depicted, may have been borrowed from the profligate manners of the Babylonian court, yet the language is not to be taken literally, as if the prophet were describing such manners, but, as the sequel shows, is applied allegorically to the state of stupefaction, prostration, and exposure, to which the conquered nations were reduced by the Chaldæans. See on Is. li. 17, 20; and comp. Ps. lxxv. 8; Jer. xxv. 15—28; xlix. 12; li. 7; Ezek. xxiii. 31, 32; Rev. xiv. 10; xvi. 6; xviii. 6. רְעֵהוּ is a collective, and thus is equivalent to רֵעֵיהוּ in the

16 Thou art filled with shame, not with glory;
   Drink thou also, and show thyself uncircumcised;
   The cup of Jehovah's right hand shall come round to thee,
   And great ignominy shall be upon thy glory.
17 For the violence done to Lebanon shall cover thee,
   As the destruction of beasts terrifieth them;

plural, which is required to agree with the suffix in מְעוֹרֵיהֶם. The latter noun is derived from עוּר, Arab. عار, to be naked, as its synonyme עֶרְוָה is from עָרָה. In הֵמָתְךָ is a change from the third person to the second, for the sake of effect. There not being anything in the ancient Greek versions corresponding to the ךְ, is no ground for its rejection, since their authors frequently took liberties even when professedly most verbal. חֲמַת is not the construct of חֵמָה or חַמַּת, bottle, but of חֵמָה, heat, or wrath. Comp. וַאֲשַׁבְּרֵם בַּחֲמָתִי Is. lxiii. 6, and li. 17; Jer. xxv. 15; Rev. xvi. 19. Delitzsch attempts in vain to set aside the signification of pour, as inhering in the root סָפַח; Arab. سفح, effudit. Cognate שָׁפַךְ. Targ. נְלַף. שַׁפֵּר is the infinitive used instead of the participle. The language of the concluding clause of the verse is expressive of the deepest humiliation on the one hand, and of the most haughty wantonness on the other.

16. The preposition in מִכָּבוֹד is negative, as in אָהַבְתָּ רָע מִטּוֹב, Ps. lii. 5. The full force of the hemistich is, "Thou art satiated, but it is with shame, not with glory." Kimchi and others, comparing כּוֹס הַתַּרְעֵלָה, Is. li. 17, and כַּף רַעַל Zech. xii. 2, suppose that in הֵעָרֵל, be thou uncircumcised, there is a transposition of the letters ע and ר, and that the verb has originally been הֵרָעֵל, reel or stagger. And thus the LXX. (καρδία σαλευθῆτι καὶ σείσθητι) have interpreted it, and have been followed by the Arab., Syr., and Vulg. There is, however, such a manifest agreement with מְעוֹרֵיהֶם, pudenda eorum, at the close of the preceding verse, that the interpretation cannot be admitted. In the mouth of a Hebrew no term could have expressed more ineffable contempt. Comp. 1 Sam. xvii. 36.

As the Chaldæans had treated the nations which they conquered in the most disgusting manner, so they, in their turn, should be similarly treated. To express the certainty of the event, the verbs are in the imperative. See on Is. vi. 10. תִּסּוֹב is the future in Niphal, and conveys the idea of the cup of suffering being transferred from one nation to another, each, in its turn, being made to drink of it. Comp. Jer. xxv. 26; Lam. iv. 21. קִיקָלוֹן, the Vul. renders, vomitus ignominiæ, as if compounded of קִי for קִיא, vomit, and קָלוֹן, shame. In nine MSS. it is read as two words, and this etymology is approved by most Jewish and Christian interpreters. It is, however, more in accordance with the genius of the Hebrew language, to regard it as a reduplicate form of קָלוֹן, employed for the sake of intensity, after the form קְלֹקֵל: only instead of קְלֹקָלוֹן we have the softer קִיקָלוֹן. Comp. the Syr. ܦ̈ܠܨ for צְלָצַל. Thus the LXX. ἀτιμία; Syr. ܙܠܝܐ; Targ. קְלָנָא. The glory of the Babylonians was to be completely eclipsed by the deep disgrace in which they should be involved.

17. חֲמַס לְבָנוֹן and חֲמַס־אֶרֶץ are genitives of object. That Lebanon is not here to be understood literally, but figuratively, of Jerusalem, seems fully established by the prophetic style in other passages, especially Jer. xxii. 23; Ezek. xvii. 3, 12. The aptness of the figure consists partly in the circumstance, that cedars from that mountain were employed in the construction of the temple and other houses in Jerusalem, 1 Kings vi. 9, 10, 18; vii. 2; ix. 10, 11; 2 Chron. i. 15; and partly in its stateliness and grandeur as the metropolis. Against this interpretation, the objections do not apply which Delitzsch makes to the opinion of those who maintain that

Because of the blood of men, and the violence done to the earth,
To the city, and all that dwell in it.

18   What profiteth the graven image which its maker graveth,
The molten image, and the teacher of falsehood?
In which the maker of his work trusteth—
Making dumb idols.

19 Wo to him that saith to the wood, Awake!
Wake up! to the dumb stone.
It teach! There it is,
Overlaid with gold and silver,
But there is no breath at all within it.

20 But Jehovah is in his holy temple;

---

by Lebanon the land of Palestine is meant. כָּפָה, *to cover,* is used emphatically to express the completeness of the destruction which should overtake the Chaldæans. Similar violence to that which they had exercised should be brought upon themselves. The ו in וְשֹׁד is a particle of comparison, retaining, indeed, its ordinary conjunctive power, but also introducing a clause designed to illustrate the preceding. Of this idiom, the following are instances: אָדָם לְעָמָל יוּלָד וּבְנֵי רֶשֶׁף יַגְבִּיהוּ עוּף, *Man is born to trouble,* AND (AS) *birds of prey fly aloft,* Job v. 7. כִּי־אֹזֶן מִלִּין תִּבְחָן וְחֵךְ יִטְעַם לֶאֱכֹל, *For the ear trieth words,* AND (AS) *the palate tasteth food,* xxxiv. 3. This construction entirely obviates the difficulty which necessarily attaches to the attempts that have been made to interpret the בְּהֵמוֹת, *beasts,* of the inhabitants of Palestine. The prophet compares the confusion and destruction, which should come upon the enemy of the Jews, to those experienced by the wild beasts when brought into circumstances from which they cannot escape. חָתַת signifies *to be broken, broken in pieces, destroyed, confounded, terrified.* In the present form יְחִיתָן, the Yod is substituted for the Dagesh in the regular form יְחִתָּן, as הֲתִימְךָ for הַתְמִיךָ, Is. xxxiii. 1. The Nun appended is not paragogic, but the verbal suffix of the third feminine plural, agreeing with בְּהֵמוֹת. There is no sufficient ground for changing ן into ך, though the authors of some of the ancient versions may have thus read. For the last clause, see on ver. 8.

18, 19. These verses expose the folly of idolatry to which the Babylonians were wholly addicted. It might be supposed, from all the other stanzas having been introduced by a denunciatory הוֹי, *wo,* that a transposition has here taken place, and that the nineteenth ought to be read before the eighteenth; and Green has thus placed them in his translation; but there is a manifest propriety in anticipating the inutility of idols, in close connexion with what the prophet had just announced respecting the downfal of Babylon, before delivering his denunciation against their worshippers themselves. כִּי, in both instances, is used as a relative pronoun, as in Gen. iii. 19; iv. 25; Is. lvii. 20. The idol is called "a teacher of falsehood," on account of the lying oracles that were connected with its worship. For these verses, compare Is. xliv. 9—20; Jer. x. In the latter part of the nineteenth verse, the language is highly and pointedly ironical. הוּא יוֹרֶה, *it teach?* is an emphatic form of putting a question which requires a negative reply. יוֹרֶה forms a paronomasia with מוֹרֶה in the preceding verse. הִנֵּה הוּא, *there it is.* Such is the force of the interjection הִנֵּה in this place —not being followed as usual by the accusative, but for the sake of making the idol more prominent, by the nominative case.

20. In striking contrast with the utter nihility of idols, Jehovah is here introduced, at the close of the prophecy, as the invisible Lord of all, occupying his

Keep silence before him all the earth.

celestial temple, whence he is ever ready to interpose his omnipotence for the deliverance and protection of his people, and the destruction of their enemies. Comp. Is. xxvi. 21. Such a God it becomes all to adore in solemn and profound silence. Ps. lxxvi. 8, 9; Zeph. i. 7; Zech. ii. 13.

CHAPTER III

Though forming a distinct whole, this chapter is intimately connected with the two preceding, the subjects contained in which it presupposes, and is evidently designed to afford consolation to the Jews during the national calamities there anticipated. It exhibits a regular ode, beginning with a brief, but simple and appropriate exordium; after which follows the main subject, which is treated in a manner perfectly free and unrestrained, as the different topics rose, one after another, in the powerfully excited mind of the prophet; and finishes with an epigrammatic resumption of the point first adverted to in the introduction, and the practical lesson which the piece was intended to teach.

With respect to the body of the ode, interpreters are greatly divided in opinion. The Fathers generally, and after them many Catholic commentators, and among Protestants, Cocceius, Bengel, Roos, and others, apply the whole chapter, with certain modifications, to New Testament times, and subject it to all the uncertainty of imaginary interpretation. But the principal point of disagreement relates to the theophania, or Divine interposition, so sublimely set forth, ver. 3—15. According to the Targum, Abarbanel, Abenezra, Tarnovius, Munster, Clarius, Drusius, Schnurrer, Herder, Michaelis, Green, Lowth, Tingstadius, Eichhorn, Justi, Hesselberg, Ackermann, and Ewald, the prophet adverts to the wonderful displays of the power and majesty of God during the early history of the Hebrews. Maurer, Hitzig, and Delitzsch, on the other hand, contend that the future interposition of Jehovah for the destruction of the Chaldæans, is what he exclusively contemplates. The last-mentioned author has not only gone at great length, and with much minuteness, into the subject, but appears to have exhausted all his critical and exegetical ingenuity in his attempt to establish his hypothesis. Taking for granted that יָבוֹא, ver. 3, cannot, by any possibility, be construed otherwise than to express the strict futurity of the advent predicated, he proceeds to show, from what he considers to be the organic structure of the ode; from the connexion of שָׁמַעְתִּי and וַתִּרְגַּז, ver. 16; and from certain features of the picture itself, that what he calls the lyric-prophetical view is alone to be admitted. I must, however, confess, that after a careful examination of his arguments, I can discover nothing in them that goes to overturn the historical position adopted by the numerous writers above mentioned. That nothing in the shape of a regular and specific recital of distinct facts is exhibited in the tableau, cannot fairly be urged against this interpretation, since such a recital would ill accord with the enthusiasm and impetuosity which are so characteristic of the ode as a species of poetry. The abrupt and rapid transitions of the prophet did not admit of more than a slight, though sublimely figurative allusion, to one or two localities, which it was necessary to specify, in order to call up the general scene of events to the mind of the reader: all the rest is left to be supplied by familiar acquaintance with the sacred national records. What he aims at is to produce a powerful impression, by condensing, within the shortest possible limits, a view of the *magnalia Dei*, as exhibited in these records. And this he does by giving utterance to the total impression which they produced upon his own mind, rather than by furnishing a detailed historical description. Regarding the composition in this light, the obscurity and apparent incoherence which attach to certain parts of it, are at once accounted for.

As parallels to this ode, we may adduce Deut. xxxiii. 2—5; Jud. v. 4, 5; Ps. lxviii. 7, 8; lxxvii. 13—20; cxiv.; Is. lxiii. 11—14. That the Holy Spirit availed himself, so to speak, of some of these passages in presenting the subject to the view of the prophet, there can, I think, be little doubt. The agreement in point of phraseology, especially as it respects Ps. lxxvii., is most palpable. Some, indeed, have maintained the priority of our ode to the Psalm; but Delitzsch has proved, by an elaborate collation of passages and expressions, that this hypothesis is entirely without foundation, and that Habakkuk had the Psalm brought to his mind, just as he had the song of Moses called up to his recollection.

The following description of this sublime ode, by the master pen of Bishop Lowth, is not more beautiful than just : "The prophet, indeed, illustrates this subject throughout with equal magnificence ; selecting from such an assemblage of miraculous incidents, the most noble and important, displaying them in the most splendid colours, and embellishing them with the sublimest imagery, figures, and diction, the dignity of which is so heightened and recommended by the superior elegance of the conclusion, that were it not for a few shades, which the hand of time has apparently cast over it in two or three passages, no composition of the kind would, I believe, appear more elegant or more perfect than this poem." (Lect. xxviii.) Whether the hand of time has really cast any shades over it, will appear in the sequel.

That it was designed for use in public worship, appears both from the inscription and the subscription, as well as from the musical term סֶלָה, *Selah*, occurring verses 3, 9, 13.

The chapter begins with the title and introduction, ver. 1, 2. Habakkuk then represents Jehovah as appearing in glorious majesty on Sinai, 3, 4; describes the ravages of the plague in the desert, 5; the consternation into which the nations were thrown by the victorious approach of the Hebrews to Canaan, and their wars with the inhabitants, 6—10; specially refers to the celestial phenomenon at Gibeon, 11; and then sets forth the auspicious results of the interposition of God on behalf of his people, 12—15. The prophet concludes by resuming the subject of the introduction, 16; and strongly asserting his unshaken confidence in God in the midst of the anticipated calamity, 17—19.

1   A PRAYER of Habakkuk, the prophet: with triumphal music.
2   O Jehovah! I heard the report of thee; I was afraid:
     O Jehovah! revive thy work in the midst of the years;

1. תְּפִלָּה, usually rendered *prayer*, comprehends all kinds of devotional composition, whether abounding in petitions, supplications, &c., or not. Hence it is applied to all the Psalms of David collectively, Ps. lxxii. 20; and is otherwise only used in the inscriptions of Psalms xvii., lxxxvi., xc., cii., cxlii. The term is derived from פָלַל, *to separate, distinguish;* cognate to פָלָה; and so *to form an opinion or judgment, to judge, give a verdict.* In Hithpael the verb signifies to apply to a judge for a favourable decision, *to supplicate, pray,* &c.; and is employed at the commencement of the song of Hannah, 1 Sam. ii. 1. Though the only precatory sentences are those contained in ver. 2, yet there are several instances of direct address to God, which impart to the ode one of the characteristic features of prayer. The Lamed prefixed in לַחֲבַקּוּק is that of authorship. עַל שִׁגְיֹנוֹת. That this is a musical term seems beyond dispute, from similar terms occurring in the titles of the Psalms, such as עַל־הַגִּתִּית, עַל יוֹנַת אֵלֶם, &c. For the explanation of the noun, which only occurs here, and in the singular שִׁגָּיוֹן, in the title of Ps. vii., different methods have been proposed. Bauer, Herder, Perschke, De Wette, Rosenmüller, Lee, Hitzig, and Maurer, have recourse to the Arabic شَجِي, *anxius, tristis, mæstus fuit,* and render עַל־שִׁגְיֹנוֹת, *after the manner of elegies,* but there seems no reason deducible either from the present ode or from the Psalm, why they should be thus characterised, or why they should be sung to a plaintive tune, but the contrary. Others, as Wahl, Justi, Gesenius, derive the word from the Syriac ܫܓܐ, in Pael, ܫܰܓܺܝ, *cecinit,* whence ܫܽܘܓܳܝܳܐ, *carmen, cantus,* to which it has justly been objected, that it is too vague and indefinite to admit of adoption. The LXX., indeed, have ψαλμὸς in the Psalm, and here ᾠδή;

but without any apparent reference to the specific meaning of the term. Other philologists more reasonably content themselves with שָׁגָה, an indigenous Hebrew verb in common use, signifying *to err, wander, reel,* &c. This interpretation Aquila, Symm., and the fifth Greek version so far support, rendering, ἐπὶ ἀγνοημάτων, which Jerome adopts, on the principle that שָׁגָה signifies *to sin through ignorance.* To this derivation Hengstenberg has recently given his adhesion (Comm. on Psalms, vol. i. p. 144), but most preposterously affirms, that in our ode the sins or crimes of the Chaldæans are intended. There is nothing either in the Psalm, or in the song of Habakkuk, to warrant the appropriation of any such signification of the term. The most probable explanation is that given by Delitzsch, who is of opinion that שִׁגָּיוֹן means a *dithyrambos,* or *cantio erratica,* a species of rhythmical composition, which, from its enthusiastic irregularity, is admirably adapted for songs of victory or triumph. It is obvious, however, from the established use of the preposition עַל, *upon, after the manner of,* or *accompanied with,* in the titles of the Psalms, that the plural שִׁגְיֹנוֹת, to which, in like manner, it is here prefixed, must be understood as describing a corresponding kind of music with which the ode was to be accompanied. The translation of Theodotion, ὑπὲρ τῶν ἑκουσιασμῶν, *i. e.* as Jerome interprets the words, *pro voluntariis,* has, in all probability, some such reference.

2. The שֵׁמַע, *report* of Jehovah, here referred to by the prophet, does not mean what God had communicated to him, but a report *respecting* Jehovah, or the punishment which he had threatened to inflict upon the Jews for their sins. The genitive is that of object. That it cannot refer to what follows in the ode is certain, since the exhibition there given of the Divine interposition for the overthrow of the enemies of his people was calculated to inspire the prophet with joy, and not with the fear

In the midst of the years make it known :
In wrath remember mercy.

3   God came from Teman ;
    Even the Holy One from Mount Paran : *Pause.*

of which he declares he. was conscious.
His prayer also, that while punishment
was being inflicted, God would exercise
pity, shows that the Jews, and not the
Chaldæans, were to be the subjects of
the infliction. It may, therefore, be
regarded as certain, that what he has in
view is the prediction chap. i. 6—11.
The fear with which the prophet was
seized, he particularly describes ver. 16.
By פָּעָלֶךָ, *thy work*, Abarbanel, Kimchi,
Schnurrer, Justi, and some others,
understand the Jews, on the ground
that they are designated the פֹּעַל, *work*
of Jehovah's hands, Is. xlv. 11; but the
simple occurrence of the same word,
irrespective of the specific claims of the
connexion, cannot justify such a construction of the meaning. In chap. i. 5,
the term is used of the Divine judgment
upon the Jews, as it also is Is. v. 12,
and of that upon their enemies, Ps.
lxiv. 10. This latter sense, which involves
the exercise of the power and goodness
of God on behalf of his people, alone
suits the present context. Comp. Ps.
xc. 16. What the prophet prays for,
is the renewal of such interposition.
This he expresses by the strong term
חַיֵּהוּ, *quicken, restore to life*, which suggests the idea of a long cessation of
the avenging and delivering power of
the Most High. It had been, in regard
to its exertion, as if it had been dead,
and required to be called forth afresh
into action. Thus Jarchi : דַּיֵּהוּ פָּעֳלֶךָ
הָרִאשׁוֹן שֶׁהָיִיתָ נִפְרַע לָנוּ מֵאוֹיְבֵינוּ בְּקֶרֶב שְׁנֵי הַצָּרָה
שֶׁאָנוּ שְׁרוּיִים בָּהּ חַיֵּהוּ כְּלוֹמַר עוֹרְרֵהוּ וְהֲשִׁיבֵהוּ.
*Thy former work, when thou didst avenge
us of our enemies, in the midst of the
years of the calamity in which we live,
revive it*, i. e. *rouse it up, cause it to return.*
Comp. Is. li. 9, 10. No stress is to be
laid on the phrase בְּקֶרֶב שָׁנִים, *in the midst
of the years*, from which Bengel deduced
so much fanciful support to his chronological calculations ; maintaining that
the middle point of the years of the
world is meant. The שָׁנִים are unquestionably the *years*, or *period of affliction*,

which was to come upon the Jewish
people. בְּקֶרֶב is not to be taken in the
strict acceptation of the middle point of
any given period of time, but is, as
frequently, only a more emphatic prepositive form, instead of בְּ, *in*. The
meaning, therefore, simply is, During
the period of suffering, or, in the course
of our punishment. by the Chaldæans,
interpose for our deliverance. Symm.
ἐντὸς τῶν ἐνιαυτῶν. To give pathos to
the language, the phrase is repeated ;
and תּוֹדִיעַ is added, as synonymous with
חַיֵּיהוּ, the suffix of which is to be understood, though not expressed. The verb
יָדַע, *to know*, is here used in the sense
of experiencing, knowing by experience.
רַחֵם, the infinitive, is to be regarded
as an accusative. Comp. Ps. xxv. 6:
זְכֹר־רַחֲמֶיךָ יְהוָה וַחֲסָדֶיךָ כִּי מֵעוֹלָם הֵמָּה. It is
merely necessary to exhibit the version
of this verse as now found in the text of
the LXX. to show that it can only
have originated in the amalgamation of
different readings, some of them probably
marginal glosses, and that it would be
most unwarrantable to attempt any
correction of the Hebrew text by it :
Κύριε, εἰσακήκοα τὴν ἀκοήν σου, καὶ
ἐφοβήθην, κατενόησα τὰ ἔργα σου, καὶ
ἐξέστην· ἐν μέσῳ δύο ζώων γνωσθήσῃ,
ἐν τῷ ἐγγίζειν τὰ ἔτη ἐπιγνωσθήσῃ· ἐν
τῷ παρεῖναι τὸν καιρὸν ἀναδειχθήσῃ, ἐν
τῷ ταραχθῆναι τὴν ψυχήν. μου, ἐν ὀργῇ
ἐλέους μνησθήσῃ.

3. אֱלוֹהַּ is not used by any of the
minor prophets except Habakkuk, and
by him only here, and chap. i. 11. It
occurs four times in Daniel, and once
in Isaiah, but never in Jeremiah or
Ezekiel. There is no foundation whatever for the position assumed by Gesenius
and some others, that this use of the
singular belongs to the later Hebrew,
though it is allowed to belong to the
poetic diction. It is employed *forty*
times in the book of Job, one of the
most ancient specimens of Hebrew composition extant, and twice by Moses,
Deut. xxxii. קָדוֹשׁ, *Holy*, which is here

His splendour covered the heavens,
And the earth was full of his praise.

parallel to אֱלוֹהַּ, God, also occurs in this application to express the absolute purity of the Divine Being, Job vi. 10; Is. xl. 25; and in the plural, קְדשִׁים, Prov. ix. 10; xxx. 3; Hos. xii. 1. Delitzsch contends, that, as יָבוֹא is uninfluenced by any preceding preterite, it cannot possibly be taken otherwise than as strictly future in signification, as it is in form. But this is not the only instance in which the future stands absolutely at the commencement of a sentence or paragraph, yet clearly indicating a past transaction. Thus Num. xxiii. 7, יִדְאָרֵם; יַנְחֵנִי בָלָק, Jud. ii. 1; אַעֲלֶה אֶתְכֶם מִמִּצְרַיִם 2 Sam. iii. 33, הַכְּמוֹת נָבָל יָמוּת אַבְנֵר; Job iii. 3, יֹאבַד יוֹם אִוָּלֶד בּוֹ; Ps. lxxx. 9, גֶּפֶן מִמִּצְרַיִם תַּסִּיעַ. The idiom, in these and similar cases, is sufficiently accounted for on the principle that the speaker places himself, in imagination, anterior to the action expressed by the verb, and thus, regarding it as still future, puts the verb in that tense. Having prayed that God would remember the mercy which he had shown to his people in ancient days, the prophet has his mind carried back to their affliction in Egypt, in their deliverance from which that mercy was signally displayed; and assuming that as his point of observation, he proceeds at once to describe the Theophania as future in regard to such position. The past, thus implied, though not expressed, as completely modifies a future tense, as if a preterite, or any qualifying particle, had preceded it. תֵּימָן, Teman, the LXX. retain as a proper name: the Targ., Syr., Theod., Vulg., and many modern versions read, the south. The word is doubtless to be taken as designating the country to the south of Judæa, and east of Idumæa, in which latter country Mount Paran (הַר פָּארָן) was situated. Some, indeed, have endeavoured to identify this mountain with Sinai, on the ground that وادي فيران Wady Pheiran, which extends north-west from Sinai, is the same as מִדְבַּר פָּארָן, the desert of Paran, mentioned in Scripture. But although this desert might have stretched

so far towards the south-west as to touch upon the Wady, and so give it the name, it is certain, from Paran being mentioned in connexion with Kadesh and Beersheba, that the wilderness of that name extended to the southern confines of Palestine, including the mountainous region to the west of the Ghor, or great valley stretching from the Dead Sea to the Élanitic Gulf. In 1 Kings xi. 18, it is spoken of as lying between Midian and Egypt. From Sinai occurring along with Seir and Paran, Deut. xxxiii. 2, and with Seir and the country of Edom, Jud. v. 4, 5, it is probable that Habakkuk here alludes to the regions to the south of Palestine generally, as the theatre of the Divine manifestations to Israel, only, like Moses and Deborah, specifying the two points nearer to that country. In this view, his omission of Sinai, which they notice, is not of material moment. The glorious displays of the power and majesty of Jehovah which had been made in that quarter occupied his thoughts, and inspired him with feelings of the most exalted devotion.—סֶלָה, Selah. This word, which occurs thrice in this ode, and seventy-three times in the Psalms, has been variously interpreted. That it is a musical sign is now almost universally admitted. It is found at the end of certain sections, or strophes, and always at the close of a verse, except Hab. iii. 3, 9; Ps. lv. 20; lvii. 4; where however, as always, it ends the hemistich. Sometimes it occurs at the end of a Psalm, as Ps. iii., ix., and xxiv. The current, and apparently the traditionary interpretation, is that of the Targ. לְעָלְמִין; Aq. ἀεί; Symm., sometimes, εἰς τὸν αἰῶνα; Theod., sometimes, εἰς τέλος; the fifth Greek version, διαπαντός; but Symm. and Theod. most commonly coincide with the LXX., who uniformly render, διάψαλμα. This last translation is decidedly entitled to the preference, in so far as it confines the idea to the music, though the exact meaning even of this Greek term has been matter of dispute. Suidas, however, seems to come nearest to the mark, when he gives as its meaning μέλους ἐναλλαγή, a change

4 For the brightness was like that of the sun ;
  Rays streamed from his hand:
  Yet the concealment of his glory was there.

of the modulation, and with him Hesy-
chius agrees, explaining it by μέλους
διαλλαγή. The hypothesis that סֶלָה is
merely an abbreviation, consisting of
the initial letters of three Hebrew words,
is altogether gratuitous, there not being
the least shadow of evidence that the
Jews, in ancient times, ever employed
abbreviations. Pfeiffer, in his work, Die
Musik der Alten Hebr. p. 17, proposes
to explain the term by the Arab. شلر,
membrum, or section; Prof. Lee, by
صلوة, صلاة, which he renders, *Dei invo-
catio*, and derives from صلرت, *he blessed;*
but neither of these derivations will suit
all the passages in which it occurs.
Indeed, *bless!* or *praise!* would come
in most incongruously in such connexions as Ps. vii. 5 ; xxxix. 5, 11; lii. 3.
Of the two Hebrew roots to which the
word has been referred, סָלַל, *to raise,
elevate*, and סָלָה, which, besides signifying *to raise*, has been supposed to be
equivalent to שָׁלָה, *to rest, pause*, the
latter, on the whole, seems to deserve
the preference. There are several instances in which the letter שׁ has been
softened into ס, as in שִׂרְיוֹן and סִרְיוֹן ;
שָׂמַר and סָמַר ; just as, in most cases, we find
it expressed in Arabic by س. This
derivation, in which Gesenius finally
acquiesced, has been approved of by
Delitzsch and Hengstenberg. The term
may be regarded as a substantive, signifying *silence* or *pause ;* designed, in all
probability, to command a cessation of
the song or chant, while the instruments
either repeated what had just been
played, or introduced an interlude between the parts. At the end of a psalm
it may have been intended to prevent
a repetition on the part of the singers,
while the instrumental music continued.
Having, by a solemn pause, prepared
the mind for the contemplation of the
manifested glory of Jehovah, the prophet
proceeds to describe this glory in the
most sublime and magnificent language.

By תְּהִלָּה is never meant *splendour* or
brightness, as the Targ., Kimchi, and
Hitzig interpret; nor does it here express
the actual praises of the inhabitants of
the earth produced by the effulgence of
Deity, for the effect of this effulgence is
described, ver. 6, to be fear and trembling; but *matter of praise*, or the glory
which was calculated to call forth universal adoration.

4. By אוֹר we are not here to understand *light* simply, but the *sun* as the
source of light. Comp. Job xxxi. 26 ;
xxxvii. 21. The Kametz of the article
in כַּ renders the noun more definite.
תִּהְיֶה, which Heidenheim would connect
with הָאָרֶץ, and Hitzig with תְּהִלָּתוֹ, in the
preceding verse, can have no other
nominative than נֹגַהּ, which, like other
substantives in the Oriental languages,
expressive of fire or light, is conceived
to be of the feminine gender, or it may
be regarded as neuter in signification,
and so taking the feminine of the verb.
That by קַרְנַיִם, *horns*, we are here to
understand *rays*, is obvious from the
connexion ; from the comparison of the
rising sun scattering his rays upon the
earth to the gazelle, Ps. xxii. 1; and
from its being common with the Arabs
to compare them to the horns of that
animal. Thus the Arab. قرن, *cornu*
*animalis, latus vel superior pars solis, pri-
mi radii solis.* Kamoos and Djauhari.
Hence, the verb קָרַן signifies to *emit rays*,
Exod. xxxiv. 29, 30, 35. Though in the
dual, the noun, like others of that
number which describe objects naturally
existing in pairs, is here expressive of
the plural. Comp. אַרְבַּע רַגְלָיִם, Lev. xi. 23 ;
שְׁלֹשׁ הַשִּׁנַּיִם, 1 Sam. ii. 13; פְּלִבְרֻכַּיִם, Ezek.
xxi. 12 ; שִׁבְעָה עֵינַיִם, Zech. iii. 9 ; and see
my note on Is. vi. 2. The phrase מִיָּדוֹ,
from his hand, is equivalent to מִפֶּנּוּ, *from
him ;* and a verb of flowing, streaming,
or the like, must be supplied. לוֹ is the
dative of possession. שָׁם, *there*, refers
to the scene of splendour just described,
which, though so excessively bright,
instead of exhibiting the Divine glory

5 Before him went the plague ;
   And the burning pestilence followed him.
6 He stood, and made the earth to tremble ;
   He looked, and caused the nations to shake ;
   Yea, the old mountains were shattered in pieces,
   The ancient hills sank down—
   His ancient ways.

only veiled or concealed it. Comp. Ps. civ. 2. The LXX., Syr., Aq., and Symm., have read וְשָׁם, *and he put*, instead of וְשָׁם, *and there*, and are followed by Hitzig and Maurer, but this rendering is less apt. עֹז in such connexion denotes *majesty* or *glory* rather than *power*. Comp. Ps. cxxxii. 8 ; lxxviii. 61. For עֻזֹּה many MSS. read עֻזֹּו, the regular affix. Whether the substratum of the vivid representation here furnished of the glorious majesty of Jehovah be the symbol of the Divine presence exhibited upon Mount Sinai, Exod. xxiv. 17, or the Shekinah which accompanied the Hebrews through the desert, chap. xvi. 7, 10 ; Lev. ix. 23 ; Exod. xl. 35, &c., cannot be determined. See on ver. 3.

5. רֶשֶׁף, from רָשַׁף, *to inflame*, has two leading significations, that of *lightning*, or *flame*, and that of *hot*, or *burning fever*. The latter is required in the present case to correspond to דֶּבֶר, *plague*, in the preceding hemistich : a circumstance which forbids the adoption of the precarious rendering, *birds of prey*, though supported by the Syr., Aq., Symm., Theod., the fifth Greek version, Michaelis, Schnurrer, Herder, Kofod, Dahl, Rosenmüller, and others ; as well as that of *lightning*, adopted by Kalinsky, Wahl, Bauer, and others ; and *burning coals*, as in our common version. Thus Kimchi : רשף כמו דבר והענין כפול במלות שונות וכן ולחומי רשף והוא חולי הקדחת שהיא חמה השורפת וממיתה מהרה, *i. e.* " רשף corresponds to דבר, the same thing being expressed in different words. The word has the same signification Deut. xxxii. 24, and denotes the fever, which consists in a burning heat, and speedily causes death." The Vulg. has, " Et egredietur *diabolus* ante pedes ejus ! " הָלַךְ or יָצָא לְרֶגֶל, means to *track* or *follow* any one. Here it is opposed to לִפְנָיו, *before him*. What the prophet has in view, would seem to be the plagues

with which the enemies of the Hebrews were visited, of which we have an instance 1 Sam. v. 9, 11.

6. עָמַד וַיְמֹדֶד, forms an easy and elegant paronomasia, and, at the same time, exhibits one of the boldest, most abrupt, and sublime turns to be found in sacred poetry. While Jehovah is marching forth for the deliverance of his people, he stops all of a sudden in his progress, the immediate effects of which are universal consternation and terror. Nature, in her strongest and most ancient formations, is broken in pieces before him. The inhabitants of the earth tremble at his look. וַיְמֹדֶד may either be the Poel of מָדַד, *to measure*, or the Pilel of מוּד, which, like the Arab. مَادَ, signifies *to be agitated*. The latter derivation best suits the connexion. LXX. ἐσαλεύθη ἡ γῆ. Targ. וְאָנִיעַ אַרְעָא. Arab. تَزَعْزَعَتِ الأَرْض. Comp. the cognate מוֹט. Thus Gesenius, Lee, Maurer, Ewald, Heidenheim, Hesselberg, Delitzsch. The primary idea conveyed by נָתַר is that of *bounding, springing up*, as a person does when overtaken by sudden fear. In יִתְפֹּצְצוּ we have all the force of intensive verbs, heightened in effect by the harsh sound of the reduplicated Tzade. פּוּץ signifies *to break* or *dash in pieces*, and also *to scatter, disperse*. For הַרְרֵי־עַד and גִּבְעוֹת עוֹלָם, comp. Gen. xlix. 26 ; Deut. xxxiii. 15. הֲלִיכוֹת עוֹלָם לוֹ, *His ancient ways*, I consider to be epexegetical of the preceding ; and הֲלִיכוֹת is to be taken in the same sense as דְּרָכִים in the sentence הוּא רֵאשִׁית דַּרְכֵי־אֵל, Job xl. 19, which describes the hippopotamus as " the first or principal of *the ways* of God," *i. e.* his creative acts, his works. The words may be resolved into הֲלִיכוֹת עוֹלָם אֲשֶׁר לוֹ, or into הֲלִיכוֹת עוֹלָמוֹ. The mountains which Jehovah had created of old, and which had resisted

7 I saw the tents of Cushan in trouble;
  The tent-curtains of the land of Midian trembled.
8 Was it against the rivers it burned, O Jehovah?
  Was thine anger against the rivers?
  Was thy wrath against the sea?
  That thou didst ride upon thy horses,
  In thy chariots of victory.

the revolutions of ages, were now shattered in pieces, and dissipated like dust before him. The irresistibility of his power, and the utter imbecility of the most formidable enemies of his people, are the ideas conveyed by the language of the prophet.

7. תַּחַת אָוֶן, "*under* affliction," is more expressive than בְּאָוֶן, "*in* affliction," as it suggests the idea of a heavy load by which those spoken of were oppressed. כּוּשָׁן, *Cushan*, is now generally admitted to be the same as כּוּשׁ, *Cush*, as לוֹטָן, *Lotan*, Gen. xxxvi. 20, is only another form of לוֹט, *Lot;* but whether it be intended to designate the African or the Arabian Cush, is disputed. Gesenius, Maurer, Delitzsch, and others, contend for the former; but the connexion of the name with that of מִדְיָן, *Midian*, is decidedly in favour of the latter. For a satisfactory refutation of the position adopted by Gesenius, that *Cush*, and all the tribes connected with this name, are only to be sought in Africa, see Robinson's Calmet, art. *Cush.* That any reference to Cushan-rishathaim, Jud. iii. 10, is intended, does not appear. *Midian* appears to have stretched from the eastern shores of the Elanitic Gulf to Mount Sinai, and the frontiers of Moab. Edrisi speaks of a town called مدين, *Madian*, about five days' journey from Ailah, or Akabah, and six from Tubuk.—The "tents" and "curtains" describe the nomadic mode of life as still found among the Bedawin of the Arabian deserts. יְרִיעוֹת, *the coverings of the tents*, so called from their tremulous motion when hanging down like curtains and affected by the wind. The word is here used merely as a synonyme of אֹהָלִים, *tents;* and both are put by metonymy for the persons dwelling in them.

8. The prophet rising in his graphic description of the ancient manifestations of Jehovah, now by a bold apostrophe inquires why the rivers were affected by them? Was it on account of any cause in the rivers? The implied answer is, No; and the true cause is assigned at the close of the verse—the safe and victorious deliverance of the Israelites from Egypt, and their introduction into Canaan. יְהֹוָה is in the vocative, and the subject of the verb חָרָה is אַפְּךָ, in the second hemistich. נְהָרִים, *the rivers*, mean the waters of the Red Sea, and the Jordan, which were dried up to allow them to pass over on foot. The former is not indeed a river, but may not inaptly be included under the term, on account of the *flowing* of the tide, which is said to rise at Suez to about the height of seven feet. On the miraculous division of the sea, recorded Exod. xiv., it was made to go or *flow* back the whole night, ver. 21. For the application of נָהָר to the stream-tide of the Mediterranean, see Jonah ii. 4. That the rivers of Cush should be intended, is altogether out of the question. Specifically, however, to mark out the Red Sea, it is afterwards expressly called יָם in the third hemistich. Comp. as parallel with the present verse, Exod. xv.; Ps. lxxvii. 13—19; cxiv. 3, 5. Jehovah is here, and in the following verses, represented as a mighty and victorious warrior, giving orders to his army, and, in triumphant progress, carrying all before him. Comp. Exod. xv. 3; xiv. 14. אַף, *anger*, and עֶבְרָה, *wrath*, are synonymes, only the latter is the stronger of the two, signifying unrestrained indignation; from עָבַר, to *pass over*, or *beyond a boundary.* By "horses" and "chariots," there is no necessity for our understanding either the angels, or thunder and lightning, as some would interpret. They are merely figurative expressions, designed to carry out the

9. Naked and bared was thy bow,
  " Sevens of spears " was the word: *Pause.*
  Thou didst cleave the earth into rivers.

metaphor adopted from military operations. In the phrase מַרְכְּבֹתֶיךָ יְשׁוּעָה, supply עַל, *upon*, before the former word, and
repeat מַרְכְּבוֹת, *chariots*, before the latter.
Comp. for instances of similar construction, כָּעֵת חַיִל, 2 Sam. xxii. 33.
Ps. lxxi. 7 ; דַּרְכֵּךְ וְזִמָּה, Ezek. xvi. 27.—
יְשׁוּעָה has, in such connexion, the specific
signification of *victory*, though the idea
of *salvation* or *deliverance*, as the result,
is not to be lost sight of.

9. The combination עֶרְיָה תֵעוֹר, which
forms a paronomasia, determines the
signification of עוּר, as here employed,
to be that of being *bare* or *naked*, and
not that of *rousing* or *exciting.* For
though the Piel עוֹרֵר is used of the lifting
up of a spear, there would be no propriety in thus applying it to a bow:
whereas the substantive עֶרְיָה, *nakedness*,
having just been employed, nothing was
more natural than to add תֵעוֹר, *to be bared*
—עוּר being thus cognate in signification
with עָרָה, from which עֶרְיָה is derived,
and with עֵר. עֶרְיָה is used adjectively,
as in וְאַתְּ עֵרֹם וְעֶרְיָה, Ezek. xvi. 7. תֵעוֹר is
not the second, but the third person
singular in Niphal, having for its nominative קֶשֶׁת, which is of common
gender. Some of the moderns have
explained קֶשֶׁת, of the *rainbow*, than
which nothing can be conceived more
incongruously out of place in a passage
containing a sublime poetical description
of warlike operations. The making
bare the bow, refers to the removal of
the cover in which it was carefully
wrapped, to prevent its receiving injury,
or of such a leathern case as the γωρυτός,
κωρυτός, *corytus*, of the Greeks and
Romans. Of the following words, שְׁבֻעוֹת
מַטּוֹת אֹמֶר, upwards of one hundred different interpretations have been proposed.
That which I have adopted, appears to
me best to suit the connexion. It keeps
up the spirit of the poem, and is fully
justified on the simplest and most legitimate etymological grounds. That שְׁבֻעוֹת
cannot signify *oaths*, is determined by
the circumstance that " the oaths of the
tribes," the rendering of our common
version, affords no tolerable sense as

here introduced, whether we regard the
tribes as the persons swearing, or as
those to whom oaths were sworn. The
other signification of שְׁבוּעָה, is *seven*, a
heptade, or what is made up of seven.
It is elsewhere literally applied only to
this number of weeks ; but in connexion
with language so highly figurative as
that of our prophet in the present
chapter, no objection can reasonably be
taken against its being used otherwise
than as a designation of time. It appears
to have been appropriated by him to
express the *perfection, fulness,* or *abundance*, of the number, instead of the
usual numeral שֶׁבַע or שִׁבְעָה, when employed symbolically as a sacred and
indefinite number. מַטֶּה signifies a *tribe*,
but also, as שֵׁבֶט, 2 Sam. xviii. 14, a
lance or *spear ;* and that the latter signification is that in which Habakkuk
here uses it, may be inferred from his
using it in this acceptation in the 14th
verse. Thus the Syr. ܐܡܪ has

been variously rendered by *word, promise,
epinicium, commander,* &c. I take it in
the first of these significations, as specifically designating the military order
or word of command. Compare Ps.
lxviii. 12. אֲדֹנָי יִתֶּן־אֹמֶר, " the Lord gave
the word," &c. Thus אָמַר, like the Arab.
ܐܡܪ, signifies to *order, command.* The

meaning of the prophet will therefore
be, that Jehovah prepared his bow for
battle, and ordered numerous spears to
be produced ; in other words, that he
brought the most formidable and effective instrumentality to bear against the
enemies of his people. The nominative
to תְּבַקַּע is not אֶרֶץ, as some would construe
the words, but יְהוָה understood from the
suffix in קַשְׁתֶּךָ. Comp. וַיְבַקַּע צֻרִים בַּמִּדְבָּר,
Ps. lxxviii. 15. Before נְהָרוֹת supply לְ or
בְּ ; to cleave *into* rivers. The effect of
the Divine command is sublimely represented under the idea of that which
is frequently produced by earthquakes,
when immense quantities of water gush
out of the fissures, and flow like rivers

10　The mountains saw thee, they were in pain;
　　The inundation of water overflowed;
　　The abyss uttered its voice,
　　It raised its hands on high.
11　Sun and moon stood back in their habitation,
　　At the light of thine arrows which flew,
　　At the glittering brightness of thy lance.

through the country. The whole verse is distinguished for its sublimity and beauty; and the sentiment conveyed in the two first lines was regarded as so weighty that a סֶלָה, *Selah*, or *pause*, is added, to give time for its producing its proper effect, before supplementing the concluding line.

10. The mountains being the most prominent objects on the surface of the globe, Habakkuk reiterates, in a somewhat different form, what he had expressed, ver. 6, in order to preserve the impression of the tremendous character of the transactions, to illustrate which they had been figuratively introduced. In the former case רָאָה is used of Jehovah: in this, of the mountains, which are, by a bold figure, represented as inspired with life, and capable of taking sensible cognizance of the manifestations of Deity. To express the instantaneous character of the effect, יָחִילוּ, *they quaked*, is put in the future. The root חוּל or חִיל properly signifies *to twist, writhe*, as with pain, and is frequently used of a woman in travail. It is also employed in the sense of *quaking* or *trembling*, which idea is conveyed by it in this place. "Juga cœpta moveri silvarum,—adventante Deo."—*Virgil*.—זֶרֶם מַיִם, *a torrent of water*, i.e. an extremely heavy rain, in contradistinction from זֶרֶם בָּרָד, *a hailstorm*, Is. xxviii. 2. רוֹם, *elevation*, is used adverbially. By יָדֵיהוּ, the elongated pronominal form of יָדָיו, *its hands*, are meant the waves of the ocean. תְּהוֹם, *the ocean*, its antecedent, is of both genders. The whole of nature is here exhibited as thrown into consternation at the approach of God. The mountains tremble; the heavens pour down sweeping torrents of rain; the sea roars, and causes its billows to "run mountains high." Comp. Ps. lxxvii. 17.

11. שֶׁמֶשׁ יָרֵחַ form an asyndeton, and are probably so put for the sake of effect. In many MSS., however, the ellipsis of the ו is supplied. The paragogic ה in וְגָלָה is that of *direction* or *motion*, and the idea which it conveys, as here used with the verb עָמַד, is not that the sun and moon remained stationary in a part of the firmament, which is represented as their dwelling or habitation, but that they *stood back* or *withdrew* into that locality. It was usual with the Arabian astronomers to assign houses or chambers to the celestial orbs. Thus منزل,

mansio, domus, is the name of the signs of the Zodiac; and فلك البروج, *the circle of the palaces* which the sun occupies. Job, likewise, speaks of חַדְרֵי תֵמָן, *the chambers of the south*, antithetically with the northern constellations, ch. ix. 9; as also of מְזָרוֹת, chap. xxxviii. 32, the same as מַזָּלוֹת, *inns* or *lodgings*, 2 Kings xxiii. 5. That specific reference is made to what is recorded Josh. x. 12, is, after the Targ., very generally admitted; but, though it were granted that the event there described may have suggested the language of the prophet, yet the point of view in which he presents the heavenly luminaries is altogether different. In the history, the construction to be put upon their standing still or being arrested in their course, is obviously their continuing to shine, in order to afford light to Joshua, while following up his victory over the enemy; whereas, in the present connexion, they are sublimely introduced as retiring into their abode before the brighter refulgence of the arrows and lances employed in the conflict. So completely were they eclipsed by

12 Indignant thou didst march through the earth ;
   Wrathful thou didst tread down the nations.
13 Thou wentest forth for the deliverance of thy people,
   For the deliverance of thine anointed ;

this refulgence, that it seemed as if they had set. Schnurrer and Justi interpret the language of their remaining in their habitation, in the sense of not rising, but the ה of motion is directly opposed to such construction. The ל in לְאוֹר and לְנֹגַהּ is the dative of cause, as in לְאֹת יֶחֱרַד לִבִּי, " at, or owing to this, my heart trembled," Job xxxvii. 1. Supply אֲשֶׁר before יְהַלֵּכוּ, which is put in Piel for the purpose of marking the velocity of the motion of the arrows. The words אוֹר and נֹגַהּ, which are elsewhere used of the light of the sun and the moon respectively, are here transferred to the glitter of the weapons specified.

12. צָעַד, to march, is used of the solemn and majestic proceeding of Jehovah before the Hebrews, Judges v. 4; Ps. lxviii. 8. דּוּשׁ, to thresh or tread down, is applied metaphorically to the destruction of enemies, Micah iv. 13.

13. Having described, in language of the most sublime and terrible import, the manifestations of Jehovah in reference to his enemies, Habakkuk now proceeds to specify in express terms the end which they were designed to answer, viz. the deliverance and safety of his chosen people ; and then depicts their fatal effects in the destruction of every hostile power. The second יֵשַׁע is employed instead of the infinitive לְהוֹשִׁיעַ, and thus governs the accusative אֶת־מְשִׁיחֶךָ. These last words Aq., and the author of the fifth Greek version, render εἰς σωτηρίαν σὺν Χριστῷ σου, and the Vulg. in salutem cum Christo tuo, which has led many interpreters, both ancient and modern, to refer מָשִׁיחַ, the anointed, to our Saviour. This construction of the passage is adopted even by Delitzsch, on the principle that as the term here designates the regal office of those who were of the Davidic dynasty, and Christ is represented as the greatest king of that family, consequently THE ANOINTED by way of eminence, he is to be regarded as included in the prophetic reference. By the law of parallelism, however, we

are compelled to identify מְשִׁיחֶךָ, thine anointed, with עַמֶּךָ, thy people, in the preceding hemistich. The noun is thus a collective, and is rendered in the plural by the LXX. τοὺς χριστούς σου, or, as in the Alex. MS., τοὺς ἐκλεκτούς σου. The plural מְשִׁיחֶךָ is actually found in two of Kennicott's MSS., and apparently in two more : in one of De Rossi's, and two more originally. It is denied, indeed, by Delitzsch, that מָשִׁיחַ, anointed, is ever used of the people of Israel ; and certainly none of the passages which have usually been adduced in support of this application of the term, can be fairly vindicated to it, except, perhaps, Ps. xxviii. 8, where מְשִׁיחוֹ corresponds to לָמוֹ, or לְעַמּוֹ according to the reading of six MSS., originally three more, and the rendering of the LXX., Syr., Vulg., and Arab. Still, as the Hebrews were מַמְלֶכֶת כֹּהֲנִים, a kingdom of priests, Exod. xix. 6, they may with as much propriety be said to have been anointed, as the patriarchs are, 1 Chron. xvi. 22 ; Ps. cv. 15. The term, as thus applied, expresses their destination. The Dagesh forte is found in the initial ר of רֹאשׁ in some editions, and is one of the few instances of its occurrence in this letter, contrary to rule. Comp. 1 Sam. i. 6 ; x. 24 ; 2 Kings vi. 32 ; Prov. iii. 8 ; xiv. 10 ; Song v. 2 ; Jer. xxxix. 12 ; Ezek. xvi. 4. Delitzsch accounts for it on the principle of the word being short, and occurring after a Milel. The prepositive מ in מִבֵּית intimates, that the ruler here spoken of as the head, was not merely over the house, which the simple construct form would have expressed, but that he sprung from it. It is most probable that one or other of the Canaanitish kings is intended ; perhaps Jabin, whose city (Hazor) is said to have been רֹאשׁ, the head of all the confederate kings, Josh. xi. 10 ; and who was the most formidable of all the kings with whom the Hebrews had to contend, Judges iv. 2, 3, 13. The general sense of the concluding hemistich is apparent ;

Thou dashedst in pieces the head of the house of the wicked,
Laying bare the foundation to the very neck : *Pause.*

14 Thou piercedst with his own spears the chief of his captains,
That rushed on like a tempest to scatter me ;
Whose joy it was to devour the poor in secret.

15 Thou wentest with thy horses through the sea,
The boiling up of many waters.

but considerable difficulty attaches to the interpretation of צַוָּאר, *neck*, as here connected with יְסוֹד, *foundation.* This connexion is so strongly marked by the force of the preposition עַד, *even to*, that the former substantive cannot be separated from the latter, and referred to some supposable higher part of the figurative building. It must, from the structure of the language, describe the very lowest part of the foundation, or that on which the foundation itself rests; but how either of these could be called *the neck*, it is impossible to conceive. There is, therefore, very great probability in the conjecture of Cappellus, which has been approved by Herder, Green, and some others, that instead of צַוָּאר, *neck*, the text originally read צִיר, *rock*, which makes all plain. Both words are derived from the same root ; and צַוָּאר occurs without the א, Neh. iii. 5. All the MSS. and versions, however, support the present reading. עָרוֹת is the infinitive absolute, which is often employed in the prosecution of a statement, instead of the finite form of the verb. The historical facts which the prophet here poetically describes, appear evidently to be those narrated Josh. xi.; Judges iv., involving the complete destruction of the Canaanitish nations, and more especially the discomfiture of Sisera, celebrated by Deborah in her splendid triumphal song, Judges v.

14. After a solemn pause, marked by סֶלָה, *Selah*, Habakkuk prosecutes his subject, which still embraces the discomfiture of the enemies of Israel. מַטָּיו, *his own spears*, the same as מַטּוֹת, ver. 9. Interpreters are divided in regard to the signification of פְּרָזָו, or, as it is in the Keri, and in the text of a great number of MSS., and of four of the early editions, פְּרָזָיו. The traditional interpretation is that of *villagers*, or the

inhabitants of the country; hence *hordes*, which Delitzsch adopts, and explains it of armies or soldiers. Thus the Vulg., *capiti bellatorum ejus.* Perschke, Gesenius, Ewald, and other moderns, however, derive the word from the Arab.

فرز, *segregavit, discrevit, modum præscripsit, statuit*, &c., and explain it of *judges, captains*, &c., which appears to be the more appropriate meaning. Thus the LXX., δυνάσται ; the Syr. ܡܚܝܠܬܐ ; just as the former in the Vatican codex render the cognate noun פְּרָזוֹן, Judges v. 7, 11, by δυναροί, and the Vulg. by *fortes.* The pronominal suffix refers to רָשָׁע, *the wicked*, in the preceding verse. Before יָכְמֵרוּ supply אֲשֶׁר. In using the first personal suffix singular in the following verb, the prophet so identifies himself with his people as to represent what was aimed at them as designed for him. Comp. ch. i. 12. The nominative to עֲלֵיצָתָם is פְּרָזָיו, *his captains.* In the last hemistich, the object of comparison is the robber who lies in wait for the poor defenceless traveller, and exults when he sees him approach. Such was the exultation of the Canaanitish chiefs when the Israelites entered the country. Comp. Ps. x. 8—10.

15. סוּסֶיךָ must either be taken as an accusative absolute, *as to thy horses ;* or it must have a בְּ supplied before it. The latter I have adopted as the easier mode of resolving the form. חֹמֶר describes here the boiling up or foaming of the sea in a storm. The immediate connexion, however, shows, that what the prophet has in view is not the Red Sea, but the hostile army of the Canaanites, which presented a furious and impenetrable aspect to the Hebrews. Through this army Jehovah is represented as

16   I heard, and my inward parts trembled,
      At the sound my lips quivered;
      Rottenness entered my bones,
      I trembled in my place:
      Yet I shall have rest in the day of distress,
      When the people that shall attack us come up.
17 Though the fig-tree should not blossom,

walking with his warriors, as if a general were coolly to march his cavalry through the thickest of a proud and vaunting foe, which he knew would prove utterly powerless in the attack. Comp. Ps. ii. 4, where Jehovah is said to *smile* at the puny attempts of his enemies.

16. Having finished the poetic rehearsal of the mighty acts of Jehovah on behalf of his people in ancient times, which he had composed in order to inspire the pious with unshaken confidence in him as their covenant God, Habakkuk reverts to the fear which had seized him on hearing of the judgments that were to be inflicted upon his country by the Chaldæans. שָׁמַעְתִּי וַתִּרְגַּז בִּטְנִי is a varied repetition of יְהֹוָה שָׁמַעְתִּי שִׁמְעֲךָ יָרֵאתִי, ver. 2. Instead of there entering into a description of his feelings, he broke out in an earnest prayer that God would exercise pity towards Israel, from which there was an easy transition to the ancient Divine interpositions. He now describes those feelings in very forcible and affecting language. קוֹל, *the voice*, is to be referred to the Divine threatening recorded chap. i. 6. The quivering of the prophet's lips is merely expressive of the effect of the fear with which he was seized, and has no reference to his delivery of the threatening. תַּחְתַּי, literally *under me*, i. e. *my under parts, limbs*, or the like. Comp. the Arab. تَحْمِس, *pars inferior*. LXX. ὑποκάτωθέν μου ἐταράχθη ἡ ἕξις μου. The Syr. ܟܘܪܒܝ, *my knees*. Jarchi and Kimchi, במקומי, *in my place*. אֲשֶׁר אָנוּחַ has been variously rendered, "That I may rest;" "That I must expect;" "O that I might rest;" "Yet I shall rest," or "have rest." The last construction is alone suitable. אֲשֶׁר, which the LXX. have entirely omitted, is here a conjunction, connecting the

following clauses with those which are antecedent to it, but obviously intended to qualify what had been there expressed. It thus forms a particle of transition from one class of circumstances to another of a different character. See Noldius, *sub voce*. Deeply as the prophet was affected, and overpowering as were the feelings of apprehension with which he anticipated the awful calamity that was coming upon his people, he did not abandon himself to despair, but, on the contrary, consoled his mind with the assurance, that God, in whom he trusted, would keep him in perfect peace in the day of trial. Nothing can be more uncritical than the emendation of אָנוּחַ into אָנִיחַ, proposed by Houbigant, the verb גּוּחַ or גִּיחַ having no such signification as that which he ascribes to it. The preposition לְ in לְיוֹם צָרָה and לַעֲלוֹת is to be taken as signifying the time when the events were to happen; in לְעַם it is the sign of the genitive; so that עֲלוֹת לְעַם is equivalent to עֲלוֹת עַם, *the coming up of the people*. The infinitive is the infinitive construct. By the *people*, the Chaldæans are meant. They are, as usual, said to *come up*, because of the elevated position of Jerusalem, both in a local and a religio-political point of view. Comp. 2 Kings xxiv. 1. Before יְגוּדֶנּוּ supply אֲשֶׁר. The verb גּוּד, like its cognate גָּדַד, signifies to *cut*, or *break in* upon an enemy, *attack*. Hence the substantive גְּדוּד, a *troop* or *band* of warriors, chiefly used of such as engage in plundering expeditions. It is the very term employed in the account given us of the fulfilment of the prophecy, 2 Kings xxiv. 2: "And the Lord sent against him אֶת־גְּדוּדֵי כַשְׂדִּים, the *bands* of the Chaldæans," &c.

17, 18. From a statement of the assurance he possessed of the mental tranquillity which he should enjoy during

And there should be no produce on the vines ;
Though the fruit of the olive should fail,
And the fields should yield no food ;
Though the flocks should be cut off from the fold,
And there should be no cattle in the stalls :

18 Yet I will exult in Jehovah ;
I will be joyful in the God of my salvation.

19 Jehovah the Lord is my strength ;
He will make my feet like those of gazelles,

the anticipated calamity, Habakkuk rises to a triumphant assertion of the holy joy and exultation that would be vouchsafed to him amidst all the desolation to which his country might be subjected. The desolation here so graphically and forcibly described, is that which was to be effected by the Chaldæans, whose army would consume or destroy the best and most necessary productions of the land; not only seizing upon the cattle, and devouring the fruits of the earth, but so injuring the trees as to render them incapable of yielding any produce. The passage contains the most beautiful exhibition of the power of true religion to be found in the Bible. The language is that of a mind weaned from earthly enjoyments, and habituated to find the highest fruition of its desires in God. When every earthly stream is dried up, it has an infinite supply in his all-sufficient and exhaustless fulness. No affliction, however severe or trying, can cut the believer off from this blessed resource. On the contrary, its tendency is to bring him into closer contact with it. מַעֲשֵׂה is not the *labour* bestowed upon the olive-tree, but the *fruit* which the tree produces. Comp. the phrase עָשָׂה פְּרִי, *to make* or *produce fruit*. The irregular construction of the singular masculine עָשָׂה with the feminine plural שְׁדֵמוֹת is to be accounted for on the principle, that in the mind of the prophet both number and gender had merged in the totality and impressiveness of his subject. Comp. שְׁדֵמוֹת אָמְלָל, Is. xvi. 8. It is what is commonly called, *constructio ad sensum.* Some would refer שְׁדֵמוֹת to an obsolete root שָׁדַם, which they take to be cognate with שָׁדַף, *to burn;* but it seems preferable to regard it as a derivative like שָׂדֶה, both signifying a *smooth* or *level field*, such as was prepared for grain or vines; from שָׂדַד, *to break*, and שָׁדַד, *to be level*, as ground is which is broken up, and levelled by the plough, the hoe, and the harrow. בָּוַר is here used intransitively, and is equivalent to the Niphal נִבְוַר. מִכְלָה stands for מִכְלָא, just as מוֹרָא for מוֹרָה, and מִקְשָׁה for מִקְשָׁא or מַקְשָׁאָה. The root is כָּלָא, *to shut up, confine.* אֲזָלֶיהָ and אֲזָנֵיהָ are synonymes in the elongated future—the ה directive expressing the strong bent of the mind towards the exercise. The words בֵּאלֹהֵי יִשְׁעִי are rendered in the Vulg. *in Deo Jesu meo !* The LXX. have ἐπὶ τῷ Θεῷ τῷ σωτῆρί μου.

19. The formula יְהוָֹה אֲדֹנָי, instead of אֲדֹנָי יְהוָה, is of infrequent occurrence. Comp. Ps. lxviii. 21; cxl. 8. The language of this verse is found in Ps. xviii. 33, 34; and in part, Deut. xxxii. 13; Is. lviii. 14. It expresses the confident hope that Jehovah would prove the support and defence of the prophet, and of all who made Him the object of their trust, and that He would grant them complete deliverance from their enemies, and restore them to the full and undisturbed possession of their own land. אֲיָּלָה, *the gazelle*, is so swift-footed, that greyhounds are liable to be killed by over-exertion in the chase. בָּמוֹתַי, *my high places*, stands for בָּמוֹת אַרְצִי, *the heights of my country.* Except for purposes of warfare, the elevated parts of a land are the last that are occupied.—The present is the only instance in which a musical direction is placed at the end of a psalm or ode. לַמְנַצֵּחַ, which occurs fifty-five times in the titles to the Psalms, is derived from the root נָצַח, *to overcome, excel, take the lead, direct, super-*

And cause me to walk on my heights.
To the precentor, with my stringed instruments.

---

intend, preside, &c.　It is used in reference to the *prefects* or *overseers*, whom
Solomon appointed over the workmen,
2 Chron. ii. 2, 18 ; and specially of the
masters or *directors* of the music employed in the temple, 1 Chron. xv. 21 ;
Neh. xii. 42.　By the LXX. לַמְנַצֵּחַ is
almost always rendered εἰς τὸ τέλος ;
Aq. τῷ νικοποιῷ ; Symm. ἐπινίκιον ;
Theod. εἰς τὸ νῖκος ; Targ. לְשַׁבָּחָא.　In
2 Chron. ii. 18, however, the LXX.
render the noun by ἐργοδιώκτης ; in
ver. 2, and xxxiv. 13, by ἐπιστάτης.
The form is that of the participle in
Piel, the ל taking the Patach of the
article—a circumstance which shows that
it cannot be, as some have supposed, an
infinitive.　נְגִינָה (from נָגַן, נָגֵן, to *strike*
the strings, *play* on a stringed instrument,
and then, generally, *to perform either
vocal or instrumental music*, but chiefly
the latter) signifies what is thus performed, *music, melody, song*, and also the
stringed instruments with which it was

accompanied.　The preposition בְּ is that
of accompaniment. Delitzsch infers from
the use of the affix in נְגִינוֹתַי, *my* music,
that the prophet himself was to take an
active part in the performance of it ; and
further, from this circumstance, that he
was of the tribe of Levi, and engaged in
carrying on the temple music.　But these
inferences cannot be sustained, since, if
the reasoning were valid, it would equally
prove that Hezekiah must have belonged
to that tribe, and been thus officially
engaged ; for he uses the very same
form : נְגִינוֹתַי, "*my* stringed instruments,"
Is. xxxviii. 20.　On what ground either
the prophet or the king claimed these
instruments, it is impossible to determine.
The conjecture of Schnurrer, that נְגִינוֹתַי
was originally נְגִינָתִי, and that the termination תִי is merely paragogic, as in
רַבָּתִי, is overturned by the fact, that this
paragogic form is never found except
when the word in which it appears is in
the construct state.

ZEPHANIAH

PREFACE

ALL that we know of Zephaniah is furnished by the title to his book, in which it is stated, that he was the son of Cushi, grandson of Gedaliah, great grandson of Amariah, and great great grandson of Hezekiah. As in no other instance do we find the pedigree of a prophet carried so far back, it has not unfairly been inferred that he must have belonged to a family of considerable respectability.* Whether, however, the Hezekiah there mentioned were the king of that name, or some other person of note so called, cannot be determined with certainty. The circumstance that the words, "king of Judah," are not added to the proper name, rather militates against the position that he was descended from that monarch, since this addition always occurs when primary reference is made to any of the Jewish kings; and, what is specially to the present point, when such reference is made to Hezekiah. See Prov. xxv. 1; Is. xxxviii. 9. The number of generations also forms an objection against the hypothesis, since it is scarcely possible to make room for them in the short space of time which elapsed between Hezekiah and Josiah.

As our prophet is stated, chap. i. 1, to have received his prophecies in the days of Josiah, he must have flourished between the year B.C. 642, and B.C. 611. This statement is corroborated by

* Οὐκ ἄσημος ὢν τὸ κατὰ σάρκα γένος.—*Cyril, Præf. ad Zeph.*

certain circumstances in the book itself. For instance, he predicts the fall of Nineveh, and the overthrow of the Assyrian empire; consequently he must have prophesied prior to the year B.C. 625, when these events took place; *i.e.* in the former half of the reign of Josiah. The mention, too, of the destruction of "the *remnant* of Baal," chap. i. 4, evidently implies, that the abolition of idolatry had been carried on to a considerable extent, but had not yet been completed. Now this exactly tallies with the state of things in Judah from the twelfth to the eighteenth year of Josiah; for though this monarch began, in the former of these years, to effect a reformation, it was not till the latter that it was prosecuted with more successful results. If, therefore, we suppose that Zephaniah delivered his predictions between these two terms, we shall not be wide of the mark. To the objection, that no mention is made of him or his labours in the historical books, which we might expect on the ground of the valuable service he must have rendered to the zealous monarch, it is sufficient to reply, that the same objection would lie against the prophetical existence of Jeremiah at the same period, though we know that he then flourished at Jerusalem, under the very eye of his sovereign. The mention made of "the king's sons," chap. i. 8, cannot be urged in favour of a later date; for it is altogether uncertain whether we are not to understand by the phrase the princes of the royal house generally, or such of the royal children as should be alive at the time of the fulfilment of the prophecy. The connexion and manner in which they are introduced favour the latter construction.

The predictions contained in the book are chiefly directed against the Jews, on account of their idolatry, and other sins of which they were guilty. The awful judgments to be executed upon them and the neighbouring nations by the Chaldæans are denounced with great force and effect. Hitzig, indeed, has recently revived the opinion advocated by Cramer and Eichhorn, that the invasion of these countries by the Scythians, about the year B.C. 630, whose incursion into Western Asia is described by Herodotus, i. 105, is what the prophet has in his eye; but the Jews appear to have been so little affected by their progress, that it by no means corresponds to that of the enemy described by Zephaniah, in the course of which not only Judæa, but the adjacent countries were to be entirely laid waste. His predictions received their accomplishment during the success of Nebuchadnezzar. Towards the close of the book the restoration and prosperity of the Jewish people are introduced.

In respect to style, Zephaniah is not distinguished either for sublimity or elegance. His rhythm frequently sinks down into a kind of prose; but many of the censures that have been passed upon his language are either without foundation, or much exaggerated. In point of purity, it rivals that of any of the prophets. He has much in common with his contemporary Jeremiah, and some, after Isidore, have regarded him as his abbreviator. A careful comparison of the two, however, proves the futility of this hypothesis. Occasionally he borrows the language of former prophets. Comp. chap. ii. 14, with Is. xiii. 21; xxxiv. 11; and chap. ii. 15, with Is. xlvii. 8.

CHAPTER I

The prophet begins by announcing the universality of the judgments which God was about to bring upon the land, 2, 3; specifies the different classes of transgressors whose conduct had merited the infliction of these judgments, 4—6; and calls attention to the speedy approach, and the features of the period of punishment, which he intermingles with further descriptions of the character of the ungodly, 7—13. He then dwells upon the awfully calamitous nature of the visitation, and points out the impossibility of escape, 14—18.

1 THE word of Jehovah which was communicated to Zephaniah the son of Cushi, the son of Gedaliah, the son of Amariah, the son of Hizkiah, in the days of Josiah the son of Amon, king of Judah:

2 I will utterly take away every thing from the face of the land, Saith Jehovah.

3 I will take away man and beast;
I will take away the birds of heaven, and the fishes of the sea;
And the causes of stumbling along with the wicked;
And I will cut off man from the face of the land,
Saith Jehovah.

1. See the Preface.

2, 3. אָסֵף, which is variously employed in Scripture in the sense of *gathering*, *collecting*, &c., is here used, as in Jud. xviii. 25; 1 Sam. xv. 6; Ps. xxvi. 9; Ezek. xxxiv. 29, to denote *the taking away* by death, or other violent means; *to destroy*. Thus Jarchi, ענין כליון, "Its signification is *destruction*." What clearly shows this, is the use of the cognate verb סוּף, *to scrape*, or *sweep off*, in the form אָסֵף = אָסִיף, which the Rabbi just mentioned erroneously takes to be the Hiphil of אָסֵף, by elision for אַאֲסֵף. The latter verb is never used in Hiphil; but the same combination of the two verbs

in the infinitive and finite forms occurs Jer. viii. 13, אָסֹף אֲסִיפֵם. Compare for similar usage אָדוֹשׁ יְדוּשֶׁנּוּ, Is. xxviii. 28; נָבֹא חֵצֵא, Jer. xlviii. 9. The enumeration of particulars is designed to augment the fearful and universal character of the punishment. מַכְשֵׁלָה does not appear to differ in this connexion from מִכְשׁוֹל, *a stumbling-block, cause of moral offence*, what occasions, excites to, or promotes sin. Syr. ܟ݂ܶܫܠܳܐ; Symm. τὰ σκάνδαλα. There can be no doubt that the different objects and rites of idolatrous worship are what the prophet has in view. Thus Jarchi, הם עבודות זרות. The

4　I will also stretch forth my hand against Judah,
　　And against all the inhabitants of Jerusalem;
　　And will cut off from this place the remnant of Baal,
　　The name of the idolatrous with that of the other priests;
5　And those that worship the host of heaven on the roofs,
　　And those that worship and swear to Jehovah,
　　And swear by their king;

repetition of אָדָם shows the prophecy had special reference to human beings, as the guilty party. The particle אֵת before רְשָׁעִים has the signification of *with*, *together with*, thus denoting accompaniment. Comp. Jud. i. 16. The idols and their worshippers were to be involved in one common destruction. Newcome improperly renders אֵת as a sign of the genitive.

4. To stretch forth the hand against any one, means not merely to threaten, but to exert one's power to his injury. הַמָּקוֹם הַזֶּה, *this place*, means *Jerusalem*. By שְׁאָר הַבַּעַל, *the remnant*, or *rest of Baal*, we are to understand the statues, images, &c., dedicated to the chief domestic and tutelary god of the Phœnicians, to whose worship the Hebrews were addicted as early as the time of the Judges, (ii. 13,) and among whom it afterwards spread more and more, especially in the ten tribes. Altars and high places were reared to this deity by Manasseh, even in the temple of Jehovah itself, 2 Kings xxi. 3, 5, 7; 2 Chron. xxxiii. 3, 7. These Josiah destroyed in the reformation which he undertook in the twelfth year of his reign, 2 Chron. xxxiv. 4; but it appears from this passage of our prophet, compared with 2 Chron. xxxiv. 8, that idols continued to be worshipped, most probably in places which were more remote from public observation, or which had been formed after the destruction of the others, and the cessation of the reformation referred to. Marckius and Gesenius interpret the phrase שְׁאָר הַבַּעַל, of *the people of Baal*, but this seems less probable. The phrase corresponds to מִכְשְׁלוֹת in the preceding verse, and is in like manner immediately followed by the אֵת of accompaniment, pointing out the persons that encouraged idolatry. For שְׁאָר the LXX., who have τὰ ὀνόματα, must have read שֵׁמוֹת, or they may have

been misled by the שֵׁם following. שֵׁם, however, is found in two of Kennicott's MSS., and in the margin of another. Upwards of twenty MSS., four ancient editions, and all the versions, read וְאֶת־שֵׁם instead of אֶת־שֵׁם. For הַכְּמָרִים, *the idolatrous priests*, see on Hos. x. 5. Both in the ancient and in the latter Hebrew, the term כֹּהֵן is used of the *priests* of idols, as well as of those belonging to Jehovah. See Gen. xli. 45, 50; 1 Kings xiii. 2, 33; 2 Kings x. 19; xi. 18. It may to some appear doubtful whether the former be not here intended; but as such are undeniably included in the כְּמָרִים, it is more probable that in using the term כֹּהֲנִים, the prophet had in his eye those who were professedly priests of the true God, but who, instead of checking, or endeavouring to eradicate idolatry, encouraged it by their indifference, or the inconsistency of their conduct in other respects. Comp. Jer. ii. 8; v. 31. The Targ. renders פָּלְחֵיהוֹן עִם כּוּמְרֵיהוֹן, *their worshippers with their priests*. Neither were to be left in the land by the Chaldæans. Their very names were to be forgotten.

5. Having directed his prophecy against the priests, the prophet now denounces those of the people who indulged in idolatrous practices. He first takes up those who were the votaries of Sabiism, or the worship of the heavenly bodies: a system which had, at an early period, become extensively prevalent, and continued to exert its influence, not only over the nomades of Arabia, but over the philosophers and wise men of the East; but which, in whatever form or degree it obtained, had the lamentable effect of deifying the creature, and obscuring the existence, claims, and glory of the Creator. That it was adopted, and its rites practised to a great extent by the Jews,

6 And those that have turned back from Jehovah,
   And that neither seek Jehovah nor apply to him.

7   Keep silence before the Lord Jehovah,
   For the day of Jehovah is near;
   For Jehovah hath prepared a sacrifice,
   He hath consecrated those whom he hath invited.

8 And it shall come to pass on the day of Jehovah's sacrifice,
   That I will punish the princes and the king's sons,
   And all that wear foreign apparel.

appears from 2 Kings xxiii. 5, 6; Jer. vii. 17, 18; xliv. 17—19, 25. The גַּגּוֹת, *roofs* or house-tops, in the East are flat, and are used for various purposes. The idolaters may have chosen them for secrecy in the time of the prophet, or they may have selected them for the purpose of obtaining a fuller view of the planetary objects of their worship. Jer. xix. 13; xxxii. 29. The planet to which they specially burned incense on the roofs of their houses is supposed to have been the moon, or it was more probably Venus, called מְלֶכֶת הַשָּׁמַיִם, "the Queen of heaven," Jer. vii. 17, 18; xliv. 17—19, 25. The prophet next instances a mongrel class of worshippers, such as professed attachment to Jehovah, as the national God, but, at the same time, were devoted to the service of *Moloch*, whom, in reality, they regarded and honoured as *their king*. For the forms מַלְכָּם, מִלְכֹּם, מַלְכְּכֶם, see on Amos. v. 26, and Gesenius under the word מֶלֶךְ. Instead of immediately connecting these opposite objects of worship with the participle הַמִּשְׁתַּחֲוִים, as he had done in the preceding clause, Zephaniah stops short, as if uncertain how to describe the persons whom he had in view, and then proceeds to characterise them as combining, by acts of solemn profession, the worship of the true God with that of Moloch. Comp. 1 Kings xviii. 21. בְּ נִשְׁבַּע, *to swear by* a deity, means to acknowledge him in a public, solemn, and binding manner; openly to pledge oneself to his service.

6. This verse is more comprehensive in its import, being descriptive of all who were in any way guilty of defection from Jehovah, and lived in total neglect of him and his ways.

7. For הַס מִפְּנֵים, comp. Hab. ii. 20; Zech. ii. 13. In the symbolical language of prophecy, a sacrifice denotes the slaughter or destruction of an army or people. In the words הִקְדִּישׁ קְרֻאָיו, *he hath consecrated his called ones*, however, there is no allusion to guests invited to partake of a sacrificial feast, as there unquestionably is, Ezek. xxxix. 17—20; Rev. xix. 17, 18. The קְרֻאִים, *called ones*, were the Chaldæans, who, as the Divine army, or the instruments of his retributive justice, were *called* into the field against the enemies of the Most High. In this sense Cyrus is said to have been *called*, Is. xli. 9; xlviii. 15. Comp. also Is. xiii. 3, and my note there, in which קָדֵשׁ, *to sanctify, consecrate*, is explained of the selection of troops for war, and the religious rites engaged in when they set out upon the military expedition.

8. That by the phrase בְּנֵי הַמֶּלֶךְ, *the sons of the king*, we are to understand the immediate children of Josiah, does not appear. He could not have had sons of an age sufficiently mature at the time the prophet uttered his prediction, to allow of their contracting guilt to such a degree as that which the connexion necessarily requires; for he could not himself have been above seventeen years old. It may either mean the princes of the royal house generally, or the children of the king who should be on the throne at the time of the accomplishment of the prophecy. That the latter supposition is the more probable, appears from 2 Kings xxv. 7, where it is stated, that the king of Babylon slew the sons of Zedekiah before his eyes. By those that wore foreign attire, the prophet means the rich and great generally, who in viola-

9　I will also punish all who leap over the threshold in that day,
　　Who fill the house of their lord with violence and deceit.

10　　And it shall come to pass in that day, saith Jehovah,
　　That there shall be the sound of crying from the fish-gate,
　　And of wailing from the second,
　　And of great crashing from the hills.

11　Howl, ye inhabitants of the Mortar!
　　For all the people of Canaan are destroyed;
　　All who are laden with money are cut off.

tion of an express ordinance relative to national costume, which was designed to preserve them distinct from other people, Numb. xv. 37—40, arrayed themselves in the more costly and gorgeous garb of idolaters, and thus more easily mixed with them in the performance of their idolatrous rites.

9. Because the priests of Dagon abstained from treading on the threshold of his temple, 1 Sam. v. 5, it has been by some inferred that Zephaniah alludes here to some such superstitious custom as practised by the Jews. Thus the Targ. כָּל דִּמְהַלְּכִין בְּנִימוֹסֵי פְלִשְׁתָּאֵי, *all who walk in the laws of the Philistines.* But this construction has little to support it beyond the simple occurrence of the word מִפְתָּן, *threshold,* in both passages; for in Samuel it is merely said,—לֹא יִדְרְכוּ עַל מִפְתַּן דָּגוֹן, "they *tread* or *walk* not over the threshold of Dagon;" whereas the language of the prophet, הַדּוֹלֵג עַל־הַמִּפְתָּן, "*him that leapeth* over the threshold," is expressive of a more violent action; and, as the parallel hemistich shows, characterises the eagerness with which the servants of the great rushed out of their palaces in order to seize upon the property of others, and thereby increase the wealth of their masters. If we may apply the signification of the cognate word in Arab. دَلَجَ, *principio* (or *sub finem*) *noctis iter fecit,* we should interpret the term as denoting their setting out on their predatory expeditions under cloud of night. Thus, as to the general sense, the Syr. ܟܠܗܘܢ ܕܥܒܕܝܢ ܚܛܘܦܝܐ, *all who commit violence and plunder.* Kimchi explains the word of

their forcibly entering the houses of the poor, and robbing them of their goods.

10, 11. These verses describe the state of Jerusalem when besieged by Nebuchadnezzar. שַׁעַר הַדָּגִים, *the fish-gate,* occurs 2 Chron. xxxiii. 14; Neh. iii. 3; xii. 39; but there is nothing in these passages by which we can determine its exact position. From the name it might be inferred, that it was situated either on the north or the north-east side of the city, that being the direction from which those would arrive who brought fish from Tiberias and the Jordan, and corresponded to what is now called the Damascus Gate, or to that of St. Stephen. It was from this side, being that which was most accessible, that Jerusalem was attacked by the enemy. That מִשְׁנֶה, *the second,* is not to be referred to שַׁעַר, *gate,* as its antecedent, but to עִיר, *city,* understood, appears from Neh. xi. 9, where we have in full הָעִיר מִשְׁנֶה, *the second city,* i.e. the second division of the city. Ewald renders the word by *Neustadt,* "Newtown." In all probability it was what was afterwards called Akra, or the lower city, which lay to the north of the ancient city on Mount Zion, and was separated from it by the Tyropœon, a valley which ran down between them to the present pool of Siloam. In our common version the word is improperly rendered *college,* 2 Kings xxii. 14; 2 Chron. xxxiv. 22; after the interpretation of the Rabbins. The גְּבָעוֹת, *hills,* here mentioned, were not those around the city, such as the Mount of Olives, the Mount of Evil Counsel, &c., but Zion, Moriah, Ophel, and other elevated localities within the walls, occupied by the temple, the royal palace, and the houses of the richer portion of the in-

12 And it shall come to pass at that time
    That I will search Jerusalem with lights,
    And punish the men who are hardened on their lees,
    Who say in their heart,
    Jehovah will not do good, neither will he do evil.

13 And their wealth shall become a spoil,
    And their houses a desolation;
    They may build houses, but they shall not inhabit them,
    And plant vineyards, but they shall not drink the wine of them.

14 The great day of Jehovah is near;
    It is near and hasteth greatly;
    The sound of the day of Jehovah:
    There the mighty man shrieketh bitterly.

habitants. The prophet graphically represents the progress of the Chaldæans, from the gate at which they entered, into the second division of the city, until they had ultimately taken possession of the whole, and destroyed the principal buildings. This destruction is very appropriately expressed by the noun שֶׁבֶר, from שָׁבַר, to break, break in pieces, 2 Kings xxv. 4, 8, 9. מַכְתֵּשׁ is not a proper name, as the article prefixed shows, but an appellative, signifying mortar, from כָּתַשׁ, to bray, pound. See Prov. xxvii. 22. It appears to have been applied, from its resemblance to that vessel, to one or other of the valleys in or about Jerusalem. Theod. ἐν τῷ βάθει. Aq. εἰς τὸν ὅλμον. According to the Targum, נַחֲלָא דְקִדְרוֹן, it was that through which the brook Kidron flows. Others think it was the Tyropœon, the locality of the bazars, where the merchants carried on their business. From what follows in the verse, the latter is most probably the true interpretation. It is thought by some that the term was purposely chosen by the prophet, on account of its resemblance in sound to מִקְדָּשׁ, a holy place, and that Jerusalem itself is meant; but this word is exclusively appropriated to the tabernacle, or temple, and other sacred places, and never to the city, though it is called עִיר הַקֹּדֶשׁ, the Holy City, just as it is still known in the East by the names القدس, El-Kuds, and بيت المقدس

Beit-el-Mukeddes, of similar signification. By עַם כְּנַעַן, the people of Canaan, the prophet does not mean the inhabitants of Canaan generally, nor Phœnician merchants in particular, who carried on trade with those of Jerusalem, but ironically the Jerusalem merchants themselves, who not only resembled the former in their modes of acquiring gain, but adopted their idolatrous manners and customs. See on Hos. xii. 8.

12. The Divine judgments were to reach those who practised wickedness in the most hidden places, and in the most covert manner. This is metaphorically expressed by searching out with lights what is concealed in the dark. The metaphor following is taken from the firm crust which is formed on the surface of fermented liquors when they have been long left in an undisturbed state. קָפָא, signifies, to contract, become concrete, hard, &c., and strikingly expresses the hardened state of the rich who have settled down into infidelity and atheism. Comp. Jer. xlviii. 11. Their practical denial of a superintending and governing providence is expressed in so many words at the end of the verse.

13. It is here implied that those of whom the prophet speaks would go on building and planting, till the judgment of God overtook them, and deprived them of all their property. Comp. Matt. xxiv. 38, 39.

14. כִּהֵר is not the participle in Piel,

15 That day is a day of indignation,
   A day of trouble and distress,
   A day of desolation and ruin,
   A day of darkness and gloom,
   A day of clouds and obscurity;
16 A day of the trumpet and the war-shout,
   Against the fortified cities,
   And against the lofty towers.
17 And I will bring trouble upon men,
   So that they shall walk as the blind;
   Because they have sinned against Jehovah,
   Their blood shall be poured out as dust,
   And their flesh shall be as dung.
18 Neither their silver nor their gold
   Shall be able to rescue them
   In the day of Jehovah's indignation;
   But the whole land shall be consumed
   By the fire of his jealousy:
   For a consummation altogether sudden will he make
   Of all the inhabitants of the land.

---

with the affirmative Mem rejected, but the infinitive of the same conjugation, used as an abbreviated form of מַהֵר יְמַהֵר. מַר, *bitter*, is here used adverbially. So irresistible should be the attack of the Chaldæans, that the Jewish warrior would be compelled to abandon himself to shrieks of hopeless grief.

15, 16. A beautiful amplification, for the purpose of aggravating the character of the calamity. Passages somewhat similar occur in the prophets, but none equal to this. צָרָה וּמְצוּקָה, as well as שֹׁאָה וּמְשׁוֹאָה, are instances of paronomasia. Comp. Job xv. 24; xxx. 3; xxxviii. 27. הַפִּנּוֹת וְהַגְּבֹהוֹת form a Hendiadys, and describe the high towers or turrets, at the angles of fortified walls. Gesenius assumes an obsolete root פָּנַן, *to separate, divide into classes*, as that from which פִּנָּה, *a turret*, is derived; but there is no occasion to depart from its usual derivation from the Piel of פָּנָה, *to cause to turn*. It thus signifies what is at the *turning, corner*, or angle of a building, and that whether at the top or the bottom. Tacitus, describing the walls of Jerusalem, says: "Per artem obliquos et introrsum sinuatos, ut latera oppugnantium ad ictus patescerent." Hist. lib. v. cap. 11, § 5.

17. לְחוּם, or, as in some MSS. and editions, לְחֻם, *flesh*. Arab. لحم, *caro*. Root לָחַם, *to eat*. שָׁפַךְ may, by zeugma, be made to govern לְחוּמָם as well as דָּמָם, but it is preferable to supply the substantive verb after לְחוּמָם. For the latter figure, comp. Job xx. 7.

18. גַּם—גַּם, *also—also*, meaning both the one and the other. As here with a negative, *neither—nor*. "Fire" is often used figuratively to denote war, because of its devastating effects; Is. x. 16; xxvi. 11. אַךְ is to be taken in the sense of *wholly, entirely, altogether*.

CHAPTER II

A solemn admonition is now given to the Jewish people to repent during the short
space of time that would be allotted them before the Chaldæan invasion, 1, 2;
followed by an exhortation to the pious to persevere in their devotedness to
God, and the interests of righteousness, 3. The prophet then proceeds to foretel the destruction of those nations which had always been hostile to the Jews,
as the Philistines, 4—7; the Moabites and Ammonites, 8—10; parenthetically,
the idols of the nations, 11; the Ethiopians, 12; and the Assyrians, 13—15.

1 BEND yourselves, and be ye bent,
   O nation not desired!
2 Before the birth of the decree;
   The day passeth away as chaff;
   Before there come upon you the burning anger of Jehovah;
   Before there come upon you the day of the anger of Jehovah.

1. הִתְקוֹשְׁשׁוּ ·וָקוֹשּׁוּ, the Hithpolel and
Kal conjugations joined for the sake of
intensity. Comp. Is. xxiv. 19. The
words have been variously rendered.
LXX. συνάχθητε καὶ συνδέθητε. Vulg.
convenite (et) congregamini. De Wette,
prüfet euch, ja prüfet. Gesenius, collect
yourselves, and be ye collected; i.e. collect
your thoughts, look into your own mind,
prove yourselves: thus agreeing with
De Wette, after the interpretation of
Pagninus, Vatablus, Cocceius, and others.
Ewald, erbleichet und bleichet. Most
refer to קָשׁשׁ as the root, which signifies
in Poel to collect stubble, wood, &c.;
but it is never used with respect to
human beings. I prefer deriving it
from קוֹשׁ, to bend, be bent. Arab.
قوس. II. incurvavit arcus more; in-
curvatus fuit senex. Hence קֶשֶׁת, a bow,
from its being bent. Bend yourselves,

and be ye bent, will then be the proper
rendering. Comp. the use of שָׁחַח, to
bow down, Is. lx. 14. The prophet calls
the Jews to deep humility before God
on account of their manifold sins. Because כָּסַף signifies to be pale, Gesenius
renders the words הַגּוֹי לֹא נִכְסָף, O nation
not ashamed! but כָּסַף never denotes to
be pale from a feeling of shame, but as
the effect of desire, the verb everywhere
else expressing the idea of pining, long-
ing, being intensely desirous of any
object. The phrase לֹא נִכְסָף, not desired,
is here used by litotes for abominated,
hated.

2. The Divine decree or purpose of
punishment announced in the preceding
chapter, is here tropically represented
as a pregnant female near the time of
her delivery. The words כְּמוֹץ עָבַר יוֹם,
as chaff the day passeth, do not refer to
the coming of the period of calamity

3　Seek ye Jehovah, all ye humble of the land,
　　Who perform his judgments;
　　Seek righteousness, seek humility,
　　If perhaps ye may be hid
　　In the day of the anger of Jehovah.

4　　For Gaza shall be forsaken,
　　And Askelon a desolation;
　　As for Ashdod, they shall drive her out at noon-day,
　　And Ekron shall be rooted up.

5　Wo to the inhabitants of the line of the sea!
　　The nation of Kerethites!
　　The word of Jehovah is against you;
　　O Canaan! the land of the Philistines,
　　I will destroy thee, that there shall be no inhabitant.

but the rapid lapse of the time of repentance. The image of chaff is always used of that which flies quickly away, never of what comes to any one. They are introduced parenthetically. The sentence בְּטֶרֶם לֹא־יָבוֹא עֲלֵיכֶם חֲרוֹן אַף יְהֹוָה is wanting in six of Kennicott's MSS., probably in two more, and originally in eight of De Rossi's. It is also omitted in the Arabic version. The declaration, with the trifling change of a single word, is properly repeated for the sake of emphasis.

3. The prophet here addresses himself to the afflicted and humble among his people, from whom some hope of a better state of things might be expected. אוּלַי, rendered *perhaps*, is not intended to express a doubt respecting the safety of the pious, but the extreme difficulty of escaping the threatened judgment. The poor of the land were left by Nebuzar-adan to be vine-dressers and husbandmen. 2 Kings xxv. 12.

4. The connective force of the particle כִּי, *for*, with which this verse commences, lies in the universality of the calamity which was about to come, not upon the Jews only, but upon all the nations with which they had been brought into contact. There would be no country to which they might flee for safety, for all were to be visited by the Chaldæans. For the cities of the Philistines here specified, see on the parallel prophecy,

Amos i. 6—8; and Is. xx. 1. צָהֳרָיִם, *the meridian* or *noon*, being the hottest part of the day, is generally spent by the Orientals in sleep, and is the less likely time for any military operations to be carried on. 2 Sam. iv. 5; Jer. vi. 4; xv. 8. The paronomasias, עַזָּה עֲזוּבָה and עֶקְרוֹן תֵּעָקֵר, are not to be overlooked.

5. This and the two following verses contain an amplification of the prediction against the Philistines. חֶבֶל הַיָּם, LXX. τὸ σχοίνισμα τῆς θαλάσσης, *the line of the sea*, i.e. the *region* or *coast* along the sea-shore, and so called from the custom of using a cord or line in measuring off or dividing a territory. Comp. with the same application, חוֹף הַיָּם, *the coast of the sea*, Jer. xlvii. 7; Ezek. xxv. 16. By גּוֹי כְּרֵתִים, *nation of Cretians*, we are not to understand the actual inhabitants of Crete, but the Philistines, a nation descended from those who originally emigrated from that island, and took possession of the south-west coast of Palestine. פְּלִשְׁתִּים, the name of *the Philistines*, properly signifies *the emigrants*, from פָּלַשׁ. Eth. ፈለሰ, *to rove, migrate*. According to Stephen of Byzantium, Gaza was originally called *Minoa*, after Minos, king of Crete, who, with his two brothers, Arakus and Rhadamanthus, undertook an expedition to the coast, and gave the city his own name. Comp. Deut. ii. 23; 1 Sam.

6 And the line of the sea shall be pastures,
  With cisterns for shepherds,
  And folds for sheep.

7 Yea, the line shall be for the remnant of the house of Judah,
  Thereupon shall they feed;
  In the houses of Askelon shall they lie down at even;
  For Jehovah their God shall visit them,
  And reverse their captivity.

8   I have heard the reproach of Moab,
  And the revilings of the sons of Ammon,
  Who have reviled my people,
  And carried themselves haughtily against their border.

9 Wherefore, as I live, saith Jehovah of hosts,
  The God of Israel:
  Surely Moab shall be as Sodom,
  And the sons of Ammon as Gomorrah;
  A region of overrunning brambles and salt pits,
  And a perpetual desolation;
  The remnant of my people shall plunder them,
  And the residue of my nation shall possess them.

10 This shall happen to them for their pride,
  Because they reproached and carried themselves haughtily,
  Against the people of Jehovah of hosts.

---

xxx. 14; Jer. xlvii. 4; Ezek. xxv. 16; Amos ix. 7. כְּנַעַן, *Canaan,* which is not only employed to designate the whole country taken possession of by the Hebrews, but more specially Phœnicia, is here to be understood as restricted to the country of the Philistines.

6. It is thought by some that there is an allusion to כְּרֹת in the word כָּרֹת, which properly signifies *wells* or *cisterns,* from כָּרָה, *to dig.* Instead of continuing to be a thickly populated and well cultivated country, the land of the Philistines should be converted into a region fit only to be occupied by nomades.

7. Instead of being any longer annoyed by the Philistines, the Jews, restored to their land, would occupy the territory as described in the preceding verse.

8—10. Comp. the parallel prophecies against Moab, Is. xv., xvi.; Jer. xlviii.; Amos ii. 1—3; and Ammon, Jer. xlix.

1—6; Amos i. 13—15. הִגְדִּיל עַל means to *carry oneself haughtily against* any one. There is no occasion to supply פֶּה or any other noun. The suffix in גְּבוּלָם has עַמִּי for its antecedent. The formulas חַי אָנִי, *I living,* or *as I live,* ver. 9, and חַי יְהוָה, חַי אֱלֹהִים, *as Jehovah, as God liveth,* are solemn modes of expression, by which the Divine Existence is pledged for the certainty of the declarations which they introduce. מִמְשַׁק, *a drawing,* or *extending out,* from מָשַׁק, cognate פָּשַׁק, *to draw out, extend.* As connected with *bramble,* it denotes the *overspreading* or *overrunning* of that shrub. מִכְרֵה־מֶלַח, *a pit* or excavation, such as are found in the vicinity of the Dead Sea, in which, when it overflows in spring, its water is collected, and pure salt obtained by evaporation. The idea conveyed by both metaphors is that of sterility and desolation.

11 Jehovah is to be feared above all the gods of the earth,
    For he will cause them to waste away;
    And all the inhabitants of the maritime regions
    Shall worship him—each from his place.

12   Also ye, O ye Cushites!
    Shall be slain by my sword.

13 And he will stretch his hand over the north,
    And destroy Assyria;
    He will also make Nineveh waste,
    An arid region like the desert.

14 And flocks shall lie down in the midst of her;
    All the wild beasts of the nations;
    Both the pelican and the porcupine
    Shall take up their abode in her capitals;
    A voice shall sing in the windows,
    Desolation shall be in the thresholds,
    For the cedar-work is laid bare.

11. This verse connects so slightly with the preceding, and, as the former part is usually rendered, affords so little suitable a sense, that I cannot but regard the suffix in עֲלֵיהֶם as possessing an anticipative pronominal reference to אֱלֹהֵי הָאָרֶץ, *the gods of the earth*, with respect to whom Jehovah was to show himself worthy of exclusive veneration by effecting their destruction. In Hebrew poetry, the pronoun or pronominal affix frequently occurs before the noun. See on Is. xxviii. 26. While announcing the destruction of the surrounding idolatrous nations, the prophet was inspired to predict the gradual, but certain destruction of idolatry universally throughout the earth. The period predicted should be one in which all peculiarity of local worship would cease, and Divine worship be acceptable wherever presented in sincerity and truth. Comp. Mal. i. 11; John iv. 21—24; 1 Cor. i. 2. For the phrase נוֹרָא עֲלֵיהֶם, comp. Ps. xcvi. 4. The מ prefixed in מִמְּקוֹמוֹ expresses simply the locality in which the persons spoken of resided. Compare מָקֵם, מִיָּמִין, מִפּוֹל, מִבַּיִת, &c. רָזָה, Arab. ﺭﺯﻯ, *to make thin, lean, diminish*, cause to waste away, and to *destroy*. LXX. ἐξολοθρεύσει. The

knowledge and worship of the true God were to be extended not only over the vast continental regions of the globe, but over those which bordered on, or existed in the sea. In אִיֵּי הַגּוֹיִם, *the isles*, or *maritime regions*, there is, as usual, a special reference to the West; though in connexion with כֹּל, *all*, the universality of such regions is intended. The passage is strictly Messianic, since the accomplishment of the prediction has been, and is being effected by means of the gospel.

12. For כּוּשׁ, *Cush*, see on Is. xi. 11; xviii. 1. The prophecy received its fulfilment when Nebuchadnezzar invaded and conquered Egypt, with whose military operations and fate the Ethiopians were more or less mixed up. Jer. xlvi. 9; Ezek. xxx. 5, 9. There is, indeed, reason to think that Egypt herself is designed to be included in the term as here employed.

13—15. From the remote South into which the prophet had carried his hearers, he turns suddenly back to the North, where there still existed a mighty empire, which must of necessity be overthrown, before the Divine sword, *i.e.* the arms of Babylon, could reach the countries against which he had denounced

15 This is the exulting city which dwelt securely,
   Which said in her heart,
   I am, and besides me there is none.
   How she is become desolate !
   A resting-place for wild beasts !
   Every one that passeth by her shall hiss,
   He shall shake his hand.

the judgments of God. This empire was the Assyrian, which was drawing towards its end, and was actually subverted when Nineveh was taken and destroyed by Cyaxares and Nabopolassar, B.C. 625. It is this catastrophe, with its disastrous consequences, which Zephaniah so graphically describes in these verses. So completely was the celebrated metropolis of the ancient world to be desolated, that not even the Nomades would seek a temporary shelter among her ruins. They should only be inhabited by the wild beasts of the desert. That by עֲדָרִים we are to understand herds of savage animals, and not flocks of sheep, goats, &c., is apparent from the mention made in the parallelism of כָּל־חַיְתוֹ־גוֹי, *every wild beast of the nation.* גּוֹי, *nation,* has by some been thought to stand poetically for a collection of animals, just as עַם, *people,* does, Prov. xxx. 25, 26; but it is rather to be regarded as synonymous with אֶרֶץ, *land,*

country ; only restricting it to the particular country in which Nineveh had been situated; so that the phrase will be equivalent to חַיְתוֹ־אֶרֶץ, Gen. i. 24. The LXX. render πάντα τὰ θηρία τῆς γῆς. Targ. כָּל חֵיוַת בָּרָא, *all the beasts of the field.* The ו in חַיְתוֹ is merely paragogic. For קָאַת and קִפֹּד, see on Is. xxxiv. 11. Some interpret קוֹל of the Arab. غُل, *the demon of the desert,* and convert חֹרֶב, *desolation,* into עֹרֵב, *raven,* but without sufficient ground. See Maurer, who, in opposition to Hitzig, takes both words in their usual acceptation. עֵרָה, the Piel of עָרָה, is here used impersonally, and is best rendered in the passive. כַּפְתֹּר, *chapiter,* see on Amos ix. 1. By אֶרְזָה is meant the wainscoting and fine carved *cedar work* with which the walls, ceiling, &c., of the houses were ornamented. For the language of pride and carnal security expressed in ver. 15, comp. Is. xlvii. 8.

---◆---

CHAPTER III

Having digressed to predict the fate of the surrounding nations, Zephaniah returns to his own countrymen, and specially directs his prophecy against Jerusalem, the leading persons in which had persevered in wickedness in spite of all the warnings which they had received, 1—7. After addressing the pious members of the theocracy, and encouraging them to wait for the development of the Divine purposes, 8, he proceeds to predict the conversion of the Gentiles, 9, and of the Jews, 10 ; describes their character when converted, 11—13 ; congratulates them on their deliverance, and enjoyment of the presence of their heavenly King, 14—17 ; and concludes by adverting to the circumstances connected with their return to Palestine after their conversion, 18—20.

1 Wo to the rebellious and polluted,
　　The oppressing city !
2 She listened not to the voice,
　　She received not instruction ;
　　She trusted not in Jehovah,
　　She drew not near to her God.
3 Her princes in the midst of her
　　Are roaring lions ;
　　Her judges are evening wolves ;
　　They gnaw no bones in the morning.
4 Her prophets are vain-glorious,
　　Hypocritical men ;
　　Her priests profane what is sacred ;
　　They do violence to the law.
5 Jehovah, the righteous One, is in the midst of her ;

1. It has been thought by some that in מוֹרְאָה, *rebellious*, as here applied to Jerusalem, there is a play upon the name of מֹרִיָּה, *Moriah*, on which the temple was built. If so, it was calculated to suggest to the minds of the Jews the gross inconsistency of their laying claim to any connexion with that sacred place, while they obstinately refused to obey the law of God. The root is מָרָא, cognate with מָרָה, *to prove refractory, rebel.* The LXX. rendering the word by ἐπιφανὴς, *illustrious*, have doubtless mistaken it as coming from רָאָה, *to see ;* as the Syr.

likewise has done, rendering مِنَبْدَآ,

noted, celebrated. יוֹנָה, the Benon. participle of יָנָה, *to rage, be cruel, oppressive*, &c. What the prophet has in his eye is the rage and cruelty with which the idolatrous inhabitants persecuted such as adhered to the worship and service of Jehovah, as well as their oppression of the widows, orphans, &c. See Jer. xxii. 3.

2—4. Not only did the inhabitants generally refuse to receive instruction from the Lord, and alienate their affections from him and his service, but the rulers, both civil and ecclesiastical, evinced the grossest dereliction of duty, and the most flagrant inconsistency of character. וְאֵבֵי עֶרֶב, *evening wolves*, i. e. wolves which come forth from the forests or other lurking places in the evening, and, greedy with hunger, seize or devour during the night, whatever animals they fall in with. Comp. Hab. i. 8; λύκοι νυκτερινοὶ, Oppian. Cyneget. 3, 266. The voracious and insatiable cupidity of the judges is further expressed by לֹא גָרְמוּ לַבֹּקֶר, *nothing is craunched in the morning ;* i. e. all is devoured in the night, and not so much as a bone left to be gnawed in the morning. גָרֵם is here used impersonally. Thus. as to the sense, the LXX. and Vulg. οὐχ ὑπελίπουτο; *non relinquebant.* The prophets, instead of evincing that gravity and humility which became those who professed to deliver Divine messages, were פֹּחֲזִים, *light* and *vain-glorious* persons, trifling with the most serious subjects, and carrying themselves haughtily towards others. The verb פָּחַז properly signifies to *boil up* like water. Comp. Gen. xlix. 4; Jud. ix. 4; Jer. xxiii. 32. Arab. فَخَرَ, *superbivit.* The priests were equally corrupt. They made no distinction between the holy and profane, and distorted the meaning of the law, when expounding it to the people. Comp. Ezek. xxii. 26, where similar language is used, and explained.

5. Jehovah had his residence in the temple, connected with the daily worship, in which were those unfailing revela-

He doeth no injustice ;
Every morning he bringeth his judgment to light,
It is not lacking ;
But the unjust know no shame.

6   I have cut off the nations ;
Their corner-stones are laid waste ;
I have made their streets desolate,
Without any one passing through them.
Their cities are destroyed ; they are without a man ;
There is no inhabitant.

7   I said : Only fear me ;
Receive instruction ;
That her habitation might not be cut off,
According to all that I had appointed concerning her :
But they rose up early ;
They corrupted all their doings.

8   Nevertheless, wait for me, saith Jehovah,

tions of the rectitude of his character that brought to view a glorious pattern, which it was the duty of the Jews to imitate; but, hardened in wickedness, they were conscious of no feelings of shame. בַּבֹּקֶר בַּבֹּקֶר, *in the morning, in the morning*, i.e. according to a common Hebrew idiom, *every* morning.

6. Besides the plentiful instruction with which the inhabitants of Jerusalem had been furnished by the public institutions that existed among them, and from which they might conclude what punishment they had to expect if they persisted in sin, they had examples from which to take warning in the desolate condition to which other nations had been reduced on account of their wickedness. Under the long and happy reign of Josiah, the Jews enjoyed rest and tranquillity until the last year, while other neighbouring nations were laid waste; for it was during his reign that the great incursion of the Scythians into western Asia took place, while Judæa was spared. Michaelis. פִּנָּה is here to be taken in its literal acceptation of *corner-stone*, but the ruin or desolation of the building resting upon it is implied. נִצְדּוּ is the Niphal of צָדָה, *to cut down, lay waste*.

7. תִּירְאִי and תִּקְחִי are both futures used

for imperatives. In מְעוֹנָהּ and עָלֶיהָ is a change, by no means uncommon, of the second person to the third. In כֹּל there is an ellipsis of כְּ, *according to*. פָּקַד עַל is not to be here taken in the sense of punishing, but of *appointing* for punishment; comp. Jer. xv. 3. The appointed and threatened judgments should be averted from Jerusalem, if the inhabitants would only turn from their evil ways, and walk in the fear of the Lord. Such was the announcement which he graciously made to them by his servants the prophets; but, instead of reforming, they addicted themselves more sedulously and entirely to the practice of iniquity. הִשְׁכִּימוּ, *to rise early*, is frequently used in the Hebrew Scriptures in a tropical sense, to indicate that a person does anything with preparedness or full purpose of mind. The primary idea conveyed by the verb seems to be that of placing the burdens on the shoulders of camels, &c., before setting out on a journey, which, in the East, is done very early in the morning. Root שְׁכֶם, *shoulder*. Eth. **ሰቀመ**: *bajulavit.* **አሰቀመ**: *onus imposuit humeris.*

8. Most expositors interpret the words חַכּוּ לִי, *expect* or *wait for me*, as if they were addressed to the profligate charac-

In the day when I rise for the prey ;
For my determination is to assemble the nations,
To gather the kingdoms ;
To pour out upon them my fury,
All the heat of my anger ;
For by the fire of my jealousy
The whole earth shall be consumed.

9 For then I will turn to the nations a pure language,
That they may all invoke the name of Jehovah ;
That they may serve him with one accord.

ters described in the preceding verse ; but this construction is admissible only on the principle of their being applied ironically, since the phrase is never used except in a good sense. Yet even this but ill suits the entire connexion. I consider them to form an apostrophe to the pious among the Jews, calling upon them to look forward, amid all the calamities which were approaching, to the glorious period which these calamities were designed to usher in, and which the prophet specially describes in the following verses. The LXX., and all the other Greek versions, as also the Syr., render עֵד, by *testimony* or *witness ;* a signification which only attaches to the letters when pointed עֵד. The signification of *prey* is more appropriate here. Compare for this signification Gen. xlix. 27 ; Is. xxxiii. 23. What is meant by rising up to the prey is explained in the following clause of the verse. Indeed, the very derivation of the word from עָדָה, *to pass on* in a hostile manner, to *rush upon, attack ;* Arab.

عَدَا, *irruit* in aliquem ; عَدُوّ, *inimici, hostes ;* at once suggests the ideas of conflict and destruction.

9. From this verse to the end of the book, the prophecy relates exclusively to Messianic times. The שָׂפָה בְרוּרָה, *purified lip* or *language*, means the profession of pure religion, a language freed from the polluted names of idols, and of every abomination connected with their worship. As this was to be realized by the nations, the עַמִּים, as distinguished from the Jews, it follows that the spread of Christianity, and the consequent subversion of idolatry throughout the world,

are here specially predicted. This prediction, however, has hitherto been only partially fulfilled. By the gospel, indeed, idolatry has been dislodged from many parts of the globe, but its place has to a great extent been occupied by the pollutions of antichristian systems of worship, while vast regions are still the scenes of varied and most degrading idolatrous abominations. And, as to the unity so strikingly expressed by שְׁכֶם אֶחָד, *one shoulder*, whatever there may be of that real substantial unity which binds all true believers to Christ as their Head, and to one another as members of the same family, there is still a deplorable want of the visible manifestation of oneness in obeying the laws of Christ, and observing the ordinances of his house. These laws are spoken of as a burden, Matt. xi. 30 ; Acts xv. 28 ; Rev. ii. 24 ; and the metaphor here employed by the prophet is taken from two persons jointly carrying a burden between them, shoulder to shoulder. Compare the use of ὁμοθυμαδὸν, Acts i. 14 ; ii. 1, 46 ; iv. 24 ; v. 12 ; xv. 25 ; Rom. xv. 6. What has prevented the outward visibility of the unity of believers has been, that some of them have added burdens of their own to that of the Redeemer, while others have submitted to those imposed by men professing to act by his authority, but who have had no scripture warranty for their pretensions. Until there is a return to an unanimous adherence to the simplicity which is in Christ, there can be no such unity as that taught in this verse. Yet for such the Bible teaches us to look ; and it behoves every Christian to do whatever lies in his

10 From beyond the rivers of Cush,
   My suppliants, the daughter of my dispersed,
   Shall bring my offering.

11   In that day thou shalt not be ashamed
   On account of all thy doings,
   By which thou hast transgressed against me;
   For then I will remove from the midst of thee
   Thy proud exulters;
   And thou shalt no more be haughty in my holy mountain.

12 And I will leave in the midst of thee
   An humble and poor people,
   And they shall trust in the name of Jehovah.

---

power, in order to bring about so blessed a consummation. Comp. 2 Cor. vi. 14, Μὴ γίνεσθε ἑτεροζυγοῦντες ἀπίστοις; and 1 Cor. i. 10, ἦτε δὲ κατηρτισμένοι ἐν τῷ αὐτῷ νοῒ καὶ ἐν τῇ αὐτῇ γνώμῃ.

10. Having foretold the conversion of the Gentiles, the prophet in this verse predicts that of the Jews; quite in accordance with other passages of Scripture, in which they are placed in juxta-position with each other. עֲתָרַי, *my suppliants*, from עָתַר, *to burn incense to a divinity*; *pray, supplicate*. Arab.

عطر, *bonos odores spiravit.* Syr. ܚܠ,

fumavit odore suavi. Comp. Rev. v. 8, where the prayers of saints are called θυμιάματα, odours or incense, and Ps. cxli. 2, where David compares his prayer to קְטֹרֶת, the Hebrew synonyme for *incense.* Who the worshippers are, the prophet explains in the following words: בַּת־פּוּצַי, *the daughter of my dispersed*, i. e. by a common Hebrew idiom, my dispersed people, the Jews; and the locality in which we are directed to look for them is מֵעֵבֶר לְנַהֲרֵי־כוּשׁ, *beyond the rivers of Cush*, i. e. Ethiopia or Abyssinia itself, the rivers of which enclose it on the north. See on Is. xviii. 1, where the same phraseology occurs, but where the Ethiopians, and not the Jews, are the subjects of the prophecy. It is a well ascertained fact, though all the historical circumstances with which it is connected have not yet been brought to light, that there has long existed in the west of Abyssinia, a people called *Falashas*, or emigrants (from the Eth. ፈለሰ: *to*

migrate; hence ፈላሲ: *a sojourner, stranger*, the root from which פְּלִשְׁתִּי, *Philistine*, is derived, and for the same reason), who maintain that they derived their origin from Palestine, and all of whom profess the Jewish religion. They are identified, as to physical traits, not with the African races living in Ethiopia, but with the tribes of Arabia. They have their own government conceded to them by the Negus, or king of Ethiopia. When Bruce was there they had a Jewish king named Gideon, and his queen, Judith. Considering how greatly the Christianity of Abyssinia has been mixed up with Judaism, there is every reason to believe that most of the early converts in that country belonged to this very people. That the Falashas are part of the dispersed people whose conversion is here predicted, I can have no doubt. They are singled out as a separate portion of the scattered seed of Abraham, most probably on account of the peculiar circumstances in which they have lived during the dispersion. Their bringing of Jehovah's offering does not necessarily imply that they are, on their conversion, to come with gifts to Jerusalem; all that is intended may only be מִנְחָה טְהוֹרָה, *the pure offering*, which, under the new dispensation, was to be presented in every place. See Mal. i. 11; and comp. ver. 9.

11—13. These verses contain a description of restored and regenerated Israel. The not being ashamed of their sinful practices does not mean their not

13　The residue of Israel shall not commit injustice;
　　They shall not speak lies;
　　Neither shall a deceitful tongue be found in their mouth;
　　But they shall feed and lie down,
　　And none shall make them afraid.

14　　Rejoice, O daughter of Zion!
　　Shout, O Israel!
　　Be joyful and exult with all thy heart,
　　O daughter of Jerusalem!

15　Jehovah hath removed thy judgments;
　　He hath cleared away thine enemies;
　　The King of Israel, Jehovah, is in the midst of thee,
　　Thou shalt see calamity no more.

16　　In that day it shall be said to Jerusalem, Fear not;
　　O Zion! let not thy hands be feeble;

17　Jehovah thy God is in the midst of thee,
　　The Mighty One, that will save;
　　He will rejoice over thee with gladness,
　　He will be silent in his love;
　　He will exult over thee with a shout of joy.

---

feeling a compunctious sense of their intrinsic odiousness and demerits, but is expressive of the great change that should take place in the outward condition of the Jews. That condition into which they have been brought by their obstinate rebellion against Jehovah and his Messiah, is one of disgrace. When recovered out of it, all the marks of shame and infamy shall be removed. The Pharisaic spirit of pride, and the vain confidence in the temple and the temple-worship, which proved the ruin of the nation, shall be taken away. The converted residue shall be a people humble and poor in spirit, Matt. v. 3; xi. 5; and of a truly righteous and upright character; who, having fled for refuge to the hope set before them in the gospel, shall be safe under the protecting care of their heavenly Father.

14. A call to the converted Israelites, restored to their own land, and especially to the inhabitants of Jerusalem, to exult in their distinguished experience of the Divine loving-kindness.

15. This and the following verses furnish the reasons why the Jews should indulge in exultation. פָּנָה, in Kal, *to turn;* in Piel, *to cause to turn out of the way, remove, destroy.* Instead of אֹיְבֵךְ, *thine enemy,* thirty-two MSS., originally six more, and two by correction, read אֹיְבַיִךְ, *thine enemies,* which reading is also supported by two early editions, the Babyl. Talmud, and all the versions. For תִּרְאִי, sixty-eight MSS., and among these some of the most accurate Spanish, read תִּירְאִי. In the full enjoyment of the presence of their God, the converted Jews should have nothing to fear.

17. A beautiful description of the delight which Jehovah shall take in his recovered people, and of their consequent and continuous happiness. The phrase יַחֲרִישׁ בְּאַהֲבָתוֹ has occasioned some difficulty to interpreters. Houbigant, after the LXX. and Syr., and following him Newcome, and recently Ewald, propose to read יְחַדֵּשׁ, "*he will renew his love;*" but this verb nowhere occurs

18 I will gather those that are grieved for the festivals,
    (They were of thee;)
    Burdened with reproach for her sake.
19 Behold! I will deal with all thine oppressors at that time,
    And will save her that halteth,
    And collect the expelled,
    And make them a praise and a name,
    In every country where they have been put to shame.
20 At that time I will bring you in,

in Hiphil, and the conjectural emendation is wholly unnecessary. חָרַשׁ, *to be
dumb, keep silence,* has the same signification in Hiphil, *to be silent, not to
speak,* and is here very appropriately
employed to express the non-remem-
brance of iniquity. Justly as God might
set the sins of his people before them,
he, in the exercise of his love, makes no
mention of them, having freely forgiven
them for the sake of the atonement
made by his only-begotten Son. Comp.
Ps. xxxii. 2; Jer. xxxi. 34; Ezek.
xxxiii. 16.

18. יָגָה, of which נוּגִים is the Niphal
participle, has two significations, that of
being *pained* or *grieved,* and that of
being *separated, removed,* &c. Both
derivations may be supported by the
Arab. وجى, *doluit,* and Conj. iv. *procul
a se removit.* The former, which is here
most approved, fully meets the exigency
of the passage, and may be said to
imply the latter. The Jews, in a state
which rendered it impossible for them
to celebrate their sacred festivals at
Jerusalem, are represented as filled
with grief when they reflected on the
privileges of their ancestors. מוֹעֵד, *festival,*
is here a noun of multitude. עָלֶיהָ, *on
her account,* is introduced, for the sake
of emphasis, between the words מַשְׂאֵת
חֶרְפָּה, *the lifting up,* or *utterance of reproach,* which would otherwise have
appeared in the construct state. By
metonymy, the Jews, who are the
objects of such reproach, are intended.
Comp. Micah vi. 16. The feminine
suffix in עָלֶיהָ refers to Jerusalem or
Zion, understood: the change of person
is, as frequently, for the sake of effect.
The various reading עָלֶיךָ, though sup-

ported by more than twelve MSS., the
Targ., and Syr., is most probably an
emendation.

19. עֹשֶׂה אֵת, means *to deal with,* in the
way of retribution or punishment. Vulg.
interficiam. Targ. אֲנָא עָבֵיד גְּמִירָא עָם, *I
will make an end of.* The restoration of
the Jews is uniformly represented as
taking place in connexion with the destruction of those nations that are hostile
to the cause of God, and that shall, in a
special manner, oppose the accomplishment of his purpose respecting the final deliverance of that long depressed and scattered, yet beloved people. Comp. Is. lix.
17—21; lxvi. 15, 16.   צֹלֵעָה, *halting,* and
נִדָּחָה, *driven away, cast out,* express the
deplorable circumstances of the Jews
during the dispersion; and the verbal
forms indicate that such shall be their
condition till the time of restoration.
The illustrious character of that restoration, however, shall redound to the
celebrity of the covenant-people in all
the countries where they have been the
objects of reproach and ignominy. אֶרֶץ,
land, is used collectively for אֲרָצוֹת, *lands;*
and אֶרֶץ בָּשְׁתָּם, *the land of their shame,*
means the countries in which they have
been the objects of contumely and disgrace. Ezek. xxxiv. 29. The occurrence
of the article in הָאָרֶץ, which is in construction with בָּשְׁתָּם, is contrary to rule,
but is otherwise not without examples.
See Josh. iii. 17; 1 Sam. ii. 13; 2 Kings
vii. 13. In such cases, however, the
article is generally repeated before the
following noun. See Josh. viii. 11;
Jer. xxv. 26. Some would account for
the irregularity by an understood repeti-
tion of the noun, thus, בְּכָל־הָאָרֶץ אֶרֶץ בָּשְׁתָּם.

20. After אָבִיא אֶתְכֶם supply בְּאִרְצְכֶם.
The י in וּבָעֵת is exegetical. The period

Even at the time when I collect you;
Yea, I will make you a name and a praise
Among all the nations of the earth,
When I reverse your captivity in your sight,
Saith Jehovah.

of the re-introduction of the Jews into their own land is here rendered distinguishingly prominent by repeated and pointed reference. So wonderful, however, shall be the circumstances connected with the event, that they shall scarcely believe it when it happens, how greatly and how long soever they may have desired it. Jehovah, to remove all doubts, declares that he will bring it about *before their eyes;* i. e. it shall certainly become the object of their delightful contemplation.

HAGGAI

PREFACE

It is generally thought that the prophet Haggai was among the Hebrew exiles who returned with Zerubbabel, and Joshua the high priest, from Babylon in the year B. C. 536, when Cyrus granted them their liberty, and ordered them to be furnished with what was necessary for the restoration of the temple at Jerusalem. His book itself vouches for the fact that he prophesied in the reign of Darius Hystaspis, who ascended the Persian throne B. C. 521. Having been interrupted in building the temple by an interdict, which the Samaritans obtained from Smerdis the usurper, the Jews became in some measure indifferent to the work; and when Darius came to the throne, an event which must have deprived the prohibition of all authority, instead of vigorously recommencing their labours, the more influential persons among them pretended that, as the prophecy of the seventy years applied to the temple as well as to the captivity in Babylon, and they were only yet in the sixty-eighth year, the proper time for rebuilding it. had not arrived, and they gave their whole attention to the erection of splendid mansions for themselves.

To rouse them from their selfish indifference to the claims of religion, Haggai and Zechariah were commissioned, in the second year of Darius, i. e. B. C. 520, to deliver to them rousing appeals from Jehovah. These appeals had the desired effect, and the work proceeded then with vigour.

The book is made up of five messages, which were all delivered, at successive periods, within the short space of three months. They are so exceedingly brief, that they are, not without reason, supposed to be only a summary or epitome of the original discourses.

The style of Haggai is not distinguished by any peculiar excellence; yet he is not destitute of pathos and vehemence, when reproving his countrymen for their negligence, and exhorting them to the performance of duty. To these, the interrogatory form which he frequently adopts, in no small degree contributes. He is not without elevation when predicting the future. Certain portions of the book are purely historical; and the rest, though exhibiting more or less of the parallelism of members which characterises the usual prophetic style, are but faintly rhythmical. The phrases, נְאֻם יְהוָה צְבָאוֹת, and שִׂימוּ לְבַבְכֶם, are frequently repeated. נְאֻם יְהוָה occurs not less than thrice in a single verse, chap. ii. 4. אֵין אֶתְכֶם, ii. 16, אַחַת מְעַט, ii. 6; כָּמֹהוּ כְאַיִן, ii. 3; are peculiar, and indicate the Chaldee age.

CHAPTER I

The prophet calls the attention of the principal civil and ecclesiastical authorities to the negligence of the people in not building the temple, 1—4; directs that of the people to this as the cause of their want of outward prosperity, 5—11; and subjoins a notice respecting the success with which the delivery of his message was accompanied, 12—15.

---

1 IN the second year of Darius the king, in the sixth month, on the first day of the month, the word of the Lord was communicated through Haggai the prophet to Zerubbabel, (the son of Shealtiel,) governor of Judah, and to Joshua, (the son of Josedech,) the high priest, saying :

1. The Darius here mentioned is Darius the son of Hystaspis, of the family of the Achæmenidæ, who, in consequence of an oracle, was raised to the throne of Persia, on the death of the usurper Smerdis, B.C. 521, and reigned thirty-six years. That this must be the monarch intended is obvious from the facts, that Darius the Mede, mentioned Dan. v. 31, and ix. 1, lived before the return of the Jews from Babylon ; and that Darius Nothus and Darius Codomannus flourished, the former ninety-three years after the completion of the temple, and the latter at a much later period. Darius Hystaspis is represented by Herodotus as a mild and benevolent ruler. He protected the Jews from the opposition of their enemies, and carried into effect the edict of Cyrus, Ezra vi. The name דָּֽרְיָ֫וֶשׁ, Daryavesh, or, as it appears in the cuneiform inscriptions of Persepolis, Daryawus, is derived by Lassen (üb. d. Keilförm. Inschriften, p. 158), from the root darh, to preserve, with the affirmative awu,

the s being the sign of the nominative ; and thus signifies conservator. Comp. Herodotus, vi. 98, where the signification ἐρξείης, coercer, is given to the name. The date in the prophecy is taken from the reign of this monarch, because at the time he swayed his sceptre over all the countries with which the Jews were brought into contact, from Lybia in Egypt, and the frontiers of Europe, to the Oxus and the Indus on the east. The months specified by Haggai and Zechariah are those not of the Persian, but of the Hebrew year. See Zech. i. 7 ; vii. 1 ; viii. 19. Zerubbabel, whose Chaldee name was Sheshbazzar, Ezra i. 8 ; v. 14 ; comp. v. 16 ; iii. 8, 10, was the grandson (בֶּן is used by Haggai in its more extended signification) of Shealtiel, of the royal house of David, 1 Chron. iii. 9—19. Cyrus committed to his care the sacred vessels of the temple, and appointed him governor of the colony which returned to Judæa. The title of פֶּחָה, prefect or governor, by which he is designated, is applied to

2   Thus saith Jehovah of hosts :
     This people say, The time is not come,
     The time for the house of Jehovah to be built.

3   Yea, the word of Jehovah was communicated through Haggai
     the prophet, saying :

4   Is it time for you, O ye,
     To dwell in your wainscoted houses,
     And this house lie waste ?

5   Now, therefore, thus saith Jehovah of hosts :
     Consider your ways.

6   Ye have sown much, but brought in little ;
     Ye have eaten, but not had enough ;
     Ye have drunk, but not to the full ;
     Ye have put on clothing, but none is warm ;

---

persons bearing rule in provinces or divisions of the Persian empire of less extent and importance than satrapies. Comp. the Pracrit. *Pakkha*, and the present Turkish *Pasha*, though the latter word باشا, *Basha*, is rather to be referred to باش, *Bash*, *head*, *commander*, *ruler*. Joshua the high priest is repeatedly mentioned in the book of Zechariah, as presiding over the Jewish affairs at the same time with Zerubbabel. That הַכֹּהֵן הַגָּדוֹל, *the high priest*, is to be connected, not with the more proximate, but with the more remote noun, *i. e.* with יְהוֹשֻׁעַ, *Joshua*, is clear, not only from the similar coherence of פֶּחָה, but from all other instances in which offices and genealogical statements are blended.

2. Simple as are the words לֹא עֶת־בֹּא עֵת "וגו, the construction is somewhat difficult, owing to the position of the infinitive בֹּא. Either we must, with Hitzig, give to the former עֵת the points עַתָּה=עַתָּ, *now*, as in Ps. lxxiv. 6 ; Ezek. xxiii. 43 ; or convert בֹּא into בָּא of the preterite, as one of De Rossi's MSS. reads, and agreeably to the rendering of the LXX., Syr., Vulg., Targ., and Arab.; or, what is preferable, regard בֹּא as put absolutely for the purpose of more emphatically expressing the sentiment that the time was not yet *really* come in which to erect the temple. As two of the seventy years' captivity had yet to elapse, the colony which had arrived at Jerusalem encouraged themselves in their neglect of present duty, by assuming that the building of the temple was included in the calculation, and that, till the full time had expired, they were under no obligation to recommence the work.

4. Repeating the word עֵת, *time*, which he had employed twice, verse 2, the prophet makes an appeal full of point and cogency to those whom he addresses. The use of אַתֶּם after לָכֶם adds to the force of the language. סָפַן signifies to *cover, cover over, wainscot*, or overlay with boards, so that what is predicated of the houses is not to be confined to the ceiling, but must be extended to the walls which were thus covered, at once for comfort and ornament. How beautifully the feelings of David, 2 Sam. vii. 2, contrast with those of the persons reproved by Haggai !

5. The וְ in וְעַתָּה is inferential, while עַתָּה is employed, not in its temporal acceptation, but argumentatively, as in Ps. ii. 10. שִׂימוּ לְבַבְכֶם עַל־דַּרְכֵיכֶם, lit. *place your heart upon your ways*, an idiomatic, but very expressive mode of speech. Comp. ver. 7, and ii. 18, twice, in the elliptical form שִׂימוּ לְבַבְכֶם.

6. הַרְבֵּה, אָכֹל, שָׁתוֹ and לָבוֹשׁ, are historical infinitives, which carry forward the force of the finite form in וּזְרַעְתֶּם at the commencement of the verse, and, at the same time, give a greater degree of prominence to the actions which they

And he that earneth wages, earneth them
To put them into a purse with holes.

7　　Thus saith Jehovah of hosts:
Consider your ways.

8　Go up to the mountain, and bring wood,
And build the house, and I will take pleasure in it,
That I may be glorified, saith Jehovah.

9　Ye looked for much, but, behold! little;
And ye brought it home, and I blew upon it.
Wherefore? saith Jehovah of hosts.
Because of my house which lieth waste,
And ye run each to his own house.

10　Therefore, it is on your account the heavens withhold the dew,
And the earth withholdeth her produce.

11　And I have called for drought,

express. Nothing prospered, and nothing could be expected to prosper, while the Jews were living in the flagrant neglect of their duty. They had brought property with them from Babylon, with which they had erected splendid houses for themselves, but God blasted their agricultural and other expectations; and they had nothing in prospect but a season of scarcity and want. The necessaries of life were already become so dear, that those who wrought for days' wages parted with all that they earned, as if they had put it into a bag or purse with holes. נָקוּב, *bored* or *perforated*.

7. A reiteration of the exhortation contained in ver. 5.

8. The reason why the Jews are called to provide wood only is thought by Jerome to be, that the walls of the temple remained standing; but this hypothesis is contradicted by repeated statements in the books of Ezra and Zechariah, as well as in Haggai ii. 18, in which express mention is made of laying its foundations. It rather seems to have been on account of the time which would be necessary to procure the article in question from Lebanon, since it required first to be hewn down, and afterwards transported by sea to Joppa. By הָהָר, *the mountain*, Rosenmüller thinks Moriah is meant; Hitzig, the mountainous country in the vicinity of Jerusalem;

but it is more natural to interpret the term of Lebanon, whence the wood was actually fetched. It is true the Jews themselves did not go to that mountain for the timber; it was conveyed by the Zidonians and Tyrians, Ezra iii. 7; but persons are often said to do what they perform through the instrumentality of others. For וְאֶבָּנֶה, the textual reading, which should be pointed וְאִבָּנֵד, the Keri has וְאֶבָּבְדָה. The copula וְ marks here the end to be obtained, or the result that would follow the performance of the enjoined duty. In such cases the future has the force of a potential mood.

9. פָּנֹה, the infinitive absolute, as in ver. 6. Even the small crop which was reaped had no sooner been brought into the barns or granaries, than it was dissipated. Their running each to his own house is expressive of the eagerness with which the Jews pursued their own affairs, and sought for self-indulgence. בֵּיתִי and בֵּיתוֹ stand here in striking contrast.

10. עֲלֵיכֶם is not to be referred to the heavens, and so rendered *over you*, but *on your account, for your sake*. Comp. לָכֵן בִּגְלַלְכֶם, Micah iii. 12. The meaning is, on account of your neglecting to build the temple. The preposition in מִמַּל, following מַל, signifies *with respect to*, but does not require to be translated.

11. In the use of חֹרֶב, *drought*, there

Upon the land, and upon the mountains,
Upon the grain, and upon the new wine,
Upon the oil, and upon what the ground bringeth forth,
Upon man and upon beast,
And upon all the labour of the hands.

12   Then Zerubbabel, (the son of Shealtiel,) and Joshua, (the son
of Josedech,) the high priest, and all the residue of the people,
hearkened to the voice of Jehovah their God, and to the words
of Haggai the prophet, according as Jehovah their God had sent
him ; and the people feared Jehovah.

13   Then spake Haggai, the messenger of Jehovah, in the message
of Jehovah to the people, saying :
I am with you, saith Jehovah.

14   And Jehovah stirred up the spirit of Zerubbabel, (the son of
Shealtiel,) governor of Judah, and the spirit of Joshua, (the son
of Josedech,) the high priest, and the spirit of all the rest of the
people, and they came and did the work in the house of Jehovah
15   of hosts, their God, on the twenty-fourth day of the sixth month,
in the second year of Darius the king.

---

is an obvious reference to חֹרֶב, dry, waste,
desolate, verses 4 and 9. They form a
paronomasia. The lengthened amplification is employed in order to add to the
force of the threatening. The LXX.,
supposing it to be incongruous to speak
of bringing a drought upon man and
beast, read חֶרֶב instead of חֹרֶב, and rendered the word by ῥομφαίαν, a sword, not
adverting to the circumstance, that the
latter term was still less applicable to
the other subjects here enumerated.
What the prophet threatens is an universal drought, the effects of which
would specially be experienced by living
creatures.
12. The prophet now describes the
happy effect which was produced by the
message which he had just delivered.
All the people who had returned united

with their rulers in rendering obedience
to the Divine command.
13. To encourage them to proceed
in the path of obedience on which they
had entered, Haggai delivers to them
the brief, but most cheering promise,
אֲנִי אִתְּכֶם נְאֻם־יְהֹוָה, I am with you, saith
Jehovah.
14. הֵעִיר רוּחַ, to excite, or stir up the
spirit of any one (comp. Ezra i. 1, 5),
means to render him inclined effectively
to undertake the performance of any act,
or to pursue a certain line of conduct.
15. From the date here assigned it
appears, that most of the month elapsed
before the work was fairly undertaken.
Several of the early editions of the
Hebrew Bible, as also the London Poly-
glot, improperly place this verse at the
beginning of the next chapter.

CHAPTER II

This chapter contains three different oracles of the prophet. The first, designed to encourage the people and their leaders to proceed with the building of the temple, by considerations derived from the Divine presence, 1—4; from their national covenant continuing in force, and that of the prophetic and gracious influences of the Holy Spirit, 5; from the advent of the person and kingdom of the Messiah, 6, 7; and from the universal proprietorship of Jehovah, the glory of the Messiah, and the reconciliation which he should effect, 8, 9. The second oracle cautions them against intermission in their labours, by showing that if they did so, nothing they did could be acceptable to God, 10—14, and by referring them to the infelicitous state of their affairs before the late revival, 15—18; and promises them prosperity, 19. The third is addressed to Zerubbabel individually, to animate and encourage him in conducting the work, 20—23.

---

1 In the seventh month, on the twenty-first of the month, the word of Jehovah was communicated through Haggai the prophet,

2 saying: Speak now to Zerubbabel, (the son of Shealtiel,) the governor of Judah, and to Joshua, (the son of Josedech,) the high priest, and to the rest of the people, saying:

3 Who is there among you that remaineth,
That saw this house in its former glory?
And how do ye see it now?
Is it not, compared with it, as nothing in your eyes?

4 Yet now be strong, O Zerubbabel! saith Jehovah;

1, 2. This oracle was delivered nearly a month after the rebuilding of the temple had commenced, and was evidently designed to remove the despondency in which some of the people indulged, and to animate them to prosecute the work.

3. It appears from Ezra iii. 12, that there were many present at the laying of the foundation of the second temple, who had seen the first. To such of them as were still alive, few as they must have been, Haggai appeals respecting the disparity between the two, in regard to the rough and unpromising appearance of the new structure, contrasted with the elegant and splendid aspect of that of Solomon, previous to its destruction by the Chaldæans. הַנִּשְׁאָר is not in apposition with בָּכֶם, but connects with the interrogative מִי. The phrase כָּמֹהוּ כְּאַיִן is peculiar, but not difficult of resolution, the word for temple being understood.

4. The comparison instituted in the

And be strong, O Joshua, (son of Josedech,) the high priest !
Be ye strong also, all ye people of the land !
Saith Jehovah of hosts, and work :
For I am with you, saith Jehovah of hosts.

5   The covenant which I made with you,
    When ye went forth out of Egypt,
    And my Spirit remain among you :
    Fear not.

6   For thus saith Jehovah of hosts :
    Yet once, within a little,
    And I will shake the heavens, and the earth,
    And the sea, and the dry land,

preceding verse, so far from being designed to discourage those to whom the
appeal was made, was on the contrary
intended to inspire them with confidence
in their covenant God, whose prerogative
it is to call things that are not as though
they were. It is tacitly implied, that
whatever might be the estimate they
might make of the work, it was very
different with respect to his. Comp.
Zech. viii. 6. And what is here only
implied is expressly declared ver. 9.

5. The government of אֶת־הַדָּבָר has unnecessarily puzzled interpreters. Ewald
thinks the sentence is incomplete, and
would supply זִכְרוּ, *remember.* Hengstenberg actually supplies the word in a
parenthesis. Maurer endeavours to make
it out to be an accusative *modi* s. *normæ,*
and explains, *secundum illud verbum:*
and connects it with the preceding verse,
thus : " I am with you, *according to that
word,*" &c. ; and so our own translators,
after Calvin. Rosenmüller would supply
עָשׂוּ from the preceding verse. The
particle אֵת I consider to be prefixed to
הַדָּבָר, in order to give it a greater degree
of prominence, and to be equivalent to
that or *the same* covenant, &c. ; while
אֶת־הַדָּבָר, together with רוּחִי, form the
nominative to the participle עֹמֶדֶת ; only,
as separated from it by the intervening
predicate "אֲשֶׁר כָּרַתִּי וגו, the participle is
put in the feminine singular, to agree
with רוּחִי, the nearer antecedent. For
this use of אֵת before the nominative,
though rare, see Neh. ix. 19. אֶת־עַמּוּד
הֶעָנָן לֹא־סָר, *the pillar of cloud did not
depart,* &c. ; ver. 34, וְאֵת־מָלְכֵינוּ—לֹא עָשׂוּ,

And our kings—have not kept, &c. :
Dan. ix. 13, אֵת כָּל־הָרָעָה הַזֹּאת בָּאָה עָלֵינוּ, *All
this evil hath come upon us.* דָּבָר, *word or
matter,* is here employed to denote the
Sinaic Covenant, as the accompanying
verb כָּרַת, *to cut,* or *make a covenant,*
obviously shows. Notwithstanding the
flagrant violation of that covenant of
which the Jews had been guilty, on
account of which they had been punished
in Babylon, it still continued in all its
force. They possessed it in its written
form, and thus had the pledge which
Jehovah had given them, that he was
their covenant God, and would confer
blessings upon the obedient. They also
had his רוּחַ, the spirit of inspiration in the
prophets who were raised up in the midst
of them to declare his will, and call them
to the discharge of duty, Ezra v. 1 ; and
of efficient influence to induce them to
listen to, and enable them to comply with
such call, Zech. iv. 6 ; Hag. i. 14.

6. In this and the following verse, the
Jews are encouraged to proceed with the
work by the assurance that Jehovah
would, as the Governor among the
nations, in a brief space, exert his Almighty power in effecting a great revolution in the state of the kingdoms of this
world, preparatory to the establishment
of the kingdom of the Messiah. This
mighty change is first described in the
usual figurative language of prophecy,
as a convulsion of the physical universe, and then literally as a convulsion of all nations. In the phrase
עוֹד אַחַת מְעַט, it is only the numeral
אַחַת which occasions any difficulty. The

7　Yea, I will shake all the nations,
　　And the things desired by all the nations shall come ;

combination עוֹד מְעַט, *yet a little*,i.e. time,
occurs more than once. See Ps. xxxvii.
10; Is. xxix. 17; Jer. li. 33. But that
here presented being peculiar to this
passage, naturally suggests some peculiarity in the meaning. Most supply פַּעַם,
time, after the LXX. ἔτι ἅπαξ, quoted
and reasoned upon, Heb. xii. 26, 27, and
the Syr. ܟܘܬ ܣܓܝܐܐ ܙܒܢ. Comp. for
פַּעַם אֶחָת, *one time, once*, Josh. vi. 3;
1 Sam. xxvi. 8; and for the ellipsis of
פַּעַם, where אַחַת stands by itself, as
here, Exod. xxx. 10; Job. xl. 5; Ps.
lxii. 12; lxxxix. 36. And certainly, as
מְעַט, *little*, is designed to express *brevity
of time*, nothing can be more appropriate
than such construction. Hengstenberg
labours hard to bring the idea of brevity
of time out of אַחַת, but fails to produce
any examples to confirm his hypothesis.
What the prophet has in view appears
to be the convulsions which were yet to
take place in the Persian and Greek
empires, some of which were soon to
commence, but all of which were more
proximately, or more remotely connected
with the complete establishment of the
Jews in their own land, and the splendour
of their temple as erected by Herod. The
previous convulsion, implied in the phrase
yet once, does not appear to be the shaking,
&c., which took place at the giving of the
law on Sinai, but the violent change
which had lately taken place in the condition of the Babylonian empire, just as
that which was yet to come is not to be
extended to the downfal of the Roman
empire, the destruction of Antichrist,
&c., but must be confined to events
which were to happen before the coming
of Christ. We have only to call to mind
the wars of the Persians in Asia Minor,
Greece, Egypt, and other parts, and
those of Alexander and his successors
which followed, till the period when the
establishment of the power of the Romans
at length gave peace to the world, in
order to read, in legible characters, the
fulfilment of the present prophecy. Nor
does the comment of the writer of the
Epistle to the Hebrews require any other
application of it. His object is to show

that the dispensation or kingdom of the
Messiah is stable and immovable; and
in order to illustrate his point, he introduces, by way of contrast, the natural
phenomena which took place on the
promulgation of the Sinaic covenant, as
described by Moses, and the political
phenomena predicted by Haggai, all of
which indicated the mutable character
of the elements upon which they were
exerted. That the prophet intended to
include the dissolution of the Jewish
state in his prediction, does not appear;
indeed, the reference to such an event
must have increased the despondency of
his people, instead of inspiring them
with hope and courage, which formed
his only object in addressing them.

7. Having figuratively set forth the
great political changes which were still
to take place among the nations before
the introduction of the kingdom of the
Messiah, Haggai here repeats his prediction in literal terms, and then at once
announces the arrival of the eagerly expected blessings of that kingdom. The
passage has long been regarded as one
of the principal prophecies relative to
the time of the Redeemer's advent.
That it was so applied by some of the
early Jewish Rabbins, is undeniable.
Thus in the chapter of the Talmudic
treatise Sanhedrin, entitled חלק, the
following interpretation is given as that
of Rabbi Akiba, who flourished before
the time of Jerome: מעט מלכות אתן להם
לישראל לאחר חרבן ולאחר מלכות הגוי
וארץ שמים מרעיש ויבא משיח, *For a little I
will give the kingdom to Israel, after our
desolation, and after the kingdom, behold
I will shake heaven and earth, and* MES-
SIAH SHALL COME. The rendering of
the Vulg. supports the same view : " Et
veniet Desideratus cunctis Gentibus."
Leo Juda: "Et veniet qui desideratur ab
omnibus gentibus." Dathe: " Et deinde
veniet gentibus omnibus expetendus."
On the other hand, Kimchi, Vatablus,
Calvin, Ribera, Drusius, Gataker, Vitringa, and others, render: "The Gentiles shall come with their delightful
things," *i. e.* their silver, gold, precious
stones, &c. Some, violently, " Come *to*

And I will fill this house with glory,
Saith Jehovah of hosts.

the desire," &c., meaning thereby Jerusalem. Most of the moderns, rejecting
this construction as altogether unwarranted, translate after the LXX. ἥξει
τὰ ἐκλεκτὰ πάντων τῶν ἐθνῶν, "the
choice things," or "the pleasant things of
all nations shall come." Ewald : "dass
die liebsten aller Völker kommen:" *i. e.*
"That the most lovely of all people may
come." Hengstenberg, who renders,
"the beauty of all the heathen," is at
great pains in endeavouring to make
good his translation, which he interprets
of what he says is always beautiful
among them—all their costly good
things. But he fails alike in his attempt
to set aside the idea of *desire* as expressed by חֶמְדָּה, and in that to prove
that the prophet here foretels the rich
contributions which the heathen would
bring into the church. That the root
חָמַד, primarily and most commonly signifies *to desire* or *covet,* both in a good
and a bad sense, must be evident to
every one who will take the trouble to
consult the Hebrew concordance ; and
that חֶמְדָּה, which is derived from it, signifies *desire, an object of desire*, see the
Lexicons of Gesenius and Lee. This
acceptation must be vindicated to 1 Sam.
ix. 20, וּלְמִי כָּל־חֶמְדַּת יִשְׂרָאֵל; to 2 Chron.
xxi. 20, בְּלֹא חֶמְדָּה; and to Dan. xi. 37,
חֶמְדַּת נָשִׁים. The want of concord in
וּבָאוּ חֶמְדַּת כָּל־הַגּוֹיִם, the verb expressing
the predicate being in the plural masculine, while חֶמְדָּה, the subject of the
proposition, is in the singular feminine,
occasions no small difficulty, and presents
an insuperable objection to the usual
Messianic interpretation. That בָּאוּ
should have been produced by zeugma
with הַגּוֹיִם, is totally unsupported by
analogy, just as a plural of excellence
in verbs is equally without example.
The only practicable solution warranted
by grammatical usage, consists in assuming חֶמְדָּה to be a collective noun,
conveying a plural idea, the gender of
which not having yet presented itself to
the mind of the prophet when he enun-
ciated the verb, he naturally expressed
it in the masculine as the more worthy
gender. The construction in such cases
is *ad sensum ;* i. e. it is not formal, but
logical. The proper translation, there-
fore, of וּבָאוּ חֶמְדַּת כָּל־הַגּוֹיִם will be, *And,*
or, *And then the things desired by all
nations shall come.* The Genitive, being
the Genitive of object, must be thus expressed. Now these objects of desire
on the part of all nations, cannot mean
their riches, for no such riches were
brought to Jerusalem by all the nations
—the gifts bestowed by some few of the
heathen princes after the time of Alexander not in any degree exhausting the
force of the language here employed.
Neither could the prospect of contributions in more remote future time have
operated in the way of encouragement
upon the minds of those whom the
prophet addressed, so as to induce them
to proceed with their work. The objects
in question, therefore, must have been of
a higher order—τὰ μέλλοντα ἀγαθά, *the
good things to come,* i. e. the blessings of
the New Covenant. There was found to
pervade the minds of the heathen, a deep
and dark feeling of the necessity of supernatural light and influence. Bewildered
in the mazes of error and superstition,
they could find nothing satisfactory respecting the Divine Being, pardon, eman-
cipation from the power of moral evil,
and a future state of existence; and
more or less earnestly desired to obtain
information in regard to these important
and necessary points. To adduce only
one testimony from among many to be
found in ancient pagan writers. Socrates, endeavouring to satisfy the mind
of Alcibiades on the subject of acceptable worship, says : ἀναγκαῖον οὖν ἐστι
περιμένειν ἕως ἄν τις μάθῃ ὡς δεῖ πρὸς
θεοὺς καὶ πρὸς ἀνθρώπους διακεῖσθαι,
*It is therefore necessary to wait till some
one may teach us how it behoves us to
conduct ourselves, both towards the gods
and men.* To which Alcibiades re-
sponds : πότε οὖν παρέσται ὁ χρόνος
οὗτος ὦ Σώκρατες; καὶ τίς ὁ παιδεύσων ;
ἥδιστα γὰρ ἄν μοι δῶκ' ἰδεῖν τοῦτον τὸν
ἄνθρωπον τίς ἐστιν; *When shall that
time arrive, O Socrates? and who shall
that Teacher be? for most eagerly do I
wish to see such a man.*—Plato, Alcibiades, ii. near the end. And, as the
time of the Redeemer's advent drew

8　Mine is the silver, and mine is the gold,
　　Saith Jehovah of hosts.
9　The glory of this latter house shall be greater than that of the
　　　　former,
　　Saith Jehovah of hosts.
　　And in this place I will give peace,
　　Saith Jehovah of hosts.

near, there was a general expectation of a Teacher and Deliverer, not only in the Jewish nation, but throughout the world. Comp. ἠθέλησαν, Luke x. 24. To Christ, as the Light of the world, and to the spiritual blessings which flow through his mediation, the prophecy strictly applies; and, with this reference, was admirably calculated to stimulate the Jews to perseverance in building the temple, with which was inseparably connected the restoration of their ancient polity, during the existence of which the Messiah was to appear. The "glory" with which the temple was to be filled, was not the rich and splendid furniture, &c., but a resplendence, consisting in the manifestation of Jehovah himself. Comp. Zech. ii. 5, with Ezek. xliii. 4, 5; Exod. xl. 34, 35; 1 Kings viii. 11.

8. The Jews needed to be under no concern about the means requisite for the erection of the temple. The earth is the Lord's and the fulness thereof, so that whatever amount of earthly riches was wanted, he would in his providence supply. The declaration contained in this verse is introduced parenthetically, to relieve their minds from any momentary anxiety, arising out of the circumstances in which, as a poor and despised people, they were placed.

9. The LXX. refer the terms הָאַחֲרוֹן, the latter, and הָרִאשׁוֹן, the former, not to הַבַּיִת הַזֶּה, this house, but to כָּבוֹד, the glory. And thus Hitzig, Maurer, and Ewald; but Ezra iii. 12, determines to the contrary. The glory here predicted was to be greater than that of the former temple, not merely in degree, but in kind. That the second temple, even as renewed and beautified by Herod, at all equalled in magnificence that of Solomon, there is no reason to believe. This must appear on comparing the description given of the former by Josephus, Antiq. Jud. lib. xv. cap. xi., with that

furnished of the latter, 1 Kings vi.; vii. 13—50. In point of size, indeed, the temple of Herod exceeded the structure erected by the celebrated Jewish monarch; but this was all. The statement made by Josephus, Bell. Jud. lib. vi. cap. iv. 8, that it was the most admirable of all the works he had seen or heard of, does not include Solomon's temple, but has respect to other erections in different parts of the world. But if the second house was inferior in point of sumptuousness to the former, and wanted, as the Jews admit, the Urim and Thummim, the ark, the pot of manna, Aaron's rod, and the visible glory, which was the symbol of the Divine presence, it follows that the greater glory by which it was to be distinguished, must denote something altogether different in kind, and which could only be supplied by Him, in whose person the glory of God appeared, 2 Cor. iv. 6, who is the "Brightness of the Divine glory," Heb. i. 2, 3, whose glory was beheld as that of the only-begotten of the Father, John i. 14; who could say of himself, "In this place is one greater than the temple," Matt. xii. 6; and who sat in it daily teaching, Matt. xxvi. 55. In support of this interpretation, and indeed of the Messianic character of the entire prophecy, ver. 7—9, the declaration made in the concluding clause of the latter verse may with all propriety be adduced. When "peace" is spoken of in an absolute sense, in the prophets, it denotes the reconciliation between God and sinful men, to be effected by the Messiah. Comp. Is. ix. 6, 7; liii. 5; lvii. 19; Micah v. 5; Zech. vi. 13; with Luke ii. 14; Acts x. 36; Rom. v. 1; Eph. ii. 14, 17. This peace was to be granted בַּמָּקוֹם הַזֶּה, in this place, i.e. in Jerusalem. It was there the Messiah made peace through the blood of his cross, Col. i. 20. It has with some been matter of dispute,

10   On the twenty-fourth of the ninth month, in the second year of
     Darius, the word of Jehovah was communicated through Haggai
11   the prophet, saying: Thus saith Jehovah of hosts: Ask now the
12   priests as to the law, saying: If any one should carry sacred flesh
     in the skirt of his garment, and touch with his skirt bread, or pot-
     tage, or wine, or oil, or any eatable, shall it be holy? And the
13   priests answered and said, No.   Then said Haggai: If any one
     who is unclean on account of a dead body, should touch any of
     these, shall it be unclean?   And the priests answered and said,
14   It shall be unclean.   Then Haggai continued, and said:

          Thus hath this people, and thus hath this nation been,
          Before me, saith Jehovah;
          And thus hath been every work of their hands,
          And what they have offered there hath been unclean.
15   And now consider, I beseech you,
          From this day and backward,
          Before one stone was laid upon another

whether the temple erected by Zerubbabel, and that built by Herod, are to
be regarded as identical, or whether the
latter is not to be considered as a third
temple.   Strictly and architecturally
considered, that of Herod was entirely
new, for he caused that of Zerubbabel to
be taken down to the very foundations;
but in the popular and religious language
they were identical; just as Josephus
speaks of those built by Solomon and
Zerubbabel as one, Bell. Jud. lib. vi. cap.
iv. 8.   Accordingly nothing is more
customary than for Jewish writers to
speak of only the first and the second
temple.   In the present verse, Haggai
is to be understood as speaking in an architectural sense, inasmuch as the second
temple was then being actually built.

10. This prophecy was delivered rather
more than two months after that contained
in the preceding verses of the chapter.

11—13. To convince his countrymen
of the impossibility of their conduct
being well-pleasing to God, and of their
obtaining his blessing, while in any one
point they neglected to comply with his
will, the prophet directs them to consult
the priests on two legal questions; the
one, relative to the communication of
ceremonial sanctity to any object, by its
having been brought into contact with

what had been sanctified; and the other,
respecting the communication of ceremonial impurity by one who was himself
impure.   The former was denied; the
latter affirmed.   Whatever the Jews
might otherwise rightly perform, would
not compensate for their neglect in
building the temple; on the contrary,
their neglect in this matter would taint
or vitiate all their other actions. Comp.
in illustration of these questions, Lev.
vi. 27 ; Numb. vi. 6 ; xix. 13 ; in which
latter passages the abbreviated form נֶפֶשׁ,
a dead body, is expressed in full by נֶפֶשׁ
מֵת, or by נֶפֶשׁ הָאָדָם אֲשֶׁר יָמוּת.

14. The application of the legal decisions of the priests to the case of the
Jews, who had neglected the building of
the temple.   It describes them, not as
they now were, engaged in the work,
but as they had been, and is designed to
put them upon their guard against falling
back into the same state.   The adverb
שָׁם, there, points graphically to the altar,
which had been erected at Jerusalem,
and which was, in all probability, within
view of the audience which the prophet
addressed.   Ezra iii. 3.

15—18. The Jews are earnestly exhorted to reflect upon the state of their
affairs during the period in which they
had intermitted the work.   God had

In the temple of Jehovah.

16 Since these days were,
　　One came to a heap of twenty sheaves,
　　And there were but ten ;
　　One came to the vat to draw fifty purahs,
　　And there were but twenty.

17 I smote you with blight, and mildew, and hail,
　　In all the labours of your hands ;
　　Yet ye turned not to me,
　　Saith Jehovah.

18 Consider, I beseech you,
　　From this day and backward,
　　From the twenty-fourth day of the ninth month,
　　From the day when the temple of Jehovah was founded,
　　Consider !

19 Is the seed still in the granary?
　　And as yet the vine, and the fig-tree,
　　And the pomegranate, and the olive have borne nothing ;
　　From this day will I bestow the blessing.

20　　And the word of Jehovah was communicated a second time to

---

frowned upon them, and rendered them infelicitous. מַעְלָה, a substantive, with the local ה, used adverbially. Properly it signifies *upward*, being derived from עָלָה, *to ascend* ; but used, as here, of time, it means *back, backwards*. In הַיּוֹם, the word יָמִים, *days*, is understood. בָּא is to be taken impersonally. At עֲרֵמַת עֶשְׂרִים, *a heap of twenty*, supply אֲלֻמּוֹת or עֳמָרִים, *sheaves*. פּוּרָה, which is used for the wine-press itself, Is. lxiii. 3, is here employed to denote a liquid measure in which the wine was drawn out. LXX. μετρητής. The quantity being unknown, I have retained the original word. For ver. 17, comp. Amos iv. 9, where we have the words לֹא־שַׁבְתֶּם עָדַי, *ye turned not unto me*, instead of אֵלַי אֶתְכֶם־וְאֵין, used by Haggai, in which there is an ellipsis of the participle שָׁבִים. For this use of אֵת, as a nominative, or as indicating the subject of discourse, see on ver. 5. In ver. 18, the exhortation is once and again reiterated for the sake of effect ; and to render it still more definite, the exact date is added to the formula הַיּוֹם הַזֶּה, *this day*, which had been employed ver. 15. מַעְלָה is here to be taken, as in

that verse, in reference to past time, and not, as the Vulg., Hitzig, &c., in reference to the future.

19. To the question put at the beginning of the verse, a negative is to be given. The seed was no longer in the granary. It had been sown in the course of the month, and there were no signs of its springing up any more than there were of the produce of the fruit-trees. Jehovah had formerly blasted their harvest ; but now that the people were diligently engaged in building his temple, they might confidently calculate upon one of plenty. He gives them a positive promise to this effect. The repetition of מִן־הַיּוֹם הַזֶּה, *from this day*, which had been twice used in the preceding verses, gives emphasis to the declaration. עַד, usually signifying *until*, is here employed in the sense of *while*, or *as yet*, as in Judges iii. 26 ; 2 Kings ix. 22 ; Job i. 18, where it corresponds to עוֹד in verses 16 and 17.

20—23. These verses contain a special message to Zerubbabel, in which there is a repetition of the prediction, somewhat amplified, respecting the revolu-

21   Haggai on the twenty-fourth of the month, saying : Speak to
      Zerubbabel, the governor of Judah, saying :
      I will shake the heavens and the earth,

22   I will overthrow the throne of kingdoms,
      I will destroy the strength of the kingdoms of the nations,
      And overthrow the chariots and those who ride in them ;
      The horses, also, and their riders shall come down,
      Each by the sword of another.

23   In that day. saith Jehovah of hosts,
      I will take thee, O Zerubbabel, the son of Shealtiel,
      My servant, saith Jehovah,
      And will make thee as a signet ;
      For in thee I take pleasure,
      Saith Jehovah of hosts.

---

tions that were about to take place, which had been delivered in verses 6 and 7. In ver. 22, the verb יֵרֵד, *to go*, or *come down*, is equivalent to נָפַל, *to fall*. That the promise made, ver. 23, cannot be viewed as having respect to Zerubbabel in his individual capacity, has been thought to be quite obvious from the fact, that he lived upwards of an hundred years before the time of Alexander, who overturned the Persian throne, and subdued the rest of Asia ; but the predicted convulsions did not commence with the conquests of that monarch. Many of them took place during the reign of Darius, whose arms were carried not only into Scythia, Asia Minor, and Greece, but, according to Herodotus, into India. It is, therefore, not at all improbable that Zerubbabel survived several of these wars, and thus lived in the beginning of הַיּוֹם הַהוּא, *that day*, or the period in the course of which the prophecy was to be fulfilled ; and as the Persians occasionally experienced serious reverses, as for instance, in the Scythian expedition, it was natural for the Jews, who were under the protection of Darius, to have their minds unsettled

by apprehensions respecting the ultimate state of their affairs. To inspire them with confidence, Jehovah here assures their governor of his regard and protection amid all the commotions that might take place in the surrounding nations. לָקַח, *to take*, is merely employed for the purpose of introducing the action expressed by the following verb. For שַׂמְתִּיךָ כַחוֹתָם, *I will place thee as a signet*, comp. Song. viii. 6 ; Jer. xxii. 24. חוֹתָם, from חָתַם, *to seal*, or *close by sealing*, signifies a *ring* with *the seal* or *signet* in it, with which the impression was made. Seals were commonly made of silver, but sometimes of the most precious stones, and, consequently, held in high estimation by their owners. Being worn on one of the fingers of the right hand, they were likewise objects of constant inspection and care. In all these points of view Zerubbabel was to be regarded by God. He was to be an object of his incessant care and delight. The latter idea is more definitely expressed by the addition בְּךָ בָחַרְתִּי, for בָּחַר signifies not only to *try* objects, and then to *select* what is valuable, but also to *take pleasure* in what is thus selected.

ZECHARIAH

PREFACE

ZECHARIAH was of a sacerdotal family. His father Berechiah
was a son of Iddo, one of the priests who returned with Zerubbabel
and Joshua from Babylon, Neh. xii. 4. When he is said to have
been the *son* of Iddo, Ezra v. 1, and vi. 14, the word בֶּן is used,
according to a common Hebrew idiom, in the sense of grandson.
He must have been born in Babylonia, and been young, rather
than otherwise, at the time of his arrival in Judæa. He was contemporary with Haggai, and, like him, received his prophetic commission in the second year of Darius Hystaspis, B. C. 520, only the
latter began his ministry two months earlier. Both prophets were
employed in encouraging Zerubbabel and Joshua to carry forward
the building of the temple, which had been intermitted through the
selfish and worldly spirit of the returned exiles—a spirit which
they boldly and variously reproved.

The most remarkable portion of the book is that containing the
first six chapters. It consists of a series of visions which were
vouchsafed to the prophet in the course of a single night, in which,
by means of symbolical representations, the dispensations of Divine
Providence relative to the nations that had oppressed the Jews, the
entire removal of idolatry from the latter, the re-establishment of
the city and temple of Jerusalem, and the certainty of the Messiah's
advent, were strikingly and impressively revealed.

The next portion comprises the seventh and eighth chapters, and contains an answer to a question which the inhabitants of Bethel had proposed respecting the observance of a certain fast, together with important ethical matter necessarily arising out of the subject.

The remaining six chapters contain predictions respecting the expedition of Alexander the Great along the west coast of Palestine to Egypt; the Divine protection of the Jews both at that time, and in that of the Maccabees; the advent, sufferings, and reign of the Messiah; the destruction of Jerusalem by the Romans, and dissolution of the Jewish polity; the sufferings of the Jews during the dispersion; their conversion and restoration; and the sacred character of their worship, in which the Gentiles shall join, after the destruction of the wicked confederacy which will be opposed to their final establishment in Canaan.

The authenticity of this last portion has been, and still is strongly contested. Not only has it been denied to be the production of Zechariah, but it has been broken up into fragments, the independent authorship of which has been vindicated to as many anonymous authors. The first who ventured upon such a denial was Joseph Mede, whose opinion was adopted by Hammond, Kidder, Whiston, and Bridge, and more recently by Secker and Newcome in this country, and on the continent by Flügge, Döderlein, J. D. Michaëlis, Seiler, Eichhorn, Bauer, Bertholdt, Forberg, Rosenmüller, Gramberg, Hitzig, Credner, Maurer, Ewald, and Knobel. The authenticity, on the other hand, has been maintained by Carpzovius, Blayney, Jahn, Beckhaus, Koester, Hengstenberg, and Bürger.

The principal objection is taken to the language and character of the materials, as being very different from those which are found to distinguish what is universally allowed to have been written by Zechariah. To this, however, it has been replied, that granting such to be the case, there may have elapsed a long period of time between the composition of the former and latter portions of the book, during which any observable change in the style of the prophet might have taken place. It is evident, from there being no reference whatever in the chapters in question to the completion of the temple and the restoration of the Jewish affairs after the captivity, that, if they had not been written previously, they must have been composed long after these events had become matter of history, and in circumstances altogether different from those which occupied the attention of the prophet at the commencement of his ministry.

That these chapters were written long before, and, indeed, during the existence of the two kingdoms of Judah and Israel, is a position maintained by most of those who dispute their authenticity; but it is based upon too feeble and precarious a foundation to recommend it to the adoption of any who will impartially examine into all the circumstances of the case. The mere mention of Judah and Ephraim, upon which so much stress is laid, can yield it no real support. Not the smallest hint is anywhere dropped which would lead us to infer the existence, at the time, of a separate political or religious establishment in the northern part of Palestine; nor is there any thing, but the contrary, to induce the conclusion that a king reigned in Judah in the days of the author. That Ephraim should be spoken of as existing after the captivity cannot be matter of surprise, when it is considered, that a very large, if not the larger, portion of the ten tribes availed themselves of the liberty granted by the Persians to the Jews in Babylon, and likewise returned to the land of their fathers. This view of the subject is confirmed by the application of the term "Israel" to all the tribes, chap. xii. 1, just as it is used in the identical formula Mal. i. 1. Compare Mal. ii. 11, 12; iii. 6. The few references to a return relate to those Jews who were in a state of banishment or slavery under the Græco-Syrian and Græco-Egyptian kings. The historical circumstances connected with the Egyptian expedition of Alexander are so strongly marked in the prophetic announcements, that they cannot without violence be identified with any previous events. The absence too of the slightest allusion to the Babylonish captivity, either in the way of threatening or warning, while the prophet minutely describes the character of the Jewish rulers, and the condition of the Jewish people, in immediate connexion with the sufferings of the Messiah, the destruction of

Jerusalem, and the consequent fate of that people, goes convincingly to show that the captivity must have taken place, and that the whole of this portion of the book has respect to times future to those in which he flourished. So strongly, indeed, has this feature of the case presented itself to Eichhorn, and other sharp-sighted critics, that, rejecting, as their neology compelled them to do, all ideas of actual prophecy, they scruple not to affirm that the disputed chapters must have been composed in the days of Alexander, Antiochus, Epiphanes, or Hyrcanus I. It also deserves notice that no reference whatever is made to the existence of royal government among the Jews, at the time the author wrote, or to any circumstances in the history of that people previous to the captivity.

When, therefore, the difference both in regard to time and subject-matter are taken into consideration, it must be regarded as sufficient to account for any difference of style that may be detected. It is, however, after all, a question whether there really does exist such a difference in this respect, as that to which it has become so fashionable to appeal. Be it that the introductory formulas which occur in the first eight chapters do not occur in the last six, the objection, if fully carried out, would go in like manner to dismember the Book of Amos, and assign its composition at least to three different authors. The first two chapters of that prophet, it may be alleged, cannot have been written by the same person that wrote the three which follow, since in the former every prediction is ushered in by the marked formula, " Thus saith Jehovah," whereas in the latter no such formula occurs, but another equally marked : " Hear ye this word." And upon the same principle, the seventh and eighth chapters must have come from the pen of a third writer, since the distinguishing formula there is, " Thus hath Jehovah showed me."

The very peculiar character of the first six chapters of Zechariah, is such as to exclude all comparison of any other portion with it, while the more adorned and poetical style of the concluding chapters, which is so admirably adapted to the subjects treated of, ought equally to be regarded as exempting them from the category of comparison. In these no dates were requisite, though they were in the former, in which they occupy their appropriate place in necessary connexion with the events which transpired at the time. With respect to the titles, chap. ix. 1, and xii. 1, they are precisely such as might be expected to mark the strictly prophetic matter to which they are prefixed. The exactly parallel title, Malachi i. 1, naturally suggests the idea, that they belong to a common period, especially as nothing analogous is found in any of the earlier prophets.

On the whole, I cannot but regard the objections to the authenticity of the disputed chapters as the offspring either of a holy jealousy for the honour of the Evangelist Matthew, who attributes chapter xi. 12, 13, to Jeremiah, and not to Zechariah,* or of a spirit of wanton and unbridled hypercriticism, which would unsettle every thing, in order to satisfy the claims of certain favourite principles of interpretation that may happen to be in vogue.

In point of style, our prophet varies, according to the nature of his subjects, and the manner in which they were presented to his mind. He now expresses himself in simple conversational prose, now in poetry. At one time he abounds in the language of symbols; at another in that of direct prophetical announcement. His symbols are, for the most part, enigmatical, and require the explanations which accompany them. His prose resembles most that of Ezekiel; it is diffuse, uniform, and repetitious. His prophetic poetry possesses much of the elevation and dignity to be found in the earlier prophets, with whose writings he appears to have been familiar; only his rhythmus is sometimes harsh and unequal, while his parallelisms are destitute of that symmetry and finish, which form some of the principal beauties of Hebrew poetry.

* See Comment. on the passage.

CHAPTER I

In the first six verses, which serve as a general introduction to the whole book, the prophet is charged to warn the Jews, by the consequences which resulted from the impenitence of their forefathers, not to be backward in complying with the Divine will. We have then the first of the prophetic visions, with which Zechariah was favoured, containing a symbolical representation of the tranquil condition of the world at the time, 7—11; followed by an expostulation respecting the desolate state of Judæa, 12, 13, and gracious promises of its restoration, 14—17. The last four verses set forth, by appropriate symbols, in a second vision, for the encouragement of the Jews, the destruction of the hostile powers by which they had been attacked, at different periods of their history.

---

1   IN the eighth month, in the second year of Darius, the word of Jehovah was communicated to Zechariah, (the son of Berechiah, the son of Iddo,) the prophet, saying:

2   Jehovah hath been greatly displeased with your fathers.

1. See preface, and on Haggai i. 1.

2. The special object which the prophet has in view in this and the following verses, is to call those Jews, who had returned from Babylon to Jerusalem, to repent of the selfish negligence which they evinced in regard to the building of the temple. Comp. Hag. i. 4, 5, 7. This repentance is urged upon them by the consideration of the severe punishment which had overtaken their fathers. The argument is of the kind called enthymeme, in which the antecedent only is expressed, and the consequent proposition is left to be supplied by the reader. "Jehovah hath been very angry with your fathers, and so he will be with you, except ye repent and reform your conduct." קָצַף קֶצֶף. The construction of a verb with a noun derived from it, is found in other languages, as μάχεσθαι μάχην, gaudere gaudium; but its frequency in the Hebrew is such as to entitle it to be regarded as one of its idioms; and generally, it expresses augmentation or intensity. Hence the LXX. render here, ὠργίσθη—ὀργὴν μεγάλην; and the Syr. ܢܪܓܙ—ܪܘܓܙܐ. In ver. 15, the intensity is still more strongly marked by the addition of גָּדוֹל, great:—וְקֶצֶף גָּדוֹל אֲנִי קֹצֵף. The persons addressed in אֲבוֹתֵיכֶם, your fathers, are the Jews to whom the prophet had been sent. There is no occasion, with Blayney, to suppose that the text is defective.

3 Say therefore unto them,
> Thus saith Jehovah of hosts :
> Return unto me, saith Jehovah of hosts,
> And I will return unto you, saith Jehovah of hosts.

4 Be not like your fathers,
> To whom the former prophets cried, saying,
> Thus saith Jehovah of hosts :
> Turn now from your evil ways,
> And from your evil practices ;
> But they did not hearken,
> Neither did they give heed to me, saith Jehovah.

5   As for your fathers, where are they?
> And as for the prophets, do they live for ever?

3. The ו in וְאָמַרְתָּ is not merely continuative, but argumentative, and inferential. For the defective form אֲלֵהֶם, twenty-eight MSS., and three editions, read אֲלֵיהֶם in full. The phrase יְהוָֹה צְבָאוֹת, *Jehovah of hosts*, is of unusually frequent occurrence in the eight first chapters of this book, and in that of Haggai, written about the same time. In the last six chapters, however, it occurs not fewer than nine times. See on Is. i. 9. Its use appears to have been designed to inspire the mind with unshaken confidence in the supreme and irresistible power of God. The ו in וְאָשׁוּב marks the apodosis, and has the force of *and then*, or, *in that case*. Comp. James iv. 8.

4. The prophets here referred to are those who lived before the captivity, and the fathers are those who lived in their time, whose wicked practices had brought upon the nation that dire calamity. The appropriation of the phrase נְבִיאִים רִאשׁוֹנִים, *the former prophets*, as a designation of the books of Joshua, Judges, Samuel, and Kings, is of much later date. The returned Jews are here reminded that the same announcement which was made to them had been made to their ancestors, and that they might have escaped all the evil by a timely repentance, to which Zechariah now urgently calls them. The former י in מַעֲלֵיכֶם is marked in the margin as redundant, and is omitted in the text of more than

twenty MSS. and some printed editions. The plural of מַעֲלָל, viz. מַעֲלָלִים, is the only form in which the word occurs. Comp. ver. 6.

5. Jerome refers הַנְּבִיאִים to the false prophets by whom the Jews who lived before the captivity had been deceived— an interpretation which appears to have been suggested by Jer. xxxvii. 19 : " Where are now your prophets, which prophesied unto you, saying, The king of Babylon shall not come against you, nor against this land ?" The most natural construction of the verse, however, is that which connects it closely with what goes before, and identifies " the prophets " here spoken of with " the former prophets " there mentioned, just as the " fathers " in both verses correspond to each other. The question, אַיֵּה־הֵם, *where are they?* is equivalent to אֵינֵּמוּ, *they are not ;* i.e. in the land of the living. This the following question clearly shows. In Hebrew, simple interrogatives frequently imply the contrary : so that the language of the prophet is equivalent to " your fathers are no more, neither do the prophets live for ever." The latter declaration seems to involve the idea, " but my words never fail," as it follows in ver. 6. This had been proved by the fulfilment of the Divine threatenings in the mournful experience of their fathers, and would again be proved in theirs, except they repented, which idea is amplified in the following verse.

6   But my words, and my decrees,
     Which I gave in charge to my servants the prophets,
     Did they not overtake your fathers?
     So that they turned and said,
     According as Jehovah of hosts purposed to do to us,
     According to our ways, and according to our practices,
     So hath he dealt with us.

7   On the twenty-fourth day of the eleventh month, which is the
     month of Shebat, in the second year of Darius, the word of
     Jehovah was communicated to Zechariah, (the son of Berechiah,
     the son of Iddo,) the prophet, saying :

8   I saw by night, and behold a man riding upon a red horse, and

6. דְּקַי, *my decrees*, i. e. my firm and determined purposes to punish your fathers, if they did not repent, which I communicated to them by the prophets. The root is דָּקַק, *to hack, cut, cut* letters, &c., *in* stone or other hard substances. Thus laws were originally written on tablets, and hung up for public inspection. The confession made in this verse is that which the captives were compelled to make by the sufferings which they endured in Babylon. How far their תְּשׁוּבָה, *conversion*, extended, we are not informed. It is, however, generally admitted that, as regards the great body of the nation, it involved the entire abandonment of idolatry. That שׁוּב is here to be strictly taken as signifying *to turn, return* from evil to good, and not according to its idiomatic usage before another verb, as simply expressing the repetition of the action described by such verb, is required by the exigency of the passage. כַּאֲשֶׁר and כֵּן are *correlates;* the כְּ repeated, qualifies a subordinate, but important part of the proposition.

7. From this part of the book to chap. vi. 8, we have a series of eight symbolical visions, the language of which is exceedingly simple, but, in many cases, the interpretation is matter of no small difficulty. The general plan on which it is constructed, is, first to present to view the symbol or hieroglyphic, and then, on a question being put respecting its import, to furnish the interpretation. Though the visions are described as distinct from each other, the one following the other in regular

succession, yet they are so closely connected as to form one grand whole; and, as we learn from ver. 8, were all presented to the mind of the prophet in the course of a single night. The period of these nocturnal revelations was between two and three months after the prophet first received his commission. Comp. ver. 1. שְׁבָט, *Shebat*, is the eleventh month of the Jewish year, extending from the new moon in February to the new moon in March. Like other names of the months, the word is Chaldee; Syr. ܫܒܛ ; Arab. شباط and شباط. The etymology is not certain; but the resemblance of the word to the Hebrew שֵׁבֶט, *a shoot, rod, staff*, suggests the idea of the month being so called because it was that in which the trees began to put forth their shoots or sprouts. As the following statement does not contain the identical words merely of the communications made to the prophet, but an account of the scenes with all their accompanying circumstances, the formula לֵאמֹר must be taken as signifying, "to the following effect," "as follows," or the like.

VISION I.

8. It has been doubted whether the article הַ in הַלַּיְלָה is to be regarded as definitely marking the particular night on which the visions were vouchsafed to the prophet, or whether it is not rather to be taken as expressing the adverbial

he stood among the myrtles in the shade, and behind him were

determination of the noun—*in the night*, or, *by night*. The latter seems preferable. Comp. בְּלַיְלָה, Job v. 14. The person here described as riding upon a red horse, is spoken of as אִישׁ, *a man*, *i.e.* in the shape or appearance of a man; for that an angel, and not a human being, is intended, is evident from verses 11 and 12, in which he is expressly called "the Angel of Jehovah." And that he was no ordinary angel, but the Divine Mediator, the Angel of the Covenant and of the presence of Jehovah, will not be denied by any who have rendered themselves familiar with the attributes and circumstances in connexion with which the Person so designated is presented to view, both in our prophet and in other parts of the Old Testament. One of the most remarkable of these circumstances, is his being identified with Jehovah himself. This Gesenius, so far from denying, or attempting to explain away, expressly asserts both in his Thesaurus, and in the last edition of his Hebrew Lexicon, under the word מַלְאָךְ. "Sometimes," he writes, "the same divine appearance, which at one time is called מַלְאָךְ יְהוָה, is afterwards called simply יְהוָה, as Gen. xvi. 7, *et seq.*, coll. ver. 13; xxii. 11, coll. 12; xxxi. 11, coll. 16; Exod. iii. 2, coll. 4; Jud. vi. 14, coll. 22; xiii. 18, coll. 22. This is to be so understood, that the *Angel of God* is here nothing else than the invisible Deity itself, which thus unveils itself to mortal eyes; see J. H. Michaelis de Angelo Dei, Hal. 1702. Tholuck, Comment. zum Ev. Johannis, p. 36. Hence Oriental translators, as Saadias, Abusaides, and the Chaldeo-Samaritan, wherever Jehovah himself is said to appear upon earth, always put for the name of God, the *Angel of God*." See the very satisfactory observations of Dr. M'Caul on this subject, in his translation of Kimchi on Zechariah, pp. 9—27, in which he has shown that there is but one being who is called in Scripture מַלְאָךְ יְהוָה, *the Angel of Jehovah;* that the proper name of this one Being is יְהוָה, *Jehovah;* that this Being says of himself, distinctly and unequivocally, that He is the God whom Jacob worshipped, the God of

Abraham, Isaac, and Jacob; and that some of the Rabbins themselves have been compelled to admit the facts. See also Dr. J. Pye Smith's Scripture Testimony to the Messiah, vol. i. pp. 445—463; and Stonard on Zechariah, pp. 15—19. In the Babylonian Talmud, Sanhedrin, fol. 93, col. 1, the following brief exposition is given of the man here referred to by the prophet: "This man is no other than the Holy One, blessed be He; for it is said, 'The Lord is a man of war.'"—The position of this Captain of the Lord's host, is stated to be "among the myrtles which were in the shady valley." Many conjectures have been advanced respecting both the myrtles and the valley, but, in my opinion, they are all gratuitous, since it does not appear that these objects were designed to be symbolically understood, but are merely added as incidental circumstances, to give vivacity and force to the representation. מְצֻלָה being always used, like מְצוּלָה and צוּלָה, of *depth* in reference to water or mire, it is clear from the connexion that such cannot be the signification of מְצֻלָה, which is a derivative, not from צוּל, *to sink, be deep,* but from צָלַל, *to be shaded, darkened;* hence *the shade* or *shady place,* probably that of a mountain. Such derivation is indicated by the Dagesh compensative in the Lamed, and is supported by the renderings of the LXX. and Syr. κατασκίων, ܡܛܠܐ. Hitzig and

Ewald, comparing the Arab. مظلة, *umbraculum, tentorium,* interpret the word as meaning tent or tabernacle, and suppose heaven, as the dwelling-place of Jehovah, to be intended; but the exegesis is far-fetched and inept. Equally unsatisfactory is the attempt of the latter of these writers to palm upon הַהֲדַסִּים the signification of הָרִים, *mountains,* by comparing the term with הֲדוּר, *height,* Is. xlv. 2. Τῶν ὀρέων of the LXX. must have originated in their having mistaken הֲדַסִּים for הָרִים, or it may be an interpretation derived from chap. vi. 1.—Behind the rider, who appears as their leader or captain, follow three companies of horsemen, distinguished from

9   horses that were red, bay, and white. Then I said, What are these, my lord? And the angel who spake with me, said to me, I will

each other by the colour of the horses. It is not to be inferred, that, because סוּסִים, *horses*, only are mentioned, we are to conceive of them as being presented to view without their riders. This is evident from the reply given by the riders, ver. 11. סוּס, like our English *horse*, is sometimes used in a military sense, to denote cavalry. Still, as the colour of the horses forms an important feature in the representation, they must have been specially prominent to the mental vision of the prophet. On a comparison of the present verse with chap. vi. 1—8, and Rev. vi. 2—8, it will appear that horses with their riders are employed in the symbolical language of Scripture to denote dispensations of divine providence. The peculiar nature of the dispensations is indicated by the colour of the horses, and the armour and appearance of the riders. *Red*, the colour first mentioned, being that of fire and blood, is the appropriate symbol of war and bloodshed. That of the second company of horses is expressed by שְׂרֻקִּים, *bay*, or *brown*, perhaps not differing from what is commonly called *chestnut*. See Bochart, Hieroz. tom. i. lib. ii. cap. 7. What induces the belief that this colour is meant is, that שְׂרֻקִּים signify vines which bear purple, or dark coloured grapes. Comp. the Arab. شَقَرَة, *rufus color*; اشقر, *valde rubens* seu *rufus* camelus. The LXX. ψαροὶ; Vulg. *varii*. The addition, καὶ ποικίλοι, in the text of the LXX. is doubtless a gloss. This colour is symbolical of a middle state of things—a dispensation neither characterised by bloodshed, nor by victory and joyous prosperity, which the *white* colour is universally allowed to represent. From what is stated, ver. 11, it is obvious we cannot interpret the dispensations, thus emblematically set forth, of events still future at the time of the vision. The different cohorts speak of their commission as already fulfilled. The colours must, therefore, denote the Medo-Persian war, in which the Babylonian empire was subverted; the mixed or transition state of affairs

which followed; and the complete establishment of the new dynasty in the room of the tyrannical power by which the Jews had been enslaved. In consideration of the awful vengeance which had been inflicted upon that power, the colour of the horse on which the commander rode is represented as being red, rather than bay or white—evidently with the design of affecting the minds of the Jews with a sense of the great deliverance which had been wrought for them by their Divine Protector.

9. Marckius, Ch. B. Michaelis, Rosenmüller, Maurer, and Ewald, are of opinion, that the angel here spoken of is identical with the man riding on the red horse mentioned in the preceding verse, but the contrary is properly maintained by Vitringa and Hengstenberg, as a comparison with ver. 10 is sufficient to show. Though the angel who made the communications to the prophet had not been formerly mentioned, he had presented himself to him, or stood beside him, ready to discharge the duties of his office. This angel is uniformly spoken of as הַמַּלְאָךְ הַדֹּבֵר בִּי, *the angel that spake with me*. See verses 13, 14; chap. ii. 2, 7, (Eng. version, i. 19, and ii. 3;) iv. 1, 4, 5; v. 5, 10; vi. 4. The language is peculiar to our prophet; and from the office specially assigned to the angel, he is usually called the *angelus interpres*, or the *angelus collocutor*. That stress is to be laid upon the use of the preposition בְּ, following the verb דָּבַר, *to speak*, as if it were designed to mark the *internal* character of the communications made by the angel to the prophet—a position maintained by Jerome, Ewald, Delitzsch, and some others— cannot be satisfactorily made out. The utmost that can be conceded respecting the force of the preposition, in such connexion, is its expressing the familiarity or intimacy of the intercourse between the Divine messenger and the prophet. See on Hab. ii. 1. When the angel says אַרְאֶךָּ, *I will show*, or *cause thee to see* these things, the reference is to a mental perception or understanding of their meaning.

10 show thee what these are. And the man that stood among the
myrtles answered and said, These are they whom Jehovah hath
11 sent to walk to and fro through the earth. And they answered
the Angel of Jehovah that stood among the myrtles, and said,
We have walked to and fro through the earth, and, behold! the
whole earth sitteth still and is tranquil.

12 Then the Angel of Jehovah answered and said: O Jehovah
of hosts! how long wilt thou not compassionate Jerusalem, and
the cities of Judah, with which thou hast been angry these
13 seventy years? And Jehovah answered the angel who spake

10, 11. עָנָה, signifies to *commence* or
proceed to speak, as well as *to answer*.
Comp. the use of ἀποκρίνομαι in the
New Testament. Instead of the requisite information being communicated
by the interpreting angel, it is imparted
by the Angel of Jehovah himself, and
by those who acted under his command.
Because the phraseology הִתְהַלֵּךְ בָּאָרֶץ is
almost identical with that employed to
describe the roaming of Satan through
the earth, Job i. 7; ii. 2, it has been
inferred that the horsemen represent
celestial spirits sent forth for the execution of the divine purposes; but the
ground is too precarious to admit of any
such theory being built upon it, as a
comparison with Rev. vi. 2—8, is sufficient to show. The simple occurrence
of the same terms cannot of itself justify
this interpretation. From the reply
being given to the Angel of Jehovah,
we may conclude, that he had signified
to them that they should make their
report for the information of the prophet.
In consequence of their several operations, the obstacles had been removed
out of the way which prevented the
restoration of the Jews; the wars in
which the Persians had been engaged
had ceased; and, at the time the prophet had the vision, in the second year
of Darius, universal peace obtained in
all the regions with which the people of
God had any connexion. For the use
of שָׁקַט to denote a state of tranquillity
after war, comp. Jud. v. 31. A similar
combination of יָשְׁבֶת with שְׁלֵוָה occurs
ch. vii. 7, and is intended to express the
profound character of the peace which
was then enjoyed.

12. עָנָה, *to answer*, is here, as in other
instances, used in the simple acceptation
of speaking, or continuing a discourse.
The language is that of intercessory
expostulation. While all the heathen
nations around Judæa enjoyed prosperity,
that country was still much in the same
state in which it had been during the
captivity. Some of the captives had
returned, but they were too few to produce anything like a marked change in
its circumstances. Vitringa, Stonard,
and some others, without sufficient
reason, think that a different term of
seventy years is here intended from that
predicted Jer. xxv. 11; xxix. 10. What
in reality were the years of indignation
upon the cities, but the years of the
captivity of their inhabitants? זֶה שִׁבְעִים
שָׁנָה, "*these* seventy years," express emphatically the period during which the
captivity had continued. Two of these
years, dating from the destruction of
Jerusalem by Nebuchadnezzar, had yet
nearly to run before the expiration of
the predicted period, so that the language
of the expostulation is most appropriate,
when viewed as calculated to meet the
feelings of the Jewish people.

13. That it is the same being who is
styled מַלְאַךְ יְהוָה, *the Angel of Jehovah*,
that is here designated by the incommunicable name יְהוָה, *Jehovah*, just as
in the passages quoted by Gesenius,
ver. 8, seems past dispute. As the
Divine Mediator, after having made
intercession with the Father, who is
addressed by the title יְהוָה צְבָאוֹת, *Jehovah
of hosts*, he communicates to the interpreting angel the consolatory answer
which was to be made to the prophet.

14 with me with good and comfortable words.   And the angel who
spake with me said to me, Cry, saying,
Thus saith Jehovah of hosts :
I am zealous for Jerusalem,
And for Zion, with great zeal ;

15 And I am very greatly displeased
With the nations that are at ease ;
Because I was a little displeased,
And they helped forward the affliction.

16 Wherefore, thus saith Jehovah :
I have returned to Jerusalem in compassion ;
My house shall be built in her, saith Jehovah of hosts,
And a line shall be stretched out over Jerusalem.

17 Cry again, saying,
Thus saith Jehovah of hosts :
My cities shall yet overflow with prosperity ;
For Jehovah will yet comfort Zion,
And will yet take pleasure in Jerusalem.

18 Then I lifted up my eyes and looked, and, behold! four horns.

דְּבָרִים נִחֻמִים, are in apposition : lit. *words,
consolations,* i. e. consolatory words.
LXX. λόγους παρακλητικούς. Comp.
Is. lvii. 18; Hos. xi. 8.

14. This and the three following
verses contain the consolatory words
just referred to, which the prophet is
commanded by the interpreting angel
to communicate to the Jews. קִנֵּא construed with בְּ, or with the accusative,
signifies *to envy, be jealous, indignant
at* any person or thing; with לְ as here,
it is taken in a good sense, *to be zealous
for* anything, *actively to interest oneself
on behalf* of any one. Comp. Numb.
xxv. 11, 13; 2 Sam. xxi. 2; 1 Kings
xix. 10.

15. The adjective שַׁאֲנָן signifies not
merely *to be at rest,* as the whole earth
is described, ver. 11, but, in a bad sense,
to live at ease, be carnally secure. The
enemies of the Jews had not simply
executed the Divine indignation against
that people, but they had done it wan-
tonly. Such seems to be the force of
עָזְרוּ לְרָעָה.

16. The building of the temple had
been begun, but it still lay for the most

part in ruins, and was not finished till
the sixth year of Darius. See Ezra vi.
15. קָוֶה, for which the Keri has, by
emendation, the more usual form קָו,
occurs 1 Kings vii. 23; Jer. xxxi. 39.

17. Few as were the inhabitants of
Judæa at the time of the vision, the
land was speedily re-occupied; and the
population had greatly increased by the
time of the Maccabees. Josephus informs
us, that overflowing with numbers, Jerusalem gradually crept beyond its walls,
till a fourth hill, called Bezetha, was
covered with habitations. פּוּץ, Arab.

فاض ,فيض, *effusus fuit,* to overflow.

That the overflowing, however, is to be
interpreted of prosperity, and not of the
inhabitants, appears from the מ, indicating the subject-matter, being prefixed to טוֹב.

VISION II.

18, 19. (Heb. ii. 1, 2.) This vision is so
intimately connected with the preceding,
that the break in the Hebrew Bible
here, occasioned by the commencement
of a new chapter, is very unhappy. As

19 And I said to the angel who spake with me, What are these? And
   he answered me, These are the horns which have scattered Judah,
20 Israel, and Jerusalem. And Jehovah showed me four workmen.
21 Then I said, What are these coming to do? And he spake, saying,
   These are the horns which have scattered Judah, so that no man

usual in these visions, the hieroglyphic is first presented. קֶרֶן, *a horn*, is the symbol of a kingdom, or political power, the figure being taken from bulls and other horned animals having their strength in their horns. Thus the ten horns of the fourth beast in Daniel's vision, are symbolical of the ten kingdoms into which the Roman empire was divided on the overthrow of the imperial throne, chap. vii. 20; and in the representation made of the same subject to John, the ten horns of the seven headed beast are said to have upon them ten crowns, Rev. xiii. 1; xvii. 3, comp. ver. 12, where it is expressly stated, that "the ten horns which thou sawest are ten kings," *i. e.* kingdoms, the ruling power being put for the whole government. The powers referred to by Zechariah were those which had been hostile to the Jews, and had scattered them abroad from their own land. Jerome, Kimchi, Abarbanel, Vatablus, and others, have been led by the occurrence of the number *four*, to interpret the horns of the Babylonian, Persian, Grecian, and Roman empires; but to this exegesis it has justly been objected, that of these powers two were not yet in existence, and cannot be prophetically spoken of, because the hostility described was that which had already taken place. Neither is it true that the Jews were scattered by the Persian power as they had been by the Babylonian. What took place under Darius Ochus cannot be taken into the account here. The number is rather to be referred to the four quarters of the earth in their immediate relation to Palestine. Comp. chap. ii. 6. Thus Theodoret, Clarius, Ribera, Sanchez, à Castro, Munster, Calvin, Newcome, Rosenmüller, Hitzig, and Maurer. "Jerusalem" is added to render the description more emphatic, being the metropolis, the site of the temple, and the royal residence.

20, 21. (Heb. ii. 3, 4.) Here, again, the same Divine Person is called יְהוָֹה, who was formerly spoken of as מַלְאַךְ יְהוָֹה. See on ver. 13. חָרָשִׁים, *workmen* in iron, brass, stone, or wood, from חָרַשׁ, *to cut, grave, fabricate*. From the special employment assigned to these artificers, we may not inaptly compare חָרָשֵׁי מַשְׁחִית, *workmen of destruction*, which is rendered in our common version, "skilful to destroy," Ezek. xxi. 36. The attempt of Blayney to justify his rendering the word by *plowmen*, first suggested by Michaelis, must be regarded as a failure. On the inquiry being made, what these artificers were coming to do, a reply is given, which further describes the tyranny exercised over the Hebrew people, and then states that they were the instruments commissioned to destroy the hostile powers. By again pressing the number *four*, interpreters have involved themselves in inextricable difficulties. All that is meant to be conveyed, is the adequacy of the means employed to effect the punishment of the nations which had afflicted the people of God. That no appeal can be made, in illustration, to the history of the four great monarchies, is proved by the fact, that the workmen are represented as distinct from the horns, whereas these monarchies successively destroyed each other. The rabbinical reference to the days of the Messiah is altogether aside from the point, as is likewise the reference which some have made to angels. There can be no doubt that the several human instrumentalities are intended, which God called into operation to crush the powers in the different countries around Palestine, by which it had been invaded, and its inhabitants carried away captive. The conjecture of Blayney, who would read הֶחָרִיר instead of הֶחָרִיד, and, changing the punctuation of אֹתָם into אֵת, renders, "to sharpen their coulter," has not been approved. Nor is anything of the kind

lifted up his head; but these are come to terrify them, to throw down the horns of the nations, which raised the horn against the land of Judah to scatter it.

necessary. Terror implies a sense of inferiority, weakness, and exposure to suffering, and is here appropriately represented as a precursor of that overthrow to which the enemies of the Jews were to be subjected. Comp. Jud. viii. 12; 1 Sam. xiv. 15; Ezek. xxx. 9. יָדָה signifies to *throw, cast, stretch*, the particular manner of which is to be determined by the context. Here that of *casting down*, or *effecting an overthrow*, is the mode most naturally suggested. The signification *to handle, exercise the hand*, which some have proposed, is less apt, יָד, *hand*, being derived from the verb, and not the verb from the noun. אֶרֶץ, *land*, is here, as frequently, put for its inhabitants.

CHAPTER II

In a third vision, a man with a measuring line is represented as going forth to take the dimensions of Jerusalem with a view to its restoration to its former condition, ver. 1—3 ; an act which is virtually declared to be unnecessary, by the prediction that such should be the increase of the population, and such their prosperity, that the city should extend, like unwalled towns, into the surrounding localities ; and that, under the immediate protection of Jehovah, walls would be altogether unnecessary, 4, 5. In the faith of this prophetic announcement, and with a view to their escape from the judgment which was still about to be inflicted upon Babylon, the Jews who remained in that city are summoned to return from their captivity, 6, 7 ; an assurance of Divine protection, and of the destruction of their enemies, is given them, 8, 9 ; and they are cheered by the promises, that Jehovah would again make Jerusalem his residence, and effect, in connexion with the restoration of his people, the conversion of many nations to the true religion, 10—12. A solemn call to universal reverence concludes the scene, 13.

---

1   THEN I lifted up my eyes, and looked, and, behold! a man
2   with a measuring line in his hand. And I said : Whither art thou going? And he said to me, To measure Jerusalem, to see how much is the breadth thereof, and how much is the length

VISION III.

1—4. (Heb. ii. 5—8.) The measurement here specified was not that of the houses, but of the whole extent of the city. Jerusalem is not here considered as already rebuilt, as Stonard supposes. The dimensions are those of the city before its destruction by the Chaldæans, and were now being taken, in order to ascertain the extent of the work that

3 thereof. And, behold! the angel who spake with me went forth,
4 and another angel came forth to meet him. And he said to him,
   Run, speak to this young man, saying,
     Jerusalem shall be inhabited into the open country,
     Because of the multitude of men and cattle in the midst of her.
5 And I will be to her, saith Jehovah,
     A wall of fire around,
     And will be the glory in the midst of her.
6   Ho! ho! flee from the north country, saith Jehovah,
     Though as the four winds of heaven
     I have spread you abroad, saith Jehovah.

---

was to be effected in its complete restoration. The symbolical action was calculated to encourage the Jews to proceed with the building of the temple which they had commenced. Who the measurer was, has been disputed. Jarchi, J. H. Michaelis, and Rosenmüller, are of opinion that the *angelus interpres* is intended. Hengstenberg thinks that, in all probability, he is none other than the Angel of Jehovah himself. But for neither of these opinions is there sufficient foundation, any more than there is for the supposition of Blayney, that he was Nehemiah. He appears to have been merely an additional person introduced into the scenic representation, for the purpose of calling forth, by the significant action which he was about to undertake, the important information contained in the following part of the chapter. יֹצֵא, as twice used here, has reference to two different localities: in the former instance, in which it is employed of the interpreting angel, the presence of the prophet is the *terminus a quo;* in the latter, that of the Angel of Jehovah. In opposition to the hypothesis of the Rabbins, Vatablus, Ribera, à Lapide, Drusius, Blayney, Rosenmüller, Hengstenberg, and Knobel, who maintain that Zechariah himself is meant by הַנַּעַר הַלָּז, *this young man,* and argue from it, that the prophet was of youthful age at the time he had the vision, I cannot but concur with Stonard, Hitzig, Maurer, and Ewald, in thinking, that the person intended is the man with the measuring line, spoken of vers.

1, 2. The verb רוּץ, *run,* implies the necessity of despatch, which could only have been occasioned by the intended procedure of the measurer. He is arrested in his progress, and virtually told, that the former dimensions of the city would be totally inadequate to contain the number of its inhabitants. פְּרָזוֹת תֵּשֵׁב יְרוּשָׁלַם, lit. *Jerusalem shall dwell,* or *inhabit open places,* i. e. the inhabitants will not confine themselves within her walls, but will occupy the localities in the open country around. Thus Symm., ἀτειχίστως; Jarchi and Jerome, מאין חומה, *absque muro.* Comp. 1 Sam. vi. 18, where כְּפַר הַפְּרָזִי, *the country village,* is contrasted with עִיר מִבְצָר, *a fortified city.* See also Esth. ix. 19; Ezek. xxxviii. 11.

5. (Heb. ver. 9.) Though "the wall of fire," and "the glory," are doubtless both to be taken figuratively, the former denoting certain protection, and the latter, illustrious displays of the Divine presence in affording all needful supplies of grace, strength, and comfort, we are not hence to conclude with Stonard, that more is meant by the city than the literal Jerusalem, as the centre of the restored theocracy. The entire connexion, and all the circumstances of the prophecy, demand this limitation.

6, 7. (Heb. 10, 11.) It is generally thought that the urgent calls here given to those Jews who still remained in Babylon, were designed to induce them to leave that devoted city before its approaching siege and capture by Darius. In all probability

7 Ho! deliver thyself, O Zion!
That dwellest with the daughter of Babylon.
8 For thus saith Jehovah of hosts:
After the glory he hath sent me
To the nations which spoiled you;
Surely he that toucheth you
Toucheth the pupil of his eye.

many of them had acquired wealth, and might have been induced to remain in the enjoyment of their possessions. It was necessary that such should take the alarm, and, with the rest of their countrymen, avail themselves without delay of the opportunity they now had of returning to their own land. The urgency of the call is expressed by the repetitious form, הוֹי הוֹי, *Ho! ho!* which occurs, so far as I am aware, in no other part of Scripture. The verbs קוּם, *arise*, שְׁמַע, *hear*, or the like, being readily suggested by the interjection, will account for the use of the conjunctive Vau in וְנֻסוּ. The land of the north is Babylon, and the regions adjacent. See Jer. vi. 22; xvi. 15. Between the former and the latter clause of the verse there seems, at first sight, a palpable discrepancy. How, it may be asked, could the scattering of the Jews like the four winds of heaven be a reason why those, in particular, who lived in the north quarter should return? But this apparent incoherence has originated in the supposition that the prophet here asserts the dispersion of that people into the four quarters of the globe. Had this, however, been his meaning, he would have employed לְ after the verb, as in Ezek. xvii. 21. Nor can such construction be supported by substituting the various reading בְּ, *viz.* בְּאַרְבַּע, instead of כְּ; for the words could then only properly be rendered, "I have scattered you *by*," and not "*in*" or "*into* the four winds." This reading, though supported by fifteen MSS., originally by seven more, and perhaps by another, by thirteen printed editions, and by the Syr. and Vulg., is inferior in point of authority to that of the Textus Receptus. The meaning seems to be, that the scattering of the Hebrew people had been so violent and extensive, that it could only be fitly com-

pared to the force and effect of the combined winds of heaven being brought to bear upon any object susceptible of dispersion. The scattering had been most severely felt by those resident at the time of the vision in Babylon, and other regions in that quarter; on which account it is described with special reference to them. כִּי is here used, not as a causative, but as a concessive participle, as in Gen. viii. 21; Exod. xiii. 17. Nothing can be more forced, or unsuited to the connexion, than the interpretation, which assumes that פְּרַשְׂתִּי is future in signification, and that the words contain a prediction of a future spreading abroad of the Jews as missionaries among the heathen. What can be conceived more incongruous, than a return of the Jews from Babylon, induced by the motive of a still more extended dispersion among the nations of the earth, without the smallest hint of this as their destination! By צִיּוֹן, *Zion*, are meant the inhabitants of Jerusalem, at that time still in Babylon. The words יֹשֶׁבֶת בַּת־בָּבֶל are not in apposition, but in construction, and are equivalent to *Habitatrix Babelis*. For this idiomatic use of בַּת see on Is. i. 8.

8. (Heb. 12.) Some suppose the prophet to be the person who here speaks of himself as having been sent; others, the angel mentioned ver. 4; but that the Messiah is intended, must be inferred from what is predicated of him, ver. 9, that he would shake his hand at the nations which had afflicted the Jews. Comp. Is. xlviii. 16, where the divine mission of the Second Person of the Trinity is described in parallel language. Blayney, Newcome, Gesenius, Hitzig, Maurer, and Ewald, strangely concur in rendering אַחַר כָּבוֹד שְׁלָחַנִי, *He hath sent me after glory*, in the

9　For, behold! I will shake my fist at them,
　　And they shall be a spoil to their slaves;
　　And ye shall know that Jehovah of hosts hath sent me.
10　Sing and rejoice, O daughter of Zion!
　　For, behold! I come,
　　And I will dwell in the midst of thee, saith Jehovah.

---

sense of, *with a view to acquire it.* In no other passage, however, is אַחַר employed, except as an adverb or preposition of place or time; nor is it ever connected as a preposition with שָׁלַח. This verb is not even here construed with it, but with the preposition אֶל immediately following. It can only, therefore, be employed to denote the posteriority of the mission specified to the restoration of the glorious presence of the manifested Jehovah to his recovered people. Thus the LXX. ὀπίσω δόξης. Syr. ܟ̇ܠܕ ܐܡܨܐ, *after the glory,* which is falsely rendered in the London Polyglott, *ad prosequendum honorem.* Targ. בָּתַר יְקָרָא דַּאֲמִיר לְאִיתָאָה עֲלֵיכוֹן *after the glory which he hath promised to bring to you.* Vulg. *post gloriam.* Such exegesis is most naturally suggested by the use of כָּבוֹד, *glory,* ver. 5. After what had been there promised should have been accomplished, the Divine Legate had a commission to punish the nations in the immediate vicinity of the Holy Land, such as the Moabites, Idumæans, Ammonites, Philistines, and Syrians, by whom the Jews had been attacked and plundered on various occasions, and especially on that of the Chaldæan invasion. The Jews in Babylon needed, therefore, to be under no apprehension from these enemies, and might return with confidence to their own land. The tender regard which Jehovah cherished for them, is expressed with exquisite beauty in the concluding clause of the verse. No member of the body is more susceptible of pain, or more vigilantly protected, than the eye, especially the pupil, or aperture through which the rays of light pass to the retina. בָּבָה, in the phrase בָּבַת עַיִן, *the pupil of the eye,* Gesenius now derives from נָבַב, *to bore, make hollow,* and considers it to stand

for נְבָבָה, *a hole gate,* like the Arab. بَاب; but his former etymology is preferable, according to which it is to be derived from בָּבָה, Arab. بَابَا, *dixit baba,* Gr. παππάζειν, to say *papa,* spoken of a child. Hence the Arab. بُوبُو, *booboo,* (the origin of our English booby,) *puellus,* boy. The phrase thus corresponds to the other Hebrew mode of expressing the same thing, אִישׁוֹן עַיִן, *the little man of the eye,* Deut. xxxii. 10; Prov. vii. 2. Both modes of expression, بُوبُو عَين and إِنْسَان الْعَين, are used in Arabic; and the Arabs say in language quite parallel to that of the prophet, هُوَ أَعَزُّ عِنْدِي مِنْ بُوبُو عَيْنِي, *He is dearer to me than the pupil of mine eye.* Both modes are more expressive than the Latin of Catullus: *multo quod carius illi est oculis,* or, *ni te plus oculis meis amarem.* The pronominal affix in עֵינוֹ, *his eye,* is to be referred to יְהוָה צְבָאוֹת, *Jehovah of hosts,* at the beginning of the verse, the nominative to שְׁלָחַנִי, and not with Kimchi, Blayney, Stonard, and others, to the enemy himself.

9. (Heb. 13.) For the phrase הֵנִיף יָד, comp. Is. xi. 15; xix. 16. It is indicative of the threatening attitude of Jehovah when about to inflict vengeance upon his enemies. By עֹבְדֵיהֶם, *their slaves,* are meant the Jews, whom the nations, either by capture or purchase, had brought into a state of slavery. Comp. Is. xiv. 2. יָדַע, here and in ver. 11, signifies, as frequently, *to know by experience.*

10, 11. (Heb. 14, 15.) The divine residence here predicted, must be interpreted of that which took place during the sojourn of the Son of God in the

11 And many nations shall join themselves to Jehovah in that day,
   And shall become my people;
   And I will dwell in the midst of thee,
   And thou shalt know that Jehovah of hosts hath sent me unto thee.
12 And Jehovah shall possess Judah his portion,
   In the holy land;
   And shall again take pleasure in Jerusalem.
13   Let all flesh be silent before Jehovah,
   For he is roused from his holy habitation.

land of Judæa. The almost entire identity of the language here employed,
with that used chap. ix. 9, where, in like
manner, the daughter of Zion is called
to hail the advent of her King, compels
to this conclusion. Comp. Ps. xl. 7;
Is. xl. 9, 10. So evidently is this the
only fair construction of the meaning,
that Kimchi himself refers the passage
לעתיד בימו המשיח, *to future events in the
times of the Messiah.* The phrases הַיּוֹם
הַהוּא and הַיָּמִים הָהֵם, *that day, those days,*
frequently point out the period of his
manifestation and reign. With this appearance and residence of the Messiah
are connected, as their consequents, the
extensive conversion of the heathen
nations, and their being constituted a
people devoted to his service and glory.
The repetition of the prediction relative
to his residence in Zion, is designed to
express the certainty of the event.

12. (Heb. 16.) As mention had just
been made of the adoption of the nations
to be the people of the Messiah, the
prophet, to preclude the idea that the
Jews were no more to enjoy that privilege, proceeds to describe a future
period, during which they should again
be the objects of the Divine favour and
delight. Restored to the Holy Land,
they shall again be the possession of the
Lord. Comp. Exod. xxxiv. 9; Deut.
iv. 20; ix. 26, 29; xxxii. 9. The ideas
suggested by their being the possession
of Jehovah are those of their being the
objects of his regard and care. Ps.
xxviii. 9.

13. (Heb. 17.) A call to universal
reverence and submission in prospect
of the wonderful interpositions of Jehovah on behalf of his church. Comp.
Ps. lxxvi. 8, 9; Zeph. i. 7.

CHAPTER III

In this chapter a fourth vision is described, in which Joshua the high priest is
   represented as occupying his official position in the Divine presence at Jerusalem, but opposed in his attempt to recommence the service of Jehovah, by
   Satan, who accused him of being disqualified for the discharge of his functions,
   ver. 1. The accusation is met by a reprimand, drawn from the Divine purpose
   to restore Jerusalem, and the narrow escape which the priesthood had had from
   total extinction, 2. The guilt attaching to the high priest, in his representative
   capacity, and its removal, are next figuratively set forth, 3—5. He has then a
   solemn charge delivered to him, followed by a conditional promise, 6, 7; after
   which we have a prediction of the Messiah, as a security that the punishment of
   the Jews would be entirely removed, their temple completely restored, and a
   period of prosperity introduced, 8—10.

1   AND he showed me Joshua the high priest, standing before
the Angel of Jehovah, and the Adversary standing on his right
hand to oppose him.

2   And Jehovah said to the Adversary,
Jehovah rebuke thee, O Adversary!
Even Jehovah that taketh delight in Jerusalem, rebuke thee;
Is not this a brand snatched from the fire?

VISION IV.

1. The nominative to וַיַּרְאֵנִי is the interpreting angel, understood. Comp. ch. i. 9. As the phrase עָמַד לִפְנֵי, *to stand before*, is sometimes used of appearing before a judge, Numb. xxxv. 12, Deut. xix. 17, 1 Kings iii. 16, it has been inferred that we have here the representation of a judicial transaction; an exegesis which is supposed to derive confirmation from the circumstance of an accuser being mentioned in the following verse. But as the person here described is the high priest, and the phrase in question is that which is appropriated to express the position of the priests when ministering to Jehovah, Deut. x. 8, 2 Chron. xxix. 11, Ezek. xliv. 15, it is more natural to conclude that Joshua is here represented as having entered the new temple which was in the course of erection, and taken his position in front of the altar before the holy of holies. The high priest not only entered the most sacred place once a year on the day of atonement, but was authorized to perform all the duties of the ordinary priests; so that he may here be conceived of as about to offer sacrifice for the people, when he was opposed by Satan. That the altar of burnt-offering was erected before the building of the temple was proceeded with, is clear, from Ezra iii. 2, 3, 6, 7. The מַלְאַךְ יְהֹוָה, before whom Joshua stood, was no other than יְהֹוָה himself, as ver. 2 evidently shows. It has been matter of dispute, whether by הַשָּׂטָן we are here to understand the great enemy of God and man, ὁ ἀντίδικος, 1 Pet. v. 8; ὁ κατήγωρ, Rev. xii. 10; or, whether a human adversary or adversaries are intended. Those who advocate the latter position think that Sanballat, or some other enemy of the Jews, is meant; but the emphatic form

of the term, investing it, as it does, with the nature of a proper name (Gesen. Heb. Gram. § 107, 2), decidedly favours the former interpretation. We find this name given to the chief of the evil spirits in the book of Job, the most ancient in the Bible. See chap. i. and ii. Some have compared Ps. cix. 6, but the parallel term רָשָׁע is against such construction in that passage. From the identity of the phraseology, however, which represents the adversary as taking his place at the right hand of the accused, it has been concluded, that it was customary in the Jewish courts for the accuser to assume this position. What the ground of opposition on the part of Satan was, we are not here informed; but if the construction put by some eminent commentators upon Jude 9, which resolves "the body of Moses," there mentioned, into the Jewish church, and supposes the apostle to refer to the passage before us, be the true one, (and of this I cannot entertain a doubt,) it will follow, that the character of the Jewish people, as not having been legally purified from their idolatries, and the backwardness which they evinced in rebuilding the temple, were urged as pleas against them. It is true, the opposition is said to have been made to Joshua; but it must be remembered that he appears here, not in his personal, but in his official character, as the representative of the whole body of the people.

2. Almost all the commentators, even Maurer and Hitzig, agree in the opinion, that the incommunicable name יְהֹוָה, *Jehovah*, is here given to the angel spoken of in the preceding verse. See on ch. i. 8. So obvious did this appear to the Syriac translator, from the spirit of the context, that he renders ܡܠܐܟܐ

3   Now Joshua was clothed with filthy garments, and he stood
4 before the Angel. And he answered and spake to those that
stood before him, saying, Remove the filthy garments from him.
And he said to him, See! I have caused thine iniquity to pass
5 away from thee, and I will invest thee with costly habiliments. He
then said, Let them place a pure mitre upon his head. And they
placed the pure mitre upon his head, and invested him with the

وَعَكَمْءَا, *the Angel of the Lord,* a rendering which Newcome would, very uncritically, have admitted into the text.
The interpretation of Rosenmüller, " vo-
catur legatus de nomine principis sui,"
is a pure fiction, and directly opposed
to Scripture usage. The verb גָּעַר signifies
to chide, rebuke, so as to silence those
who are the objects of the reproof, and
restrain them from carrying their designs
into effect. It is repeated for the sake
of emphasis, to express the absolute
certainty that the machinations of Satan
should prove utterly abortive. In the
reference to the Divine choice of Jerusalem, there is a recognition of the
promise, ch. i. 17 ; ii. 12. The pointed
interrogation has respect to Joshua, and
forcibly, though tacitly, conveys the
idea, that his deliverance, and that of
the people whom he represented, from
the destruction which threatened them
in Babylon, was the result of sudden
and efficient interposition on the part
of Jehovah. It was not, therefore, for
a moment to be supposed that he would
now withdraw his favour from them, and
abandon them to their enemies. He
had rescued them, in order that they
might be preserved.

3, 4. Because the Romans used to
clothe persons who were accused in a
sordid dress, Drusius and others have
imagined that the idea of a criminal is
still kept up. That the filthy garments
in which Joshua appeared were symbolical of the guilt and punishment of
the Jews, seems beyond dispute ; just
as their removal, and his investment
with splendid attire, indicates a state
of restoration to the full enjoyment of
their religious privileges. צוֹאָה, *filth,* is
used metaphorically to denote the moral
pollution contracted by sin. See Prov.
xxx. 12 ; Is. iv. 4. He is represented

as appearing in the squalid garments
in which he had returned from a state
of captivity in Babylon, and as having
restored to him the gorgeous dress of
the high priest. מַחֲלָצוֹת, *costly* or *splendid
habiliments,* such as were worn on special
occasions, and put off as soon as the
occasion was over. See on Is. iii. 22.
Those who are here commanded to
change the dress of Joshua are not, as
Ewald supposes, attendant priests, but
attendant angels. The nominative to
הָעֹמְדִים and וַיֵּן is לִפְנֵי, יְהֹוָה, and not יְהוֹשֻׁעַ.
עָוֹן does not mean, as Gesenius interprets,
to let iniquity or sin pass by, but to
remove its guilt or *punishment,* and thus
effectively to remit or forgive. This
guilt or punishment is represented as
having lain as a heavy load upon Joshua,
and to have been removed מֵעַל, *from
upon* him. הַלְבֵּשׁ is not to be changed
into אַלְבֵּשׁ, as in the Targ. and Syr., but
is to be regarded as a not unusual
elliptical form of the idiomatic הַלְבֵּשׁ אַלְבֵּשׁ.

5. The punctuation וָאֹמַר is obviously
incorrect, since it introduces the prophet
as taking a part in the transactions
exhibited in the vision, which is altogether foreign to the position he occupied.
The word should be pointed וְאָמַר, and
has been so read by the Targ., Syr., and
Vulg. translators. צָנִיף, *tiara,* or *turban,*
is used instead of מִצְנֶפֶת, the term employed in the Pentateuch to denote this
part of the high-priest's dress. LXX.
κίδαρις. At בְּגָדִים the adjective טְהֹרִים is
to be supplied from the preceding,
or the article may be understood. עָמַד is
more appropriately rendered " stood up,"
than, as in our common version, " stood
by." The latter rendering presents the
Angel of Jehovah to view as a simple
spectator ; the former, in the solemn
posture of one who is about to deliver
an important charge. And this, as the
following verses show, was precisely the

6 habiliments. Then the Angel of Jehovah stood up. And the
    Angel of Jehovah protested to Joshua, saying :
7   Thus saith Jehovah of hosts :
    If thou wilt walk in my ways,
    And if thou wilt observe my charge,
    Then thou shalt both judge my house,
    And keep my courts,
    And I will give thee guides among these who are standing by.
8 Hear now, O Joshua ! the high priest,
    Thou and thy companions that sit before thee ;

character in which he appeared. He
had been sitting upon his throne,
but now rises to announce the divine
decree respecting the responsible duties
which devolved upon Joshua in his
sacerdotal capacity. I do not agree
with Dr. Stonard, who supposes that
the Angel assumed the character and
position of a witness. The participial
form of the verb is adopted for the
purpose of varying the style.

6, 7. עֵד, as here used in Hiphil, signifies *to make a solemn declaration.*
LXX. διεμαρτύρατο. Targ. and Syr.
אַחִיד. Vulg. *contestabatur.* מִשְׁמַרְתִּי,
my charge, means the laws, prescriptions,
or rites, which I have given in charge,
namely, the Mosaic Institute. Obedience
to this the high priest was bound to
render himself, and upon him supremely
devolved the obligation to see that it
was obeyed by others. מִשְׁמֶרֶת, from
שָׁמַר, *to guard, keep, observe,* is frequently
used by Moses to denote the *office, duty,*
or *charge,* to which the priests were to
attend. See Lev. viii. 35 ; Numb. i. 53 ;
iii. 28, 31, 32, 38. By the "house" of
the Lord here, we are not to understand
the temple, as some have imagined, but
the people of Israel, viewed as composing
his household or family. Comp. Numb.
xii. 7 ; Hos. viii. 1 ; ix. 15. דִּין, *to judge,*
is always employed in reference to
persons : never with respect to things.
There appears to be in the declaration
here made, an anticipation of the part
which the sacerdotal family of Joshua
was to take in the government of the
Jewish state. מַהְלְכִים is the Hiphil participle of הָלַךְ, just as מַחְלִמִים is of חָלַם, Jer.
xxix. 8 ; and מְעוֹרִים of עֵוּר, 2 Chron.
xxviii. 23. It must, therefore, signify

those who cause to go or *walk, leaders,
conductors, guides.* Who these were we
are not informed, farther than that they
were standing in the presence of the
Angel, and were pointed at by him.
Some have thought that the subordinate
priests who attended upon Joshua are
intended ; but such interpretation is
altogether unsuitable to the dignified
character which, as high priest, he
sustained. As none but superior beings
could be his leaders or conductors, it
follows that the angels must be meant.
This view is confirmed by the circumstance of their being represented as
"standing," namely, in the presence of
Jehovah, ready to execute his behests,
whereas the subordinate priests are
spoken of in the following verse as
"sitting" before Joshua. The import
of the promise is, that he and his
successors in office should enjoy the
care, direction, and aid of celestial
spirits in the management of the national
affairs. Munster, Vatablus, Rosenmüller, Ewald, and Hitzig, take מַהְלְכִים
to be the plural of the noun מַהֲלָךְ, *a
walk,* or *walking place ;* but this affords
no appropriate sense, except it be referred to the heavenly state—a construction put upon the clause by the
Targum, Kimchi, and several Christian
interpreters, but which is little suited to
the language of the connexion, and is a
mode of representation otherwise foreign
to Scripture.

8. The companions of Joshua were
the ordinary priests, who were associated
with him for the purpose of carrying
on the service of the temple. They are
represented as "sitting before" him,
not at the time the words are addressed

(For they are typical persons,)
For, behold! I will introduce my servant THE BRANCH.
9 For, behold! the stone which I have laid before Joshua,
Upon the one stone shall be seven eyes:
Behold! I will form the sculpture thereof,
Saith Jehovah of hosts;
And I will remove the punishment of that land in one day.

to him, for they are spoken of in the third person, but usually, when consulting together about religious matters. On such occasions he occupied a more elevated seat or throne as their president, while they sat on chairs or benches before him. By אַנְשֵׁי מוֹפֵת, *men of sign* or *portent*, are meant *symbolical men*, persons prefiguring, or foreshadowing some person or persons still future. Comp. Is. viii. 18; xx. 3; Ezek. xii. 6; xxiv. 27. That only one person is here referred to as typified by the Jewish priests, and that this one person is none other than the Messiah, the following clause of the verse incontrovertibly shows. In their sacerdotal character, and in the presentation of sacrifices before Jehovah, they foreshadowed the High Priest of our profession, Christ Jesus, and the one sacrifice which he offered for sins, when he presented himself as a propitiatory victim in the room of the guilty. For the derivation of מוֹפֵת, see on Joel ii. 30. Though הֵפָּה, *they are*, refers immediately to the subordinate priests, we are not to suppose that Joshua is excluded, or that he was not a symbolical person as well as they. This use of the third person of the pronoun instead of the second is not without example. See Zeph. ii. 12.—The author of the Targum admits that by צֶמַח, *Branch*, the MESSIAH is meant. His words are, יָת עַבְדִּי מְשִׁיחָא וְיִתְגְּלֵי, "My Servant, the Messiah who shall be revealed." The same interpretation is found in other Jewish authorities, as both Kimchi and Rashi admit. Some few Christian interpreters, among whom Grotius and Blayney, adopting the opinion of the two Rabbins just mentioned, suppose Zerubbabel to be intended; but, in my opinion, very preposterously, for that prince was already in existence, and in the full exercise of

his official duties; whereas the person to whom Jehovah refers had not yet appeared. Even Gesenius, Hitzig, and Maurer, make no scruple in applying the title to the Messiah. It is that given to him, Is. iv. 2; Jer. xxiii. 5; xxxiii. 15; and Zech. vi. 12; and is equivalent to *Son*. See on Is. iv. 2, where it is shown that in the writings of the ancient Persians, "the *branch*" of any one means his son, or one of his posterity. The verb צָמַח, from which the noun is derived, signifies to *spring forth* or *up*, as plants; but the LXX. have adopted the word ἀνατολή, which expresses the *sun-rise*. Hence the Saviour is called ἀνατολὴ ἐξ ὕψους, "the Day-spring from on high," Luke i. 78. Comp. Mal. iv. 2, where וְזָרְחָה שֶׁמֶשׁ צְדָקָה, "the Sun of righteousness shall arise," is rendered by the LXX. ἀνατελεῖ ἥλιος δικαιοσύνης. The Vulg. *adducam servum meum orientem*. For עַבְדִּי, *my servant*, as a designation of the Messiah, comp. Is. xlii. 1—7; xlix. 1—9; l. 5—10; lii. 13—liii.; and see my Comm. on the first of these passages.

9. Most interpreters regard this verse as a continuation of the subject treated of at the close of the preceding, and explain the אֶבֶן, *stone*, of the Messiah, in accordance with such passages as Ps. cxviii. 22; Is. xxviii. 16. This view is largely insisted upon by Stonard; but what, in my judgment, renders it altogether untenable, is the circumstance that the stone is spoken of as having been laid *before*, or *in the presence of* Joshua—language which can with no propriety be employed with reference to the Messiah. Neither can the reference be to הָאֶבֶן הַבְּדִיל, *the plummet*, spoken of ch. iv. 10, that being represented as in the hand of Zerubbabel, and not placed or laid before his associate in the government. I cannot, therefore,

10 In that day, saith Jehovah of hosts,
　　Ye shall each invite his neighbour,
　　Under the vine, and under the fig tree.

imagine any other stone to be here intended than the foundation-stone of the
temple, which had been laid by Zerubbabel in the presence of Joshua and
his brethren the priests, who celebrated
the joyful event in songs of praise to
Jehovah ; Ezra iii. 8—13. When it is
said, that upon this "one stone" were
"seven eyes," we are not to conclude
that they were exhibited upon it. The
meaning is, that they were directed
towards it, or intent and fixed upon it,
as an object of special attention and care.
While with us an eye is the hieroglyphic
of Divine Providence, the Hebrews, to
express the perfection of knowledge and
wisdom in which all its affairs are conducted, employed the hieroglyphic of
"*seven* eyes,"—seven, in the Oriental
style, denoting fulness or perfection.
Such symbolic representations were
common among the Persians. Comp.
Rev. i. 4; v. 6. Jehovah here declares,
that the erection of the temple, the commencement of which had been made, in
the course of his providence, by the
laying of the foundation, should be an
object of his special care and regard.
For עַל עַיִן, *the eye being upon* any person
or thing, as denoting the exercise of kind
and vigilant care, see Ps. xxxii. 8. The
attempt of Vitringa and Blayney to explain עֵינַיִם, of *fountains*, and so apply
the passage to living waters flowing
from Christ as the antitype of the rock
smitten in the wilderness, is a complete
failure. The singular עַיִן, signifies, indeed, *fountain* as well as *eye*, but it is a
settled principle of Hebrew grammar
that when *fountains* are intended, the
plural feminine is uniformly employed,
just as the dual עֵינַיִם is as uniformly and
exclusively used to express *eyes*. See
for the principle, Gesen. Lehrgeb. pp.
539, 540. That the dual is employed to
express things that exist in pairs, even

when more than two is intended, see on
Is. vi. 2, and Hab. iii. 4. הִנְנִי מְפַתֵּחַ פִּתֻּחָהּ,
Behold! I will form the sculpture thereof :
lit. "I will *open the opening thereof.*"
What kind of architectural ornaments are
hereby intended, it is impossible to say ;
but that they were cut out or engraven
in the foundation-stone, the exigency of
the place requires, except we regard the
stone as here used by synecdoche for
the whole temple, in which case reference
will be had to the finishing off of the
structure, the foundation of which had
been laid in the presence of Joshua.

LXX. ὀρύσσω βόθρον. Syr. ܘܗܐ ܦܬܚ

ܐܢܐ ܬܪܥܘ̈ܗܝ, "Behold, I open the gates
of it." מוש is here used in Kal, but with
a causative signification, *to remove, cause
to depart.* עָוֺן is to be understood, not
of iniquity, but of the punishment of
iniquity, the troubles and sufferings to
which the Jews were subjected on
account of it. Thus the iniquity of
Sodom, Gen. xix. 15, was the punishment to be inflicted upon it ; and that
of Babylon, Jer. li. 6, the same. The
land of Judæa had borne its punishment
during the captivity, but was now to be
occupied and cultivated. To sufferings
the Jews were still exposed on the part
of their enemies, who caused an interruption of the building of the temple,
and prevented the comfortable settlement of the people in their own land.
For their encouragement Jehovah promises to put an end to their distress,
בְּיוֹם אֶחָד, *in one day ;* i. e. soon, in the
shortest space of time. הָאָרֶץ הַהִיא is
specifically the land of Palestine.

10. A promise of the tranquillity and
social enjoyment that were to be experienced by the restored Hebrews. See
on Mic. iv. 4.

CHAPTER IV

Under the symbol of a golden candlestick is represented the pure and flourishing
state of the Jewish church as restored after the captivity, 1—3. The signification
of this symbol the prophet is left to find out, 4, 5 ; only a clue is given him in
the message which he was commissioned to deliver relative to the completion of
the temple, in spite of the formidable difficulties which interposed, and to the
Messiah who was to come after the temple was in a finished state, 6, 7. He
was further instructed to announce the certainty of the former event, on the
ground that Zerubbabel, who superintended the work, was under the special
care of Divine Providence, which should so arrange the course of human affairs
as to render them subservient to the undertaking, 8—10. Under the additional
symbol of two olive trees, which supplied the candlestick with the necessary oil,
are represented Joshua and Zerubbabel, the two principal official persons in the
new state, 11—14.

---

1   AND the angel who spake with me awoke me again, like one
2   who is waked out of his sleep. And he said to me, What dost thou
     see ? And I said, I see, and behold! a candlestick wholly of gold,
     and its bowl upon the top of it, and its seven lamps upon it, and

VISION V.

1. We are not to conclude from the
use of the verb שׁוּב at the beginning of
this verse, that the communicating angel
had removed to a distance from the
prophet, and now returned to him.
When employed by itself, שׁוּב certainly
signifies *to return ;* but, according to a
common Hebrew idiom, when used before another verb, it merely indicates
the repetition of the action expressed
by such verb. See Gen. xxvi. 18 ; xxx.
31; 2 Kings i. 11, 13. Connecting the
verb in this manner with וַיְעִירֵנִי, reference
will be had, not to any absence of the angel, but to his renewed excitement of the
prophet to give his attention to another
vision which was to be presented to his
view. He had become so absorbed in

the contemplation of the preceding vision,
that he required to be roused, as in the
case of a person in profound sleep.

2. Instead of the second וַיֹּאמֶר, a vast
number of the MSS. read correctly
וָאֹמַר, as the word is found also in some
of the earliest editions. Many MSS.
and several printed editions exhibit גֻּלָּה
without Mappick in the ה, and thus
bring the word into accordance with the
feminine form, as occurring in the
following verse. It has been thus read
by the LXX. and Syr. ; still it seems
preferable to regard it as a masculine
noun, and read גֻּלָּהּ, with the pronominal
affix. It signifies an oil-cup, bowl, or
bason, and was placed at the top of the
candlestick for the purpose of supplying
with oil the small tubes or pipes leading

3 seven pipes to the lamps which are upon the top of it. And two olive-trees beside it, one on the right side of the bowl, and one
4 on the left side of it. And I addressed myself farther to the angel who spake with me, saying, What are these, my lord?
5 And the angel who spake with me answered and said to me, Dost thou not know what these are? And I said, No, my lord.
6 And he answered and spake to me, saying, This is the word of Jehovah to Zerubbabel, saying:

Not by might, nor by power,
But by my Spirit, saith Jehovah of hosts.

to the several lamps. Considerable difficulty has been found in endeavouring to account for the double numeral form שִׁבְעָה וְשִׁבְעָה, seven and seven. Some think the number is to be multiplied by itself, and rendered forty-nine; but this is not only abhorrent from the representation otherwise given of the candlestick, but is unwarranted by Hebrew usage. Others, as Stonard, take the words in a distributive sense, and make the number to be fourteen, understanding by seven and seven, twice seven. To this hypothesis, however, the copulative Vau forms an insuperable objection, since it conveys the idea not of distribution merely, but also that of diversity or variety. The instance adduced from 1 Kings viii. 65, is not exactly parallel, as the noun is there repeated, which is not the case in Zechariah; nor, so far as I can find, do we meet with any instance parallel to שִׁבְעָה וְשִׁבְעָה מוּצָקוֹת. Our translators remove the one seven, and place it before "lamps;" but such construction is altogether unwarranted, and, indeed, they appear to have placed only a qualified reliance upon it, for they render in the margin, seven several pipes. There is every reason to suspect that the former שִׁבְעָה is an interpolation which has found its way into some ancient MSS. and been copied into all the rest. This suspicion is confirmed by two circumstances. The word occurs only once both in the LXX. and the Vulg. The former renders: καὶ ἑπτὰ ἐπαρυστρίδες τοῖς λύχνοις τοῖς ἐπάνω αὐτῆς; the latter, et septem infusoria lucernis, quæ erant super caput ejus. The other circumstance is, that, as in conformity to the number of lamps belonging to the candelabrum in the taber-

nacle, Exod. xxv. 37, from which the symbol was evidently borrowed, it is expressly stated, that there were only שִׁבְעָה נֵרוֹת, seven lamps attached to that presented to view in the vision, we cannot conceive of there being to each two pipes or conductors for the oil. The קָנִים, reeds or tubes of Moses, Exod. xxv. 32, 33, 35; xxxvii. 18, and the מוּצָקוֹת, pipes or tubes of Zechariah, both signify the same objects, viz. those used for conveying the oil into the lamps. The latter word is derived from יָצַק, to pour or flow. Vulg. infusoria. That the candlestick was symbolical of the Jewish church cannot be doubted. Comp. Rev. i. 20; xi. 4, where the same symbol is used in reference to Christian churches. The idea which it conveys is that such churches are placed in the world for the sake of its illumination. Thus it was with the Jewish church in the midst of the surrounding darkness of Paganism; and thus it hath been with Christian churches in every age of their history.

3. Of what the two olive-trees were emblematical, we learn from ver. 14.

4, 5. עָנָה, like ἀποκρίνομαι in the New Testament, signifies to proceed or begin to speak, as well as to answer. It is obviously thus used at the beginning of ver. 4. Comp. chap. i. 10. While the angel had it in commission to explain what was meant by these trees, he was to reserve the explanation till after he had made certain communications relative to the building of the temple, and the advent of Messiah.

6. From the purport of the message which the prophet was to deliver to Zerubbabel, it may be inferred that he was labouring under despondency, produced

7 Who art thou, O great mountain?
   Before Zerubbabel thou shalt become a plain:
   And he shall bring forth the Chief Stone,
   With shouts of Grace! Grace to it!

by the consideration of the powerful op-position with which he had to contend, the greatness of the undertaking in which he had embarked, and the inadequacy of the human means which he had at his disposal. Between חַיִל and כֹּחַ there is no clearly defined difference of meaning. They are both used equally of physical and of mental and moral *power ;* and are here employed as synonymes, to ex-press the idea that human might, of whatever description, was of no account with the Almighty; that he can effect his purposes by few as well as by many, by those whom the world accounts foolish as well as by those of superior intellect; and that it is by the exercise of his own spiritual agency exciting to action, and sustaining and giving efficiency to it, that its performance is secured. There seems to be here a reference to what we read, Haggai ii. 5: "My Spirit re-maineth among you: fear ye not." The truth, however, is of universal applica-tion, and is clearly taught in the New Testament in reference to the conversion of sinners. 1 Cor. iii. 6; 2 Cor. x. 4; Eph. i. 19; Col. i. 12.

7. However lowly the feelings enter-tained by Zerubbabel, he is here taught by the sublime and noble figure of the depression of a large mountain into a level plain, that none of the formidable impediments which he apprehended, should, in the smallest degree, obstruct his progress. מִי, *who,* sometimes refers to things, yet so as to include the idea of the human agency connected with them. Before לְמִישׁוֹר supply הָיָה or תִּהְיֶה. The interpretation of Stonard, who applies the mountain to the Christian church, is altogether forced and inept. By אֶבֶן הָרֹאשָׁה is meant, not any stone uniting the two sides of a building at the top, but the *lapis angularis,* or foundation stone, on which at the angle both rest, and which, being necessarily much larger and more ponderous, as well as more serviceable than any other, was fully entitled to the distinctive character of *the chief* or *principal stone.* The foun-

dations of the literal temple having already been laid by Zerubbabel, it must be obvious, that the language is merely borrowed from that event, and that his attention is directed to Him of whom David had prophesied as אֶבֶן רֹאשׁ פִּנָּה, the *chief* or *principal corner stone,* Ps. cxviii. 22, and who is called in the New Testament, Κεφαλὴ γωνίας, and Λίθος ἀκρογωνιαῖος. Symm. renders: τὸν λίθον τὸν ἄκρον ; Theod. τὸν λίθον τὸν πρῶτον ; Aq. τὸν λίθον τὸν πρωτεύωντα ; all conveying the idea of the primary or principal stone of the building. The LXX. mistaking הָרֹאשָׁה for יְרֻשָּׁה, render, τὸν λίθον τῆς κληρονομίας. The nomi-native to הוֹצִיא is not Zerubbabel, but Jehovah. This was perceived by the Targumist, who puts the same Messianic interpretation upon the passage, para-phrasing it thus: וִיגַלֵּי יָת מְשִׁיחֵיה דַאֲמִיר שְׁמֵיה מִלְּקַדְמִין וְשַׁלִּיט בְּכֹל מַלְכְוָתָא, *And he shall reveal his Messiah, who was named of old, and he shall rule over all kingdoms.* The introduction of this stone was to be accompanied with acclamations of "Grace, Grace to it." תְּשֻׁאוֹת, *shouts* or *acclamations,* from שָׁאָה, *to make a noise, shout aloud,* cry as a crowd; hence the noun came to signify the shouting of a multitude. The repetition of חֵן, *favour* or grace, is for the sake of intensity ; and the ascriptions of this favour to the stone (לָהּ) implies that it was possessed of this quality, and was to be the medium or means of its conveyance to others. This prediction was clearly fulfilled in our Redeemer. " *Grace,*" or *favour,*" was poured through his lips." Ps. xlv. 2. At his birth the תְּשֻׁאוֹת, accla-mations of the heavenly choir, were, " Glory to God in the highest, on earth peace, goodwill toward men." Luke ii. 14. As he approached Jerusalem, the multitudes were loud in their acclaims of " Hosannah to the Son of David. Blessed be he that cometh in the name of the Lord! Hosannah in the highest." Nor is the phrase, " The *grace* of our Lord Jesus Christ," of unfrequent occur-rence in the New Testament. The usual

8 And the word of Jehovah was communicated to me, saying,
9 The hands of Zerubbabel have founded this house,
  And his hands shall finish it :
  And ye shall know that Jehovah of hosts hath sent me to you.
10 For who hath despised the day of small things?
  For those seven eyes of Jehovah
  Which run to and fro through the whole earth rejoiced,
  When they saw the plummet in the hand of Zerubbabel.
11   Then I proceeded and said to him, What are these two olive-
  trees on the right side of the candlestick, and on the left of it ?

application of the words to the completion of the work of grace in the soul of
a believer, or to the addition of the last
convert to the church, is quite incongruous. Whatever grace is possessed
by the people of God is altogether derived, and is not to be ascribed to themselves, but to Him to whom alone they
are indebted for its communication. It
may farther be observed, that perhaps
the repetition in the phrase חֵן חֵן, *Grace,
Grace,* may have been intended to express the infinite value of the Corner
Stone. In Prov. xvii. 8, we read that "a
gift is אֶבֶן חֵן, *a precious stone* in the eyes
of him that hath it;" and one of the qualities of the stone laid for a foundation
in Zion is, that it is יְקָרָה, *precious,* Is.
xxviii. 16.

9, 10. יִסְּדוּ is the Preterite of Piel.
בָּצַע signifies *to cut, cut off, bring to an
end, finish,* in which last acceptation it
is here used. The verse contains a
positive assurance that the temple should
be completed by Zerubbabel. "The
day of small things" means the short
period which had elapsed since the Jews
had begun to rebuild the temple, and
the commencement, which had been
inconsiderable and inauspicious. The
efforts bore no proportion to the magnitude of the undertaking, and could only
provoke the scorn and contempt of unbelievers. בַּז is derived from בָּזַז, as סָב
is from סָבַב; only with the signification
of בוז and בָּזָה, *to despise.* בָּזַז otherwise
signifies *to plunder, spoil.* With the
human estimate of the enterprise, forcibly expressed in the interrogative form,
that of Jehovah is strikingly contrasted.
His eyes rejoiced when they saw the
work marked out by Zerubbabel with

the plummet. This instrument was
called אֶבֶן הַבְּדִיל, *the stone of separation,*
because it consisted of the alloy of lead
or tin, which was *separated* by smelting
from the silver ore with which it was
combined. The Vau prefixed in וְרָאוּ is
to be rendered *when,* as in וִיכָלֶף, Judges
xix. 1. The nominative to וְשָׂמְחוּ וְרָאוּ is
שִׁבְעָה־אֵלֶּה, with which עֵינֵי יְהֹוָה, as expletive,
is in apposition. This, which appears to
me to be the only tenable construction,
is that given in the margin by our
Translators. It relieves the passage
from the burden of fanciful conjectures
which have been advanced in regard to
the meaning, and brings out the simple
but encouraging truth, that, how much
soever men might despise the commencement of the work in which Zerubbabel
and his compatriots were engaged, it
was the object of peculiar regard and
delight to Divine Providence, which was
acquainted with all human designs, and
from its universal activity could not only
defeat the machinations of enemies, but
command the agency of those who should
help forward the cause of truth and
righteousness. Comp. chap. iii. 9; 2
Chron. xvi. 9; Prov. xv. 3.

11, 12. It is not a little remarkable
that the prophet had to put the question
three times respecting the two olive-trees,
before he received any reply; first, ver.
4; a second time, ver. 11; and a third
time, ver. 12. The question is varied
each time, and becomes at last minute
and particular. The reason seems to
be, that it could scarcely be conceived
possible for him not to understand their
symbolical reference to the two most remarkable persons with whom he was conversant, Joshua and Zerubbabel. שִׁבֹּלֶת,

12 And I proceeded a second time, and said to him, What are the
   two branches of the olive-trees, which, by means of the two
13 tubes of gold, empty the golden liquid out of themselves? And
   he spake to me, saying, Knowest thou not what these are? And
14 I said, No, my lord. Then he said, These are the two anointed
   ones, that stand before the Lord of the whole earth.

a branch. LXX. κλάδος, so called from its resemblance to an *ear* of grain. צַנְתְּרוֹ, *a tube* or *canal*, through which oil or any other liquid is poured. The etymology of this quadriliteral is uncertain. LXX. μυξωτήρ. With the tubes the two branches were exhibited as connected, to indicate the source whence the candlestick was supplied with oil. By הַזָּהָב, *the gold*, is meant the oil, which is so called because its purity and brightness resembled those of gold.

14. שְׁנֵי בְנֵי־הַיִּצְהָר, *two sons of oil*, i. e. two anointed ones, Joshua and Zerubbabel, who are so called, because, when installed into office, they had oil poured upon their heads as a symbol of the gifts and influences of the Holy Spirit, which alone could fit them rightly to discharge their important functions. Their services to the new state were of such value that they might well be represented as furnishing it instrumentally with what was necessary for enabling it to answer the purposes of its establishment. הָעֹמְדִים עַל is elliptical for—הָעֹמְדִים עַל פְּנֵי, *who stand before*. The phrase expresses the posture of servants waiting to receive orders from their masters.

CHAPTER V

The two visions exhibited in this chapter are of a very different character from any of the foregoing, and were designed to furnish striking and instructive warnings to such of the Jews as might refuse to render obedience to the law of God, and might not have been thoroughly weaned from idolatry. In verses 1—4, is the description of a flying roll, presented to the view of the prophet, on which were inscribed the threatenings of the Divine law, which still remained in all their force, and were ever ready to be executed upon transgressors. In verses 5—11, the means are emblematically set forth which Jehovah had employed for the entire removal of idolatry from the Holy Land, and its abandonment to mingle with its native elements in Babylon—the land of graven images.

---

1   AND I again raised my eyes, and looked, and, behold! a flying

VISION VI.

1. For the adverbial use of שׁוּב see on chap. iv. 1. מְגִלָּה, *a volume* or *roll*, from the root גָּלַל, *to roll*. The ancients wrote upon the inner bark of trees, which was rolled up for the sake of convenience, and for the better preservation of the writing. They also used rolls of papyrus and of the dressed skins of animals. Aq. and Theod. render the word by διφθέρα, a skin or parchment; Symm. by κεφαλίς, the term by which the LXX. have rendered it, Ps. xl. 8. Mistaking מְגִלָּה for מַגָּל, they have here translated it δρέπανον, *a scythe* or *sickle*.

2　roll. And he said to me, What seest thou? And I said, I see
　　a flying roll, the length of which is twenty cubits, and the breadth
3　of it ten cubits. And he said to me, This is the curse which
　　goeth forth over the face of the whole land; for every one that
　　stealeth shall be cleared away on this side, according to it, and
　　every one that sweareth shall be cleared away on that side, ac-
4　cording to it. I bring it forth, saith Jehovah of hosts, and it
　　shall enter the house of him that stealeth, and the house of him

2. The roll here described was of large dimensions, more than ten yards in length, by upwards of five in breadth. To compose such a roll, several skins had to be sewed together, as we find to be the case with the Jewish Megillahs, or rolls containing the Pentateuch and other portions of the Old Testament, read in the synagogue at the present day. One of these synagogue-rolls, preserved in the British Museum, contains the Pentateuch, written on forty brown African skins. In the Rabbinical division of the books of the Old Testament, the title of the five Megilloth is given to those of the Song of Solomon, Ruth, Lamentations, Ecclesiastes, and Esther; but in Ps. xl. 8, the term מְגִלָּה is applied by way of eminence to the roll or book of the law. The large size of the roll seems to have been intended to indicate the number of the curses which it contained. The circumstance, that the dimensions of the roll correspond to those of the porch of the temple, 1 Kings vi. 3, seems rather to be accidental than intended to convey any specific instruction. The participle עָפָה, flying, expresses the velocity with which the judgments denounced in the volume would come upon the wicked.

3. וֹאת הָאָלָה, this is, or signifies, represents the curse, a phrase altogether parallel with that used by our Lord when instituting the sacred supper: τοῦτό ἐστι τὸ σῶμά μου; in Heb. וֹאת גְּוִיָּתִי, this is, i. e. represents my body. אָלָה, curse, is to be taken as a collective, comprehending all the curses denounced against transgressors of the Divine law. After הַיּוֹצֵאת supply מִלִּפְנֵי יְהֹוָה, "from the presence of Jehovah." Because מִזֶּה וּמִזֶּה, on this side and on that, is used when the writing of the law on both sides of the

tables is spoken of, Exod. xxxii. 15, Abenezra, Kimchi, Rosenmüller, Hengstenberg, and some other interpreters, have argued in favour of the position, that the roll, like that of Ezek. ii. 9, 10, was also written in this manner; but the immediate construction of the pronoun with נִקָּה in both instances, shows that it cannot be maintained. Reference is had to the place where the transgressor may be. From that place, whether on the right hand or on the left, he should be swept away by the Divine judgment. Nowhere should he find protection. The curse went forth over the whole land. It has been properly remarked, that an individual example of transgression is selected from each of the two tables of the law: הַגֹּנֵב, he who stealeth, standing for those who break the rule of duty in regard to their neighbour; and הַנִּשְׁבָּע, he who sweareth, for those who are guilty of a violation of such duties as have immediate reference to God. נִקָּה is not to be taken here in the sense of treating as innocent, but with the signification of emptying, clearing, sweeping clean away. Comp. Is. iii. 26. It is in the Niphal conjugation, the form of which is the same as that of Piel. The ancient translators are at fault here, having mistaken נִקָּה for נָקָם. Thus the LXX. ἐκδικηθήσεται; Symm. δίκην δώσῃ. Nor can the rendering of Stonard, "pleadeth not guilty," be sustained. כָּמוֹהָ, like, or according to it, if fully expressed, would be כַּאֲשֶׁר כָּתוּב, according as it is written, referring to the curse or threatening inscribed upon the roll. Thus Jerome, sicut ibi scriptum est.

4. The pronominal affix in הוֹצֵאתִיהָ refers to הָאָלָה in the preceding verse. וְנִשְׁבָּע לַשֶּׁקֶר is an aggravation of וְנִשְׁבָּע. The

that sweareth falsely by my name, and it shall continue in the midst of his house, and destroy it, and its wood, and its stones.

5   Then the angel who spake with me came forth, and said to me, Raise thine eyes, now, and look what this is that cometh forth.

6 And I said, What is it? And he said, This is the ephah that cometh forth. He said, moreover, This is their appearance in all

7 the land. And, behold! a round piece of lead, and there was a

---

punctuation of לָנֶה is irregular for לָנֶה the third feminine of the preterite of לִין, which one of De Rossi's MSS. exhibits. לִין not merely signifies to *turn aside and spend the night* in any place, but also to *remain permanently.* See Ps. xlix. 13, (Eng. version, 12).— כִּלְתָהוּ = כִּלְתִּי. A like curse was pronounced by the Delphic oracle against perjury:

———Κραιπνὸς δὲ μετέρχεται, εἰσόκε πᾶσαν, Συμμάρψας ὀλέσει γενεήν, καὶ οἶκον ἅπαντα.   *Herodot.* vi. 86.

VISION VII.

5. וַיֵּצֵא, *came forth,* i.e. came again into view to explain the new vision.

6. The ephah was one of the larger Jewish corn measures, containing about an English bushel, or seven gallons and a half. The LXX. give it simply by τὸ μέτρον. Symm. leaves it untranslated, οἰφὶ, which presents it pretty much in its original Egyptian form, which was ωIΠI. Comp. the Arab.

ويبة. Some have supposed that it is not to be specifically understood of the measure so called, on the ground that such a measure could not have contained the woman mentioned ver. 7; but the assumption is altogether gratuitous, since there is no necessity for maintaining that the female represented was actually in appearance of the ordinary size. There is equally little foundation for the interpretation of the Targum, that the use of false measures was intended by this item of the vision. עֵינָם, literally *their eye,* has been variously regarded by different translators and expositors. The LXX., Arab., and Syr., have read עֲוֹנָם, *their iniquity,* which many think much more suited to the connexion, but this reading is supported by only one of De Rossi's MSS. It is clear from what

Jerome says on the subject, that the text was the same in his day as we have it at present. The latter reading is adopted by Houbigant, Newcome, and others of the same school. That עַיִן signifies *appearance.* or that which presents itself to the *eye,* is fully established by reference to Lev. xiii. 55, Numb. xi. 7, Ezek. i. 4, 7; x. 9; and this signification is appropriately applicable in the present passage. Hengstenberg, taking the word in its primary acceptation, considers the meaning to be that *their eye* was universally set on evil; it was the effort of the whole people to fill up the measure of their sins, and thereby bring upon themselves a full measure of divine punishment. When it is said that the ephah (for this is the nominative to the latter זֹאת, *this is,*) was their appearance, the language is metonymical, the container being used for the thing contained, *i.e.* הָרִשְׁעָה, *wickedness,* or idolatry, as further explained, ver. 8.

7. The כִּכָּר contracted for כְּרִכַּר, *what is round* or *globular,* from כָּרַר, *to go round,* was the heaviest weight in use among the Hebrews, being equal to 3,000 shekels, or, according to Jahn, 125 pounds, English troy weight. Luther renders it here by *Centner,* or *hundredweight;* but it is obviously to be taken, not in its strict estimate as a measure, but in its etymological import, as signifying a' flat, roundish lump or cake of lead, yet not without some respect to its heaviness, in consideration of the end it was designed to serve—the security of the woman in the vessel over which it was placed. To express the idea of weight it is called אֶבֶן, *a stone,* in the following verse. נִשֵּׂאת is the feminine participle in Niphal. זֹאת does not refer to the talent or weight going before, but to אִשָּׁה immediately following, and is equivalent to *there was.* The woman

8 woman sitting in the midst of the ephah. And he said, This is
wickedness. And he threw her down in the midst of the ephah,
9 and threw the weight of lead on the mouth of it. Then I raised
my eyes, and looked, and, behold! two women came forth, and
the wind was in their wings, for they had wings like the wings
of a stork; and they bore away the ephah between earth and
10 heaven. Then I said to the angel who spake with me, Whither
11 are these conveying the ephah? And he said to me, To build
for it a house in the land of Shinar; for it shall be set up, and
placed there on its own base.

was placed in the ephah in order to be conveyed to Babylon.

8. By וְשָׁעָה in this place is meant idolatry, which was the most flagrant kind of *wickedness* with respect to God, and the fruitful parent of every other species of iniquity. To mark it more emphatically, the article is prefixed. הַשְׁלִיךְ, as used both times, conveys the idea of a forcible action. In the preceding verse the woman is represented as already sitting in the midst of the ephah; the action here described may either be carried back to a period preceding the vision, or it may be intended to indicate what was further done, in order to cause her to occupy a lower position in the vessel, so as to allow of the leaden cover being thrown over her. The latter is the more probable interpretation. Jarchi is of opinion that the feminine suffix in פִּיהָ, *her mouth*, refers to the woman; but it can alone with propriety be referred to the ephah.

9. The two females here mentioned are regarded by Maurer and Hengstenberg as merely belonging, by way of colouring, to the symbol as such, two persons being required to carry so large a measure as the ephah. I should rather, however, infer that the Assyrian and Babylonian powers are intended, by which, as instruments, God removed idolatry in the persons of the apostate Hebrews out of the holy land. By their having the wind in their wings is conveyed the idea of the celerity of their motion. חֲסִידָה, *the stork*, so called from the affection which both the parent

bird and her young show to each other. Aq., who frequently gives the etymology of Hebrew words, renders it Ἐρωδιός, in which he is followed by Theod. and Symm. This Greek term is derived from ἔρως, *love*. The large wings of the stork greatly accelerate its flight, when aided by the wind. In וַתִּשֶּׁנָה is an elision of the letter א, the third radical, for וַתִּשְׂאֶנָה, which is found in a great number of MSS. and some of the earliest printed editions.

10. Instead of the defective orthography מוֹלְכוֹת, many MSS. and some editions read in full, מוֹלִיכוֹת.

11. אֶרֶץ שִׁנְעָר, *the land of Shinar*, is rendered in the LXX. γῆ Βαβυλῶνος, and in the Targ. מְדִינַת בָּבֶל, which is the proper interpretation. הוּכַן is to be construed with בַּיִת, and הִנִּיחָה with אֵיפָה, including the idea of the woman, or of idolatry, of which she was the symbol. To the latter also the affix in מְכֻנָתָהּ belongs.

In this striking hieroglyphic we are taught how idolatry, with all its accompanying atrocities, was removed from the land of the Hebrews, which it had desecrated, to a country devoted to it, and where it was to commingle with its native elements, never to be re-imported into Canaan. How exactly has the prediction been fulfilled! From the time of the captivity to the present, a period of more than two thousand years, the Hebrew people have never once lapsed into idolatry! The whole vision was intended to convince them of the greatness of the evil.

CHAPTER VI

Having warned the Jews against indulging in the evil practices which had
occasioned their removal to Babylon, Jehovah now, in another vision, exhibits
to their view the warlike and unsettled state of political affairs in the immediate
future, during the reigns of Darius, and his successors, 1—8. Most commentators seem to have concurred in the opinion expressed by Munster: "Hæc
visio est valde obscura." The symbols are in themselves simple, consisting of
four chariots drawn by horses of different colours, which issue from between
two mountains of copper, and proceed in different directions with respect to the
land of Palestine. That they betoken certain dispensations of Divine Providence,
in reference to the nations by which the Jews were immediately surrounded, and
by whose fate they were more or less affected, appears to be the most consistent
position that can be assumed in interpreting them, especially as such is the
application of similar symbols elsewhere in the prophetic records. The colours
of the horses denote, as usual, the character of these dispensations, as either
calamitous, prosperous, or mixed. Comp. chap. i. 8; Rev. vi.

This vision, which is the last, is followed by a splendid prophecy of the
Messiah in his co-ordinate offices of Priest and King, to typify which the
symbolical action of making two crowns and placing them upon the head of
Joshua, is ordained by Divine authority, 9—15.

---

1   AND I raised my eyes again, and looked, and, behold! four
     chariots came forth from between two mountains, and the moun-

VISION VIII.

1. For the idiom וָאָשֻׁב וָאֶשָּׂא, see on ch.
iv. 1. Considering that the events referred to are those of war, it is most
natural to infer that war-chariots are
here intended. By mountains of copper
are meant solid, strong and durable
mountains, such as those in which copper
and other metals are ordinarily found.
Comp. Jer. i. 18. Of what these mountains were designed to be the symbols,
or whether they are introduced merely

as an ornamental part of the vision, have
been matters of dispute. I am strongly
inclined to regard them as emblems of
the Medes and Persians, and thus corresponding to the two horns of the ram
which are employed by Daniel to denote
the same people; chap. viii. 3, 4. From
between these, or from the powerful
empire which they formed, the instruments of Divine Providence were
to proceed to execute his purposes in
punishing the nations. That mountains
are employed in the figurative language

2 tains were mountains of copper. In the first chariot were red horses ;
3 and in the second chariot black horses ; and in the third chariot
white horses ; and in the fourth chariot were piebald grey horses.
4 I then proceeded and said to the angel who spake with me, What
5 are these, my lord? And the angel answered and said to me, These
are the four spirits of heaven, coming forth from presenting them-
6 selves before the Lord of the whole earth. That and the black
horses in it are going forth into the north country ; and the white
go forth to the west of them ; and the piebald go forth to the

of prophecy to signify kingdoms or
governments, see Is. ii. 2 ; xli. 15 ; Jer.
li. 25 ; Dan. ii. 35.

2, 3. The *red* horses are symbolical
of war and bloodshed ; the *black*, of
general calamity and distress ; the
white, of victory and prosperity ; and
the *piebald greys*, of a dispensation,
mixed in its character, partly prosperous, and partly adverse. The last
word, אֲמֻצִּים, would seem most naturally
to be referrible to the root אָמַץ, *to be
strong, active*, &c. ; and this mode of
solution would at once be satisfactory,
were there no qualifying circumstances
in the immediate context to require
another interpretation. But as all the
other terms here employed in describing
the horses are expressive of colours, we
should expect something of the same
character to be intended by the word in
question. I, therefore, prefer adopting
a derivation from the Arab. ومض
leviter splenduit, and regard it as qualifying בְּרֻדִּים, immediately preceding.
Thus the Targ. קִמְצָנִין, *ash-coloured,
grey ;* so that the most appropriate rendering of the two terms will be *spotted*,
or *piebald greys*.

5. Though the phrase אַרְבַּע רוּחוֹת הַשָּׁמַיִם
is that employed chap. ii. 10 (Eng. 6), to
denote the four quarters of the horizon,
yet, that it cannot have this meaning in
the present instance, is evident from its
being added that the רוּחוֹת are such as
had taken their station, or presented
themselves before the Lord, in order to
receive their commissions for the execution of his will. In our common version, therefore, the words are properly
rendered as to the meaning, *spirits of
the heavens ;* or, as we now commonly

say, *celestial spirits*, thereby meaning
angels. These are represented, (as in
Job i. 6 ; ii. 1,) as employed by God to
carry into effect his high behests, which
they receive in his immediate presence,
and then proceed to the different quarters
of the globe in which the special operations of Divine Providence are to be
carried forward.

6. By אֶרֶץ צָפוֹן, *the north country*, we
are to understand, as usual, the land of
Babylon. Comp. Jer. iii. 18 ; vi. 22 ;
x. 22 ; xlvi. 10 ; Zech. ii. 10 (Eng. 6).
Though that empire had been subdued by
Cyrus, yet the Babylonians revolted in
the beginning of the fifth year of Darius,
on which that monarch besieged them
with all his forces ; and, after much
devastation, completely depopulated it,
and reduced it to solitude. To set forth
symbolically this fearful event, black-
coloured horses are represented as conveying into the country the executioner
of the Divine indignation upon that
devoted people. It is remarkable that
the red-coloured horses, which had been
introduced into the vision, ver. 2, are
entirely passed over. The reason may,
perhaps, be, that, disastrous as was the
final destruction of Babylon, it was un-
accompanied with any thing like the
quantity of bloodshed which characterised the battles of conflicting armies in
the open field, though at the commencement there was every appearance of
much blood being shed. Although
therefore, the chariot with the red horses
appeared along with the others, it seems
to be intimated, by no further notice
having been taken of it, that it was not
employed.—The *white* horses, denoting
victory and prosperity, point out the
successes of Darius in different parts

7 south country. And the greys went forth, and asked to go to walk to and fro through the land; and he said, Go, walk to and fro through the land; and they walked to and fro through the land.

8 Then he summoned me and said to me, See, those that went to the north country have appeased my anger in the north country.

9, 10 And the word of Jehovah was communicated to me, saying: Take from the captivity, from Heldai, from Tobijah, and from Jedaiah,

of Greece, which, though checked by the battle of Marathon, contributed to the strengthening of his power in that quarter. The phrase, אֶל־אַחֲרֵיהֶם, literally means *behind them*, but geographically, *to the west of them.* That it is to be so taken here, the use of אֶל, *to*, corresponding with the use of the same preposition after the verb, both before and after in the verse, sufficiently shows. The dappled horses were symbolical of the varied condition of the Persian affairs, which followed the battle of Marathon, especially the changes which took place on the death of Darius, and the expedition of Xerxes for the reduction of Egypt. This last circumstance is particularly pointed at in the reference, אֶרֶץ הַתֵּימָן, *the country of the South.* That by תֵּימָן, *Teman,* we are not here to understand the city or region so called on the east of Idumæa, but a land to the south of Palestine, is obvious from the article being prefixed, and from a comparison of the use of the term in such passages as the following, Job ix. 9; Is. xliii. 6. It is synonymous with יָמִין, *on the right hand,* which geographically means *the South,* and here specifically signifies Egypt, to express which Daniel uses the word נֶגֶב, chap. xi. 40.

7. הָאָרֶץ, *the land* here referred to, but not described by any qualifying epithet, must be understood of the country of Palestine, the peculiar features of the dispensation of Providence with respect to which are marked by two circumstances: the grey colour of the horses, which indicated the mixed state of the Jewish affairs till the time of Artaxerxes Mnemon; and the form of the verb הָלַךְ, *to go* or *walk,* which is in Hithpael, and signifies *to go about,* or *to walk up and down.* They were not to be molested by the hostile incursions of foreign armies, but neither were they to be free from annoyances. Accordingly, we find them

involved in troubles by Sanballat, and other chiefs of the Samaritans; and, as the Persian army marched through Palestine to attack the Egyptians in the reign of Darius Nothus, the inhabitants must have been exposed to numerous inconveniences, which they could not but feel the more severely, owing to their having only just begun to take possession of their patrimonial inheritances. On the other hand, the appointment of Nehemiah to be governor of Judæa, and other favours conferred by the Persian monarch, were calculated to mitigate their distress, and inspire them with the hope of a complete and happy restoration to the enjoyment of their ancient privileges. These dappled horses supply the place of the red, specified ver. 2, but omitted in the explanation, ver. 6, so that the number of chariots is still four.

8. The nominative to וַיִּזְעַק must either be Jehovah, or the Angel of Jehovah, understood as the pronominal affix in רוּחִי, "*my* anger," shows. That among other significations רוּחַ has that of *anger,* see Jud. viii. 3; Eccles. x. 4; Is. xxxiii. 11. The phrase, הֵנִיחַ רוּחַ, *to cause anger to rest,* is equivalent to הֵנִיחַ חֵמָה, Ezek. v. 13; xvi. 42; xxiv. 13; and means *to satisfy, pacify.* The final judgment having been inflicted upon Babylon, the Divine displeasure should no more be manifested in that direction.

The tendency of the whole vision was to assure the Jews of the care and protection of their covenant God, and thus lead them to exercise confidence in him, while prosecuting the restoration of the temple and their former institutions.

9—11. Here commences a separate prophecy, calculated, like the preceding vision, to stimulate the Jews in their work. That what was commanded was actually performed by the prophet, and that it was not done in vision, seems the

who are come from Babylon, and enter thou on that day, yea,
11 enter the house of Josiah the son of Zephaniah; yea, take silver
   and gold, and make crowns, and place them upon the head of
12 Joshua, (the son of Josedech,) the high priest; and speak to
   him, saying, Thus speaketh Jehovah of hosts, saying:

Behold the Man whose name is THE BRANCH,
For he shall grow up out of his place,
And he shall build the temple of Jehovah.

only tenable construction that can be put upon it. The infinitive לָקוֹחַ, at the beginning of the 9th verse, is to be taken in connexion with the finite form of the same verb at that of the 11th, both having כֶּסֶף וְזָהָב for their object. The preposition which is prefixed to the following nouns is not to be taken partitively, as if *some* of the captivity, and *one* of each of the families, the heads of which are supposed to be here specified, were meant, but is used in its primary and most common signification. The persons named appear to have formed a deputation from the גּוּלָה, *captives* still remaining in Babylon, who had sent them with contributions in gold and silver to help forward the building of the temple at Jerusalem. These deputies had deposited their gifts in the house of Josiah, to which the prophet is commanded to repair and take what was necessary for making the two crowns which were to be placed on the head of the high priest. It is not improbable that Josiah was public treasurer at the time. The language of Zechariah is here more heavy and verbose than usual, which has occasioned some difficulty to interpreters. Instead of אֲשֶׁר בָּאוּ מִבָּבֶל, two of Kennicott's MSS., the LXX., Syr., and Targ., read בָּא in the singular, and restrict the declaration to Josiah, mentioned immediately before; but there can be little doubt that this various reading is merely an emendation of some copyist, who took Josiah, and not the three persons spoken of at the beginning of the verse, to be the subject of the predicate. To remove the ambiguity, our translators have properly connected the words immediately with the names of the persons to whom they belong. Hengstenberg contends that only *one* crown is intended, and that

the plural form, עֲטָרוֹת, is to be referred to several small crowns or diadems of which it consisted. With many other interpreters, he adduces in support of the opinion the διαδήματα πολλά, *many crowns,* which are described as being upon the head of the Saviour, Rev. xix. 12; but the reference there is purely to the crown of a conqueror, composed of many diadems, which Christ is represented as wearing, as a symbol of the numerous victories he had won over the enemies of his church. It appears, however, essential to the thing signified, namely, the priestly and regal offices, that they should have been distinct crowns, in which case either the one may have been placed upon the head of Joshua after the other, or they may have been joined together so as to form a double crown, and so placed upon his head at once. What favours the latter view of the subject is the circumstance, that the plural עֲטָרֹה is construed with תִּהְיֶה, the singular of the substantive verb, ver. 14. Maurer not inaptly illustrates this by a reference to the triple crown or the tiara of the popes, by which they arrogate to themselves a higher degree of dignity than that of Him whose servants they profess to be.

12. The symbolical action performed upon Joshua as representative of the Messiah, is here followed by an explanatory prophecy, in which his person, offices, and work are distinctly set forth. For the signification of צֶמַח, BRANCH, see on Is. iv. 2. That the Messiah is meant must be evident to all who will impartially compare Is. iv. 2; Jer. xxiii. 5; xxxiii. 15; Zech. iii. 8. Thus the Targ. expounds: הָא גַּבְרָא מְשִׁיחָא שְׁמֵיהּ עָתִיד דְּיִתְגְּלֵי, "Behold the Man, MESSIAH is his name; who is to be revealed." The same view is taken by Moses Hadarsan: הגואל אשר

13　Even he shall build the temple of Jehovah,
　　And he shall bear the glory;
　　And he shall sit and rule upon his throne,
　　And shall be a priest upon his throne,
　　And the counsel of peace shall be between them both.

אקים מכם אין לו אב שני" הנה איש צמח שמו
ומתחתיו יצמה, " The Redeemer whom
I will raise up from you shall have no
father, as it is said; Behold the man,
whose name is Zemach, and he shall
grow up from his place." The Rabbins
Jarchi, Abenezra, and Kimchi, and after
them, Bauer and Ewald, suppose Zerubbabel to be intended. The last-
mentioned writer, after the example of
Eichhorn and Theiner, conjectures that,
instead of בְּרֹאשׁ יְהוֹשֻׁעַ, on the head of
Joshua, the text has originally read,
בְּרֹאשׁ זְרֻבָּבֶל וּבְרֹאשׁ יְהוֹשֻׁעַ, on the head of
Zerubbabel, and on the head of Joshua.
But who does not perceive that this
conjecture is to be traced to the mere
love of hypothesis? Maurer scruples
not to regard it as doing violence to the
passage. The application of the words
to Zerubbabel is decidedly rejected by
Abarbanel, notwithstanding his bigoted
hostility to the Messianic interpretations.
The words of the text can apply to no
one who was not a priest; for it is expressly declared that such was to be
the official character of him who is the
subject of discourse. And that neither
Joshua nor any of his descendants could
be meant, is evident from the fact, that
they could not exercise the regal power,
none of them being entitled to occupy
the throne. Simon Maccabæus, to whom
Michaelis applies the prophecy, never
filled the kingly office; he was merely
commander of the army, and civil governor, subject to the kings of Syria.
Instead of building the temple, as is
here predicted of the Branch, he erected
a splendid palace for himself on the
mountain on which the temple stood.
Nor did the work of repairing it, after
it had been pillaged by Antiochus
Epiphanes, devolve upon him, but upon
his brother Judas. Besides, the declaration that the Branch should be invested
with the honour or glory connected with
the building of the temple, would be at
variance with the uniform ascription of

the glory of all great undertakings to
Jehovah and not to man, wherever in
Scripture such works are represented as
carried on under the special direction of
the Most High. In the phrase, וּמִתַּחְתָּיו
יִצְמָח, and he shall sprout forth from his
place, while there is a direct reference
to the name צֶמַח, here given to the Messiah, there seems to be no very indistinct
allusion to the miraculous conception.
תַּחְתָּיו, his place, the place which was
peculiar to him. The interpretation,
that "under him there shall be growth,"
which is adopted by Cyril, Jerome,
Luther, Calovius, Hitzig, Maurer, and
Ewald, applying it to the church, the
body of believers, or the affairs of Messiah's kingdom, is to be rejected on the
ground of its not being warranted by
Scripture usage. By הֵיכַל יְהוָה, the temple
of Jehovah, which the Messiah was to
build, the material temple then in the
course of erection cannot be understood,
for that was to be carried on and completed by Zerubbabel, chap. iv. 9. But,
as we have just seen, Zerubbabel and
the Branch are not identical. We are,
therefore, compelled to interpret the
phrase in application to the New Testament church, which is frequently spoken
of as a temple, 1 Cor. iii. 17; 2 Cor.
vi. 16; Eph. ii. 22; 2 Thess. ii. 4; and
respecting which the Messiah himself
declares, "Upon this rock will I build
my church, and the gates of hell shall
not prevail against it." Matt. xvi. 18.
13. The repetition וְהוּא יִבְנֶה אֶת־הֵיכַל יְהוָה
is not, as has been conjectured, to be
ascribed to an error of some transcriber,
and on the authority of the LXX., Arab.,
and Syr., to be expunged as superfluous,
but is singularly in its place, as giving a
high degree of emphasis to the statement
made respecting the personal work of
the Messiah. The erection of the spiritual temple was to be effected exclusively
through his mediation. With the declaration, that he should "bear the glory,"
compare Ps. xxi. 5; cii. 16; Is. lii. 13;

14   And the crowns shall be for Helem and for Tobijah, and for
Jedaiah, and for Hen the son of Zephaniah, for a memorial in the
15 temple of Jehovah. And those who are far off shall come and
build in the temple of Jehovah; and ye shall know that Jehovah
of hosts hath sent me to you. And it shall come to pass, if ye
will diligently obey the voice of Jehovah your God * * * *

Heb. ii. 9. The declaration has reference to the crowns, the insignia of glory and majesty, which were to be placed on the head of Joshua. In the following clauses of the verse, the union of the regal and sacerdotal offices in the person of the Messiah is distinctly set forth, thus exhibiting the peculiar feature of the Melchizedekian priesthood, Gen. xiv. 18; Ps. cx. 4; Heb. v. 6, 10; vi. 20; vii. While our Lord continues to officiate in the heavenly temple as the Great High Priest of his people, ever living to make intercession for them, he exercises his mediatorial rule over the world and the church—that over the former being rendered subservient to the administration of that which he exercises over the latter. Vitringa, Reuss, Dr. M'Caul, and others, refer the pronominal affix in כִּסְאוֹ, "his throne," to Jehovah, or the Deity absolutely considered, but, in my opinion, without sufficient ground. The natural construction requires the person who is prominently before the reader to be the object of reference. The rendering of Newcome, Hitzig, and Ewald, "and a priest shall be upon his throne," is forced and unwarranted; the Vau clearly connecting the substantive verb with the preceding verbs יִשָּׂא and יִבְנֶה, the nominative to which is הוּא, the Branch, or Messiah. The nominatives to שְׁנֵיהֶם, "them both," are neither Jehovah and the Messiah, as maintained both by ancient and by many modern interpreters; among others, Cocceius, De Dieu, Vitringa, Bengel, Reuss, Dr. M'Caul, and Dr. J. Pye Smith; nor Jews and Gentiles, as Dr. Stonard strangely interprets; but the כְּהֻנָּה, priesthood, and the מְמְשָׁל, regal dignity, which had just been mentioned as unitedly exercised by the Branch. Thus Jerome, Marckius, Drusius, Lowth, Dathe, Rosenmüller,

Hengstenberg, and others. The reason assigned by Dathe forms an insurmountable objection to the first opinion: "Quoniam enim Deus in toto hoc loco loquitur, affixum tertiæ personæ in שְׁנֵיהֶם non potest ad Jovam referre." The same objection lies against the reference of the affix in כִּסְאוֹ to Jehovah. By עֲצַת שָׁלוֹם, the counsel or purpose of peace, is to be understood the glorious scheme of reconciliation between God and man, effected by the joint exercise of the sacerdotal and regal offices of the Lord Jesus Christ. Comp. Is. ix. 6; Micah v. 5; Eph. ii. 14—17; Col. i. 20, 21; Heb. xiii. 20.

14. *Helem* is, in all probability, the same as *Heldai*, ver. 10, and *Hen* another name of *Josiah*, there also mentioned. There seems no ground for rendering חֵן, *favour*, and interpreting it of the hospitality shown to the deputies by Josiah; the construction adopted by Hengstenberg, Maurer and Ewald. The words הָעֲטָרֹת תִּהְיֶה לְחֵלֶם, *the crowns shall be to Helem*, &c., do not mean that they were to belong to the persons specified, but that they were to be for a memorial to them of the symbolical act that had just taken place, and were for this purpose to be deposited in the temple, where it is possible they remained till the Messiah, as high priest and king of his people, had taken possession of his mediatorial throne, when temple, and crowns, and the whole Jewish polity, were taken or destroyed by the Romans.

15. This verse contains a striking prophecy of the calling of the Gentiles, together with a solemn warning to the Jews, in which, the sentence being left unfinished, their rejection in consequence of unbelief is forcibly implied. It is a striking instance of ἀποσιώπησις.

CHAPTER VII

This and the following chapter are occupied with replies to questions which had
been proposed for solution, relative to certain fasts which the Jews had observed,
but which they supposed might no longer be binding after the restoration of
their prosperity, 1—3. From this circumstance Zechariah is commanded to
take occasion to reprove them for their selfish observance of the days appointed
for fasting, 4—7; to enforce attention to the weightier matters of the law,
8—10; and to warn them, by placing before them the rebellious conduct of
their fathers, and the punishment with which it had been visited, 11—14.

---

1   AND it came to pass in the fourth year of Darius the king, that
     the word of Jehovah was communicated to Zechariah on the
2 fourth day of the ninth month, which is Chislev; when Bethel
     sent Sherezer, and Regem-melech, and his men, to conciliate the

1. The occurrence here described took place two years later than those described in the preceding chapters. כִּסְלֵו, *Chislev*, the name of the ninth month of the Hebrews, which corresponds to part of November and part of December. Some think it is of Persic origin; but the idea of *torpor, rigidity, stiffness*, which is conveyed by the Heb. כָּסַל, is sufficient to justify its being referred to this root, such being the character assumed by nature in the course of this month. The ב prefixed may be regarded as the *Beth essentiæ*.

2. The words וַיִּשְׁלַח בֵּית־אֵל have occasioned considerable perplexity to interpreters. Some of the earlier Jews took *Bethel* to be the name of a person. Lightfoot supposes that it means the congregation of the Jews who had remained in Babylon. To the same effect Michaelis, "The congregation of God at Sharezer," though he acknowledges he had no idea of the geographical position of the city so called. Heng-

stenberg and Maurer think the people of the Jews are intended. The Vulg., Grotius, Dathe, Newcome, De Wette, and Arnheim, supply אֶל before the word, and render, "to the house of God." The LXX., Syr., Targ., Drusius, Blayney, Hitzig, and Ewald, regard it as the name of the city so called, in the tribe of Benjamin; only the ancient versions just specified represent it as the place to which the deputation was sent. Against the interpretation which explains it of the temple, there lies the insuperable objection, that that sacred edifice is uniformly called בֵּית יְהוָה, *the house of Jehovah*—never בֵּית־אֵל, *the house of God*; and that it should have been so designated after the recovery of the Jews from idolatry is altogether incredible, considering the infamy attached to the city so named. I entirely concur in the last opinion, which refers it to the city of Bethel, which is used by metonymy for its inhabitants. The word occupies its proper place as the nominative to

3 regard of Jehovah, speaking to the priests which were in the
house of Jehovah of hosts, and to the prophets, saying : Shall I
weep in the fifth month, separating myself as I have done these
many years?

4   Then the word of Jehovah of hosts was communicated to me,
5 saying: Speak to all the people of the land, and to the priests,
saying, When ye fasted and mourned in the fifth and in the
seventh month, even those seventy years, was it at all to me that
6 ye fasted? And when ye ate, and when ye drank, was it not ye
7 that ate, and ye that drank? Are not these the words which
Jehovah proclaimed by the former prophets, when Jerusalem
was inhabited and at peace, and her cities around her, when both
the south and the plain were inhabited?

8   And the word of Jehovah was communicated to Zechariah,
saying,

---

the verb, which cannot here be taken
impersonally, as such construction would
exclude all reference to those who sent
the deputation, a circumstance not to
be reconciled with the express specification of the names of the persons who
composed it. לְחַלּוֹת, lit. *to stroke the
face, to ingratiate oneself with another,
conciliate his regard.*

3. The city having been introduced
in the preceding verse as sending the
deputation, speaks here in the first
person singular. Comp. 1 Sam. v. 10 ;
2 Sam. xx. 19; Zech. viii. 21. The
question related to the continuance of
the fast in the *fifth* month, which had
been instituted to commemorate the destruction of Jerusalem by the Chaldæans.
2 Kings xxv. 8, 9; Jer. lii. 12—14.
As the city was now being restored, it
was presumed there would no longer
be any necessity for keeping up the
humiliating memorial. הַאֶבְכֶּה is not
simply, *Shall I fast?* but, *Shall I continue to fast?* The following words
indicate, that it was felt to be a tedious
and irksome performance of duty. The
persons speaking were thoroughly weary
of it. הִנָּזֵר, the infinitive in Niphal of נזר,
to separate, consecrate, vow ; in Niphal,
to *abstain* from food, and the ordinary
employments of life.

5, 6. Though the question had been
proposed by the leading men of a single
city only, yet the burden was generally

felt, on which account the prophet is
directed to address the Divine reply to
all the inhabitants of the land, the priests
not excepted, who appear to have been
desirous of getting rid of the fast as well
as others. Their fasts had not been
performed from a purely religious motive,
but were self-righteous and hypocritical.
While they observed them, they neglected
the weightier matters of the law. At
צוֹם is an ellipsis of the finite form of
the same verb. In הֲצוֹם צַמְתֻּנִי אָנִי there
is a double idiom, which renders it
peculiarly emphatic. Not only is the
finite form used after the infinitive of
the same verb; but the nominative of
the personal pronoun is employed after
the usual verbal suffix. Comp. Gen.
xxvii. 34, בָּרֲכֵנִי גַם אָנִי. The fast in the
seventh month was in commemoration
of the murder of Gedaliah, and those
who were with him at Mizpah. See
2 Kings xxv. 25, 26; Jer xli. 1—3.
Neither in fasting nor in feasting had
the Jews any regard to Jehovah, but
did all from self-interested motives.
The feasting referred to is that which
took place on the festival-days, which
were always days of rejoicing.

7. The former prophets had taught the
worthlessness of attention to meats and
drinks, while God was forgotten, and
the weightier matters of his law neglected.
If the Jews had listened to, and complied
with the messages of the prophets, none

9　Thus spake Jehovah of hosts, saying:
　　Execute true judgment,
　　And show kindness and mercy one to another;
10　Oppress not the widow and the orphan,
　　The stranger and the poor;
　　And think not in your heart of the injury
　　Which one hath done to another.
11　But they refused to attend,
　　And turned their back rebelliously;
　　And they made their ears heavy,
　　That they might not hear.
12　Yea, they made their heart an adamant,
　　That they might not hear the law,
　　Nor the words which Jehovah sent by his Spirit
　　Through the former prophets;
　　And there was great wrath from Jehovah of hosts.
13　And it came to pass,
　　When he called, and they would not hear,
　　So they called, and I would not hear,
　　Saith Jehovah of hosts,
14　But I tossed them among all the nations which they knew not,
　　And the land was desolate after them;
　　No one passed through or returned,
　　For they had made the land of delight desolate.

of the evils which had come upon them would have been inflicted. For "the former prophets," see on chap. i. 4. By the "south and the plain," are meant the southern and western parts of Judah.

9. אָמַר is here to be taken in the strictly past tense, as the beginning of the 11th verse clearly shows.

10. Though אִישׁ intervenes between רֵעַ and אָחִיו, they are to be regarded as in construction. Comp. Is. xix. 8; Hos. xiv. 3 (Eng. version, 2). No one was to harbour any feelings of resentment against another for any injury he might have done him.

11. נָתַן כָּתֵף, to give the shoulder, is equivalent to turning the back upon any one. The cause of such action is traced to a refractory, rebellious, and intractable disposition. The מ prefixed in מִשְּׁמוֹעַ is privative.

12. שָׁמִיר signifies both a thorn and a diamond, from the Arab. ‎سمر, to pierce. Here the idea of hardness is that conveyed by its use. In בְּרוּחוֹ בְּיַד הַנְּבִיאִים the double agency by which the Divine will was communicated is recognised— that of the inspiring Spirit, and that of the instruments inspired.

14. אֲסָעֲרֵם is an anomalous form, after the Aramæan manner, according to which Zêre is placed where there would otherwise be a moveable Sheva. Regularly, it would be אֲסָעֲרֵם. It is of the Piel conjugation. אֶרֶץ חֶמְדָּה, the land of delight, Canaan. Comp. Jer. iii. 19. Maurer proposes to take וַיָּשִׂימוּ impersonally. Others more properly consider the Jews to be the nominative, who, by their crimes, had brought judgments upon the land.

CHAPTER VIII

This chapter is a continuation of the subject introduced and treated of in the preceding. Having shown the awful consequences of disregarding the Divine will, which had been clearly announced by the prophets, God promises the renewal of his favour towards those who had returned from the captivity, 1, 2. Restored to purity, 3, Jerusalem should enjoy security and prosperity to a degree far exceeding the conceptions of those whom the prophet addressed, 4—6. Those who were still in heathen countries should be brought back, and share in the general prosperity, 7—17. The chapter closes with a direct answer to the question relating to the fasts, and a prediction of the great number of proselytes that should be made to the true religion by the display of the Divine goodness towards the Jews, 18—23.

———————

1　AND the word of Jehovah was communicated to me, saying:
2 · Thus saith Jehovah of hosts:
　　　I have been zealous for Zion with great zeal,
　　　Yea, with great indignation have I been zealous for her.
3　　　Thus saith Jehovah, I am returned to Zion,
　　　And will dwell in the midst of Jerusalem;
　　　And Jerusalem shall be called, The city of truth,
　　　And the mountain of Jehovah of hosts, The holy mountain.
4　　　Thus saith Jehovah of hosts:
　　　Aged men and aged women shall yet be sitting in the
　　　　　streets of Jerusalem,
　　　Each man with a staff in his hand for very age;
5　And the streets of the city shall be filled

1. Before אמר the word אֱלַי, to me, is found in thirty-three Heb. MSS.; it has been in ten more originally, and is now in three by correction; it is the reading of the Soncin., Brixian, and Complutensian editions, and is supported by the Syr. and Targ.
2. Comp. i. 14, 15.

3. Comp. Is. i. 26, and the remarks there made on the idiomatic use of קָרָא to call.
4, 5. These verses beautifully depict the security and happiness of the inhabitants of Jerusalem. Longevity and a numerous offspring were specially promised under the old dispensation,

With boys and girls, playing in the streets of it.

6   Thus saith Jehovah of hosts :
Though it shall be wonderful
In the eyes of the remnant of this people in those days,
Should it also be wonderful in my eyes ?
Saith Jehovah of hosts.

7   Thus saith Jehovah of hosts :
Behold, I will deliver my people
From the land of the rising,
And from the land of the setting of the sun,

8   And I will bring them, and they shall dwell in the midst of
      Jerusalem,
And they shall become my people,
And I will become their God,
In truth and in righteousness.

9   Thus saith Jehovah of hosts :
Let your hands be strong,
Ye that hear in these days
These words from the mouth of the prophets,
Which were spoken on the day when the foundation was laid

but uniformly in connexion with obedience to the law. Deut. iv. 40; v. 16, 33; vi. 2; xxxiii. 6, 24; Is. lxv. 20. The idea conveyed by מְשֻׁחֲדֶּם in such connexion is exquisite. What can be more gratifying to the uncorrupted simplicity of human feelings, than to witness a number of young children enjoying their innocent gambols ? For a contrary state of things, see Jer. vi. 11; ix. 21.

6. Though פָּלָא, like its cognate פָּלָה, is not used in Kal, yet, from its significations in Niphal, Piel, Hiphal, and Hithpael, it cannot be doubted that it must have conveyed the idea of *separation, distinction, difficulty;* hence in Niphal, it signifies *to be distinguished, to stand out prominently,* from common events, to be *impossible* to human power, to be *miraculous.* נִפְלָאוֹת, the participial noun, is often used for miraculous occurrences. ‏בַּיָּמִים הָהֵם‎, *in those days,* i. e. at the time when I fulfil my promise. To justify the rendering of our common version, " in *these* days," the Hebrew should have been בַּיָּמִים הָאֵלֶּה. See ver. 9.

7. The east and west are here put as parts for the whole. The meaning is, I will deliver my people from every region whither they have been scattered. Were there any reason to believe that the prophecy has respect to a restoration of the Jews yet future, there would be a singular propriety in the use of מְבוֹא הַשֶּׁמֶשׁ, *the setting of the sun,* the Jews being now, for the most part, found in countries to the west of Jerusalem; but there is every reason to conclude that it has an exclusive reference to what was to take place soon after it was delivered. Vast numbers were carried away captive after the time of Alexander. Not fewer than 100,000 were carried by Ptolemy to Egypt, and were settled in Alexandria and Cyrene.

8. The words בֶּאֱמֶת וּבִצְדָקָה belong to both the members of the sentence, and express the reality and sincerity of the relation on both sides.

9. תֶּחֱזַקְנָה יְדֵיכֶם, *let your hands be strong,* a figurative mode of expression, denoting *courage, resolution, effort.* Jud. vii. 11 ; 2 Sam. xvi. 21. The prophets here

Of the house of Jehovah of hosts,
The temple, in order to its being built.

10 For before those days
There was no hire for man,
Neither was there any hire for beast;
And to him that went out or came in
There was no peace, because of the enemy:
Yea, I sent all men each against another.

11 But now I will not be as in the former days
To the residue of this people,
Saith Jehovah of hosts.

12 For the seed shall be prosperous,
The vine shall yield her fruit,
And the earth shall yield her produce,
The heavens also shall yield their dew,
And I will cause the residue of this people
To possess all these things.

13 And it shall come to pass,
As ye have been a curse among the nations,
O house of Judah, and house of Israel,
So I will deliver you, and ye shall be a blessing:
Fear not, let your hands be strong.

referred to were Haggai and Zechariah. See Ezra v. 1, 2. The words which the people heard were those of consolation and encouragement. Haggai ii. 18, 19. After אֲשֶׁר, subaud. דִּבְּרוּ.

10. Such was the danger to which the Jews were exposed before the actual commencement of building the temple, that all intercourse between the city and the country was interrupted. The Samaritans pressed sore upon them, and annoyed them in every possible way. See Ezra iv. 1—5. By צַר is not meant *affliction*, θλίψις, *tribulatio*, as the Eng., LXX., and Vulg.; but the *enemy*, or as we have it, צָרֵי יְהוּדָה וּבִנְיָמִין, *the enemies of Judah and Benjamin*, Ezra iv. 1. In the last clause of the verse, reference is had to the intestine broils and contentions which prevailed.

11, 12. וְעַתָּה stands forcibly in contrast with לְפְנֵי at the beginning of the preceding verse. The providence of God brought about a complete change

in the circumstances of the Jews who had returned. As they obeyed his voice and prosecuted his work, he gave them outward tranquillity, and prospered their agricultural pursuits. After זֶרַע הַשָּׁלוֹם, *the seed of prosperity*, i. e. healthy, prosperous seed, such as would not fail, supply יִהְיֶה, *there shall be*. Their fields should not be trodden down by the enemy, nor suffer from drought, mildew, locusts, and other calamities.

13. By the Jews being a curse and a blessing, is not meant that they were the instruments of communicating either evil or good to the nations, but that they themselves experienced either the one or the other. They were subjects of the curse and the blessing. "The house of Israel," or the ten tribes, as distinguished from "the house of Judah," shared in the happy fulfilment of the prophecy. It follows, that they also returned to Palestine, בַּיָּמִים הָאֵלֶּה, in the very days to which it refers. All attempts to discover

14 For thus saith Jehovah of hosts:
    As I purposed to afflict you,
    When your fathers provoked me to wrath,
    Saith Jehovah of hosts, and I repented not;
15 So again I have purposed, in these days,
    To do good to Jerusalem and the house of Judah:
    Fear ye not.
16 These are the things which ye shall do:
    Speak truth one to another;
    Execute true and sound judgment in your gates.
17 And think not in your hearts of the injury
    Which one hath done to another;
    And love not the false oath;
    For all these things are things that I hate,
    Saith Jehovah.
18 And the word of Jehovah of hosts was communicated to me,
19 saying, Thus saith Jehovah of hosts: The fast of the fourth
month, and the fast of the fifth, and the fast of the seventh, and
the fast of the tenth, shall become joy and gladness to the house
of Judah, even cheerful festivals; but love ye truth and peace.
20 Thus saith Jehovah of hosts:

them at more recent periods have proved utterly fruitless; and the idea that they must still exist somewhere in the world, and are still to be restored in their tribal state, has arisen from a misconstruction of those prophecies which refer to the return from Babylon.

14, 15. An amplification of what had been stated in the preceding verse.

16, 17. These verses contain a virtual and instructive reply to the question relative to the celebration of the fast, chap. vii. 3. It was not in such merely external, ritual, or ceremonial observances that Jehovah delighted, but in the love and practice of moral rectitude. The "gate" was, and still is, the forum in the East. מִשְׁפַּט שָׁלוֹם means *sound*, *wholesome* judgment. אֲשֶׁר, in ver. 17, is wanting in three MSS., originally in two more, and now by correction in one; in the LXX., Syr., and Arab.

19. Now follows a formal reply to the question just referred to. The fast of the *fourth* month was on account of

the taking of Jerusalem, Jer. xxxix. 2; lii. 5—7; that of the *tenth* was in commemoration of the commencement of the siege, Jer. lii. 4. For the other two fasts, see on chap. vii. 3 and 5. The Jews are distinctly informed that these fasts should be turned into festivals of joy. The ו in וְהָאֱמֶת is adversative, having the force of, But in order that ye may enjoy the predicted and promised blessing, see that ye be sincere before me, and live in harmony among yourselves.

20. The prophecy concludes with the announcement that, in consequence of the distinguished favour shown to the Jewish people after their restoration to their own land, multitudes of Gentiles should be induced to embrace the worship of Jehovah. Just before the appearance of Christ, the heathen began powerfully to feel the emptiness of their false religions, and the unsatisfactoriness of their systems of philosophy, and many of them, who were brought into contact

There shall yet come people,
And the inhabitants of many cities,

21 And the inhabitants of one shall go to another, saying,
Let us go speedily to conciliate the regard of Jehovah,
And to seek Jehovah of hosts :
I will go, even I also.

22 Yea, many people and mighty nations shall come
To seek Jehovah of hosts in Jerusalem,
And to conciliate the regard of Jehovah.

23 Thus saith Jehovah of hosts :
In those days ten men,
Out of all the nations,
Shall take hold, shall even take hold
Of the skirt of a Jew, saying,

---

with the people of God, found in their religion, with all its imperfections, a satisfaction which they had sought in vain from any other quarter. It is evident, from various parts of the Acts of the Apostles, that proselytes were numerous in their day. Between עֹד and אֲשֶׁר, supply יִהְיֶה. Two MSS., the LXX., and Arab., read רַבִּים, *many*, after עַמִּים, which in all probability existed originally in the text.

21. The second אַחַת is equivalent to אַחֶרֶת. Comp. Exod. xvii. 12 ; xviii. 4.

23. אֲשֶׁר is redundant. *Ten* is put as a round number, or a definite for an indefinite, but indicating many rather than few. Comp. Gen. xxxi. 7 ; Mic. v. 5. מִכֹּל לְשֹׁנוֹת הַגּוֹיִם, *of all the languages of the nations*, means, of all the nations speaking different languages. Comp. כָּל־הַגּוֹיִם וְהַלְּשֹׁנוֹת, *all the nations and the languages*, Is. lxvi. 18. See also Gen. x. 5, 20 ; Dan. iii. 7 ; Rev. v. 9 ; vii. 9 ; xiii. 7. *To take hold of the skirt*, is not intended to convey the idea of entreaty, or the gesture of application for assistance, but is significant of a feeling of inferiority, and a desire to enjoy the happy privileges possessed by another. The Gentile nations would be anxious to participate in the blessings of the theocracy. The repetition of the verb הֶחֱזִיק is emphatic. אִישׁ יְהוּדִי, *a man, a Jew*, is merely a periphrasis for *a Jew*. Comp. ἀνὴρ Ἰουδαῖος, Acts x. 28. The prophecy is generally regarded as having

respect to something yet future, and is often interpreted of the instrumentality of the Jews, when converted, in effecting the conversion of the world. I can find no such reference in the passage. "Jerusalem" cannot be understood otherwise than literally, just as the term "Jew" is to be so understood ; but, according to our Lord's doctrine respecting the New Dispensation, that city is no longer the place where men are exclusively to worship the Father, John iv. 21—23. Incense and a pure offering are now presented to his name in every place where his people assemble in the name of Jesus and with a view to his glory, Mal. i. 10, 11. It was otherwise before the advent of Christ. Jerusalem was the place which Jehovah had chosen to put his name there, and thither all his true worshippers were expected to come to the great festivals, in whatever country they might reside. Thus, the treasurer of Candace went all the way from Abyssinia, Acts viii. 27 ; and thus numbers from all parts of the Roman empire assembled in that city at the first Pentecost after our Saviour's resurrection. As the Hellenistic Jews and the Gentile proselytes travelled along in companies, they could not but excite the curiosity of the pagans through whose countries and cities they passed ; and celebrated as the metropolis of Judæa had become for the favours conferred upon it by some of the greatest monarchs of the times

> We will go with you;
> For we have heard that God is with you.

immediately gone by, and for the prosperity and warlike prowess of the Jewish people, it was impossible that it should not attract the attention of the surrounding nations to the character and claims of the God who was there adored, and who accorded such blessings to his worshippers.

———◆———

CHAPTER IX

For the arguments in opposition to, and those in favour of, the authenticity of that portion of the book of Zechariah which begins with this chapter, and comprises it and the remaining chapters, see the Preface.

Having in prophetic vision exhibited some of the more remarkable events connected with the continued rule of the Persians, Zechariah now proceeds to predict those which were to take place under that of the Greeks, during the military expeditions of Alexander and his successors, in so far as they had a bearing upon the affairs of the Jews. He describes the conquest of Syria after the battle of Issus, 1; and the progress of the army of Alexander along the coast of the Mediterranean, involving the capture of the principal cities of the Phœnicians and Philistines, but leaving the Jews unmolested, through the protecting care of Jehovah, 2—8. He then contrasts with the character and military achievements of that conqueror the qualities which should distinguish the Messiah and his kingdom, whom he expressly predicts, 9, 10. After which he resumes the thread of his historical discourse, and describes the wars of the Maccabees with Antiochus Epiphanes, and the victory and prosperity with which they were followed, 11—17.

———

> 1 THE sentence of the word of Jehovah,
>   Against the land of Hadrach,
>   And Damascus shall be its resting place,
>   When towards Jehovah shall be the eye of man,
>   And of all the tribes of Israel.

1. For the signification of מַשָּׂא, see on Is. xiii. 1. The combination מַשָּׂא דְּבַר־יְהֹוָה, occurs only here, chap. xii. 1, and Mal. i. 1. As דָּבָר occurs in the sense of oracle, and מַשָּׂא signifies what is taken up and uttered by the voice, the phrase might be rendered, *The announcement of the oracle of Jehovah;* but it is better for the sake of uniformity to retain the term *sentence,* which I have adopted in my translation of Isaiah. With respect to חַדְרָךְ, *Hadrach,* it is uncertain whether it was intended to denote a country, a city, or a king. The last is the most probable, on the ground that it is not likely that the name either of a country or its metropolis, in a region near Damascus, would have entirely disappeared from the pages of history. But no such name has been found in any Arabic work

2　Hamath also which is contiguous to it;
　　Tyre and Zidon, though she be very wise.

either of history or geography. Joseph
Abassus, indeed, a native of that country,
informed Michaelis that there was a place
so called at the distance of some miles
from Damascus; that it was now of small
consequence, but had once been a city
of great celebrity; but there is every
reason to believe that if he did not intend
to impose upon his learned interrogator,
the place he had in view was אֶדְרֶעִי, in
Arabic ادرعات, called by Eusebius
'Αδραά, and by Ptolemy 'Αδρα. It lay
about thirty miles from Damascus. The
same remark applies to the statement of
Rabbi Jose, mentioned by Kimchi in his
Comm. on this verse, that he was from
Damascus, and that there was a place
there, of which the name was Hadrach.
The Rabbins consider the term to be a
compound appellative of the Messiah,
who was to be חַד, sharp or severe towards
the Gentiles, but רַךְ, tender towards
Israel! Hengstenberg, who treats on
the subject at large in his Christology,
vol. ii. pp. 69—77, Keith's Translation,
denies that it is a proper name at all,
and regards it as a symbolical appellation
of the Persian empire, which he thinks
Zechariah would not designate by its
proper name for fear of offending the
government under which he lived. His
reasoning in support of his hypothesis is
very unsatisfactory, and his construction
of לֵב קָמָי, Jer. li. 1, is perfectly ridiculous.
I am compelled to acquiesce in the
opinion, that a king of this name is
meant, as the most probable of those
that have been advanced, especially as
the phrase, "the land of a king," is not
without example in Scripture; see Neh.
ix. 22; and very much suspect that the
word חַדְרָךְ, Hadrach, is after all only a
corruption of חֲדָד, the common name of
the kings of Syria, though such corruption must have taken place at a very
early period, for it was found in the copy
from which the version of the LXX. was
made.—The affix in מְנֻחָתוֹ refers to דְּבַר in
the preceding hemistich. Damascus was
to be the place in which the Divine word
or sentence was to rest or settle; in other
words, where the threatened punishment

would permanently be inflicted. That
ancient city was taken by Alexander the
Great after the battle at Issus, and formed
part of the kingdom of the Seleucidæ,
from whom it passed into the hands of
the Romans. The native rule, which
thus ceased on the Greek conquest, was
never afterwards recovered. Several
commentators, following the ancient versions, render the words, כִּי לַיהוָה עֵין אָדָם וְכֹל
שִׁבְטֵי יִשְׂרָאֵל, for the eye of Jehovah is
upon men and all the tribes of Israel,
and explain them with reference to the
universal judgments which the providence of God had brought or would
bring upon the people in and around
Palestine. But it is more natural to
regard עֵין in construction with אָדָם וגו'.
The reference will then be to the effect
produced upon the minds of others as
well as of the Israelites, by the success
and progress of the army of Alexander.
Apprehensive of danger, they should be
compelled to look to Jehovah alone for
deliverance. When Alexander threatened to punish the Jews on account of
the refusal of Jaddua the high priest to
swear fealty to him, they were thrown
into the greatest consternation, and
offered many sacrifices and prayers to
God for deliverance. כִּי is here used as
a particle of time.

2. *Hamath* was the capital of a kingdom of the same name, which lay between
Zobah and Rehob, and to the north of
Damascus. It was called by the Greeks
Epiphania, but is now known by its
ancient name, which it has all along retained among the natives. That the kingdom was conterminous to that of which
Damascus was the metropolis, is here
expressed by תִּגְבָּל־בָּהּ, the feminine affix
referring to אֶרֶץ, *land*, in the preceding
verse. The whole of Syria was subjugated by the Greeks, or submitted to
Alexander. *Tyre* and *Zidon*, which lay
directly in the way of that monarch,
as he marched along the coast of the
Mediterranean towards Egypt, are next
mentioned. See on Is. xxiii. The
latter city voluntarily surrendered, and
had Abdolonymus appointed as viceroy.
Though originally the chief of all the

3 Yea, though Tyre hath built a fortress for herself,
  And heaped up silver as dust,
  And fine gold as the mud of the streets;
4 Behold, Jehovah will dispossess her,
  And strike her wealth into the sea,
  And she herself shall be burned with fire.
5 Askelon shall see it, and be afraid;
  Gaza also, and shall be in great pain;
  And Ekron, because her expectation hath made her ashamed;
  For the king shall perish from Gaza,
  And Askelon shall not be inhabited.

Phœnician cities, and the mother of many colonies, yet at the time here referred to, she had become far inferior to Tyre, and quite sunk in comparison with her; on which account the predicate חָכְמָה מְאֹד, *she is very wise*, though, in point of position, it might seem to belong to צִידוֹן, *Zidon*, is nevertheless to be referred to צֹר, *Tyre*, as the more important of the two cities. The Tyrians, who had long been celebrated for their worldly wisdom, Ezek. xxviii. 3, 4, 5, 12, 17, gave a specimen of it on the approach of the Grecian monarch. On his intimating that he wished to offer sacrifice in the temple of Hercules, they replied that the ancient and true temple of that god was at Old Tyre on the continent, and sent him a crown of gold in testimony of their respect for so great a conqueror; hoping by these means to induce him to pass on without visiting their island.

3. This verse is graphically descriptive of the insular and strongly fortified position of New Tyre, at the distance of seven hundred paces from the shore, and of the immense stores of wealth which it contained as the great emporium of Phœnician commerce. Ezek. xxvi.; xxvii.

4. Instead of אֲדֹנָי, many MSS., and some of them the best of the Spanish, read יְהֹוָה, which I have adopted as the true lection. Here is set forth the conquest of Tyre by Alexander, who constructed a causeway with the rubbish of Old Tyre from the shore to the island, and after a siege of seven months took the city by storm, put eight thousand of the inhabitants, who had not taken flight to Carthage, to the sword, sold thirteen

thousand into slavery, crucified two thousand, and after plundering the city, burned it to ashes. Jahn's Heb. Commonwealth, sect. 70.

5. It may easily be imagined what terror the news of the fall of Tyre must have struck into the inhabitants of the cities further along the coast southward, who knew the destination and route of the victorious army. The prophet accordingly predicts the march of the conqueror from Phœnicia into Philistia. The principal cities of the Philistines are here enumerated. *Gath* only is omitted, owing, probably, to its being farther inland, and thus lying somewhat out of the route of the army. For *Ashkelon* and *Ekron*, see on Amos i. 8. For *Gaza*, on Amos i. 6. Ekron, lying farthest north of these cities, is represented as exercising confidence in Tyre. While that city withstood the attack, she might expect Alexander to be arrested in his course, and hope that he would give up his plan of invading Egypt. But when it fell, her hopes were gone. History is silent respecting the fate of these cities on occasion of the present expedition, but of Gaza it is recorded, that it resisted, and was captured after a siege of two months. Not fewer than ten thousand of the inhabitants were put to death, and the rest were sold into slavery. Betis, the commander or governor of the city, was bound to a chariot with thongs thrust through the soles of his feet, and in this manner dragged around the city. It is not improbable, that it is specially to this circumstance that the words אָבַד מֶלֶךְ

6 A foreigner also shall sit as ruler in Ashdod,.
   And I will cut off the pride of the Philistines.
7 I will remove his blood from his mouth,
   And his abominations from between his teeth ;
   And he, even he, shall be left for our God,
   And shall be as a prince in Judah,
   And Ekron shall be as a Jebusite.
8 And I will encamp about my house because of the army,
   Both when it passeth through, and when it returneth ;
   And no oppressor shall pass through them any more.
   For now do I look with mine eyes.

מִעַזָּה, *the king shall perish from Gaza,*
refer. The title of king is frequently
used in Scripture in a subordinate sense,
to denote any chief ruler or governor.
See Gen. xiv. 2.

6. For *Ashdod,* see on Amos i. 8.
The word מַמְזֵר, which occurs only here
and Deut. xxiii. 3 (Eng. version, 2), has
been considered of uncertain etymology.
Lee thinks it may probably be a compound of מִן, *from,* עַם, *a people,* and זָר, *a
foreigner ;* but this conjecture, however
ingenious, is not warranted by Hebrew
usage. In Deut., the LXX. render it by
ἐκ πόρνης, *one born of a whore ;* but ἀλλο-
γενὴς, *of a different race or people,* best
suits both passages. See Blayney. According to the form, it must be regarded
as the Hiphil participle of מָזַר, a root not
occurring in the Hebrew Scriptures,
but signifying in more modern Hebrew,
to mix. Comp. the Arab. مَذَر, *corruptus
fuit.* Hengstenberg renders, *rabble.*
By גָּאוֹן, *the pride* of the Philistines, we
are to understand the splendour of their
cities, especially of their temples.

7. This verse contains a prediction of
the future conversion of the Philistines
to the knowledge and service of the true
God. The pronominal affix ו refers to
מַמְזֵר, the foreign prince, as does הוּא, *he,*
further on in the verse. Their abandonment of idolatry, and their embracing
the true religion, is represented by their
no longer drinking blood, and eating
things sacrificed to idols, both of which
were common among the pagans, but
prohibited by the Mosaic law, Numb.
xxv. 2 ; Lev. vii. 26 ; xvii. 10, 12 ; and

by the apostles, Acts xv. 29. It is
implied that what the ruler did, would
be done by the citizens subject to his
power. He was to belong to God, as
one who had joined himself to him by
an act of self-dedication. Comp. Is.
xliv. 5 ; lvi. 3. On his becoming a
Jewish proselyte, he should be regarded
as sustaining the dignity of one of the
princes of Judah ; no distinction should
exist between them. The same idea is
expressed in the parallel clause. The
Jebusites were the original inhabitants
of Jerusalem, who, on their subjugation
by David, were incorporated among the
Jews, and enjoyed their privileges,
2 Sam. xxiv. 16, &c.

8. For צָבָה, the Keri has the proper
orthography צָבָא, *a host,* or *army.* Jehovah here promises to afford protection
to the Jews (called, as in Hos. viii. 1,
בֵּית יְהוָה, *the house of Jehovah*). They
were not to be injured by the army of
Alexander, either on its march to or
from Egypt, a promise which was fulfilled to the letter ; for while that
monarch punished the Samaritans, he
showed great favour to the Jews. Nor
was any foreign oppressor to invade
their land, as the Assyrians and Chaldæans had done, during the period which
was to intervene before the advent of
the Messiah, predicted in the verse
immediately following. They were,
indeed, subject to much suffering, both
from the Egyptian and the Syrian kings,
especially from Antiochus Epiphanes,
but their nationality was not destroyed,
and the evils to which they were
exposed only paved the way for the

9　Rejoice greatly, O daughter of Zion!
　　Shout aloud, O daughter of Jerusalem!
　　Behold, thy King will come to thee;
　　Righteous, and having salvation,
　　Lowly, and riding upon an ass,
　　Even upon a colt the foal of an ass.

Maccabæan victories, and the establishment of the Asmonæan dynasty. For this preservation they were indebted to the providence of God which watched over them for good. This is emphatically expressed in the last clause of the verse.

9. From the great Grecian conqueror, and the temporal protection which Jehovah would accord to his people, the prophet abruptly, and in the most sublime and animated strain, calls the attention of the Jews to a Royal Personage of a very different character, the MESSIAH, meek and righteous, the Prince and pattern of peace, and the Author of spiritual salvation to all his subjects. His advent was to be accompanied by such glorious results, that it was to be hailed with the most joyful anticipation. That the subject of the prophecy is the Messiah, is not only established by the inspired authority of the Evangelist Matthew, chap. xxi. 4, but has the suffrages of all the early Jewish authorities. It was not till the twelfth century that it was otherwise interpreted. Thus the Book of Zohar: ובגיניה אתמר על משיח עני ורוכב על חמור. "On this account it is said of Messiah, Lowly and riding upon an ass;" a statement which is repeated in the same work. The same construction is put upon the passage by Joshua Ben Levi, Saadias Gaon, and others. The testimonies will be found in Wetstein on Matt. xxi. 4, who says in reference to them: "Magno consensu Judæi dictum Zachariæ de Messia interpretantur." And Solomon Jarchi has the ingenuousness to acknowledge, אי אפשר לפותרו אלא על מלך המשיח, that "it is impossible to interpret it of any other than the King Messiah." Of Him as the king of Zion it is predicated that he should be צדיק, righteous, a quality frequently ascribed to him in the Old Testament. See Is. xlv. 21; liii. 11; Jer. xxiii. 5; xxxiii. 15; Mal. iv. 2. With respect to נושׁע, or, as it is pointed in some copies, נושָׁע, of which Kimchi

approves, on the ground of its being the preterite converted into the future by the ו conversive, most modern commentators construe it as strictly passive in signification, and the more orthodox interpret it with reference to Christ's deliverance from the grave, after his sufferings upon the cross, rendering the passage, "righteous and saved." But to such construction it must be objected, first, that the passive signification does not suit the connexion. If the people had been the nominative to the verb, this signification would have been admissible; but it is the king who is here described, and to speak of him as saved or delivered without any reference to previous danger or suffering would be most inappropriate. There is, therefore, a real *exigentia loci:* the context imperatively requires the verb to be understood in an active sense. Secondly, though the usual signification of Niphal is passive, yet there are numerous instances in which verbs of that conjugation have a reflexive signification, which represent the agent as showing himself possessed of the quality of the action, or in which the signification is purely active, especially verbs, which are not used in Kal. Thus נֶאְדָּר, *to show oneself glorious;* נָלוֹן, to show oneself *obstinate, to murmur, complain;* נִבָּא, *to prophesy;* נִכְסָף, *to desire greatly;* נִקְרַב, *to approach;* נִשְׁבַּע, *to swear;* נִשְׁמַע, *to obey,* show oneself obedient; נִשְׁעָן, *to lean,* &c. And thus in the present case נוֹשָׁע, *showing himself a Saviour, having salvation, saving, a Saviour.* Thirdly, that the verb is so to be interpreted here, the combination of the term with צַדִּיק, *righteous,* clearly shows; for it occupies the same position in relation to that adjective, which the active participle רֹכֵב, *riding,* does to עָנִי, *lowly,* in the following clause of the verse. As in the latter case the Messiah's riding upon an ass was a proof or manifestation of his humility, so, in the former, his

10 And I will cut off the chariot from Ephraim,
    And the horse from Jerusalem;
    The battle-bow also shall be cut off;
    And he shall speak peace to the nations;
    And his rule shall be from sea to sea,
    And from the river to the ends of the earth.

actually having salvation for others was a manifestation of his possessing that righteousness which was indispensable for the justification of the guilty. See 1 Cor. i. 30; 2 Cor. v. 21; Phil. iii. 8, 9; 1 John ii. 1, 2. As the one feature contrasted with the haughty character of the Grecian conqueror, so the other contrasted with the cruelties that were inflicted by him on the cities which he captured. The Son of Man came not to destroy men's lives, but to save them. Fourthly, all the ancient versions render the verb actively. LXX. σώζων; Targ. פְּרִיק; Syr. ܦ݂ܵܪܘ̇ܩ; Vulg. *Salvator*. That עָנִי is here to be taken in the sense of *meek, lowly*, and not in that of *poor*, or *afflicted*, the connexion sufficiently shows. Thus the LXX., πραΰς. In proof of the mild and gentle character of the Messiah's reign, he is represented as riding upon an ass, which, though not in the East the degraded and despised animal which it is with us, being used by princes and other persons of rank, is nevertheless comparatively so as it regards the horse, and specially contrasts with the war-horse in the following verse. It was proverbially the symbol of peace, so that what the prophet here describes was at once calculated to inspire the mind with the conviction that the King of whom he spake was none other than the Prince of Peace, predicted Is. ix. 6. The ו in וְעַל עַיִר, " *and* upon a colt," is exegetical of the preceding. Comp. Gen. xlix. 11. אֲתֹנוֹת, *she-asses*, does not, as Michaelis would have it, convey the idea of the pedigree of the colt, as one of excellent breed, whose mothers could be traced back through several generations, but is merely an idiomatic form, the plural being used for the singular. Comp. הָרֵי אֲרָרָט, *mountains of Ararat*, i. e. *one* of the mountains, &c., Gen. viii. 4; עָרֵי גִלְעָד, *cities of Gilead*, i. e. *one* of them, Jud. xii. 7; and see on

Jonah i. 5. For the fulfilment of the prophecy, see Matt. xxi. 4, and the Commentators on that passage.

10. This verse contains a distinct announcement of the nature and extent of the Messiah's reign. Instead of leading forth the Jews to battle and conquest, as their Rabbins have long taught them to believe, he was in his providence completely to disarm them, and render them incapable of engaging in hostile conflict. How literally this was accomplished, their history subsequent to the destruction of Jerusalem by the Romans convincingly shows. The reign of the Messiah was not to be that of a worldly conqueror, like Alexander, nor was it to be confined, as to its boundaries, within the narrow limits of Palestine; but it was to be that under which the inestimable blessing of peace was pre-eminently to be enjoyed; it was to embrace the Gentiles, who had been excluded from the commonwealth of Israel; and, in point of extent, was to cover a vastly greater portion of territory than ever was possessed by the warrior of Macedon. On the circumstance that *Ephraim* is here mentioned, no valid argument can be built in favour of the hypothesis that this prophecy must have been delivered before the captivity of the ten tribes, since it is evidently the design of the prophet merely to describe the whole land of Canaan, the northern part of which still went by the ancient name, in contradistinction from *Judah*, which is here designated from Jerusalem, the capital. דִּבֶּר שָׁלוֹם, *to speak peace*, means to announce the message of the reconciliation effected by the Messiah. From the express inclusion of the גּוֹיִם, *nations*, among those who were to enjoy the benefits of the spiritual reign of the King of Zion, it is manifest that whatever may have been the originally restricted sense of מִיָּם עַד־יָם וּמִנָּהָר עַד־אַפְסֵי־אָרֶץ, as descriptive of the utmost bounds of the

11   As for thee also, by the blood of thy covenant,
      I will send forth thy prisoners out of the pit
      In which there is no water.
12 Return ye to the strong-hold, ye prisoners of hope,
      Even to-day I declare I will render to thee double;
13 For I have bent Judah for myself,
      I have filled the bow with Ephraim,

Hebrew kingdom, the words must here be taken in the widest possible extent of meaning, just as in Ps. lxxii. 8, where it is declared in the connexion, that *all nations* should serve the Messiah.

11. Having been led by his predictions respecting the expedition of Alexander in the direction of Egypt, to exhibit in boldest contrast the character and reign of the Prince of Peace, Zechariah returns to the subject which he had in hand—the state of the Jewish people in the times succeeding the captivity in Babylon. גַּם, *also*, connects what follows with verses 6—8. The feminine pronoun אַתְּ refers to בַּת־צִיּוֹן, or בַּת־יְרוּשָׁלַ͏ִם, ver. 9. The covenant here called בְּרִיתֵךְ, *thy covenant*, means the covenant made with the Hebrews at Sinai, and ratified by the sprinkling of the blood of the victims slain upon the occasion. By that act the nation was consecrated as a peculiar people to Jehovah, and taken under his special protection. The covenant is called theirs, because it had their government and happiness for its object. In virtue of the blood then shed, it is here declared that their covenant-God would release such of them as were still captives in foreign lands. By אֲסִירַיִךְ is meant, not prisoners whom the Jews had taken, but such of their own nation as were in the condition just described. After the death of Alexander many thousands of Jews were in a state of exile in Egypt, and many thousands more in that of actual slavery in Greece and other parts of the East. Their condition is described as that of prisoners confined in dungeons, which were commonly cisterns without water. See Jer. xxxviii. 6; Gen. xxxvii. 24. In consequence of the mud which remained in them, they were exceedingly noxious to health, and those consigned to them were considered as subjects of the deepest misery. שִׁלַּחְתִּי is

not here the proper preterite, as some interpreters construe it, but the prophetic future, which is thrown into the form of the preterite to express the certainty of the event.

12. With the Divine promise of release is connected the duty of the captives to embrace the opportunity afforded them of returning to their own land, where they should enjoy the protection and favour of the Most High. בִּצָּרוֹן occurs only in this place. It is derived from בָּצַר, *to cut off*, to prevent the approach of an enemy, to erect an inaccessible fortification; hence the signification of the noun, *strong-hold*, or *fortress*. LXX. ὀχύρωμα. It forcibly contrasts with בּוֹר, *the pit*, in the preceding verse, and for this reason is not to be interpreted of Jerusalem considered as again fortified, but is used figuratively to express the security and prosperity which those should enjoy who returned from captivity. Though captives, their condition was not hopeless. They were not to abandon themselves to despair, but to exercise confidence in the promise of God that he would assuredly deliver them, nor were they to wait for the arrival of any distant period when they might return as a body; even then (גַּם הַיּוֹם) they might individually avail themselves of the invitation, and share in the blessings. The abundance of these blessings is expressed by the term מִשְׁנֶה, *double*, which is elsewhere similarly employed to convey the idea of full or ample compensation, Is. lxi. 7. There is no foundation for the opinion of Michaelis, adopted by Blayney, who takes מַגִּיד to be a noun having the signification of מֶגֶד, *something precious*, and not the participle of Hiphil.

13. The declaration here made, that Jehovah would lead forth the Hebrews to military operations, and crown these operations with success, cannot be recon-

　　And raised up thy sons, O Zion!
　　Against thy sons, O Greece!
　　And made thee as the sword of a hero.

14　And Jehovah shall appear on their behalf,
　　And his arrows shall go forth as lightning;
　　Yea, the Lord Jehovah shall blow the trumpet,
　　And march in the storms of the south.

15　Jehovah of hosts shall protect them,
　　And they shall devour, and tread down the sling-stones;
　　They shall drink, they shall be noisy, as those who drink wine;
　　They shall be full as the bowl,
　　As the corners of the altar.

16　And Jehovah their God shall save his people,

---

ciled with the statement made ver. 10, on any other principle but that which refers them to two totally different periods of time. The one, as explained above, is predictive of the condition to which the nation was to be reduced after the advent of Messiah, instead of having become, under his reign, as they vainly expected, the conquerors of the world; the other sets forth the successful wars in which they would engage with the Grecian rulers of Syria under the command of the Maccabees. The prophecy is parallel with that of Daniel, chap. xi. 32. For the fulfilment, see 1 Macc. i. 62; ii. 41—43; iii. 43, &c. By a bold and expressive figure, the Hebrews are represented as the bows and arrows of Jehovah, the military implements which he would employ in resisting and overcoming the Grecians under Antiochus Epiphanes. By בְּנֵי־יָוָן, the sons of Greece, we are to understand, not the Greeks resident in Ionia or Greece, but those composing the army of the monarch just mentioned. Grotius remarks, that at the time here referred to, the Jews were accustomed to call the kings both of Syria and Egypt, מַלְכֵי־יָוָן, kings of Greece, because they were of Grecian extraction.

14. Here commences a number of special promises of Divine interposition and protection. Considering what the Jews had experienced from hostile armies, it was necessary to disarm their fears by such assurances, that God was on

their side. He is represented as appearing in the thunderstorm, with the lightnings of which his arrows are compared, and with the noise of its thunders, the sound of his trumpet, summoning to the attack. For "the storms of the south," see on Is. xxi. 1.

15. After אָכְלוּ, they shall eat, supply בָּשָׂר, flesh, i. e. of their enemies; and after שָׁתוּ supply דָּם, their blood. This highly figurative language is frequently employed in Scripture to express the destruction of enemies in battle. כְּמוֹ־יַיִן, like wine, is elliptical for כְּמוֹ־שֹׁתֵי־יַיִן, like those who drink wine. Before חָמוּ, thirty-two MSS., originally four more, three by correction, eight printed editions, and the Rabbins Nathan, Kimchi, and Abarbanel, supply the conjunctive ו. By אַבְנֵי קֶלַע, sling-stones, the enemies are meant, as clearly appears from the contrasted form of expression, אַבְנֵי נֵזֶר, stones of a crown, descriptive of the Jews, in the following verse. The phrase conveys the idea of feebleness and contempt. The stones used for slinging are otherwise of no use or value. Carrying forward the idea of blood, reference is made to מִזְרָק, the bowl, which was used to receive that of the sacrifices, and to זָוִית, the corners of the altar, on the horns of which it was sprinkled. Abundant as was the blood thus shed and sprinkled should be that of the enemies of the Hebrews.

16. For כְּצֹאן עַמּוֹ, as sheep, his people, comp. כְּצֹאן עֲמֵהּ. The words are neither

He shall save them as sheep in that day ;
For they shall be as the stones of a crown,
Carrying themselves highly over his land.

17 For how great is his goodness! and how great his beauty!
Corn shall cause the young men to thrive,
And new wine the maids.

in construction, nor in apposition, but are to be separated, so as to connect עִמּוֹ with הוֹשִׁיעַ, understood as repeated from the beginning of the verse. By אַבְנֵי־נֵזֶר, *crown-stones*, are meant the precious stones or gems which were set in crowns, and were of great value. The elevation of these, and consequently of the crown which contained them, was strongly indicative of victory. For נָסַם in the acceptation of being *high*, comp.

the Arab. نَصَّ, *elevavit rem ;* in the viii. Conj. *elatus fuit ;* نَصّ, *elevatus thronus.*

17. The affix in מִּוּבוֹ and יָפְיוֹ is most naturally to be associated with that in אַדְמָתוֹ at the close of the preceding verse, and referred to Jehovah. The meaning is,

the goodness and beauty which he bestows. Compare Jer. xxxi. 12 ; Ps. xxv. 7. יְנוֹבֵב, though occurring in the latter half, is common to both parts of the sentence. Piel has here the causative power of Hiphil. The root is נוּב, to *sprout, germinate, grow up.* The prophet refers to the plenty which there should be in the land after the destruction of the enemy. The drinking of must by young females is peculiar to this passage; but its being here expressly sanctioned by Divine authority, furnishes an unanswerable argument against those who would interdict all use of the fruit of the vine. תִּירוֹשׁ, *new wine* or *must*, so called from יָרַשׁ, *to take possession of,* because when taken to excess, it gains the mastery over the person who indulges in it.

CHAPTER X

This chapter continues the subject with which the preceding concluded. The Hebrews are exhorted to apply to Jehovah for the constant supply of temporal blessings, 1, and are warned against an imitation of the conduct of their forefathers, who had recourse to false oracles, on account of which they and their rulers had been carried into captivity, 2, 3. Promises are then made of government by rulers of their own nation, and the victorious operations of their armies, 4, 5 ; the complete re-establishment of the theocracy, 6, 7 ; the restoration of such of the nation as still remained in foreign countries, especially in the East, and in Egypt, 8—11 ; and the chapter concludes with an assurance of the security and happiness which they should enjoy under the divine protection, 12.

---

1 ASK ye from Jehovah rain in the time of the latter rain :

1. This verse stands in the closest connexion with the preceding. חֲזִיזִים, *lightnings*, the precursors of rain. מְטַר גֶּשֶׁם, lit. *rain of heavy rain,* i. e. *plentiful*

Jehovah maketh the lightnings,
And giveth them the heavy rain,
To every one grass in the field.

2 Surely the household gods spake vanity,
And the diviners saw a lie ;
Yea, they told false dreams,
They gave vapour for comfort;
Therefore they wandered as sheep ;
They were afflicted because there was no shepherd.

3 My anger burned against the shepherds,
And I punished the he-goats;
Nevertheless Jehovah of hosts hath visited his flock, the house
     of Judah,
And made them as his splendid horse in war.

4 From him shall be the corner-stone,
From him the peg,

---

rain. Comp. Job xxxvii. 6, where the same words occur, only their order is inverted.

2. הַתְּרָפִים, *the teraphim,* or household gods, are opposed to Jehovah in the preceding verse. The term occurs only in the plural, and is of uncertain derivation. Gesenius refers it to the Arab.

تَرَف, *to live in comfort,* and considers it as signifying the indicators or givers of pleasure or happiness; Lee to the Eth. ፕርፋ : *reliquus fuit, superfuit,* and thinks *relics* are meant. They appear to have had the form of the human body, and to have been consulted as oracles. See on Hos. iii. 4. The preterites and futures, which are intermixed, are all to be taken in the strictly past time, reference being had to the evils which had prevailed among the Jews, on account of which they had been carried away to Babylon, and against any further indulgence in which they are here warned. They were exposed afresh to the influence of idolatrous practices by their intercourse with the Syro-Grecian and Egyptian troops, which repeatedly traversed the land. Antiochus Epiphanes actually set up a heathen idol in the temple at Jerusalem, and ordered temples

and altars to be erected in the different cities throughout the country.

3. The verb פָּקַד is here used both in a good and a bad sense; followed by the preposition עַל, it signifies to *visit for evil, to punish;* governing the accusative, to *visit with good.* The ו in וְעַל is properly the ו conversive, so that אֶפְקוֹד is to be rendered in the preterite, to agree with חָרָה. By "he-goats" are meant the chiefs or leaders of the nation. יֶעֱנוּ, ver. 2, all the versions render, as if it had been וְעָנוּ, in the preterite, which the connexion requires. The "shepherds" and "he-goats" are used synonymously of the civil rulers. In the middle of this verse is a sudden transition from the calamitous condition to which the Jews had been reduced as a punishment for their sins, to that of prosperity and military prowess to which they were raised in the time of the Maccabees. In the preceding chapter they had been set forth under the images of the bows and arrows ; here they are represented under that of the battle-horse. The horse selected by the commander of an army on which to ride at its head, was stately and richly caparisoned. The כ in כְּסוּס is the Caph veritatis.

4. מִמֶּנּוּ thrice repeated, possesses much emphasis. The nominative is יְהוָה in the

From him the battle-bow,
From him shall go forth each and every rule
5 And as heroes shall they trample the enemy
In the mud of the streets in battle;
They shall fight, for Jehovah is with them,
And put to shame the riders on horses.
6 For I will strengthen the house of Judah,
And deliver the house of Joseph,
And will settle them, because I have pitied them;
And they shall be as if I had not cast them off;
For I Jehovah am their God, and will answer them.
7 And Ephraim shall be as a hero,
And their heart shall rejoice, as those who drink wine;
Their sons also shall see it and be glad;
Their heart shall exult in Jehovah.

preceding verse. The Hebrews were not now to be subject to governors of foreign extraction or appointment, but were to be independent, enjoying the benefits of a native rule. By פִּנָּה, *corner-stone*, is meant the prince or governor, on whom the political edifice may be said metaphorically to rest. The word is derived from פָּנָה, *to turn*, and primarily signifies a *turning-point, angle* or *corner* of a building. With us a nail would be an insignificant image; but יָתֵד, the Oriental nail, is a large peg in the inside of a room, wrought into the wall when the house is built, and on which are hung all kinds of household stuff, together with the different implements of war. See on Is. xxii. 23. One of these, *the bow*, is mentioned immediately after, and stands for the whole. נוֹגֵשׂ is used here simply in the sense of *ruler*. Compare the Eth. ሠርጉ : *king*.

5. Supply אֹיְבִים, *enemies*, as the object to בּוֹסִים, *trampling*, and compare Is. xiv. 25; lxiii. 6. רֹכְבֵי סוּסִים refer to the numerous cavalry which composed the chief strength of the Syro-Grecian army (see 1 Macc. iii. 39), but which were put to the rout by a mere handful of Jews.

6. "The house of Joseph" stands for the ten tribes, in contradistinction to those of Judah and Benjamin, to which is given the name of "Judah" as the more important of the two. It is clear from the reference thus made, that part, if not most of all the tribes, returned and took possession of their patrimonial lands after the captivity. הוֹשְׁבוֹתִים is a mixed form, supposed by Kimchi, Abarbanel, and some others, to have been artificially compounded of הֲשִׁיבֹתִים, the Hiphil of שׁוּב, *to return*, and הוֹשַׁבְתִּים, the Hiphil of יָשַׁב, *to sit* or *dwell*, in order to express in one word both verbs as used by Jeremiah, וַהֲשִׁיבֹתִים אֶל־הַמָּקוֹם הַזֶּה וְהֹשַׁבְתִּים לָבֶטַח, chap. xxxii. 37; but it is far more probable that the word is a corruption of הוֹשַׁבְתִּים, introduced through inadvertence by some transcriber. Such is, indeed, the reading of many MSS. and of four printed editions, and is supported by the LXX. κατοικιῶ. The reading הֲשִׁיבֹתִים, has the support of the Syr., Vulg., and Targ., but is less suitable to the connexion.

7. As the state of things here described was brought about by the heroic conduct of Ephraim, it is obvious the return from the captivity cannot be intended, for the Hebrews were altogether passive on that occasion. The reason why special mention is here made of the ten tribes may be their longer rejection by the Lord, and the exiled state in which many of them still were in the days of the prophet. אֶפְרַיִם, as a collective noun, is the nominative to הָיָה. For כְּמוֹ־יַיִן see on chap. ix. 15.

8 I will whistle for them and gather them,
  For I have redeemed them,
  And they shall increase, as they did increase.
9 Though I have scattered them among the nations,
  Yet they shall remember me in the distant regions,
  And shall live with their children, and return.
10 I will bring them back from the land of Egypt,
  And gather them from Assyria;
  And I will bring them to the land of Gilead and Lebanon,
  And room shall not be found for them.
11 And He shall pass over the sea,
  He shall cleave and smite the waves of the sea,
  And all the deeps of the river shall dry up;
  Yea, the pride of Assyria shall be brought down,
  And the sceptre of Egypt shall depart.

8. An express promise of the restoration, settlement, and increase of the ten tribes, many of whom were still at that time in a state of exile. They were to be brought back to Palestine, and placed in a condition in which they should be able to act valiantly in defence of their country. The verb שָׁרַק signifies *to whistle*, or give a shrill sound, as those who keep bees do, who, by means of a whistle, or pipe, call them out from and back to their hives. See on Is. v. 26. Josephus informs us, that two hundred years after the time here referred to, Galilee was peopled to an amazing extent, studded with cities, towns, and villages; and adds, that the villages were not what were usually called by that name, but contained, some of them, fifteen thousand inhabitants. Jewish Wars, book iii. ch. iii. § 2.

9. The first two Vaus are employed antithetically, the former having the signification of *though* or *indeed*; the latter, that of *but* or *yet*. זָרַע cannot here mean *to sow*, as Hengstenberg contends, but must be rendered *scatter*, which the verb primarily signifies, and the connexion here requires. The last clause of the verse indicates the settled enjoyment of chartered privileges as before the dispersion, when the Hebrews should return to their own land.

10. We have no historical account of any specific removal of any belonging to the ten tribes into Egypt, but it cannot be doubted that, as in the case of the Jews in the time of Jeremiah, many of them betook themselves to that country for refuge on the invasion of Tiglath-pileser; and when Ptolemy attempted to seize the whole of Syria, and carried away 100,000 captives, whom he settled in Alexandria and Cyrene, vast numbers of them must have consisted of the descendants of those Israelites who had returned from the Eastern captivity. Those who had remained in the East were also to return. Comp. Is. xi. 11. נִמְצָא has here the signification of there being *sufficient* or *enough*, as in Kal, Numb. xi. 22; Jud. xxi. 14. מָקוֹם, *room*, or *place*, is understood. So great should be the number of inhabitants, that the territory, however ample and fertile, would not be able to furnish them with the necessary supplies.

11. There is here an allusion to the original deliverance of the Hebrew people at the Red Sea. Comp. Is. xi. 15. The Divine interposition in behalf of those who were still in Egypt is not expressly compared with what then took place, but such comparison is implied. צָרָה has been variously rendered. The LXX. στενῇ; Vulg.. *freto*; Syr. أَوْدَخِنُ, *angustia*; Calvin, *afflictio*; Hengstenberg, *the distress*; Blayney, *Tyre*; Hitzig, *Zara*, by which he understands the Nile. The

12 And I will strengthen them through Jehovah,
And they shall walk up and down in his name,
Saith Jehovah.

difficulty is at once removed by taking צָרָה as a verb, with the Aramaic signification of צְרָא, زرّ, *cut, cleave, divide.* Comp. the Arab. صرى, *resecuit, amputavit.* In which case three verbs, having Jehovah understood as their nominative, will follow in regular order : וְעָבַר בַּיָּם צָרָה וְהִכָּה בַיָּם גַּלִּים. *And he shall pass over the sea ; he shall cleave and smite the waves of the sea.* The last words are literally, *he shall smite the sea into waves ;* or, *as to the sea, he will smite its waves.* Comp. Exod. xiv. 16, 21 ; Is. xi. 15, 16. That by "the river," the Nile, and not the

Euphrates, is meant, the use of the Egyptian word יְאוֹר places beyond dispute. See on Is. xix. 6. With respect to אַשּׁוּר, *Asshur,* it may justly be queried whether the Syro-Greek kingdom be not intended—that kingdom occupying not only the territory which belonged to ancient Assyria, but extending still further towards the east. The pride of that power, as well as the Egypto-Greek sceptre, was to be swept away.

12. The phrase, הִתְהַלֵּךְ בְּשֵׁם, *to walk in the name* of a deity, is a Hebrew mode of speech, descriptive of a course of action pursued in accordance with his character and will. Comp. Micah iv. 5.

CHAPTER XI

It is obvious, from the nature of the predictions contained in this and the following chapters, that they must have been delivered at a time subsequent to the erection of the temple. As they are exclusively occupied with denunciations of evil against the Jews, with the exception of interjected prophecies of the Messiah, and one relative to the final deliverance of the covenant people, they would have dispirited rather than encouraged those who were engaged in building the sacred edifice. It may be said, indeed, that there were many carnal and secure persons among the Jews, who required to be warned, and that the following denunciations were designed for their benefit ; but, as the predictions do not relate to the times in which those persons lived, it is not conceivable how they could have so appropriated them as to derive effectual advantage from them. Besides, they contain no instances of direct address, or personal application of the truths delivered, such as we find in the other prophets when addressing themselves to their contemporaries for their immediate benefit. It may, therefore, be concluded, that they were communicated by Zechariah on some occasion or occasions of which we have no knowledge.

The scenes here depicted lay in the more distant future. In the present chapter the prophet furnishes a bold figurative description of the destruction of the temple by the Romans, and the utter consternation into which the priests and rulers of the people should thereby be thrown, 1—3. He then describes certain symbolical actions performed by him in vision, by which he personated the Messiah, who had been promised as the Shepherd of his people, setting forth his commission to teach and rule them, 4 ; their deplorable condition in consequence of the rapacious disposition of their leaders, 5 ; and the judgments that should over-

take them in consequence of their wickedness, 6.   Under the emblems of two
staves, the relation of the whole nation to God, as their protector, and the relation of the different tribes among themselves, are exhibited, and the cessation of
these relations is pointed out by the act of breaking the staves, 7—14. The
three last verses set forth the character of Herod, and the judgment of God
upon him for his wickedness, 15—17.

---

1 OPEN, O Lebanon! thy gates,
      That the fire may devour thy cedars.
2 Howl, ye cypresses! for the cedars have fallen,
      Because the magnificent are destroyed;
      Howl, ye oaks of Bashan! for the fortified forest hath come down.
3 There is the sound of the howling of the shepherds,
      Because their magnificence is destroyed;
      There is the sound of the roaring of young lions,
      Because the pride of Jordan is destroyed.

1. Some interpret this verse literally
of the locality so called; others understand it figuratively, but apply it either
to Jerusalem, or to the whole land of
Palestine. The construction which most
commends itself is that which applies it
to the temple restrictively. Such is the
ancient rabbinical interpretation. To
the same effect is the remarkable declaration of Rabbi Johanan Ben Zakkai:
"O sanctuary, sanctuary! why dost
thou trouble thyself? I know of thee
that thine end is to be left desolate,
for Zechariah, the son of Iddo, has
prophesied against thee long ago. Open
thy doors, O Lebanon, that the fire may
devour thy cedars." Talmud, Bab.
Yoma. fol. 39, col. 2. This interpretation seems to be referred to by Josephus,
in his Jewish Wars, bk. vi. ch. v. § 3.
The temple might with all propriety be
figuratively called Lebanon, not only
because the cedars with which it was
built were brought from that mountain,
but because as Lebanon was the most
stately and magnificent of all in the
vicinity of Palestine, so the temple was
the most glorious of all objects in or
about Jerusalem. Its gates were kept
carefully shut against all who had no
right to tread its courts. Now it was
to become a prey to the flames. The
prediction received its literal fulfilment
in spite of the utmost solicitude of the
Roman general to preserve the edifice.
In vain did he attempt to save it from
the flames, so that in a short time it
was entirely consumed.

2. בְּרוֹשׁ, *the cypress*, was greatly inferior to the *cedar*, but was employed
for the floors and ceilings of the temple.
"The oaks of Bashan" were also used
for purposes of building. These terms,
however, are likewise to be interpreted
figuratively of the priests and rulers of
the temple, its superior and inferior
officers, together with the judges of the
people. אַדִּיר is used both of animate
and inanimate objects. It is here
employed to denote those who were
elevated in dignity and magnificent in
apparel. Comp. אַדִּירֵי הַצֹּאן. By יַעַר הַבָּצוּר,
the fortified or *inaccessible forest*, is
meant Jerusalem, the houses of which
were numerous and close together as
the trees of the forest, and round which
the Jews had thrown up a wall of great
strength. Comp. Micah iii. 12. For בָּצוּר,
many MSS., and two early editions, read
בָּצִיר, which is only another form to express
the same thing.

3. The Jewish rulers are called
"shepherds," with reference to their
office, and "young lions," in regard to

4   Thus saith Jehovah my God,
     Feed the sheep of slaughter;
5 Whose possessors kill them, and are not held guilty;
   And each of those who sell them saith,
   Blessed be Jehovah, I am enriched;
   And none of whose shepherds spareth them.

their fierce and rapacious disposition. The אַדֶּרֶת, was the *magnificence* of the temple of which they boasted. Comp. Mark xiii. 1; Luke xxi. 5. גְּאוֹן הַיַּרְדֵּן, *the pride of Jordan,* i. e. the thickets which ornament its banks, and furnish excellent lairs for lions, has the same figurative reference, and is selected to correspond to the young lions immediately preceding. Comp. Jer. xii. 5; xlix. 19. The leaders of the Jews are represented as indulging in loud wailings of despair, on account of the destruction of their temple and polity.

4, 5. The prophet now proceeds to point out the cause of the destruction which he had figuratively described, and that of the people which was connected with it—the obstinate refusal of their rulers to receive the doctrine of the Messiah. By צֹאן הַהֲרֵגָה, *the sheep of slaughter,* are meant the people devoted to destruction. Comp. צֹאן טִבְחָה, Ps. xliv. 23. At the fall of Jerusalem not fewer than 1,100,000 Jews perished, and near a million and a half altogether in the course of the war. It has been questioned, who is the person directed in this verse to assume the office of a shepherd, and who declares, ver. 7, that he performed the duties of that office? Frischmuth, Marckius, Michaelis, and others, are of opinion that it is the Messiah, and, unquestionably, if ultimate reference be had to him, this is the true interpretation; but it is equally clear that the prophet is to be regarded as having received the commission, and performed, in vision, what was enjoined upon him. What proves this, is the putting into the hands of the same person the instruments of a foolish shepherd, ver. 15, an action which can with no propriety be referred to the Messiah. On this principle, most of the difficulties connected with the exegesis of the intervening verses vanish. Zecha-

riah had all the transactions presented to his view in prophetic vision, but what he describes was actually done, not in his own personal history, nor in any outward occurrences between him and the Jews of his time, but in the personal history and office of the Messiah whom he personated. He did not really feed or teach those who were to be slain, but the Messiah and his apostles did; and had the Jews believed their message, the awful calamity would have been averted. The hypothesis of a prophetic vision was first advanced by Maimonides, and is ably supported by Hengstenberg, in his Christology, and by Dr. M'Caul, in his translation of Kimchi on our prophet. That by the buyers and sellers of the Jewish people, we are not to understand the Romans, but their own unprincipled teachers and rulers, the facts of the case show. The corresponding term רֹעֵיהֶם, *their shepherds,* is merely expletive of what the same persons were officially. The avarice of the Pharisees was excessive, yet they had the barefaced hypocrisy to thank God for their ill-gotten wealth; and because they were not punished, they imagined they might persevere with impunity. The construction of the plural nouns קֹנֵיהֶן, מֹכְרֵיהֶן, and רֹעֵיהֶם, with the singulars יֹאמַר and יַחְמוֹל, cannot, with any propriety, be accounted for on the principle advanced by Hengstenberg, that Jehovah himself was the principal actor, and that the wicked rulers were merely his instruments. It is only a more emphatic mode of construction, by which each of the individuals specified in the plural is represented as performing the action, see Gen. xxvii. 29; Exod. xxxi. 14; Prov. iii. 18. The masculine affix הֶם refers to the people, strictly so taken; the feminine הֶן, refers to them as considered under the idea of the sheep that were to be fed, צֹאן being of the common

6   For I will no more spare the inhabitants of the land, saith Jehovah,
But behold! I will deliver the men,
Each into the hand of his neighbour, and into the hand of his king;
And they shall destroy the land,
And I will not deliver them out of their hand.

7   And I fed the sheep of slaughter, truly miserable sheep! And
I took to myself two crooks; the one I called Grace, and the

gender. There is, therefore, no ground for correcting the text by changing רֹעֵיהֶם into רֹעִיהֶן, the reading of fifteen MSS. and some printed editions.

6. The particle כִּי, *for*, connects what follows with the command, ver. 4. The Jews were no longer to have Divine pity extended to them, but were to be abandoned to all the evils of civil discord, and to the oppressions of a foreign rule. That the king here referred to was the Roman emperor, is obvious from the acknowledgment of the Jews themselves: "We have no king but Cæsar." John xix. 15. The verb כָּתַת, *to beat*, or *dash in pieces*, is most appropriately chosen to express the destructive measures adopted by the Romans, by which the Jewish polity was broken up. The nominative is the troops of the foreign ruler that had just been spoken of.

7. The prophet declares, in the name of the Messiah, that he executed the task committed to him. This was fulfilled during the personal ministry of our Lord. לָכֵן עֲנִיֵּי הַצֹּאן have been variously rendered. LXX. εἰς τὴν Χαναανίτιν· Syr. ܠܡܣܟܢܐ ܕܥܢܐ, *the little ones on account of the collection of the sheep*. Vulg. *propter hoc, ó pauperes gregis*. Leo Juda, *adeoque pauperes gregis*. Tremellius and Junius, *vos inquam. ó pauperes gregis*. Schmid, J. H. Michaelis, Newcome, Hitzig, and others, *propter vos, o miseri gregis*. Maurer, *pavi igitur miserrimas ovium*. Arnheim, fürwahr die elendesten der Heerde. Ewald, wirklich die unglücklichsten Schafe. The only real difficulty lies in the word לָכֵן. The LXX. have read it, and the following word, as one, thus, לִכְנַעֲנִי, and made *Canaanite* of it. This rendering is adopted by Blayney, only he attaches to the term the idea

of *merchant*, which it sometimes has (*among those who trafficked with the flock*), and explains it of the buyers and sellers of the flock, described ver. 5. The interpretation is so far specious, and is approved by Jahn, but cannot be philologically sustained. Some take לָכֵן for the infinitive in Hiphil of כּוּן, which furnishes no tolerable sense; others, for the dative of the second personal feminine pronoun, supposing the Segol to have been changed into a Tzêre, but this is liable to the same objection. Most regard it as the particle לָכֵן, and construe it either with its causal, or its adversative signification; but neither do any of the interpretations thus brought out satisfactorily meet the exigencies of the case. I cannot help thinking that the ל is here redundant, as it is in many instances, and that we must construe כֵּן, as in ver. 11, where it occurs without the ל. The term is properly a participial noun, derived from כּוּן, in the sense of the Arab. كون, *esse*, and implies *reality*, *certainty*, or the like, but admits of being variously rendered, according to the context in which it is found. See Lee's Heb. Lex. *in voc*. And thus it is understood by Kimchi, Jarchi, Castalio, De Dieu, Drusius, Storr, Dathe, Arnheim, De Wette, and Ewald. Even were the ל retained, the same result would be brought out, the rendering in this case being, *with respect to truth*, i.e. *truly*; just as in לָנֶצַח, *with respect to perpetuity*, i.e. *for ever*. The words עֲנִיֵּי הַצֹּאן are the superlative of construction, as in רְעֵי גוֹיִם, *the most wicked of nations*, Ezek. vii. 24; מִבְחַר בְּרוֹשָׁיו, *the choicest of his cypresses*, Is. xxxvii. 24; or, what is quite parallel with the present case, צְעִירֵי הַצֹּאן, rendered in our common version, *the least of the flock*, Jer. xlix. 20. The article is as usual to be referred to the

8 other I called Bands, and I fed the sheep. And I cut off
   the three shepherds within one month; and my soul loathed
9 them, and their soul also rejected me. So that I said:
     I will not feed you;
     That which is dying, let it die;
     And that which is being cut off, let it be cut off;
     And as for the rest, let them eat each the flesh of another.
10   I then took my crook Grace, and cut it asunder, in order to break

former of the two nouns, and both might
be rendered, *the most miserable of sheep*,
or *the most miserable sheep*. Such was
the state to which the Jewish people
were reduced in the days of our Lord.
They were ἐσκυλμένοι καὶ ἐῤῥιμμένοι,
ὡσεὶ πρόβατα μὴ ἔχοντα ποιμένα, Matt.
ix. 36. They were *worried* and *harassed*
in every possible way, πρόβατα ἀπολω-
λότα, Matt. x. 6. The two staves were
symbolical of the different modes of
treatment which the Hebrews had experienced under the guidance and protection of the providence of God. One
of them was called נֹעַם, *Grace*, or *Favour*,
to indicate the kindness of Jehovah to
them in restraining the surrounding
nations from overpowering them, and
carrying them again into captivity. See
ver. 10. To the other was given the
name of חֹבְלִים, which Drusius, Marckius,
the Dutch translators, and others, render
Binders, but better, *Bands*, expressing
the ties which unite parties together.
The LXX., Aq., Symm., σχοίνισμα;
Vulg. *funiculi;* Maurer, *conjuncti, fœde-
rati.* Reference is had to the fra-
ternal confederacy into which the Jews
and Israelites had entered with each
other after the return from Babylon.
See ver. 14. The last clause of the
verse is a repetition of the first, for the
sake of emphasis.

8. Who were " the three shepherds "
here definitely pointed out, cannot be
determined with certainty. All kinds
of interpretations have been given, from
Moses, Aaron, and Miriam, (suggested
to Jerome by his Hebrew Rabbi,) to
the Roman emperors Galbus, Otho, and
Vitellius, in Calmet. The only construction which is at all entitled to any
notice, is that which regards the language
as descriptive of the three orders of rulers
in the Jewish state—the priests, the

teachers of the law, and the civil magistrates. These were the persons of
influence by whom the affairs of the
nation were conducted, and to whose
wickedness, which reached its culmi-
nating point when they crucified the
Lord of Glory, the destruction of the
state is to be ascribed. יֶרַח אֶחָד, *one
month*, doubtless refers to the last period
of the siege of Jerusalem, when everything was thrown into confusion, and
all authority came to an end. כָּחַד, *to
hide, conceal;* in Hiphil, as here, ἀφα-
νίζειν, *to cause to disappear, to cause to
cease with respect to office, to remove
from it.* The last two lines of the verse
point out the mutual dissatisfaction and
disgust with which the wicked rulers
and the Messiah regarded each other.
בָּחַל, occurs only here, and Prov. xx. 21.
Comp. the cognate root גָּעַל, *to reject*,
and the Arab. بَحَلَ, *impulsus validus,
propulsio vehemens;* بَهَلَ, *maledixit*, III.
execratus fuit.

9. The entire abandonment of the
Hebrew people is here most affectingly
set forth. For the threefold destruction
here predicted, comp. Jer. xv. 1, 2;
xxxiv. 17; Ezek. vi. 12. And for the
fulfilment, see Josephus.

10. By this symbolical action, the
removal of the restraint which Jehovah
had exercised over the nations, whereby
the destruction of the Jewish people
had been prevented, is strikingly represented. The exercise of restraint with
respect to hostile forces is elsewhere
spoken of under the idea of a covenant.
See Job v. 23; Ezek. xxxiv. 25; Hos.
ii. 18. When this restraint was removed,
the Romans invaded Judæa, and destroyed the city and polity of the ancient
people of God. That by עַמִּים, *people*,

11 my covenant which I had made with all the nations. And it was
broken in that day, and the miserable sheep that gave heed to
12 me, knew of a truth that it was the word of Jehovah. And I
said to them, If it be good in your eyes, give my reward; and
if not, forbear. So they weighed my reward, thirty pieces of
13 silver. And Jehovah said to me, Cast it to the potter, the

or *nations*, we are to understand foreign nations, and not the Hebrew tribes, is now agreed among the best interpreters.

11. The anticipated accomplishment of the prediction, and the conviction wrought in the minds of the pious portion of the Jewish people, that the prediction was indeed divine. For the force of פֶּן see on ver. 7. The LXX. again join the two words, and render, οἱ Χαναναῖοι.

12, 13. On the question of the application of these verses to the circumstances narrated Matt. xxvii. 7—10, a very decided difference of opinion has obtained. This difference has been occasioned, partly by the fact of certain discrepancies existing between the accounts which they furnish of the transactions, and partly by the more important consideration that the Evangelist expressly ascribes the words which he quotes to Jeremiah, and not to Zechariah. With respect to the former of these points, it may, to a considerable extent, be obviated by the general observation, that the discrepancies are not greater than we meet with in several other quotations made from the Old Testament by the writers of the New, and are by no means such as to affect the end which either the prophet or the Evangelist had in view. In producing the citation, the latter had his eye more intent upon the historical circumstances which he had just detailed, than upon the strict grammatical construction and verbality of the language employed in the prophecy. He fixes upon the principal points, the despicable price at which the Messiah had been sold, and the appropriation of the money as a compensation to the potter for the possession of his field; and having faithfully exhibited these to the view of his readers, he is less solicitous about the wording of the prophet. The very changes which he introduces into the phraseology are

such as his position in the character of an historian required. Thus, instead of אֲשֶׁר יָקַרְתִּי מֵעֲלֵיהֶם, *at which I was estimated by them*, Matthew has ὃν ἐτιμήσαντο ἀπὸ υἱῶν Ἰσραὴλ, *at which he was estimated by the sons of Israel.* Instead of וָאֶקְחָה שְׁלֹשִׁים הַכָּסֶף, *And I took the thirty pieces of silver*, we find, καὶ ἔλαβον τὰ τριάκοντα ἀργύρια, *and they took the thirty pieces of silver.* Instead of וָאַשְׁלִיךְ אֹתוֹ, *and I threw it*, the Gospel has, καὶ ἔδωκαν αὐτά, *and they gave them.* The freedom with which the Evangelist renders שְׁלֵךְ by δίδωμι is the more noticeable, since he employs the participle ῥίψας in reference to the same subject in the fifth verse, where, at the same time, he renders בֵּית יְהֹוָה by ἐν τῷ ναῷ. The conjecture of some that יוֹצֵר, *potter*, is a corruption of אוֹצֵר, *treasurer*, is worse than gratuitous, as the latter word nowhere occurs in Hebrew in reference to such an office, and as the potter was the most suitable person to whom to cast the despicable sum, occupying as he did a workshop in the valley of Hinnom, (Jer. xviii. 2, 3; xix. 2,) which was held in abomination by the Jews. That the Evangelist should have ascribed the prediction to Jeremiah has proved a source of great perplexity to critics. No person who has read the passage in Zechariah can peruse that in Matthew without at once being reminded of it. And so exactly do they tally in every important point, that no doubt of their relationship can for a moment be entertained. On the other hand, no such passage is to be found in any part of the prophecies of Jeremiah. The solution of the difficulty proposed by Hengstenberg, that it was the object of our prophet to bring forward to view the predictions contained in Jer. xviii. and xix., in order to point out the destruction of Jerusalem by the Romans, and that on this ground the Evangelist might, with all propriety, ascribe the authorship to Jeremiah, is very unsatisfactory; and

splendid price at which I was estimated by them! And I took
the thirty pieces of silver, and cast them into the house of
Jehovah, to the potter..

14 Then I cut asunder my second crook Bands, in order to break
the brotherhood between Judah and Israel.

we are shut up to one or other of the
following conclusions: First, that the
one name was substituted for the other
by a *lapsus memoriæ*. Secondly, that
the portion of the book of Zechariah,
in which the words are found, though
now bearing his name, was actually
written by Jeremiah, and by some means
or other, to us unknown, has been appended to the real prophecies of Zechariah. Thirdly, that the citation is made
from an apocryphal book of the prophet
Jeremiah. Or lastly, that there is a
corruption of the name in the Greek
text of Matthew. The first of these
positions will not be admitted by any
who believe in the plenary inspiration
of the Apostles; a doctrine fully established on Scripture authority, and which,
if denied, would completely annihilate
our confidence in their testimony, since
if their memory might fail, or they might
be mistaken in one instance, such might
be the case in hundreds. For a refutation of the second hypothesis, see the
Preface, in which it is shown that there
is no solid foundation for the opinion,
that the last six chapters of Zechariah
were not written by that prophet. With
respect to the third supposition, it cannot
be denied that there was an apocryphal
book of Jeremiah, containing an analogous passage. Jerome found it among
the Nazarenes, and a portion of it still
exists in a Sahidic Lectionary, in the Codex Huntingtonianus 5, in the Bodleian
Library, Oxford, and in the Coptic
language in the MS. 51 fol. in the
library of St. Germain in Paris. The
words are as follows: "Jeremiah spake
again to Pashur, Ye and your fathers
have resisted the truth, and your sons,
which shall come after you, will commit
more grievous sins than ye. For they
will give the price of him that is valued,
and do injury to him that maketh the
sick whole, and forgiveth iniquity: And
they will take thirty pieces of silver, the
price which the children of Israel have
given. They have given them for the
potter's field, as the Lord commanded.

And thus it shall be spoken: The sentence
of eternal punishment shall fall upon
them, and upon their children, because
they have shed innocent blood." But
who does not perceive in this fragment
the clumsy attempt of one of the early
Christians to support the cause of truth
by what was deemed a harmless fraud?
Jerome at once rejected it as spurious,
and expresses his belief that Matthew
made his citation from Zechariah. It
only remains, that we assume a corruption in the Greek text of the Evangelist.
That a variety of reading exists, has long
been matter of notoriety. Augustine
mentions, that in his time some MSS.
omitted the name of Ἰερεμίου. It is
also omitted in the MS. 33, 157; in the
Syriac, which is the most ancient of all
the versions; in the Polyglott Persic,
and in a Persic MS. in my possession,
bearing date A.D. 1057; in the modern
Greek; in the Verona and Vercelli Latin
MSS., and in a Latin MS. of Luc. Brug.
The Greek MS. 22, reads Ζαχαρίου, as
also do the Philoxenian Syriac in the
margin, and an Arabic MS. quoted by
Bengel. Origen and Eusebius were in
favour of this reading. I think it very
probable that Matthew did not insert
either name, but simply wrote in his
Hebrew Gospel, הנביא ביד, *by the prophet*,
just as in chap. i. 22; ii. 5, 15; xiii. 35;
xxi. 4; xxvii. 35; and that his Greek
translator, mistaking ד in ביד for ר, read
ביר, which he considered to be a contraction for בירמיהו, and so rendered it
διὰ Ἰερεμίου τοῦ προφήτου. This reading
having thus found its way into the first
Greek MS., will account for its all but
universal propagation. Another conjecture supposes Ἰρίου to have been
written by some early copyist instead
of Ζρίου. I only add, that there can be
no doubt the passage in question existed
in the book of Zechariah in the Jewish
canon in the days of the Evangelist,
since it is found to occupy that place in
the text of the LXX. which was formed
three hundred years previously.

14. For the meaning of חֹבְלִים, *Bands*,

15   And Jehovah said to me, Take to thee yet the instruments of
          a foolish shepherd ;
16   For, behold, I will raise up a shepherd in the land ;
          Those which are perishing he will not visit,
          That which strayeth he will not seek,
          That which is wounded he will not heal,
          That which standeth he will not nourish ;
          But he will eat the flesh of the fat,
          And will break off their hoofs.

see on ver. 7. The circumstances here predicted were those of the utter breaking up of the social condition of the Hebrews. This dissolution was in no small degree brought about by the internal dissensions which prevailed among themselves, the rage of the different parties against each other, and the barbarities that they practised, which none could have indulged in but such as had their hearts steeled against every feeling of brotherhood or humanity. "Yet by these men," says Josephus, "the ancient prediction seemed rapidly drawing to its fulfilment: That when civil war should break out in the city, and the temple be profaned by the hands of native Jews, the city should be taken, and the temple burned with fire."

15. עוֹד, *again*, refers back to what is recorded ver. 7. The כֵּלִים, here as a collective in the singular כְּלִי, were the articles usually belonging to shepherds, viz. a crook, a bag or wallet containing food, a pipe or reed, a knife, &c. Instead of כְּלִי, one of De Rossi's MSS., the Halle Bible of 1720, the Vatican copy of the LXX., the Syr., Vulg., and Arab., read כְּלֵי, the punctuation of the plural. אֱוִלִי, *foolish*, by implication *wicked*, as wickedness is often represented in Scripture as folly.

16. מֵקִים is employed here, like similar verbs in Hiphil, to denote not any direct moral excitement to action, but the operation of concurring circumstances, under the Divine government, in consequence of which certain events are brought about by responsible human agency. הַנִּכְחָדוֹת, *those that are perishing*, the Niphal participle of כָּחַד, which in Hiphil and Niphal signifies *to cut off* or *be destroyed*. נַעַר is not to be taken in the sense of *young*, as it is interpreted

by Kimchi and Hitzig, since it is never so used, except with reference to human beings, but signifies *expulsion*, that which has been *cast out*, by implication, *strayed*, *wandered*. Comp. the Arabic نعار, *repulsus, in fugam versus*. הַנִּצָּבָה, *that which standeth still*. נָצַב properly signifies *to set* or *place*, in Niphal, *to stand, stand firm, be strong, firm, sound ;* and thus the LXX. here ὁλόκληρον, but this interpretation is quite at variance with the exigency of the place, which requires the idea of *weakness* rather than *strength* to be expressed. And this the verb naturally suggests, reference being had to the *standing*, or *standing still* of sheep that are obliged, through weakness or faintness, to lag behind. Comp. the Arabic نصب, *posuit, fixit*, and then *dolore affecit, lassus fuit, laboravit*. Such it devolves upon the shepherd to provide with necessary nourishment, or, as it is here expressed, לְכַלְכֵּל, *to sustain, furnish with provisions.*. Root כּוּל, *to measure grain*. The words פְּרָסֵיהֶן יְפָרֵק are expressive of the greatest cruelty, being descriptive of an act which must not only occasion the most acute pain, but disable the animals, and prevent their going about in quest of pasture. Who the ruler here depicted is, cannot with certainty be determined. If taken as pointing to an individual king, there is none to whom it will more aptly apply than to Herod, who was totally regardless of the real interests of the Jews, and whose reign was marked by the perpetration of the most shameful and barbarous cruelties. What goes to confirm this view is the circumstance of his being said to be raised up "*in* the land."

17 Wo to the worthless shepherd, that leaveth the flock,
 The sword shall be upon his arm,
 And upon his right eye ;
 His arm shall be utterly palsied,
 And his right eye utterly darkened.

17. This denunciation seems to be directed against the wicked rulers of the Jews who might be in office between the time of the prophet, and that of the dissolution of the Jewish state, rather than against the person referred to in the preceding verse. The י in רֹעִי is not the pronominal affix, but the poetic paragogic, as in the following עֹזְבִי, and other participles. See Gen. xlix. 11; Deut. xxxiii. 16 ; Ps. cxiv. 8 ; cxxiii. 1.

רֹעִי הָאֱלִיל, *the worthless* or *good-for-nothing shepherd.* Comp. Job xiii. 4. The root must unquestionably have been אֱלַל. Comp. כְּלִיל from בָּלַל ; סָבִיב from סָבַב. The character described is that of negligence, arising from the total absence of a sense of official claims, and of personal responsibility. The rest of the verse from חֶרֶב onward, is to be taken optatively. The doom imprecated is truly awful—an utter deprivation of power and intelligence.

CHAPTER XII

This chapter contains a series of predictions, which relate to the future restoration of the scattered people of the Jews, the destruction of whose national polity, and their consequent wretchedness, had been so graphically set forth in that which precedes it. On their return to their own land, Jerusalem shall prove formidable to the nations that oppose them, 2—4, having a regular government, by which, in reliance upon Jehovah, the inhabitants shall be protected, 5, 6. To prevent the inhabitants of the metropolis from glorying over their brethren in the country, the latter shall be first delivered from their invaders, 7 ; but Jerusalem being the principal point of attack, special promises of deliverance are made to it, 8, 9. When the Jews shall have been collected, and delivered from the opposing powers, there will be a remarkable effusion of the influences of the Holy Spirit, in consequence of which a season of great and universal mourning, on account of the crucifixion of the Messiah, will be observed, each family bewailing separately the guilt entailed upon it by the nefarious deed, 10—14.
As might be expected to be the case with unfulfilled prophecy, a considerable degree of obscurity necessarily attaches to certain portions of this and the two following chapters ; but the leading features of the Divine dealings with the Jews in times yet future, are marked with a sufficient degree of distinctness to enable us to form a general idea of the circumstances in which they will be placed.

1 THE Sentence of the word of Jehovah concerning Israel;
  Saith Jehovah, who stretcheth forth the heavens,
  And layeth the foundations of the earth,
  And formetn the spirit of man within him:
2 Behold, I will make Jerusalem a cup of intoxication
  To all the people around;
  And also with Judah it shall be thus,
  In the siege of Jerusalem.
3 And it shall be in that day, I will make Jerusalem
  A burdensome stone to all people,
  All that lift it shall be cut in pieces:
  Yet all the nations of the earth shall be gathered against it.

1. For the entire phrase, מַשָּׂא דְבַר יְהוָֹה, see on chap. ix. 1. That מַשָּׂא does not necessarily involve a sentence of judgment, see on Is. xiii. 1. That it cannot be so taken here, is manifest from the connexion. Hengstenberg, in order to establish the contrary hypothesis, is obliged to have recourse to the desperate resort of interpreting *Israel* of the enemies of God! The term is obviously employed in its original acceptation, as designating the whole Hebrew people. With no other reference could it have been introduced. To remove all the doubts which unbelief might suggest respecting the possibility of the deliverance here predicted, a sublime description is given of the omnipotent Creator by whom it would be effected, than which no introduction could have been more appropriate. For יֹצֵר וְחֹדָאָדָם, compare Πατὴρ τῶν πνευμάτων, Heb. xii. 9, and Numb. xvi. 22; xxvii. 16; and for the several predicates, Is. xlii. 5.

2. סַף רַעַל, some render a *shaking threshold*, in imitation of the LXX. ὡς πρόθυρα σαλευόμενα, and interpret the declaration here made of the concussion which Jerusalem should receive from the attack of the enemy; but it is more natural to regard the phrase as only another form for כּוֹס הַתַּרְעֵלָה, Is. li. 17, 22, by which is meant a cup filled with intoxicating liquors, causing those who drink it to *reel* and stagger to their injury. Root רָעַל, *to shake, reel, stagger*. The attempt of Hengstenberg to deny that סַף is ever used to denote *a cup*, is

a complete failure, as must be obvious to any one who will take the trouble to consult the Concordance. The second part of the verse has occasioned no small perplexity to interpreters. The chief difficulty is created by the position of the preposition עַל in the phrase וְגַם עַל־יְהוּדָה. The Targ., Jerome, Kimchi, Drusius, Rosenmüller, Hitzig, Maurer, and Ewald, suppose the meaning to be, that the inhabitants of Judah would be compelled to join the enemies in the attack upon Jerusalem, and with them share in the punishment: making סַף־רַעַל the nominative to יִהְיֶה. But this interpretation ill suits the context, in the whole of which Judah is represented as triumphant, and not as placed in the degrading position of auxiliaries in a war against its own capital. I consider the preposition to be here used for the purpose of conveying the idea of addition or accompaniment, so that, connecting Judah with Jerusalem, it represents the former, as well as the latter, as a cup of intoxication to the invaders. See for this use of עַל, Gen. xxxii. 12; Exod. xxxv. 22; Job xxxviii. 32. In support of this interpretation, see especially ver. 6. The same result will be brought out, if we take עַל in the acceptation *in reference to, with respect to;* thus: "And with respect to Judah it shall also be in the siege;" *i. e.* Judah shall also be a cup, &c.

3. Another metaphor employed like the preceding to represent the victory

4 In that day, saith Jehovah,
   I will smite every horse with consternation,
   And his rider with madness ;
   But upon the house of Judah I will keep my eyes open,
   While I will smite every horse of the people with blindness.

5   And the chiefs of Judah shall say in their heart,
   My strength is the inhabitants of Jerusalem,
   Through Jehovah of hosts, their God.

6 In that day I will make the chiefs of Judah
   Like a fire pot among sticks of wood,
   And like a torch of fire in a sheaf,
   And they shall consume all the people around,
   On the right hand and on the left ;
   For Jerusalem shall yet occupy her place in Jerusalem.

7 And Jehovah shall deliver the tents of Judah first,
   In order that the splendour of the house of David,
   And the splendour of the inhabitants of Jerusalem,
   May not be magnified above Judah.

which the Jews shall obtain over their enemies, whose attack will only issue in their own injury. Jerome mentions it as a custom, which still obtained in his time, in Palestine, for young men to try their strength by lifting enormous stones so high from the ground, as to place them upon their heads. It may be from such an exercise that the metaphor is borrowed. שָׂרַט describes the inflicting of cuts or gashes by the sharp edges or corners of the stones thus employed. Though exposed to the punishment here predicated, the nations shall confidently advance to the attack. The confederacy against the Jews will be universal in its character.

4. While Jehovah will specially interpose for the discomfiture of the enemy by rendering their cavalry incapable of performing any effective service, he will exercise the greatest watchfulness over his people.

5. אַמְצָה is a substantive, but occurs only this once. The LXX. have read אַמְצָא, and render εὑρήσομεν. The successful resistance offered to the enemy by the inhabitants of the metropolis, will inspire those of the country

with the assurance, that, through the Divine aid, they shall obtain deliverance. לִּי, which is the Dative of advantage, stands collectively for לָנוּ. Two MSS. and the Targ. read לִישְׁבֵי, but no doubt from correction. In two other MSS. לִי is omitted.

6. *Jerusalem*, in the first instance, stands for the inhabitants. After the Jews shall have completely routed their enemies, they shall dwell in peace in their own land, and in the city of their ancient solemnities. Houbigant proposes to change יְרוּשָׁלַם, as occurring the second time, into בְּשָׁלוֹם, but, like most of his other conjectures, the change is not based upon any authority. One MS., the Arab., and the Greek MS. Pachom, omit the word altogether.

7. The inhabitants of the country being more exposed to the evils of the war than those in the fortified city, shall be the first to experience the Divine help. Standing in antithesis with the capital, their comparative helplessness is clearly implied ; and the reason for the preference being given to them is assigned to be the prevention of that spirit of pride and self-exaltation, in

8 In that day Jehovah shall protect the inhabitants of Jerusalem;
　 So that he that stumbleth among them in that day shall be as David,
　 And the house of David shall be as God,
　 As the Angel of Jehovah before them.
9 And it shall be in that day,
　 I will seek to destroy all the nations
　 That come against Jerusalem.
10 And I will pour out upon the house of David,
　 And upon the inhabitants of Jerusalem,
　 A spirit of grace and of gracious supplications,
　 And they shall look unto me whom they have pierced,
　 And they shall lament for him,

which the inhabitants of a royal metropolis are too prone to indulge. The reading פְּרִאשֹׁנָה, "as at the first," which is found in two MSS., and is the original reading of three more, and is favoured by the LXX., Arab., Syr., and Vulg., is not entitled to consideration.

8. A gracious promise of Divine assistance, supported, with admirable effect, by a beautiful climax. From the circumstance, that the LXX. have in several instances rendered אֱלֹהִים, by *angels*, some interpreters have supposed that the term is to be so understood here. The more enlightened moderns, however, discard this signification altogether. See Gesenius, Thesaurus Ling. Heb. p. 95, and Lee's Heb. Lex. p. 32. What clearly shows that no such idea can attach to the word in this place is the corrective phrase, כְּמַלְאַךְ יְהוָה, *as the Angel of Jehovah*, immediately following. The house of David was to be as God, yet not as God in the abstract, of which no proper conception can be formed, but as God manifested to men in his glorious forthcomings under the ancient dispensation, in the Divine Person of the Son, who went before the children of Israel as their Almighty Leader and Protector, and to whom are vindicated the sum total of the Divine attributes. See Exod. xxxii. 34; where the words מַלְאָכִי יֵלֵךְ לְפָנֶיךָ form the type of כְּמַלְאָךְ יְהוָה לִפְנֵיהֶם, here adopted by Zechariah. Compare also Exod. xxxiii. 15; xxiii. 21; Is. lxiii. 9; Mal. iii. 1; and my Comment. on Zech. i. 11.

9. אֲבַקֵּשׁ לְהַשְׁמִיד, *I will seek to destroy*, is spoken *more humano*, but conveys no

idea of weakness in the speaker. "Summo studio ero attentus." Calvin.

10. We have here a clear and definite prophecy of the future conversion of the Jews, in consequence of a special and extraordinary outpouring of the influences of the Holy Spirit. Nothing that has hitherto taken place in the history of that people can be regarded as in any degree answering to the description here furnished, not even the numerous conversions that accompanied the Apostolic preaching on the day of Pentecost, and subsequently as narrated in the Acts. By רוּחַ, *spirit*, is not meant a gracious and prayerful disposition produced in the minds of the Jews, but the Divine influence itself by which that disposition will be created. It is called "spirit" by metonymy of cause for effect. חֵן and תַּחֲנוּנִים are from the same root, חָנַן, *to regard with favour, exercise mercy*, &c. The verb נָבַט, here used in Hiphil, is intensive in signification: *to look to*, or *regard with fixed attention*, to contemplate *with deep interest*, and with believing expectation. Such is the nature of that act of the mind which is exerted by every converted sinner; when the Saviour is spiritually discerned. In the case of the Jews there will be a special recognition of him as the Messiah whom their ancestors crucified, and whose deed they have appropriated by their personal unbelief and opposition to the truth of the Gospel, but whom they will then regard as all their salvation and all their desire. The textual reading אֵלַי, in the phrase הִבִּיטוּ אֵלַי, "they shall look to Me,"

As one lamenteth for an only son,
And be in bitterness for him,
As one is in bitterness for a first-born.

has been the subject of much controversy. It is found in most MSS., and among these the best, and is supported by the LXX., Aq., Symm., Theod., Syr., Targ., Vulg., and Arab. It is the more difficult reading, and one which has always proved revolting to the mind of a Jew, as there is no other antecedent to whom it can be referred than יְהֹוָה, JEHOVAH, verses 1 and 4. In order to avoid this reference, Kimchi gives to the following words, אֵת אֲשֶׁר דָּקָרוּ, the interpretation, *because they pierced*, leaving it undetermined who was pierced. But this construction is altogether inadmissible, as it deprives the verb of its accusative case, which is expressed in every other instance in which it occurs. It has accordingly been condemned by Abenezra, Abarbanel, Alschech, and other Rabbins. The rendering given to דָּקָר by the LXX. κατωρχήσαντο, *they insulted*, has been eagerly seized upon by some, especially by Theiner, Rosenmüller, Eichhorn, Gesenius, De Wette, Winer, and by none more than Maurer, who is at great pains to prove that, like נָקַב and קָבַב, the verb דָּקָר is to be taken in the metaphorical sense of *blaspheming* or *cursing*. Against such interpretation it is justly objected that this verb, which occurs in ten other passages, is never used except in the literal acceptation of piercing the body. It is thus used in chap. xiii. 3, of this very book. The same objection lies against the metaphorical sense of *grieving* or *provoking*, which even Calvin has adopted, though he admits that the prophecy was literally fulfilled in Christ.

That the passage has a Messianic reference has been admitted both by the ancient and the more modern Jews. In the Gemara of Jerusalem, written sometime in the third century, we read: תרין אמורין חד אמר זה הספידו של משיח וחורנה אמר זה הספידו של יצר הרע. *Two opinions are expressed: one states that they mourned on account of Messiah, and another that they mourned on account of corrupt nature.* A similar passage occurs in the Gemara of Babylon, Tract Succoth, fol. 52, col. 1, in which the words of Zecha-

riah are cited, after the declaration respecting the mourning: בשלמא למאן דאמר על משיח בן יוסף שנהרג. *May he be in peace who refers it to Messiah the son of Joseph, who shall be slain.* See also the commentaries of Abarbanel and Abenezra, who give the same interpretation, as also does the Talkut Chasdash, fol. 24: כי אחר שידקר יונה שהוא משיח בן יוסף אחרי כן יבא דויד דהיינו משיח בן דויד. *For after they have pierced Jonah, who is Messiah the son of Joseph, then David will come, Messiah the son of David.* Hengstenberg's Christol. vol. ii. p. 222. The fiction of two Messiahs, one the son of Joseph, who should suffer and die, and another the son of David, who should prove victorious and reign for ever, was invented purely with a view to reconcile those passages which describe the Messiah now as suffering, and now as reigning in glory, and thus to evade the Christian application of them to our Saviour.

It only remains to inquire how the Jews, who did not acquiesce in the interpretation adopted by Kimchi, have endeavoured to get rid of the pronominal reference in אֵלָי. To this the reply is: By changing the reading into אֵלָיו, which, however, they did not at first venture to insert into the text, but merely gave it as the Keri, or corrected reading in the margin. This Keri, however, is only found in sixteen of Kennicott's and De Rossi's MSS.; but at length a more daring step was taken by receiving it into the text itself, in which it is found in thirty-four of Kennicott's MSS., originally in three more, perhaps in five others, and now by correction in six; in six of De Rossi's own, in two more originally, now in five others, and in twenty collated by him in other libraries. Of this insertion a serious complaint is made by Raymundus Martini, in his Pugio Fidei, p. 411, Leipsic, 1687, fol. And so ashamed have Lipmann, Abarbanel, and other Rabbins been of it, that they pass it entirely by in their controversies with the Christians, or candidly acknowledge that it is not

11 In that day there shall be great lamentation in Jerusalem,
　　As the lamentation of Hadad-rimmon in the valley of Megiddon.
12 And the land shall lament, every family apart ;
　　The family of the house of David apart, and their wives apart ;
　　The family of the house of Nathan apart, and their wives apart ;
13 The family of the house of Levi apart, and their wives apart ;
　　The family of Shimei apart, and their wives apart ;
14 All the families that are left,
　　Every family apart, and their wives apart.

to be regarded as forming any part of the sacred text. It is much to be regretted, that while it has been rejected by the best Jewish and Christian critics, the most free-thinking of the German school not excepted, it should have been adopted by Newcome and Boothroyd, who accordingly translate : " They shall look unto HIM whom they have pierced." It is true, they may seem to have the sanction of the Evangelist John, who quotes the passage thus : "Οψονται εἰς ὃν ἐξεκέντησαν, xix. 37, and employs the words, καὶ οἵτινες αὐτὸν ἐξεκέντησαν, Rev. i. 7 ; but it must be obvious that he gives the prophecy historically, as having been literally fulfilled in Jesus of Nazareth, without designing to exhibit the exact wording of the prophet. See on Zech. xi. 12, 13. It might be supposed that אֵלַי being the true reading, עָלַי, and not עָלָיו, would be required in the following sentence ; but the use of the expletive phrase אֵת אֲשֶׁר, necessarily led to the change of construction.· הָמֵר is the infinitive of Hiphil, which carries forward the description instead of the finite form. It is here used intransitively ; the root is מָרַר. The verb סָפַד signifies primarily to beat ; then, as a sign of intense grief, to smite or beat the breast. There being usually great wailing and lamentation connected with such significant action in the East, it is also used to denote the noise made by mourners. The instances selected for illustration are of the most tender and touching kind.

11. To represent the greatness and universality of the lamentation which he describes, the prophet compares it to the greatest· ever known among the Jews, viz. that which took place on the death of the excellent king Josiah, the result of the wound which he received at Hadad-rimmon. 2 Kings xxiii. 29 ; 2 Chron. xxxv. 23—25. Hadad-rimmon was the name of a place in the great plain of Esdraelon, near Megiddo, and was probably so called after the Syrian idol of that name. In the time of Jerome it was called Maximianopolis.

12—14. In these verses the universal character of the mourning is described, while, at the same time, its particular and individual features are likewise set forth. To show that all will be the subjects of it, the prophet begins with the descendants of David, and then proceeds to those of the priests, on account of the influence which their example would have on the rest of the people. Instead of Shimei, the LXX. have Συμεὼν, supposing that a tribal division was intended ; and some have thought that שַׁמּוּעַ, Shammua, one of the sons of David, 2 Sam. v. 14, is meant ; but it is more natural to regard the individual as one of the sons of Levi, who is classed along with that patriarch, just as Nathan, one of the sons of David, is with him, ver 12. For שִׁמְעִי, Shimei, see Numb. iii. 18, 21, in which latter verse מִשְׁפַּחַת הַשִּׁמְעִי, the family of the Shimeites, occurs just as in Zechariah. It is implied in the last verse, that some families shall have become extinct at the period referred to. The men and women mourning apart has reference to the Jewish custom, according to which not only did the females dwell in separate apartments from the males, but also worshipped separately.

CHAPTER XIII

This chapter contains a continuation of the prophecy respecting the future conversion of the Jews, ver. 1; predictions relating to the entire abolition of idolatry and false doctrine, 2—6; a resumption of the subject of the Messiah's sufferings, 7; and an account of the destruction of the greater part of the Jews during the Roman war, the preservation of the rest, and their ultimate restoration, 8, 9.

1 IN that day there shall be a fountain opened
   To the house of David, and to the inhabitants of Jerusalem,
   For guilt and for uncleanness.
2 And it shall be in that day, saith Jehovah of hosts,
   I will cut off the names of the idols from the earth;

1. This verse is intimately connected with the subject of the concluding verses of the preceding chapter. It is designed to relieve the anxious and troubled minds of the penitents there described. מָקוֹר, a *well*, or *fountain*, from קוּר, *to dig;* not, perhaps, without reference to chap. xii. 10. חַטָּאת, *guilt*, from חָטָא, *to miss a mark* or *way, to sin;* hence the substantive comes to signify the *guilt* contracted by sinning, the *punishment* to which it exposes the transgressor, and *a sin-offering*, for the purpose of making expiation. That it is here to be taken in the sense of *guilt*, is shown by the accompanying term נִדָּה, *uncleanness*, or the impurity contracted by sin. That moral, and not ceremonial guilt and pollution are intended, the circumstances of the case evince; and the Jews are taught, that their deliverance from these is not to be effected by the Levitical sacrifices and purifications, but by the cleansing influence flowing from the death of the Messiah. See Heb. ix. 13, 14; 1 John i. 7. The verse exhibits the two grand doctrines of the gospel: justification and sanctification. The fountain here spoken of was opened when the Redeemer presented his sacrifice on the cross; but the Jews, with comparatively few exceptions, after the apostolic age, have shut it against themselves by their impenitence and unbelief. When, however, these shall be removed by the outpouring of Divine influence, promised, chap. xii. 10, they shall find it נִפְתָּח, *opened*, full, and overflowing with all spiritual blessings.

2. As no idolatry has existed among the Jews since their return from Babylon, and it is in the highest degree improbable that they will ever fall into it again, הָאָרֶץ should not be rendered, as in our common version, *the land*, but *the earth;* so that this and the following verses

And they shall not be remembered any more.
And I will also cause the prophets and the unclean spirit
To pass away from the earth.

3 So that should any one still prophesy,
His father and his mother—his parents
Shall say to him, Thou shalt not live,
For thou speakest falsehood in the name of Jehovah;
And his father and his mother—his parents
Shall thrust him through when he prophesieth.

4 And it shall be in that day,
That the prophets shall be ashamed,
Every one of his vision, when he prophesieth;
And they shall not wear a hairy garment to deceive.

5 But each shall say, I am not a prophet,
I am a tiller of .the ground;
For I have been in a state of slavery from my youth.

6 Then shall it be said to him,
What are these wounds in thy hands?

describe the total extinction of that horrible evil, and all the other systems of superstition and false religion which now impose upon the human family, together with those who teach and defend them. By רוּחַ הַטֻּמְאָה, *the spirit of impurity,* is meant a person pretending to inspiration, and in league with Satan, the god of this world, to whom, in contradistinction to רוּחַ הַקֹּדֶשׁ, *the spirit of holiness,* the designation may well be applied. Compare πνεῦμα πύθωνος, Acts xvi. 16; τὸ πνεῦμα τῆς πλάνης, 1 John iv. 6; and especially, καὶ ἐκ τοῦ στόματος τοῦ ψευδοπροφήτου πνεύματα τρία ἀκάθαρτα, Rev. xvi. 13.

3. There is in this verse a recognition of the law against those who seduced others to idolatry, Deut. xiii. 6—11. לְדִים, *parents.* יָלַד, signifies both to *beget,* and to *bear* children. The evil here denounced will not be connived at even by the nearest relatives. The tenderest parental feelings shall give place to the infliction of merited punishment.

4, 5. The shame with which false teachers shall be covered is here set forth. The hairy mantle, the garb of the ancient prophets, and that of certain orders of monks still, which is assumed in order to inspire the multitude with an impression of the superior sanctity of those by whom they are worn, shall be thrown aside, as dangerous to appear in. The false prophets wished to pass off as those who had really been invested with a Divine commission. The form of the infinitive הִנָּבְאֹתוֹ, is according to the analogy of verbs in לה. To the singular וְאָמַר, at the beginning of ver. 5, each of the prophets previously mentioned is the nominative. הִקְנַנִי, lit. *one sold me as a slave,* but taken in connexion with the following, מִנְּעוּרָי, *from my youth,* it signifies to be held in a state of slavery, to be a slave. The speaker declares that he had always been in a condition of life with which the exercise of the prophetic office was altogether incompatible. אָדָם, which some translators have preposterously retained as the proper name, *Adam,* is here used impersonally, precisely as the German *man,* and is best rendered into English by the passive of the accompanying verb.

6. This verse is commonly applied to the sufferings of Christ, but without any

And he will say,
Those with which I have been wounded in the house of my friends.
7   Awake, O sword! against my shepherd,
And against the man who is united to me,
Saith Jehovah of hosts:
Smite the shepherd, and the sheep shall be scattered,
But I will turn back my hand upon the little ones.

further ground than its mere proximity to that which follows, in which he and his sufferings are clearly predicted. In no tolerable sense could the Jews be called his מְאַהֲבִים, *lovers*, or *friends*; on the contrary, they hated both him and his Father. The words connect with the preceding thus: The false prophet, though he might rid himself of his idolatrous vestments, would not be able to efface the marks that had been made on his hands in honour of the idol which he served, yet as it was customary to cut and maim the body, especially the hand, in token of grief for departed relatives, he might hope to escape detection by attributing his scars to the latter cause.

7. Various opinions have been formed respecting the person here referred to. Calvin thought he was Zechariah himself, as representative of all the prophets, and that the prophecy referred only indirectly to Christ. Grotius, Eichhorn, Bauer, and Jahn, apply it to Judas Maccabæus; Maurer to Jehoiakim; Ewald to Pekah; Hitzig to the pretended prophets spoken of in the preceding verses! The only satisfactory solution of the question is that which regards the words as directly and exclusively prophetic of the person and sufferings of the Messiah. This solution is induced not only by our Saviour's express appropriation of them to himself, Matt. xxvi. 31, but also by the manifest identity of the subject treated of with that exhibited chap. xi. 4, 7, 10—14. The same subject there handled is resumed, and treated, just as it is there, in connexion with the downfal of the Jewish state. The prophecy contained in this and the following verses has no coherence with what immediately precedes, and was evidently delivered upon

a different occasion. A new section may, therefore, be considered as commencing here, though it only extends to chap. xiv. 5. The language employed is altogether peculiar. Not only is the Messiah designated the Shepherd of Jehovah, to indicate the relation in which he stood to the Father in the economy of redemption, but he is described as גֶּבֶר עֲמִיתִי, *the man of his union*; *i.e.* conjoined or closely united to him. The term translated *man*, is not that usually employed in Hebrew, which in such construction would merely be idiomatic, but גֶּבֶר, *a strong*, or *mighty man*, one who is such by way of eminence. עָמִית is used elsewhere only in the Pentateuch, namely, in Lev. v. 21; xviii. 20; xix. 11, 15, 17; xxiv. 19; xxv. 14, 15, 17; in all which passages it is employed to denote persons who were united together under common laws, for the enjoyment of common rights and privileges. It is derived from עָמָה, cognate with עָמַם, *to bind, bind together, unite in society;* Arab. عمّ, *communis fuit res, communem fecit rem:* hence the derivatives עַם, *a people,* i.e. those united for their common interest; עֻמָּה, *conjunction, communion, association;* עִם, the conjunction *with*, indicating *accompaniment, society.* The renderings of the versions vary. LXX. ἄνδρα πολίτην μου. Aq. ἄνδρα σύμφυλόν μου. Symm. ἄνδρα τοῦ λαοῦ μου. Theod. ἄνδρα πλησίον μου. Syr. ܐܢܫ ܚܒܪܝ, *the man my friend.* Targ. שִׁלְטוֹנָא חַבְרֵיהּ דְּכַוָתֵהּ דְּכָמֵי לֵיהּ, *the ruler his companion, his associate who is like him.* Vulg. *virum cohærentem mihi.* Leo Juda, *virum coæqualem mihi.* Heng-

8 And it shall be that in all the land,
 Saith Jehovah,
 Two parts therein shall be cut off and expire,
 But the third part shall be left in it.
9 And I will cause the third part to go through the fire,

stenberg, *a man, my nearest relation.* Burger, *mon confident.* De Wette, **den Mann meines Gleichen,** *the man my equal.* Arnheim, **dem Manne, den ich mir zugesellt,** *the man whom I have associated with myself.* The two last are the more remarkable, coming, as they do, the one from a Rationalist, and the other from a Jew. The idea expressed by the latter I conceive to be precisely what was intended by the Holy Spirit, by whom the words were indited. But of whom can this association be predicated, except of Him whose human nature was assumed into the most intimate and perfect union with the Divine—IMMANUEL, who was one with the Father, and who could say, "He that hath seen me, hath seen the Father!" The union or association is that of the two natures, and not that of the Divine nature or substance. This the use of the word גֶּבֶר, *man,* clearly proves. To the objection, that the words cannot be applied to our Saviour, since he was not cut off by a *sword,* it has been sufficiently replied, that חֶרֶב, *sword,* is here used figuratively for any means of taking away human life, just as in Exod. v. 21; 2 Sam. xii. 9, compared with 2 Sam. xi. 24. That the wicked Jews are intended, see Ps. xvii. 13, where the wicked are called the sword of Jehovah. They are regarded as in a state of sleep or inactivity, and are summoned to perpetrate the awful deed. According to an idiom common in the Hebrew prophets, the imperative is used instead of the future, in order to express with greater force the certainty of the event. See my note on Is. vi. 10. For a parallel instance of the personification of the sword, see Jer. xlvii. 6, 7. As חֶרֶב is feminine, and הַךְ masculine, Hitzig would refer the latter to the human agent handling the sword, but the irregularity in point of gender is sufficiently accounted for by the remoteness

of the antecedent. הַךְ, *smite,* is quoted, Matt. xxvi. 31, as if it were אַךְ, *I will smite,* the first person singular of the future in Hiphil. There is no diversity of reading in the Hebrew MSS., but the Ald. and Pachom. MSS. of the LXX. read πατάξον, instead of πατάξω, which the Evangelists Matthew and Mark have copied. The difference is unimportant, yet there seems to be more propriety in the reading הַךְ, with reference to the sword addressed in the preceding clause, than in connecting this verb, whatever may be supposed to have been its form, with what follows in the verse. Comparing the present verse with chap. xi. 4, 7, and especially with what is predicted in the two following verses of the present chapter, in which the same subject is continued, it is evident the צֹאן, *sheep,* or *flock,* cannot be restricted to the disciples of Christ. The circumstances, however, in reference to which our Saviour appropriated the prophecy, afforded a striking type of the dispersion of the Jewish people, which is that intended by Zechariah. The disciples as Jews formed part of the flock which the good shepherd was commissioned to feed, but they, together with the Jewish Christians, converted by their ministry, who formed the first church at Jerusalem, were the צְעִירִים, *little ones,* on whom the Lord promises to turn back his hand, in order to protect them in the time of calamity. That the phrase הֵשִׁיב יָד עַל, *to turn,* or *turn back the hand,* upon any one, is used in a good as well as in a bad sense, see on Is. i. 25.

8, 9. In these verses are predicted the destruction of two-thirds of the inhabitants of Judæa by the Roman arms, and by the famine and pestilence, the usual concomitants of war in the East, and the preservation of the remaining third part, which, after having been submitted to very trying and afflictive

And will refine them as silver is refined,
And will try them as gold is tried;
It shall invoke my name, and I will answer it;
I will say, It is my people;
And it shall say, Jehovah is my God.

processes, should come forth out of the furnace a regenerated and spiritual people. The former was fulfilled not only during what is commonly called the Jewish war, but also, to a fearful extent, under more than one of the succeeding emperors; the processes pointed at in the latter have been more or less carried forward ever since, but are, it is to be hoped, soon to terminate in the conversion of the Jews to God. Then shall they enter into a new relation to him, according to the terms of the better covenant, Jer. xxxi. 33; Heb. viii. 10, 11.

CHAPTER XIV

In the first two verses of this chapter the destruction of Jerusalem by the Romans and the calamities consequent upon that event are set forth; after which the destruction of the forces composing the hostile army is predicted, 3. A promise of special interposition in behalf of the people of God is then given, by which effectual provision is made for their escape, 4, 5. The prophet next describes a period of great calamity, which is to give place to one of unmixed and perennial happiness, 6, 7; when the means of spiritual life and enjoyment shall be universal and continual, 8; and the true God the exclusive object of obedience and worship, 9; and while every barrier to the free intercourse of Christians throughout the world shall be removed, special honour will be conceded to Jerusalem as the metropolis of converted Israel, 10, 11. The dreadful judgments to be inflicted on their final enemies, and the complete discomfiture of these enemies, are depicted, 12—15; after which follow predictions respecting an annual visit which all the nations shall pay to Jerusalem, 16; the punishment of those that neglect to perform it, 17—19; and the universally holy character which shall distinguish her inhabitants, their occupations and services, 20, 21.

---

1 BEHOLD the day of Jehovah cometh,
  And thy spoil shall be divided in the midst of thee.

1. For the phraseology יוֹם בָּא לַיהוָה, comp. Is. xxii. 5. The criticism of Hengstenberg, who denies that it is equivalent to בָּא יוֹם יְהוָה, is without any foundation. By the day of Jehovah is meant the period of the infliction of judgment. See, in reference to the same event which is here predicted, Joel ii. 31; iii. 14; Mal. iv. 1, 5. By the spoil of Jerusalem is meant all that her inhabitants had accumulated, and which would be fit spoil for the enemy, especially the treasures of the temple. Notwithstanding all that was consumed by fire,

2 For I will collect all the nations against Jerusalem to battle,
   And the city shall be taken,
   And the houses plundered, and the women ravished ;
   And half the city shall go forth into captivity,
   But the rest of the people shall not be cut off from the city.
3   And Jehovah shall go forth,
   And fight with those nations,
   As in the day when he fought
   In the day of battle.
4 And his feet shall stand in that day
   On the mount of Olives, which is before Jerusalem on the east;
   And the mount of Olives shall be split in its midst,
   Toward the east, and toward the west,
   Into a very great valley ;
   For half of the mountain shall recede towards the north,
   And half of it towards the south.
5 And ye shall flee to the valley of my mountains,
   For the valley of the mountains shall reach to Azal ;
   Yea, ye shall flee as ye fled from the earthquake,
   In the days of Uzziah, king of Judah ;

the plunder obtained by the Romans was so great, that gold fell in Syria to half its former value.

2. *All the nations* here mean soldiers from all the different nations forming the Roman empire, which composed the army of Titus. The verse contains a fearful description of the capture of Jerusalem under the command of that general. After its destruction the more distinguished, handsome, and able-bodied Jews were sold into slavery, or condemned to work in the mines; but the poorer and more contemptible sort were permitted to remain among the ruins. As usual, where תִּשָּׁגַלְנָה occurs in the text, the Keri has תִּשָּׁכַבְנָה, for the sake of euphemism. The latter word has found its way into a great many MSS.

3. The Roman power was doomed in its turn to destruction. Formidable as it might appear, Jehovah would in his providence overthrow it, as he had done the enemies of his people in former ages. Comp. Exod. xiv. 14; xv. 3, &c.

4, 5. These verses convey in language of the most beautiful poetical imagery

the assurance of the effectual means of escape that should be provided for the truly pious. We accordingly learn from Eusebius, that on the breaking out of the Jewish war, the Christian church at Jerusalem, in obedience to the warning of our Saviour, Matt. xxiv. 16, fled to Pella, a city beyond Jordan, where they lived in safety. As the mount of Olives lay in their way, it is represented as cleaving into two halves, in order to make a passage for them. Comp. chap. iv. 7. הָרַי is not to be considered as the less usual form of the masculine plural, but as a proper plural with the pronominal affix. Jehovah calls them *his*, because he had formed them, by cleaving Olivet into two. The valley lay between them. אָצֵל was the proper name of a place, close to one of the gates on the east side of Jerusalem, to which the cleft or valley was to extend westward, so as at once to admit those who should flee from the enemy. Most commentators think of some locality to the east of the Mount of Olives, but far less aptly. The word properly signifies to *join* or *be*

For Jehovah my God shall come,
And all the holy ones with thee.

6   And it shall be in that day
That there shall not be the light of the precious orbs,
But condensed darkness.

7   But there shall be one day,

joined to, be at the side, near. Its proximity to the city must have originated the name. For וְנַסְתֶּם, *ye shall flee,* we find the reading וְנִסְתַּם, *shall be stopped up,* in four of De Rossi's MSS. and in the margin of Bomberg's Hebrew Bible; but, though supported by the LXX., Arab., Targ., Symm., and the other Greek interpreters, it is utterly to be rejected, as unsuited to the connexion. The very opposite of what would thus be expressed, is required. Yet it is adopted by Blayney and Boothroyd! We have nothing in Scripture relative to the earthquake here referred to except as a date, Amos i. 1. Instead of עִמָּךְ, *with thee,* nearly forty MSS. and all the versions read עִמּוֹ, *with him;* and instead of קְדֹשִׁים, *the holy ones,* one MS., the Syr., Arab., and Targ., read קְדֹשָׁיו, *his holy ones.* To refer עִמָּךְ, with the Rabbins, Drusius, and Blayney, to Jerusalem, is quite inadmissible, since such construction affords no tolerable sense. The change of person was occasioned by a sudden transition in the mind of the prophet to the Lord, whom he addresses as present. For the application of this part of the prophecy, compare the parallel prediction of our Lord himself, Matt. xxiv. 30, 31, where those whom Zechariah designates קְדֹשִׁים, *holy ones,* are called τοὺς ἀγγέλους αὐτοῦ. That a future personal and pre-millennial advent of the Redeemer is here taught, I cannot find.

6. Now follows the prediction of a period of unmitigated calamity, which may be regarded as comprehending the long centuries of oppression, cruelty, mockery, and scorn, to which the Jews have been subjected ever since the destruction of Jerusalem. It has also, for the most part, been a period during which the gross darkness of superstition and delusion has reigned over the land of their fathers. יְקָרוֹת יִקְפָּאוּן have been variously rendered and interpreted. LXX. ψῦχος καὶ πάγος; Vulg. *frigus et*

gelu; Syr. إِذَا خِنْمَا ٥ خِنْمَا, *cold and ice.* Thus also Maurer, and several other moderns. But whatever connexion there may be between the absence of light and the production of cold and ice in the depth of winter, the contrast is not so natural as that between light and darkness. Besides, יְקָרוֹת cannot with any show of truth be rendered *cold.* It is an adjective plural from the root יָקַר, *to be precious, valuable, costly.* The idea of *cold* rests upon no better authority than a mere Rabbinical conjecture embodied in the Keri of Prov. xvii. 27, which exhibits יְקַר רוּחַ, instead of יְקַר רוּחַ, the proper and only term suitable in such connexion. That יְקָרוֹת may fitly be understood as designating the celestial luminaries, whence we obtain what, in common parlance, we call "the *precious* light of heaven," will appear on comparing Job xxxi. 26, where the moon is described as יָקָר הֹלֵךְ, *walking preciously* or *splendidly* across the heavens. With Prof. Lee, (Heb. Lex. p. 533,) I read יְקָרוֹת אוֹר in construction, placing the accent on the latter of the two words, instead of retaining it over the former. קָפָא properly signifies *congelation, condensation, excessive density,* from קָפָא, *to draw together, contract, become thick, dense,* and the like. Blayney renders, *thick fog.* The textual reading יִקְפָּאוּן *they shall withdraw themselves,* is inferior to that of the Keri יִקְפָּאוּן, which is found in the text of one hundred and thirty-four of Kennicott's MSS., and in twenty-two more originally, in nine of De Rossi's Spanish MSS., which are reckoned the best, in the Soncin., Brixian, and Complutensian editions, and in Machzors of the fifteenth and sixteenth centuries. None of the ancient versions employ a verb.

7. Another period is here predicted, but one entirely different from the preceding—a day altogether *unique,* יוֹם אֶחָד,

(It is known to Jehovah,)
When it shall not be day and night;
For at the time of the evening there shall be light.

8 And it shall be in that day
That living waters shall proceed from Jerusalem,
Half of them to the Eastern sea,
And half of them to the Western sea;
In summer and in winter shall it be.

9 And Jehovah shall become king over all the earth;
In that day Jehovah alone shall be,
And his name alone.

one peculiar day, the only one of its kind. See Gesenius in אֶחָד, No. 5. Its peculiarity is to consist in the absence of the alternations of day and night. It is to be all day—a period of entire freedom from war, oppression, and other outward evils which induce affliction and wretchedness, interrupt the peace of the church, and prevent the spread of truth and righteousness. Νὺξ γὰρ οὐκ ἔσται ἐκεῖ, Rev. xxi. 25. צֵת־עֶרֶב, *the time of the evening*, does not refer to the close of the happy period just described, but to that of the preceding period of afflictive darkness. At the very time when a dark and gloomy day is expected to give way to a night of still greater darkness and obscurity, light shall suddenly break forth, the light of the one long day, which is to be interrupted by no night. That this period is that of the Millennium, or the thousand years, the circumstances of which are described Rev. xx. 3—7, I cannot entertain a doubt. The time of its commencement has been variously but fruitlessly calculated. The knowledge of it the Father hath reserved in his own power. "It is known to Jehovah," and, by implication, to him alone.

8. מַיִם חַיִּים, *living*, i. e. *running*, *perennial*, *refreshing*, and *salubrious water*, in opposition to that which is stagnant and noxious. יָם הַקַּדְמוֹנִי, *the Eastern sea*, i.e. the Asphaltitic Lake; and יָם הָאַחֲרוֹן, *the Western sea*, i. e. the Mediterranean; so called because when a person resident at Jerusalem faces the East, which is the primary point of the horizon with the Orientals, the Dead Sea is *before* him

(קַדְמוֹנִי), and the Mediterranean (אַחֲרוֹנִי) *behind* him. The more important portions of the globe lying to the east and west of Jerusalem, there is an obvious propriety in the selection of these two directions. The declaration that these waters are to flow בַּקַּיִץ וּבָחֹרֶף, is expressive of constancy. They shall neither be dried up by the heat of summer, nor congealed by the frost of winter. The LXX. have ἐν θέρει καὶ ἐν ἔαρι, "in summer and in *spring*," which is to be accounted for on the ground that what was winter in more northerly regions, was spring in Egypt, in which country that version was made. In the figurative language of Scripture, water is not only used as an emblem of purification, but also for the purpose of representing the means of spiritual life, refreshment, and fertility—the doctrines and ordinances of the gospel. The descendants of Abraham, restored to their own land, and become his children in the faith, will go forth, full of zeal and spiritual activity, as missionaries to other nations, to promote revivals in the churches of Christ by rehearsing what great things God hath done for them, and to carry on the work of conversion among those nations and tribes that shall not then have been turned to the Lord.

9. In consequence of the universal spread of the Gospel, the multiplicity of heathen gods will be swept away from the face of the earth, the unity of Jehovah universally acknowledged, and the glorious harmony of those attributes which constitute his one Divine character (שְׁמוֹ, *his name*) clearly discovered, and

10 And all the earth shall be changed
　　As it were into the plain from Geba to Rimmon,
　　South of Jerusalem;
　　And she shall be exalted,
　　And be inhabited in her place,
　　From the gate of Benjamin
　　To the place of the former gate,
　　To the gate of the corners;
　　And from the tower of Hananeel
　　To the king's wine-vats.
11 And they shall dwell in her,
　　And there shall be no more curse,
　　And Jerusalem shall dwell in safety.

heartily adored. According to the ordinary mode of translating the words יִהְיֶה יְהֹוָה אֶחָד וּשְׁמוֹ אֶחָד, *there shall be one Lord and his name one*, they may seem clogged with little or no difficulty, as the true God is thus set forth in opposition to the "gods many and lords many" of the heathen; but we have only to introduce the incommunicable name JEHOVAH into the translation when the greatest incongruity at once appears. If we then render, *there shall be one Jehovah*, the conclusion is inevitable, that previous to the predicted period, there must have existed more Jehovahs than one. Or, if we render, *Jehovah shall be one*, we make the passage teach either that Jehovah was not one before, or, that he will no longer be three, or triune—Father, Son, and Holy Ghost, in the undivided unity of the Godhead. All ambiguity, however, will at once be removed, if אֶחָד be taken adverbially, and rendered *only*, *alone*, or the like. And thus I conceive it must be rendered in the primary article of the inspired creed of the Hebrews: יְהֹוָה אֱלֹהֵינוּ יְהֹוָה אֶחָד, JEHOVAH *is our God*, JEHOVAH *alone*. The doctrine, therefore, taught in the present verse is simply that Jehovah shall be the only existing object of religious worship and obedience, and no characteristics but his be any longer recognised as divine.

10, 11. These verses intimate that every obstruction shall be removed which prevents the free and full flow of the living waters throughout the world. What is high shall be levelled, and what is low shall be elevated. This idea was suggested by the natural impossibility of water flowing in a westerly direction from Jerusalem to the Mediterranean, owing to the hilly country which intervenes. In יִסֹב we have a rather unusual signification of סָבַב, *to be turned*, i. e. *changed*. The verb הָפַךְ is ordinarily used to express what is here intended. גֶּבַע, *Geba*, was a Levitical city in the tribe of Benjamin, near to Gibeah, on the northern border of the kingdom of Judah. רִמּוֹן, *Rimmon*, was a town in the tribe of Simeon, in the south of Palestine, and to be distinguished from the rock Rimmon, to the north-east of Michmash. הָעֲרָבָה, *the Arabah*, is the level or plain of the Jordan, extending from the lake of Tiberias to the Elanitic Gulf, though in the present day this name is only applied to that part of it which lies to the south of the Dead Sea. The nominative to רָאֲמָה and יָשְׁבָה, is not הָאָרֶץ, but יְרוּשָׁלַם, immediately preceding. For the orthography of רָאֲמָה, comp. Hos. x. 14, and other passages in which the א is inserted as a *mater lectionis*. Great uncertainty exists relative to the exact position of some of the places here mentioned.—חֵרֶם is used as in Mal. iii. 24, (Eng. ver. iv. 6,) in the acceptation, *curse*; LXX. ἀνάθεμα. Comp. πᾶν κατάθεμα οὐκ ἔσται ἔτι, Rev. xxii. 3. There will be no more any civil or national punishments inflicted on account of sin, these having been ren-

12　And this shall be the plague
　　With which Jehovah will plague all the people
　　That shall fight against Jerusalem ;
　　Their flesh shall consume away
　　While they stand upon their feet,
　　And their eyes shall consume away in their sockets,
　　And their tongue shall consume away in their mouth.

13　And it shall be in that day
　　There shall be great confusion from Jehovah among them,
　　So that each shall seize the hand of another,
　　And his hand shall be raised against the hand of another ;

14　And Judah also shall fight in Jerusalem,
　　And the wealth of all the nations around shall be collected,
　　Gold, and silver, and garments, in great abundance.

15　And the plague of the horses,
　　The mules, the camels, and the asses,
　　And all the cattle which shall be in those camps,
　　Shall be even as this plague.

16　And it shall be
　　That the whole residue of all the nations
　　That shall come up against Jerusalem,

---

dered unnecessary by the universal prevalence of righteousness and truth.

12—15. The hostile powers whose
punishment is here denounced are those
which shall form the great final confederacy. Comp. Is. lix. 19 ; Rev. xix.
The representation of the punishment
is the most horrible that can be imagined
—a living skeleton, rapidly wasting
away ! From what is stated ver. 14, it
appears that the Jews (יְהוּדָה, *Judah*,)
shall not only defend themselves at
Jerusalem, but make a successful attack
upon the enemy. נִלְחַם בְּ, when used in
reference to place, signifies to fight *at*
or *in* such place. LXX. παρατάξεται ἐν
Ἰερουσαλήμ. וְנִלְחֲמוּ—בְּתִיכֵךְ, Jud. v. 19.
The collection of the wealth of the surrounding nations, refers to the gathering
of the rich spoil of the contingents furnished by them to compose the hostile
army. The entire encampments of the
enemy, including the cavalry and beasts
of burden, were all to share in the awful
catastrophe. Whether God will employ

the plague and other destructive diseases
for the annihilation of the enemies of
his people, time must show. The
genitive in מְדֻמַת יְהוָה is that of cause,
a consternation sent or *produced by
Jehovah.*

16—18. מִדֵּי שָׁנָה בְשָׁנָה, lit. *from the
sufficiency of a year in a year,* i. e. when
time has fully satisfied the claims of one
year and enters upon another. It is
only an idiomatic mode of expressing
from year to year, or *annually.* What
is here predicted is expressly restricted
to the particular nations which shall
have engaged in the last great attack
upon the Jews. And, though the language of the following verse may appear
to be more general, yet the circumstances
of the context require the restriction to
be carried forward beyond the limits of
the present. Still, however, even with
this restriction, the prophecy cannot,
without manifest absurdity, be interpreted of the totality of the inhabitants
of the nations in question. Let steam-

Shall go up from year to year
To worship the king, Jehovah of hosts,
And to celebrate the feast of tabernacles.

17 And it shall be that those who go not up
Of the families of the earth to Jerusalem,
To worship the King, Jehovah of hosts,
Upon them there shall be no rain.

vessels and railroads be multiplied to any imaginable extent, the idea of the possibility of conveying such immense numbers to Palestine cannot be entertained. Or, supposing them to have been conveyed thither, few of them would after all have an opportunity of worshipping at Jerusalem during the short period allotted for the Feast of Tabernacles. Not only would the country be too small to contain their encampments, and to furnish them with necessary provisions, but the pressure, noise, and bustle of the crowds would be such as to destroy everything in the shape of devotional propriety and enjoyment. I cannot, therefore, but take the meaning to be, that the nations in question will go up to Jerusalem in the persons of their representatives, just as in former times the Jews resident in foreign countries had those who went to the annual festivals in their name, or on their behalf. Why the Egyptians should be specially introduced, ver. 18, it is difficult to determine, except it be, that as their country is watered by the Nile, and is not dependent for fertility upon rain falling in the country itself, they might be considered as exempt from the threatened plague of drought. But, if the rains fail in Ethiopia, it will in effect be the same as if they fail in Egypt itself. After the words וְלֹא עֲלֵיהֶם, the repetition of הַגֶּשֶׁם, *the rain*, from the end of the preceding verse, is understood.

It is worthy of notice, that the Feast of Tabernacles or Booths is the only one of all the Jewish festivals which is represented in this prophecy as being observed at the period therein specified. No mention is made of the great day of Atonement, the Passover, the Pentecost, &c. These have all been superseded by their fulfilment as types in the substantial blessings of the Christian economy. Their re-establishment would be a denial of the reality or efficacy of their antitypes. It may, however, be asked, Why should the Feast of Tabernacles form an exception? To this it may be replied, first, that such a festival may be observed without any compromise of the principles of the New Dispensation. Secondly, it may be considered as peculiarly adapted to the retrospections of the converted Jews, who will have to commemorate the sojourn of their fathers, not merely for forty years in the wilderness, but their sojourn for two thousand years in the countries of the dispersion. And thirdly, it may serve as a striking memento to them, that, though they have been restored to the rest of Canaan, they are still only strangers and pilgrims upon the earth, and that there yet remaineth a rest for the people of God. In this point of view, believing Gentiles, who may go up to the festival, can find no difficulty in celebrating it with them to their mutual edification. That the sacrifices which were offered at that feast, or any other animal sacrifices, will then be renewed, is a position, to maintain which would be to counteract the express design, and contradict the express declarations of the dispensation of grace.

It may be said, that Ezekiel gives a full description of the re-establishment of the sacrificial system and of the whole of the temple worship. Nothing can be more certain. But when was this re-establishment to take place? Any one who will only cursorily examine the commencement of the fortieth chapter of that prophet will at once perceive, that, though it follows immediately after chapters relating to the destruction of Gog and Magog, it was nevertheless delivered to the prophet at another time, (not fewer than *thirteen* years afterwards,

18 And if the family of Egypt should not go up, nor come,
Upon them also there shall be none ;
There shall be upon them the plague,
With which Jehovah shall plague the nations,
That will not go up
To celebrate the feast of tabernacles.
19 This shall be the punishment of Egypt,
And the punishment of all the nations
That will not go up
To celebrate the feast of tabernacles.
20   In that day there shall be upon the bells of the horses,
HOLINESS TO JEHOVAH ;
And the pots in the house of Jehovah
Shall be as the bowls before the altar.
21 Yea, every pot in Jerusalem and in Judah
Shall be holiness to Jehovah of hosts ;

if we reckon from the date in chap. xxxii. 1,) and may, therefore, naturally be expected to refer to a subject altogether different. That subject I conceive to be the restoration of the temple and the temple worship after the return from Babylon—a subject which cannot but have lain near the heart of the exiles, and worthy to be made the theme of prophecy, but which is nowhere else referred to in the book of Ezekiel. Difficulty there may be in making the measurements there given agree with those specified by Josephus as the dimensions of the second temple; but far greater difficulties attach to every attempt to refer them to a temple still future, or to view them as wholly emblematical.

19. The connexion shows that חַטָּאת is not here to be taken in the sense of *sin*, but of the *punishment of sin*. Comp. Lam. iii. 39; iv. 6.

20. The מְצִלּוֹת were small metallic plates, suspended from the necks or heads of horses and camels, for the sake of ornament, and making a tinkling noise by striking against each other like cymbals. Root צָלַל, to *tingle, tinkle*. As the inscription קֹדֶשׁ לַיהוָה, HOLINESS TO JEHOVAH, was the sacred symbol engraven upon the golden crown of the Jewish High Priest, the design of the prophecy is evidently to teach, that when

the Jews shall be restored to their own land, there shall be no greater degree of holiness attaching to what was formerly accounted most sacred, than what will attach to the ornamental trappings of the horses. Devotion of person and property to the service of God will be the only holiness then recognised. Ceremonial sanctity shall no longer exist. The same thing is expressed in the second clause of the verse. The vessels in which the flesh was cooked, and which were accounted the meanest about the temple, shall, as to the degree of holiness, be upon a par with those which had been destined for the most sacred purpose, namely, the reception of the blood of the sacrificial victims. All distinction shall be done away.

21. The same idea is here more fully carried out. Not only the common utensils used by the priests, but those employed for cooking in private houses, both at Jerusalem and throughout the country, shall all be regarded as equally holy. From its being expressly stated, that the flesh of the animals to be slaughtered is to be boiled in the pots, and no mention being made of the sprinkling of the blood, it must be inferred that killing for food, and not for sacrifice, is what the prophet has in view. Considering what a stumbling-block a mer-

And all who slaughter shall come,
And take of them and boil in them,
And there shall no more be a Canaanite
In the house of Jehovah of hosts in that day.

cenary and covetous priesthood has ever proved to the world, and to what a fearful extent the ministry in holy things has been made a matter of merchandise, there is great force in the declaration with which the prophet closes : " There shall no more be a *Canaanite* in the house of Jehovah ! "

By כְּנַעֲנִי, *Canaanite,* is meant a *merchant,* the Phœnicians, who inhabited the northern part of Canaan, having been the most celebrated merchants of antiquity. See for this acceptation of the term, Job xl. 30 ; Prov. xxxi. 24 ; Is. xxiii. 8. It is here used metaphorically.

MALACHI

PREFACE.

MALACHI (מַלְאָכִי, *Messenger*,) is the last of all the Hebrew prophets, but we are left in profound ignorance respecting his personal history, and can only judge of the circumstances of his times from what is contained in his book. According to the tradition o the synagogue, he lived after the prophets Haggai and Zechariah, and was contemporary with Nehemiah. This statement is fully borne out by the affinity of the book written by the prophet, with that written by the patriot. Both presuppose the temple to have been already built. The same condition of the Jews is described. They both condemn foreign marriages, and enforce the due payment of tithes, which had been neglected. They likewise correct abuses which had crept in with respect to the sacrifices, and reprove their countrymen for their want of sympathy with the poor.

In all probability, Malachi occupied the same place with respect to Nehemiah, which Haggai and Zechariah did with respect to Zerubbabel. That the former was assisted in the discharge of his duties by prophets, may be inferred from the charge brought against him by Sanballat, Neh. vi. 7. Malachi may therefore be conceived of as having flourished about the year B. C. 440. His book is composed of a series of spirited castigations, in which the persons accused are introduced as repelling the charges, but thereby only affording occasion for a fuller exposure, and a more severe reproof of their conduct. Both priests and people are unsparingly reprimanded; and while they are threatened with divine judgments, encouragement is held out to such as walked in the fear of the Lord. His predictions respecting John the Baptist, the Messiah, and the destruction of the Jewish polity, are clear and unequivocal.

Considering the late age in which he lived, the language of Malachi is pure; his style possesses much in common with the old prophets, but is distinguished more by its animation, than by its rhythmus or grandeur.

CHAPTER I

With a view to work a conviction of ingratitude in the minds of his countrymen, the prophet begins by setting forth the peculiar favour which Jehovah had shown to them as a people in contradistinction to the Edomites, 1—5. He then reproaches the priests for their unworthy conduct in presenting the refuse of the animals in sacrifice, 6—8; charges them with a mercenary spirit, and threatens to reject them, and supply their place with true worshippers from among the most distant heathen, 9—11; and concludes with a renewed reprimand, and the denunciation of a curse upon those who practised deception with respect to the offerings, 12—14.

---

1 THE Sentence of Jehovah's oracle to Israel by Malachi.

2 I have loved you, saith Jehovah,
   Yet ye say, Wherein hast thou loved us?

1. For the formula מַשָּׂא דְבַר יְהֹוָה, see on Zech. ix. 1. That מַלְאָכִי, *Malachi*, is the proper name of the prophet, and not a mere official appellative, as the LXX., Vitringa, and others, interpret, may safely be inferred from the analogy of the title with others prefixed to the prophetical writings. As for the form of the name, Vitringa, Hiller, Michaelis, and Gesenius, take it to be compounded of מַלְאָךְ and יָה, of which they consider ' to be a contraction, and accordingly explain the name as meaning *The Messenger of Jehovah*. To this, however, it has been objected, that no examples of an abbreviation of the Divine name to this extent are to be found ; and, therefore, it has been deemed more natural to regard the ' as the pronominal affix of the first person singular, and to render, *My Messenger*. This latter solution has been adopted by Hengstenberg, who labours in vain to establish a connexion between the name of the prophet, and the same word as occurring in its official signification, chap. iii. 1. The form appears to be really nothing more than an instance of what Ewald calls "the last and newest mode of deriving adjectives from nouns," and denoting origin or source. Compare רַגְלִי, נָכְרִי, סוֹדִי, סִתְרִי, עָמְרִי, עַבְדִּי, &c. יִשְׂרָאֵל, *Israel*, is here used to denote the whole of the twelve tribes, which had returned to their native land, Jer. l. 4, 5, 19, 20.

2, 3. The sovereign benevolence of Jehovah, and the ingratitude of the Hebrews in the time of the prophet, are strikingly contrasted. To the petulant

Was not Esau brother to Jacob? saith Jehovah,
   Yet I loved Jacob,
3 But I hated Esau,
   And made his mountains a desolation,
   And his heritage abodes of the desert.
4 Because Edom saith, We are impoverished,
   But we will rebuild the desolate places;
   Thus saith Jehovah of hosts,
   They may build, but I will overthrow;
   And men shall call them, The border of wickedness,
   And, The people against whom Jehovah is indignant for ever.
5 And your eyes shall see, and ye shall say,
   Let Jehovah be magnified, from the border of Israel.
6   A son honoureth his father,

question, "Wherein hast thou loved us?" which is only the first of a series which are put in the course of the book, the answer is direct and conclusive—in showing greater kindness to their progenitor Jacob, than he had done to his brother Esau. The temporal advantages of Palestine were vastly superior to those of Idumæa, which was comparatively a sterile and desert country; and the Jews had, besides, experienced distinguished favour in having been restored to their land, and had prosperity conferred upon them, while the Edomites, who had suffered from the invasion of their country by the Chaldæans, five years after the capture of Jerusalem, had not been restored. It is to the desolations occasioned by this invasion that reference is made, ver. 3. שָׂנֵא, to hate, is here used in a comparative sense, qualifying the preceding verb אָהֵב, to love. As the opposite of love is hatred, when there is only an inferior degree of the former exhibited, the object of it is regarded as being hated rather than loved. See for this idiom, Gen. xxix. 30, 31; Deut. xxi. 15, 16; Prov. xiii. 24; Matt. vi. 24; Luke xiv. 26, compared with Matt. x. 37. תַּנּוֹת is considered by some to be the feminine of תַּנִּים, and is rendered, serpents, jackals, or the like; but it is preferable to adopt the derivation from the Arabic, تَسّ, substitit, habitavit. Hence تَنَاة,

habitatio, mansio. By the "habitations of the desert," are meant deserted, ruined dwellings, such as are still found in great abundance in Idumæa. The phrase is parallel to שְׁמָמָה in the preceding hemistich, and corresponds to the חֳרָבוֹת, waste places, or ruins, ver. 4.

4, 5. Every attempt on the part of the Idumæans to recover themselves, and enjoy permanent prosperity, should prove abortive, and their continually depressed condition should afford additional proof to the Israelites of the kindness of God towards his own people. גְּבוּל, boundary, is here used in the sense of territory, or the space marked out by the surrounding boundaries. Comp. Gen. x. 19; Numb. xxi. 24. מֵעַל לִגְבוּל יִשְׂרָאֵל, according to Rosenmüller, Hitzig, Maurer, and Ewald, means beyond the Hebrew territory,—construing the words with יַגְדִּל, but it seems more natural to connect them with אַתֶּם תֹּאמְרוּ: Ye who dwell upon the land of Israel shall say from the locality you occupy, and to which, through the Divine goodness, ye have been restored, Jehovah be magnified. The לְ prefixed to גְּבוּל, adds nothing to the force of the preceding preposition. See Gesen. in מֵעַל.

6. Upon the fact of the respect usually shown by inferiors to their superiors, Jehovah founds proof of his right to expect that honour and reverence which corresponded to the high position he

And a servant his master :
If then I be a father, where is my honour ?
And if I be a master, where is my fear ?
Saith Jehovah of hosts to you, O ye priests,
That despise my name; yet ye say,
Wherein have we despised thy name ?

7 In offering polluted bread upon my altar ;
But ye say, Wherein have we polluted thee?
In your saying, The table of Jehovah is contemptible.

8 When ye offer the blind for sacrifice, is it not evil?
And when ye offer the lame and the sick, is it not evil?
Present it now to thy governor ;
Will he be satisfied with thee,
Or accept thy person ? saith Jehovah of hosts.

9 Now, then, conciliate the regard of Jehovah, that he may pity us:
This hath been by your means ;
Will he accept your persons ? saith Jehovah of hosts.

10   Who is there even among you that would shut the doors?
Yea, ye will not kindle the fire on my altar for nought.
I have no pleasure in you, saith Jehovah of hosts,
Neither will I accept an offering at your hand.

11 But from the rising of the sun to its setting,
My name shall be great among the nations ;
And in every place, incense shall be offered to my name,

---

occupied as Author and Moral Governor of the universe. These having, however, been withheld, chiefly owing to the irreligious and profane conduct of the priests, the charge is principally laid against them.

7. That לֶחֶם, *bread*, or *food*, is here to be taken as the Arab. ‎, *caro*, in the sense of *animal flesh*, is obvious, from its being presented on the מִזְבֵּחַ, *altar of sacrifice*, to which also the שֻׁלְחָן, *table*, must be referred, and not to the table of shew-bread. Contempt of sacred things involves contempt of Him to whom they appertain.

8. Another *argumentum ad hominem.* The priests had the effrontery to present to Jehovah what they would not have dared to offer to their civil governor. To offer animals with any blemish, was expressly prohibited in the law. Lev. xxii. 22, 24; Deut. xv. 21.

9. How much soever the words וְעַתָּה חַלּוּ־נָא פְנֵי־אֵל וִיחָנֵנוּ, may at first sight appear to contain a serious exhortation to the priests to repent of their wicked conduct, and to pray for the Divine favour to themselves and the people, yet the connexion requires them to be understood ironically. No prayers or supplications of theirs could avail anything while they presented such unlawful sacrifices. This is expressly declared in the form of a pointed interrogation at the close of the verse. הֲיִשָּׂא מִכֶּם פָּנִים is a more emphatic form, instead of הֲיִשָּׂא פְנֵיכֶם.

10, 11. The rendering of the LXX., adopted by Newcome, " Surely the doors shall be closed against you," cannot be admitted. The authority for the change

And a pure offering;
For my name shall be great among the nations,
Saith Jehovah of hosts.

12 But ye have profaned it by your saying,
The table of Jehovah is polluted,
And its fruit, even his food, is contemptible.

13   Ye have also said, Behold, what a weariness!
And have contemned it, saith Jehovah of hosts;
And ye have brought the torn, the lame, and the sick,
Yea, ye have brought the offering;
Should I accept it at your hand? saith Jehovah.

14 But cursed be the deceiver, who hath a male in his flock,
And voweth, and sacrificeth to Jehovah that which is corrupt;
For I am a great king, saith Jehovah of hosts,
And my name shall be feared among the nations.

---

of מִי, *who*, into כִּי, *surely*, is of no weight; and the verb סָחַר is never construed with בְּ, in order to express the idea of exclusion. Such was the avaricious disposition of the priests, that they would not perform even the most trivial services without payment. How could such expect to be acceptable to God? These verses contain an explicit prediction of the rejection of the Jewish worship, and of the reception of the Gentiles to perform spiritual worship in the Church of the Lord. His name, which the priests had treated with contempt, ver. 6, should receive universal homage among the nations that had been addicted to idolatry, and who were now the objects of abomination on the part of the Jews. The sacrificial terms are transferred from their original application to ceremonial objects and acts, to such as are spiritual, agreeably to the nature of the new economy. Comp. John iv. 20—24; Heb. xiii. 10, 15, 16; 1 Pet. ii. 5. All that Hitzig can discover in these verses is, that God was worshipped by all nations, under the different names of Jehovah, Ormuzd, Zeus, &c.!!!

12—14. A renewal of the charge against the priests, nearly in the same words. מַתְלָאָה is an abbreviated form for מַה תִּלָאָה. Comp. מִדָּה, Exod. iv. 2; מָלָּכֶם, 1s. iii. 15. אוֹתוֹ, *it*, after הִפַּחְתֶּם, refers to אֲכָלוֹ in the preceding verse, and is not to be changed into אוֹתִי, *me*, as proposed in the Tikkun Sopherim. The וְ in וְאֶת־הַפֶּסַח is omitted in ninety-three MSS., in seven printed editions, and in all the versions except the Syriac. Though it is not said that the מִנְחָה, *meat offering*, consisted of inferior ingredients, yet it is either implied, or the idea is intended to be conveyed, that the presentation of the other sacrifices rendered this, however pure in itself, unacceptable to God. Hitzig and Maurer regard מָשְׁחָת to be a contraction of the feminine מָשְׁחָתְ; but I should rather think it ought to be pointed מָשְׁחָת, as in Lev. xxii. 25, where it occurs, in application to the same subject, in the masculine gender. Many MSS. and some of the early editions read לַיהוָה instead of לְאלֹנָי, which has no doubt been substituted for it by some superstitious Jewish scribe.

CHAPTER II

The prophet continues to urge the charge against the priests, warning them that if they did not reform, they should be deprived of all enjoyment, and rendered the objects of shame and contempt, 1—4. The original institution, and the sacred nature and obligations of the priestly office, are then brought forward, with which to contrast the baseness of their conduct in violating its responsibilities; and the section closes with another threatening of punishment, 5—9. In a new section the prophet takes up the subject of divorce, and marriage with foreign women, and severely reproves the priests for the evil example which they had set in this respect, 10—16. They are finally charged with teaching immoral doctrine, 17.

----

1 AND now, unto you is this charge, O ye priests!
2 If ye will not hearken, nor lay it to heart,
　To give glory to my name, saith Jehovah of hosts;
　I will send the curse among you, and will curse your blessings,
　Yea, I will curse them singly,
　Because ye lay it not to heart.
3 Behold! I will rebuke the seed to your hurt,
　And I will scatter dung upon your faces,
　The dung of your festivals;
　And ye shall be taken away with it.
4 And ye shall know that I have sent to you this charge,
　Because my covenant was with Levi, saith Jehovah of hosts.

2. הַמְּאֵרָה is emphatic, and doubtless has reference to Deut. xxvii. 15, &c. The feminine suffix in אֲרוֹתִיהָ is to be taken distributively, with reference to the בְּרָכוֹת, blessings, immediately preceding.

3. The לְ in לָכֶם is that of the Dativus incommodi, "to your detriment or disadvantage." זֶרַע, seed, is not to be changed into זְרוֹעַ, and rendered shoulder, as Houbigant and Newcome do, merely on the authority of the LXX. There is great force in the reference to the dung of the festivals, as the maw, which contained it, belonged to the priests. Deut. xviii. 3. אֵל in אֲלֵיכֶם has the signification of with, together with, as in Lam. iii. 41. Such usage, however, is rare. נָשָׂא is to be taken impersonally.

4. יָדַע, to know, has here the significa-

5 My covenant of life and peace was with him,
   And I gave them to him,
   For the fear which he showed for me,
   And the awe in which he stood of my name.

6 The law of truth was in his mouth,
   And no iniquity was found in his lips;
   He walked with me in peace and uprightness,
   And turned many from iniquity.

7 For the lips of the priest should preserve knowledge,
   And men should seek the law at his mouth,
   For he is the messenger of Jehovah of hosts.

8 But, as for you, ye have departed from the way,
   Ye have made many to stumble in the law;
   Ye have corrupted the covenant of Levi, saith Jehovah of hosts.

---

tion, to *know by experience,* to feel the consequences of transgression. From the words which follow, we must infer that knowledge issuing in reformation of conduct is meant. On no other condition could the Levitical covenant continue in force.

5. In this and the following verses the prophet forcibly contrasts with the base and unworthy conduct of the priests, the noble character of their progenitor, with whom officially Jehovah had entered into covenant. The reference, however, is not to Levi personally, but to Phinehas, Numb. xxv. 12, 13, where we have an account of this covenant, there called בְּרִיתִי שָׁלוֹם, *my covenant of peace,* and בְּרִית כְּהֻנַּת עוֹלָם, *the covenant of an everlasting priesthood.* Both ideas are expressed in the present verse, and the meaning is, that the covenant was secured in perpetuity. Before הַחַיִּים וְהַשָּׁלוֹם, the word בְּרִית is understood from the preceding. מוֹרָא, *fear* or *reverence,* is here the accusative absolute. נִחַת is the Niphal of חָתַת, *to be terrified, dismayed.* This verb is here purposely employed to express the extraordinary degree of profound and holy awe with which Phinehas was inspired when zealously vindicating the honour of Jehovah.

6, 7. A comprehensive and beautiful description of the character and spiritual duties of Phinehas, which ought to have been realized in the persons and ministrations of all his successors in office, and which suggests topics for the most serious self-examination to all who engage in the work of the Christian ministry. The higher and more important functions of the sacerdotal office are here recognised, to the exclusion of such as were merely ceremonial. These the priests in the days of Malachi had neglected, while they discharged the latter in a perfunctory and niggardly manner. That תּוֹרָה is not here to be rendered *doctrine,* but is to be taken in its appropriated sense of *law,* appears from the use of the term in the two following verses. תּוֹרָה is in the accusative case, with which נִמְצָא, as in other instances of passive verbs, does not agree in number. See Gesen. Gram. § 140, 1, b. The priests were the ordinary expounders of the law to the people; it was only on special and extraordinary occasions that the prophets gave their decision. Each of them was, therefore, to be regarded as מַלְאָךְ, a *messenger,* or interpreter of the Divine will.

8. The character of the priests whom Malachi was sent to reprove was the very reverse of that exhibited by Phinehas. Not only did they violate the law themselves, but, as is universally the case, induced others by their bad example to violate it likewise. They thus forfeited all right to the sacerdotal immunities of the Levitical covenant.

9 Therefore have I also rendered you contemptible and base to all
    the people ;
  Forasmuch as ye have not observed my ways,
  And have acted partially in the law.
10   Have we not all one Father?
  Hath not one God created us ?
  Wherefore do we act unfaithfully one to another,
  Profaning the covenant of our fathers ?
11 Judah hath acted unfaithfully ;
  And an abominable thing hath been done in Israel and in
    Jerusalem ;
  For Judah hath profaned that which was holy to Jehovah,
  That which he loved,
  And hath married the daughter of a strange god.
12 Jehovah will cut off the man that doeth this,
  Him that watcheth, and him that answereth,

9. וְנָסִאֲנִי is strikingly antithetical to אַתֶּם at the beginning of ver. 8. The priests are here threatened with a retribution corresponding to their base and contemptible character, an additional and aggravating feature of which is added, viz. partiality in the decisions which they gave on points of law. Instead of הָעָם, *the people,* twenty-three MSS., and a few printed editions, the LXX., Targ., Vulg., Arab., and Hexapl. Syr., read הָעַמִּים, *the peoples* or *nations,* but much less appropriately.

10. The prophet now proceeds to administer reproof to the people, and especially to the priests, for their flagrant violation of the law, which prohibited intermarriages with foreigners. See Exod. xxxiv. 16 ; Deut. vii. 3. For the historical account of this violation, see Ezra ix. 1, 2 ; Neh. xiii. 23—31. That by אָב אֶחָד, *one Father,* we are to understand *Jehovah,* and not *Abraham,* or *Jacob,* as some have supposed, is determined by the force of the parallelism, in which we have the corresponding and elucidatory phrase אֵל אֶחָד, *one God.* As the Jews put away their wives, that they might marry others, they are here distinctly taught that both males and females stood in the same relation to God as their common Father and Creator. He had an equal propriety in them, and when the men acted the part for which

they are here reproved, they acted unjustly by their Maker. But, in addition to this, they broke the covenant made with their fathers, which interdicted such practices. אָח, *brother,* is not here to be pressed, as if reference were had to the father of the female who had been repudiated. אִישׁ בְּאָחִיו is the usual idiom, *one against another.* Comp. 1 Thess. iv. 6. The questions so pointedly put at the commencement of this verse are highly condemnatory of that degradation which is experienced by Oriental females. Not only do most of the Mohammedans deny them the privilege of immortality, but the Jews universally to this day give thanks every morning—the man, that God has not made him a woman ; and the woman, that God has made her כִּרְצוֹנוֹ, *according to his pleasure.*

11. The nominative to בָּגְדָה is אֶרֶץ, understood in יְהוּדָה. By קֹדֶשׁ יְהוָה, *the holiness of Jehovah,* is meant the people of the Hebrews, who were separated to be a people devoted to his service. Comp. זֶרַע הַקֹּדֶשׁ, *the holy seed;* Ezra ix. 2 ; and קֹדֶשׁ יִשְׂרָאֵל לַיהוָה, *Israel is holiness,* i.e. *holy to Jehovah,* Jer. ii. 3. For אֲשֶׁר אָהֵב comp. Ps. xlvii. 5. "The daughter of a strange god" means an idolatress, a female addicted to the worship of a false deity.

12. עֵר וְעֹנֶה עֵר has been variously rendered. The LXX. mistaking עֵר for עַד, have ἕως καὶ ταπεινωθῇ. Vulg. *magis-*

From the tents of Jacob,
And him that presenteth an offering to Jehovah of hosts.
13 And this ye have done a second time,
Covering the altar of Jehovah with tears,
With weeping and groaning,
So that there is no longer any regard paid to the offering,
Nor is it favourably received at your hand.
14 Yet ye say, Wherefore?
Because Jehovah was witness
Between thee and the wife of thy youth;
To whom thou hast acted unfaithfully,
Though she was thy companion and thy covenanted wife.
15 Yet did he not make one?
Though he had the residue of the spirit.

---

trum et discipulum. Targ. בַּר וּבַר בַּר, *son and son's son.* Syr. ܟ݂ܒܪܗ ܘܟܒܪ ܒܪܗ, *both his son and his son's son.* Thus also Abarbanel, Sachs, Ewald, and others. The phrase is obviously, from its very form, like עָצוּר וְעָזוּב, נִין וָנֶכֶד, proverbial, and has its parallel in the Arabic, وليس بها داع ولا مجيب, *There is not in the city a caller, nor is there a responder.* Life of Timur, quoted by Gesenius in his Thesaur. p. 1004. Turkish, هم اويانغ هم جواب ايدنى, both the *watcher, and the answerer.* The meaning is, that *none* should be left alive; all should be cut off. Gesenius thinks that the reference is probably to the Levites who kept watch in the temple by night, and who called and responded to each other at certain intervals; but the mention that is made of "the tents of Jacob" immediately after, shows that the words are not to be thus restricted. עֵר is the participle of עוּר, *to wake, be awake.*

13. שֵׁנִית is to be taken strictly in the sense of *a second time.* Measures had been adopted to cure the evil in the time of Ezra, chap. ix., x.; but the Jews had relapsed into the same sin of marrying foreign wives in that of Nehemiah, and it is this latter which the prophet

here reproves. Neh. xiii. 23—31. The language implies an aggravation of the offence. The crying and weeping were those of the Jewish wives who had been repudiated by their husbands.

14. The legitimate marriages had been contracted with special appeal to Jehovah as witness of the transaction. The phrase אֵשֶׁת נְעוּרֶיךָ, *the wife of thy youth,* has reference to the early marriages among the Hebrews. In Poland, at the present day, they marry at the age of thirteen and fourteen, and the females still younger.

15. Michaelis, Hitzig, Maurer, and Hengstenberg, concur in the opinion expressed in the Targum, and adopted by most of the Rabbins, that by אֶחָד, *one,* and הָאֶחָד, *the one,* Abraham is intended; and maintain, that what is here stated, was designed to repel an objection raised by the priests, viz. that Abraham took an Egyptian female in addition to Sarah. The prophet, according to them, admits the fact, but denies the consequence, by showing that Abraham still retained the Spirit of God, because his object in contracting this alliance was to obtain the seed which God had promised him, and not to gratify carnal passion, to which the evil here condemned was to be traced. Ewald refers אֶחָד, *one,* to God, considering the term to be used here in the same sense as in ver. 10, but he fails in giving

And why the one?
That he might seek a godly seed.
Therefore take heed to your spirit,
That none act unfaithfully to the wife of his youth.

16 For I hate divorce, saith Jehovah, the God of Israel,
And for a man to cover over his garment with violence,
Saith Jehovah of hosts.
Therefore take heed to your spirit,
That ye act not unfaithfully.

17   Ye have wearied Jehovah with your words,
Yet ye say, Wherein have we wearied him?
In your saying, Every one that doeth evil
Is good in the sight of Jehovah, and he delighteth in them;
Or, Where is the God of justice?

---

a satisfactory explanation of the passage. Nor does the other interpretation at all do justice to its claims; so that we are shut up to the conclusion, that by הָאֶחָד, *the one*, we are to understand בָּשָׂר אֶחָד, the *one flesh*, or conjugal body into which the first couple were formed, Gen. ii. Instead of forming only two into one, the Creator might have given to Adam many wives. There was no lack of spiritual existence from which to furnish them with intelligent souls. When he gave to Eve such an existence, he did not exhaust the immense fountain of being. There remained all with which the human race hath been furnished throughout its generations. What then, the prophet asks, was the design of the restriction? to this he replies, The securing of a pious offspring. Divorces and polygamy have ever been unfavourable to the education of children. It is only by the harmonious and loving attention bestowed by parents upon their children, that they can be expected to be brought up in the fear of God. The reply bore hard upon the priests who had married idolatrous wives.

In such a connexion there was everything to counteract and destroy the interests of piety.

16. שָׂנֵא should be pointed שֹׂנֵא, with the personal pronoun אֲנִי understood. By לְבוּשׁ, *garment*, it is now generally admitted we are to understand the *wife*, who had the most glaring injustice done to her by giving her a divorce, or by taking one or more in addition to her. Thus the Arab. لبس, *texit, induit;* لباس, *vestimentum*, " *conjux*, tum mulier viri, tum vir mulieris, quod sibi invicem pro tegumento sunt;" Freytag. Accordingly we read in the Koran, Sur. ii. 183, respecting the wives: هن لباس لكم ولنتم لباس لهن, *they are your garment, and you are theirs*. In the ecclesiastical language of the East, matrimony was called τὸ θνητὸν καὶ δουλικὸν ἱμάτιον.

17. The old objection taken against the providence of God from the afflictions of the righteous, and the prosperity of the wicked.

CHAPTER III

This chapter commences with a lucid prophecy of John the Baptist, as the forerunner of the Messiah, and of the Messiah himself, who was, as he had long
been, the object of delightful expectation to the Jews, 1. The aspect of his
advent in regard to the wicked, and especially to the ungodly priesthood, is next
introduced, together with the severe judgments that were to be brought upon
the nation, 2—6. The people are then reproved for having withheld the legal
tithes and offerings, and are promised a profusion of blessings in case of repentance, 7—12. To the infidel objection that there is no utility in religion, seeing
the wicked prosper, while the godly are oppressed, the prophet replies by pointing to the day of retribution, when all should be treated according to their character, which would then be fully disclosed, 13—18.

---

1 BEHOLD! I will send my messenger,
And he shall prepare the way before me,
And suddenly there shall come to his temple
The Lord whom ye seek,

1. That by מַלְאָכִי, *my messenger*, we
are to understand John the Baptist, is
placed beyond dispute by the appropriation of the words of the prophecy
to him, Mark i. 2. Comp. Is. xl. 3.
Hengstenberg strangely gives in to the
notion of Eichhorn and Theiner, that
the collective body of the prophets is
intended, though he thinks that the idea
of the messenger chiefly concentrates in
John. Not one of his five reasons is at
all satisfactory. The office of this messenger is described as preparing the way
for the Messiah. The language is borrowed from the custom of sending pio-
neers before an Eastern monarch, to cut
through rocks and forests, and remove
every impediment that might obstruct
his course. פָּנָה, which in Kal is never
transitive, signifies in Piel *to clear, clear*

away, put in order, prepare. This John
did by preaching repentance, and announcing the near approach of the
kingdom of God. Comp. chap. iv. 5.
In this prophecy of the Messiah are
three palpable and incontrovertible
proofs of his divinity. First, he is identified with Jehovah : " he shall prepare
the way before ME "—" saith Jehovah."
Secondly, He is represented as the Pro-
prietor of the temple. Thirdly, He is
characterised as הָאָדוֹן, THE SOVEREIGN,
a title nowhere given in this form to any
except Jehovah. In its anarthrous state
the noun אָדוֹן is applicable to any owner,
possessor, or ruler, and it is applied
in the construct state to Jehovah as
אֲדוֹן כָּל־הָאָרֶץ, *the Possessor of the whole
earth,* Josh. iii. 11, 13; but when it
takes the article, as here, it is used κατ'

Even the Messenger of the covenant, in whom ye delight,
Behold! he shall come, saith Jehovah of hosts.

2   But who may endure the day of his coming?
And who may stand when he appeareth?
For he is like the fire of the refiner,
And like the soap of the fullers;

ἐξοχὴν, and exclusively, of the Divine
Being. See Exod. xxiii. 17; xxxiv. 23;
Is. i. 24; iii. 1; x. 16, 33; xix. 4. See
Dr. J. Pye Smith's Messiah, vol. i. pp.
442—444. Abenezra thus explains the
term, and identifies the Sovereign Lord
with the angel spoken of immediately
after : כי הברית מלאך הוא הכבוד הוא האדון
כמול הטעם, *The Lord is both the Divine
Majesty, and the Angel of the Covenant,
for the sentence is doubled.* It is likewise admitted in Mashmiah Jeshua,
fol. 76, המשיח מלך על האדון לפרש אפשר,
*The Lord may be explained of the King
Messiah;* and Kimchi not only, with
Abenezra, identifies the Lord and the
Angel, but applies both to the Messiah:
הברית מלאך הוא המשיח מלך הוא האדון, *The
Lord is the King Messiah, he is also the
Angel of the Covenant;* though, in order
to elude the Christian application of the
passage, he suggests another interpretation, according to which Elijah is
meant. It has been questioned, whether
the phrase הַבְּרִית מַלְאַךְ, *the Messenger of
the Covenant,* is to be viewed retrospec-
tively or prospectively ; in other words,
whether it be the Old or the New Covenant to which reference is made. Considering the fact, that in such parallel
forms as הַבְּרִית לוּחֹת, *the tables of the
covenant,* הַבְּרִית אֲרוֹן, *the ark of the covenant,* הַבְּרִית סֵפֶר, *the book of the covenant,*
הַבְּרִית דַּם, *the blood of the covenant,* &c.,
the ancient dispensation which Jehovah
granted to the Hebrews at Sinai is intended, it would seem natural to infer
that הַבְּרִית מַלְאַךְ is to be understood in the
same way. This view of the subject
would seem to be corroborated by the
circumstances, that a מַלְאָךְ, *Angel* or
Messenger, who is said to possess the
Divine name, *i. e.* whatever is distinctive
of Deity, is frequently spoken of under
that economy; that He is represented
as leading the Israelites out of Egypt,
giving them the law, and superintending

the whole of the theocracy. All the
theophanies or manifestations of the
invisible Deity were made in his Person.
He was the proper nuncius sent to
reveal the will of the Father. Moses
was only a θεράπων, עֶבֶד, or servant employed by him, while he was God manifested in glory. I can put no other consistent construction upon such passages
as the following: Gen. xlviii. 15, 16;
Exod. iii. 2—15; xxiii. 20, 21; Is. lxiii.
9; Zech. i.; ii.; iii.; vi.; Acts vii. 38;
Heb. xi. 26; xii. 26. In strict consistency with the representations of Scripture, therefore, the Messiah may be
called the *Messenger* of that ancient
economy of which he was the Founder
and Head. Most interpreters, however,
understand the New Covenant, or the
dispensation of grace, with special reference to Heb. ix. 15, where our Saviour
is called διαθήκης καινῆς μεσίτης, *the
Mediator of the New Covenant;* among
others, Grotius, Rosenmüller, and Gesenius. The Jews may be said to have
sought and delighted in the Messiah,
because he was the object of national
expectation and desire, though the great
body of them formed no higher conception of him than that of an earthly monarch, under whose reign they should
enjoy a profusion of temporal blessings.
When it is declared that he should come
" *suddenly* " to his temple, it is not implied that he was to come in or near the
times of the prophet, but merely that
his coming would be sudden and unexpected in the circumstances under which
it took place.

2—4. Employing a strong metallurgic
metaphor, the prophet shows that the
office of the Covenant Messenger would
be very different from that which the
carnal Jews expected. Instead of flattering their prejudices, and gratifying
their wishes, he would, by his pure and
heart-searching doctrines, subject their

3 And he shall sit, refining and purifying the silver;
   Yea, he shall purify the sons of Levi,
   And refine them like gold and like silver,
   That they may present to Jehovah an offering in righteousness.
4 Then shall the offering of Judah and Jerusalem
   Be pleasing to Jehovah,
   As in the days of old,
   And as in the former years.
5   But I will draw nigh to you for judgment,
   And will be a swift witness
   Against the sorcerers, and against the adulterers,
   And against those who swear to a falsehood,
   And against those who wrest the wages of the hireling,
   The widow and the orphan,
   Who turn aside the stranger as to his right,
   And fear not me, saith Jehovah of hosts.
6 Because I am Jehovah, I change not;
   Therefore ye sons of Jacob are not consumed.
7   Even from the days of your fathers
   Ye have departed from my statutes, and have not kept them;
   Return to me, and I will return to you,
   Saith Jehovah of hosts.
   But ye say, Wherewith shall we return?

principles and conduct to the severest test. Those of the priests should specially be tried. The object he was to have in view in this trial, was their purification, that they might serve him in righteousness. Matt. iii. 12; John xv. 3. And such was the result with respect to many of them. "A great company of the priests were obedient to the faith," Acts vi. 7. The influence of their conversion upon the people must have been very great, though we have no information respecting it in the Acts. The religious services of the churches composed of Jewish converts in Jerusalem and throughout Judæa, are represented as peculiarly well-pleasing to God. For the meaning of מִנְחָה, offering, as here used, comp. chap. i. 10, 11.

5. Malachi here returns to his own times, and threatens his ungodly contemporaries with divine judgment, speedily to be executed upon them. Magic greatly prevailed among the Jews after the captivity, as did also the other crimes here specified. How much they obtained in the time of our Lord, we learn from the Evangelists and Josephus. The prophet traces them all back to their true source—absence of the fear of God. After וּבִנְשָׁעִים, the phrase בִּשְׁמִי is found in nineteen MSS., in some printed editions, and in the LXX., Syr. Hexapl., and Arab.

6. As the incommunicable name יְהוָֹה, JEHOVAH, implies a futurity of reference with respect to the communication of blessings, (see on Hos. xii. 5,) the Divine immutability secured the preservation of the Jewish people from destruction, notwithstanding their flagrant wickedness, till he had accomplished all his purposes of mercy.

7. The ל in לְמִימֵי is prosthetic, with

8 Will a man defraud God?
   Yet ye have defrauded me.
   But ye say, Wherein have we defrauded thee?
   In the tithes and the oblations.

9 Ye are cursed with the curse;
   For ye—the whole nation—have defrauded me.

10 Bring ye all the tithes into the storehouse,
   That there may be meat in my house,
   And try me now with this, saith Jehovah of hosts,
   Whether I will not open for you the windows of heaven,
   And pour out a blessing for you,
   Till there shall be a superabundance.

11 And I will rebuke the devourer for your sake,
   And he shall not destroy the fruits of your ground;
   Neither shall your vine in the field be unfruitful,
   Saith Jehovah of hosts.

12 And all the nations shall pronounce you happy,
   For ye shall be a delightful land,
   Saith Jehovah of hosts.

13 Your words against me have been hard, saith Jehovah;
   But ye say, What have we spoken against thee?

14 Ye have said:
   It is vain to serve God;
   And what profit is it that we keep his ordinance,
   And that we walk mournfully before Jehovah of hosts?

15 For now ye pronounce the proud happy;
   They also that work wickedness are built up;
   They even tempt God, yet they are delivered.

---

somewhat of its temporal signification. There was still mercy in store for the Jews, if they would only repent.

8. בָּקַע, which occurs only in our prophet, and in Prov. xxii. 23, signifies *to cover, do anything covertly, defraud.* Comp. the Arab. قبع, *retraxit.* قابع, *occultus.*

9. Comp. chap. ii. 2.

10. עַד־בְּלִי־דָי, *usque ad defectum sufficientiæ,* i.e. not as Gesenius explains it, till my abundance be exhausted, which being impossible, the phrase is equivalent to, *for ever, without end;* but where

sufficiency can have no more place, more than sufficient, superabundantly. To this effect Jerome, Winer, De Wette, Hitzig, and Maurer.

11. By the אֹכֵל, *devourer,* noxious animals and insects are meant, especially the locusts. שִׁכֵּל properly signifies *to cause abortion, render childless,* and metaphorically, to make *barren* or *unfruitful,* when spoken of trees.

13—15. חָזַק signifies to *bind fast, make firm,* and, in a bad sense, *to be hard, obstinate,* or the like. Such was the language of the Jews against Jehovah. Comp. Jude 15, περὶ πάντων τῶν σκληρῶν,

16   Then they that feared Jehovah
Conversed one with another;
And Jehovah hearkened, and heard,
And a book of remembrance was written before him,
For those that feared Jehovah,
And that thought upon his name.

17   And they shall be a peculiar treasure to me, saith Jehovah of hosts,
In the day which I have appointed;
And I will be kind to them
As a father is kind to his son who serveth him.

18   Then shall ye again perceive the difference
Between the righteous and the wicked,

ὧν ἐλάλησαν κατ' αὐτοῦ. Some awful specimens of their hard speeches are here exhibited, in which the usual objection against the rectitude of Providence is dressed up in some of its more taking forms. Comp. Job xxi. 14, 15; Ps. lxxiii. 1—14. בָּחַן is here used like נִסָּה in the bad sense of tempting, or braving the Most High by presumptuous speeches and conduct. The walking mournfully has reference to their going about in sackcloth and ashes, pretending to sorrow on account of their sins. קָדַר, to be dirty, to go about in filthy garments, like persons who mourn; such being universally the custom in the East.

16. אָז, then, specially marks the time in which the impious conversations were being held. Here נִדְבְּרוּ beautifully contrasts with the same term in the thirteenth verse. The verb is in Niphal, to express the reciprocal or conversational character of the language. As the ungodly did not confine their hard speeches to the mere utterance of them to such individuals as they might happen to meet, but made their infidel objections the subject of mutual discussion, so the pious are here represented as holding mutual converse respecting the interests of truth and godliness. It does not appear that Niphal ever has the frequentative signification, expressed in our common version. The writing of a book of remembrance is a metaphor borrowed from the custom at the Persian court of entering in a record the names

of any who have rendered service to the king, with an account of the nature of such service. See Esther vi. 1, 2.

17. סְגֻלָּה is to be construed with וְהָיוּ לִי, and עֹשֶׂה is connected by means of אֲשֶׁר with יוֹם. The phrase עֹשֶׂה יוֹם, to make a day, which occurs chap. iv. 3, and Ps. cxviii. 24, means to fix, ordain, appoint such a period for the execution of a special purpose. סְגֻלָּה, signifies private, special, or peculiar property. סָגַל, like the kindred root סָגַר, has the primary signification of shutting up, closing, and then, secondarily, that of getting, or acquiring what is shut up, in order to its being carefully preserved. Hence the idea of what is peculiarly valuable or precious. The term is applied to the people of Israel, Exod. xix. 5; Deut. vii. 6; xiv. 2; xxvi. 18. It is used of the choice treasure of kings, &c., Eccles. ii. 8. It is expressive of the high estimation in which God holds his people, and, in this connexion, of their perfect safety in the day of judgment.

18. שׁוּב is used idiomatically in connexion with רָאָה to express the repetition of the action, the idea of which is conveyed by the latter verb. Notwithstanding the charge brought by the wicked against the providence of God, as if he treated all alike, the righteous had already had opportunities of perceiving, from observation and experience, that the position was false, viewed in application to the entire state and circumstances of the different characters; but they should have another and most

Between him that serveth God,
And him that serveth him not.

convincing proof in the salvation of all who loved and feared the Lord, and in the overthrow and destruction of his enemies.

CHAPTER IV

Most editions of the Hebrew Bible, and most of the MSS., exhibit this concluding portion of the book as a continuation of the third chapter. Not a few MSS., however, leave a blank space before it, and several editions make a separate chapter of it. As this division obtains in all the versions, it is more convenient to retain it.

The chapter continues the threatenings against the Jewish unbelievers, 1; exhibits a luminous prophecy of the Messiah, and the prosperity of his people, 2, 3; and concludes with a solemn call to the Jews, to observe the institutes of the old economy, till the forerunner of the Messiah should appear, when the Jewish polity should be destroyed, and a new and better dispensation established, 4—6.

---

1 For, behold! the day cometh, it shall burn as an oven,
　　And all the proud, and every one that doeth wickedly, shall be
　　　　stubble,
　　And the day that cometh shall burn them up,
　　Saith Jehovah of hosts,
　　That it may not leave them either root or branch.
2　　But unto you that fear my name,
　　The Sun of righteousness shall arise,
　　And there shall be healing in his wings;
　　And ye shall go forth and leap as calves of the stall.

1. Instead of עֹשֵׂה רִשְׁעָה, nearly eighty MSS., the most ancient and several other editions, the Babylon. Talmud, the LXX., Syr., and Targ., read עֹשֵׂי רִשְׁעָה in the plural. The phrase שֹׁרֶשׁ וְעָנָף, root or branch, is proverbial, and signifies any, the least remnant. The persons referred to were to be consigned to utter destruction. The Targum has בַּר וּבַר בַּר, son or son's son.

2. The term שֶׁמֶשׁ, Sun, is metaphorically applied to God, Ps. lxxxiv. 11, on account of that luminary being the most glorious and beneficent object which meets the human eye. It is with good reason supposed to be thus used of the Messiah in the declaration, 2 Sam. xxiii. 4:

וּכְאוֹר בֹּקֶר יִזְרַח־שָׁמֶשׁ,

"And as the morning light he shall arise—a Sun."

In the present verse there can be no doubt with respect to the application. Our Lord is elsewhere called אוֹר, Light, which in Hebrew poetry is used of the sun, as the source of light. See Is. ix. 1, (Eng. version, 2); xlix. 6; John i. 9; viii.

3   And ye shall tread down the wicked;
     Surely they shall be ashes under the soles of your feet,
     In the day which I have appointed, saith Jehovah of hosts.

4   Remember ye the law of Moses my servant,
     Which I gave him in charge in Horeb for all Israel,
     The statutes and the judgments.

5   Behold! I will send to you Elijah the prophet,

12. What the sun is to the natural world, that the Messiah is to the moral. The invaluable spiritual blessings which he dispenses are all comprehended under the two heads here specified—righteousness and moral health. Comp. Is. lvii. 19. Both of these are indispensably requisite to the happiness of our guilty and depraved race, and from no other quarter can they be obtained, than from Him, "who of God is made unto us wisdom, and righteousness, and sanctification, and redemption." 1 Cor. i. 30. By "wings" we are to understand the *beams* of the sun, on account of the velocity and expansion with which they spread over the earth. Comp. Ps. cxxxix. 9. Those for whose immediate benefit the Sun of righteousness was to arise, were such as "feared the name" of Jehovah—like Simeon, who was δίκαιος καὶ ευλαβης ς, righteous and *devout*, waiting for the consolation of Israel, Luke ii. 25. אצי, *to go forth*, is here used in the sense of escaping from the judgment to be inflicted upon the unbelieving part of the Jewish nation. This the Jewish Christians did when they left Jerusalem, and proceeded to Pella, where they were preserved in safety. שׁוּפ, signifies *to spread, take a wide range*, and is used of the proud prancing of horses, and as here of the leaping and sporting of calves. The simile is designed to convey the ideas of freedom from outward restraint, and enjoyment of self-conscious hilarity.

3. This verse expresses the depressed condition to which the Jews were to be reduced after the destruction of their polity, contrasted with the prosperous condition of those who embraced Christianity, and who were no longer subject to oppression on the part of their unbelieving brethren.

4. As the law and the prophets were to remain in force till the appearance of John the Baptist, no prophet intervening

after Malachi to make any further communications of the Divine will, it was necessary to pay the closest attention to the enactments and observances of the Mosaic institute. That there were no more inspired messengers under the Old Economy may be inferred, not only from the nature of the injunction here given, especially as taken in connexion with the promise of a new messenger in the following verse, but also from Ecclesiasticus xlix. 10, where, after mentioning Jeremiah and Ezekiel, the author closes with τῶν δώδεκα προφητῶν, *the twelve prophets*, as the last in the category.

5. The coherence of this verse with the first clause of chap. iii. is too palpable to be overlooked. Accordingly, the Jews in the time of Jerome interpreted the messenger of Jehovah there predicted, of Elijah the Tishbite, as they explain the present verse to this day, believing, that as the ancient prophet ascended into heaven both as to body and soul, he is destined to reappear in the same upon earth before the advent of Messiah, the Son of David. That Elijah here presented to view is to be understood ideally and not historically, and that the individual personally intended is John the Baptist, are positions the certainty of which is rendered indubitable by the repeated declarations of our Lord. When John denied that he was Elias, John i. 21, he is to be understood as making the denial in reference to the personal sense of the term as employed in the question that had been proposed to him. The historical theory is entirely set aside by the express testimony of the angel, Luke i. 17, according to which all that is meant by Malachi is, that the forerunner of the Messiah was to come "in the spirit and power of Elias." Like that prophet, he was to be endowed with extraordinary power and energy, to fit

> Before the great and terrible day of Jehovah come :
> 6 And he shall turn the heart of the fathers to the children,
> And the heart of the children to their fathers,
> Lest I come and smite the land with a curse.

him for the great work of reformation which his ministry was designed to effect. Adverting to the erroneous Jewish notion which even then obtained, relative to the appearance of Elijah in person, our Lord says of John, "If ye will receive it, αὐτός ἐστιν Ἠλίας ὁ μέλλων ἔρχεσθαι, *he is Elias who was to come,*" Matt. xi. 14. And when the disciples asked him, "Why do the Scribes then say that Elias must first come?" he replied, "Elias shall, indeed, first come and restore all things : but I say unto you that Ἠλίας ἤδη ἦλθε, *Elias is already come,* and they knew him not, but have done unto him whatsoever they listed." Matt. xvii. 10—13. Upon the circumstance that our Lord uses the future tense, ἔρχεται, *shall come,* some Christian interpreters have attempted to establish the hypothesis, that the prophecy is still to be fulfilled before his second advent; but he is obviously speaking in the style of language employed by the prophet, to whom the event was future, and in adaptation to the opinion of the Scribes, though he immediately corrects what was erroneous in their notion, declaring that the event was no longer future, but had actually taken place in the person and ministry of John. It is truly surprising that any should persist in giving to the prophecy an aspect still future, in the very face of an exposition at once positive and infallible. That John the Baptist was נָבִיא, *a prophet,* Christ admits, though he at the same time declares, that he was "more than a prophet." Matt. xi. 9. The "great and terrible day of Jehovah" was the dreadful period of his judgment, effecting the destruction of Jerusalem by the Romans. Comp. Joel ii. 31.

6. The design of the ministry of John is described as consisting in the production of universal peace and concord. Family feuds had increased to an enormous extent by the time of John the Baptist, the removal of which by genuine repentance and reformation of conduct

might be taken as a specimen of the ἀποκατάστασις, or restoration of things to a better state throughout Judæa. Some have proposed to take the preposition עַל, *to,* as equivalent to עִם, *with,* a signification which it sometimes has, and so to explain the passage as simply predicting the universality of the conversion spoken of; but such an interpretation would introduce an intolerable tautology into the language of the prophet, and be at variance with the construction put upon it by the angel, Luke i. 17, in which only one member of the sentence is quoted. With respect to the extent of the effects produced by John's ministry, there can be no doubt it was very great. Not only did immense multitudes come to his baptism, confessing their sins, but the great body of the common people appear to have been prepared by him for the labours of our blessed Lord himself, and thus the foundation was laid for the recovery of tens of thousands from Judaism to the faith of the gospel, previous to the destruction of Jerusalem. See Acts xxi. 20.

The prophecy, and with it the entire Old Testament, closes with the awful alternative—the denunciation of the Divine curse, to be realized in the extermination of the impenitent Jews from their own land. חֵרֶם signifies *utter destruction,* from חָרַם, *to shut or stop up,* exclude from common use, place under a ban, devote to destruction. It is one of the most fearful words in use among the Jews, and was specially applied to the extermination of the Canaanites, whose cities were razed to the foundations, and their inhabitants utterly destroyed. Under this ban, the land of Palestine has lain ever since the capture of Jerusalem; and the sufferings to which, in consequence, the Jews have been subjected are truly appalling; but incomparably more dreadful is the New Testament חֵרֶם—ANAΘEMA, MAPAN AΘA! 1 Cor. xvi. 22.

DATE DUE

11.8.2006		